P9-DOG-190

READINGS IN MORAL THEOLOGY No. 8

Dialogue About Catholic Sexual Teaching

Edited by
Charles E. Curran
and
Richard A. McCormick, S.J.

PAULIST PRESS
New York/Mahwah

Copyright © 1993 by Charles E. Curran
and Richard A. McCormick

All rights reserved. No part of this book may be reproduced or transmitted in any
form or by any means, electronic or mechanical, including photocopying, recording
or by any information storage and retrieval system without permission in writing
from the Publisher.

Library of Congress Cataloging-in-Publication Data

Dialogue about Catholic sexual teaching / edited by Charles E. Curran
    and Richard A. McCormick.
        p.   cm. — (Readings in moral theology ; no. 8)
    Includes bibliographical references.
    ISBN 0-8091-3414-4 (paper)
    1. Sex—Religious aspects—Catholic Church.   2. Sexual ethics.
3. Catholic Church—Doctrines.   I. Curran, Charles E.
II. McCormick, Richard A., 1922–   .   III. Series.
BX1795.S48D53   1993
241'.66'08822—dc20   93-4370
                                                                        CIP

Published by Paulist Press
997 Macarthur Boulevard
Mahwah, New Jersey 07430

Printed and bound in the
United States of America

Contents

PART THREE:
STERILIZATION

PART FOUR:
ARTIFICIAL INSEMINATION AND
IN VITRO FERTILIZATION

PART FIVE:
HOMOSEXUALITY

PART SIX:
MASTURBATION

Official Teaching may be found in Part Seven, *Declaration on Certain Questions Concerning Sexual Ethics* (1975), no. 9.

PART SEVEN:
CHASTITY, SIN, AND SEXUALITY OUTSIDE MARRIAGE

ACKNOWLEDGMENTS

The articles reprinted in *Moral Theology No. 8* appeared in the following publications and are reprinted here with permission:

André Guindon, "A Theory of Sexual Ethics for Concerned Christians," in *The Sexual Creators: An Ethical Proposal for Concerned Christians* (Lanham, Maryland: University Press of America, 1986) pp. 21–41; Joan Timmerman, "Sex, Sacred or Profane?" in *The Mardi Gras Syndrome: Rethinking Christian Sexuality* (New York: The Crossroad Publishing Company, 1984) pp. 1–9; John Gallagher, "Magisterial Teaching from 1918 to the Present," in *Human Sexuality and Personhood* (St. Louis: Pope John Center, 1981) pp. 191–210 [Pope John Center, 186 Forbes Road, Braintree, MA 02184, (617) 848–6965]; J. A. Selling, "Magisterial Teaching on Marriage 1880–1986: Historical Constancy or Radical Development?" in Réal Tremblay and Dennis J. Billy (eds.), *Historia: Memoria futuri Mèlanges Louis Vereecke* (Roma: Accademia Alfonsiana, 1991), pp. 397–402 of 351–402; John T. Noonan, Jr., "Use of the Sterile Period," in *Contraception: A History of Its Treatment by the Catholic Theologians and Canonists* (Cambridge: Belknap Press of Harvard University Press, Copyright 1965, 1986 by the President and Fellows of Harvard University), pp. 438–447; Dietrich von Hildebrand, "The Meaning of Marriage and the Principle of Superabundant Finality," in *The Encyclical Humanae Vitae: A Sign of Contradiction* (Chicago: Franciscan Herald Press, 1969), pp. 29–49 [with the permission Alice von Hildebrand]; Germain Grisez, Joseph Boyle, John Finnis, and William E. May, "NFP: Not Contralife, in *The Teaching of Humanae Vitae: A Defense* (San Francisco: Ignatius Press, 1988), pp. 81–92; Rosemary Radford Ruether, "Birth Control and the Ideals of Marital Sexuality," in *Contraception and Holiness: The Catholic Predicament* (New York: Herder and Herder, 1964), pp. 72–92 [with the permission of the author]; Bernard Häring, "The Inseparability of the Unitive—Procreative Functions of the Marital Act," in Charles E. Curran, ed., *Contraception, Authority and Dissent* (New York: Herder, 1969), pp. 176–192 [with the permission of The Crossroad Publishing Company]; John P. Boyle, "Church Teaching on Sterilization," in *The Sterilization Controversy: A New Crisis for the Catholic Hospital?* (New York: Paulist Press, 1977), pp. 5–29; John P. Kenny, "Sterilization," in

Principles of Medical Ethics, 2nd ed., (Westminster, Maryland: Newman Press, 1962), pp. 166–174; Richard A. McCormick, "The Sisters of Mercy of the Union and Sterilization," *Notes on Moral Theology 1981 through 1984* (Lanham, Maryland: University Press of America, 1984), pp. 187–192; John R. Connery, "Tubal Ligation: Good Medicine? Good Morality?" *Linacre Quarterly* 48 (May 1982), pp. 112–114; Gerald T. Kelly, "Artificial Insemination," in *Medico-Moral Problems* (St. Louis: Catholic Hospital [Health] Association, 1957), pp. 228–244; John Mahoney, "Human Fertility Control," in *Bioethics and Belief: Religion and Medicine in Dialogue* (London: Sheed and Ward, 1984), pp. 11–26; Kevin T. Kelly, "What the Churches are Saying About IVF in *Life and Love* (London: HarperCollins Publishers Limited, 1987) pp. 15–36; John F. Harvey, "Arguments from Revelation and Reason in Favor of the Official Teaching of the Church," in *The Homosexual Person: New Thinking in Pastoral Care* (San Francisco: Ignatius Press, 1987), pp. 95–107; John J. McNeill, "Epilogue," in *The Church and The Homosexual,* updated edition, (Boston: Beacon Press, 1988), pp. 196–200; Margaret A. Farley, "An Ethic for Same Sex Relations," in Robert Nugent, ed., *A Challenge to Love: Gay and Lesbian Catholics in the Church* (New York: The Crossroad Publishing Company, 1983), pp. 93–106; Anthony Kosnik et al., "Masturbation," in *Human Sexuality: New Directions in American Catholic Thought* (New York: Paulist Press, 1977), pp. 219–229; Ronald Lawler, Joseph M. Boyle, Jr., and William E. May, "Masturbation," in *Catholic Sexual Ethics: A Summary, Explanation, and Defense* (Huntington, Indiana: Our Sunday Visitor Press, 1985), pp. 187–195 [with the permission of the authors]; Gerald Kelly, S.J. "Practical Moral Principles," from *Modern Youth and Chastity* (St. Louis: Queen's Work, 1941), pp. 72–84; Charles E. Curran, "Sexuality and Sin: A Current Appraisal," in *Contemporary Problems in Moral Theology* (Notre Dame, Indiana: Fides Publishers, 1970), pp. 159–170 [with the permission of the author]; Philip S. Keane, "Heterosexual Expression, Marriage, and Morality," in *Sexual Morality: A Catholic Perspective* (New York: Paulist Press, 1977), pp. 92–113; Jack Dominion, "Marriage Under Threat," *Tablet* 246 (July 4, 1992) 834–835; Leslie Griffin, "American Catholic Sexual Ethics, 1789–1989" in *Perspectives on American Catholicism,* ed. by Stephen Vicchio and Virginia Geiger (Westminster, Md.: Christian Classics, 1989), pp. 231–252; William E. May, "The Liberating Truth of Catholic Teaching on Sexual Morality," *Homiletic and Pastoral Review* (July 1983), pp. 21–28; Lisa Sowle Cahill, "Current Teaching on Sexual Ethics," *Studies* 76 (Spring 1987), 20–28; Charles E. Curran, "Official Catholic Social and Sexual Teachings: A Methodological Comparison," in *Tensions in Moral Theology* (Notre Dame, Indiana: University of Notre Dame Press, 1988), pp. 87–109; Richard A. McCormick, "Declaration on Certain Questions Concerning Sexual Ethics," in *Notes on Moral Theology 1965 through 1980* (Washington, D.C.: University Press of America, 1981), pp. 668–682; Susan L. Secker, "Human Experience and Women's Experience: Resources for Catholic Ethics," in *The Annual: Society of Christian Ethics* (1991), pp. 133–150.

FOR JOSEPH FUCHS, S.J., AND
FOR BERNARD HÄRING, C.SS.R.,

MENTORS, COLLEAGUES AND FRIENDS,
WHO TURNED EIGHTY IN 1992.

Foreword

In this volume we have followed the policy that prevails in our other volumes. This means that we have attempted to include as many points of view as possible in a limited space, including, of course, those that we do not share. The reason for this is not a kind of deferential etiquette eager to please all parties. Rather, it is an attempt to achieve three goals. First, it tries to be a realistic reflection of the pluralism of opinion in the church. Second, it provides the opportunity to display development in a particular area. For instance, it is for this reason that we have included a selection from Gerald Kelly's *Modern Youth and Chastity* (1941). Kelly was one of the most highly respected moralists of his time and his booklet was very influential with counselors and confessors. But it is safe to say that contemporary sexuality education would reveal rather different emphases. Third, it gently suggests the desirability, even the necessity, of continued conversation and interaction between those who disagree, a particular need of our day.

When we have reproduced sections of official church documents, we have left footnote references intact rather than try to renumber them. Not only is this editorially easier, but it indicates to the reader in a general way where the excerpt occurs relative to the overall text.

These readings include selections that have been criticized by the Holy See. We include such selections in no spirit of provocation or endorsement, but only because they display various attempts to formulate more meaningfully sexual morality in our time. In each case we have included the critique of the Holy See so that the state of the question would be clear and complete. We ask the reader to be attentive to the date of the article since it is entirely possible that an author has a modified opinion since the time of its original composition.

Charles E. Curran
Richard A. McCormick, S.J.

Part One

GENERAL PERSPECTIVE

1. Pastoral Constitution on the Church in the Modern World (1965) nn. 47–52

Marriage and Family in the Modern World

47. The well-being of the individual person and of human and Christian society is intimately linked with the healthy condition of that community produced by marriage and family. Hence Christians and all men who hold this community in high esteem sincerely rejoice in the various ways by which men today find help in fostering this community of love[152] and perfecting its life, and by which spouses and parents are assisted in their lofty calling. Those who rejoice in such aids look for additional benefits from them and labor to bring them about.

Yet the excellence of this institution is not everywhere reflected with equal brilliance. For polygamy, the plague of divorce, so-called free love, and other disfigurements have an obscuring effect. In addition, married love is too often profaned by excessive self-love, the worship of pleasure, and illicit practices against human generation. Moreover, serious disturbances are caused in families by modern economic conditions, by influences at once social and psychological, and by the demands of civil society. Finally, in certain parts of the world problems resulting from population growth are generating concern.

All these situations have produced anxious consciences. Yet, the power and strength of the institution of marriage and family can also be seen in the fact that time and again, despite the difficulties produced, the profound changes in modern society reveal the true character of this institution in one way or another.

Therefore, by presenting certain[153] key points of Church doctrine in a clearer light, this Council wishes to offer guidance and support to those Christians and other men who are trying to keep sacred and to foster the natural dignity of the married state and its superlative value.

The Sanctity of Marriage and the Family

48. The intimate partnership of married life and love has been established by the Creator and qualified by His laws. It is rooted in the conjugal covenant of irrevocable personal consent. Hence, by that human act whereby spouses mutually bestow and accept each other, a relationship arises which by divine will and in the eyes of society too is a lasting one. For the good of the spouses and their offspring as well as of society, the existence of this sacred bond no longer depends on human decisions alone.

For God Himself is the author of matrimony, endowed as it is with various benefits and purposes.[154] All of these have a very decisive bearing on the continuation of the human race, on the personal development and eternal destiny of the individual members of a family, and on the dignity, stability, peace, and prosperity of the family itself and of human society as a whole. By their very nature, the institution of matrimony itself and conjugal love are ordained for the procreation and education of children,[155] and find in them their ultimate crown.

Thus a man and a woman, who by the marriage covenant of conjugal love "are no longer two, but one flesh" (Mt. 19:6), render mutual help and service to each other through an intimate union of their persons and of their actions. Through this union they experience the meaning of their oneness and attain to it with growing perfection day by day. As a mutual gift of two persons, this intimate union, as well as the good of the children, imposes total fidelity on the spouses and argues for an unbreakable oneness between them.[156]

Christ the Lord abundantly blessed this many-faceted love, welling up as it does from the fountain of divine love and structured as it is on the model of His union with the Church. For as God of old made Himself present[157] to His people through a covenant of love and fidelity, so now the Savior of men and the Spouse[158] of the Church comes into the lives of married Christians through the sacrament of matrimony. He abides with them thereafter so that, just as He loved the Church and handed Himself over on her behalf,[159] the spouses may love each other with perpetual fidelity through mutual self-bestowal.

Authentic married love is caught up into divine love and is governed and enriched by Christ's redeeming power and the saving activity of the Church. Thus this love can lead the spouses to God with powerful effect and can aid and strengthen them in the sublime office of being a father or a mother.[160]

For this reason, Christian spouses have a special sacrament by which they are fortified and receive a kind of consecration in the duties and dignity of their state.[161] By virtue of this sacrament, as spouses fulfill their conjugal and family obligations, they are penetrated with the spirit of Christ. This spirit suffuses their whole lives with faith, hope, and charity. Thus they increasingly advance their own perfection, as well as their mutual sanctification, and hence contribute jointly to the glory of God.

As a result, with their parents leading the way by example and family prayer, children and indeed everyone gathered around the family hearth will find a readier path to human maturity, salvation, and holiness. Graced with the dignity and office of fatherhood and motherhood, parents will energetically acquit themselves of a duty which devolves primarily on them,[162] namely education, and especially religious education.

As living members of the family, children contribute in their own way to making their parents holy. For they will respond to the kindness of their parents with sentiments of gratitude, with love and trust. They will stand by them as children should when hardships overtake their parents and old age brings its loneliness. Widowhood, accepted bravely as a continuation of the marriage vocation, will be esteemed by all.[163] Families will share their spiritual riches generously with other families too. Thus the Christian family, which springs from marriage as a reflection of the loving covenant uniting Christ with the Church,[164] and as a participation in that covenant, will manifest to all men the Savior's living presence in the world, and the genuine nature of the Church. This the family will do by the mutual love of the spouses, by their generous fruitfulness, their solidarity and faithfulness, and by the loving way in which all members of the family work together.

Conjugal Love

49. The biblical Word of God several times urges the betrothed and the married to nourish and develop their wedlock by pure conjugal love and undivided affection.[165] Many men of our own age also highly regard true love between husband and wife as it manifests itself in a variety of ways depending on the worthy customs of various peoples and times.

This love is an eminently human[166] one since it is directed from one person to another through an affection of the will. It involves the good of the whole person. Therefore it can enrich the expressions of body and mind with a unique dignity, ennobling these expressions as special ingredients and signs of the friendship distinctive of marriage. This love the Lord has judged worthy of special gifts, healing, perfecting, and exalting gifts of grace and of charity.

Such love, merging the human with the divine, leads the spouses to a free and mutual gift of themselves, a gift proving itself by gentle affection and by deed. Such love pervades the whole of their lives.[167] Indeed, by its generous activity it grows better and grows greater. Therefore it far excels mere erotic inclination, which, selfishly pursued, soon enough fades wretchedly away.

This love is uniquely expressed and perfected through the marital act. The actions within marriage by which the couple are united intimately and chastely are noble and worthy ones. Expressed in a manner which is truly human, these actions signify and promote that mutual self-giving by which spouses enrich each other with a joyful and a thankful will.

Sealed by mutual faithfulness and hallowed above all by Christ's sacrament, this love remains steadfastly true in body and in mind, in bright days or dark. It will never be profaned by adultery or divorce. Firmly established by the Lord, the unity of marriage will radiate from the equal personal dignity of wife and husband, a dignity acknowledged by mutual and total love.

The steady fulfillment of the duties of this Christian vocation demands notable virtue. For this reason, strengthened by grace for holiness of life, the couple will painstakingly cultivate and pray for constancy of love, largeheartedness, and the spirit of sacrifice.

Authentic conjugal love will be more highly prized, and wholesome public opinion created regarding it, if Christian couples give outstanding witness to faithfulness and harmony in that same love, and to their concern for educating their children; also, if they do their part in bringing about the needed cultural, psychological, and social renewal on behalf of marriage and the family.

Especially in the heart of their own families, young people should be aptly and seasonably instructed about the dignity, duty, and expression of married love. Trained thus in the cultivation of chastity, they will be able at a suitable age to enter a marriage of their own after an honorable courtship.

The Fruitfulness of Marriage

50. Marriage and conjugal love are by their nature ordained toward the begetting and educating of children. Children are really the supreme gift of marriage and contribute very substantially to the welfare of their parents. The God Himself who said, "It is not good for man to be alone" (Gen. 2:18) and "who made man from the beginning male and female" (Mt. 19:4), wished to share with man a certain special participation in His own creative work. Thus He blessed male and female, saying: "Increase and multiply" (Gen. 1:28).

Hence, while not making the other purposes of matrimony of less account,[168] the true practice of conjugal love, and the whole meaning of the family life which results from it, have this aim: that the couple be ready with stout hearts to cooperate with the love of the Creator and the Savior, who through them will enlarge and enrich His own family day by day.

Parents should regard as their proper mission the task of transmitting human life and educating those to whom it has been transmitted. They should realize that they are thereby cooperators with the love of God the Creator, and are, so to speak, the interpreters of that love. Thus they will fulfill their task with human and Christian responsibility. With docile reverence toward God, they will come to the right decision by common counsel and effort.

They will thoughtfully take into account both their own welfare and that of their children, those already born and those which may be foreseen. For this accounting they will reckon with both the material and the spiritual conditions of the times as well as of their state in life. Finally, they will consult the interests of the family group, of temporal society, and of the Church herself.

The parents themselves should ultimately make this judgment, in the sight of God. But in their manner of acting, spouses should be aware that they cannot proceed arbitrarily. They must always be governed according to a conscience dutifully conformed to the divine law itself, and should be submissive toward the Church's teaching office, which authentically interprets that law in the light of the gospel. That divine law reveals and protects the integral meaning of conjugal love, and impels it toward a truly human fulfillment.

Thus, trusting in divine Providence and refining the spirit of sacrifice,[169] married Christians glorify the Creator and strive toward fulfillment in Christ when, with a generous human and Christian sense of responsibility, they acquit themselves of the duty to procreate. Among the couples who fulfill their God-given task in this way, those merit special mention who with wise and common deliberation, and with a gallant heart,[170] undertake to bring up suitably even a relatively large family.[171]

Marriage to be sure is not instituted solely for procreation. Rather, its very nature as an unbreakable compact between persons, and the welfare of the children, both demand that the mutual love of the spouses, too, be embodied in a rightly ordered manner, that it grow and ripen. Therefore, marriage persists as a whole manner and communion of life, and maintains its value and indissolubility, even when offspring are lacking—despite, rather often, the very intense desire of the couple.

Harmonizing Conjugal Love with Respect for Human Life

51. This Council realizes that certain modern conditions often keep couples from arranging their married lives harmoniously, and that they find themselves in circumstances where at least temporarily the size of their families should not be increased. As a result, the faithful exercise of love and the full intimacy of their lives are hard to maintain. But where the intimacy of married life is broken off, it is not rare for its faithfulness to be imperiled and its quality of fruitfulness ruined. For then the upbringing of the children and the courage to accept new ones are both endangered.

To these problems there are those who presume to offer dishonorable solutions. Indeed, they do not recoil from the taking of life. But the Church issues the reminder that a true contradiction cannot exist between the divine laws pertaining to the transmission of life and those pertaining to the fostering of authentic conjugal love.

For God, the Lord of life, has conferred on men the surpassing ministry of safeguarding life—a ministry which must be fulfilled in a manner which is worthy of man. Therefore from the moment of its conception life must be guarded with the greatest care, while abortion and infanticide are unspeakable crimes. The sexual characteristics of man and the human faculty of reproduction wonderfully exceed the dispositions of lower forms of life. Hence the acts themselves which are proper to conjugal love and which are exercised in accord with genuine human dignity must be honored with great reverence.

Therefore when there is question of harmonizing conjugal love with the responsible transmission of life, the moral aspect of any procedure does not depend solely on sincere intentions or on an evaluation of motives. It must be determined by objective standards. These, based on the nature of the human person and his acts, preserve the full sense of mutual self-giving and human procreation in the context of true love. Such a goal cannot be achieved unless the virtue of conjugal chastity is sincerely practiced. Relying on these principles, sons of the Church may not undertake methods of regulating procreation which are found blameworthy by the teaching authority of the Church[172] in its unfolding of the divine law.[173]

Everyone should be persuaded that human life and the task of transmitting it are not realities bound up with this world alone. Hence they cannot be measured or perceived only in terms of it, but always have a bearing on the eternal destiny of men.

All Must Promote the Good Estate of Marriage and the Family

52. The family is a kind of school of deeper humanity. But if it is to achieve the full flowering of its life and mission, it needs the kindly communion of minds and the joint deliberation of spouses, as well as the painstaking cooperation of parents in the education of their children. The active presence of the father is highly beneficial to their formation. The children, especially the younger among them, need the care of their mother at home. This domestic role of hers must be safely preserved, though the legitimate social progress of women should not be underrated on that account.

Children should be so educated that as adults they can, with a mature sense of responsibility, follow their vocation, including a religious one, and choose their state of life. If they marry, they can thereby establish their family in favorable moral, social, and economic conditions. Parents or guardians should by prudent advice provide guidance to their young with respect to founding a family, and the young ought to listen gladly. At the same time no pressure, direct or indirect, should be put on the young to make them enter marriage or choose a specific partner.

Thus the family is the foundation of society. In it the various generations come together and help one another to grow wiser and to harmonize personal rights with the other requirements of social life. All those, therefore, who exercise influence over communities and social groups should work efficiently for the welfare of marriage and the family.

Public authority should regard it as a sacred duty to recognize, protect, and promote their authentic nature, to shield public morality, and to favor the prosperity of domestic life. The right of parents to beget and educate their children in the bosom of the family must be safeguarded. Children, too, who unhappily lack the blessing of a family should be protected by prudent legislation and various undertakings, and provided with the help they need.

Redeeming the present time,[174] and distinguishing eternal realities from their changing expressions, Christians should actively promote the values of marriage and the family, both by the example of their own lives and by cooperation with other men of good will. Thus when difficulties arise, Christians will provide, on behalf of family life, those necessities and helps which are suitably modern. To this end, the Christian instincts of the faithful, the upright moral consciences of men, and the wisdom and experience of persons versed in the sacred sciences will have much to contribute.

Those, too, who are skilled in other sciences, notably the medical, biological, social, and psychological, can considerably advance the welfare of marriage and the family, along with peace of conscience, if by pooling their efforts they labor to explain more thoroughly the various conditions favoring a proper regulation of births.

It devolves on priests duly trained about family matters to nurture the vocation of spouses by a variety of pastoral means, by preaching God's Word, by liturgical worship, and by other spiritual aids to conjugal and family life; to sustain them sympathetically and patiently in difficulties, and to make them courageous through love. Thus families which are truly noble will be formed.

Various organizations, especially family associations, should try by their programs of instruction and action to strengthen young people and spouses themselves, particularly those recently wed, and to train them for family, social, and apostolic life.[175]

Finally, let the spouses themselves, made to the image of the living God and enjoying the authentic dignity of persons, be joined to one another[176] in equal affection, harmony of mind, and the work of mutual sanctification. Thus they will follow Christ who is the principle of life.[177] Thus, too, by the joys and sacrifices of their vocation and through their faithful love, married people will become witnesses of the mystery of that love which the Lord revealed to the world by His dying and His rising up to life again.[178]

Notes

152. A notable feature of the Council's teaching on Christian marriage is the repeated emphasis on the centrality of conjugal love. It is important, of course, to recall that Pius XI made much the same emphasis in a less-known passage of his encyclical "Casti Connubii." The present treatment is nonetheless remarkable.

153. It is important to an understanding of the entire section on Christian marriage and family life to realize that the Council intends to discuss "certain" key points only and not to give an exhaustive treatment of all matters in this area. Thus, it clearly intended to leave untouched those aspects of birth control and related themes that are under debate in the special commission set up by Paul VI to study them.

154. Cf. St. Augustine, "De bono coniugii": PL 40, 375–376 and 394; St. Thomas, "Summa Theol.," Suppl. Quaest. 49, Art. 3 ad 1; Decretum pro Armenis: Denz.-Schoen. 1327; Pius XI, encyclical letter "Casti Connubii": AAS 22 (1930), pp. 547–548; Denz.-Schoen. 3703–3714.

155. Here, as elsewhere when the question arises, the Council sedulously avoids the terminology of primary and secondary ends of marriage. It insists on the natural ordering of marriage and conjugal love to procreation but without recourse to such formulations. The same teaching is repeated in Art. 50, and the Council's care to avoid distinguishing "primary" and "secondary" is again evident.

156. Cf. Pius XI, encyclical letter "Casti Connubii": AAS 22 (1930), pp. 546–547; Denz.-Schoen. 3706.

157. Cf. Os. 2; Jer. 3, 6–13; Ezek. 16 and 23; Is. 54.

158. Cf. Mt. 9:15; Mk. 2:19–20; Lk. 5:34–35; Jn. 3:29; cf. also 2 Cor. 11:2; Eph. 5:27; Apoc. 19:7–8; 21:2 and 9.

159. Cf. Eph. 5:25.

160. Cf. Second Vatican Council, dogmatic constitution "Lumen Gentium": AAS 57 (1965), pp. 15–16; 40–41; 47.

161. Pius XI, encyclical letter "Casti Connubii": AAS 22 (1930), p. 583.

162. The Council speaks also of the primary right and duty of parents

with respect to the education of their children in its Declaration on Christian Education.

163. *Cf. 1 Tim. 5:3.*

164. *Cf. Eph. 5:32.*

165. *Cf. Gen. 2:22–24; Pr. 5:15–20; 31:10–31; Tob. 8:4–8; Cant. 1:2–3; 1:16; 4:16; 5:1; 7:8–14; 1 Cor. 7:3–6; Eph. 5:25–33.*

166. The emphasis on conjugal love necessarily involves a strong personalist tone in this section of the Constitution and thus brings once more to the fore a major theme of the entire document.

167. *Cf. Pius XI, encyclical letter "Casti Connubii": AAS (1930), p. 547 and 548; Denz.-Schoen. 3707.*

168. The Commission charged with drafting this text made every effort to avoid any appearance of wishing to settle questions concerning a hierarchy of the "ends" of marriage. Thus, the passage includes a beautiful reference to children as "the supreme gift of marriage," but this sentence makes it clear that the present text cannot be read as a judgment on the relative importance or primacy of ends. Since the clause has been phrased with so much care, it may be useful to cite the Latin: "non posthabitis ceteris matrimonii finibus."

169. *Cf. 1 Cor. 7:5.*

170. The following reference to a text of Pius XII could be confirmed by citing similar statements from John XXIII's addresses on a number of occasions.

171. *Cf. Pius XII, Address "Tra le visite," Jan. 20, 1958: AAS 50 (1958), p. 91.*

172. Widely published reports indicated that this passage and the official footnote appended to it were the subject of considerable debate within the drafting commission in the last days of the Council's fourth session. It seems certain that Pope Paul submitted a recommendation that the text take note explicitly of statements by his predecessors, Pius XI and Pius XII, on birth control. It is evident, however, that the reference in the present footnote in no way alters the state of debate that had existed in the Church since Paul VI's own announcement of June 23, 1964, of his creation of a commission to study the questions in dispute. The Council states clearly that, with matters standing thus, it has no intention of proposing concrete solutions here.

173. *Cf. Pius XI, encyclical letter "Casti Connubii": AAS 22 (1930), Denz-Schoen., 3716–3718; Pius XII, Allocutio Conventui Unionis Italicae Inter Obstetrices, Oct. 29, 1951: AAS 43 (1951), pp. 835–854; Paul VI, address to a group of cardinals, June 23, 1964: AAS 56 (1964), pp. 581–589. Certain questions which need further and more careful investigation have been handed over, at the command of the Supreme Pontiff, to a commission*

for the study of population, family, and births, in order that, after it fulfills its function, the Supreme Pontiff may pass judgment. With the doctrine of the magisterium in this state, this holy Synod does not intend to propose immediately concrete solutions. [In the Latin text this is footnote 14 of Chap. I, in Part 2 of the document.—Ed.]

174. *Cf. Eph. 5:16; Col. 4:5.*

175. Examples of such organizations are the Christian Family Movement and the various types of Cana and Pre-Cana Conference programs conducted in the United States.

176. *Cf. Sacramentarium Gregorianum: PL 78, 262.*

177. *Cf. Rom. 5:15 and 18; 6:5–11; Gal. 2:20.*

178. *Cf. Eph. 5:25–27.*

Humanae Vitae (1968) nn. 7-12

Paul VI

A TOTAL VISION OF MAN

7. The question of the birth of children, like every other question which touches human life, is too large to be resolved by limited criteria, such as are provided by biology, psychology, demography or sociology. It is the whole man and the whole complex of his responsibilities that must be considered, not only what is natural and limited to this earth, but also what is supernatural and eternal. And since in the attempt to justify artificial methods of birth control many appeal to the demands of married love or of "responsible parenthood," these two important realities of married life must be accurately defined and analyzed. This is what We mean to do, with special reference to what the Second Vatican Council taught with the highest authority in its Pastoral Constitution *Gaudium et spes.*

MARRIAGE IS A SACRAMENT

8. Married love particularly reveals its true nature and nobility when we realize that it derives from God and finds its supreme origin in him who "is Love,"[6] the Father "from whom every family in heaven and on earth is named".[7]

Marriage, then, is far from being the effect of chance or the result of the blind evolution of natural forces. It is in reality the wise and provident institution of God the Creator, whose purpose was to establish in man his loving design. As a consequence, husband and wife, through that mutual gift of themselves, which is specific and

17

exclusive to them alone, seek to develop that kind of personal union in which they complement one another in order to co-operate with God in the generation and education of new lives.

Furthermore, the marriage of those who have been baptized is invested with the dignity of a sacramental sign of grace, for it represents the union of Christ and his Church.

MARRIED LOVE

9. In the light of these facts the characteristic features and exigencies of married love are clearly indicated, and it is of the highest importance to evaluate them exactly.

This love is above all fully *human,* a compound of sense and spirit. It is not, then, merely a question of natural instinct or emotional drive. It is also, and above all, an act of the free will, whose dynamism ensures that not only does it endure through the joys and sorrows of daily life, but also that it grows, so that husband and wife become in a way one heart and one soul, and together attain their human fulfilment.

Then it is a love which is *total*—that very special form of personal friendship in which husband and wife generously share everything, allowing no unreasonable exceptions or thinking just of their own interests. Whoever really loves his partner loves not only for what he receives, but loves that partner for her own sake, content to be able to enrich the other with the gift of himself.

Again, married love is *faithful* and *exclusive* of all others, and this until death. This is how husband and wife understand it on the day on which, fully aware of what they were doing, they freely vowed themselves to one another in marriage. Though this fidelity of husband and wife sometimes presents difficulties, no one can assert that it is impossible, for it is always honourable and worthy of the highest esteem. The example of so many married persons down through the centuries shows not only that fidelity is conatural to marriage but also that it is the source of profound and enduring happiness.

And finally this love is *creative of life,* for it is not exhausted by the loving interchange of husband and wife, but also contrives to go beyond this to bring new life into being. "Marriage and married love are by their character ordained to the procreation and bringing up of children. Children are the outstanding gift of marriage, and contribute in the highest degree to the parents' welfare."[8]

RESPONSIBLE PARENTHOOD

10. Married love, therefore, requires of husband and wife the full awareness of their obligations in the matter of responsible parenthood, which today, rightly enough, is much insisted upon, but which, at the same time, should be rightly understood. Hence, this must be studied in the light of the various inter-related arguments which are its justification.

If first we consider it in relation to the biological processes involved, responsible parenthood is to be understood as the knowledge and observance of their specific functions. Human intelligence discovers in the faculty of procreating life, the biological laws which involve human personality.[9]

If, on the other hand, we examine the innate drives and emotions of man, responsible parenthood expresses the domination which reason and will must exert over them.

But if we then attend to relevant physical, economic, psychological and social conditions, those are considered to exercise responsible parenthood who prudently and generously decide to have a large family, or who, for serious reasons and with due respect to the moral law, choose to have no more children for the time being or even for an indeterminate period.

Responsible parenthood, moreover, in the terms in which we use the phrase, retains a further and deeper significance of paramount importance which refers to the objective moral order instituted by God,—the order of which a right conscience is the true interpreter. As a consequence the commitment to responsible parenthood requires that husband and wife, keeping a right order of priorities, recognize their own duties towards God, themselves, their families and human society.

From this it follows that they are not free to do as they like in the service of transmitting life, on the supposition that it is lawful for them to decide independently of other considerations what is the right course to follow. On the contrary, they are bound to ensure that what they do corresponds to the will of God the Creator. The very nature of marriage and its use makes this clear, while the constant teaching of the Church affirms it.[10]

RESPECT FOR THE NATURE AND PURPOSE OF THE MARRIAGE ACT

11. The sexual activity, in which husband and wife are intimately and chastely united with one another, through which human life is transmitted, is, as the recent Council recalled, "honourable and good."[11] It does not, moreover, cease to be legitimate even when, for reasons independent of their will, it is foreseen to be infertile. For its natural adaptation to the expression and strengthening of the union of husband and wife is not thereby suppressed. The facts are, as experience shows, that new life is not the result of each and every act of sexual intercourse. God has wisely ordered the laws of nature and the incidence of fertility in such a way that successive births are already naturally spaced through the inherent operation of these laws. The Church, nevertheless, in urging men to the observance of the precepts of the natural law, which it interprets by its constant doctrine, teaches as absolutely required that *in any use whatever of marriage* there must be no impairment of its natural capacity to procreate human life.[12]

TEACHING IN HARMONY WITH HUMAN REASON

12. This particular doctrine, often expounded by the Magisterium of the Church, is based on the inseparable connection, established by God, which man on his own initiative may not break, between the unitive significance and the procreative significance which are both inherent to the marriage act.

The reason is that the marriage act, because of its fundamental structure, while it unites husband and wife in the closest intimacy, also brings into operation laws written into the actual nature of man and of woman for the generation of new life. And if each of these essential qualities, the unitive and the procreative, is preserved, the use of marriage fully retains its sense of true mutual love and its ordination to the supreme responsiblity of parenthood to which man is called. We believe that our contemporaries are particularly capable of seeing that this teaching is in harmony with human reason.

Notes

7. Cf. Eph. 3:15.
8. Cf. II Vat. Council, Pastoral const. *Gaudium et Spes,* No. 50.
9. Cf. St. Thomas, *Summa Theologica,* I–II, q. 94, art. 2.
10. Cf. Pastoral Const. *Gaudium et Spes,* nos. 50, 51.
11. *Ibid.,* no. 49.
12. Cf. Pius XI, encyc. *Casti Connubii,* in AAS XXII (1930), p. 560; Pius XII, in AAS XLIII (1951), p. 843.

2. A Theory of Sexual Ethics for Concerned Christians

André Guindon, O.M.I.

This chapter first appeared in *The Sexual Creators* in 1986.

Four basic elements make up the theory of sexual ethics for concerned Christians propounded in this chapter. Each one of them examines a fundamental question which a coherent theory of sexual ethics must discuss. The first question deals with sexual *anthropology:* How is a virtuous sexual self structured? The second deals with sexual *activity:* How is virtuous sexual practice structured? The third deals with moral *efficiency:* How is a virtuous sexual deed begotten? The fourth deals with sexual *historicity:* How is a virtuous sexual deed experienced by social human beings? In other words, the theory must explain what a sexually successful person looks like; what kind of sexual activity is conducive to such a goal; what sort of moral power is needed for this activity to produce its fruits; under what conditions of responsibility do these moral fruits ripen. The first two questions address the issue of ontological structures, that of sexual selfhood and that of sexual activity. The third question attends to the very foundation of moral normativity. The fourth question raises the issue of contextuality and, therefore, of moral responsibility.

The following claims are made concerning the four components of the theory. First, each of those components manifests what has been called, in the Catholic tradition, its "natural law." The discussion of each component starts, therefore, with an analysis of sexual reality as human reason is able to perceive it. Secondly, each of the answers given to the four basic questions is influenced by and, in turn, influences the author's Christian Posture. In this sense, the theory is theological and speaks to the Christian project as such even though a non-Christian may very well (because of the first claim) find it acceptable on its own merits. The discussion of each component ends, therefore, with an examination of the Christian perspectives which the sexual experience is liable to open.[1] Thirdly, the responses form a fourfold criterion for moral decision-making concerning sexual dilemmas and for assessing the moral quality of our sexual life. This third claim will be examined in the fourth chapter after a criticism of dualistic interpretations of fecundity in chapter three.

1. INTEGRATION OF SENSUALITY AND TENDERNESS

Before venturing any kind of ethical statement on human sexuality, one must have at least a vague notion of the essential or formal features of a successful sexual self. How is anyone going to decide which model of sexual behaviour is, in the long run, humanizing if one does not know how a humanized sexual person is structured?[2] The basic choice to be made in this regard is, as the history of sexual ethics clearly manifests, between a dualistic interpretation and a unitive or wholistic view of sexual selfhood.

The initial and most decisive option is linked with the problematic of the structure of human "beinghood." Whatever vocabulary or philosophy is utilized to argue this point, there is widespread agreement to conceptualize human beinghood as "composed" of two elements: matter-form, body-soul, physical-cognitive, body-mind, organic-symbolic, and so forth. For the purpose of the present overview, the vocabulary of body and spirit will be retained.

The problematic raised by the dual nature of human beinghood lies less, it seems to me, with acknowledging the existence of this long-celebrated duality of sorts than with conceiving its mode of existence. There are various and quite opposite ways of doing so. At one end of the spectrum, dualistic currents of thought have the tendency to view two separate and separable substances,[3] mysteriously glued together for the time of our earthly pilgrimage. Depending on one's life options and orientations, ascendancy is generally attributed to one of the two substances. The dominant substance becomes the essential self, the most valuable "part," that which, even at the expense of the expendable portion of the composite, we must care for and bring to its fulfillment. It is, perhaps, due to the fact that Descartes is so representative of this dualism of "body thing" and "acosmic spirit," that French contemporary philosophers have instituted an ongoing criticism of dualistic anthropology and have argued quite convincingly against a tandem model of the human self.[4]

At the other end of the spectrum, wholistic views explain, in one way or another, that corporality and spirituality designate only two complementary aspects of one human reality; that they never exist as human, one without the other; that they are mutually pervasive, forming one, indivisible, whole, human person. As long as we subsist, we are body as well as spirit. If, as Blaise Pascal claims, we do no better acting bestially than we do acting angelically, it is because a human spiritless body would be nothing more than a corpse while a human bodiless spirit would have no means of knowing and of doing anything in this world of ours.

Few people stand at one or the other pole of the spectrum. Most of us are somewhere in between, with a penchant to indulge either in dualistic thinking or in unitive thinking. We may even have a tendency to shift from one pole to the other as we pass from one issue to the next. One should not be astonished to find, therefore, that many who theoretically stand for a wholistic view of the human person yield to dualistic thinking and language in the concrete realm of human sexual realities. Because moralists, until recently, identified sexuality with the genitals and their functions, sexuality is regarded by the majority of people as a mere bodily element, subject (though with difficulty) to the control of the "spiritual faculties."

Since we have finally recognized that the human self necessarily exists as male or female, is kneaded of chromosomal, hormonal, and gonadal ingredients which affect every particle of the self, develops wholesomely through a psycho-sexual process, maintains with the cosmos, with others, and with God relationships which are marked by sexuality, etc., the proof has been established beyond all possible doubt that whole persons, not bodies, are sexed and sexual.[5] This wholistic view is not an entirely new phenomenon caused by "Freudian pansexualism." As Philippe Ariès remarks, in Saint Theresa's mysticism, for instance, or, again, in baroque art, spirit and sexuality are never separated. The new phenomenon is that, today, we are conscious of it while they were not.[6]

In a wholistic view of selfhood, human sexuality necessarily comprises, like the being it qualifies, two aspects. They have been called the affectionate and the sensual currents,[7] affection and desire,[8] tenderness and eroticism,[9] the tender and the daimonic,[10] love and desire.[11] I intend to use the terms tenderness and sensuality. The sensual aspect is linked with this facet of the self called body. Body, here, is not meant as a mere organic system, as an object separated from personal activity. It refers to the body as flesh, as having an affective life, as the originator of erotic movements, of sensations, of desires, of pleasures, and so forth. The tender aspect is linked with this side of the self called spirit, creator of significance or of symbols and originator of movements from within such as love, attention, care, delight, amazement, and other meaningful sentiments.

Since sensuality and tenderness, like body and spirit, never exist separately in a human being,[12] they live in a tensional and dynamic unity. The moral task, on this level of being, consists essentially in sensualizing tenderness, as befits an em(=in)-bodied spirit. Thus, intentionality is incarnated and the word becomes flesh. Correspondingly, sensuality becomes tender, as is proper to an enspirited body. Corporeity expresses what is human. The flesh becomes a human word. As the sexual virtue accomplishes its integrative work, sensuality and tenderness blend more and more into one another. They energize one another, forming integrated sexual selves whose spirits are enfleshed, perfectly at home in their sexual bodies, and whose bodies are spiritualized, expressive of their sexual selves' genuine identity. This sexual virtue was called "chastity" by the theological wholistic tradition led by Thomas Aquinas. Chastity is a properly moral category which evokes the idea of integrity. For contemporary ears, this virtue is probably best referred to as sexual integration.

In a wholistic perspective, sexual *dis*integration represents, then, a failure of tenderness and of sensuality to merge into an integrated human wholeness. This occurs in two basic ways which are well documented in the history of dualistic theories and practices. One consists in giving sensuality priority. Fun moralities, more technically called hedonistic ethics, are structured on this corporealist ideology. The other failure occurs when tenderness is favoured at the expense of sensuality. Shame moralities and, specifically in Christianity, "purity ethics," advocating will-power or prayer control, are built on this spiritualist interpretation.[13]

Both those ethical formulations, primarily the latter, have always lived and keep on living in the Christian Churches. "Sex is dirty, save it for someone you love" has often been the enigmatic message Christians have heard from sexually confused (or inhibited) Christian teachers. Yet, we must also acknowledge the fact that when, in the course of history, the dualistic premises of such ethical positions were clearly articulated in certain circles, mainstream Christianity took its distance from such systems and looked upon them as sects. Why? Surely not because all Christians would necessarily disagree on philosophical grounds as such. Christian faith is not a philosophy, but an assent and a commitment to the God of Jesus the Christ. If Christianity cannot accommodate itself to sexual ethics structured on a well-defined dualistic sexual anthropology, it is because it knows instinctively, with an instinct which is inspired by the Holy Spirit, that in such ethics the faith experience of God is distorted. The *sensus fidelium,* which in the course of history has constantly manifested the Christian instinct on this point, is correct. To regard either tenderness or sensuality as evil, or even as less good, and to construct a theory of sexual ethics which despises either aspect militates against Christian faith in a God whose parenthood is benevolent and from whom nothing despicable proceeds.[14]

Judeo-Christian faith experiences God as the loving, caring, and merciful Father, the giver and protector of human life.[15] He is not, as in juridically inspired ethics where God and the Law are mistaken one for the other, a deity whose demands are infinite and, therefore, never satisfied. The God of Jesus affirms the goodness of finite, incarnated human existence.[16] Has He not created sexual, mutually attracted persons, and seen that "it was very good" (*Gn* 1:31)? Is it not true that the admirable and God-like nudity[17] of those who live in God's friendship is freed from all culpability (*Gn* 2:25)? The paradisiac myth expresses the harmony of a well-integrated humanity, at peace with its own truth, a truth reflecting that of its Creator. The shameful fig leaf cover-up operation (*Gn* 3:7–8 and 20–21), on the contrary, is clearly part and parcel of the broken-down world of sin, of a self-withdrawal syndrome. Because of who the Creator is, the sensuous flesh is linked with the condition of creature, not with that of sinner. The sinful condition is characterized, on the contrary, by a diminished and guilty sexuality.[18]

Sinless, Jesus, like the first Adam before the Fall, never manifests shame when confronted with sexual facts or gestures. Nor does he ever participate in the sexually insecure and culpabilizing censorship of sexual delinquents. Risen from the dead, he becomes in his glorified body the token of the resurrection of our own flesh endowed with incorruptibility and immortality (*Rm* 1:4; 6:4–5; *1 Co* 15:54; *Ph* 3:21). With the promise of eternal life (*Rm* 8:11), our own corporality must let itself be pervaded and transformed by the Spirit so as to become, in the risen Lord, a *soma pneumaticon,* a spiritualized body (*1 Co* 15:44–49). If not, body and soul will perish. Nothing will remain but a disintegrated and broken-down self (*Mt* 10:28). This integrative process is already at work in our earthly body which, having received the first-fruits of the Spirit (*Rm* 8:23), is already the temple of the Spirit (*1 Co* 6:19–20), the locus where the image of the first-born Son is gradually formed (*Rm* 8:29). The children of God can live their corporality with thanksgiving (*1 Tm* 4:1–5) since they are integrally redeemed (*Rm* 8:23), a living host truly pleasing to God (*Rm* 12:1).

Christian faith refuses the ambivalence of the deity confessed by Gnostic dualisms. The One revealed through the Jesus-event is not the God whom Maurice Bellet rightly calls perverse, a deity whose parenthood would be both the cruel principle of a damned sexual flesh and the benevolent generatrix of a pure, spiritual soul.[19] To experience human sexuality as shameful, following a body-negating ethics, is an obstacle to the existential knowledge of "God, the Father all-mighty, Creator of heaven and earth."

In his autobiographical novel, *A Portrait of the Artist as a Young Man,* James Joyce captures well the birth of the "perverse God" in the anxious sexual questioning of his sixteenth year. After a

college retreat in which each sermon ends with morbid exposures of
THE SIN, "impurity," Stephen Dedalus reflects on his sexual
experience:

> But does that part of the body understand or what? The
> serpent, the most subtle beast of the field. It must under-
> stand when it desires in one instant and then prolongs its
> own desire instant after instant, sinfully. It feels and under-
> stands and desires. What a horrible thing! *Who made it to
> be like that,* a bestial part of the body able to understand
> bestially and desire bestially?[20]

Yes, the sexual experience does raise the question of God. Why
would any healthy human being want to believe in a God who created her or him with a bestial part?[21]

2. LANGUAGE OF INTIMACY

To state that the fully energized sexual self is one in which
sensuality and tenderness are harmoniously integrated is to take a
decisive stance for a wholistic view in sexual anthropology. How this
integration occurs, however, is still left unexplained. In other words,
an ethical model is still needed for understanding sexual *practice.*
How are we to conceive a sexual activity which is formative and
expressive of our fundamental way of existing as both, and inseparably, sensuous and tender? Based on certain cues which point in the
direction of a close rapport between sexual behaviour and a child's
learning of his native language,[22] I have proposed the use of a language model. The idea is gaining ground in the ethical as well as in
the sexological literature.[23]

Human sexuality is irreducible to a mere physiological or psychological or social capacity. Sex, as a consequence, is not adequately understood merely in terms of orgasms or, for that matter,
of personal or social interactions. As the very condition of our be-
ing-in-the-world as enfleshed spirits, sexuality affects our whole personality and is symbolic of it.[24] Pope John Paul II is right when he
states that "sexuality [. . .] is by no means something purely biologi-

cal, but concerns the innermost being (*nucleum intimum*) of the human person as such."[25] Sexuality is an ontological reality, a word (*logos*) of being (*onto*).[26] Of itself, it speaks of who we are. Philosopher Edmond Barbotin calls it "the language of being itself."[27] How, indeed, will a carrier of an enfleshed meaning express his or her unutterable experience of personal uniqueness to others without the sensually tender connotations of sexual expression? Any other form of language is inadequate to express human selfhood.

When gestural language[28] is used to express ourselves not about things, but about our intimate selves, about our experience of tender-sensuous existence, we are speaking the sexual language. Of itself, human sexual communication tends towards the establishment of a relationship based on the totality of who we are. This is what we call intimacy.[29] To experience and live human sexuality under the sign of usefulness (*e.g.,* for producing babies) or of pleasurableness (*e.g.,* for having fun) is a betrayal of its very nature. Of the order of *being* and not of *having,* sexuality's activities are gratuitous. Sexual activity finds in itself, in the truthful communication of intimate selves, its very meaning.

Like all other forms of human communication, the sexual language has a wide variety of expressions, tonalities, emotions and sentiments at its disposal. Do we seem to be talking exclusively about things? We seldom do so without letting out a few words about our selves. In fact, is it not when we are willing to surrender something of our selves to others that what we are saying about things is recognized by those who listen as "truly true?" True human words call on the other to share something with the one who speaks. Nor have human words reached their goal when they are merely spoken. They are yet in need of a receiver, that is to say of a person who listens carefully, who is trusting and consenting. The reception of the human word and the quality of this reception depend, to a great extent, on whether or not the receiver has been reached in his or her identity. This can never be realized so integrally as in the sexual language where words of intimate selfhood are spoken, words which convey the other in an intimate dialogue. Sexual modes of behaviour are subject to moral qualification insofar as they are "gestures," as they convey intimate meaning from one person to another.

Does the fact of granting that sexual acts are open to different personal meanings lead us into some whimsical "personalism" or "situationism" in which human actions would have no internal laws of their own independently of the agent's motivations? The very idea of sexuality as language should be enough to discard this fear of subjectivism voiced so readily against the emerging paradigm by code moralists. They themselves rely on legislation to secure a sacrosanct order which they take to be "objectivity." They do not seem to reflect that legislators are *subjects,* enunciating what *they* perceive or will to be the right thing to do. Their being "empowered" to enounce certain rules of social conduct does not give their own interpretation more "objectivity" than anyone else's interpretation. It merely confers upon this interpretation an authority which, given the conditions for its legitimate exercise, is functional for the common good. Properly speaking, "objectivity" can only be produced by the "object." The object, in the domain we are concerned about, is the sexual language, the language of intimacy which is being spoken by human persons.

This object, the sexual language, is, like any other human language, used by a subject. Considered in its relation to its user, it constitutes behaviour. This behaviour, as we have seen, is that of a subject who fills it with different emotions, who speaks it more or less fluently and gracefully, who adapts it to fit the situation, who invites others to share their own selves intimately, and so forth. However, if this language, more than any other language, is spoken with subjectivity, like all other languages it also has an objectivity of its own. Considered in its relation to the community of its users, it is a cultural reality with a structure of its own. Regardless of its user, it has a grammar, it represents an organized system. Not to comply with the objective rules of a language is to condemn oneself not to be understood or, at least, to be misunderstood. "Objects" which are not handled in accord with their internal law cannot be expected to produce what they are meant to produce.

If, therefore, an individual uses human sexuality in such a fashion that nothing significant is conveyed, one way or other, to someone else, then this person uses the sexual language in violation of its true relational nature. We could call this vice "sexual solipsism."[30]

Instead of becoming a human gesture, namely the embodiment of one's intention to meet and learn to know someone else, the carnal word of one's desire to share something significant with this other person, sexual behaviour is degraded to the unhuman status of a raw sensuous pulsion, of a mere movement *in* one's body. Far from establishing a proximity between two persons, from being a mutual word of presence, from creating the openness of one person to another, the sexual caress becomes a way of appropriating another's body and of transforming the other into a mere object of desire. Men and women with their lovable uniqueness, their preferences and dislikes, their joys and sorrows, their daring creativity and their doubts, do not emerge from mere sexual games.

The call to share one's intimate life with others may, on the contrary, be totally repressed. Repressed persons may feel a longing for an absent someone, but they are unable to respond. By getting rid of sensuality, they have gotten rid of the only human vehicle of tenderness.

For Christians, a language model is not the only possible way of understanding human sexual practice. Montreal theologian Guy Durand, for instance, suggests an "encounter" model which proves most rewarding.[31] Whichever model is put forward, though, its theological plausibility should be established in the light of God's self-revealed personhood and intimate communication as these are grasped in the faith experience of the Christian community.

When *Genesis* 1:27 speaks about human beings as the image of God, it evokes their sexual make-up:

God created man [*adam:* human being] in the image of himself,
in the image of God he created him
male [*ish*] and female [*ishshah*] he created them.[32]

In the ninth-century B.C. Yahwist narrative of creation, indications similar to those spelled out more theoretically in the later fifth-century B.C. Priestly source, quoted above, are already found. Woman is not presented, like other creatures, as man's property (*Gn* 2:19–20). She is Adam's counterpart (2:18, 20), the one who faces or confronts him, the one in whom man recognizes bone of his bones and flesh from his flesh (2:23).[33] The sexual split (*sexus*) is that whereby the relational nature of human selfhood and interaction is symbolized.

Neither male nor female, human nature in each one of us is, in its very sexual structure, relational. Only by interpersonal communion are women and men humanized. This is the means by which they carve in themselves the image of God. Guy Durand remarks appropriately that "a human being is relational, he is 'for the other' as he is 'by the other.' In this, he is God's image: human selfhood in 'relation' as God himself is pure 'relationality.' "[34] Relational sexuality reflects and teaches the relational personhood and activity of the Triune God, a God who generates the Word in Love and through the Word creates all things which have life in Him (*Gn* 1: "God said: . . ."; *Jn* 1:1–14). The profound truth of all creation is the Word (*Col* 1:15–16). Those in whom the creative Word dwells are empowered to speak a sexual language whose life-serving function far surpasses their wildest human expectations. The speechless God once again becomes Word through the sexual stories of their own lives. Otherwise, God would remain the unreachable Other, characterized by a transcendence which would imply pure and insurmountable "strangeness."

The drama which is described in *Genesis* 3 and the following chapters is the story of the failure of the language of intimacy to express the truth of the human condition. Refusing to accept that the Word comes from God, the right relationship between Yahweh and his creature is distorted (*Gn* 3:1–7). When God comes "walking in the garden in the cool of the day" for a moment of intimacy with his creatures, Adam and Eve hide among the trees (*Gn* 3:8) Truthful relationships have broken down. This human alienation from God (*Gn* 3:23–24) has repercussions on the whole of their relational life: Adam and Eve start accusing each other (*Gn* 3:12–13); their relation to their world loses much of its former smoothness (*Gn* 3:14–19); their children are at each others' throats (*Gn* 4); their descendants lose the social ability to communicate well with each other (*Gn* 11:1–9). Like the Story of creation and redemption, the Story of sin also speaks, in a sad way, of intimate human communications.

Jesus lays claim to the creation narrative on relational humanity (*Gn* 1:27 and 2:24 in *Mt* 19:4–5). The old perspectives are even interpreted by him in their widest sense, for Jesus makes it clear that "when people rise from the dead, they neither marry nor are given in marriage" (*Mt* 22:30). While he assumes integrally the human condition—and therefore the sexual condition—Jesus himself does not seem to have been married during his earthly existence. Furthermore, he probably calls some "who can accept it" to a charismatic celibacy for the sake of the Kingdom (*Mt* 19:3–12; *Lk* 18:29–30). The sexual condition which no one is without and which makes of us relational beings does not aim essentially at the establishment of a conjugal bond. It calls for interpersonal communication.[35]

In Jesus, the full significance of the Covenant, celebrated throughout Biblical times in terms of a sexual bond, becomes manifest. We are gratified with a sexuality which is eternally linked with our quest of "blissful perfection"[36] because sex is that whereby we share our intimate life with others and, by the same token, learn to recognize the face of a God who is relational. To experience sexuality as "private property" and sexual virtue as a power of self-refusal and of uninvolvement in intimate relationships would be to mold in one's being an image of a God who is so transcendent that he is unrelated to us, the Totally Separated Other. Through their sexuality, Christians ought to live, on the contrary, the enlightening experience of a God whose Word became flesh so that the flesh might resume its dialogue with Him in the communion of all the saints. I leave it to the reader to judge whether or not the language model makes good Christian sense, whether or not it is in tune with his or her Christian instinct.

3. CREATIVE LOVE

As a generator of intimate interpersonal relationships, human sexuality opens up a space for personal freedom to enhance the personality of others through love and, indivisibly, to be created anew by love.[37] Well spoken, the sexual language does not aim exclusively at this or that quality of another person's body or mind. To be attracted to a person for her or his physical features, power-position, sharp wits, or cooking aptitudes is to *like* this person functionally, to like this person for my own pleasure or usefulness, to covet what he or she can bring me. Since the qualities a person *has* never express adequately who this person *is,* to be attracted by them is not to be attracted to a person for whom this person is. The ensuing interaction would not be the language of being itself.

This is not to say that interrelating with others in a merely "liking" fashion is necessarily evil. We meet some people exclusively on the tennis court or on the ski slopes because we enjoy playing tennis or skiing with them. We visit our dentist because of her skill at repairing our teeth. We follow a professor's lectures because he can teach us something. We watch a ballet company for the aesthetical enjoyment the dancers provide us. Nothing more may and need be involved in these and similar human transactions. But as long as they remain of this nature, the rapport between human beings is not properly sexual. They become humanly sexual when some degree of intimacy exists, when sharing is involved at the level of the person's whole being.

The love of friendship, the primary sense of love according to Aquinas,[38] effectively establishes this kind of wholistic bond since its object is the other's own good. Aristotle describes this "friendly feeling towards any one" as "wishing for him what you believe to be good things, not for your own sake but for his, and being inclined, so far as you can, to bring this thing about."[39] Awakened by the attraction of the good, by being as alluring, love is always stimulated by what, rightly or wrongly, it perceives the other's qualities to be. Since it cannot be really *satis-fied* (full-filled) with pretense and illusions, love aims, beyond appearances, at the whole reality of the other's being.

Mere infatuation, writes Thomas Tyrrell, "is disrespectful because it falsifies the existence of the beloved."[40] Real love, on the contrary, is, following Beverly Harrison's expression, "the power to act-each-other-into-well-being."[41] Because love of friendship avoids transforming reality into illusion, it reverently accepts the other in his or her weakness and vulnerability as well as in his or her strength. But real love, as Aristotle points out in the text quoted above, also seeks to create in the other what is still longing to be: the fullness of life.

Love is the utopia of the sexual encounter where the intimate well-being of each person is strengthened in the very act which offers to share it gratuitously with another. As Albert Donval remarks, love exerts over all other meanings given to human sexual transactions (organic relief, psychic relaxation, ecstatic pleasure, reproduction of the species, etc.) a critical function: none of them can make an absolute claim on sexuality at the expense of love.[42] Love is the afflatus which harmonizes the multiple sexual values, from pleasure to fertility, with the ever renewed modulations of the amorous poem of our lives.

It follows that, from an ethical point of view, sexual perversion cannot consist in specific modes of behaviour (such as incest, bestiality, or necrophilia) defined in their materiality. "To pervert" means to cause to turn from what is good to what is evil, to overturn, to distort, to corrupt. If the sexual language is meant, basically, to convey love in ways which are specifically human, to corrupt it is obviously to use it for suppurating hatred, the corrosion of love. An ethicist can only agree with Robert J. Stoller's title: *Perversion: the Erotic Form of Hatred.*[43] All forms of sexual exploitation, from violent outbursts, like rape, to disguised manifestations in attitudes of dominance and censorship are, morally speaking, sexual perversions.

Christian theology carries this analysis still further. Breaching the communion of love is that whereby a *sin* properly so called is distinguished from a moral fault, that is to say, a lack, by defect or excess, of "proper measure" in reference to the objective of the act.[44] To distort the language of loving intimacy into a spurious discourse, a discourse made with the intention of abusing someone, of using someone in ways which lead him or her astray from the paths of self-fulfillment, goes directly against man's Godlike reality.[45] Lacking the generosity of love, such a sexual language is an ugly corruption of the Father's language saying Love in his Word made flesh. This is, in point of fact, a perversion of the central Christian mystery.[46]

Here again, therefore, the stakes are high for Christians who cannot doubt that the radical meaning of human sexuality is to create loving bonds. As for every other human activity, love is ultimately normative for sexual practices.

> For God's Word—proclaims the second Vatican Council
> —,through whom all things were made, was Himself made
> flesh and dwelt on the earth of men. [. . .] He Himself
> revealed to us that "God is love" (*1 Jn* 4:8). At the same
> time He taught us that the new command of love was the
> basic law of human perfection and hence of the world's
> transformation.[47]

Pregnant with love's generosity, human sexuality discloses, for those who have the experience of truly being cared for or of actively caring for another, the fecundity of a God who *is* love.[48] Saint Anselm of Canterbury drew our attention to the fact that the Holy Spirit is the *cry of love* uttered by the Father and the Son before the immensity of the infinite plenitude of God. It is this Love which also makes our God burst into the creation of women and men so that He may adopt them in his first-born Son as his children, children of light and of freedom.

Moved by the experience of a loving God, the author of the oldest narrative of creation represents sexuality as a function of loving reciprocity. Lived, on the contrary, as a closing in on oneself, sexuality manifests the broken-down world of sin. To mutual self-disclosure and admiring acceptance (*Gn* 2:23–25) the Yahwist Tradition opposes self-refusal, symbolized by the attempt to hide in the shameful awareness of one's vulnerable nakedness (*Gn* 3:8–11). The lack of generosity in sexual practice explains, thereafter, Onan's condemnation because his sexual services to Thamar are voluntarily short-circuited so that Judah's heritage will pass into his own lineage (*Gn* 38),[49] as well as the Biblical interdiction of incest inasmuch as the latter signifies the refusal of the gift of one's children to society (*Lv* 18:10 and 17: see *Gn* 2:24).

To object that, with the advent of Jesus of Nazareth, "real love," the one which builds Christian fellowship, is *agape,* a totally "spiritual" love, and not *eros* or sexual love, is to commit theology to dualistic thinking.[50] Moreover, this view is also totally out of character with Jesus of Nazareth's own life style. His celibacy never strikes one as being an asexual condition which would facilitate the expression of disembodied divine love. Towards adulterers, prostitutes, and all the others who are pronounced contagious and outcasts by the laws of purity, his attitude manifests a Son of God who lives the agape of the covenant in our carnal condition. Besides, how would authentic love be expressed between human beings without the carnal accents of eros?[51] In Jesus, divine love has taken this law of incarnation upon itself. More religious than true believers in a God who is Love, the righteous Jews in Jesus' surroundings are scandalized when the Father's Witness sits down with those who are poorly loved, drinks and eats with them, listens to them, understands them, accepts them for who they are.[52] In the intimacy of Jesus of Nazareth, those who are in need rediscover their full truth and learn anew to love themselves and to love others as themselves "for the love of God."

These sayings and gestures of Jesus set generous sexuality back on its right course, that of the Kingdom where eternal life is celebrated in a communion of love. There can be no doubt left in the minds of Christians that the ultimate intent of the sexual language is to say love. Its primary purpose is to promote love and the reciprocal giving and receiving which love implies. As Francis Mugavero, Bishop of Brooklyn, puts it: "Sexuality is that aspect of personhood which makes us capable of entering into loving relationships with others."[53]

4. HISTORICAL CONDITION

Because the sexual language is the instrument of creative love, views which would reduce sexual life to genital activities directed "by nature" toward the production of limited goals such as orgasmic pleasure, organic hygiene or reproduction are clearly unsatisfactory. The inadequacy of such narrowly functional views are further demonstrated today by the philosophically richer strand of sexual anthropology which sees sexuality as that whereby human persons have the capacity to adhere to various environments and to acquire adapted structures of interpersonal conduct. Sexuality is that which gives human beings an interpersonal and social history and that which makes them responsible for its development.[54]

By their sexuality, human beings are males or females. They must identify their core gender identity, learn certain socially prescribed gender roles (and later on unlearn some of them!), and cope successfully with the sameness and the differentness of human dimorphism. By their sexuality, human beings are also differentiated from one another and they interrelate among themselves following a complex developmental sequence. Social scientists of all brands are busy plotting the course of sexual development. By their sexuality, finally, human beings establish intimate, but socially significant covenants with each other following elaborate cultural norms. Thus, culture permeates their sexual self. Their sexual behaviour, in turn, permeates the whole fabric of their culture. Such is the sexual condition of embodied spirits, a highly personalized and socialized way of existing dynamically in time.[55]

The significance of the historical condition of sexuality is paramount for an ethical consideration. This condition implies, in point of fact, that the sexual language can never be true when it contradicts the historical consistency and thrust of the partners. To abstract from one's historically conditioned self, to "have sex" with this or that individual and come back to "real life" as if nothing had happened is a sexual lie. Sexual language is true to the extent that one says one's intimate self to other intimate selves following one's own and the others' historical actuality and intentionality. In the presence of others, the sexually integrated person knows how to devise a sexual expression which is adapted to the global reality of a personal and a social situation lived in time.

To behave sexually without engaging one's historically conditioned identity is sexual exhibitionism. Sexual exhibitionism is characterized (not unlike artistic exhibitionism) by a representation of forms in which there is no real encounter, no commitment to historical realities.[56] In this sense, we could say that Platonician erotics, for instance, suffer from this sexual pathology. They regard the beloved as a mere springboard which provides one with the necessary momentum for a soaring erotico-mystical experience. Sexual partners serve merely as enfleshed mediums for what Plato calls the "divine frenzy."[57] A-historical sex also runs counter to the Judeo-Christian tradition because in this illusory experience of impersonal and uncommitted sex the very notion of God is once more at stake.

If the sexual institutions of Ancient Israel do not differ substantially from the institutions shared by the inhabitants of the Near East,[58] nonetheless, the very anthropological status of sexuality is profoundly altered by the monotheistic revolution.[59] The myths concerning divine sexual unions are overthrown. In their downfall, they drag down with them the orgiastic rites which are meant to actualize the myths so as to exorcize daimonic forces and to communicate with the divine mana. Freed from such sacral pseudo-finalities, human sexuality is restored by the Jewish faith to its human integrity. The sexual paradigm born out of Israel's experience of a Covenantal God is a *human prototype,* that of Adam and Eve, of worldly loves and fecundities. The original couple and their descendants are seen as responsible for sexual behaviour which is linked with human historical becoming. Sexuality is not a mysterious energy which enables human beings to communicate mystically with the gods. It is a human dynamism of interpersonal relationships and historical development.

We touch here upon a crucial point for a religiously inspired ethic. The originality of the faith in the God of the Covenant depends to a great extent on the rapport which it establishes between God's Design and Man's History. Contrary to what is found in other Canaanite religions, Israel does not deify cosmic powers. It rejects the idea of a sacral universe which imposes its blind Destiny on human beings. Men and women are seen as being responsible for their world.[60] It is their task as well as their duty to bring it to its completion. Judeo-Christian faith contends, therefore, with obscure gods for autonomy over the world of man and woman, the location of human decisions and endeavours. Faith in the God of the Covenant gives back to men and women what is theirs, this earth which has been entrusted to their care by the Creator. Only the true presence of men and women to the world is capable of unveiling to their own eyes God's presence, his creative and redemptive action, the ongoing gift of Himself to us. The only way to be in touch with the transcendence of God is in living the most ordinary realities of human existence. This is the reason why morality is the location where man meets God.

The favoured Witness of the Covenant, Jesus of Nazareth, illustrates perfectly, by his own sexual attitudes and behaviour, this understanding of responsible human stewardship and the way in which a sexual praxis reveals a liberating God. Confronted with "sexual sinners," he displays neither incantatory proclivities nor disguised erotic interests. On the contrary, those are the evangelical scenes in which he is shown to be exquisitely (or should we say divinely?) human. Contrary to those around him who judge others because of this or that act against the law, he is sensitive to the whole truth of the persons who need someone to listen to them and to confirm in their own eyes that their personal history is meaningful. For Jesus, persons are not faceless objects with no historical depth, sinful perpetrators to be exorcised, or interchangeable sexual mediums with whom to get high on God. Every single person has his or her own historical worth because God made a covenant of love with each one of us. By his responsible sexual attitudes towards others, Jesus opens us to the knowledge of *this* God, the covenantal God.

The Judeo-Christian experience of sexuality as a historical reality is not without dangers of its own. The sexual ethics we have sometimes elaborated bear that out. When the meaning of "history" is taken to be that of a species rather than that of a community of persons, sexuality is turned into a mere reproductive function; its pleasurable and playful dimensions are forsaken; its gratuitous aspects are ignored.[61] To acknowledge the historical nature of sexuality is not to deny its festive character. The issue is whether or not sexual pleasure itself creates humanity.

Notwithstanding excessive and sometimes erroneous expressions, the longstanding opposition of the Church to a contraceptive *mentality*[62] and to sexual pleasure *sought for its own sake*[63] follows the logic of faith in the God of the Covenant. The Christian experience of sexuality refuses to see any likeness between itself and a sexuality lived as the dreary repetition of orgasmic instants which would periodically draw us away from our existential truth in order to help us forget our daily chores and the insignificance of an existence without a History. The sexually integrated Christian lives in a world in which God seeks people who are accountable for themselves and for each other, people who speak an historically truthful sexual language. Such is the God of the Covenant revealed in the faith experience of those who seek Her.

The sexual ethic sketched out in this chapter and proposed as acceptable to Christians does not stand out as the one, universal, and irreformable model. The paradigm in which it is couched takes seriously both contemporary sexological findings and God's self-revelation. Of necessity, therefore, it is open to an ongoing revision. As the human sexual script is better understood and as the Christian experience of God's presence unfolds itself in historical communities through time, the implications for sexual ethics have to be continually discerned and reappraised.

The theory of sexual ethics suggested here radically transforms the fundamental question which should be addressed to our sexual conduct. This question cannot bear, as prescriptive moral theology understands it, on the "doings" and the "non-doings": "May I touch here or there, look at this or that, practice such or such a coital position, utilize this or that means of birth control?" It ought to seek the truthfulness of the "sayings" and the "non-sayings": "What am I saying about myself to this or that person in such or such circumstances when I behave in this or that fashion? Is it true to who we are in ourselves and for each other?" A sexually intimate self-saying which is integrative of sensuality and tenderness, relational, loving, and historically and socially responsible is truthful. Otherwise it is disintegrating, solipsistic, perverse, or illusory. This way of raising the question is likely to yield a formally moral response and to open Christians to the mystery of a God in whose image they are created and who seeks to reveal his truth in his Word made flesh.

Notes

1. The theory presented in this chapter is more fully developed and its ethical ramifications are examined at length in *The Sexual Language*. However, the influence of a Christian Posture on the elaboration of a "Paradigm of Human Sexuality" (pp. 7–220) and the Christian implications of the

theory were not clearly exposed in that work. Since then, two consecutive essays have helped me articulate this important aspect: "Le sens chrétien de la sexualité," *Communauté Chrétienne,* 17/101 (1978), pp. 444–452, and "Gestuelle sexuelle et révélation de Dieu," *Eglise et Théologie,* 11 (1980), pp. 371–398. Nonetheless, the approach used in these articles has been substantially modified in the present chapter.

2. F. CHIRPAZ, *Difficile rencontre* (Paris: Cerf, 1982), pp. 11–29.

3. "Substance," here, is understood in the Scholastic sense, expressing the basic characteristic of that which exists: a being which has the capacity to exist by and in itself and not merely as a modification of some other reality.

4. See, *e.g.,* M. MERLEAU-PONTY, *Phenomenology of Perception* (London: Routledge and Kegan Paul, 1962); J. SARANO, *The Meaning of the Body* (Philadelphia: Westminster Press, 1966); E. BARBOTIN, *The Humanity of Man* (Maryknoll: Orbis, 1975).

5. See also X. THEVENOT, "Christianity . . . ," p. 53.

6. P. ARIES, "Réflexions sur l'histoire de l'homosexualité," in *Sexualités occidentales. Communications No. 35* (Paris: Seuil, 1982), p. 61.

7. S. FREUD, "On the Universal Tendency to Debasement in the Sphere of Love (1912)," in J. STRACHEY (ed.), *The Standard Edition of the Complete Psychological Works of Sigmund Freud* (London: The Hogarth Press and the Institute of Psycho-analysis, 1953–1966), Vol. XI, p. 180.

8. T. REIK, *Sex in Men and Women. Its Emotional Variations* (New York: Noonday Press, 1960).

9. P. RICOEUR, "Wonder, Eroticism, and Enigma," *Cross Currents,* 14 (1964), pp. 133–166.

10. R. MAY, *Love and Will* (New York: W. W. Norton, 1969).

11. E. FUCHS, *Sexual Desire . . .* ; P. AUDOLLENT *et al., Sexualité . . .*

12. This view is implied in Vatican II's statement to the effect that "the sexual characteristics of man and the human faculty of reproduction wonderfully exceed the dispositions of lower forms of life." See *GS,* par. 51 (p. 1072; tr., p. 256).

13. See the criticism of these philosophically poor traditions in A. PLE, *Chastity and the Affective Live* (New York: Herder and Herder, 1966).

14. P. S. KEANE, *Sexual Morality. A Catholic Perspective* (New York: Paulist Press, 1977), pp. 3–4, is right in founding his ethical reflection on the radical goodness of the sexual condition.

15. See, also, D. BAKAN, *And They Took Themselves Wives. The Emergence of Patriarchy in Western Civilization* (San Francisco: Harper and Row, 1979), pp. 12–22.

16. See E. FUCHS, "Loi et Evangile: de l'anthropologie à l'éthique," in *Loi et Evangile. Héritages confessionnels et interpellations contemporaines* (Geneva: Labor et Fides, 1981), p. 237.

17. G. VON RAD, *Genesis. A Commentary* (London: SCM Press, 1961), p. 56, shows how "the marvel of man's bodily appearance is not at all to be excepted from the realm of God's image."

18. D. LYS, *La chair dans l'Ancien Testament: "bâsâr"* (Paris: Editions universitaires, 1967), in particular the summary, pp. 135-139; S. SAPP, *Sexuality, the Bible, and Science* (Philadelphia: Fortress Press, 1977), pp. 1-21.

19. M. BELLET, *Le Dieu pervers* (Paris: Desclée de Brouwer, 1979), p. 117.

20. J. JOYCE, *A Portrait of the Artist as a Young Man* (New York: Penguin Books, 1977), pp. 139-140 (italics are mine).

21. J. B. NELSON, *Embodiment. An Approach to Sexuality and Christian Theology* (Minneapolis: Augsburg Publishing House, 1979), p. 44, is right: "Most basically, body alienation is alienation from God." Scores of biographies could be quoted to illustrate this statement. This book by Nelson is, in my judgment, one of the best essays on sexual ethics written in the 1970s.

22. A child, *e.g.,* begins to learn how to speak as he or she begins to establish his or her gender identity. See J. MONEY, "Psychosexual Differentiation," in J. MONEY (ed.), *Sex Research. New Developments* (New York: Holt, Rinehart and Winston, 1965), pp. 3-23; A. McCUMBER, "Development of Sexual Identity in Children," in J.-M. SAMSON (ed.), *Childhood and Sexuality* (Montreal: Etudes Vivantes, 1980), p. 222. Children raised with animals and without human contact regularly show a double deficiency: an incapacity to speak and an inability to establish a significant sexual rapport with others. See the 36 cases studied by R. M. ZINGG, "Feral Man and Extreme Cases of Isolation," *American Journal of Psychology,* 530 (1940), pp. 487-517; and the 30 cases studied by L. MALSON, *Wolf Children* (London: NLB, 1972).

23. In sexology, see, *e.g.,* J. MONEY, "Human Hermaphroditism," in F. A. BEACH (ed.), *Human Sexuality in Four Perspectives* (Baltimore: The Johns Hopkins University Press, 1976), pp. 77-79; W. H. DAVENPORT, "Sex in Cross-Cultural Perspective," *ibid.,* pp. 120-121; B. SCHLESINGER, *Sexual Behaviour in Canada. Patterns and Problems* (Toronto: University of Toronto Press, 1977), pp. X-XI; E. J. HAEBERLE, *The Sex Atlas* (New York: Seabury, 1978), pp. 146, 150, 280. In ethics, see, *e.g.,* J. DOMINIAN, *Proposals . . . ,* pp. 61-63; J. B. NELSON, *Embodiment . . . ,* pp. 25-30 and 105-106; B. HARING, *Free and Faithful in Christ* (New

York: Seabury, 1979), vol. II, pp. 492–571; A. AUDOLLENT *et al., Sexualité . . .* , pp. 99–102.

24. J. LACROIX, *Force et faiblesses de la famille* (Paris: Seuil, 1948), p. 55; A. DONVAL, *Un avenir pour l'amour. Une nouvelle éthique de la sexualité dans le changement social aujourd'hui* (Paris: Centurion, 1976), p. 47. This is why sexual self-expression is akin to an artistic language: see R. MAY, *The Courage to Create* (New York: W. W. Norton, 1975), p. 85.

25. *FC,* par. 11 (p. 92; tr., p. 20).

26. P. RAMSEY, "A Christian Approach to the Question of Sexual Relations Outside of Marriage," *The Journal of Religion,* 45 (1965), pp. 102–103.

27. E. BARBOTIN, "La sexualité d'un point de vue anthropologique," *Supplément,* 27 (1974), pp. 445–457 (my translation).

28. For a good overall study of the human gestural language, see D. MORRIS, *Manwatching. A Field Guide to Human Behavior* (New York: H. N. Abrams, 1977).

29. The idea of intimacy will be developed in the fourth chapter.

30. "Solipsism" is the philosophical doctrine which holds that the individual conscious self is the whole of reality and that other selves have the status of mere imaginary constructions.

31. G. DURAND, *Ethique de la rencontre sexuelle. Essai* (Montreal: Fides, 1971). The model was subsequently used in a theological context in *Sexualité et foi. Synthèse de théologie morale* (Montreal: Fides, 1977).

32. See the remarkable comment of this text in *GS,* par. 12 (p. 1034; tr., p. 211).

33. For the history of this text's interpretation see M. DE MÉRODE, "Une aide qui lui corresponde: l'exégèse de Gn 2, 18–24 dans les écrits de l'Ancien Testament, du judaisme et du Nouveau Testament," *Revue Théologique de Louvain,* 8 (1977), pp. 329–352; also, W. VOGELS, "It is not Good that 'Mensch' Should Be Alone; I Will Make Him/Her a Helper Fit for Him/Her (Gen 2:18)," *Eglise et Théologie,* 9 (1978), pp. 9–35.

34. G. DURAND, *Sexualité . . .* , pp. 114–115 (my translation). That it is the relational aspect rather than the idea of incompleteness and of complementarity which is signified in the male-female humanity in God's image is convincingly demonstrated in P. K. JEWETT, *Man as Male and Female. A Study in Sexual Relationships from a Theological Point of View* (Grand Rapids: W. B. Eerdmans, 1975).

35. E. FUCHS, *Sexual Desire . . .* , gives, following the Calvinist tradition of ethics, a highly "conjugal" interpretation of human sexuality. This interpretation is not questioned sufficiently, in my opinion, by the works and the life of the celibate Jesus.

36. *GS,* par. 17 (p. 1037; tr., p. 214).

37. N. PITTENGER, *Love and Control . . .* , pp. 21–22; A. DONVAL, *Un avenir . . .* , p. 54.

38. THOMAS AQUINAS, *ST,* Iᵃ-IIᵃᵉ, q. 26, a. 4.

39. ARISTOTLE, *Rhetoric,* II, chap. 4 (1380b35–1381a1), in R. McKEON, *The Basic Works of Aristotle* (New York: Random House, 1941), p. 1386.

40. T. J. TYRRELL, *Urgent Longings. Reflections on the Experience of Infatuation, Human Intimacy, and Contemplative Love* (Whitinsville: Affirmation Books, 1980), p. 82.

41. B. W. HARRISON, "The Power of Anger in the Work of Love: Christian Ethics for Women and Other Strangers," *Union Seminary Quarterly Review,* 36, Supplementary Issue (1981), p. 47.

42. A. DONVAL, *Un avenir . . .* , p. 49.

43. (New York: Pantheon Books, 1975).

44. THOMAS AQUINAS, *ST,* Iᵃ-IIᵃᵉ, q. 72, a. 5; q. 88, a. 2. See a good introduction to the distinction between moral faults and sins in L. MONDEN, *Sin, Liberty and Law* (New York: Sheed and Ward, 1965).

45. *FC,* par. 11 (pp. 91–92; tr., p. 19).

46. See the excellent remarks of E. FUCHS, *Sexual Desire . . .* , p. 173, on the "dramatic of sexuality," this violence of desire in which Christianity has refused, by branding it a sin, to recognize a fatal power. On p. 197, he also designates the violent products of sexuality as "perverse behavior."

47. *GS,* par. 38 (pp. 1055–1056; tr., pp. 235–236).

48. See B. W. HARRISON, "The Power . . . ," p. 51.

49. T. and D. THOMPSON, "Some Legal Problems in the Book of Ruth," *Vetus Testamentum,* 18 (1968), pp. 79–99, particularly pp. 93–94.

50. See the judicious remarks of J. B. NELSON, *Embodiment . . .* , pp. 109–114.

51. This position is clearly that of the Second Vatican Council. See, *e.g., GS,* par. 49 (pp. 1069–1070; tr., pp. 252–253).

52. J. POHIER, "Preaching on the Mountain or Dining with Whores?" *Concilium,* 110 (1977), pp. 62–70.

53. F. J. MUGAVERO, Pastoral Letter "Sexuality—God's Gift," (February 11, 1976), *Origins,* 5 (1976), p. 581.

54. M. MERLEAU-PONTY, *Phenomenology . . .* , p. 158, interprets Sigmund Freud's own thought in this sense.

55. Those three aspects of the sexual condition—gender, growth, and culture—are exposed in more detail in *The Sexual Language . . .* , pp. 113–162.

56. See J. W. MOHR, R. E. TURNER, and M. B. JERRY, *Pedophilia*

and *Exhibitionism* (Toronto: University of Toronto Press, 1964), pp. 111–170, in particular, pp. 162–164.

57. PLATO, *Phaedrus,* 244a, in *The Collected Dialogues of Plato, including the Letters* (Princeton: Princeton University Press, 1961), p. 491. For Plato's mind on this, see F. BUFFIERE, *Eros adolescent. La pédérastie dans la Grèce antique* (Paris: Belles Lettres, 1980), pp. 409–422.

58. R. DE VAUX, *Ancient Israel. Its Life and Institutions* (London: Darton, Longman and Todd, 1962), pp. 19–55.

59. See W. G. COLE, *Sex . . .* , pp. 161–192; W. EICHRODT, *Theologie des Alten Testaments* (Leipzig: J. C. HINRICH, 1962), Vol. I, pp. 91–92 and 143; P. GRELOT, *Le couple humain dans l'Ecriture* (Paris: Cerf, 1962), pp. 17–36; E. SCHILLEBEECKX, *Marriage. Secular Reality and Saving Mystery* (London: Sheed and Ward, 1965), Vol. I, pp. 33–51; G. VON RAD, *Old Testament Theology* (Edinburgh: Oliver and Boyd, 1967), Vol. 1, pp. 27–28); J. BLENKINSOPP, *Sexuality and the Christian Tradition* (Dayton: Pflaum Press, 1969), pp. 16–41.

60. *FC,* par. 34 (p. 123; tr., p. 66).

61. See D. DE ROUGEMONT, *The Myths of Love* (London: Faber and Faber, 1963).

62. Is this not what stands out most clearly in the masterly study of J. T. NOONAN, Jr., *Contraception. A History of its Treatment by the Catholic Theologians and Canonists* (New York: The New American Library, 1967)?

63. See the insightful essay of J.-M. POHIER, *Le chrétien, le plaisir et la sexualité* (Paris: Le Cerf, 1974).

3. Sex, Sacred or Profane?

Joan Timmerman

This chapter originally appeared in *The Mardi Gras Syndrome* in 1984.

Sex is a *sacramental* reality. By sex I mean the whole range of feeling and acts that embodied persons engage in their processes of relating to each other, from walking around museums together to hand holding, kissing, necking, petting, intercourse of various kinds, and afterplay. I do *not* mean solely that part of feeling that has been called venereal pleasure or lust or eros—this would connote less than the truth. I also do not mean solely the genital activity that characterizes procreative intent. That is also less than the truth.

A great breakthrough in our theological thinking about this topic occurs when it dawns on us that our sexuality is in our *being* and not just in the functions of certain of our organs. There is sexuality in each and every word and act, just as there is spirituality in each and every act of the incarnate persons we are. Once we realize this, it makes no sense to try to single out a section of ourselves as the focus of our sin and guilt; nor does it make sense to imagine sexuality as a separable section, a kind of luxury that we can deny we have and refuse to deal with in any conscious way. Our sexuality is our embodiment and it pervades every act of our body-selves. To be embarrassed about it or ashamed of it would be as absurd and self-defeating as shame at our noses or hands or relatedness.

The word *sacramental* refers to the function that all of nature has borne since the revelation of God in Christ and is derived from the Latin word for symbol. In this context, a sacramental reality, a symbol of God's love, is any action or thing that delivers to us the experience of God's presence or places us in touch with the basic mystery—the mystery that we are loved by God. Happily, there is today a stress on the religious dimension of ordinary human experiences. This stress does not deny God's freedom to intervene in special ways, but it cultivates an awareness of the reality, the mystery, that permeates all human events.

About all we can do at this point is appeal to our experience, including our sexual experience. Is there not a dimension of mystery that undergirds our experience? At the depths of the significant things that we do or undergo, is there not an occasional awareness of something that could be called the More, the Whole, the Transcendent, the Other? Any human interaction is and should be capable of revealing our relationship to this mystery. When I play with children I grasp *in* and *through* the playing a momentary glimpse of the "wonder of it all," the ultimate gift of love. When my father sits by the side of the lake, in and through the watching he is lost in an awareness of the rhythms of life and death and of his own living inside this reality. Our *faith* is faith that the ultimate loving reality, the mystery, is there all around us. Our *experience* is that in and through these common but special human interactions we are catapulted into an awareness of our relationship with that reality.

Theology has traditionally affirmed that certain experiences reveal the source and destiny of human life. The accompanying of Christ in his suffering, and the experience that he through his Spirit remained with them as consoler, strengthener, and advocate were such experiences to the disciples of Jesus—men and women—whose stories are recounted in the New Testament. When we look at the small pieces that made up those stories, we see that they are actions like ours—dining, talking, caressing with oil, caring for each other. These actions made up the rites and ceremonies that Christians soon began to do in the name of the Lord Jesus, and that they called sacraments. They were sacramental because in doing them the mystery of God's love revealed in Jesus was experienced once again as transparent, as the reality of the water, the food, the anointing, and the forgiving. The human things aren't *done away with* to get at the mystery—rather, it is *in* and *through* them that the love of God is made present and active in the life of this people.

But why is it that some types of experience have not brought with them an awareness of this holy mystery within which we "live and move and have our being." Sexual experience has by and large been characterized (at least by the writers who achieved ascendancy in the Christian theological tradition) as at worst a place of demonic impulses and forces that pull us against our will and as at best an ambiguous reality that inspires fear, guilt, humor, and some often regretted pleasure. For traditional religious humanity, prior to the widespread desacralization of sex, sex was an experience of the divine; but for modern Christian and post-Christian Westerners, it is often opaque and has little significance beyond the two individuals, their bodily pleasures, and their possible offspring.

Why should this be so? Where was a pearl of such great price lost? Why should an integral aspect of our humanity be excluded from our religious experience? After all, if faith is the attitude that tells us how much we're going to see, why do we see so little in sex? The question moves one to reflect on the historical sources to find out if the pearl might yet be recovered.

In the Gospels two images are used, one female, one male, that seem appropriate to the attempt to appreciate how sex is sacramental. There was a woman who swept the house from attic to alley to find a coin that she had lost. She found it, and called her neighbors to celebrate her good (rewon) fortune. There is another story about a man who heard about a field in which a treasure was buried. To those who had no knowledge of the treasure it seemed a foolish idea, but after selling all he had and buying the field, he found the treasure. He won not only the treasure, but praise from the skeptics.

The theological reconsideration of sex has gained much of its impetus from the renewal of biblical study and improved historical methods but it is also indebted to the feminist movement and the entrance into theological schools of large groups of men and women who do not interpret purity to mean sexual abstinence. They find enough clues in their houses and fields to make them devote their lives to the critical study of the tradition.

In Old Testament times, sex was a prominent symbol of union with the gods and goddesses in the cult religions which surrounded Israel. This led the Israelites to reactionary views on any attempt to relate sexual practices to worship or to the spiritual (religious) life. Yahweh, God of the Hebrews, was conceptualized as a creator without consort who, contrary to the creation stories of the other religions, brought forth all of life by word only, without any sexual partnership or imagery: in this creating there was no paradigm for human sexual life. Yahweh was sole sovereign, leader of the chosen people in their historical exodus and journey, but the symbols of his presence and his power were historical symbols not symbols from nature. War, not sex, was sacralized; struggle to transcend or overcome enemies of Yahweh, not the search for ecstatic union, was the mode of salvation. The practical effect of this concept of God's self-revelation in historical acts, in the building of the holy city and the kingdom, was the desacralization of sex and nature for the Hebrews.

But this, of course, does not mean that the Hebrew tradition considered sex to be profane or evil or especially pervaded by sinfulness. The positive attitudes toward sex of Genesis, the Song of Songs, and the Book of Hosea are well-known. For the Hebrews sexuality was a *human* matter, to be regulated for practical and political necessities, but not a religious reality with absolute value or disvalue. The human experience of sexual love was seen to be natural and good, and a matter of human responsibility. So it was that the new bride and groom were guaranteed a year together for special enjoyment. The man, even the king, who sent a husband into battle so he could take liberties with the wife, was punished. Adultery was reprehensible and the spilling of seed was to be avoided because of the social importance of procreating the chosen people and of the orderly distribution of property. One acted responsibly in one's sexual life, but sexual activity was not an imitation of God's activity for there was nothing in the concept of Yahweh to serve as a model for this aspect of created life. Sex was not God's affair, it was man's.

But then quite a new situation emerged as the developing community of Christ's followers struggled with the new concept of God that was revealed through Jesus. In Jesus the Christ there is a God who is a model for human life!

In the Father, Christ, and the Spirit, there is a God who is in dynamic interpersonal relation. The Old Testament used sexual images, but its basic purpose was religious: to tell something about God. The New Testament gradually developed a religious language whose basic purpose was existential: to reveal something about human life. For Christians' understanding of sex the result was ambiguous. On the one hand a devotion to the imitation of Christ may be patterned after his martyrdom and may find its fulfillment in bodily asceticism and abstinence from sexual relations. Such abstinence was not an imitation of Jesus' own sexual abstinence; rather, it was based upon a theological view of the "end time" and the passing away of all temporal concerns. Nonetheless, it produced a spirituality in which the highest goal was thought to be a life without sex in imitation of a sexless Christ and a sexless God. The injunction in 1 Corinthians 7:1, "It is good for a man not to touch a woman," might be the first written evidence of Christian asceticism.

On the other hand there is a baptismal and marital theology in the epistles attributed to Paul that, in effect, resacralized the sexuality of Christians. In such passages as ". . . in all that you do, whether you work or play, do all in the name of the Lord Jesus" and "this is the great mystery; in the love of a man and woman is the love of Christ for his church" the resacralization of natural life takes place. It is said that the great passage from Galatians 3, "In Christ there is neither Jew nor Gentile, slave nor free, male nor female," is a baptismal formula that reflects the conviction, shared by the early Christians, that Christian existence transcends the cultural world, including its sexual distinctions. For some this transcendence meant the freedom to do any sexual act, like the man who married his stepmother; for others it meant rejection of all sexual acts. Even in these early times there was wide variation in behaviour among groups of Christians and a variety of beginning theologies of how one should live who had in effect entered into the resurrection with the Lord Jesus.

Although the theologizing that these passages call for—on sexual love as the sanctifying symbol of marriage—did not take hold until the twentieth century, the church did accept, in practice, the sacramentality of marriage. More important than the sanctity of sexual love, however, was fidelity (that is, a lifelong, exclusive relationship) and parenthood (that is, the procreation and education of children).

Consciousness of the sacredness of sex seems to be a fragile thing indeed. It appears to emerge in brief periods of insight only to be overwhelmed once more by asceticisms and philosophies hostile to the body.

The danger confronting our contemporary age with regard to the human experience of meaning in sexual life seems to be just the opposite of the threat apparent to the great prophets of Israel. Then the religious meaning assigned to sex was so numinous that it endangered—or seemed to endanger—the singleness of devotion exacted by Yahweh from the covenanted people. In our time, sexuality has been so completely desacralized that it is in danger of being depersonalized. There is no mystery, no union, expected by many people for whom sex is no more than release of tensions and a few minutes of closeness with one other warm body. Christians can discover a message that may help people today to find the meaning that is *already there.* This message is not: "transcend this—avoid this—use this unholy thing only as a means to the holy thing of childbearing," but rather: "Expect connecting love to be holy love. Expect to find here the experience of that Other who calls you out of yourself to love and to relationship and to a creative task in society. Know that your bodies, even as they symbolize or make present your person, also symbolize God. And where you make his love present, God is present and active."

What are some practical effects of taking seriously the sacramental character of our capacity for sexual love?

First, with a sacramental reality all the difference is made by the *meaning* that is perceived. Moreover, it's a kind of meaning that cannot be conveyed in words, but one into which one is initiated experientially. I think one of the reasons that sex is so rarely a religious experience is because the sex education Christian children receive is so rarely a religious formation in self-esteem, reverence for the other as already loved, and an experience of the Christian community as a place of expansion and growth of life.

Second, to recover the insight that our sexual lives and our spiritual lives are not mutually exclusive should not lead us to discard the wisdom that resides in our tradition—whether in its preventive morality or in its practical leniency. But we should have the courage to apply a corrective. Pride and exploitation constitute the biblical notion of sin and are the proper theological definition of concupiscence. Erotic passion or the pleasure drive or the abandon that characterizes the ecstasy of sexual climax is not accurately represented by the category "concupiscence."

Third, sacramental realities are as open to abuse in their natural symbolism as all other realities are. But the possibilities of abuse—in this case, the demonic element of sex—should not be used as a reason for avoiding them altogether, or for constructing an image of redemption and grace that exclude them. They are no more or less dangerous and destructive than food, that other symbol of union that human beings also experience in its demonic properties. The insight of the Old Testament is that sex is not demonic but human; the insight of the New Testament is that faithful, relational sex is sacramental.

Fourth, when the sacramental attitude toward sexual expression replaces the presupposition that sexuality is best left unexpressed, then the Christian has a different obligation. The virtue is not in repressing but in cultivating the human capacity to respond sexually. While extremely significant, this aspect of personal development is not altogether different from intellectual, physical, or spiritual development. One does not come into life fully developed; one has an obligation to grow toward full adulthood. The Christian community shares the responsibility of preparing its members for the fullest possible expression of intimacy and love. Love, after all, is the greatest of the gifts of the Spirit, and the Incarnation remains the central mystery of our faith.

Abraham Maslow, speaking of love and sexuality in "self-actualizing people" characterized their sexuality as follows:

- They enjoy genital sex wholeheartedly, *far above* average, yet specific sex acts or goals do not play any central role in their lives.
- Sex itself may bring on mystical experience at times, yet at other times is simply experienced as lighthearted and playful.
- Their talk about sex is considerably more free, casual, and unconventional than the average.
- They are aware of their sexual attractiveness but are less driven to secretive affairs precisely because their own sexual partnerships are profoundly satisfying.
- They make no sharp differentiation between the roles and personalities of the two genders. They are so certain of their maleness or femaleness that it is no threat to them to take on some cultural aspects of the opposite sex role.
- Their love relationships are characterized by elation, merriment, a feeling of well-being, gaiety.

- They affirm the other's individuality, are eager for the growth of the other, respect the other's unique personality.

While posed in psychological language, this is a remarkable portrait of grace and freedom at work in an individual. These people are so, says Maslow, because their needs have already been met: they have been loved and are thus free to love in response. Grace, according to Saint John, is experienced in that one has first been loved by God and knows that love in Christ and the community. Reclaiming the graced meaning of sexual love could give new meaning to the impression made by some of the early Christians: "See how they love one another!" It is not sexual activity in itself that is scandalous, but precisely that Christians have come to be characterized in the popular mentality as repressed, rigid, legalistic, and incapable of responding humanly to a human need or situation.

Fifth and last, the understanding of what constitutes religious experience—prayer—needs to be reformulated to include the sexual aspects of life. Images of prayer and meditation have come through a monastic tradition that is inseparable from its historical ideal of sexual abstinence. But God's presence is known by the *effects* in one's life of the encounter with the sacred. We might say that wherever one is given a new beginning, wherever something is made real or realized in a new way, wherever that happens, the reality of God has been present to us. If God can only be found where God is supposed to be—in the churches or in the present order of things—then there is no mystery left, and not even the churches are sacramental. God's free and ever outpouring love finds its way through every seam and crack in our personal universes. The false dichotomies between body and spirit, sexuality and sacredness, cannot remain unchallenged.

Part Two

RESPONSIBLE
PARENTHOOD AND
CONTRACEPTION

4. *Casti Connubii* (1930) nn. 53–56

Pius XI

CONTRACEPTION

53. Turning now, Venerable Brethren, to treat in detail the vices which are contrary to each of the blessings of matrimony, we must begin with the consideration of offspring, which many nowadays have the effrontery to call a troublesome burden of wedlock—a burden which they urge married folk carefully to avoid, not by means of a virtuous continence (which is permissible even in marriage with the consent of both parties) but by vitiating the act of nature. This criminal abuse is claimed as a right by some on the ground that they cannot endure children, but want to satisfy their carnal desire without incurring any responsibility. Others plead that they can neither observe continence nor, for personal reasons or for reasons affecting the mother, or on account of economic difficulties, can they consent to have children.

54. But no reason whatever, even the gravest, can make what is intrinsically against nature become conformable with nature and morally good. The conjugal act is of its very nature designed for the procreation of offspring; and therefore those who in performing it deliberately deprive it of its natural power and efficacy, act against nature and do something which is shameful and intrinsically immoral.

55. We cannot wonder, then, if we find evidence in the Sacred Scriptures that the Divine Majesty detests this unspeakable crime with the deepest hatred and has sometimes punished it with death, as St Augustine observes: "Sexual intercourse even with a lawful wife is unlawful and shameful if the conception of offspring is pre-

vented. This is what Onan, the son of Judah, did, and on that account God put him to death."

A Renewed Condemnation

56. Wherefore, since there are some who, openly departing from the Christian teaching which has been handed down uninterruptedly from the beginning, have in recent times thought fit solemnly to preach another doctrine concerning this practice, the Catholic Church, to whom God has committed the task of teaching and preserving morals and right conduct in their integrity, standing erect amidst this moral devastation, raises her voice in sign of her divine mission to keep the chastity of the marriage contract unsullied by this ugly stain, and through Our mouth proclaims anew: that any use of matrimony whatsoever in the exercise of which the act is deprived, by human interference, of its natural power to procreate life, is an offence against the law of God and of nature, and that those who commit it are guilty of a grave sin.

Humanae Vitae (1968) nn. 14–18

Paul VI

---

14. Therefore we base our words on the first principles of a human and Christian doctrine of marriage when we are obliged once more to declare that the direct interruption of the generative process already begun and, above all, direct abortion, even for therapeutic reasons, are to be absolutely excluded as lawful means of controlling the birth of children.[14]

Equally to be condemned, as the Magisterium of the Church has affirmed on various occasions, is direct sterilization, whether of the man or of the woman, whether permanent or temporary.[15]

Similarly excluded is any action, which either before, at the moment of, or after sexual intercourse, is specifically intended to prevent procreation—whether as an end or as a means.[16]

Neither is it valid to argue, as a justification for sexual intercourse which is deliberately contraceptive, that a lesser evil is to be preferred to a greater one, or that such intercourse would merge with the normal relations of past and future to form a single entity, and so be qualified by exactly the same moral goodness as these. Though it is true that sometimes it is lawful to tolerate a lesser moral evil in order to avoid a greater or in order to promote a greater good,[17] it is never lawful, even for the gravest reasons, to do evil that good may come of it[18]—in other words, to intend positively something which intrinsically contradicts the moral order, and which must therefore be judged unworthy of man, even though the intention is to protect or promote the welfare of an individual, of a family or of society in general. Consequently it is a serious error to think that a whole married life of otherwise normal relations can justify sexual inter-course which is deliberately contraceptive and so intrinsically wrong.

LAWFULNESS OF THERAPEUTIC MEANS

15. But the Church in no way regards as unlawful therapeutic means considered necessary to cure organic diseases, even though they also have a contraceptive effect, and this is foreseen—provided that this contraceptive effect is not directly intended for any motive whatsoever.[19]

LAWFULNESS OF RECOURSE TO INFERTILE PERIODS

16. However, as We noted earlier (n. 3), some people today raise the objection against this particular doctrine of the Church concerning the moral laws governing marriage, that human intelli-gence has both the right and the responsibility to control those forces of irrational nature which come within its ambit and to direct them towards ends beneficial to man. Others ask on the same point whether it is not reasonable in so many cases to use artificial birth control if by so doing the harmony and peace of a family are better served and more suitable conditions are provided for the education of children already born. To this question we must give a clear reply. The Church is the first to praise and commend the application of human intelligence to an activity in which a rational creature such as man is so closely associated with his Creator. But she affirms that this must be done within the limits of the order of reality established by God.

If therefore there are reasonable grounds for spacing births, arising from the physical or psychological condition of husband or wife, or from external circumstances, the Church teaches that then married people may take advantage of the natural cycles immanent in the reproductive system and use their marriage at precisely those times that are infertile, and in this way control birth, a way which does not in the least offend the moral principles which we have just explained.[20]

Neither the Church nor her doctrine is inconsistent when she considers it lawful for married people to take advantage of the infertile period but condemns as always unlawful the use of means which directly exclude conception, even when the reasons given for the latter practice are neither trivial nor immoral. In reality, these two cases are completely different. In the former married couples rightly use a facility provided them by nature. In the latter they obstruct the natural development of the generative process. It cannot be denied that in each case married couples, for acceptable reasons, are both perfectly clear in their intention to avoid children and mean to make sure that none will be born. But it is equally true that it is exclusively in the former case that husband and wife are ready to abstain from intercourse during the fertile period as often as for reasonable motives the birth of another child is not desirable. And when the infertile period recurs, they use their married intimacy to express their mutual love and safeguard their fidelity towards one another. In doing this they certainly give proof of a true and authentic love.

GRAVE CONSEQUENCES OF ARTIFICIAL BIRTH CONTROL

17. Responsible men can become more deeply convinced of the truth of the doctrine laid down by the Church on this issue if they reflect on the consequences of methods and plans for the artificial restriction of increases in the birth-rate. Let them first consider how easily this course of action can lead to the way being wide open to marital infidelity and a general lowering of moral standards. Not much experience is needed to be fully aware of human weakness and to understand that men—and especially the young, who are so exposed to temptation—need incentives to keep the moral law, and it is an evil thing to make it easy for them to break that law. Another effect that gives cause for alarm is that a man who grows accustomed to the use of contraceptive methods may forget the reverence due to a woman, and, disregarding her physical and emotional equilibrium, reduce her to being a mere instrument for the satisfaction of his own desires, no longer considering her as his partner whom he should surround with care and affection.

Finally, grave consideration should be given to the danger of this power passing into the hands of those public authorities who care little for the precepts of the moral law. Who will blame a Government which in its attempt to resolve the problems affecting an entire country resorts to the same measures as are regarded as lawful by married people in the solution of a particular family difficulty? Who will prevent public authorities from favouring those contraceptive methods which they consider more effective? Should they regard this as necessary, they may even impose their use on everyone. It could well happen, therefore, that when people, either individually or in family or social life, experience the inherent difficulties of the divine law and are determined to avoid them, they may be giving into the hands of public authorities the power to intervene in the most personal and intimate responsibility of husband and wife.

Consequently, unless we are willing that the responsibility of procreating life should be left to the arbitrary decision of men, we must accept that there are certain limits, beyond which it is wrong to go, to the power of man over his own body and its natural functions—limits, let it be said, which no one, whether as a private individual or as a public authority, can lawfully exceed. These limits are expressly imposed because of the reverence due to the whole human organism and its natural functions, in the light of the principles, which we stated earlier, and according to a correct understanding of the so-called "principle of totality," enunciated by Our Predecessor, Pope Pius XII.[21]

THE CHURCH, GUARANTOR OF TRUE HUMAN VALUES

18. It is to be anticipated that not everyone perhaps will easily accept this particular teaching. There is too much clamorous outcry against the voice of the Church, and this is intensified by modern means of communication. It should cause no surprise that the Church, any less than her divine Founder, is destined to be a "sign of contradiction."[22] She does not, because of this, evade the duty imposed on her of proclaiming humbly but firmly the entire moral law, both natural and evangelical.

Since the Church did not make either of these laws, she cannot be their arbiter—only their guardian and interpreter. It can never be right for her to declare lawful what is in fact unlawful, because this, by its very nature, is always opposed to the true good of man.

By vindicating the integrity of the moral law of marriage, the Church is convinced that she is contributing to the creation of a truly human civilization. She urges man not to betray his personal responsibilities by putting all his faith in technical expedients. In this way she defends the dignity of husband and wife. This course of action shows that the Church, loyal to the example and teaching of the divine Saviour, is sincere and unselfish in her regard for men whom she strives to help even now during this earthly pilgrimage "to share as sons in the life of the living God, the Father of all men."[23]

Notes

14. Cf. Council of Trent Roman Catechism, Part II, ch. 8; PIUS XI, Encycl. *Casti Connubii,* AAS 22 (1930), pp. 562–564 (C.T.S. translation, nn. 62–66); PIUS XII, Address to the Medico-Biological Union of St Luke, *Discorsi e Radiomessaggi,* VI, pp. 191–192; Address to Midwives, AAS 43 (1951), pp. 842–843 (C.T.S. translation, nn. 20–26); Address to the "Family Campaign" and other Family Associations, AAS 43 (1951), pp. 857–859 (C.T.S. translation, nn. 6–15); JOHN XXIII, Encycl. *Pacem in terris,* AAS 55 (1963), pp. 259–260 (C.T.S. translation, nn. 8–13); VATICAN COUNCIL II, Pastoral Constitution on the Church in the World of Today *Gaudium et spes,* n. 51, AAS 58 (1966), p. 1072.

15. Cf. PIUS XI, Encycl. *Casti Connubii,* AAS 22 (1930), p. 565 (C.T.S. translation, nn. 67–70); Decree of the Holy Office, 22 Feb. 1940, AAS 32 (1940), p. 73; PIUS XII, Address to Midwives, AAS 43 (1951), pp. 843–844 (C.T.S. translation, nn. 24–28); to the Society of Haematology, AAS 50 (1958), pp. 734–735.

16. Cf. Council of Trent Roman Catechism, Part II, ch. 8; PIUS XI, Encycl. *Casti Connubii,* AAS 22 (1930), pp. 559–561 (C.T.S. translation, nn. 53–57); PIUS XII, Address to Midwives, AAS 43 (1951), p. 843 (C.T.S. translation, n. 24); to the Society of Haematology, AAS 50 (1958), pp. 734–735; JOHN XXIII, Encycl. *Mater et Magistra,* AAS 53 (1961), p. 447 (C.T.S. translation, n. 193).

17. Cf. PIUS XII, Address to the National Congress of the Italian Society of the Union of Catholic Jurists, AAS 45 (1953), pp. 798–799.

18. Cf. Rom 3:8.

19. Cf. PIUS XII, Address to the twenty-sixth Congress of the Italian Association of Urology, AAS 45 (1953), pp. 674–675; to the Society of Haematology, AAS 50 (1958), pp. 734–735.

20. Cf. PIUS XII, Address to Midwives, AAS 43 (1951), p. 846 (C.T.S. translation, n. 36).

21. Cf. PIUS XII, Address to the Association of Urology, AAS 45 (1953), pp. 674–675; to Leaders and Members of the Italian Association of "corneae" donors and the Italian Association of the Blind, AAS 48 (1956), pp. 461–462.

22. Lk 2:34.

23. Cf. PAUL VI, Encycl. *Populorum Progressio,* AAS 59 (1967), p. 268 (C.T.S. translation, n. 21).

Familiaris Consortio (1981) nn. 28–32

John Paul II

28. With the creation of man and woman in his own image and likeness, God crowns and brings to perfection the work of his hands: he calls them to a special sharing in his love and in his power as Creator and Father, through their free and responsible cooperation in transmitting the gift of human life: "God blessed them, and God said to them, 'Be fruitful and multiply, and fill the earth and subdue it.' "[80]

Thus the fundamental task of the family is to serve life, to actualize in history the original blessing of the Creator—that of transmitting by procreation the divine image from person to person.[81]

Fecundity is the fruit and the sign of conjugal love, the living testimony of the full reciprocal self-giving of the spouses: "While not making the other purposes of matrimony of less account, the true practice of conjugal love, and the whole meaning of the family life which results from it, have this aim: that the couple be ready with stout hearts to cooperate with the love of the Creator and the Saviour, who through them will enlarge and enrich his own family day by day."[82]

However, the fruitfulness of conjugal love is not restricted solely to the procreation of children, even understood in its specifically human dimension: it is enlarged and enriched by all those fruits of moral, spiritual and supernatural life which the father and mother are called to hand on to their children, and through the children to the Church and to the world.

29. Precisely because the love of husband and wife is a unique participation in the mystery of life and of the love of God himself, the Church knows that she has received the special mission of guarding and protecting the lofty dignity of marriage and the most serious responsibility of the transmission of human life.

Thus, in continuity with the living tradition of the ecclesial community throughout history, the recent Second Vatican Council and the magisterium of my predecessor Paul VI, expressed above all in the Encyclical *Humanae Vitae,* have handed on to our times a truly prophetic proclamation, which reaffirms and reproposes with clarity the Church's teaching and norm, always old yet always new, regarding marriage and regarding the transmission of human life.

For this reason the Synod Fathers made the following declaration at their last assembly: "This Sacred Synod, gathered together with the Successor of Peter in the unity of faith, firmly holds what has been set forth in the Second Vatican Council (cf. *Gaudium et Spes,* 50) and afterwards in the Encyclical *Humanae Vitae,* particularly that love between husband and wife must be fully human, exclusive and open to new life (*Humanae Vitae,* 11; cf. 9, 12)."[83]

30. The teaching of the Church in our day is placed in a social and cultural context which renders it more difficult to understand and yet more urgent and irreplaceable for promoting the true good of men and women.

Scientific and technical progress, which contemporary man is continually expanding in his dominion over nature, not only offers the hope of creating a new and better humanity, but also causes ever greater anxiety regarding the future. Some ask themselves if it is a good thing to be alive or if it would be better never to have been born; they doubt therefore if it is right to bring others into life when perhaps they will curse their existence in a cruel world with unforeseeable terrors. Others consider themselves to be the only ones for whom the advantages of technology are intended and they exclude others by imposing on them contraceptives or even worse means. Still others, imprisoned in a consumer mentality and whose sole concern is to bring about a continual growth of material goods, finish by ceasing to understand, and thus by refusing, the spiritual riches of a new human life. The ultimate reason for these mentalities is the absence in people's hearts of God, whose love alone is stronger than all the world's fears and can conquer them.

Thus an anti-life mentality is born, as can be seen in many current issues: one thinks, for example, of a certain panic deriving from the studies of ecologists and futurologists on population growth, which sometimes exaggerate the danger of demographic increase to the quality of life.

But the Church firmly believes that human life, even if weak and suffering, is always a splendid gift of God's goodness. Against the pessimism and selfishness which cast a shadow over the world, the Church stands for life: in each human life she sees the splendour of that "Yes," that "Amen," who is Christ himself.[84] To the "No" which assails and afflicts the world, she replies with this living "Yes," thus defending the human person and the world from all who plot against and harm life.

The Church is called upon to manifest anew to everyone, with clear and stronger conviction, her will to promote human life by every means and to defend it against all attacks, in whatever condition or state of development it is found.

Thus the Church condemns as a grave offence against human dignity and justice all those activities of governments or other public authorities which attempt to limit in any way the freedom of couples in deciding about children. Consequently any violence applied by such authorities in favour of contraception or, still worse, of sterilization and procured abortion, must be altogether condemned and forcefully rejected. Likewise to be denounced as gravely unjust are cases where, in international relations, economic help given for the advancement of peoples is made conditional on programmes of contraception, sterilization and procured abortion.[85]

31. The Church is certainly aware of the many complex problems which couples in many countries face today in their task of transmitting life in a responsible way. She also recognizes the serious problem of population growth in the form it has taken in many parts of the world and its moral implications.

However, she holds that consideration in depth of all the aspects of these problems offers a new and stronger confirmation of the importance of the authentic teaching on birth regulation reproposed in the Second Vatican Council and in the Encyclical *Humanae Vitae.*

For this reason, together with the Synod Fathers I feel it is my duty to extend a pressing invitation to theologians, asking them to unite their efforts in order to collaborate with the hierarchical Magisterium and to commit themselves to the task of illustrating ever more clearly the biblical foundations, the ethical grounds and the personalistic reasons behind this doctrine. Thus it will be possible, in the context of an organic exposition, to render the teaching of the Church on this fundamental question truly accessible to all people of good will, fostering a daily more enlightened and profound understanding of it: in this way God's plan will be ever more completely fulfilled for the salvation of humanity and for the glory of the Creator.

A united effort by theologians in this regard, inspired by a convinced adherence to the Magisterium, which is the one authentic guide for the People of God, is particularly urgent for reasons that include the close link between Catholic teaching on this matter and the view of the human person that the Church proposes: doubt or error in the field of marriage or the family involves obscuring to a serious extent the integral truth about the human person, in a cultural situation that is already so often confused and contradictory. In fulfillment of their specific role, theologians are called upon to provide enlightenment and a deeper understanding, and their contribution is of incomparable value and represents a unique and highly meritorious service to the family and humanity.

32. In the context of a culture which seriously distorts or entirely misinterprets the true meaning of human sexuality, because it separates it from its essential reference to the person, the Church more urgently feels how irreplaceable is her mission of presenting sexuality as a value and task of the whole person, created male and female in the image of God.

In this perspective the Second Vatican Council clearly affirmed that "when there is a question of harmonizing conjugal love with the responsible transmission of life, the moral aspect of any procedure does not depend solely on sincere intentions or on an evaluation of motives. It must be determined by *objective standards.* These, *based on the nature of the human person and his or her acts,* preserve the full sense of mutual self-giving and human procreation in the context of true love. Such a goal cannot be achieved unless the virtue of conjugal chastity is sincerely practised."[86]

It is precisely by moving from "an integral vision of man and of his vocation, not only his natural and earthly, but also his supernatural and eternal vocation,"[87] that Paul VI affirmed that the teaching of the Church "is founded upon the inseparable connection, willed by God and unable to be broken by man on his own initiative, between the two meanings of the conjugal act: the unitive meaning and the procreative meaning."[88] And he concluded by re-emphasizing that there must be excluded as intrinsically immoral "every action which, either in anticipation of the conjugal act, or in its accomplishment, or in the development of its natural consequences, proposes, whether as an end or as a means, to render procreation impossible."[89]

When couples, by means of recourse to contraception, separate these two meanings that God the Creator has inscribed in the being of man and woman and in the dynamism of their sexual communion, they act as "arbiters" of the divine plan and they "manipulate" and degrade human sexuality—and with it themselves and their married partner—by altering its value of "total" self-giving. Thus the innate language that expresses the total reciprocal self-giving of husband and wife is overlaid, through contraception, by an objectively contradictory language, namely, that of not giving oneself totally to the other. This leads not only to a positive refusal to be open to life but also to a falsification of the inner truth of conjugal love, which is called upon to give itself in personal totality.

When, instead, by means of recourse to periods of infertility, the couple respect the inseparable connection between the unitive and procreative meanings of human sexuality, they are acting as "ministers" of God's plan and they "benefit from" their sexuality according to the original dynamism of "total" self-giving, without manipulation or altercation.[90]

In the light of the experience of many couples and of the data provided by the different human sciences, theological reflection is able to perceive and is called to study further *the difference, both anthropological and moral,* between contraception and recourse to the rhythm of the cycle: it is a difference which is much wider and deeper than is usually thought, one which involves in the final analysis two irreconcilable concepts of the human person and of human sexuality. The choice of the natural rhythms involves accepting the cycle of the person, that is the woman, and thereby accepting dialogue, reciprocal respect, shared responsibility and self-control. To accept the cycle and to enter into dialogue means to recognize both the spiritual and corporal character of conjugal communion, and to live personal love with its requirement of fidelity. In this context the couple comes to experience how conjugal communion is enriched with those values of tenderness and affection which constitute the inner soul of human sexuality, in its physical dimension also. In this way sexuality is respected and promoted in its truly and fully human dimension, and is never "used" as an "object" that, by breaking the personal unity of soul and body, strikes at God's creation itself at the level of the deepest interaction of nature and person.

Notes

80. *Gen* 1:28.

81. Cf. *Gen* 5:1–3.

82. Second Vatican Ecumenical Council, Pastoral Constitution on the Church in the Modern World *Gaudium et Spes,* 50.

83. *Propositio* 21. Section 11 of the Encyclical *Humanae Vitae* ends with the statement: "The Church, calling people back to the observance of the norms of the natural law, as interpreted by her constant doctrine, teaches that each and every marriage act must remain open to the transmission of life (*ut quilibet matrimonii usus ad vitam humanam procreandam per se destinatus permaneat*)": *AAS* 60 (1968), 488.

84. Cf. 2 *Cor* 1:19; *Rev* 3:14.

85. Cf. the Sixth Synod of Bishops' Message to Christian Families in the Modern World (24 October 1980), 5.

86. Pastoral Constitution on the Church in the Modern World *Gaudium et Spes,* 51.

87. Encyclical *Humanae Vitae,* 7: *AAS* 60 (1968), 485.

88. *Ibid.,* 12: *loc. cit.,* 488–489.

89. *Ibid.,* 14: *loc. cit.,* 490.

90. *Ibid.,* 13: *loc. cit.,* 489.

5. Magisterial Teaching from 1918 to the Present

John Gallagher, C.S.B.

This chapter originally appeared in *Human Sexuality and Personhood* in 1981.

THE CODE OF CANON LAW

This paper traces the teaching of the Roman Catholic magisterium from 1918 to the present. It was in the year 1918 that the modern Code of Canon Law came into force. The code contains certain theological statements about marriage. One such statement concerns the ends of marriage. Paragraph One of Canon 1013 states: "The primary end of marriage is the procreation and education of children; its secondary end is mutual help and the allaying of concupiscence."

In view of the subsequent controversy it is well to look closely at what the code actually says. There is a widespread impression that the code says that the mutual love of spouses is only a secondary end of marriage. In fact, however, the code does not speak of the mutual love of spouses as an end of marriage in either way, as a secondary end or as a primary end.

This raises an interesting point. An end is the object of an act of will. One can, no doubt, have as one's purpose in marriage a growth in love. Love then can be said to be an end of marriage. However, it is an end in a special way. The love in question is itself an act of will responding to those further ends and goods which are the objects of love—namely, the persons who are loved and their welfare. Love is in this case an end which is a response to a more ultimate good or end. For this reason some thinkers who hold that love is central to Christian marriage may not wish to express that centrality by calling love an end of marriage.

The code does not give mere biological generation as the principal end of marriage. That end is procreation and education. Canon 1113 explains this. It states: "Parents are bound by a most serious obligation to provide to the best of their power for the religious and moral as well as for the physical and civil education of their children, and also to provide for their temporal welfare." The code sees marriage as an institution whose principal end is the total human good of the next generation.

What is the authority of the code's theological teaching about marriage? By including certain theological principles in the code the Church was not interested primarily in settling theological disputes. She was interested primarily in providing some theological background for law. For this purpose she adopted certain theological principles commonly accepted in the Church at the time. Some of these principles had already been taught authoritatively by popes and councils. Some had not. The inclusion of a theological principle in the code need not mean that the principle was being taught with new authority.

CASTI CONNUBII

On December 31, 1930, Pope Pius XI published the encyclical, *Casti Connubii,* on Christian marriage. To some extent this encyclical was a response to the Lambeth Conference of 1930, at which for the first time the Church of England withdrew its official objections to artificial contraception. *Casti Connubii* does not limit itself to the problem of artificial contraception, however. It covers a wide range of topics concerning which the modern world either rejects or ignores the traditional teaching of the Catholic Church.

This encyclical seems to presuppose what one might call an organic notion of marriage. Some "reformers" would like to get rid of the institution of marriage or at least radically restructure it. Such efforts are suspect to those who have an organic notion of social institutions. A medical doctor does not begin with an abstract idea of what a rationally constructed human body should be, and then proceed to tear apart the human body and put it together along more rational lines. The human body exists and functions before any physician studies it. Analogously, marriage exists and functions before any theorist studies it. Marriage draws upon and channels certain human energies and instincts, it fulfills certain needs, and it embodies certain principles learned by trial and error, long before it is studied theoretically. In the organic view, the reformer of marriage should not try to destroy the existing institution and rebuild a substitute according to some abstract and partial view of what is needed and what is possible. The reformer of marriage, like the physician, should be humble, learning from the existing thing and respecting the requirements which flow from its nature.

Casti Connubii does not explicitly adopt this organic view, but it seems to imply it. Paragraph 6 states: "The nature of matrimony is entirely independent of the free will of man, so that if one has once contracted matrimony he is thereby subject to its divinely made laws and properties."[1] Paragraphs 49 and 50 argue that matrimony was instituted by God who is the author of nature. The argument seems to be that it was in creating the nature of things that God created marriage. Marriage is not something arbitrarily set up by God but an institution which arises because of the nature of human beings. The encyclical draws from this, that because matrimony is created by God it has laws which human beings should obey, laws which they cannot change. The point is elaborated in Paragraph 95, which contains a quotation from Pope Leo XIII.

> It is a divinely appointed law that whatsoever things are constituted by God, the author of nature, these we find the most useful and salutary, the more they remain in their natural state, unimpaired and unchanged; inasmuch as God, the Creator of all things, intimately knows what is suited to the constitution and the preservation of each, and by his will and mind has so ordained all things that each may duly achieve its purpose. But if the boldness and wickedness of men change and disturb this order of things, so providentially disposed, then indeed things so wonderfully ordained will begin to be injurious, or will cease to be beneficial, either because, in the change, they have lost their power to benefit, or because God Himself is thus pleased to draw down chastisement on the pride and presumption of men.

Of special interest to our purpose is Pius's discussion of the ends of marriage. He quotes Canon 1013. "The primary end of marriage is the procreation and the education of children."[2] Elsewhere he reemphasizes the primacy of procreation. "Thus, amongst the blessings of marriage, the child holds first place."[3] The child is destined not only for a noble and dignified life in this world but also for eternal life. The sublime end of matrimony is to bring forth children who will become members of Christ and who will enjoy eternal life with God.[4]

Among the secondary ends of marriage Pius XI includes the two mentioned by canon law, mutual aid and the quieting of concupiscence. To these he adds a third, the cultivation of mutual love.[5]

It is clear that Pius does not consider these unitive aspects (mutual love, mutual aid) to have only minor importance. Concerning the union of spouses he speaks of "the generous surrender of his own person made to another for the whole span of life."[6] Furthermore:

> By matrimony, therefore, the minds of the contracting parties are joined and knit together more intimately than are their bodies, and that not by any passing affection of sense or heart, but by a deliberate and firm act of the will.[7]

The mutual love of spouses motivates them to help each other. Pius expands the scope of this traditional category, mutual help.

> This outward expression of love in the home demands not only mutual help but must go further; must have as its primary purpose that man and wife help each other day by day in forming and perfecting themselves in the interior life, so that through their partnership in life they may advance ever more and more in virtue, and above all that they may grow in true love toward God and their neighbor.[8]

There is some reason to believe that Pius XI was not completely satisfied with calling these unitive elements merely secondary ends of matrimony. Of the love between husband and wife he says that it "pervades all the duties of married life and holds pride of place in Christian marriage."[9] Of the mutual help of spouses he says:

> This mutual inward moulding of husband and wife, this determined effort to perfect each other, can in a very real sense, as the Roman Catechism teaches, be said to be the chief reason and purpose of matrimony, provided matrimony be looked at not in the restricted sense as instituted for the proper conception and education of the child, but more widely as the blending of life as a whole and the mutual interchange and sharing thereof.[10]

It seems that Pius XI is insisting on two points which, in the theology of the day, were not easily expressed in one simple formula. The first point is that marriage has an essential orientation to children. The second point is that the mutual love and aid between spouses has an importance which is not adequately expressed by calling them secondary ends of marriage. To add a second primary end to marriage presents its own difficulties, however, as we shall see in discussing a later document. Pius XI resorts to the vague formula of two primacies according to two different points of view.

On sexual relations outside of marriage, the encyclical restates the Church's traditional teaching as follows:

> Nor must we omit to remark, in fine, that since the twofold duty entrusted to parents for the good of their children is of such high dignity and of such great importance, every lawful use of the faculty given by God for the procreation of new life is the right and the privilege of the marriage state alone, by the law of God and of nature, and must be confined absolutely within the sacred limits of that state.[11]

The order of the argument here is worth noting. Pius does not base his rejection of fornication and adultery only on an analysis of biological sexuality. His basis is the nature and end of the institution of marriage. That sex should be properly oriented toward procreation is a truth seen in the context of the orientation of marriage toward procreation.

In Paragraphs 53 to 59, Pius XI condemns artificial contraception as gravely sinful, and instructs confessors to hold to this teaching. Some writers have complained that here Pius resorts to biologistic reasoning. Biologistic reasoning in moral matters begins by discovering in a physical faculty an orientation toward some goal, and then makes that orientation into a moral principle. In sexual ethics, the biologistic approach sees that the sexual organs and sexual responses are so constituted as to produce offspring, and concludes that therefore the production of offspring is the proper good of sex, and that any use of sex for any other purpose is immoral. Biologistic reasoning in ethics is open to serious objections.

Does Pius XI actually resort to a biologistic approach in condemning artificial contraception? Certain passages could suggest that he does. He states that artificial contraception is "intrinsically against nature," and that, "since, therefore, the conjugal act is destined primarily by nature for the begetting of children, those who in exercising it deliberately frustrate its natural power and purpose sin against nature and commit a deed which is shameful and intrinsically vicious."[12] In the context of the whole encyclical, however, it seems that what is "according to nature" is to be determined not by considering the physical aspect by itself but by looking at the nature and purpose of matrimony.

Paragraph 59 states that one partner in a marriage has a duty to try to convince the other not to use artificial contraceptives. However, one is not bound to refuse to have sexual intercourse with a spouse who insists on using contraceptives. The same paragraph states that spouses may have sexual intercourse when for natural reasons either of time or defect conception cannot occur. Intercourse at such times may be for such ends as mutual aid or the cultivation of mutual love, and one is free to pursue such secondary ends so long as they are subordinated to the primary end and so long as the intrinsic nature of the act is preserved. Pius thus rejects the rigourist opinion of some earlier theologians who allowed sexual intercourse only for the purpose of procreation and only when procreation is possible. In 1930 the researches of Ogino and of Knaus into periodic infertility had not yet led to widespread use of periodic continence as a way to prevent pregnancy. It is not clear, then, that in *Casti Connubii* Pius XI is thinking of periodic continence as a long-term strategy for avoiding pregnancy.

As the encyclical situates the meaning of sex in the context of marriage, so it briefly situates marriage in the context of society as a whole. The stability of matrimony is a fruitful source of habits of integrity and guards the well-being of the nation.[13] "The prosperity of the state and the temporal happiness of its citizens cannot remain safe and sound where the foundations on which they are established, which is the moral order, is weakened, and where the very fountain-head from which the state draws its life, namely wedlock and the family, is obstructed by the vices of its citizens."[14]

HERBERT DOMS AND THE MEANING OF MARRIAGE

The 1930's saw a lively controversy in the Catholic Church regarding the position expressed in the code of Canon Law regarding the primary and secondary ends of marriage. In 1935 Herbert Doms, a German diocesan priest, published a book[15] which appeared in 1939 in an English translation as *The Meaning of Marriage*.[16] Doms objected that Canon Law seemed to say that the meaning of marriage comes only from what is called its primary end, the procreation and education of children. Doms does not deny that marriage has this end, but he insists that it has a meaning in itself apart from this end.

> The constitution of marriage, the union of two persons, does not consist in their subservience to a purpose outside themselves for which they marry. It consists in the constant vital ordination of husband and wife to each other until they become one. If this is so, there can no longer be sufficient reason, from this standpoint, for speaking of procreation as the primary purpose (in the sense in which St. Thomas used the phrase) and for dividing off the other purposes as secondary . . . perhaps it would be best if in the

future we gave up using such terms as "primary" and "secondary" in speaking of the purpose of marriage.[17]

Doms distinguishes the meaning of marriage from the ends of marriage. The meaning of marriage and of sexual activity within marriage consists in the actual realization of the unity of the two persons. Besides this meaning there are two ends of marriage. The personal end is the mutual completion and perfection of the spouses on every level. The specific end (i.e., that which gives marriage its distinctive nature) is the child. These two ends are equally primary, and one is not subordinate to the other.

THE ROMAN ROTA, 1944

The views of Doms stirred up considerable reactions. They failed, however, to convince Rome on the central point. A decree of the Holy Office on April 1, 1944,[18] stated that the procreation and education of children is to be considered the primary end of marriage and no other ends are to be considered as equally principal ends. Other ends are to be considered secondary and subordinate to the one primary end. In this decree, and in a "sentence" of the Holy Roman Rota earlier in the same year,[19] Doms is not named, but it is clear that his position is being rejected.

The sentence of the Rota appeals to a principle which can be found in St. Thomas, that the end specifies a reality. Applied to activity it means that the end determines the nature of the activity. If your end is to remove a brain tumor this requires one type of activity. If your end is to pass an examination in mathematics this requires a different type of activity.

One activity may serve two ends at the same time. You may run home from work both as a means to keep fit and as a means to get home. Doms claimed that marriage has two ends, both equally primary, and one is not subordinate to the other. In the view of the Rota this would mean that in marriage there are two distinct aspects, the marriage as directed toward the mutual completion and perfection of the spouses, and the marriage as directed toward the child; these two aspects would be only accidentally, not essentially, united. If they had no essential relation to each other there would be no theological reason for keeping them together. If someone wanted to have one without the other, there would be no reason not to do so. This is a consequence which the Rota would not accept.

In summary, the Rota seems to have rejected the notion that marriage has two primary ends, because this would destroy the essential relationship between the ends and leave the way open for allowing marriage with no procreative orientation. It is noteworthy that the acceptance by many Catholic theologians of two primary ends of marriage has been followed, a few years later, by the acceptance of deliberately childless marriages.

One may ask: what is wrong with deliberately childless marriages? The 1944 sentence of the Rota did not discuss this question, because Doms and his followers had not denied that marriage has procreation and education of children as an essential end.

If the two ends of marriage are not independent, how are they united? The Rota states that the secondary end is subordinate to the primary end. That is, the mutual help and perfecting of spouses is ordered to the procreation and education of children. This raises a question. May spouses pursue these secondary ends not only insofar as they are ordered to procreation but also for other reasons? Surely they may; in fact, to develop one's love for one's spouse and to help one's spouse *only* as ordered to procreation seems to offend against the very meaning of the love of one's spouse. However, if one can pursue these unitive ends not merely as subordinate to procreation, do they not thereby become primary ends? Here the Rota's explanation of the relation between the unitive and the procreative aspects of marriage left room for controversy.

Pope Pius XII

When Pope Pius XII enters the discussion he expresses concern that the secondary end be shown to be very important.[20] On the other hand he holds firmly to the notion of primary and secondary ends as expressed in canon law. He states also that the secondary end is subordinate to the primary end. The unitive aspects are placed by the will of nature and of the creator at the service of the offspring.[21]

In the address to the midwives Pius XII repeats the Church's rejection of artificial contraception, and adds that this moral teaching is valid for all time, a law which is natural and divine. Why is artificial contraception wrong? In some passages Pius XII seems to argue biologistically, from the nature of the physical sexual faculty considered in itself.[22] Elsewhere he seems to argue from the nature of marriage.[23] Further study is needed to show whether these two approaches can be fitted together.

Pius XII dealt with a number of practical moral questions concerning sex and marriage. In the address to the midwives he discussed periodic continence. There he first repeats the teaching of Pius XI that spouses may engage in sexual intercourse when the wife cannot conceive. May a couple restrict the marital act to only infertile periods in order to avoid conception? Pius XII replies that married couples who engage in sexual intercourse have a general duty to provide for the conservation of the human race. However, he says, "serious reasons, often put forward on medical, eugenic, economic and social grounds, can exempt from that obligatory service, even for a considerable period of time, even for the entire duration of the marriage."[24]

Pius XII rejected the use of artificial insemination.[25] He considers three situations. In the first the mother is not married. In this case the use of artificial insemination offends against the requirement that procreation take place within marriage. In the second situation the mother is married but the semen is from a man other than her husband. This is immoral because only the husband and wife have rights over the body of the other for purposes of generating new life. The bond of origin created by physical paternity creates a duty to protect and educate the child, but this cannot take place properly in this second type of situation. In the third type of situation the semen is from the husband of the woman. Artificial insemination is wrong even in this case because marriage and the marital act are not merely organic functions for the transmission of seed. The marital act is a personal act which expresses the mutual giving of spouses. This makes it the proper context for conception. Here, interestingly, Pius XII appeals explicitly to an aspect of the sexual act which is beyond the merely physical. Finally, according to Pius

XII, artificial means may be used to facilitate conception after natural intercourse.

Pius XII rejects experiments in *in vitro* fertilization as immoral and absolutely illicit.[26] His reasons for rejecting artificial insemination using semen from the husband would rule out *in vitro* fertilization.

In an address on September 12, 1958 Pius discusses some moral issues related to genetics.[27] When genetic factors are likely to cause a couple to produce defective offspring, a prenuptial examination to discover the likelihood of such a result is licit. If the likelihood of defective offspring is great, authorities may even make such examinations obligatory. For genetic reasons one may advise a couple not to marry but one may not forbid them to marry. "Marriage is one of the fundamental human rights, the use of which may not be prevented." If the discovery of the genetic difficulty comes after marriage one may advise the couple not to have children but one may not forbid them to have children.

VATICAN II

The Second Vatican Council dealt with marriage and the family in *The Constitution on the Church in the Modern World* (*Gaudium et Spes*), sections 46–52. There were differences of opinion among the Council Fathers concerning earlier drafts of this document. One group wanted the document to follow closely the formulations of canon law and of papal documents on such crucial matters as the ends of marriage. Another group wanted to depart quite sharply from such formulations. Some wanted to open for discussion the question of artificial contraception. Pope John XXIII set up a commission to study the question. Pope Paul VI instructed the council not to pronounce on the question. He himself would pronounce on it after studying the report of the commission.

The treatment of marriage in *Gaudium et Spes* contains much from earlier papal statements, but the council gives its own particular emphasis to the material. Central to its discussion of marriage and family is what it calls "married love" or "spousal love." As a matter of human will, this love is much more than physical desire, but it includes physical expression. It is distinct from other types of friendship in that it is expressed and perfected through the physical marital act which both signifies and promotes the mutual self-giving of the spouses.[28] This spousal love wells up from the fountain of divine love, and is structured on the model of Christ's love for the Church. This spousal love is caught up in the divine love and can lead the spouses to God.

Spousal love leads to mutual help and service.

> Thus a man and a woman, who by the marriage covenant of conjugal love "are no longer two, but one flesh" (Mt. 19, 6), render mutual help and service to each other through an intimate union of their persons and of their actions. Through this union they experience the meaning of their oneness and attain to it with growing perfection day by day. As a mutual gift of two persons, this intimate union, as well as the good of the children, imposes total fidelity on the spouses and argues for an unbreakable oneness between them.[29]

The council expresses clearly the orientation of marriage toward children.

> By their very nature, the institution of marriage itself and conjugal love are ordained for the procreation of children, and find in them their ultimate crown.[30]

Clearly the Council Fathers are arguing not from a narrowly biological basis. It is the nature of marriage itself and of conjugal love to be oriented toward procreation.

Although it does not state whether or not artificial contraception is licit, the Constitution does discuss the problem. It stresses that parents are to procreate responsibly, taking account of their own welfare and that of their children. They are to consider the material and the spiritual condition of the times, the interests of the family group, of temporal society and of the Church. In some situations there will be a conflict between different factors. There may be strong reasons to limit the number of children. At the same time sexual abstinence can create problems. It may, for example, make it difficult to maintain the faithful exercise of love and the full intimacy of spousal life. The judgment about whether to have children is to be made by the parents, but it is not to be made arbitrarily. Moral duty involves not motive only, but the observance of objective standards. These standards, in the area of sexual behaviour, are those which "based on the nature of the human person and his acts, preserve the full sense of mutual self-giving and human procreation in the context of true love."[31] Parents are to reject abortion. They are to have an informed conscience, one conformed to the divine law and submissive to the teaching of the Church which interprets divine law.

Possibly the most controversial points about the treatment of marriage and the family in *Gaudium et Spes* concern what the document does not say. In at least one case an omission was a triumph for one point of view at the council. This case is the omission in the document of the old terminology of primary and secondary ends of marriage and the omission of any explanation of mutual help of spouses as merely subordinate to the procreation and education of children.

The conciliar text on marriage and the family left several questions unanswered. The problem of artificial contraception was, of course, deliberately left unresolved. Another question concerns whether there is an intrinsic relationship between the unitive and procreative ends of marriage. If there is no such intrinsic relationship then the way is open, as we have seen, to allow a type of marriage which is deliberately not oriented toward children.

THE PAPAL COMMISSION, 1966

In June, 1966, the papal commission on birth control reported to Pope Paul VI. Four documents eventually came to light. One was the "Theological Report of the Papal Commission on Birth Control." This document, which has since become known as "the majority report," was signed by nineteen of the theologians and by a number of the other experts on the commission. It represents the view of a substantial majority of those on the commission. A second document, "Pastoral Approaches," is in agreement with the majority report. They both advocate a change in the Church's official teaching in order to allow artificial contraception in some cases. A third document, the so-called "minority report," was signed by four theologians on the commission who disagreed with the majority report and who advised that no change be made in the Church's teaching. A fourth document is a working paper by some of the theologians who advocated change in the Church's teaching. It defends their position against arguments in the third document.[32]

The position of the first document, the majority report, can be summarized in six points. First, although it would allow artificial contraception in some cases, yet it insists that sex and marriage are properly oriented toward the procreation and education of children. The union of spouses is not to be separated from the procreative finality of marriage. Conjugal love and fecundity are in no way opposed, but complement each other. The community of life of spouses provides the proper framework for the procreation and education of children.

Second, the majority report approaches the problem from the point of view of the totality of the marriage. It wishes to take its moral direction not from a consideration of the sexual act or faculty by itself but from a consideration of what is good for the marriage as a whole. This allows the majority report to allow artificial contraception in certain cases while insisting on the procreative orientation of all sexual acts. In other words, the majority report does not fall into the trap of separating two independent ends for marriage and then justify artificial contraception as a pursuit of one end while excluding the other. It insists that if artificial contraception is used it must respect the procreative finality of marriage. How can it do so? The union of spouses, their mutual help, their love and their life together all have a procreative orientation. That is, they exist not only for their own sake, but for the sake of children. Therefore, if artificial contraception in a particular situation helps the union of the couple it indirectly serves the procreative end of marriage. Furthermore, if artificial contraception helps parents to provide for the proper care of already existing children it serves the procreative end of marriage.

Third, the majority report is somewhat situationist in approach. It does not see artificial contraception as intrinsically morally evil. (It does refer to a physical evil which is present in artificial contraception.) To decide what is morally good in a particular case one must consider the different values involved and try to harmonize them as well as possible. The majority report advocates this situationist approach in the case of artificial contraception, but this need not mean that it would suggest such an approach in all areas of ethics. Its outright and apparently universal rejection of abortion suggests that it does not adopt a situationist approach to that question.

Fourth, the authors of the majority report believe that they are being faithful to tradition. They hold that the values which the Church in the past protected by a universal exclusion of artificial contraception can now best be protected by allowing it in certain cases. They seem to be distinguishing two levels of moral norms. On one level are basic values which are seen to endure from century to century. Concerning contraception, one such value, apparently, is the orientation of marriage to children. On another level are the more specific rules by which such values are applied in particular times and situations. As conditions and available information change, so the Church's teaching on this second level may change.

Fifth, the majority report condemns any contraceptive mentality. It states that couples should be willing to raise a family with full acceptance of the various human and Christian responsibilities that are involved. The marriage as a whole should be procreative.

Sixth, the majority report stresses education. It expects couples to make their own judgment about what is best in their particular situation. To do so properly, they need a profound knowledge and appreciation of the values involved. There is an obvious danger of conforming not to Gospel values but to popular opinion and pressure.

The minority report argues at some length against various positions in the majority report. Clearly, however, for the four authors of the minority report the questions of tradition and authority are crucial. They maintain that the question of artificial contraception cannot be solved by reason alone. They seem to believe that reasons put forward by either side cannot settle the matter. The matter is to be settled then by tradition and authority. The Catholic Church has traditionally rejected each and every act of artificial contraception as gravely wrong. The Church could not have erred on so important a matter.

The minority report denies that the traditional teaching of the Catholic Church against contraception was based on a biologistic argument. It states that the traditional teaching does not appeal to some general principle that man must use all physical faculties in accord with the biological orientation of the faculty. Artificial contraception is wrong not because it goes against the biological orientation of simply any faculty, but because it goes against the orientation of the generative faculty. The generative faculty is concerned with the generation of new life, and life is not under man's dominion. By analogy, just as human life once constituted *in facto esse* is inviolate, so is the process inviolate in which the human life is *in fieri.*

HUMANAE VITAE

In August, 1968, more than two years after receiving the commission reports, Pope Paul VI published the encyclical letter *On Human Life* (*Humanae Vitae*). He begins by acknowledging that a new state of affairs has given rise to questions which necessitate a re-examination of the Church's traditional teaching on artificial contraception.

In his relatively brief discussion of marriage and conjugal love, Pope Paul incorporates much of the material on marriage and the family in *Gaudium et Spes.* Much of what he says conforms with the majority report. Marriage, he states, is the wise institution of the Creator to realize in mankind His design of love. "By means of the reciprocal gift of self, proper and exclusive to them, husband and wife tend towards the communion of their beings in view of mutual perfection, to collaborate with God in the generation and education of new lives."[33] Conjugal love is fully human, of the senses and of the spirit at the same time. Not only an instinct or a sentiment, it is an act of will intended to endure and to grow so that husband and wife become one only heart and one only soul. This love is not exhausted by the communion between husband and wife, but is destined to continue, raising up new lives. As Vatican II has said, the pope notes, marriage and conjugal love are by their nature ordained for the begetting and educating of children.

Paul VI proceeds then to rule out the use of artificial contraception, and repeats the traditional teaching that each and every marriage act must remain open to the transmission of life. He continues:

> That teaching, often set forth by the magisterium, is founded upon the inseparable connection willed by God and unable to be broken by man on his own initiative, between the two meanings of the conjugal act: the unitive meaning and the procreative meaning. Indeed, by its intimate structure, the conjugal act, while most closely uniting husband and wife, capacitates them for the generation of new lives, according to laws inscribed in the very being of man and of woman. By safeguarding both these essential aspects, the unitive and the procreative, the conjugal act preserves in its fullness the sense of true mutual love and its ordination towards man's most high calling to parenthood. We believe that the men of our day are particularly capable of seizing the deeply reasonable and human character of this fundamental principle.[34]

The sequence of the argument seems to be as follows: first, marriage and conjugal love have both a unitive and a procreative meaning, the two being essentially bound together. Marital sexual relations should preserve the full meaning of conjugal love, and so should combine both unitive and procreative meanings. Artificial contraception prevents this from happening.

Why does Pope Paul's conclusion regarding artificial contraception differ from the conclusion of the majority report? On the nature of marriage and of spousal love, Paul VI seems to be in general agreement with the majority report. The difference seems to lie in two opposed ways of applying general norms to particular cases. Specifically, Pope Paul holds that artificial contraception is intrinsically evil and can never be allowed. This rules out any appeal to the totality of a marriage for reasons to justify artificial contraception in particular cases. It rules out allowing artificial contraception as a lesser evil in certain situations.

The encyclical does not give reasons for adopting the notion of intrinsic evil or for rejecting an appeal to the total good of the marriage or for not allowing contraception as a lesser evil. These provide an important area for theological investigation, because they constitute the apparent reasons for Pope Paul's rejection of the conclusions of the commission.

Why did he hold to these views against the advice of the majority report? He states that the conclusions of the commission were not definitive, but required his personal further study ". . . above all because certain criteria of solutions had emerged which departed from the moral teaching on marriage proposed with constant firmness by the teaching authority of the Church."[35] Therefore, although he does not dwell at length on the question of tradition and magisterial authority, this seems to be an important reason, perhaps the primary reason, for his conclusions concerning contraception.

Paul VI agrees with *Gaudium et Spes* that parents should be responsible in deciding the number of children ". . . either by the deliberate and generous decision to raise a numerous family, or by the decision, made for grave motives and with due respect for the moral law, to avoid for the time being, or even for an indeterminate period, a new birth."[36] When there are legitimate reasons for avoiding pregnancy, periodic abstinence may be used for that purpose. Paul VI argues that periodic abstinence is significantly different from artificial contraception. The former makes legitimate use of a natural process, whereas the latter impedes the development of a natural process.

DECLARATION ON SEXUAL ETHICS

In December, 1975, the Congregation for the Doctrine of the Faith published the *Declaration on Certain Questions Concerning Sexual Ethics.* Its main purpose was to warn against certain contemporary errors.

The declaration insists that there are objective moral standards which accord with the nature of human beings. These standards are known by a natural law written in the hearts of men. Revelation gives further knowledge of moral standards. Certain moral norms, including certain sexual moral norms, are immutable exigencies of human nature, not mere products of a culture which change as cultures change.

According to the declaration (and here it is following *Gaudium et Spes,* Section 51) the objective moral standards governing sexual acts are those which preserve the full sense of mutual self-giving and human procreation in the context of true love. That is, sexual norms are valid if they preserve the full sense of mutual self-giving and human procreation in the context of true love. Once again, the unitive and the procreative are bound together.

From this basis the declaration proceeds to an evaluation of various types of sexual behavior. It condemns premarital sex, because only in stable marriage can the full sense of mutual self-giving and human procreation in the context of true love be maintained. Premarital sex cannot be properly procreative because it lacks the stable family unit in which children can be properly nurtured. Only in the stable commitment of marriage is there assurance of sincerity and fidelity, protection against whim and caprice.

The same basis is used to condemn homosexual actions. They are wrong because they do not provide for a full sense of mutual self-giving and human procreation in the context of true love. The same criteria rule out masturbation, which, the declaration teaches, is intrinsically and seriously disordered.

The declaration points out that psychology can help to show how various factors, such as adolescent immaturity, may reduce responsibility in the case of sexual sin. However, one should not go so far as to presume easily that people are not seriously responsible when they transgress in sexual matters. If responsibility is to be evaluated in particular cases, one should take account of the person's habitual behavior and his or her sincere use of the means necessary to overcome sexual sin. In other words, the declaration seems to say, if the person normally tries sincerely to do what is right, and seriously makes use of prayer and other means, then there is some reason to believe that a particular failure may not be fully responsible and so should not be considered a serious sin.

The declaration comments on the notion of fundamental option. It opposes the idea that mortal sin occurs only in a formal refusal of love of God or in a complete and deliberate closing of oneself to love of neighbor. Mortal sin can occur because of the rejection of God which is implied in choosing anything which is seriously morally disordered. Thus, a sexual sin can be a mortal sin.

Furthermore, it is possible for a mortal sin to occur in one act. On the other hand, the declaration points out, "it is true that in sins of the sexual order, in view of their kind and their causes, it more easily happens that free consent is not fully given."

The declaration goes on to point out that chastity as a virtue does not consist only in avoiding faults. It involves something positive. It is a virtue of the whole personality, regarding both interior and outward behaviour. An important point, in the declaration's view, is that chastity frees the person to more fully follow Christ.

QUESTIONS

From this brief outline of official Roman Catholic teaching since 1918, several questions emerge. I will note only three questions which bear on the tasks of this workshop.

First, what is the relation between the unitive and procreative aspects of marriage? More generally, why are sex and marriage essentially directed towards procreation? Vatican II, the majority report of the papal commission, and *Humanae Vitae* all agree that sex and marriage are essentially ordered towards procreation. Such agreement is not automatic today, however, among Catholic theologians. Outside of the Church there is relatively little support for the Church's official teaching on this point.

The second question is: given the general orientation of sex and marriage towards procreation, why must we conclude that artificial contraception is wrong in each and every case? Why must we accept that artificial contraception is intrinsically evil? Why may we not appeal to the total good of marriage, to other values in a particular situation, to allow artificial contraception in particular cases, at least as a lesser evil? More generally, may not the demands of the situation justify exceptions to other rules of sexual ethics?

The third question is: what weight is to be given to the traditional teaching of the Roman Catholic Church in sexual and marriage ethics? Some hold that the condemnation of artificial contraception has been taught infallibly.[37] Others would limit the scope of the Church's authority to teach on morals infallibly to the area of general principles and to things certainly revealed in Scripture. The majority report seemed to distinguish two levels. On a level of fundamental values the Church's teaching continues unchanged. On another level change can be accepted without being unfaithful to tradition. Is this an acceptable middle position?

Notes

1. *Casti Connubii,* Paragraph 5. Quotations from *Casti Connubii* used in this paper are taken from the translation in *The Church and the Reconstruction of the Modern World, The Social Encyclicals of Pius XI,* edited by Terence P. McLaughlin (Garden City, N.Y.: Doubleday, 1957).

2. Paragraph 17.

3. Paragraph 11.

4. See Paragraphs 11–13.

5. Paragraph 59.

6. Paragraph 9.

7. Paragraph 7.

8. Paragraph 23.

9. Paragraph 23.

10. Paragraph 24.

11. Paragraph 18.

12. Paragraph 54.

13. Paragraph 37.

14. Paragraph 123.

15. *Vom Sinn Und Zweck Der Ehe* (Breslau: Osterdeutsche Verlag).

16. Published in New York by Sheed and Ward.

17. *The Meaning of Marriage,* pp. 87–88.

18. *Acta Apostolicae Sedis* 36 (1944): 103.

19. An English translation of the relevant parts of this sentence is available in *Love and Sexuality,* edited by Odile M. Liebard (Wilmington, N.C.: McGrath, 1978), pp. 71–83.

20. See, for example, his allocution to the Sacred Roman Rota on Oct.

29, 1941, *Clergy Review* 22 (1942): 84–88; his address to the midwives, Oct. 29, 1951, in *Love and Sexuality*, p. 117.

21. See address to midwives, *Love and Sexuality*, p. 117, and address of May 19, 1956, *ibid.*, p. 175–76.

22. See, for example, his address of Nov. 12, 1944, in *Love and Sexuality*, p. 92.

23. See the address to the midwives, *Love and Sexuality*, p. 116.

24. *Love and Sexuality*, p. 113.

25. Address on Sept. 29, 1949, *Love and Sexuality*, pp. 96–100; address to the midwives, Oct. 29, 1951, *Love and Sexuality*, 117–18.

26. Address on May 19, 1956, *Love and Sexuality*, p. 177.

27. *Love and Sexuality*, pp. 240–41.

28. *Gaudium et Spes*, Section 49.

29. *Gaudium et Spes*, Section 48. Quotations from *Gaudium et Spes* in this paper are taken from *The Documents of Vatican II*, edited by Walter B. Abbott (London-Dublin: Geoffrey Chapman, 1966).

30. Section 48. See also section 50.

31. Because these words are central to our discussion and are often quoted, it will be useful to quote the Latin of the original text. That text, having noted that the moral judgment must not depend only on a sincere intention or an evaluation of motives continues: ". . . *sed objectivis criteriis, ex personae eiusdemque actuum natura desumptis, determinari debet, quae integrum sensum mutuae donationis ac humanae procreationis in contextu veri amoris observant.*" It might be argued that in emphasizing that the couple must preserve the *full* sense of mutual self-giving and human procreation in the context of true love, this text rules out artificial contraception. However, that can hardly have been the general understanding of the text by the Council Fathers. Having been instructed by Pope Paul VI not to pronounce on the issue of artificial contraception, they would not be likely to try to settle the issue even in principle.

32. The first, third and fourth documents were published in *The Tablet* 221(1967):449–54; 478–85; 510–13. The first and second documents are available in *Love and Sexuality*, pp. 296–320.

33. *On Human Life* (Jamaica Plains, Boston: Daughters of St. Paul, 1968), Section 8.

34. Section 12.

35. Section 6.

36. Section 10.

37. See "Contraception and the Infallibility of the Ordinary Magisterium" by J. C. Ford and G. Grisez, *Theological Studies* 39 (1978): 258–312, esp. 312.

6. Magisterial Teaching on Marriage 1880–1986: Historical Constancy or Radical Development?

J.A. Selling

This article first appeared in *Historia: Memoria futuri Mèlanges Louis Vereecke* in 1991.

Important questions have been asked and continue to be asked with respect to marriage and conjugal life. The magisterium has attempted to give some clear answers to these questions, but has not always succeeded in its efforts. Often laypersons find themselves more confused than convinced, a phenomenon that was not un-known at the time of the *Humanae vitae* event. One response to this confusion has been that the faithful have been deprived of reason-able explanations on the part of priests and theologians whose role it supposedly is to interpret the judgments of the magisterium in a manner that is understandable and acceptable for all persons. It would be short-sighted to deny that in the case of the debate over the responsible regulation of fertility there was a certain hesitation on the part of many to provide such an "acceptable" interpretation of the 1968 encyclical. Up until the present time, few have suggested that perhaps one of the reasons for this hesitation might have been a similar state of confusion on the part of those priests and theolo-gians. An explanation for this state of affairs might be that what the magisterium has taught on these subjects over the past one hundred years has gone through such profound change that it is difficult to discern precisely what that teaching might be.

The above survey reflects upon only five sources since 1880, although these five have been recognized as pre-eminently expres-sive of what the magisterium has taught in this area. What we have found in these sources is a continuous development in magisterial teaching that is hard to recognize as "constant." Leo XIII's *Arcanum divinae sapientiae* was concerned primarily with legislative jurisdiction with respect to marriage and the evil of divorce. The source of common errors about marriage, he suggested, was the notion that marriage was a "natural institution," one that was not determined and defined by God himself. In correcting this error, Leo XIII put forth his concept of marriage which he saw as complete at the time of creation, only to be raised to the dignity of a sacrament by Christ. Marriage, he wrote, had two essential properties, "unity and perpetuity." All its other characteristics belonged to the "natural order" of creation, including its orientation to the procreation and education of children and the submission of the wife to her husband as the head of the conjugal unit and the family. The "rights and duties" of marriage were attributed to conjugal and family life in general and were not equated with the performance of sexual acts. Leo XIII did not characterize procreation as a duty, nor did he ascribe any meanings or purposes to "the conjugal act," even though his teaching presumes that the natural purpose of this act would be procreation alone.

The 1917 codification of canon law was concerned to describe the nature of the marital contract as accurately as possible in order to insure that marital consent would be fully and freely given. To this end, marriage is defined functionally as having a primary and a secondary end. These ends, however, apply to marriage alone and are not said to be realized through the marriage act, which itself is euphemistically characterized merely as "apt" for procreation. The contract of marriage entails rights and duties. However, these are not described in the same way that *Arcanum* had suggested, but rather are restricted to the *ius in corpus.* There is not even a "right" to a specifically procreative act spelled out in the text since at that time distinguishing between fertile and infertile acts of sexual intercourse was virtually impossible.

Pius XI's *Casti connubii* represents one of the most elaborate teachings of the magisterium on marriage and conjugal life. In it we find for the first time the appropriation of Augustine's *tria bona* for explaining the meaning of marriage, although there is some ambiguity with respect to whether these *bona* should be interpreted in a hierarchical fashion. Overall, Pius XI's teaching resembles that of Leo XIII, especially in his understanding of domestic life. However, this pope was forced to deal with the question of known infertility when judging the moral permissibility of the conjugal act. In response to this question, he stated that the couple could engage in sexual intercourse known to be infertile because doing so would have significance for the secondary ends of marriage which the couple could intend in their activity. Nevertheless, Pius XI was careful to avoid the notion that these secondary ends alone could function as a sufficient justification, leaving the hierarchy of ends intact and applying them exclusively to marriage, not to the performance of the marital act as such.

In 1951, in his "Address to the Midwives," Pius XII addressed the difficult question of periodic continence and the licitness of the procreation-excluding intention. In doing so, he shifted the question away from the meaning or purpose of the marital act and onto the "duty" of a married couple to contribute to the propagation of the human race when they engage in this "right of marriage." However, he characterized this as a positive duty from which the couple could be excused because of "serious reasons" ("indications"). At the same time, neither the willingness of the couple to accept a child, should their efforts fail, nor the mere integrity of the sexual act were considered to be sufficient to justify this practice. No vague "openness to procreation" provided any moral justification.

The concern of Pius XII to counteract the setting forth of "personal values" in marriage as primary for the relationship caused him to withdraw from the possible opening that had been suggested by his predecessor for transferring the ends of marriage onto the purposes or meanings of the marriage act. In fact, he became very explicit about the absolute subordination of these secondary ends and understood sexual intercourse in marriage to have only one purpose: "the great and unique law, *generatio et educatio prolis.*"

While Pius XII solved the problem of the relationship between the practice of periodic continence and the realization of the primary end of marriage, his teaching eventually opened new questions about the meaning of marriage itself and eventually about the possibility of inducing infertility while maintaining the integrity of the sexual act. However, before these questions entered into public debate, the Second Vatican Council took place and substantially changed the entire understanding of marriage and conjugal life.

Gaudium et spes made a significant contribution in defining marriage and conjugal life in quite different terms than the previous magisterial teaching. The conciliar teaching effectively abandoned the doctrine of the ends of marriage and opted for a scripturally inspired notion of covenant to describe the conjugal relationship. This was seen as a relationship between equal partners, having a meaning and purpose in itself, regardless whether children were forthcoming. The procreation of children was described as a supreme gift and the ultimate crown of both marriage and conjugal love, while the task and the project of having and raising children was to be taken on with a "generous human and Christian sense of responsibility."

Within the perspective of the Pastoral Constitution, sexual acts were understood to be an expression of conjugal love and were characterized as "noble and worthy." Conjugal love itself, and not specifically the marital act, was "unitive" in the sense of involving the whole person in a lasting and exclusive relationship. Marital sexual behavior, therefore, must always be understood in terms of the whole of conjugal life. Its "meaning" or "purpose" was in service to that relationship, a covenant (*foedus*) which served as the basis for speaking of marriage as a sacrament.

When *Humanae vitae* was published in 1968, its primary concern was to pass judgment on the practice of "artificial" contraception. The resulting perspective adopted by this papal letter placed a heavy emphasis upon the structure, meaning and purpose of sexual acts. However, in place of continuing the development that magisterial teaching had taken from 1880 to 1965, Paul VI took up the option that Pius XII had left behind and completed the transfer of the ends of marriage onto the conjugal act. In doing so, he changed the vocabulary from "ends" (*fines*) to "meanings" (*significationes*). The subsequent teaching, on the "two meanings of the conjugal act" (*Humanae vitae, 12*) may have followed the line from Pius XI to Pius XII, but it did so by developing this teaching a step further, not by repeating a teaching that was "constant." In fact, the position of Paul VI clearly goes beyond that of Pius XII in that the "serious reasons" argument is substituted by the council's notion of "responsible parenthood." Then, Paul VI implied that the mere integrity of the act of sexual intercourse was sufficient to guarantee the moral acceptability of the couple's behavior. The new norm became "openness to procreation," going considerably beyond what Pius XII had explicitly taught.

Unfortunately, this development, even though it might somehow be connected with "previous magisterial teaching," now appeared out of place, *Gaudium et spes* having abandoned the structure that had already proven itself inadequate. It is not surprising that some received the teaching of *Humanae vitae* as a virtually "new" teaching of the magisterium. However, in the light of the history of the teaching of the magisterium on marriage and conjugal life, *Humanae vitae* can be better characterized either as a radical development of the line of teaching of Leo XIII, Pius XI and Pius XII, or a departure from the developing teaching of Leo XIII, Pius XI, Pius XII and the Second Vatican Council. It would demand stretching one's imaginative capabilities to understand this encyclical—and the subsequent teaching that has emerged from the magisterium—as typical of "constant teaching" in most any sense of that term.

7. Permitted and Disputed Means of Controlling Conception

John T. Noonan, Jr.

This chapter first appeared in *Contraception* in 1965.

When means are developed to reach a result whose achievement by other means is prohibited, several questions arise. Does the logic of the prohibition require condemnation of the new alternatives, or does the existence of the alternatives require rethinking of the prohibition, or can prohibition and permitted alternatives coexist? Is it the means and not the end which is objectionable? What is the purpose of the prohibition? All of these questions, so characteristic of the development of rules, appeared in the course of controversy over the means by which conception might be regulated.

Prior to the mid-nineteenth century, it was admitted that conception might be avoided by abstinence; no obligation to procreate was ever imposed. It was debated whether *amplexus reservatus* was permissible, and this debate continued. But never had it been admitted by a Catholic theologian that complete sexual intercourse might be had in which, by deliberation, procreation was excluded. It was, then, a capital event when use of a sterile period, even one wrongly calculated in fact, was permitted in theory. In the twentieth century the significance of this permission was to become apparent.

USE OF THE STERILE PERIOD

In 1845, Felix Archimedes Pouchet had won the prize for experimental physiology of the French Royal Academy of Sciences for his report, on the basis of observations of animals, that conception in all mammals occurred only during menstruation and one to twelve days after menstruation.[1] In 1853, Antoine de Salinis, the bishop of Amiens, reported that some married persons, "relying on the opinion of skilled doctors," were persuaded that there were "several days each month in which conception by a woman could not take place." The bishop asked the Penitentiary if those who had intercourse on such days were to be disturbed, "if at any rate they had legitimate reasons for abstaining from the conjugal act." The Penitentiary replied that "those about whom you ask are not to be disturbed provided they do nothing by which conception is prevented."[2] Evidently there was no one who recalled St. Augustine's opinion that intercourse only on sterile days was a prime way of doing something to prevent conception. The Penitentiary did not restrict its answer to those who in good faith believed they were acting lawfully, so that its decision seemed to indicate more than mere tolerance. The practice was accepted although its apparent purpose was to make conception impossible.

The reply of 1853 was not given publicity, and in 1867 a Dr. Avard of La Rochelle asked Cardinal Gousset whether it was lawful for couples to use the period they believed to be absolutely sterile according to the Pouchet theory. Noting that the question needed further study, Gousset replied that such couples should not be disturbed; he seemed himself to favor permitting such usage, but did not commit himself.[3]

There was no theoretical development of support for deliberate use of the sterile period before 1873. Then a theologian at Louvain with a knowledge of biology, Auguste Joseph Lecomte (1824–1881), published *L'Ovulation spontanée de l'espèce humaine dans ses rapports avec la théologie morale.*[4] This was the first attempt to take theological account of the nineteenth-century discoveries about ovulation. In 1827 Karl Ernst von Baer had published his discovery of the human ovum, which revolutionized the understanding of human reproduction.[5] But the moral theologians were still speaking about female "seed" and female "semination." Part of Lecomte's work was directed to showing the consequences of the new account of reproduction for the traditional theological views on feminine "pollution," part to showing that menstrual blood had no effect on offspring and that intercourse in menstruation was not certain to be sterile, and part to relating the Pouchet theory to moral theology.[6]

Citing Pouchet and other medical authors, Lecomte concluded that in the period which was sterile by Pouchet's calculations fecundation was improbable, although exceptions had been noted and their cause debated. He then argued that married couples having "reasonable and proportionate causes" for avoiding children might morally choose to have intercourse only in this period.[7] Lecomte emphasized the dilemma presented by the large number of ovulations which might occur if, "as often happens," a girl married under the age of twenty. Either she would be burdened "by a most numerous abundance of offspring" or the couple would practice "onanism." Lecomte believed that use of the sterile period was the way out of the dilemma. Confessors should insinuate the method in discreet language, not appearing "over-learned" in these matters.[8]

Lecomte's book was published with the permission of the archbishops of Malines and Bourges.[9] Large extracts from it were reprinted in the *Analecta juris pontificii,* a clerical journal addressed to a clerical audience. That a book presenting such a breakthrough in theory then received comparatively little attention must be attributed to the prevailing torpor in moral theology. Its thesis on the intentional use of the sterile period was well received by an anonymous reviewer for the *Nouvelle revue théologique.*[10] It was, however, violently attacked in 1874 by an anonymous priest in a Madrid weekly, *Consultor de los parrocos.* This critique is an index to the continued existence of one current of thought in the Church. The anonymous author accused Lecomte of defending intercourse in marriage "not to generate children, but only to have pleasure. This pernicious sensualism is entirely contrary to the laws of God and the good of society. It constitutes the horrible crime against nature." The vital point was made: "Coitus indeed takes place, but at a time at which conception is known to be almost impossible. And is this not to prevent generation? Without doubt." The author admitted that intercourse might lawfully be had by the pregnant or the aged for the lawful purpose of quieting concupiscence. What was the difference between such intercourse and the use of the sterile period? He answered that the obstacle to procreation in the former cases was not put by human design, whereas "in this will of avoiding generation is found the great difference between the two cases." The author's parting shot was to invite Lecomte to submit his theses to the Roman congregations.[11]

Another review of the book in 1874 in the *Revue des sciences ecclésiastiques* (27:594ff), published in Amiens, was more restrained. The reviewer, one Craisson, former vicar-general of the diocese, said that the deliberate choice of the sterile days in order to avoid children "was contrary to the principal end which the Creator had in view in authorizing the conjugal act." However, as a lesser evil, the method might be suggested by a confessor to lead habitual onanists from their mortal sin.

Lecomte was apparently under more serious pressure than from these two unfavorable reviewers. "By order of his superiors," he withdrew his book from circulation.[12] He also submitted his thesis on the sterile period to the Penitentiary. He asked a series of questions:

I. 1. Is it permitted to act in this way without sinning mortally?
   2. Is there any venial sin because of the intention of not conceiving?
II. May a confessor counsel use of this means:
   1. To a wife who detests and reproves the onanistic action of her husband without being able to correct it?
   2. To two spouses who are willful onanists in order not to have the care of a numerous family?
III. 1. Is there any danger which decency [*l'honnêteté*] reproves in counseling this means which would procure the diminution of the family more surely than onanism?
   2. Would not the resulting danger be compensated for by the advantage of avoiding mortal sin and of giving tranquility to numerous Christian women who are alienated from the sacraments by the fault of their husbands or their own fear?

The Penitentiary replied on June 16, 1880. Without characterizing them, it referred to the positions of Gousset, the *Analecta juris pontificii,* and the two reviews. It then said: "Spouses using the aforesaid way of marriage are not to be disturbed, and a confessor may, though cautiously, insinuate the opinion in question to those spouses whom he has vainly tried with other reasons to lead from the detestable crime of onanism."[13]

This answer was indirect and ambiguous. In saying that confessors could recommend use of the sterile period, the Penitentiary could have meant to indicate that the practice was not sinful. On the other hand, some authority supported the position that a confessor might tolerate a sinful act to lead a penitent from a greater sin. This was the position of Craisson, which the Penitentiary refers to in the preliminary discussion. Consequently, it may also have meant to adopt his view. Grudging as the answer seemed, this official Roman act gave the theologians enough ecclesiastical backing to enable them to maintain the new position.

No advance beyond the cautious position of the Penitentiary appeared in such typical works as Lehmkuhl's *Moral Theology* (2-1.8.4.1.1.1, *ad* 5) or De Smet's *Les Fiançailles et le mariage* 2.1.3.1.1, annex 2). Both authors observed that the method was not certain, and followed the Penitentiary in saying that its use was not to be recommended indiscriminately to everyone. Somewhat greater enthusiasm appeared in the work of C. Capellmann, an Aachen doctor, who wrote one of the first treatises explicitly devoted to the moral theology of medicine. He said that "he and others" had observed that impregnation was improbable, although not impossible, in the third week after the beginning of menstruation. No moral law prevented coitus at that time.[14] On the other hand, by 1900 it could be noted in the *Nouvelle revue théologique* that "the improbability of fecundation at the so-called sterile times had been exaggerated by the doctors." "Who has not heard penitents who adhered to the observance of these times and yet did not avoid fecundation?"[15] As the formula for sterility involved having intercourse at the time subsequent research indicated that fertility would be apt to be greatest, it was perhaps fortunate that no greater attention was paid this method.

By the time of *Casti connubii* the lack of success with the Pouchet period made it far from a burning question. New discoveries had been made, but they had not made their way into practice. Accordingly, Pius XI made only a passing reference to couples who have intercourse "even though, through natural causes either of time or of certain defects, new life cannot thence result" (*AAS* 22:561). Such intercourse, the Pope held, was lawful, "provided always the intrinsic nature of that act is preserved, and accordingly its proper relation to the primary end." There was nothing in the Pope's address dealing with the deliberate avoidance of births through such use in a systematic way.

Meanwhile, research had been going on which made the use of a truly sterile period a possibility. In 1924 Kyusaku Ogino published in Japan a work presenting new data on the time of the sterile period. His work was not at once known in Europe, and in 1929, independently of Ogino's research, Hermann Knaus, an Austrian doctor, published the results of research reaching the same conclusion.[16] According to these studies, ovulation occurred sixteen to twelve days before the anticipated first day of the next menstrual period. For a woman with a regular menstrual cycle it was possible to avoid intercourse at the time when fecundation of the ovum might occur.

These results were widely circulated in Europe and the United States in the early 1930's. In Europe, J. N. J. Smulders was the chief popularizer. His *Periodische Enthaltung in der Ehe: Methode Ogino-Knaus* was published in Regensburg in 1931. In the United States there appeared Leo Latz's *The Rhythm of Sterility and Fertility in Women* (Chicago, 1932) and Valère Coucke and James J. Walsh's *The Sterile Period in Family Life* (New York, 1933). The first two works were by doctors; the last was written in collaboration by Canon Coucke and Dr. Walsh. All carried imprimaturs from the dioceses in which they were published.

The principal Roman authority was still the 1880 response of the Penitentiary. Writing for American priests, John A. Ryan recognized that this response dealt with a different question: Could intercourse be sought on days when fertility was improbable? What was proposed now was a method whereby sterility was certain. If successfully employed, the method might substantially decrease the population. But, pending that time, and stressing the ideal of fecundity, Ryan thought that deliberate use of the method was acceptable.

Further, Ryan believed that the 1880 answer of the Penitentiary could be liberally construed to permit confessors to suggest the sterile period not only to those already practicing contraception, but to any married person with a serious reason for avoiding offspring.[17] Asked directly about the new method, the Penitentiary on July 20, 1932, replied by simply citing the response of 1880. This answer was not, however, immediately published.[18]

From the cautions that soon followed, it is apparent that many priests found in the Ogino-Knaus method an answer to pressing pastoral problems. In reaction, Ignatius Salsmans, a Belgian Jesuit, protested against the "rash promotion" of "Oginoism," a system which Salsmans seemed to feel was but one remove from onanism. Pius XI in *Casti connubii,* he contended, had not thought of rhythm when he approved the use of a sterile "time"; he had had in mind only intercourse after the menopause.[19] A still more influential warning voice was raised by Arthur Vermeersch. He quoted the outraged cry of an American priest that the "heresy of the empty cradle" was now being promoted by the Church as priests recommended use of the sterile period to space births. He noted as an evil the dissemination of the view that the Church had its own method of achieving sterility contrary to the primary end of marriage. He further observed that widespread use of the method would diminish the population, contrary to "the common good of men and the particular good of states." In the light of these risks, Vermeersch taught that the subject should not be treated in special books devoted to the Ogino-Knaus method, but only in the context of a treatise on marriage where the Church's ideal of fecundity was set out. He did not move an inch beyond the 1880 answer of the Penitentiary. Confessors should, cautiously and prudently, suggest the method to obstinate onanists, not commending the method to them but permitting it as a lesser evil.[20]

Several bishops followed Vermeersch's lead and counseled restraint in the diffusion of the rhythm method. As enlightened a body as the provincial council of Malines under Cardinal Van Roey said in 1937 that (1) the use of the sterile period presents dangers, such as the encouragement of egotism, the unilateral denial of marriage rights in the fertile period, the lessening of conjugal love, the willingness even to abort a child conceived by mistake; (2) the method is consequently not to be proposed except to onanists, to wean them from their sin, and to others who have adequate reasons for avoiding conception; (3) adequate reasons for avoiding conception are danger to the wife from childbirth, or "truly serious economic difficulty in feeding numerous offspring."[21]

A doctoral dissertation in 1942 at The Catholic University of America by a diocesan priest, Orville N. Griese, reviewed the authorities and concluded that the Church neither approved nor disapproved the use of rhythm. Griese himself contended that the use of rhythm was per se illicit, but under some circumstances might be justified.[22] In the face of criticism, he later explained that he was speaking of rhythm chosen as "a way of life."[23] His position was generally rejected. However, in rejecting it, one of the leading American Jesuit moralists, Gerald Kelly, professor of moral theology at St. Mary's Seminary, Kansas, wrote: "Only exceptional couples can take up the practice of the 'rhythm-theory' without exposing their married lives to grave dangers; and even these couples usually need the special grace of God. If this is true, and I believe it is, then the *per se illicitum, per accidens licitum* is also true—though not, it seems, in the sense in which he [Griese] explains it."[24]

There was recognition among the theological writers that the method would not work in all cases to prevent procreation. Confessors were counseled not to try to tell the penitent when the sterile period occurred.[25] An instruction from the Holy Office, dated May 16, 1943, reminded confessors that they were not to give medical advice.[26]

Medical doubts, pastoral caution, general suspicion, still surrounded the practice of rhythm two decades after it had been popularized. In 1950, however, the fourth national convention of the Association of Italian Catholic Physicians, recognizing that the method was not secure, approved the method in particular cases where it was desirable to avoid childbirth.[27] A year later, on October 29, 1951, Pius XII spoke to the Italian Catholic Society of Midwives, a group of nurses specializing in maternity cases. The Pope chose the occasion to make the fullest statement on marriage since *Casti connubii.* In this address a new spirit was visible. For the first time rhythm was referred to by Roman authority not as an alternative to be cautiously proffered to onanists, but as a method open to all

Christian couples. The group Pius XII addressed were specialists, but the public character of the address and its publication in the *Acta Apostolicae Sedis* proclaimed that Pius XII had moved far from the 1934 counsels of Vermeersch. The Pope taught that rhythm, for a reason, could be used. To have intercourse and avoid the duty of procreation without serious reason would, he said, be a sin. But there might be serious motives (*seri motivi*) for avoiding procreation. These motives might be "not rarely present in the so-called 'indications'—medical, eugenic, economic, and social." Given these serious motives, "it follows that observance of the sterile period can be licit" (*AAS* 43:845–846).

The papal statement was not only public approval of rhythm. It recognized "economic" motives without restricting them to serious poverty. It recognized "social" motives, and such motives would seem to have embraced consideration of the world population or at least consideration of the population of a given society. The Pope's speech was far from being as serious or solemn an act as, say, the adoption of the decretal *Si aliquis* or the approval of the Roman Catechism. But as the sign of a new attitude it was a major step.

One month later Pius XII underlined the authoritativeness of the October statement and at the same time left no doubt of his intention by using the word *regolazione,* regulation, to describe what might be accomplished by use of the sterile period. This was the first time that a Pope had spoken with approval of the regulation of birth. Referring to the October address, Pius XII declared, "We have affirmed the lawfulness and at the same time the limits—in truth quite broad—of a regulation of offspring. . . Science, it may be hoped, will develop for this method a sufficiently secure base" (*AAS* 43:859). This second address, of November 26, 1951, was given to an even more significant audience than the midwives: to two Italian societies, the Association of Large Families and the Family Front. Not only was regulation of births publicly expounded to these lay groups; the Pope hoped that the method for securing sterility would be made certain.

A dozen years after the Pope had asserted leadership in approval of regulation of births, the American Jesuit John Lynch in an address to the Catholic Theological Society reviewed the evolution from 1930. Up until the allocution of Pius XII the "standard authors [were] still treating quite gingerly the pastoral aspects of periodic continence." Even after the allocution, theologians "lagged." It was still, "often carelessly," stated that a large family is the Christian ideal. "However, this maxim is not universally applicable to each individual marriage; it obtains, in truth, only in circumstances wherein the decent raising of a large family is reasonably possible." It was time to recognize that the education of children might require spacing of births, time to recognize that "the average couple of normal fertility over the average span of married life can virtually always adduce more than sufficient reason for at least periodic recourse to periodic continence." Lynch called attention to the operation, beginning in 1961, of a Family Life Clinic by the Catholic diocese of Buffalo. He plainly implied that instruction in the use of rhythm should be undertaken with the support of ecclesiastical organizations.[28]

Use of the sterile period, once attacked by Augustine when used to avoid all procreation, approved in 1880 for cautious suggestion to onanists, guardedly popularized between 1930 and 1951, was now fully sanctioned. The substantial split between sexual intercourse and procreation, already achieved by the rejection of Augustinian theory, was confirmed in practice.

Notes

1. F. A. Pouchet, *Théorie positive de l'ovulation spontanée et de la fécondation des mammifères et de l'espèce humaine, basée sur l'observation de toute la série animale* (Paris, 1847). Pouchet was an admirer of St. Albert the Great and later wrote a book on his contributions to experimental science.

2. *Decisiones Sanctae Sedis de usu et abusu matrimonii,* ed. Hartmann Batzill, 2nd ed. (Rome, 1944), p. 130.

3. Answers of Gousset summarized in *Revue de thérapeutique médico-chirurgicale,* February 15, 1867, and July 15, 1867.

4. Paris and Louvain, 1873. My citations are from the excerpts therefrom in *Analecta juris pontificii,* Recueil de dissertations sur différents su-

jets de droit canonique, de liturgie, de théologie, et d'histoire, 12th series (Paris, Brussels, Rome, 1873). Lecomte published his book anonymously as by "Abbé A. L., docteur en sciences naturelles." He is identified as the author in the Index to the *Nouvelle revue théologique* for the years 1869–1880. Lecomte also had written a work on human evolution.

5. Charles Singer and E. Ashworth Underwood, *A Short History of Medicine,* 2nd ed. (Oxford, 1928), p. 204.

6. Lecomte noted that the ancient theory by which intercourse in menstruation had been treated as a mortal sin had been refuted in 1774 by De Lignoir, *De l'homme et de la femme consideré physiquement dans l'état du mariage* (Lille, 1774).

7. Lecomte, in *Analecta juris pontificii* (1873), col. 721.

8. *Ibid.,* cols. 722–723.

9. *Ibid.,* col. 706, n. 1.

10. "Bulletin bibliographique," *Nouvelle revue théologique* 5 (1873), 527. The reviewer notes that he himself defended the same theory in 1857, but that there were and are substantial doubts about its scientific foundation.

11. Anonymous review of *L'Ovulation spontanée de l'espèce humaine dans ses rapports avec la théologie morale,* reprinted from *Consultor de los parrocos* in *Analecta juris pontificii,* 13th series (1874), cols. 995–997. This anonymous critic was even more shocked at Lecomte's view that a woman could commit a mortal sin of autoerotic excitement, but that this sin could not be described as a "sin against nature" because no emission of seed for generation was involved (col. 997).

12. *Ibid.,* col. 993. It is not clear whether the withdrawal was ordered because of the thesis on the sterile period or the thesis on "the sin against nature" in the case of women.

13. The French text of the questions is given in *Decisiones Sanctae Sedis,* p. 26, and *Nouvelle revue théologique* 13 (1881), 459–460. In its answer, the Penitentiary puts the questions in Latin (*Decisiones,* pp. 24–26).

14. C. Capellmann, *Medicina pastoralis* (Aachen, 1890) D.4.1.

15. E. de Gryse, "Théologie pastorale," *Nouvelle revue théologique* 32 (1900), 581. In the United States the method was apparently recommended by some priests to parishioners even in the 1920's, for Monsignor John A. Ryan comments wryly on the complaints and jokes about the method's failure to work; "The Moral Aspects of Periodical Continence," *Ecclesiastical Review* 89 (1933), 29.

16. Ogino's work appeared in an English translation by Yonez Miyagawa ten years later: *Conception Period of Women* (Harrisburg, Penn.,

1934). Hermann Knaus, *Die periodische Fruchtbarkeit und Unfruchtbarkeit des Weibes: Der Weg zur natürlichen Geburtenregelung* (Vienna, 1934), translated into English by D. H. and Kathleen Kitchin as *Periodic Fertility and Sterility in Woman* (Vienna, 1934).

17. Ryan, "The Moral Aspects of Periodical Continence," p. 28.

18. Text of the reply of the Penitentiary in Francis X. Hürth, *De re matrimoniali,* Pontificiae universitatis Gregorianae series theologica, 30 (Rome, 1955), p. 111.

19. Ignatius Salsmans, "Sterilitas facultativa licita?" *Ephemerides theologicae lovanienses* 11 (1934), 563–564.

20. Arthur Vermeersch, "De prudenti ratione indicandi sterilitatem physiologicam," *Periodica de re morali, canonica, liturgica* 22 (1934), 246–247.

21. Fifth Provincial Council of Malines, Resolution 47, set out in J. Goeyvaerts, "De moralitate usus matrimonii ad tempus ageneseos restricti," *Collectanea mechliniensia* 33 (1948), 704. Somewhat similarly, Patrick Cardinal Hayes in September 1936 sent to every priest of his diocese a letter entitled "Official Monitum on the Rhythm Theory," in which he said that in teaching and preaching priests "must insist on the Church's ideals of the purpose of marriage, rather than what is allowed in particular cases for upright and holy motives." Quoted in Orville N. Griese, *The Morality of Periodic Continence* (Washington, 1942), p. 41.

22. Griese, p. 18. Griese said that if a newly married couple asked a priest, they should be told that the practice can be justified, but only in cases where married persons are in such unfavorable circumstances as poor health or genuine poverty (*ibid.,* p. 110). The actual use of the method should be adopted only with the approval of a confessor (*ibid.,* p. 95).

23. Orville N. Griese, "Objective Morality of the Rhythm Practice," *Ecclesiastical Review* 120 (1949), 475.

24. Gerald Kelly, "Notes on Moral Theology, 1946," *Theological Studies* 7 (1946), 105–106. See also John C. Ford, S. J., "Notes on Moral Theology, 1944," *Theological Studies* 5 (1944), 509. Hugh J. O'Connell, C.S.S.R., "Is Rhythm *Per Se* Illicit?" *Ecclesiastical Review* 119 (1948), 336; Gerald Kelly, S.J., "Notes on Moral Theology," *Theological Studies* 11 (1950), 71–77; J. McCarthy, "The use of the 'Safe Period,' " *Irish Ecclesiastical Record* 67 (1946), 259–263.

25. John C. Ford, S.J., "Current Moral Theology and Canon Law," *Theological Studies* 2 (1941), 537; P. Ahearne, "The Confessor and the Ogino-Knaus Theory," *Irish Ecclesiastical Record* 61 (1943), 1–14.

26. "Normae quaedam de agendi ratione confessariorum circa VI decalogi praeceptum," *Periodica de re morali, canonica, liturgica* 33 (1944),

130. John Ford interpreted this instruction as not preventing the confessor from answering to a direct question by indicating "when the sterile period generally takes place, making it quite clear that only professional advice can give any real assurance in the matter." "Notes on Moral Theology, 1943," *Theological Studies* 4 (1943), 584.

27. "L'Opinione dell'Associazione de' Medici Cattolici Italiani sulla continenza periodica," *Perfice munus* 26 (1951), 8–14.

28. John J. Lynch, S.J., "Changing Pastoral Emphases on the Practice of Periodic Continence," in *The Catholic Theological Society of America, Proceedings of the Eighteenth Annual Convention* (St. Louis, 1963), pp. 110, 112, 114–115.

It was widely felt by doctors experienced with rhythm that many people who were instructed in its use were badly instructed, and that much greater accuracy in its use could be obtained by combining the simple method of keeping track of the dates of menstruation with the taking of temperature in order to note the slight temperature rise indicative of ovulation. The first international symposium on the use of rhythm was held October 20–22, 1964, in Washington, D.C.; see Martin Boler, O.S.B., "Symposium on Rhythm," *American Ecclesiastical Review* 152 (1965), 13.

8. The Meaning of Marriage and the Principle of Superabundant Finality

Dietrich von Hildebrand

This chapter first appeared in *The Encyclical Humanae Vitae: A Sign of Contradiction* in 1969.

To this sublime love union God has confided the coming into being of a new man, a cooperation with His divine creativity. Could we think of any thing more beautiful than this connection between the deepest love communion, the ultimate self-donation out of love, and the creation of a new human being? A deep mystery is here offered to us, which calls for reverence and awe. But we can grasp the grandeur and depth of this connection only if we first understand the meaning and value of marriage as a love communion and the meaning and value of the marital act as the consummation of this ultimate union to which spousal love aspires. We can appreciate the mysterious character of the link between the marital act and the birth of a new person only if we have understood its finality as an instance of the principle of superabundance and not as an instrumental finality in which the conjugal act is looked at as a mere means for procreation. And it must be most emphatically stated that understanding the meaning and value of marriage as a love union *does not minimize but rather enhances the link between marriage and procreation.*

This will become clear as we examine briefly the nature of the principle of superabundance and its difference from merely instrumental finality.

We cannot deny that one end of knowledge is to enable man to act; our entire practical life, from the most primitive activities to the most complicated ones, presupposes knowledge. Moreover, a still more sublime end of knowledge is to enable us to attain the moral perfection and sanctification which is the presupposition for our eternal welfare. And yet, if these can rightly be called the ends to which knowledge is destined, knowledge has undoubtedly also a meaning and value of its own; and the relation to the ends it serves has the character of superabundance. This is a typical case of a finality in which the end is not the exclusive *raison d'être* of something.

This kind of finality differs patently from the instrumental finality which is in question when we call a surgical instrument a means for operating, or money a means for procuring ourselves a good, or teeth a means for the mastication of food. The main difference between instrumental finality and the finality that we have called the principle of superabundance consists in the fact that in instrumental finality the being which is considered as a means is in its meaning and value completely dependent upon the end, whereas in superabundant finality, it has a meaning and value independently of the end to which it leads.

In the instrumental finality the *causa finalis* determines the *causa formalis;* in the superabundant the *causa formalis* differs from the *causa finalis.*

In the case of a knife, the end (cutting) determines its entire nature; its meaning is identical with serving this end, and its value depends upon its function as a means. Its only *raison d'être* is to be a means for cutting. This is a typical instrumental finality.

In instrumental finality, the end is the exclusive *raison d'être* of the means; in superabundant finality, the good serving the end has also a *raison d'être* in itself.

We saw above that the intrinsic meaning and value of marriage consists in its being the deepest and closest love union. We saw that in its mutual self-donation and in its constitution of a matchless union, the conjugal act has the meaning of a unique fulfillment of spousal love. But to that high good, which has a meaning and value in itself, has been entrusted procreation. The same act, which in its meaning is the constitution of the union, has been superabundantly made the source of procreation; thus, we must speak of procreation as the end—but not in the sense of mere instrumental finality.

Though we may consider the sexual instinct in animals as a mere means for the continuation of the species, as an end in the sense of an instrumental finality, this is patently impossible with respect to the love between man and woman or to their union in marriage.

Occasionally, it has been conceded that in their subjective approach the spouses need not look at marriage and the conjugal union as a mere means in the instrumental sense; but the claim continues to be made that objectively the relation between a union of love and procreation has the character of an instrumental finality. It is claimed that God has implanted in their hearts the love between man and woman and the desire for a conjugal union as a mere means for procreation. But in arguing thus, one has not understood the real character of the link between marriage and procreation.

We touch here on a general and dangerous tendency to overlook the very nature of the person and to assume that the kind of instrumentality that is to be found in the biological realm can be extended to the spiritual realm of man. As long as instincts or urges are in question, their inner logic and *ratio* goes, so to speak, over the head of the person. It is true that neither man's intelligence nor his free will establishes the meaningful direction of an instinct such as thirst or the desire to sleep. God has given to these instincts and urges their meaningfulness without involving man's intelligence; this finality is similar to the one found in merely unconscious physiological processes. In so far as the experienced urge or instinct of thirst, for instance, is at stake, we thus rightly say that its *raison d'être* is to procure for the body the necessary liquid, and that God has installed it as a means to that end.

But when it comes to the spiritual acts of the person, such as willing or loving or experiencing contrition, we can no longer assume that in the eyes of God they have no meaning in themselves but are only means linked to an end by a finality similar to that of the instincts or urges. We must not forget that God takes man as person so seriously that He has addressed Himself to man, and that it depends on man's free response whether or not he will attain his eternal destiny. St. Augustine expressed this when he wrote: "He who made you without you, will not justify you without you." The spiritual attitudes of man have a meaning and a *ratio* in themselves, and they can never be treated as having their real significance independently of the person; they involve a person's intelligence and his freedom, his capacity to respond meaningfully, and not an impersonal, automatic finality going over the person's head. Consequently, it is impossible to see them as having their real significance beyond and independently of the person's conscious experience. Man is not a puppet for God, but a personal being to whom God addresses Himself and from whom He expects a meaningful response.

This devalorization and degradation of the spiritual human attitudes is incompatible with the character of man as a person, his character of *imago Dei;* it ignores the very fact that God has revealed Himself to man and also the way in which man's redemption took place.

It may be objected: Does not God often use an evil attitude as a means for something good in the life of the individual and especially in the history of mankind? May not an attitude which is evil in itself become a means leading to something good? Yes, indeed, but the *felix culpa* does not remove from the fault its morally negative character and does not entitle us to look at a moral decision as something which acquires its real meaning only in its possible function as *felix culpa,* instead of seeing its primary meaning in its moral value or disvalue.

The kind of finality which we have in mind when we say that God's providence makes out of evil something leading to a good differs obviously also in a radical way from the instrumental finality with which we are confronted in the biological sphere. It is not a finality which is rooted in the nature of something, but a free intervention of God's providence, using something in a direction which is even opposed to its nature and meaning. It would obviously make no sense to say that the end of moral evil is to lead to something good; that would be to claim that the very nature of a moral fault makes it a means for bringing about a good. The *culpa* is as such *infelix,* and that it may become *felix* is owing to an intervention of God, which never entitles us to say that this is the objective, valid meaning of moral guilt in God's eyes. God does not judge man according to whether or not his sins later on prove to be a *felix culpa* but according to their intrinsic sinfulness. Thus, we see that the merciful intervention of God, making a good grow out of evil, in no way reduces the role of man to that of a puppet.

2. THE MEANING OF MARRIAGE AND ITS PRIMARY END

Coming back to our topic, we must state that it is incompatible with the very nature of the person to consider the deepest human spiritual experiences as mere subjective aspects of something that, in God's eyes, is a means for an extrinsic end. It would be seeing man in a merely biological light if we assumed that love between man and woman, the highest earthly good, is a mere means for the conservation of the species, that its objective *raison d'être* is exclusively to instigate a union which serves procreation. The God-given, essential link between love of man and woman and its fulfillment in the marital union, on the one hand, and the creation of a new person, on the other hand, has precisely the character of superabundance, which is a much deeper connection than would be one of merely instrumental finality.

But let it be stated again emphatically: to stress the meaning and value of marriage as the most intimate, indissoluble union of love does not contradict the doctrine that procreation is the primary end of marriage. The distinction we have made between meaning and end, as well as the insight that marriage has a value of its own besides its sublime value as source of procreation, in no way diminishes the importance of the link between marriage and procreation; it rather enhances the link and places it in the right perspective.

3. WHY ARTIFICIAL BIRTH CONTROL IS SINFUL

We can now see more clearly the difference between natural and artificial birth control. The sinfulness of artificial birth control is rooted in the arrogation of the right to separate the actualized love union in marriage from a possible conception, to sever the wonderful, deeply mysterious connection instituted by God. This mystery is approached in an irreverent attitude. We are here confronted with the fundamental sin of irreverence toward God, the denial of our creaturehood, the acting as if we were our own lords. This is a basic denial of the *religio,* of our being bound to God; it is a disrespect for the mysteries of God's creation, and its sinfulness increases with the rank of the mystery in question. It is the same sinfulness that lies in suicide or in euthanasia, in both of which we act as if we were masters of life.

Every *active* intervention of the spouses that eliminates the possibility of conception through the conjugal act is incompatible with the holy mystery of the superabundant relation in this incredible gift of God. And this irreverence also affects the purity of the conjugal act, because the union can be the real fulfillment of love only when it is approached with reverence and when it is embedded in the *religio,* the consciousness of our basic bond to God.

To the sublime link between marriage and procreation Christ's words on the marriage bond also apply: "What God has joined together, let no man put asunder." This becomes still clearer when we consider that the mystery of the birth of a man not only should[1] be essentially linked to wedded love (through the conjugal act, which is destined to be the expression and fulfillment of this love), but is always linked to a creative intervention of God. Neither wedded love nor, still less, the physiological process of conception is *itself capable* of creating a human being with an immortal soul. On this point Pope Paul VI quotes the encyclical *Mater et Magistra:* " 'Human life is holy,' Pope John XXIII reminds us, 'and from conception on it demands the immediate intervention of God!' " (*Humanae Vitae,* 13). Man always comes forth directly from the hand of God, and therefore there is a unique and intimate relation between God and the spouses in the act of procreation. In a fruitful conjugal act we can say that the spouses participate in God's act of creation; the conjugal act of the spouses is incorporated into the creative act of God and acquires a serving function in relation to His act.

We thus see that artificial birth control is sinful not only because it severs the mysterious link between the most intimate love union and the coming into existence of a new human being, but also because in a certain way it artificially cuts off the creative intervention of God, or better still, it artificially separates an act which is ordained toward co-operation with the creative act of God from this its destiny. For, as Paul VI says, this is to consider oneself not a servant of God, but the "Lord over the origin of human life" (*Humanae Vitae,* 13).

This irreverence, however, is exclusively limited to *active* intervention severing the conjugal act from its possible link with procreation.

The conjugal act does not in any way lose its full meaning and value when one knows that a conception is out of the question, as when age, or an operation for the sake of health, or pregnancy excludes it. The knowledge that a conception is not possible does not in the least taint the conjugal act with irreverence. In such cases, if the act is an expression of a deep love, anchored in Christ, it will rank even higher in its quality and purity than one that leads to a conception in a marriage in which the love is less deep and not formed by Christ. And even when for good and valid reasons conception should be avoided, the marital act in no way loses its *raison d'être,* because its meaning and value is the actualization of the mutual self-donation of the spouses.[2] The intention of avoiding conception does not imply irreverence as long as one does not actively interfere in order to cut the link between the conjugal act and a possible conception.

Nor is the practice of rhythm to avoid conception in any way irreverent, because the existence of rhythm—that is to say, the fact that conception is limited to a short period—is itself a God-given institution. In Section 6 we shall show in greater detail why the use of rhythm implies not the slightest irreverence or rebellion against God's institution of the wonderful link between the love union and procreation; it is in no way a subterfuge, as some Catholics tend to believe. On the contrary, it is a grateful acceptance of the possibility God has granted of avoiding conception—if this is legitimately desirable—without preventing the expression and fulfillment of spousal love in the bodily union.

4. TWO CONCEPTS OF NATURE IN "HUMANAE VITAE"

In order to understand the decisive difference between natural and artificial birth control we must be aware that the concept "nature" can have various meanings.

On the one hand, "nature" can signify the purely factual order of creation, especially material and biological creation. On the other, however, the same word can signify the essence of profoundly significant relations endowed with a high value.

That the time between the conception and birth of a man is nine months and not eight or ten months is merely a factual datum. It could just as well be otherwise, and this fact bears no significant value. That the openings of the esophagus and the windpipe are so close together in man that one can choke easily is certainly a fact, but it is not a deeply meaningful relation which has a value. On the contrary, injuries could be averted were this not the case. But quite different, for instance, is the fact that love brings happiness. This is not something merely factual; it is deeply meaningful and bears a high value. This is also true of the fact that a deep union of two persons is constituted in mutual love. Indeed, it is of meaning and value that this reciprocal love is the only path leading to a spiritual union that is much deeper and more authentic than any amalgamation, any fusion, in the impersonal world. This fact, which is rooted in the nature of love and the personal I-thou communion, is the bearer of a high value. No one can reasonably say that this fact could be otherwise. It could not be otherwise, because it is a significant, intelligible, and necessary intrinsic relation. Similarly, it would betray extraordinary value-blindness not to see the depth and sublimity of this relation, but to regard it as something indifferent.

However, the *essential* difference between the two concepts of nature is not that in the one case we are confronted with an intelligible necessary fact and in the other with a mere empirical fact, but rather that in the one relations are deeply meaningful and possess a high *value,* and in the other they are only factual.

It is certainly true that for the faithful Christian both kinds of "nature" proceed from God and are therefore reverently accepted. Nevertheless, nature in the purely factual sense does not constitute something in which man ought not to intervene when there are reasonable grounds for seeking a change (in some circumstances he is even *obliged* to intervene). But intervention in nature in the second sense, where meaning and value are grounded in the essence of a thing, has a completely different character. For this nature contains in its very meaning and value a unique message from God and calls upon us to respect it.

This applies most of all to relations which constitute a deep mystery. Any violence done to these is particularly presumptuous on the part of man the creature. It is the usurpation of a right which man does not possess; it reflects a desire to play the role of God and Providence.

The confusion of these two concepts of nature has kept many from a proper understanding of the encyclical Humanae Vitae. They do not understand that it is not a merely factual or exclusively biological connection but rather a great and sublime mystery that God has entrusted the generation of a human being to the intimate union of man and wife who love each other in wedded love and who in becoming "two in one flesh" participate in the creative act of God. This is gloriously expressed by a prayer of an ancient Fulda ritual: "O Lord our God, who created man pure and spotless and thereafter ordained that in the propagation of the human race one generation should be produced from another by the *mystery of sweet love.*" The relation expressed here is thus not a merely factual one, but a staggering mystery, an ineffably deep and glorious fact. It is therefore a false argument to say: Why shouldn't man be allowed to regulate birth by artificial means, when God, after all, gave man control and dominion over nature and in the Old Testament made him the master of creation? Why is it allowed in medicine to take out the uterus, to transplant hearts, and perform many kinds of operations, but forbidden to intervene and modify nature in the case of the regulation of births? All those who argue in this way do not understand the radical difference between these two cases, because they confuse the two concepts of nature. As long as we remain within the realm of the purely "factual,' we are not morally forbidden to intervene. But when we deal with meaningful relations which possess a high value in themselves, and when, as in this case, we deal with a mystery which we can contemplate only with the deepest reverence, then every artificial intervention is a flagrant moral wrong.

A Static or a Dynamic Concept of Nature?

It is more than regrettable that the terms "dynamic" and "static" have been used in the polemic against the encyclical and its concept of nature. These typical shibboleths have taken on a particularly demagogic character in contemporary philosophical discussions. They appeal to irrational emotions and muddle the objective state of affairs. I have treated extensively the various confusions that lie behind these concepts in my book *Trojan Horse in the City of God.*[3]

5. THE RELATION BETWEEN BIOLOGICAL NATURE AND THE PERSON

One might object: Co-operation in the creation of a new human being is, after all, confined to the *physical act;* this co-operation can even take place when no union of love is present; therefore, it is a purely biological datum; it is bound neither to reciprocal love nor to the consensus of marriage, and can even be the result of the crime of rape.

But this objection overlooks the deep connection between biological nature and the person, and in two ways. First, the fact that in human nature many things are *de facto* the result of physical processes does not in the least cancel the truth that these physical processes *should* be the expression of *spiritual* attitudes. Secondly, not everything that is *connected* with biological conditions is itself biological.

The Order of What Is and the Order of What Ought to Be in Marriage

The *meaning* of the conjugal act is, as we have said, the ultimate fulfillment of the union desired by spousal love. It represents a unique gift of self, a gift that presupposes not only love, but also consensus—the volitional act necessarily aspired to by the type of love we termed spousal love and initiating the irrevocable bond of marriage. We have seen the grave sin in every profanation of the conjugal act, every isolation of it from mutual love and the consensus. This is the source of all *impurity*. On the other hand, the *active,* artificial isolation of this act from the possible generation of a human being constitutes a sin of *irreverence* towards God. This is usurping a right not given to the creature.

That conception is possible even when the sanctioned love union is absent does not deny that God has entrusted procreation to the wedded act, which ought to be a love union sanctioned by consensus.

Here we touch upon a profoundly mysterious area of creation, where what is can either coincide with what ought to be or deviate from it. This is most clearly seen in human freedom: man *can* do what he *ought not* do. He can freely initiate a causal sequence independently of whether he should or should not do so. He can use his freedom in a way opposed to that for which his freedom was granted to him. On the one hand, a causal sequence is not deprived of its efficacy because men abuse it. On the other hand, the fact that this causal sequence *should* serve an end endowed with value is in no way suspended by this abuse. This relation of oughtness remains unchanged and keeps its full validity and reality. Precisely for this reason, every deviation from it is a sin.

When, therefore, someone enters into marriage for, let us say, financial reasons and thereby separates the consensus from its proper context, the marriage is certainly valid; but this does not deny that marriage should be the most intimate union of love, that this union is its meaning, and that God has given it as such to man.

Similarly, the superabundant finality of this union of love remains a relation ordained by God, one which *ought* to exist between the union of love and the generation of a new human being, even though sexual intercourse performed without any love or outside of marriage can lead to conception.

We must endeavor to understand more deeply this mysterious structure of the cosmos: *an infraction of a moral obligation does not in itself cancel the factual order*—that is, the causal efficacy inherent in physical and physiological processes will not be destroyed when we do not act as we ought to; *but neither is the fact that something is morally binding affected by its not being done.*

We must acknowledge this great gift, which God grants to men: He entrusts to man's free will the task of harmonizing things as they are with things as they ought to be. This is man's great dignity and awesome responsibility. In order to divine the meaning of the cosmos in the light of God and understand His message in it, we must take into account how things ought to be and not restrict ourselves to the mere factual order. Therefore, the fact that a man can be generated through sexual intercourse without any love in no way nullifies the mysterious truth that God has entrusted the coming into being of a man to an indissoluble love communion.

Physiological Processes and the Creation of Human Life: Is Artificial Birth Control Ever a Merely "Biological" Intervention?

Moreover, the conception of a human being, even when it takes place without the prescribed connection with marital love, is not a mere biological fact. Our entire spiritual and personal life is bound to physiological conditions in various ways, but it is not for this reason a biological reality. Indeed, even baptismal grace or the Real Presence of Christ is attached to an outward sign. In the entire cosmos, then, we repeatedly find this dispensation of divine Providence: realities of a very high order are connected with inferior conditions. But this does not permit us to see only the latter.

The creation of an immortal human person by God through the cooperation of the married couple is therefore in itself never a biological occurrence, though it requires biological conditions. Therefore, the fact that biological laws connect the conjugal act with the creation of a human person does not justify our considering the rupture of the connection only a biological intervention. An extreme case makes this immediately clear: a fatal shot through a man's head is not simply a "biological intervention" but a murder, because a man's life was connected with the physiological processes that were frustrated.

Artificial birth control is thus no mere biological intervention but the severing of a bond which is under the jurisdiction of God alone.

Biological vs. Personal Values

In order to justify artificial birth control some people invoke the superiority of personal values over biological values. It is undoubtedly true that personal values rank higher than biological values. But the generation of a new human being, a spiritual person who is an image of God, clearly bears not only a biological value but also an eminently personal value. Whoever is blind to this cannot speak meaningfully of personal values. Again, the fact that the coming into being of a new person is bound by God to the most tender love union is a great mystery which obviously also cannot be regarded as the bearer of a merely biological value. The superabundant finality that binds the becoming of a new human being to the love union in a special way even draws the one who understands it *in conspectu Dei*—before the face of God.

6. WHY ARTIFICIAL BIRTH CONTROL IS SINFUL BUT THE RHYTHM METHOD IS NOT

The distinctions we have made above between the two concepts of nature shed new light upon the whole problem of artificial birth control. Above all, we are now in a position to see more clearly the decisive difference between rhythm and artificial birth control. We can now meet more decisively the objection: "Is it not also irreverent to have the explicit intention of avoiding the conception of a new human being without totally abstaining from the conjugal act?"

In the first place the value and meaning of the conjugal act is not affected by the married couple's certainty that it cannot lead to conception. Having seen that this act in its very meaning is a unique expression of spousal love and a mutual donation of self, grounded in consensus, we now understand more clearly that this act is not only allowed, but is possessed of a high value even when conception is not possible. This meaning and value is explicitly recognized in the addresses of Pius XII, in the Council decree *Gaudium et Spes,* as well as in the encyclical *Humanae Vitae.*

In the second place it is definitely allowed *expressly* to avoid conception when the conjugal act takes place *only* in the *God-given* infertile time—that is, only by means of the rhythm method and for legitimate reasons. One would have to be blind to the meaning and value of the conjugal act to say that complete abstinence is morally required when conception is to be avoided for legitimate reasons.

It is clear, therefore, that in the intention itself of avoiding another child for serious reasons there is not the least trace of irreverence toward the mysterious fact that God has entrusted the birth of a person to the spousal love union. We see that only during relatively brief intervals has God Himself linked the conjugal act to the creation of a man. Hence the bond, the active tearing apart of which is a sin, is realized only for a short time in the order of things ordained by God Himself. This also has a meaning. The fact that conception is restricted to a short time implies a word of God. It not only confirms that the bodily union of the spouses has a meaning and value in itself, apart from procreation, but it also leaves open the possibility of avoiding conception if this is desirable for serious reasons. The sin consists in this alone: the sundering by man of what God has joined together—the *artificial, active* severing of the mystery of bodily union from the creative act to which it is bound at the time. Only in this artificial intervention, where one *acts against* the mystery of superabundant finality, is there the sin of irreverence—that is to say, the sin of presumptuously exceeding the creatural rights of man.

Analogously, I may very well wish (and pray) that an incurably sick and extremely suffering man would die. I may abstain from artificially prolonging his life for a matter of hours or days. But I am not allowed to kill him! There is an abyss between desiring someone's death and euthanasia. In both cases the *intention* is the same: out of sympathy I desire that he be delivered from suffering. But in the one case I do nothing that might prolong his suffering, whereas in the other I actively intervene and arrogate to myself a right over life and death that belongs to God alone.

Only when we see the *divinely ordained limits to our active intervention,* the limits that define what is allowed and that play a great role in the whole moral sphere, can we perceive the abyss separating the rhythm method from the use of all kinds of contraceptive devices.[4]

It is therefore desirable that science discover improved methods for ascertaining the infertile days. Pope Pius XII said that he prayed for this, and so should all Christians. Paul VI expresses this wish in *Humanae Vitae,* 24.

As soon as we see the abyss separating the use of rhythm from artificial birth control, we have answered the question: why should artificial birth control be a sin if the use of rhythm is allowed? And as soon as we see clearly the sinfulness of artificial birth control, we can and must repudiate the suggestion that it is the proper means of averting dangers that menace marital happiness or averting overpopulation. No evil in the world, however great, may be avoided through a sinful means. To commit a sin in order to avoid an evil would be to adhere to the ignominious principle: the end justifies the means.

Notes

1. See under 5 below, "The Order of What Is and the Order of What Ought to Be in Marriage."

2. Even when conjugal love has grown cold, the marital act remains morally allowed, as long as worthily fulfilled and not desecrated by an impure attitude, since the right of the partner to one's body was granted in the marital consensus.

3. Chicago: Franciscan Herald Press, 1968.

4. This distinction between *active intervention* on our part and *letting things* take their course is also drawn in another situation: though no Catholic spouse is allowed to use contraceptive means, he is still not allowed to refuse the marital act even when his partner employs contraceptive means. Here also the distinction between the active and passive attitude is morally decisive.

9. NFP: Not Contralife

Germain Grisez, Joseph Boyle, John Finnis, and William E. May

This chapter first appeared in *Humanae Vitae: A Defense* in 1988.

Ethical considerations apart, NFP can be described roughly but sufficiently for our purpose here as a practice adopted by couples who abstain from sexual intercourse at times when they believe conception is likely and engage in sexual intercourse only at times when they believe conception is unlikely. (The techniques of NFP are equally valuable for increasing the likelihood of conception; couples then choose to engage in marital intercourse when they believe conception is most likely.)

Many argue: How can NFP be chosen without contraceptive intent? Couples using NFP studiously abstain on the "baby days" and have intercourse only during the "safe" periods. It certainly seems that they do not *want* to have another baby and are doing what is necessary to avoid having one. Thus, the argument will go: Those who choose NFP must have exactly the same contralife will as those who choose to contracept. So, the argument will conclude, if contraception really is, morally unacceptable, NFP is no less unacceptable.

We concede that NFP can be chosen with contraceptive intent.[1] But we hold that NFP also can be chosen without the contralife will that contraception necessarily involves. To understand the second point, it will help to understand the first.

To see that NFP can be chosen with a contralife will, imagine a married couple who rightly judge that they should not have another baby. But they feel they are entitled to regular satisfaction of their sexual desire and so are not willing to accept long-term abstinence. They choose to use some form of birth prevention. Looking into methods, they find something they do not like about each of them. IUDs and pills can be dangerous to a woman's health. Condoms and diaphragms interfere with the sexual act and pleasure. Jellies and lotions are messy and often ineffective. And so on. Then they hear about NFP. They will have to abstain for a longer stretch than they would like but still will be able to have intercourse during a week to ten days each cycle. Even the abstinence will have its advantages from their point of view: They know it will increase desire and intensify their pleasure. So they decide to use NFP as their method of contraception.

For them, choosing to use NFP is not essentially different from choosing any other method of contraception. They project the coming to be of another baby, want that possible baby not to come to be, and act accordingly. Their will is contralife and no less against reason than if they had chosen some other method of contraception. If pregnancy occurs, the baby will be unwanted.

In our example, the couple rightly judge that they should not have another baby. Of course, couples who have no reason to avoid pregnancy also can choose NFP with contraceptive intent. But the opposite is not the case: No couple can choose NFP without contraceptive intent unless they have a reason not to have another baby.

Now, if a couple's reason not to have another baby excludes contraceptive intent, that could be so only because their reason does not include the very not-being of the baby. It must include only the burdens that having another baby would impose with respect to other goods, and/or the benefits that might flow from avoiding those burdens.

Thus, the first step in the deliberation and choice that lead to a morally acceptable practice of NFP is to become aware of a reason not to have another baby. Recognizing that intercourse during a fertile time might lead to having another baby, contrary to such a reason, one judges that intercourse during that time is to be avoided. Thus, abstinence is chosen.

This first step plainly is different from a first step toward a choice to contracept based on merely emotional motivations either of hatred of the prospective baby or selfishly not wanting another baby. For here there is a reason.

But the reason not to have another baby when NFP is chosen to avoid the consequences of the possible baby's coming to be might equally well be a reason to choose to use contraception. For a couple who otherwise would welcome another baby might for that very reason choose contraception with a view to preventing the consequences that the couple who choose NFP equally are trying to avoid. How, then, does the practice of NFP differ from the use of contraception in such a case, when the reason not to have another baby is exactly the same?

They differ not in the *reason* for the choices which are motivated, but in the *choices* which that reason motivates and in those choices' relationships to the benefits and burdens which such a reason represents. When contraception is chosen, the choice is to impede the baby's coming to be in order that the goods represented by that reason be realized and/or the evils represented by it be avoided. When NFP is noncontraceptively chosen, the choice is to abstain from intercourse that would be likely to result in both the baby's coming to be and the loss of goods and/or occurrence of evils represented by that same reason in order that the goods represented by that reason be realized or the evils represented by it be avoided.

Even when based on good reasons, the contraceptive choice by its very definition is contralife. It is a choice to prevent the beginning of the life of a possible person. It is a choice *to do something,* with the intent that the baby not be, as a means to a further end: That the good consequences of the baby's not-coming-to-be will be realized and the bad consequences of the baby's coming to be will be prevented. The noncontraceptive choice of NFP differs. It is a choice *not to do something*—namely, not to engage in possibly fertile sexual intercourse—with the intent that the bad consequences of the baby's coming to be will be avoided, and with the *acceptance as side effects* of both the baby's not-coming-to-be and the bad consequences of his or her not-coming-to-be. In this choice and in the acceptance of its side effects, there need be no contralife will. The baby who might come into being need not be projected and rejected.[2]

In general, those who consider choosing to do something for a certain good but decide *not to do it* in order to avoid bad side effects do not thereby reject the good that they do not pursue. True, not choosing to realize that good—and, indeed, choosing to avoid the burdens one anticipates if one were to realize it—means *not willing* that the good *be realized,* but it does not mean *willing* that the good *not be realized.* In other words: The will's not bearing on the realization of a good is not the same as its bearing on the nonrealization of that good, even if in both cases the will bears on the nonrealization of side effects anticipated if that good were realized.

Not to choose to realize a good—such as the coming to be of a possible person—that offers of itself a reason for its realization can be in harmony with reason. The choice precisely of such a good's nonrealization necessarily is contrary to a reason.

Because the contraceptive choice is contralife, it is in itself contrary to a reason and only seems reasonable insofar as it appears possible to establish that the reason not to have a baby is rationally preferable to the value of the baby's life. But, as we showed, that preferability never can be rationally established.

Because the choice of NFP need not be contralife, that choice need not be contrary to a reason. There is a reason to choose to practice NFP: the bad side effects, which one wills to avoid, of having another baby. There also is a reason to choose to go on having intercourse during fertile and infertile times alike: the prospect of having the baby with all the goods associated with that and/or the bad side effects of his or her not coming to be. Whether one chooses the practice of NFP or not, one chooses to act for one reason and does not choose to act for the other, but in both cases one can choose in harmony with both reasons, and need not choose contrary to either. Thus, the choice of NFP need not be immoral. It is merely a case of something common in human life: choosing not to realize something one has a good reason to choose to realize, but whose realization would conflict with avoiding something else one has a good reason to avoid.

Couples who choose to practice NFP do consider what the future will be like if they have another baby. They foresee certain bad effects—for example, they will not be able to fulfill both their present responsibilities and their new ones, and so judge that they should not assume new ones. So they choose to abstain. But they do not have to judge that the possible future without the baby will be rationally preferable to a possible future with it. For their choice to abstain need not be contrary to any reason, and so, assuming it is not, they need not try to justify it by reasoning that their reason for abstinence is rationally preferable to the reason to have another baby—namely, the inherent goodness of a possible person's coming to be.

Apart from the choice to abstain during fertile times, the non-contraceptive practice of NFP involves only two other morally significant elements: the choice to engage in intercourse during infertile times and the choice to adopt a systematic policy of periodic abstinence and intercourse. Neither of these elements need involve a contralife will. The choice to engage in intercourse by those who think they are naturally sterile, permanently or temporarily, cannot involve a contralife will; thinking they are sterile, they cannot choose to do anything whatsoever to impede what they believe to be impossible—the coming to be of a possible person—and so they cannot choose to engage in intercourse with that intent. The adoption of the policy of periodic abstinence could be made to implement a contraceptive choice, as the earlier example showed. But if the adoption of the policy of periodic abstinence does not implement a prior contraceptive choice, the systematization of choices—none of which is contralife in itself—to abstain and to engage in intercourse does not require any additional choice that would be contralife.

Those who defend the morality of contraception will object: The preceding abstract argument simply tries to obscure NFP's obvious moral identity with contraception. It has been admitted, they will point out, that people can have the very same reason for choosing both, and that the reason in some cases can constitute a strict moral obligation not to have another baby. Moreover, in both cases, the purpose is identical: to avoid having that baby. Therefore, they will continue, those who choose NFP and those who choose contraception when NFP would be justified necessarily want the same thing. In either case, the couple do not want to have another baby. And in either case, they will conclude, if pregnancy occurs, the baby is unwanted.

In reply, we agree that there is a sense in which the wanting and the not wanting are the same in both cases. The couples' emotional motivations can be very similar. People practicing NFP often fear pregnancy and, when they think an unexpected pregnancy has occurred, react with acute feelings of sadness toward the prospect of the new baby. They may hope and pray that a menstrual period will come as welcome evidence that no baby is coming. It is fair to say: They do not (emotionally) want that baby. But feelings and wishes are not morally determinative. The wanting that counts morally is willing: choosing, intending, and accepting.

What the abstract argument makes clear is that the willing that relates to the prospective baby's not-coming-to-be is not the same in (1) the choice of NFP with contraceptive intent or any other method of contraception as in (2) the noncontraceptive choice of NFP. In (1) the intention precisely is the will that the possible baby not-come-to-be. Even when their intention that the baby not-come-to-be is for some further end, those who make this choice do *not want the baby,* in the precise sense that, as a means to their further end, they choose the possible baby's not-coming-to-be. But in (2), the noncontraceptive choice of NFP, the choice is to not-cause-the-side-effects-of-the-baby's-coming-to-be by abstaining from causing the baby to come to be. Those who make this choice precisely do *not want to cause the baby,* but they do not choose the baby's not-coming-to-be, although they do accept that not-coming-to-be as a side effect of what they intend.

This fact makes a great difference if pregnancy does occur. Since couples who practice NFP noncontraceptively never will a prospective baby's not-coming-to-be, they do not have to change their will toward the new baby to accept or love him or her. They may find the new baby's coming to be emotionally repugnant, but, whatever their feelings might be, the baby is not unwanted in the sense that counts morally. For, using the word "want" to refer to volitions rather than feelings, the baby does not come to be as unwanted. Thus, there is a real and very important difference between *not wanting to have a baby,* which is common to both (1) and (2) above, and *not wanting the baby one might have,* which is true of (1) but not of (2).

Those who agree that there is a morally significant difference between the noncontraceptive practice of NFP and the use of contraception and find the preceding explanation otherwise acceptable might still remain unsatisfied with it as an account of what the Church actually teaches about the difference between NFP and contraception. For, on our account, all that is required to make abstinence noncontraceptive is *a* reason not to have another baby other than one that precisely is or includes the baby's not-coming-to-be. But the Church's teaching is that the upright choice of NFP requires *a serious* reason.[3] Thus, the objection will conclude, the choice to practice NFP is not justified merely by having *some* reason other than the baby's not-coming-to-be to avoid pregnancy.

The answer: Any reason, other than the baby's not-coming-to-be, for not wanting to have a baby is sufficient to distinguish the choice to abstain from the choice to contracept. However, the choice to practice NFP requires more for its justification than that it not be contraceptive. In marrying, Christian couples who do not know they will be sterile undertake to accept parenthood and its responsibilities, for the sake of giving life to new members of the human community and the heavenly Kingdom. If a husband and wife are physically or morally unable to carry out that undertaking, they do not fail morally in not carrying it out. But if they are physically able to carry it out and have no serious reason not to have another baby, yet choose to avoid pregnancy by practicing NFP, they fail morally to fulfill the vocation they accepted in marrying. Therefore, the Church teaches that a serious reason is necessary to choose uprightly to practice NFP. But this teaching is entirely compatible with our analysis according to which a less than serious reason can distinguish NFP from contraception.

The ethics of responsible parenthood is the same as the ethics of responsible care for the dying. Christian morality requires the same reverence for life in its coming to be as in its passing away. Just as the cherishing of human life in its coming to be does not mean that one always must bring a possible person into being, so the cherishing of human life in its passing away does not mean that one always must keep a dying person in being. Just as abstinence from marital intercourse *can* be justified to avoid side effects of bringing possible persons into being and of their being, so the limitation of medical treatment *can* be justified to avoid side effects of keeping persons alive and of their continuing life. Just as the contralife will involved in the contraceptive choice to prevent another person's coming into being never can be justified by any further end, so the contralife will involved in the choice to bring about someone's death never can be justified by any further end. Just as the reasons for the upright practice of NFP and for the use of contraception can be the same, although in many cases they are not, so the reasons for limiting medical treatment and for euthanasia can be the same, although in many cases they are not. Just as one can choose NFP with contraceptive intent, so one can choose to limit medical treatment with homicidal intent—that is, precisely in order to bring about the patient's death. Finally, just as a reason other than precisely not wanting another baby is sufficient to distinguish the choice of NFP from the choice of contraception, although only a serious reason justifies the former choice, so a reason for limiting medical treatment other than the very ending of the patient's life is sufficient to distinguish nonmurderous letting die from euthanasia, although only a good reason for limiting medical treatment is sufficient to justify abstaining from possible life-prolonging treatment. For, just as a couple, without a contraceptive will, can fail to fulfill their responsibility to give life to possible persons, so those who care for the dying, without a murderous will, can fail to fulfill their responsibility to sustain the lives of actual persons.

Before concluding this section, another important difference between contraception and NFP is worth noting. As the preceding section showed, the choice of contraception, besides being contralife, is inconsistent with marital chastity. Not only is the upright choice of NFP not contralife but it also is conducive to marital chastity and fosters marital love. In using abstinence to avoid having another baby, couples who uprightly choose NFP reject the assumption that they are entitled to regular and frequent satisfaction of their sexual desire. The result is that although they may find ten to twenty days' abstinence during each cycle difficult and frustrating, they do not understand abstinence as some sort of arbitrary imposition.

Moreover, such couples' practice of restraint actually increases their control, and so their freedom, and so the meaningfulness of their marital acts. Their personalities become more integrated rather than self-disintegrated. Their communication improves. And their sense of the dignity of their bodily selves grows.[4]

Notes

1. See John Paul II, General Audience, Sept. 5, 1984; *Insegnamenti di Giovanni Paolo II,* vol. 7, pt. 2 (Rome: Libreria Editrice Vaticana, 1984), 321; *L'Osservatore Romano,* Eng. ed., Sept. 10, 1984, 10; Giovanni Paolo II, *Uomo e Donna lo creò: catechesi sull'amore umano* (Rome: Libreria Editrice Vaticana, 1985), 474.

2. For a fuller treatment than we offer here of the distinction between choosing and accepting the effects of one's choice, see Grisez and Boyle, *Life and Death with Liberty and Justice,* 381–92; Grisez, *Christian Moral Principles,* 233–36, 239–41.

3. Paul VI, *Humanae vitae,* 16, *AAS* 60 (1968): 492: "If, then, there are serious reasons to space out births, which derive from the physical or psychological conditions of the husband and wife, or from external conditions, the Church teaches that it is then licit to take into account the natural periodicity immanent in the generative functions, for the use of marriage in the infecund periods only, and in this way to regulate birth without offending the moral principles which have been recalled earlier."

4. For an interesting psychological study of the difference between contraception and NFP, see Wanda Poltawska, "The Effect of a Contraceptive Attitude on Marriage", *International Review of Natural Family Planning* 4 (1980): 187–206. A sound and useful practical treatment of NFP: John Kippley and Sheila Kippley, *The Art of Natural Family Planning,* 3d ed. (Cincinnati: Couple to Couple League, 1987). (The address of the Couple to Couple League is P.O. Box 111184, Cincinnati, Ohio 45211.)

10. Statement by Catholic Theologians Washington, D.C., July 30, 1968

As Roman Catholic theologians we respectfully acknowledge a distinct role of hierarchical magisterium (teaching authority) in the Church of Christ. At the same time Christian tradition assigns theologians the special responsibility of evaluating and interpreting pronouncements of the *magisterium* in the light of the total theological data operative in each question or statement. We offer these initial comments on Pope Paul VI's Encyclical on the Regulation of Birth.

The Encyclical is not an infallible teaching. History shows that a number of statements of similar or even greater authoritative weight have subsequently been proven inadequate or even erroneous. Past authoritative statements on religious liberty, interest-taking, the right to silence and the ends of marriage have all been corrected at a later date.

Many positive values concerning marriage are expressed in Paul VI's Encyclical. However, we take exception to the ecclesiology implied and the methodology used by Paul VI in the writing and promulgation of the document: they are incompatible with the Church's authentic self-awareness as expressed in and suggested by the acts of the Second Vatican Council itself. The Encyclical consistently assumes that the Church is identical with the hierarchical office. No real importance is afforded the witness of the life of the Church in its totality; the special witness of many Catholic couples is neglected; it fails to acknowledge the witness of the separated Christian Churches and Ecclesial Communities; it is insensitive to the witness of many men of good will; it pays insufficient attention to the ethical import of modern science.

Furthermore, the Encyclical betrays a narrow and positivistic notion of papal authority, as illustrated by the rejection of the majority view presented by the Commission established to consider the question, as well as by the rejection of the conclusions of a large part of the international Catholic theological community.

Likewise, we take exception to some of the specific ethical conclusions contained in the Encyclical. They are based on an inadequate concept of natural law: the multiple forms of natural law theory are ignored and the fact that competent philosophers come to different conclusions on this very question is disregarded. Even the minority report of the papal commission noted grave difficulty in attempting to present conclusive proof of the immorality of artificial contraception based on natural law.

Other defects include: overemphasis on the biological aspects of conjugal relations as ethically normative; undue stress on sexual acts and on the faculty of sex viewed in itself apart from the person and the couple; a static worldview which downplays the historical and evolutionary character of humanity in its finite existence, as described in Vatican II's *Pastoral Constitution on the Church in the Modern World;* unfounded assumptions about "the evil consequences of methods of artificial birth control"; indifference to Vatican II's assertion that prolonged sexual abstinence may cause "faithfulness to be imperiled and its quality of fruitfulness to be ruined"; an almost total disregard for the dignity of millions of human beings brought into the world without the slightest possibility of being fed and educated decently.

In actual fact, the Encyclical demonstrates no development over the teaching of Pius XI's *Casti Connubii* whose conclusions have been called into question for grave and serious reasons. These reasons, given a muffled voice at Vatican II, have not been adequately handled by the mere repetition of past teaching.

It is common teaching in the Church that Catholics may dissent from authoritative, noninfallible teachings of the magisterium when sufficient reasons for so doing exist.

Therefore, as Roman Catholic theologians, conscious of our duty and our limitations, we conclude that spouses may responsibly decide according to their conscience that artificial contraception in some circumstances is permissible and indeed necessary to preserve and foster the values and sacredness of marriage.

It is our conviction also that true commitment to the mystery of Christ and the Church requires a candid statement of mind at this time by all Catholic theologians.

11. Birth Control and the Ideals of Marital Sexuality

Rosemary Radford Ruether

This chapter first appeared in *Contraception and Holiness* in 1964.

The present controversy in the Catholic Church over the licitness or illicitness of various methods of birth control is so heated and fraught with polemic that it seems increasingly difficult to think through the whole issue in a simple and same fashion, and yet such simple and sane thinking is desperately needed on this issue, now more than ever. The Church can scarcely afford to perpetuate the present muddle much longer without the gravest danger to the consciences of thousands of sincere persons within the Church as well as the general disrespect and contempt which the situation is engendering among non-Catholics both Christian and non-Christian.

Much of the difficulty which impedes clear thinking on this issue is a frightful semantic muddle. Words used by one person to mean one thing are used by another school of thought to mean another. Thus the present author wrote in the *Saturday Evening Post* (April 10, 1964) that the Church should clearly recognize that the relational aspect of the marital act is a genuine value and purpose in itself, and cannot just be subsumed as a means to the end of procreation. The critics immediately replied that this meant promiscuity and extra-marital intercourse, since, for some strange reason, procreation in their minds necessarily implied marriage whereas the relational aspect of the marital act did not seem to imply any permanent bond between two human beings. Now obviously one can have babies outside of marriage just as well as one can have sexual relationships outside of marriage. If we are to have any intelligent discussion of this problem at all, we must be convinced that we are talking about *marriage* and not promiscuity. Within this context we must then make clear that the procreational and the relational aspects of the sexual act are two semi-independent and interrelated purposes which both are brought together in their meaning and value within the total marriage project, although it is not only unnecessary but even biologically impossible that both purposes be present in every act.

Another semantic muddle exists in regard to the term "procreation" or, more specifically "procreativeness." The present proponents of the rhythm method have redefined procreativeness until it simply means a kind of formal structure of the sexual act, irrespective of whether that act can procreate or not. Thus, since rhythm doesn't interfere with this formal procreative structure, it is licit, while mechanical contraceptives, which supposedly interfere with this procreative structure, are illicit. Now it is very strange that procreativeness should be defined only in terms of the operation of the sperm as it travels into the uterus, but the presence or absence of the ovum is deemed irrelevant to the definition of procreativeness. One almost suspects some hangover of the medieval notion that the sperm alone was the generative agent, the existence of the ovum being then unknown. In any case it is obvious that procreative means nothing less than the actual possibility of the act procreating, although this may not always occur, and this capacity to procreate entails the presence of ovum just as much as the viability of the sperm. Hence, sexual acts which are calculated to function only during times of sterility are sterilizing the act just as much as any other means of rendering the act infertile. It is difficult to see why there should be such an absolute moral difference between creating a spatial barrier to procreation and creating a temporal barrier to procreation.

In any case it is necessary to clear away these semantic squabbles and rethink clearly and succinctly the various values that are at stake in the birth control controversy, and how these various values ought to be related to each other within an understanding of the total nature of the marital relationship; then, in terms of this evaluation of the nature of the marital relationship, to consider the various methods of birth control and how they may be conducive to or destructive of these values.

First, let us think about marital morality in terms of the full expression of its ideal nature. The sexual act exists on several levels of meaning and purpose. First of all, it is a biological act whose purposive goal is the generation of a new human being. Secondly, it is an act of love in which the married couple express their union with each other. In this union they both express their union and make this union; that is, the sexual act does not merely express the union of their persons, but in this expression it also makes this union, and so it is the cement that holds together the relationship, and not only of the couple to each other, but also as the parents of their children. This union does not just exist on a physiological level, but it expresses the mutuality of their union on all levels of their being, their total I and Thou with each other.

The sexual act would be expressed ideally when all these purposes and meanings could be present in a total and harmonious whole. This would mean that the couple truly give themselves to each other in deep devotion and love; that from this act of love a child should actually spring, as its natural fruition, and that the act of love and the biological cause and effect that produce the child be no mere chance coincidence, but, in loving each other, the couple should also choose to create a child as an authentic act of will. For man is not just an animal, and should not just procreate as an animal does as the servant of biological chance, but he should choose his own existence, and the effects of his own acts in an authentically human way.

This, then, would be the nature of the sexual act under ideal circumstances. This is, perhaps, the way it might have been before the fall of Adam, when nature was as God intended it to be before it became disordered and its existence as a created image of God was blurred. However, in actual reality, under our present situation, this complete unification of all the goals of marriage in a single and harmonious act can only occasionally occur at best. First of all, man never knows when his sexual acts will procreate, so that he cannot will a sexual act to be an act of procreation and know that he has actually effected this end. In the order of fallen nature, the sexual act is used many hundreds of times and only procreative occasionally. Secondly, the limitations of man's social life, particularly in the modern world, are such that man feels less and less free to procreate.

The psychological demands of living within a sexual union impel a relatively frequent use of the sexual act, and yet man, particularly in our urban society, only feels really free to allow himself, perhaps, between two and five children. Many couples may have more than that, and society today will make these couples feel (and with some reason since we cannot ignore the realities of economic and social life) that they have produced more children than is in the common good. Thus we see that the actual use of the sexual act and the number of children that can be positively desired are radically out of tune with each other.

We have discussed the sexual act from the point of view of its ideal completion in procreation and shown how the limitations imposed upon man, both from biological nature and the social structure, create a radical and inevitable falling away from the ideal in practice. Let us now consider the marital act from the point of view of its expression of the person to person relationship of the couple. This purpose of the sexual act also has its inner laws of perfection. Above all an authentic act of love should be given freely, without external force. The couple should not feel forced to love when they are not genuinely drawn together, or forced not to love for reasons external to their personal well being. Above all it should be an act arising from the total communion of the couple, without calculation, so that, for example, a conversation in the evening which brings with it a deepened sense of person to person understanding might lead on into the expression of their relationship in physical union. All traces of lust should be expelled, so that one partner never approaches the other as a mere thing to be used for his own gratification, but the pleasure of the sexual act should arise as a by-product of their mutual self-giving to each other.

However, in actual practice, the limitations of a man's lack of charity, preoccupation with selfish concerns or mere day to day business create a falling away from this ideal. Most couples do not express the full mutuality of their persons in the sexual act for the simple reason that they have not achieved such mutuality, because their understanding of each other is distorted and fraught with petty tensions and dislikes. A thousand concerns press upon them and fragment the wholeness of their persons and thus impede their communion. The sexual act, in practice, may seldom be an expression of deeper commingling, but may be a casual thing, or even forced upon the one partner by the desires of the other. Seldom are the moments when the two turn equally to each other in full openness to the spirit of each other. The sexual natures themselves of man and woman make union difficult, for the two are not temperamentally compatible, but the man's sexual desires are more constant, while the woman's are more variable, and the two have different cycles of crescendo in the act itself. Thus many factors, both in the biological nature and in the social nature of the relationship, tend toward a falling away from the ideal of full mutuality.

Having accepted the fact that, in actual life, the achievement of the ideal nature of the sexual act at all times is impossible, because man can neither desire nor have a child with each sexual act, nor can he give himself to his partner as lovingly as he ought, what should be our guidelines in coming as close as possible to the various ideals and purposes of marital sexuality? When we spoke of the perfection of the procreative nature of the sexual act, it was clear that this purpose of the act is best expressed when man does choose to procreate as an authentic act of desire. But man, as we have seen, can only desire perhaps three, four or five children (and there is no point telling people they ought to have more children when the circumstances of their life mitigate against it). The second best expression of the ideal would then be that those children which are born are genuinely desired and authentically chosen; that is, at the time they are begotten, the couple is actually making use of the sexual act with a desire to procreate. Now we come to the ironic fact that in our present situation man is only able fully to say "yes" to procreation if he is also able to say "no." If, on the other hand, he has at his disposal only an ineffective method of birth control which does not give him the freedom to say "no," then he will not really have the freedom to say "yes" either, because his efforts will be expended on trying to prevent the birth of more children than he feels he can provide for, and to space those children with an insecure method; and so the children that he does have tend to be "accidents" rather than products of authentic human will. Only when he can be confident that the "accident" will not occur is he then able to feel free to stop holding his procreative powers in abeyance at appropriate intervals and to make love with the full intention of creating a child, although, of course, he can never be absolutely sure when or if a child will be conceived. Therefore, we arrive at the paradox that, in man's present situation, his ability to approach the ideal of marital sexuality, where all the purposes of the sexual act can be present harmoniously, is dependent on his ability to hold his procreative powers in abeyance at other times.

Having shown that man's ability to choose procreation authentically is dependent on his ability not to choose it at other times, let us look at the various methods for holding the procreative powers in abeyance, to see which are suited to the best ordering of the primary and auxiliary purposes of the marital act. Looking at the question from one point of view we might be inclined to feel that man should only make love when he can really desire a child, and when he does not so desire, he should dispense with the sexual act altogether. This might be the ideal situation from the standpoint of radical morality, but in actual practice it is both impossible and inadvisable for most couples. As we have seen, man's sexual desires and his desire for procreation are not actually in tune, and this is a fact of his nature which he cannot well overcome. The demands of living in the sexual union are real and meaningful demands which impose a far more frequent use of the sexual act for its relational function than could ever be brought into harmony with procreation itself. Man needs to express his mutuality with his partner, and in the sexual act this mutuality is both expressed and recreated; and in this sense the sexual act as a relational act is a genuinely purposeful act, and not mere play or unleashing of passion. Since this is the case, the couple cannot well dispense with the act and yet continue to live in a sexual relationship without doing extensive emotional damage to the basic stability of their marriage. Since the firmness of their relational cohesion with each other is the cement that holds the marriage together, and this, in turn, is the milieu in which the children which have been born are nurtured, the first ideal of marriage, the ideal of procreation itself mitigates against the use of a method of birth control which would undermine the stability of the sexual union of the couple. Thus the continued use of the sexual act for its relational purpose, even when its procreational purpose is impeded, may be said to be required by the procreational purpose itself, because the procreational purpose extends to the nurture of the child; and if the continued use of the sexual act is necessary in order to maintain the union of the couple and their ability to carry out their continued responsibility to the child, then the primary purpose of marriage itself points to the use of the sexual act for its purely relational function.

Thus in actual practice man has no real choice (except perhaps in the case of a couple both called to a life of virginity), but to find some method of birth control which allows him to continue to use the sexual act for its relational purpose and to do this under as ideal emotional circumstances as possible. Among these methods there are four main types: permanent sterilization, periodic continence, the mechanical or chemical contraceptive and the oral-steroid pill.

Permanent sterilization is undesirable chiefly because of its finality. It takes from man his ability to choose in favor of procreation and leaves him only with his previous choice against it. It thus dehumanizes him by depriving him of his freedom to make authentically human choices.

The rhythm method (which I shall examine in greater detail below) has several defects which cause a falling away from the ideals we have outlined. First, the method forces a mechanization of the affections of the couple who must artificially "schedule" their mutual affection at the time of the infertile period, and this takes from the couple their freedom to choose to love as an expression of true mutuality, and makes them subservient to an impersonal biological cycle which has no genuine relationship to their human expression of mutual love. Secondly, this method is very insecure and so forces a constant calculation and worry which is psychologically debilitating and tends to undermine the couple's stability and introduces fear and conflict into their relationship. Thus the rhythm method is undesirable for the same reasons as total abstinence, that its demands upon the psychological cohesion of the couple often exceed what can be reconciled with the stability of their relationship, and thus not in the best interests of the family as a whole. Thirdly, this method does not give fully effective control over procreation, but the natural fluctuations of sterility are such that the most careful use of the method (and we must remember that the method is being practiced by human beings, and not laboratory rats, and that the psychological tensions created by the method also are a permanent contributing factor to its ineffectiveness) will produce many accidental babies, often exceeding the total number of children the couple feels they can accept, and so it does not give the couple the freedom to fully affirm their desire for children—rather, in practice, the couple has to spend so much energy in trying to make the method work, i.e. to get it to effectively impede procreation, that the freedom authentically to desire a child and plan for his conception is lost.

The third method is that of the traditional contraceptive: condom, diaphragm, spermicidal jelly and the like. All have the undesirable quality that they tend to intrude themselves into the psychological dynamics of the sexual act itself, because the couple must calculate the time of the sexual act in order to be armed in advance, and they are made psychologically aware of the means being used to impede procreation in a way esthetically distasteful to many people. However, one must make distinctions within this general group of mechanical and chemical means. Certain means, such as condom and *coitus interruptus,* definitely do not allow for the full completion of the sexual act as a relational act, and so they may be said to devalue the relational aspect of the act in a way which is morally intolerable. Other methods, such as the diaphragm, operate at the base of the cervix, or even within the womb. They do not prevent the full and natural sexual play between the couple and the depositing of the seed in the vagina. Thus they can be condemned only if one condemns any method which prevents the procreative fulfillment of the act, and this, as we have said, is equally true of all methods of birth control, including the rhythm method. Some of these mechanical means are still inesthetic, and this may cause some falling away from the ideal of marital mutuality, but it is questionable whether esthetic criteria alone can brand these methods as absolutely immoral. The esthetic criterion is a highly subjective one, and many persons do not feel such methods are inesthetic or that they prevent the full expression of mutual self-giving (in the relational rather than the procreational sense of the word). These people simply accept such means in the same way that one accepts a pair of reading spectacles, as an aid to nature which one uses but psychologically ignores.

Finally, there are the new oral-steroid pills, which, assuming that they are medically safe, would seem to hold out the best possibility for a reasonable balance of goals and ideals in marriage. First, this method is fully effective, and gives to the couple the power to hold their procreative powers in abeyance when this is necessary, and, in turn, to release these powers to create a child, when they can and do desire to so choose (—and this choice may often require a great sacrificial effort. We do not intend to suggest that this voluntary choice of procreation by which man dares to live up to the highest ideal of the sexual act will existenially be an easy one to make). Furthermore, when the woman discontinues the use of the pills, she has a jump-back of heightened fertility and so receives a "bonus" of added assurance that the desire for a child may actually be brought to fruition. Thirdly, the method is totally divorced from the physical and psychological setting of the sexual act, and as such it is preferable from the esthetic point of view. Finally, it allows the couple full freedom to use or control the sexual act according to the true laws of their love and respect for each other, without being forced into subservience to its external considerations, such as the "safe period," or the need to calculate the relationship in order to have the contraceptive in place.

I would like now to examine in greater detail the flaws in the use of what is known as the "safe period." The theoretical understanding of fertility upon which the rhythm method has been based assumes too simple and schematic a functioning of human fecundity. It has been assumed, for example, that the sperm could live only about forty-eight hours, so that a couple had only to abstain for about two days before this time. Recent studies have shown that forty-eight hours is only the *average* life of the sperm, and that actually this is only the mid-point in a spectrum. Some of the spermatozoa may live only a few hours. Others have been found to be still viable in the mucus of the cervix after intercourse for as long as seven or eight days, and it is unknown how much longer they might live in particular instances.

The ovarian cycle of the woman is equally unpredictable. The twenty-eight day cycle is only a statistical *average,* but real women are not statistical averages. Many women have cycles which vary considerably, but it is absolutely normal for the woman's cycle to vary somewhat, that is from twenty-six to thirty-one days. When we try to put all these facts together: the variations in the woman's cycle, the difficulty in predicting the exact terminus in the life cycle of the sperm, the possibility of second ovulations, which occur quite often in some women, it becomes obvious that for the more fecund couple there may be no time when they can be sure whether an act of intercourse will result in conception. Fecundity is not a phenomenon which exists in the same way in all people. It is rather a group of variables which go from the very infecund couple, the couple where the husband has a very low sperm count, although not low enough to be classed as sterile, where the wife ovulates very irregularly to the highly fecund couple, where the man's spermatozoa may have a very high count and long durability, and the wife be subject to short cycles or perhaps to second ovulations. The relatively infecund couple may be able to use the rhythm method quite well; in fact, they might be surprised to discover that they would have done almost as well to have used no method at all. The highly fecund couple, on the other hand, may abstain for long periods during every cycle and still find that the method has inexplicably failed. The method, in effect, rewards the sterile, and penalizes the fertile.

R. E. Lebkicker, a biologist from Philadelphia, has done research on the ovarian cycle which indicates that the time of ovulation has no calculable relationship with the onset of menstruation and, therefore, that the Ogino-Knaus rhythm method, which attempts to predict the probable time of ovulation from the beginning of menstruation, has been operating under a fallacy. According to Lebkicker, ovulation is related to hormone changes which take place previous to menstruation at the end of the cycle at a time difficult to determine by overt signs. Depending on when these changes occur and depending on variables in the hormone structure of different women which create various patterns in the time of menstruation, the time of ovulation may take place as early as the fifth day after the onset of menstruation. This means that a woman could be ovulating and menstruating at the same time, a thing which is considered impossible according to the rhythm methods now being taught, which take the menstrual period as absolutely infertile. According to this research, however, even this period may not be infertile, but a woman who carefully followed the present calculation of the "infertile" period could actually become pregnant while still menstruating. Whether Lebkicker is correct in his criticism or not, in any case it indicates how little agreement there is even among experts as to when the infertile period actually is and how it is to be determined.

Another common fallacy found in discussions of the rhythm method, particularly by the clergy, lies in the attempt to promote periodic abstinence as a kind of ascetic discipline. Yet the clerical moralists themselves are somewhat of two minds about this. On the one hand, they try to laud the virtue obtained by abstinence as "heroic sacrifice" and, on the other hand, to denigrate any real hardship involved, so that they may not be thought to be imposing something beyond the reach of the average person. Now it is obvious that no married couple either needs or wants to make love every night, and it is perfectly normal to go weeks at a time without making use of the sexual act. The typical clerical query: "Can't you abstain for just a few days?" really misses the point of the criticism of the rhythm method. The present author, for example, is presently living alone while her husband works on a scholarship in India for twelve months. It is certainly a hardship to be separated from him, but it is *him* and not the sexual act which is the essence of the deprivation. The mistake which the clerical moralists tend to make in this matter is to assume that married people have some purely bodily drive which needs to be satisfied. This drive is seen on the animal level essentially as an egotistic need of each of the members of the partnership individually. In other words, the drive is understood by the clerical moralist primarily under the rubric of lust. Therefore he tends to assume that it would be "good for them" to repress this drive for a while, that periodic continence will "help" them to "humanize" their lust; otherwise they would be given over to unrestrained self-indulgence.

This point of view totally misses the essence of the marital relationship. This is so primarily because the clerical moralist unconsciously has patterned his description of the sexual drive on his own position, which requires the repression of a need, which, for him, is totally egotistic. If the priest has experienced the sexual drive at all, it is as a need of his own body, and without any specific link to another person. In other words, the sexual drive outside the context of marriage is and can be nothing else but a purely egotistic drive, because it does not exist in the context and as an expression of a specific I-Thou relationship with a particular person.

Unconsciously, the clerical moralist tries to apply some of the rationale of his own celibate existence to his understanding of the marital relationship. His line of reasoning goes something like this: "I have sublimated my sexual drive entirely. Why can't they do it for a little while each month?" What this kind of thinking fails to grasp is that the married person, if he is really a morally developed person, already has sublimated his sexual drive, but in a different manner from the celibate, and in a manner which makes any half-way application of the celibate's kind of asceticism quite irrelevant for the best fulfillment of the married person's state of life. The married person has sublimated the sexual drive into a *relationship* with another person. The sexual drive, for him, ceases to have any meaning or urgency simply as an egotistic drive, or self-centered bodily appetite. It is rather the intimate expression of one's relationship with this particular other person, this unique and irreplaceable other person. Thus it is quite clear that once my husband is gone, the sexual act is simply no longer relevant. It no longer has a purpose or need in my life. I don't miss it or need it at all because it is not a thing which I need to satisfy an appetite of my own, but it is entirely subsumed into a means of expressing my relationship with him. Once we are reunited, however, it again will become important as the act of communion by which that relationship is expressed.

Rhythm is debilitating to this relationship not because it is difficult in itself for a couple to abstain for a few days. Most couples tend to do this even without thinking about it. In fact, couples who use contraceptives and who know that they can use the sexual act without fear of pregnancy whenever they wish may well be far less preoccupied with sex than those who use the rhythm method. From my discussion with Catholics using the rhythm method and with Protestants who use contraceptives, I have noticed a kind of obsession among the Catholics which seems to be absent in many of the Protestants of comparable social and moral development. The very tension created by the rhythm method may make the Catholic couple more rather than less taken up with sex. By being constantly forced to worry about when "it is safe" to use the sexual act, they may well be being forced into a hyper-consciousness of the need for sexual expression which would not exist with some other method. Thus the rhythm method may really have an effect for many couples which is the opposite of the supposed ascetic virtues commonly predicated of it.

Essentially the rhythm method is debilitating because it imposes an abnormal regime on the expression of marital love. It treats marital love as an appetite which can be scheduled, like eating and sleeping. But marital love, if it is really developed, has been sublimated from the appetite level. It has been raised into the expression of a relationship, and therefore needs to follow the laws of that relationship, and to flow with the dynamics of that relationship. When a couple are busy, tired, caught up with other concerns, they may go for considerable periods without even thinking of using the sexual act. But at the moments when they need to turn to each other for solace, reassurance, renewal of their bonds with each other, it is precisely at this moment and not ten days later that they need to be able to use the sexual act.

It is this essential kind of psychological naturalness which the rhythm method destroys, when a couple must try to hold their sexual relationships to some rigid calendar schedule. Thus the effort to interpret rhythm as a kind of half-way celibacy is misconstrued and rests on an inability to understand the sexual act as the expression of the relationship, rather than merely the satisfaction of an egoistic appetite. Now it is obvious that if a couple were to really practice continence as a spiritual discipline, the last way they would do it would be according to the woman's monthly cycles of fertility. They would perhaps abstain for the forty days of Lent, or something of this kind, and meanwhile devote themselves to some special regime of prayer and contemplation. In this way abstinence might have a genuine spiritual function in their lives. But to abstain according to the woman's monthly cycle can scarcely be subsumed into an authentic spiritual discipline. It serves primarily to disrupt the natural psychological dynamics of the sexual life, and to reveal itself at every turn as a blatant method for avoiding pregnancy. Anyone who has tried to live by the temperature-taking, glucose-testing, chart-making routine imposed by the rhythm method with its artificial manipulation of the whole relationship can scarcely be led to see this as any real spiritual discipline. The motivation is obviously all wrong to begin with. It is like being asked to fast during Lent not for any ascetic value, but because a ten-ton block had been placed over the ice box which would fall on your head if you opened the door. Obviously such a situation, far from promoting the ascetic values, would simply make a person obsessed with hunger and filled with a sense of personal degradation. He would feel that he was being treated like a rat in a laboratory, and rightly so. Let this ten-ton block stand for the fear and uncertainty which accompany the rhythm method, and one may see why the rhythm method is a debilitating rather than an elevating adjunct to the normal marital relationship; and one must recognize also that this ten-ton block will grow space with each failure of the method to produce the kind of control over fertility that the couple wants and needs.

One might use this kind of analogy to explain the dehumanization created by such a method of regulating fertility. Suppose one were not allowed to smile when one really felt happy. The smile was not allowed to function as a spontaneous expression of *joie de vivre.* Rather the smile was treated as if it were some kind of appetite which had to be kept in check, although being a forceful appetite, one must condescend and satisfy it periodically. The satisfaction of this animal smiling-drive was linked by some Grand Inquisitor with a lunar stopwatch which flashed red and green at intervals. When it flashed green the person could smile, when red he must stop. In addition to this, the stopwatch had a few kinks in its mechanism so that it functioned very irregularly and inefficiently. The person therefore was not quite sure when it was flashing red and when green and he lived in constant dread of smiling at the wrong time, in which case he would be hit on the head with the aforementioned ten-ton block. Let the clerical moralist contemplate this analogy with care. Let him consider honestly what effect such a regime would have on his own psychic life, and perhaps he will have an inkling of why many Catholic married people object to the rhythm method.

As we have indicated at the outset of this essay, the ability to love and to procreate is a union of will and act governed only by the discipline of love itself: this is the full ideal of marital sexuality. But, in the existential situation, this cannot be attained at all times. Failing this full ideal in every act, it would seem that some such method as we have outlined earlier might give the couple the second best possibility of experiencing their full union and harmony of purpose from time to time, until they can give themselves to procreation in full generosity of spirit; and, on the other hand, it gives them the maximum freedom to develop the auxiliary perfections of their married life as much as possible. In the words of Augustine: "*Ama et fac quod vis.*"

12. The Inseparability of the Unitive-Procreative Functions of the Marital Act

Bernard Häring, C.SS.R.

This chapter first appeared in *Contraception, Authority and Dissent* in 1969.

The encyclical *Humanae Vitae* rests chiefly on the assertion that the procreative and unitive elements of the conjugal act are inseparable, and evinces optimism and confidence that all men of good will can accept this proposition: "We believe that men of our day are particularly capable of seizing the deeply reasonable and human character of this fundamental principle" (*H.V.* 12). Our attention will therefore be given to that part of the encyclical.

1. Openness of Each Marital Act to Procreation

For centuries the Church shared the common belief that each conjugal act was, by its very "nature," procreative and could only accidentally fail to be so. It was not until the nineteenth century that medical scientists posited the ovule of the woman as a condition for procreation; closer scientific investigation revealed a certain rhythm in nature which set limits on fecundity. It was further found that natural rhythm, unreliable as it may be, tends to separate the procreative and unitive functions of the marital act by restricting biological fecundity to few conjugal acts only. It was then evident that the "procreative good," at least in the sense of an actual transmission of life, could not be truly obtained during infertile periods. Thus it was only with great reluctance that the Church accepted marital intercourse to be good when it was intentionally limited to the infecund periods.

Indeed, a long tradition in the Church had consistently maintained that conjugal intercourse was truly and fully good only when it intended procreation explicitly or implicitly. It followed logically that marital intercourse during a pregnancy was immoral. St. Ambrose reflected the thinking of many theologians over the centuries when he stated, "God does the marvels of creation in the secret sanctuary of the mother's womb, and you dare to desecrate it through passion! Either follow the example of the beasts or fear God."[1]

The marital intercourse of sterile persons was generally condoned by the bishops and theologians on the basis of the persons' desire for fecundity. The biblical stories of women who had been considered definitively sterile and who became blessed with offspring could be used as supportive arguments for the lawfulness of intercourse. However, where there was neither hope nor desire for fecundity, the general trend was to discourage intercourse; not only was it considered most imperfect behavior but it indicated a lack of self-control and mortification.

The encyclical *Humanae Vitae* reaffirms the positive value of the marital act as expressive of conjugal love; such valuation was not at all common before St. Alphonsus of Liguori, or even before Pius XII and Vatican II. Conjugal acts, the encyclical states, "do not cease to be lawful if, for causes independent of the will of husband and wife, they are foreseen to be infecund, since they remain ordained towards expressing and consolidating their union. In fact, as experience bears witness, not every conjugal act is followed by new life. God has wisely disposed natural laws and rhythms which, of themselves, cause a separation in the succession of births" (11). Thus the simplistic alternative, "either the spouses have the explicit or at least implicit intention to transmit life or they are indulging in lustful desires," is finally eliminated. On this point, *Humanae Vitae* marks a tremendous progress over *Casti Connubii*. The question is raised, however, as to whether *Humanae Vitae* is as consistent as was *Casti Connubii* in its own way since such an important presupposition has now been eliminated.

Paul VI follows an ancient tradition when he asserts that each individual marital act must manifest readiness to transmit life: "The Church, calling men back to the observance of the norms of the natural law, as interpreted by her constant doctrine, teaches that each and every marriage act must remain open to the transmission of life" (*H.V.* 11). This main thesis of the new encyclical is rightly introduced by the word "nonetheless." Attention is called to the fact that apparently the same conclusion is reached in spite of the changed general premises. Moreover, the thesis not only stands on different premises but has a very different and most limited meaning. In the older tradition, the thesis was taken literally and absolutely; therefore, according to many Church Fathers, intercourse during a pregnancy was considered a kind of sacrilege. The majority of theologians before St. Alphonsus maintained the necessary intent to transmit life; if, somehow, they approved the lawfulness of a marital act when chiefly motivated by the "remedy to concupiscence," they insisted on the inclusion of the intention to procreate.

The expression "open to the transmission of life" has much less meaning now. The marital act during pregnancy is acknowledged as being "open to new life," and so is the conjugal act in the infecund periods despite the fact that scientific calculations might practically eliminate the probability of any transmission of life. It is unfortunate that Pope Paul uses the same phrase in referring to the "constant doctrine" of the Church when historically the expression originated at a time when scientific theories on infecund periods were unknown. Today the same expression refers to a totally different reality. According to *Humanae Vitae,* the calculated use of infecund periods is not contraceptive; rhythm keeps the marital act open for procreation but in a totally new sense, namely, it follows "the natural laws and rhythms of fecundity which, of themselves, cause a separation in the succession of births" (*H.V.* 11). The openness is still asserted relative to "each and every marital act," but the openness remains as long and only as long as the "laws of the generative process" (*H.V.* 13), "the natural laws and rhythms of fecundity" (*H.V.* 12), are observed, although this is done to avoid a new pregnancy.

In the past it was generally asserted that the conjugal act could not be free from sinfulness unless it truly sought the transmission of life. The same teaching is emphatically maintained now but with a different wording: "An act of marital love, which is detrimental to the faculty of propagating life . . . is in contradiction to both the divine plan according to whose norm matrimony is instituted, and the will of the Author of life. To use this divine gift destroying, even if only partially, its meaning and its purpose is to contradict the nature both of man and woman and of their most intimate relationship" (*H.V.* 13). But in context, the malice is not in the unwillingness to propagate life while engaging in the conjugal act; rather it now lies in intercourse without absolute respect for "the laws of the generative process" (*H.V.* 13), namely, the "natural laws and rhythms of fecundity which, of themselves, cause a separation in the succession of births" (*H.V.* 11). For good reasons or motives, those natural laws and rhythms can lawfully be exploited for the unitive meaning of the marriage act while assuring that the procreative meaning is respected only by eliminating it through the use of calendar, temperature charts, or other means. It is evident that "openness to the transmission of life" is not necessarily synonymous with "readiness to transmit life" through intercourse; rather it lies in the observance of the "natural laws and rhythms of fecundity" in order to exclude transmitting new life as effectively as possible through the use of "natural rhythms" and by no other means.

2. RESPECT FOR BIOLOGICAL LAWS

Humanae Vitae confines the procreative meaning of the marital act to the faithful observance of biological laws and rhythms. It implied therein that God's wise and divine plan is revealed to the spouses through these absolutely sacred physiological laws. This is undoubtedly the philosophy underpinning the argumentation of the whole encyclical. It goes so far as to declare biological laws as absolutely binding on the conscience of men.

"In relation to the biological processes, responsible parenthood means the knowledge and respect of their functions; human intellect discovers in the power of giving life biological laws which are part of the human person" (*H.V.* 10). Does it follow that God governs the human person through the same biological laws as animals? The answer is: No! In animals, the biological laws are linked to instinct. As for man, the encyclical cautions strongly, "In relation to the tendencies of instinct and passion, responsible parenthood means the necessary dominion which reason and will must exercise over them" (*H.V.* 10). Instinct is not a natural law in man; rather it is a questionable theory that has been superseded by motivation theories of drive or passion. The absoluteness of biological laws can apply to the human person to the extent that he knows them; he then has to observe them, even against the proddings of passion.

Some of the questions which arise spontaneously are: How did God govern man during the thousands of years when the biological laws relative to the separate unitive and procreative functions of the marital act were unknown? How does he govern those for whom the "natural laws and rhythms" do not function properly? And what about the less educated people who are incapable of acquiring and using the modern knowledge of these rhythmic tendencies? How absolute can "natural laws and rhythms" be if we can prove that over long periods of history they are undergoing slow but deep changes? How can one ascribe absoluteness to biological laws if they are "inscribed in the very being of man and woman" (*H.V.* 12) not as absolute laws but as changing and unreliable trends? The fundamental question remains: Is man to be absolutely subjected to biological laws and rhythms or is he and should he be their wise administrator?

The response of *Humanae Vitae* is apodictic: "In fact, just as man does not have unlimited dominion over his body in general, so also, with particular reason, he has no such dominion over his generative faculties as such, because of their intrinsic ordination towards raising up life, of which God is the principle" (13).

The premise "man does not have unlimited dominion over his body" cannot be denied. Modern medicine is based on a *reasonable, limited* dominion over the organism. Good medical art rejects any *arbitrary* interference with the biological functions, but it does intervene whenever it is to benefit not only the biological organism but *the whole person.* It would have seemed logical to pursue the thought to its proper conclusion: ". . . so also, with particular reason, he has *no unlimited dominion* over his generative faculties . . ." Man must be a wise—never an unwise or arbitrary—steward of his generative faculties as such; this would mean that any *arbitrary* interference is against the moral natural law. But *Humanae Vitae* seems to say: Although man has a real but limited dominion over his body, he has *no* dominion over the biological functions related to the transmission of life. In my opinion, this total difference between "limited dominion" and "no such dominion" demands a special proof. The quote from Pope John's encyclical *Mater et Magistra* seems intended for this purpose: "Human life is sacred; from its very inception it reveals the creating hand of God" (*H.V.* 13). Here again we encounter unequal members in the comparison: the absolute sacredness of the *biological laws and rhythms* is compared and equated with the sacredness of *human life.* The difference is as great as between "no dominion" and "limited dominion." Biological functions, including the human sperm and ovule, are not human life nor the inception of human life.

In spite of the unreliability of biological laws and rhythms, the encyclical seems to consider them as a part of the human person. It seems to go so far as thoroughly to subordinate the whole human person and the marriage itself to the absolute sacredness of biological laws which have only recently become better known. It has, in fact, been learned that they are not "unchangeable" but are constantly subject to change. We know, for example, that certain animals capable of begetting offspring two or three times a year adjust rapidly when transferred from tropical or subtropical regions to northern areas with a long winter. By a change in their biological "laws and rhythms" they adjust the process of begetting to once a year. Man's biological nature differs from that of lower animals; it is slower in its changes. However, man survives precisely because he can make use of such artificial means as clothing, modern technology, and, most importantly, medicine in adjusting in a typically human way.

3. MINISTER OF THE CREATOR'S DESIGN (H.V. 13)

The expression "minister of the design established by the Creator" has or can have a deep meaning. All can agree that man must act in wisdom as a faithful steward in submission to the loving will of

God. Man must not be the "arbiter of the sources of human life." In our interpretation, it becomes: man must never act arbitrarily; he must make the best possible use of all the gifts of God; he must administer his biological and psychological heritage in generous responsibility to the best of the whole person, of himself, and of his closest neighbor, especially of the marriage as a community of persons. However, *Humanae Vitae* intends an entirely different meaning: it seems to say that any effort of man to be the steward of biological reality is arbitrary; man is expected to be simply and absolutely submitted to biological "laws and rhythms," at least insofar as "each and every marriage act must remain open to the transmission of life." Human biology, not human reason, determines whether a conjugal act is to become fruitful or not, even at times and in situations when a new pregnancy or total continence would destroy persons or the marriage itself. There is no doubt left that respect for biological laws must be absolute: "It is not licit, even for the gravest reasons, to do evil so that good may follow therefrom . . . even when the intention is to safeguard or promote individual, family, or social well being" (*H.V.* 14).

Humanae Vitae seems to allow only one exception to the absolutely binding power of "natural laws and rhythms of fecundity" and it refers to the correction of the biological functions themselves. It appears to be the intended meaning of the principle: "The Church does not at all consider illicit the use of those therapeutic means truly necessary to cure diseases of the *organism,* even if an impediment to procreation, which may be foreseen, should result therefrom, provided such impediment is not, for whatever motive, directly willed" (*H.V.* 15). Medicine is generally based on the principle that biological functions may be interfered with and even destroyed if it is necessary for the well being of the *person.* It is evident that the final perspective of an anthropologically grounded medicine is not the mere restoration of the *organism* but the wholeness of a *person* in community. Medical practices of the last century often tended to focus on the organism instead of the person as a person; today, however, the trend has been reversed and corrected by the best of medical thought.

Let us consider the case of a postpartum psychosis or of a psychotic fear of pregnancy. How else can a woman in either instance be helped and her capacity to render the marital due be restored if not by an interference into her biological "laws and rhythms" so as to ascertain avoidance of a pregnancy? A literal interpretation of *Humanae Vitae,* and this in the whole context, condemns such an interference because it seeks directly to impede procreation; the intervention is not intended to cure a disease of the organism but to help the whole person. While the cure of organic ailments is allowed, the wholeness of the person does not seem to justify the treatment.

It is quite clear that in *Humanae Vitae* "the natural laws and rhythms" are considered as "the established order of the Creator"; therefore, the only way to regulate births is to follow "the natural rhythms immanent in the procreative functions" by "the use of marriage in the infecund periods only" (*H.V.* 16). The text is emphatic in elaborating the difference between "recourse to infecund periods" and "the use of means directly contrary to fecundation": "In reality, there are essential differences between the two cases: in the former, the married couple make use of a natural disposition; in the latter, they impede the development of natural processes" (*H.V.* 16).

The only solution for the difficulties, according to *Humanae Vitae,* is to bring rhythm to perfect functioning and to let married people determine their infecund days. This frame of reference truly suggests a place for a "catholic pill," namely, one that would ascertain or fix the time of ovulation; such regulation would respect "the established order of the Creator" and "the natural laws and rhythms," while a pill that postpones ovulation would be intrinsically evil and immoral since it does not respect these laws.

I think that modern man is particularly incapable of grasping the total difference in the moral import of these two means of interference. Today man thinks much more in terms of the good of the whole person than in terms of absolutely sacred but often dysfunctional "natural laws and rhythms." I must humbly confess that for me it is impossible to come to an understanding of

(1) how and in what realistic sense the marriage act can truly remain "open to the transmission of life" when a perfectly calculated use of rhythm—and, if needed, an artificial correction of the improperly functioning

"natural laws and rhythms"—guarantees no new life
in the marriage act;

(2) why such a difference in the morality of
   (a) interference in the organism for the restoration of
       the organism or the correction of improperly func-
       tioning "natural rhythm";
   (b) the responsible use of other means of birth regula-
       tion with even less interference into the biological
       functions.

Why should a pill that fixes the date of ovulation and guarantees the
loss of the ovule be more "catholic" than a pill that preserves the
ovule which, here and now, is not needed because procreation
would be irresponsible? One point emerges clearly: in the first case
the treatment respects the "law" of rhythm, while in the other it
does not respect the absolute validity of the natural rhythm. Yet it is
common knowledge today that in millions of cases "the natural law
of rhythm" by itself is not functioning or is at least unreliable.

Should the salvation of a marriage or even the eternal salvation
of a person depend so greatly on whether or not the "natural
rhythm" is functional? Should heavy and very dangerous burdens
be shouldered by couples who simply cannot rely on natural rhythm
while others go justified because they can operate "safely" within
such bounds and thereby avoid pregnancy?

4. DISREGARD FOR BIOLOGICAL FUNCTIONS
AND DESTRUCTION OF MARITAL LOVE

The encyclical *Humanae Vitae* marks an advance over earlier
teaching by its acknowledgment of the true meaningfulness of the
marriage act èven when childbirth is not desired, but it remains
adamant in the assertion that a marriage act bespeaks genuine love
only when the biological laws and rhythms are fully observed and
respected. It argues that "the dignity of man and wife" must be
defended in this way; where man relies on technical means he is no
longer a responsible being: the Church "engages man not to abdicate
from his own responsibility in order to rely on technical means"

(*H.V.* 18). I agree: if man were to *rely* on technical means *alone* without discernment in the proper use of technical means, mankind would be degraded. But the argument runs differently: any use of technical means relative to "natural processes" would necessarily destroy the integrity of conjugal love. Such a thesis finds no basis in experience; it assumes that biological laws and rhythms best protect man's dignity and capacity to love if dutifully followed, if observed with absolute respect and submission. How can such an assumption stand without proof?

The encyclical attempts to prove the unavoidably destructive character of all artificial means of birth control by signaling the "necessary" consequences: "Let men consider, first of all, how wide and easy a road would thus be opened up towards conjugal infidelity and the general lowering of morality. Not much experience is needed in order to know human weakness. . . . (*H.V.* 17). Pope Paul VI is convinced that nothing can better express the unitive and procreative meaning of marriage, can better check immorality, infidelity, and promiscuity, than the absolute sacredness of biological processes: "Consequently, if the mission of generating life is not to be exposed to the arbitrary will of men, one must necessarily recognize insurmountable limits of the possibility of man's domination over his own body and its functions. . . . Such limits cannot be determined otherwise than by the respect due to the integrity of the human organism and its functions" (*H.V.* 17).

Somehow, a strange counter-argument could run something like this: Unmarried couples who, by an accurate observance of the natural rhythm, let their intercourse be open to transmitting life while being, at the same time, absolutely sure that they do so only in infecund periods, can express mutual love while respecting "the integrity of the human organism and its functions." This argument cannot be disregarded if the "natural laws and rhythms" are the chief cornerstone of sex morality. Such argumentation, however, is immediately seen as fallacious if we come to a deeper understanding of the need to preserve the unitive and procreative meaning of the marital life; application of the principle of totality encompasses the nature of the *person* and the *personal* acts.

5. A PERSONALISTIC APPROACH
TO THE UNITIVE-PROCREATIVE MEANING OF MARRIAGE

There is need for a thorough study of the problem raised by the encyclical *Humanae Vitae,* namely, that of the relationship between the unitive and the procreative meaning of the marriage act. The encyclical could have been worded very differently had this problem received adequate attention in Catholic moral theology of the past decades. There is and must be a close linkage of the two meanings, and great care must be exercised never to separate them unduly or totally in any aspect of sex morality.

Moralists of the past did touch upon the problem, however, when they declared that extra-marital intercourse was immoral because it did not respect the "*bonum prolis,*" the good of procreation; if a child should result, it would not be born into a family. This argument could be developed along the following lines of thought: the unitive meaning of marriage is also disregarded because the partners do not look upon one another as a spouse or a possible parent of his/her children; they do not want to unite as spouses nor in view of the parental vocation. However, the old argument emphasizing only responsibility towards possible offspring when partners are unmarried does not go far enough; these two people do not want to be now and forever "two in one flesh." Their union is casual and superficial, not truly sincere; they lie in becoming "one flesh" while remaining separated.

Adulterers who use the rhythm method with the greatest skill and certainty observe the biological laws and relate the unitive and procreative meaning in the unrealistic and tenuous sense of "openness to the transmission of life" as emphasized in *Humanae Vitae.* From the personalistic point of view, they have totally divorced the two meanings because they do not bind themselves in a covenant uniting the conjugal and parental vocation. Indeed, they have fully neglected both meanings while respecting the biological laws and rhythms.

It is not easy to explain the relationship of the procreative to the unitive good in the marriage of proven sterile partners. Their marriage can fulfill the unitive meaning while it cannot truly and really fulfill a procreative role. However, I think the combined functions are not totally excluded in such marriages, in which the partners truly consider each other as spouses, and love each other in a way that would keep them open for the parental vocation were such within the range of possibility. One who sincerely loves his spouse as spouse would not refuse to have him or her as parent of his or her child if the choice were given.

Homosexuality is by no means a union of two *persons* "in one flesh," not only because sex activity of this kind is totally and absolutely opposed to any kind of parental vocation, but also because the sexual behavior of the partners fails to convey that love which is the gift of God for married people. The unitive semblance of homosexual behavior has nothing in common with the covenant of loves between man and woman. Not only is there lacking the biological basis for the unitive-procreative functions, but also the basic criteria of true love which are taken from an understanding of married love and union.

Premarital intercourse is another instance where the unitive and procreative functions of marriage are separated; it is a case of seeking the unitive meaning before uniting themselves in a lasting covenant of love, before a marriage that would assure a family setting for expected offspring. The two meanings are separated in spite of the fact that the partners could be observing the "natural laws and rhythms."

A husband who imposes a new pregnancy every year on his sick and nervous wife, doing so at the expense of proper family care, also separates the unitive from the procreative meaning of marriage. While the conjugal act may observe "the integrity of the human organism and its functions" (*H.V.* 17), it totally disregards genuine love for the wife and responsibility for the family. The unitive function is destroyed by this lack of love and responsibility while the procreative function is used irresponsibly.

6. Pastoral Considerations

Both the communicative-unitive good of the marriage and the good of the children impose constant sacrifices on the spouses who strive incessantly to do their best for the family. These sacrifices cannot be determined and motivated by a biological understanding of natural law or by mere respect for badly functioning rhythm. There are higher, more demanding but less frustrating criteria of "natural law." I am referring to the very nature of the persons as persons and the meaning of the acts of persons.

Vatican II was explicit in setting the direction for all future research relative to preserving the genuine human connection between the unitive and procreative meanings of marriage: "The objective standards, based on the nature of the human person and the acts of the person, preserve the full sense of mutual self-giving and human procreation in the context of true love" (*Pastoral Constitution on the Church in the Modern World,* 51). The Latin text emphasizes "*personae eiusdemque actuum natura. . . .*" The genuine relationship is broken whenever the conjugal act becomes sexual exploitation. It does not matter, then, whether such exploitation is done in conformity with biological laws and rhythms or against them; an irresponsible act of procreation can destroy the unitive meaning of marriage as well as the irresponsible use of contraceptive means.

It can positively be said that when a couple strives in the best possible way to grow in mutual affection, to promote the unity and stability of the marriage so as better to fulfill the parental vocation as regards good education and readiness to desire as many children as they can responsibly accept, then they preserve the human connection between the two meanings. Total continence can undermine a whole marriage. The *Pastoral Constitution* points to a dangerous disregard for the psychological and moral connection between the communicative-unitive good and the procreative good. It states: "Where the intimacy of married life is broken off, it is not rare for its faithfulness to be imperiled and its quality of fruitfulness ruined. For then the upbringing of the children and the courage to accept new ones are both endangered" (51).

When an absolute respect for improperly functioning, changing, or unknown biological laws and rhythms imposes total continence or an anguished, anxiety-arousing periodic continence, the unitive-procreative meanings of marriage can be severed. The procreative good is not obtained by a procreation which is against genuine human responsibility. The unitive good of the conjugal acts is not observed when total continence does, in fact, separate what God has joined together. Much human experience and, above all, shared experience is necessary in order to determine how, in the totally new situation of this day and age, the closely related unitive and procreative goods can remain effectively welded together. The encyclical seems to say that in this matter that "not much experience is needed" (17). It should be a matter of factual truth, a question of shared experience whether or not total continence imposed on the other spouse out of absolute respect for the natural biological functions and rhythms carries greater risks for conjugal fidelity and generous fecundity than a moderate and responsible use of some artificial means of birth regulation.

There is one point of the encyclical that should not be overlooked: "It is also to be feared that the man, growing used to the employment of anti-contraceptive practices, may finally lose respect for the woman and, no longer caring for her physical and psychological equilibrium, may come to the point of considering her a mere instrument of selfish enjoyment, and no longer his beloved companion" (17). I would not dare deny that this danger can arise. Everyone should be fully aware, however, that the danger cannot be dismissed by teaching the meaning of natural law, in a biological frame of thought, but the risk can at least be reduced by a better understanding of the nature of the person and his actions as a person. Countless spouses and marriage counselors testify to the fact that users of artificial means of birth regulation can be most attentive to the feelings of the spouse, caring in a very special way for the physical and psychological equilibrium of the spouse. There lurks the danger that they will not care or not enough; therefore, the moral teaching must alert them. I do not think that the doctrine of the absolute sacredness of the biological laws provides sufficient help in this direction. The close relationship between the unitive and procreative good of the marriage and of the conjugal act must be explained at a much higher, more demanding, and less frustrating level than that of an absolute respect for biological "laws and rhythms" which are anything but absolute.

Notes

1. Saint Ambrose, *Expositio Evangelii secundum Lucam,* liber I, Migne *PL* 15, 1552.

Part Three

STERILIZATION

13. Remarks to the Congress of Hematologists (September 12, 1958)

Pius XII

Several times already we have taken a position on the subject of sterilization. We have stated in substance that direct sterilization is not authorized by man's right to dispose of his own body. When, about ten years ago, sterilization began to be more widely applied, it became necessary for the Holy See to declare expressly and publicly that direct sterilization, permanent or temporary, of a man or woman is illicit by virtue of the natural law from which the Church herself, as you know, has no powers to dispense. By direct sterilization we mean an act whose aim is to make procreation impossible. (*The Pope then turned to the question of the Pill*). . . . In these cases the use of medication has as its end the prevention of conception by preventing ovulation. They are instances therefore of direct sterilization.

Sterilization in Catholic Hospitals (March 13, 1975)

Congregation for the Doctrine of the Faith

This sacred congregation has carefully examined the problem of therapeutic preventive sterilization and the various opinions put forward on how to solve it. It has also examined the problems posed by requests for collaboration in such sterilizations in Catholic hospitals. It offers the following replies to the questions asked of it:

1. Any sterilization whose sole, immediate effect, of itself, that is of its own nature and condition, is to render the generative faculty incapable of procreation is to be regarded as direct sterilization, as this is understood in statements of the pontifical magisterium, especially of Pius XII.[1] It is absolutely forbidden, therefore, according to the teaching of the Church, even when it is motivated by a subjectively right intention of curing or preventing a physical or psychological ill-effect which is foreseen or feared as a result of pregnancy. The sterilization of the faculty itself is even more strongly prohibited than is the sterilization of individual acts, since it is nearly always irreversible. Nor can any public authority justify the imposition of sterilization as being necessary for the common good, since it damages the dignity and inviolability of the human person.[2] Neither can one invoke the principle of totality in this case, the principle which would justify interference with organs for the greater good of the person. Sterility induced as such does not contribute to the person's integral good, properly understood, "keeping things and values in proper perspective."[3] Rather does it damage a person's ethical good, since it

deprives subsequent freely-chosen sexual acts of an essential element. Hence article 20 of the ethical code published by the Conference held in 1971 faithfully reflects the correct teaching and its observance should be urged.

2. The congregation re-affirms this traditional Catholic teaching. It is aware that many theologians dissent from it, but it denies that this fact as such has any doctrinal significance, as though it were a theological source which the faithful might invoke, forsaking the authentic magisterium for the private opinions of theologians who dissent from it.[4]

3. With regard to the administration of Catholic hospitals:

   a. The following is absolutely forbidden: co-operation, officially approved or admitted, in actions which of themselves (that is of their own nature and condition) have a contraceptive purpose, the impeding of the natural effects of the deliberate sexual acts of the person sterilized. For the official approval of direct sterilization and, all the more so, its administration and execution according to hospital regulations is something of its nature—that is, intrinsically—objectively evil. Nothing can justify a Catholic hospital co-operating in it. Any such co-operation would accord ill with the mission confided to such an institution and would be contrary to the essential proclamation and defence of the moral order.

   b. The traditional teaching on material co-operation, with its appropriate distinctions between necessary and freely-given co-operation, proximate and remote co-operation, remains valid, to be applied very prudently when the case demands it.

   c. When applying the principle of material co-operation, as the case warrants it, scandal and the danger of creating misunderstanding must be carefully avoided with the help of suitable explanation of what is going on.

This sacred congregation hopes that the criteria outlined in this document will meet the expectations of this episcopate, so that having removed the doubts of the faithful they may the more easily perform their pastoral duty.

Notes

1. See especially the two allocutions to the Catholic Union of Obstetricians and to the International Society of Hematology; see also *Humanae Vitae.*
2. See Pius XI, *Casti Connubii.*
3. Paul VI, *Humanae Vitae.*
4. See Vatican Council II, *Lumen Gentium,* n. 25.

Statement on Tubal Ligation (July 3, 1980)

National Conference of Catholic Bishops

Since we note among Catholic health care facilities a certain confusion in the understanding and application of authentic Catholic teaching with regard to the morality of tubal ligation as a means of contraceptive sterilization (cf. nos. 18 & 20, *Ethical and Religious Directives for Catholic Health Facilities*) the National Conference of Catholic Bishops makes the following clarification:

1) The traditional teaching of the Church as reaffirmed by the Sacred Congregation for the Doctrine of the Faith on March 13, 1975 clearly declares the objective immorality of contraceptive (direct) sterilization even if done for medical reasons.

2) The principle of totality does not apply to contraceptive sterilization and cannot be used to justify it.

3) Formal cooperation in the grave evil of contraceptive sterilization, either by approving or tolerating it for medical reasons, is forbidden and totally alien to the mission entrusted by the Church to Catholic health care facilities.

4) The reason for justifying material cooperation as described in the NCCB Commentary on the SCDF response refers not to medical reasons given for the sterilization but to grave reasons extrinsic to the case. Catholic health care facilities in the United States complying with the *Ethical and Religious Directives* are protected

by the First Amendment from pressures intended to require material cooperation in contraceptive sterilization. In the unlikely and extraordinary situation in which the principle of material cooperation seems to be justified, consultation with the Bishop or his delegate is required.

5) The local Ordinary has responsibility for assuring that the moral teachings of the Church be taught and followed in health care facilities which are to be recognized as Catholic. In this important matter there should be increased and continuing collaboration between the Bishop, health care facilities and their sponsoring religious communities. Local conditions will suggest the practical structures necessary to insure this collaboration.

6) The NCCB profoundly thanks the many physicians, administrators and personnel of Catholic health care facilities who faithfully maintain the teaching and practice of the Church with regard to Catholic moral principles.

14. Church Teaching on Sterilization

John P. Boyle

This chapter first appeared in *The Sterilization Controversy* in 1977.

The practice of sterilization is not new.[1] The court eunuch who looked after the king's harem is a familiar figure in biblical and other ancient literature. In fact the most practicable form of permanent sterilization known to the ancient world was castration of the male. The anatomical information and surgical techniques that would have made possible the permanent sterilization of the female were not available.

The ancients did, of course, have crude forms of contraception, some of which were thought to have a temporary sterilizing effect, and there are references from time to time to "poisons of sterility" in Christian literature, apparently referring to these contraceptives, and all the references are condemnatory.[2]

The possibility of surgical sterilization for the control of fertility is not, however, a very old one. If one looks at the *Theologia moralis* of St. Alphonsus Liguori,[3] who died in 1787 but whose works continued to appear in numerous editions during the nineteenth century, one will find no discussion whatever of surgical sterilization as we know it. What one does find is a discussion of the morality of castrating singers for Church choirs—a practice not unknown in St. Alphonsus' time and even well into the nineteenth century. Curiously, St. Alphonsus does not reject the practice, although he reviews the opinions of moralists who think it wrong and calls their opinion "more probable." But the opinion of moralists who thought the practice permissible to improve the quality of Church music and provide a good living for the singers is described as "probable" and the point is made that the Church in fact tolerated the practice.

Church tradition was also aware of the early condemnation of castration for religious reasons, such as it had been practiced by Origen, who made himself a eunuch for the Kingdom of God.

I mention these somewhat bizarre problems to make the point that the setting in which the sterilization question arose in moral theology was in terms of the liceity of mutilation. The decision was that it is not permissible to mutilate oneself, as Origen had, for religious reasons; but it was not so clear that mutilation was ruled out completely, if the motivation was partly religious, as in the case of the Church singers.

Of course moralists did recognize the permissibility of mutilating a part of the body for the good of the whole, e.g., by amputation, although there is a curious silence in St. Alphonsus about medicine and surgery in this context. But for the moment I merely note that the question of the *castrati* is discussed under the heading of mutilation and that the principle of bodily totality does not seem to be enough to explain or justify the castration of healthy male singers. There is no discussion of sterilization performed to protect the life of a woman which would be threatened by pregnancy.

The silence of moralists on therapeutic sterilization is not mysterious. The workings of the human reproductive system were not well understood until at least the second quarter of the nineteenth century, when von Baer published his discovery of the female ovum in 1827.[4] And despite the fact that Fallopius had described the tubes which bear his name in the sixteenth century, and van Leeuwenhoeck had discovered the male sperm in 1677, basic reproductive facts were simply unknown until the nineteenth century. Combine that with the fact that antiseptic surgery and anesthesia were not developed until the middle of the nineteenth century by Morton and Long for anesthesia and Lister for antisepsis, and it becomes clearer why modern surgical sterilization is not discussed by moralists. It was in 1834 that James Blundell suggested the sectioning of the fallopian tubes, but it was only between 1880 and 1910 that successful techniques of tubal ligation were developed.

That produced a different kind of moral evaluation.

The first attention to surgical sterilization seems to have come from canonists who had to deal with the problem of sterility and impotence as possible impediments to matrimony. John Noonan has found a description of surgical sterilization in Cardinal Pietro

Gasparri's canon law text on matrimony from 1894, but Gasparri limits his discussion to the problem of a possible marriage impediment. There is no discussion of sterilization among the major moralists of the nineteenth century. It is not until the first decades of the twentieth century that moralists began to write about surgical sterilization.

When they saw the procedure as contraceptive, their opinions were condemnatory, and in this they were but following an opinion of the Holy Office of May 22, 1895. The Holy Office was asked:

Whether the practice is permissible either actively or passively of a procedure which intentionally proposes as an express purpose the sterilization of the woman?

The Congregation responded in the negative.[5]

Sabetti and Barrett, who cite this response, explain the condemnation not in terms of mutilation but in terms of contraceptive effect, which they find opposed to the primary purpose and good of matrimony, i.e., children, to the purpose of the matrimonial contract, to the purpose of the seed, and therefore contrary to the natural law, so that it can in no way be justified.

The position of Sabetti and Barrett is consistent with the traditional condemnation of contraception and also with the natural law doctrine which flourished under Leo XIII after the publication of the encyclical *Aeterni Patris* on the revival of Thomism in 1879. However, I think it is important both to note the shift from the older treatment of sterilizing surgery as mutilation to such surgery as contraception and to appreciate the historical situation in which the discussion began. Two factors are to be considered: one, the purpose for which surgical sterilization was used, and the other, the population question. We begin with a word about the eugenic use of sterilization.

In this connection, the development of techniques of vasectomy is instructive.[6] The early technique was developed at the Indiana State Reformatory by Dr. Harry C. Sharpe, using reformatory inmates as his experimental subjects. The purposes for which these techniques were employed were clearly eugenic. Sterilizations had also been carried out in Pennsylvania—without benefit of any legal authorization—apparently by a superintendent who wished to deliver his male inmates from self-abuse. Whatever the motivations of the first practitioners of eugenic sterilization, the movement gained ground rapidly after Indiana passed in 1907 a law providing for the involuntary sterilization of the mentally defective. The U.S. Supreme Court in *Buck vs. Bell* in 1927 declared such laws constitutional, with the ringing dictum of Mr. Justice Holmes that "three generations of imbeciles are enough." At one point twenty-seven states had laws providing for involuntary eugenic sterilization. Many such laws are still on the books.

The program of eugenic sterilization that was carried on in Germany under the Nazi regime beginning in 1933 is still remembered. The involuntary sterilization of thousands of men and women for eugenic reasons reached its peak in the 1930's, but the movement was underway earlier, perhaps as a result of the social Darwinism that had its origins in the nineteenth century.

The point is that the popes' moral evaluation of the new surgical techniques for the sterilization of both men and women had its origins in a climate which is regarded today even in legal circles as inimical to human freedom. The scientific arguments advanced for eugenic sterilization are recognized today as largely unfounded, despite the fact that the Supreme Court and many state legislatures presumably acted on that basis.[7]

There was another factor too: the population problem.

In his monumental study of the moral and canonical aspects of contraception, John Noonan has noted the relationship, often expressed, between declining population levels and opposition to contraception. Such arguments appear in the late nineteenth century in France, for example, after the debacle of the Franco-Prussian War.[8] Society—both Church and state—had a need for children which became another argument against contraception, one explicitly cited by bishops in Belgium, France and Germany in the period between the Franco-Prussian War and World War I—precisely the period when the eugenic sterilization movement was growing. In the period between 1880 and just prior to World War II, the birth rate declined in almost all Western European and North American countries to less than twenty per thousand, and England, Switzerland and Sweden just before World War II had net rates of reproduction of less than one, while Belgium and France in 1939 had rates slightly over one. Noonan comments:

> Western society seemed to be seeking stability of population and achieving it. In most countries this achievement appears to have been through contraception.[9]

Malthus' warnings had apparently been taken seriously over a period of many years.

But many countries perceived their population situation as a national threat. I have already mentioned France. The German Nazis and the Italian Fascists attempted to increase the populations of their respective countries, and I noted the eugenic dimension of their efforts.

Perhaps these indications are enough to suggest the climate in which the modern discussion of sterilization, especially through surgical techniques, arose. The Holy See condemned in eugenic sterilization what is properly viewed as the violation of the natural rights of those who were being involuntarily sterilized, even though the techniques were more sophisticated than castration. Sterilization by cutting or tying the fallopian tubes for contraceptive purposes was condemned as well, although it is important to note the circumstances, so different from our own in concern for population, in which the prohibition of contraception was restated. It should be noted too that Rome did not reject sterilization as punishment for crime. But it was in a generally disapproving climate that there occurred the earliest modern discussion of surgical sterilization to prevent even a pregnancy that would be life-threatening or at least seriously health-threatening to the mother.

The condemnation of eugenic sterilization took its most solemn form in the encyclical *Casti Connubii* of Pius XI in 1930. The same condemnation was repeated by Pius XI, Pius XII, and Paul VI, and by Roman Congregations.[10] These statements extend the condemnation to contraceptive and eugenic sterilization, but not always to punitive sterilization. They also make it clear that sterilization for therapeutic reasons can be permissible under the principle of double effect.

Sterilization was treated, except for contraceptive sterilization, as a form of mutilation, and moralists applied their usual rules. Or at least they tried. Mutilations are permissible for the good of the whole, under what Pius XII called the "principle of totality," the theological tradition said. Or sterilization might be the unavoidable side-effect of quite legitimate procedures such as prostate surgery or a hysterectomy demanded by some pathology of the reproductive system. These latter cases are called "indirect" sterilizations, because the primary intention is not sterilization but the treatment of the pathology of the reproductive system.

But neither the popes nor the moralists applied the principle of totality to the reproductive system itself. They did not recognize the legitimacy of sterilizing, if the pathology was located outside the reproductive system and the threat to life or health would arise only if a pregnancy occurred. It seemed easy enough to say that there is simply no such thing as an unavoidable pregnancy, except perhaps in the case of rape. In that case precautions against an unwanted pregnancy were permitted so long as they were not clearly abortifacient. The moralists, and the pronouncements of the Church authorities which they were following, explained this stance by declaring that the reproductive system, unlike other bodily organs, is ordered not to the good of the individual who possesses it, but to the good of the species. Thus the principle of totality may not be invoked but only the principle of double effect. Pius XII spoke to that effect in 1953.[11]

With the development of the anovulant pills in the 1950's, the same pope extended his prohibition of contraceptive sterilization to include temporary sterilization induced by the pill. Thus sterilization, whether produced by surgery or by drugs, whether permanent or temporary, whether of the male or the female, was proscribed when done for eugenic, contraceptive and even for therapeutic reasons, unless the sterilization was only the indirect effect of a procedure which had other direct therapeutic effects. Punitive sterilization, however, was still defended. That was the state of the discussion when Pius XII died in 1958.

Since the death of Pius XII and the election of Pope John XXIII, a great discussion has taken place in the Church on the meaning of marriage and the morality of regulating births. In the following pages I turn to several positions that have been taken on sterilization. I have tried to choose authors whose views are broadly representative of Church teaching, and I have also tried to present evidence drawn from a number of countries and language groups.

In March 1963, Pope John XXIII created a commission to study the question of birth control. The study commission was continued and enlarged by Pope Paul. I will turn below to its recommendations, but the task may be simpler if we treat Pope Paul's position first.

The pope's comment on the work of the commission, and the key to his own position, can be found in n. 6 of the encyclical *Humanae Vitae* (1968):

> The conclusions at which the commission arrived could not, nevertheless, be considered by us as definitive, nor dispense us from a personal examination of this serious question; and this also because, within the commission itself, no full concordance of judgments concerning the moral norms to be proposed had been reached, and above all because certain criteria of solutions had emerged which departed from the moral teaching on marriage proposed with constant firmness by the teaching authority of the Church.[12]

The encyclical then goes on to describe four characteristics of conjugal love, i.e., that it must be human, total, faithful and exclusive, and fecund. While the pope acknowledges the need for responsible parenthood, his conclusion is:

> Nonetheless the Church, calling men back to the observance of the norms of the natural law, as interpreted by their constant doctrine, teaches that each and every marriage act must remain open to the transmission of life.[13]

The encyclical recognizes the legitimacy of using rhythm to regulate births, but of sterilization it says:

> Equally to be excluded, as the teaching authority of the Church has frequently declared, is direct sterilization,

whether perpetual or temporary, whether of the man or of the woman.[14]

Generally, since the teaching of *Humanae Vitae* is a restatement of the teaching of Pius XI and Pius XII, the encyclical does not provide lengthy arguments for its position. But there is one facet of the argument that is touched upon. In defending the use of rhythm while at the same time forbidding the use of artificial means of birth control, the pope writes:

> In reality, there are essential differences between the two cases; in the former, the married couple make legitimate use of a natural disposition; in the latter they impede the development of natural processes. It is true that, in the one and other case, the married couple are concordant in the positive will of avoiding children for plausible reasons, seeking the certainty that offspring will not arrive; but it is also true that only in the former case are they able to renounce the use of marriage in the fecund periods when, for just motives, procreation is not desirable, while making use of it during the infecund periods to manifest their affection and to safeguard their mutual fidelity. By so doing they give proof of a truly and integrally honest love.[15]

The point to note in this paragraph is that it distinguishes between the moral and the immoral on the basis of a "natural process," i.e., on the basis of reproductive biology. And obvious importance is attached to the opportunity afforded by the use of rhythm to make abstinence an expression of conjugal love.

Briefly, I mention too another series of arguments, mostly on the basis of negative consequences, offered in *Humanae Vitae*. The pope fears that artificial birth control would open the road to conjugal infidelity and the general lowering of morality. Fear is expressed of a lowering of respect for women: men will become careless of the physical and psychological equilibrium of women and make of women instruments of selfish enjoyment rather than respected and beloved companions.

Moreover, Pope Paul fears the power that would be placed in the hands of public authorities if they seek to remedy population problems by immoral means and thus invade the most private sector of conjugal intimacy. On the basis of these grave consequences, the pope reaches the following conclusion:

> Consequently, if the mission of generating life is not to be exposed to the arbitrary will of men, one must necessarily recognize insurmountable limits to the possibility of man's domination over his own body and its functions, limits which no man, whether a private individual or one invested with authority, may licitly surpass. And such limits cannot be determined otherwise than by the respect due to the integrity of the human organism and its functions, according to the principles recalled earlier, and also according to the correct understanding of the "principle of totality" illustrated by our predecessor Pope Pius XII.[16]

The encyclical then has sought to define the limits of a person's licit intervention in the processes of one's own body, and it has sought those limits in the natural biological processes themselves, which the pope has described as grounding the natural moral law.

I need hardly say that the teaching of *Humanae Vitae* is the authoritative view of the pope; it is shared too by bishops and theologians. I have not attempted to count heads or to determine the extent to which the encyclical's doctrine has been accepted. In the review of various views on sterilization being given here, it is enough to say that the teaching of the pope and the reasons offered in support of it are accepted by significant numbers of people in the Church. But there are other views, and I turn now to them.

In the turbulence which followed the publication of *Humanae Vitae* in 1968, the work of the papal commission to which the encyclical was reacting has not received much attention. The substance of its reports has, however, been published.[17] From the various published documents, I wish to comment only on what pertains to the question of sterilization.

The report adopted by the majority of the commission says this about sterilization:

> Sterilization, since it is a drastic and irreversible intervention in a matter of great importance, is generally to be excluded as a means of responsibly avoiding conceptions.[18]

While this is hardly a ringing endorsement, it must be noted that what is "generally to be excluded" might, given the proper circumstances, be permitted. The position of the commission therefore represented a modification of the position taken by the Holy Office in 1936 and 1940, which declared direct sterilization intrinsically immoral.[19]

How did the commission arrive at its position? The teaching of the Holy Office, which was repeated by *Humanae Vitae*, was that sterilization is intrinsically evil *ex defectu juris*, i.e., because it was an action which the agent had no right to perform. In 1953 Pius XII had explained at some length why the principle of totality ought not to be invoked when the danger to the total human life and health arose not from some pathology of the reproductive system but from the threat posed by a future pregnancy. The pope held that since pregnancy is voluntary, the principle of totality could not apply.[20]

In brief, the argument of the commission runs this way: The fundamental principle is that of responsible parenthood. In the discharge of their responsibility the couple may find the regulation of conception necessary. To this end some intervention in physiological processes, ordained to the essential values of marriage and first of all to the good of children, is to be judged according to the fundamental and objective principles of morality.

> A right ordering toward the good of the child within the conjugal and familial community pertains to the essence of human sexuality. Therefore the morality of sexual acts between married people takes its meaning first of all and specifically from the ordering of their actions in a fruitful

married life, that is, one which is practiced with responsible, generous and prudent parenthood. It does not then depend upon the direct fecundity of each and every particular act. Moreover, the morality of every marital act depends upon the requirements of mutual love in all its aspects. In a word, the morality of sexual actions is thus to be judged by the true exigencies of the nature of human sexuality, whose meaning is maintained and promoted by conjugal chastity, as we have said.[21]

The reader will note, I think, that a fundamental difference of approach exists about human dominion over biological processes and whether and to what extent those processes can be considered *morally* normative. The reader will also note that the commission insists that there are objective criteria for the moral evaluation of interventions in physiological processes. The commission wrote:

The objective criteria are the various values and needs duly and harmoniously evaluated. These objective criteria are to be applied by the couples, acting from a rightly formed conscience and according to their concrete situation.[22]

There are also objective criteria as to the means to be employed. Thus Vatican II altogether rejected abortion or procedures that are thought to be abortifacient. Then there follows the comment that sterilization is generally to be excluded because it is a drastic and irreversible intervention. As to other means the commission writes:

Moreover, the natural law and reason illuminated by Christian faith dictate that a couple proceed in choosing means not arbitrarily but according to objective criteria. These objective criteria for the right choice of methods are the conditions for keeping and fostering the essential values of marriage as a community of fruitful love. If these criteria are observed, then a right ordering of the human act according to its object, end and circumstances is maintained.[23]

First, then, the action must correspond to the nature of the person and his acts so that the meaning of procreation is kept in the context of true love.[24] Second, the means chosen must have an effectiveness proportionate to the necessity of averting a new conception temporarily or permanently. Third, since every method, even abstinence, has certain negative effects, the means chosen must carry the least possible negative effects for the concrete couple. Fourth, the means chosen must be considered in the light of what is available to the couple in their specific situation, including its economic factors.[25]

Thus, the commission insists, couples properly instructed are to make their decision "not arbitrarily, but as the law of nature and of God commands; let couples form a judgment which is objectively founded, with all the criteria considered."[26]

The commission also devoted a section to indicating what is considered the continuity of its position with the previous teaching of the Church more profoundly understood. Noting that the rhythm method has been approved by the popes, despite the fact that the use of it separates the reproductive from the other aspects of marital acts, the commission wrote:

> The tradition has always rejected seeking this separation with a contraceptive intention for motives spoiled by egoism and hedonism, and such seeking can never be admitted. The true opposition is not to be sought between some material conformity to the physiological processes of nature and artificial intervention. For it is natural to man to use his skill in order to put under human control what is given by physical nature. The opposition is really to be sought between one way of acting which is contraceptive and opposed to a prudent and generous fruitfulness, and another way which is in an ordered relationship to responsible fruitfulness and which has a concern for education and all the essential, human and Christian values. In such a conception the substance of tradition stands in continuity and is respected.[27]

I conclude this review of the commission's stand with another citation, this one from a document on "pastoral approaches" prepared for the pope by some of the bishop members of the commission:

> What has been condemned in the past and remains so today is the unjustified refusal of life, arbitrary human intervention for the sake of moments of egoistic pleasure; in short, the rejection of procreation as a specific task of marriage. In the past, the Church could not speak other than she did, because the problem of birth control did not confront human consciousness in the same way. Today, having clearly recognized the legitimacy and even the duty of regulating births, she recognizes too that human intervention in the process of the marriage act for reasons drawn from the finality of marriage itself should not always be excluded, provided that the criteria of morality are always safeguarded.
>
> If an arbitrarily contraceptive mentality is to be condemned, as has always been the Church's view, an intervention to regulate conception in a spirit of true, reasonable, and generous charity does not deserve to be, because if it were, other goods of marriage might be endangered. So what is always to be condemned is not the regulation of conception, but an egoistic married life, refusing a creative opening-out of the family circle, and so refusing a truly human—and therefore truly Christian—married love. This is the anti-conception that is against the Christian ideal of marriage.[28]

Although the commission's view did not win the pope's acceptance, I have dealt with it at length both for the approach to the natural law which it employs, which is rather different from that of the encyclical, and also for its view of the relationship between its viewpoint and that of the tradition. In the words of a theologians' report to the study commission, "Man is the administrator of life and consequently of his own fecundity."[29] The commission, therefore, sees human physiology as being at the disposal of human reason and not as a norm-giver to it, even in matters of reproduction.

The commission also has a rather different view of human sexuality than has often been found in the Christian tradition, and it stresses the interpersonal dimensions of sexual love, even as it insists on the ordering of love to a prudent and generous fecundity. And, finally, the commission claims to preserve the *values* traditionally proclaimed by the Church's teaching authority, even though it recognizes that it proposes new *norms* with respect to contraception.

With these contrasting views in mind, I turn to some current theological writing on the subject of sterilization. I have tried to locate materials which would reflect not only the work of American theologians and practice in this country, but also that of other places.

In the November 1974 issue of the German periodical *Stimmen der Zeit*,[30] Franz Böckle, professor of moral theology in the University of Bonn, published an article on "Ethical Aspects of Voluntary Sterilizing Operations."

Böckle's treatment is in two parts. The first treats sterilization as a mutilation, and the second deals with sterilization as contraceptive. As to the first, Böckle notes that the principle of totality has traditionally been applied. When a physical pathology is involved the case is obvious enough and is really not in dispute. But Böckle points out that the principle has been extended to justify the voluntary castration of men guilty of sexual misconduct. The totality then must therefore include more than just the physical totality of the body and extend at least to psychic totality as well.[31]

Böckle also refers to the use of the principle of totality when prophylactic sterilization was under consideration. He mentions in particular the situation of the nuns in the Congo, in which the use of sterilizing pills was justified by theologians held in high esteem in Rome on the ground that contraception was prohibited *only* when sexual relations were voluntary, and in the Congo situation they were most involuntary. Hence the principle of totality could be invoked to avoid the consequences of involuntary sexual relations. This reading of the 1958 allocution of Pius XII on the principle of totality is thoroughly ingenious and representative of a legal model of morality in the hands of real experts.

Böckle has another situation too. He distinguishes between "infertility" and "sterility." "Infertility" means that a woman is unable to carry a child to viability. "Sterility" means that a conception is not possible. Böckle then argues that the moral order is violated only by the destruction of a healthy fertility. Therefore in cases of infertility a directly sterilizing operation does not violate the moral order but instead is therapeutic. Böckle notes that after consultation among German moral theologians, this opinion was included in a book of principles and counsels in marriage matters for German physicians and he calls it a *sententia probata,* which I take to mean not only probable but officially approved. And he concludes:

> On the basis of this fact we could say that the official teaching of the Catholic Church does not oppose a medically indicated sterilizing operation in concrete cases.[32]

But Böckle has more. He then suggests that the principle of totality can be extended even to the marriage, so that a husband could be sterilized in place of the wife. Böckle says that in the relationship of the individual to society the individual human being can never simply be sacrificed to human society. But, he argues, the fertility of a marriage is in a certain degree an indivisible whole related to the unity and indissolubility of the marriage itself. Therefore, when there are weighty reasons for not sterilizing the woman, and where the age and life situation of the man would make it a responsible action, the principle of totality could be applied to the marriage and the husband vicariously sterilized for his wife. All this, of course, assumes that fertility as defined has been destroyed. Böckle is of the opinion that even this latter case is not contrary to the position of *Humanae Vitae* on contraception.

Then Böckle turns to sterilization as a form of contraception. Noting the widespread disagreement among German Catholics with the position of *Humanae Vitae* (sixty-one percent disagreed in a poll) and the action of various bishops' conferences in pointing to the possibility and the obligation of the faithful to make their own decision in conscience—an event without parallel in modern Church history—Böckle proceeds to a critique of the encyclical's position. In brief, Böckle rejects the notion of "intrinsically evil acts" that underlies the encyclical's position on contraception and which in turn is grounded in the encyclical's position on the normative character of biological processes as willed by God. Böckle's formulation of a moral rule is this: "It is immoral actively to exclude birth from sexual love *(Hingabe),* unless avoiding conception is indicated by weighty reasons and abstinence would be injurious to the well-being of the couple."[33]

Given sufficient grounds for contraception, the choice of means depends on the health and the personal values of the couple. Böckle then applies this analysis to sterilization:

> Whoever holds with *Humanae Vitae* that every artificial contraceptive act is intrinsically evil must reject also every sterilization for simply prophylactic reasons. But whoever, counter to *Humanae Vitae,* treats contraception as not an evil in every case (and this could be a considerable part of the bishops and theologians) must treat sterilization as a "last resort" for an indicated prevention of contraception. The moral judgment will conscientiously weigh the positive and negative consequences for the integral good of the person. Where a lasting avoiding of children is indicated, there the sterilization could be included in the same consideration.[34]

Böckle, like the papal commission, holds that the choice of contraceptive methods, including sterilization as a last resort, must be made by the couple according to objective criteria. And he ends his article with the statement:

> Where contraception by drugs is tolerated by Catholic hospitals, it follows that sterilizing operations as a last resort in a necessary and lasting prevention of conception should be permitted as well.[35]

Employing rather different moral criteria and methods, Böckle has arrived at a quite different conclusion from the encyclical's. It is difficult to know how widely his ideas are shared in Germany, especially with regard to prophylactic sterilizations. He does refer in the course of his discussion to recent synods, including the recent German synod, in which a position similar to his on birth regulation seems to be at work.[36]

The lines of quite different positions are appearing by this time, so I will summarize more briefly other discussions, largely for the purpose of indicating the spread of the point of view they represent.

Even prior to the publication of *Humanae Vitae,* Eugène Tesson had published an examination of a number of situations in which sterilization, either permanent or temporary, might be considered, as well as some situations in which the anovulant pill might be used for other than directly sterilizing purposes, e.g., the control of irregular cycles, etc.[37]

Tesson describes the situation in which Catholic moralists concluded that it was legitimate to perform a hysterectomy to remove a uterus that *would* pose a problem if a pregnancy occurred but which is not otherwise a health problem. The case of the uterus after multiple Caesarean sections is an example. Although not all theologians agreed, the opinion of Gerald Kelly, S.J., who defended a hysterectomy in such a case, was widely accepted.

Tesson presses the case further. If a hysterectomy could be performed in such cases, could not a physician achieve the same effect by tying the woman's tubes, a much less drastic procedure? Tesson agrees that a tubal ligation and sterilization in such a case is justified, either by surgery or the use of the anovulant pill. What has come to be called an "isolation procedure" of this sort is justified by the argument that *qui maius potest, minus potest,* the sterilization being the less drastic action.

In Canada the practice of Catholic hospitals can be measured by the codes of ethics that some of them have adopted. In London, Ontario, St. Joseph's Hospital adopted a "Policy Manual for a Committee To Advise on Requests for Obstetrical/Gynaecological Sterilization Procedures."[38] The policy is this:

A. There are medical instances in which a tubal ligation may be considered as a final procedure to be used in the total treatment of a woman who is judged unable to support a future pregnancy.

B. The only reason for allowing sterilization in this hospital is the presence of a pathological condition in the woman.

C. Only those medical indications will be considered which pose a permanent major threat to the life and health of a woman.

The moral underpinning of this position is explicitly the principle of totality, understood as the physical totality of the woman, which would be threatened by a future pregnancy. The policy modifies the position of *Humanae Vitae* and Pius XII by extending the principle of totality to the reproductive system, but it does not envision sterilization for purely contraceptive reasons.

The Ottawa General Hospital[39] performs sterilization for obstetrical, gynecological, surgical, and psychiatric reasons without prior committee review, provided that the indications are verified in a consultation with colleagues in the field. Ottawa does seem to have periodic post-operative review. It is of some interest that among the indications is one for the case of a mother with a retarded, psychotic or epileptic child, when the woman must still act as mother and wife. The policy statement says: "In certain cases a sociological evaluation is almost indispensable to carry out a decision." Thus the principle of totality has been extended.

Two hospitals in Toronto[40] have adopted policy statements based on two basic values: (1) the commitment of the hospitals to their Roman Catholic status and to the obligations which result from this status vis-à-vis their constituency; (2) the respect of the hospital for the individual religious and moral convictions and family relationships which influence the patient's decision concerning the number of their children and the time in their marriage when they decide to opt for permanent forms of family planning. The policy is a statement about the conditions under which the hospital will *cooperate*. That framework is noteworthy.

In cases of conflict between these two sets of values, the hospitals will decide whether or not to cooperate on the basis of: (1) informed consent of the patient; (2) marital status, age of the couple and the number of children; (3) assurance that the medical, psychological or socio-economic indications warrant limitation in the size of the family on a permanent basis; (4) a signed statement by the couple that it is their conviction that they are making a conscientious decision.

The policy requires that persons to be sterilized in these hospitals be thirty years of age, and with at least three children, if the decisive arguments are socio-economic. Single persons will not be sterilized unless there is a strict medical counter-indication to pregnancy.

It is hardly necessary to point out the increasingly broad grounds, especially socio-economic ones, which are indicated here. But there is also explicit reference to a rather new factor: the individual religious and moral convictions of the person or couple requesting sterilization. The influence of discussions about moral and religious liberty since Vatican II is obvious. It should also be noted that Ontario has a health-care plan which involves the hospitals.

The precise moral ground for these policies is not indicated, but there is reason to think that in addition to the principle of totality, which may be operative in some cases, there are at least two other considerations. One is a conflict of parental obligations. On this point the bishops of Canada expressed themselves in their statement on *Humanae Vitae*[41] when they noted a possible "clear conflict of duties, e.g., the reconciling of conjugal love and responsible parenthood with the education of children already born or with the health of the mother." It is possible, although I am unable to document it, that the judgment in some cases may simply be that permanent means of contraception are needed in view of some other and broader principle of morality than the principle of totality.

With that I turn to the position taken by Father Charles E. Curran in his article "Sterilization: Roman Catholic Theory and Practice"[42] and by Richard McCormick, S.J. Father Curran discusses the position of the popes on sterilization and various interpretations put upon it by theologians, including the famous Congo situation. He also mentions again punitive sterilization, and yet another situation of the incompetent female who cannot provide for her hygienic needs or who is in danger of being impregnated. Sterilization for hygienic reasons he regards as indirect sterilization since its purpose is not contraceptive at all but hygienic, and thus it falls well within traditional limits, provided that important questions of adequate and informed consent are met. Sterilization in the case of the incompetent in danger of being impregnated Curran regards as parallel to the Congo situation and also falling well within traditional limits, again if important questions of informed consent are satisfied.[43]

Generally, however, Curran wished to handle the whole subject in a rather different framework. For one thing Father Curran would extend the principle of totality to include the good of the whole person, not just his physical being. The good of the whole person would include his relationship to his family, community and the larger society. Curran also knows of the opinion that totality might be extended to the marriage.

But in addition to the principle of totality, Father Curran would invoke the principle of man's stewardship over his sexuality and his generative organs. Rather than consider sterilization in terms of mutilation, with its traditional emphasis on totality, and indirect and direct effects, Curran would consider it in the same basic terms as contraception. Thus surgical sterilization and the use of anovulant pills belong in the same discussion, since both are sterilizing and the difference is only in duration of effects. Whenever contraception can be justified on a permanent basis, Father Curran would see the moral possibility of a sterilization, provided that the usually permanent and irreversible effects are understood. The weight of the reasons needed to justify a sterilization under the principle of stewardship should be in proportion to the permanent effects of the procedure. Richard McCormick, S.J., has published what is fundamentally a similar opinion.

The Code of Ethical and Religious Directives for Catholic Health Facilities of course repeats the statements of *Humanae Vitae* prohibiting any direct sterilization. The Code was adopted in 1971 by an overwhelming majority of the American bishops (232 to 7) and has been promulgated in a number of dioceses.

In a curious development, however, Father Anthony Kosnick, who is a member of the Advisory Committee to the Bishops' Committee on Health Affairs of the U.S. Catholic Conference, did a survey of dioceses in the U.S. The responding dioceses represent those in which a large portion of Catholic health facilities are found. In his report[44] on procedures being followed with regard to Directive 20 on sterilization, Father Kosnick writes:

The matter is urgent for medical men who insist that concern for the welfare of the total person as well as the practice of responsible medicine requires recourse to sterilization procedures in some instances. Diverse interpretation of this Directive 20 has led to widely divergent practices and applications with regard to sterilization procedures in Catholic hospitals. In one diocese it was indicated that prior to the promulgation of the Directives a policy had been in effect that permitted sterilizations for medical purposes, including psychiatric reasons, under the principle of totality.[45]

Confusion of course followed the apparently restrictive policy declaration of Directive 20. But what is telling in Kosnik's report is his description of sterilization committees set up in Catholic hospitals and at work without complications or difficulties for a year in early 1973! Note that these are explicitly sterilization committees, which must mean that, despite Directive 20, tubal ligations for medically indicated reasons are being and have been done since the new Code was published in a significant number of American dioceses. Just how many Kosnik does not say, but he has enough information to provide three different models for such committees. I omit the details. What is significant is that a policy approved 232 to 7 by the American bishops' conference has not been strictly observed in American Catholic hospitals. The indications for sterilizations, however, seem to be limited to medical ones. Policy in the U.S. is apparently stricter than in Canada.

In summary then, the development of surgical techniques of sterilization and the Church's reaction to them has taken place since the 1890's. While castration of Church singers had been defended and practiced for centuries, the problem had been considered one of mutilation by moralists. But when sterilization became available as a contraceptive technique, it was forbidden along with other forms of contraception. Both *Humanae Vitae* and the recent Roman reply are restatements of this doctrine, which is explained as an application of the natural law.

But other opinions have gained adherents in the Church. The papal commission and many contemporary theologians urge that contraception and sterilization can be morally justified under some circumstances.

That raises two additional questions: (1) How does one go about making a moral judgment about sterilization—or anything else? (2) What is the authority of Church officials to make pronouncements about moral questions?

Notes

1. See Jonas Robitscher (ed.), *Eugenic Sterilization* (Springfield: Charles C. Thomas, 1973): J. Robitscher, "Introduction: Eugenic Sterilization: A Biomedical Intervention," pp. 3–16; J. Paul, "State Eugenic Sterilization History: A Brief Overview," pp. 25–40.

2. See John T. Noonan, Jr., *Contraception: A History of Its Treatment by the Catholic Theologians and Canonists* (Cambridge: Harvard, 1965).

3. *Theologia moralis,* ed. by Michael Heilig (Malines: P. J. Hanicq, 1852), esp. vol. 3, p. 99.

4. See Arturo Castiglioni, *A History of Medicine,* trans. and ed. by E. B. Krumbhaar (New York: Knopf, 1941); and Theodore Cianfrani, *A Short History of Obstetrics and Gynecology* (Springfield: Thomas, 1960); B. E. Finch and Hugh Green, *Contraception Through the Ages* (Springfield: Thomas, 1963); Larry L. Langley (ed.), *Contraception* (Benchmark Papers in Human Physiology) (Stroudsburg, Pa.: Dowden, Hutchinson and Ross, 1973).

5. Cited in A. Sabetti, S.J. and T. Barrett, S.J., *Compendium theologia moralis,* 22nd ed. (New York: Pustet, 1915), p. 250. See Noonan, *Contraception,* p. 429; and T. J. O'Donnell, S.J., "Sterilization," in *New Catholic Encyclopedia,* XIII, pp. 704–5.

6. See note 4.

7. See *Relf v. Weinberger* 372 US 1196ff. (1974) and *Wyatt v. Aderholt* 368 Fed Supp 1382 (1974); and also Robitscher. HEW regulations on the use of federal funds for sterilization were published in the *Federal Register,* 39 (1974), 4730–33 and 13872–73.

8. Noonan, p. 414.

9. *Ibid.,* p. 410.

10. The materials are assembled by John C. Ford, S.J., and Gerald Kelly, S.J., *Contemporary Moral Theology,* II, pp. 315–37, 2 vols. (Westminster: Newman, 1963). See also *Litterae encyclicae de matrimonio christiano,* ed. by F. Hürth, S.J., Textus et Documenta, series theologica, n. 25 (Rome: Gregorian University Press, 1953) for text and commentary on *Arcanum* (Leo XIII, 1880) and *Casti Connubii* (Pius XI, 1930). See also *The Human Body,* ed. by the Monks of Solemnes (Jamaica Plains: Daughters of St. Paul, 1960) for various papal statements.

11. Text in Ford and Kelly, p. 322–24. See also 1958 address cited at pp. 341–42. *The Human Body,* p. 279, n. 501.

12. *Humanae Vitae,* USCC edition, n. 6.

13. *Ibid.,* n. 11, with footnote to *Casti Connubii,* p. 560, cited in Hürth, pp. 48–49, and to Pius XII, *Allocution to Midwives,* October 29, 1951, AAS 43 (1951), p. 853, cited in Hürth, pp. 90–91. The 1951 allocution is also in *The Human Body,* n. 268, p. 160.

14. *Humanae Vitae,* n. 14, with note to *Casti Connubii,* p. 565, and to the Decree of the Holy Office, Feb. 22, 1940 (DB 2283), and to *Roman Catechism,* II, 8.

15. *Humanae Vitae,* n. 16.

16. *Humanae Vitae,* n. 16, with note to AAS, 45 (1953), pp. 674–75 (Allocution to Urologists), and AAS, 48 (1956), pp. 461–62 (Allocution to Congress on Sterility and Fertility).

17. *The Birth Control Debate,* ed. by Robert G. Hoyt (Kansas City: National Catholic Reporter, 1968).

18. *Ibid.,* p. 93.

19. Texts in Hürth, pp. 114–16.

20. Allocution to Urologists, Oct. 8, 1953; *The Human Body,* nn. 500–501.

21. Hoyt, p. 87–88.

22. *Ibid.,* p. 92, with note to GS, nn. 50 and 87.

23. *Ibid.,* pp. 93–94.

24. Note to GS, n. 51.

25. Hoyt, p. 94.

26. *Ibid.*

27. *Ibid.,* pp. 90–91.

28. *Ibid.,* pp. 106–107.

29. *Ibid.,* p. 74.

30. Franz Böckle, "Ethische Aspekte der freiwilligen operativen Sterilisation," *Stimmen der Zeit,* 99 (1974), 755–60.

31. The principle of totality has been analyzed by John M. Cox, *A Critical Analysis of the Roman-Catholic Medico-Moral Principle of Totality and*

Its Applicability to Sterilizing Mutilations, a dissertation from the Claremont Graduate School (Ann Arbor: University Microfilms, 1972). Cox concludes that contemporary circumstances require a modification of the ban on direct sterilizations.

32. Böckle, p. 756.

33. *Ibid.,* p. 759.

34. *Ibid.*

35. *Ibid.,* p. 760.

36. *Ibid.,* p. 759.

37. E. Tesson, "Discussion morale," *Cahiers Laennec,* 24 (1964), 64–73.

38. St. Joseph's Hospital, London, Ontario, 1973.

39. "Indication for a Sterilization, Committee of Hospital Morality, Ottawa General Hospital" (n.d.).

40. "Suggested Medico-Moral Guidelines," St. Joseph's Hospital, Toronto, Sept. 27, 1974. The same are in force at St. Michael's Hospital.

41. Text in Hoyt, pp. 165–74, n. 26 at p. 172.

42. *Linacre Quarterly,* 40 (1973), 97–108. See Richard McCormick, S.J., "Vasectomy and Sterilization," a reply to a letter of L. L. deVeber, M.D., *Linacre Quarterly,* 38 (1971), 7 and 9–10.

43. Curran, pp. 100–101.

44. Anthony R. Kosnik, "The Present Status of the Ethical and Religious Directives for Catholic Health Facilities," *Linacre Quarterly,* 40 (1973), 81–90.

45. *Ibid.,* p. 85. Directive 20 reads: "Procedures that induce sterility, whether permanent or temporary, are permitted when: a. they are immediately directed to the cure, diminution, or prevention of a serious pathological condition and not directly contraceptive (that is, contraception is not the purpose); and b. a simpler treatment is not reasonably available. Hence, for example, oophorectomy or irradiation of the ovaries may be allowed in treating carcinoma of the breast and metastasis therefrom; and orchidectomy is permitted in treatment of carcinoma of the prostate." Directive 18 reads: "Sterilization, whether permanent or temporary, for men or for women, may not be used as a means of contraception."

15. Sterilization

John P. Kenny, O.P.

This chapter first appeared in *Principles of Medical Ethics* in 1962.

Sterilization is a specific type of mutilation. In medical ethics, sterilization refers to *any mutilating procedure which deprives man or woman of the power of generation.* It is a grave mutilation because of the functional importance of this faculty.

In the past fifty years, the morality of sterilization has been widely discussed, since it has been advocated and practiced as a punitive and eugenic measure. Eugenical sterilization originated in the United States. A bill advocating it was introduced to the State of Michigan legislature in 1897. Though not adopted at the time, it was the forerunner of similar bills in other states. Pennsylvania was the first state to pass a sterilization bill in 1905, but it was vetoed by the governor. The first law was enacted by the State of Indiana in 1907. This statute was eventually declared unconstitutional as were all other sterilization laws which came before the courts prior to 1925. In that year, the courts of Michigan and Virginia ruled that their sterilization laws were valid enactments. The Virginia case was appealed to the United States Supreme Court which upheld the decision of the lower court. Many states subsequently passed legislation similar to that of the State of Virginia. The following report indicates the current status of eugenical sterilization laws:

> At present twenty-eight states have eugenic sterilization laws, twenty-six of which are compulsory. Mentally-deficient persons are subject to the laws in all of these states and in all but two they are also applicable to the mentally-ill. Seventeen states include epileptics in the groups designated by such laws. Nineteen of these laws apply to per-

sons confined in hospitals or other institutions caring for afflicted persons with the named conditions while the remaining laws include persons who are not confined.

Various reasons are given to justify such legislation. In general, these laws are based on the assumption that sterilization will reduce the number of feeble-minded, insane and epileptics, and will save the state the expense of supporting these persons in institutions.

The function of procreation can be destroyed in many ways. Sterilization of the male is generally accomplished by a vasectomy. In this operation, the vasa deferentia (which convey the spermatozoa from the testicles to the seminal vesicles) are either excised or thoroughly ligated. The spermatozoa are thus deprived of their normal outlet and are absorbed. In the female, sterilizing operations are more varied and more serious. They are more serious because of the physical consequences which may result from such operations. In general, it can be stated that the female nervous system is often affected by operational interference with the organs of reproduction. The following operations are performed to sterilize women: hysterectomy, which consists in the removal of the uterus; the surgical excision of the ovaries. termed an ovariotomy or oöphorectomy; and fallectomy or salpingectomy, which consists in ligating or removing part of the fallopian tubes. The generative function of the ovaries can be inhibited by the administration of drugs or destroyed by the use of radium or X rays.

The moral aspect of operational procedures which result in sterilization is of the utmost importance because fundamental rights are involved. This aspect of sterilization is often disregarded by legislators, eugenists, and even by members of the medical profession. The determination of the morality of sterilization rests upon the distinction between a direct and an indirect mutilation. Sterilization is termed *direct* when it is intended as an end in itself, or as a means to an end. *Indirect* sterilization is the direct result of some action, but follows indirectly from the act of the will. Sterilization is indirectly willed when it occurs as one of the normal effects of a surgical operation or a therapeutic treatment which is necessary for the health of the whole body. The morality of sterilization may be stated as follows:

Moral Principles: Direct sterilization is not lawful. Indirect sterilization is lawful if a proportionately grave cause is present.

These principles follow from what has been said concerning man's natural right to life and from the doctrine on mutilation. The first principle states that sterilization which is directly intended is unlawful. Every human being possesses a natural right to life and the consequent obligation of preserving that life. God alone has absolute dominion over life and over the human body. Human jurisdiction is subordinated to that of the Creator. The human body with all its faculties is given to us for our use. We do not possess the jurisdiction to mutilate the body in any way, except to maintain the health of the whole body or to preserve life itself.

Sterilization which occurs as a consequence of a necessary surgical operation is termed indirect, because the evil effect is not directly willed. The morality of such operations must be judged by the four conditions laid down in the principle of the double effect. It is especially important that there be a proportionately grave cause, i.e., that the operation be necessary for the person's bodily health. There must be a proportion between this necessity and the evil effect of sterilization. Some moralists refer to this type of sterilization as "curative or therapeutic." This designation is liable to lead to confusion, since medical authorities use the term "therapeutic sterilization" in a different sense. It is sometimes used in connection with the sterilization of a woman, at the time of a Caesarean section, as a prevention against future pregnancies; or as a designation for any operation which is performed to prevent pregnancy in certain cases of heart and lung ailments. Hence, in determining the morality of any such mutilating operations, the distinction between direct and indirect sterilization must be used.

Medical research has produced new drugs which are being used to treat functional abnormalities of the female generative system. Certain menstrual disorders, such as amenorrhea and menorrhagia, can be corrected by the use of synthetic progestational compounds. Stilbestrol, a synthetic estrogen, is used in the treatment of endomitriosis and dysmenorrhea. Drugs have been used successfully to effect conception in cases of anovulatory menstruation. Basically, these medications achieve their effects through the temporary suppression or modification of the ovarian function. If these drugs inhibit ovulation, then concomitant temporary sterility results. Hence the moral problem arises as to the lawfulness of administering such medications. Concerning treatments that induce sterility, the *Ethical and Religious Directives for Catholic Hospitals* states:

> Procedures that induce sterility, whether permanent or temporary, are permitted when:
> a) they are immediately directed to the cure, diminution, or prevention of a serious pathological condition;
> b) a simpler treatment is not reasonably available; and
> c) the sterility itself is an unintended and, in the circumstances, an unavoidable effect.[2]

The use of progestational compounds as a therapeutic measure is lawful if these three conditions are fulfilled. In such cases, the induction of sterility is indirectly willed and is ultimately justified by the principle of the double effect.

Pope Pius XII, in one of his last allocutions, discussed the morality of administering drugs which induce temporary sterility. Speaking to a group of blood specialists attending the Seventh International Hematological Congress, he introduced this portion of his address by proposing two questions. He said:

> It also answers the question that is very much discussed today by doctors and moralists: Is it licit to prevent ovulation by means of pills used as remedies for the exaggerated reaction of the uterus and the organism, when this medicine, while preventing ovulation, also renders fecundation impossible? Is its use permitted to married women, who in spite of this temporary sterility, desire to have relations with their husbands?
>
> The answer depends on the intentions of the person.
>
> If the woman takes the medicine, not to prevent conception, but only on the advice of the doctor as a necessary remedy because of the condition of the uterus or of the

organism, she provokes indirect sterilization which is permitted according to the general principles governing acts with a double effect. But a direct and, therefore, illicit sterilization is provoked when the ovulation is stopped so as to protect the uterus and the organism from the consequences of pregnancy which it is not able to sustain.

Some moralists maintain that it is permissible to take medicines for this reason, but they are wrong.

It is likewise necessary to refute the opinion of several doctors and moralists who permit the use (of such medicines) when a medical symptom makes conception (in the near future) undesirable, or in other similar cases which it is impossible to speak of here. In these cases the use of medicines has as its end the prevention of conception by preventing ovulation. Therefore, it is a question of direct sterilization.[3]

It is important that every physician and nurse know the extent of the state's power regarding the imposition of sterilization as a means of punishment or for eugenical reasons. The limitations of this power should be evident from the doctrines presented in the preceding chapter. As rational creatures, we have been endowed with certain inalienable and inviolable rights by our Creator. These natural rights are not bestowed upon us by the state. They exist prior to the formation of any civil society; they arise from our rational nature. The state, therefore, may not interfere with the exercise of natural rights unless they are forfeited by the individual. On the contrary, the state has a grave obligation to protect and safeguard each citizen and his rights.

Sterilization is sometimes advocated as a punishment for the more serious sexual crimes. Such a mutilation is not in itself unlawful. The state has the power to inflict severe penalties for violations against society. A convicted criminal may forfeit his right to life and be executed by lawfully constituted authority. From this it follows that the state may inflict the lesser punishment of mutilation, and prevent the exercise of man's natural right, if it is necessary for the public welfare. In either case, the penalty must be proportioned to the crime. The question is raised as to whether or not punitive sterilization is an adequate and effective punishment for sexual crimes. It seems that it is not, since the sexual tendency remains. Such criminals are merely prevented from propagating, a fact which least concerns them. Isolation is a more effective penalty for heinous sexual crimes.

The power of the state to inflict penalties upon its subjects is restricted to those who are convicted of crime. It does not follow that the state may sterilize any of its citizens merely because it possesses this power over criminals. The jurisdiction of the state is not absolute. Just as it is unlawful for the state to take the life of an innocent person, so also it is morally unlawful to sterilize anyone who is not guilty of crime. Neither is it within the jurisdiction of the person himself to seek such a mutilation voluntarily. Eugenical sterilization has been widely publicized under a variety of guises as a means of improving the nation both physically and mentally. According to some persons, it is the only practical solution for ridding the nation of such undesirables as the mentally defective and the physically incurable. It is thought that these evils would eventually be banished, or at least greatly decreased, if these unfortunate creatures were sterilized either at their own request or by command of the state. Defective offspring would thereby be prevented; the race would improve; and the state would be relieved of supporting such persons in institutions at public expense.

Eugenical sterilization is morally unlawful, for it is a grave mutilation which deprives a person of the power of procreation. When there is no question of removing a diseased organ or of imposing sterilization as a punitive measure, the immediate effects are evil, namely, mutilation and sterility. The possibility of future good effects, either for the individual or for society itself, is no justification for its lawfulness.

It is interesting to note that the scientific and legal bases of eugenical sterilization legislation are being questioned. The proponents of eugenical sterilization, the state legislatures, and the courts have assumed that the inheritability of mental illness, mental deficiency, epilepsy, and similar defects has been scientifically proved. Recent scientific studies, including two by committees of the American Medical Association and the American Neurological Association, have contradicted this opinion.[4] Moreover, the legal bases are not universally accepted. In general, there are two opinions concerning the constitutionality of eugenical sterilization statutes. One theory maintains that the constitutionality of these laws depends upon their scientific validity. If these premises are erroneous, then compulsory sterilization is an unreasonable deprivation of liberty. The proponents of the second opinion consider these laws to be unconstitutional because they violate a person's liberty by depriving him of the fundamental right of procreation. In view of these facts, a study made in 1960 by the Legal and Socio-Economic Division of the American Medical Association included the following recommendation:

> The fact that scientific opinion differs as to the value of sterilization certainly indicates that the merits of this type of legislation should be re-evaluated. Since court decisions have assumed that the conditions included in sterilization statutes are hereditary, the constitutionality of such statutes is questionable if scientific opinion is divided concerning the effectiveness of this procedure. A study of sterilization statistics indicates that its use is steadily decreasing. However, it is not known whether this stems from doubts concerning the constitutionality of the laws, public reaction or a change in medical opinion.[5]

Finally, the Church has condemned eugenical sterilization and compulsory sterilization legislation on many occasions. In his *Encyclical on Christian Marriage,* Pope Pius XI wrote:

> For there are some who oversolicitous for the cause of eugenics, not only give salutary counsel for more certainly procuring the strength and health of the future child—which, indeed, is not contrary to right reason—but put eugenics before aims of a higher order, and by public authority wish to prevent from marrying all those who, even though naturally fit for marriage, they consider, according to the norms and conjectures of their investigations, would through hereditary transmission, bring forth defective off-

spring. And more, they wish to legislate to deprive these of that natural faculty by medical action despite their unwillingness; and this they do not propose as an infliction of grave punishment under the authority of the state for a crime committed, nor to prevent future crimes by guilty persons, but against every right and good they wish the civil authority to arrogate to itself a power over a faculty which it never had and can never legitimately possess . . .

Public magistrates have no direct power over the bodies of their subjects; therefore, where no crime has taken place and there is no cause present for grave punishment, they can never directly harm, or tamper with the integrity of the body, either for the reasons of eugenics or for any other reason. St. Thomas teaches this when, inquiring whether human judges for the sake of preventing future evils can inflict punishment, he admits that the power indeed exists as regards certain other forms of evil, but justly and properly denies it as regards the maiming of the body. "No one who is guiltless may be punished by a human tribunal either by flogging to death, or mutilation, or by beating." (*Summa Theologica,* 2a2ae, q. 108, a. 4, ad 2um.)[6]

Pius XII, in his discourse to the Italian Catholic Union of Midwives, reiterated this teaching of his predecessor:

Direct sterilization, that which aims at making procreation impossible as both means and end, is a grave violation of the moral law, and therefore illicit. Even public authority has no right to permit it under the pretext of any "indication" whatsoever, and still less to prescribe it or to have it carried out to the harm of the innocent. This principle has been already stated in the Encyclical of Pius XI which We have quoted. Therefore, ten years ago, when sterilization came to be more widely applied, the Holy See found itself in need of stating expressly and publicly that direct sterilization, either permanent or temporary, of man or of woman, is illegal by virtue of the natural law from which, as you are aware, the Church has no power to dispense.[7]

Notes

1. "A Reappraisal of Eugenic Sterilization Laws," prepared by the Legal and Socio-Economic Division of the American Medical Association, May, 1960, p. 6. Reprinted with the permission of the American Medical Association.

2. *Ethical and Religious Directives for Catholic Hospitals,* No. 31. Cf. *Appendix,* p. 244.

3. Pius XII, "Address to the Seventh International Hematological Congress," September 12, 1958, National Catholic Welfare Conference News Service Translation, pp. 3–4. Cf. *The Pope Speaks,* 6 (1960), 395.

4. "A Reappraisal of Eugenic Sterilization Laws," pp. 9–10.

5. *Ibid.,* p. 13.

6. Pius XI, *op. cit.,* pp. 23–24.

7. Pius XII, "Address to the Italian Catholic Union of Midwives," October 29, 1951, *Moral Questions Affecting Married Life,* p. 12. Cf. also "Address to the Primum Symposium Geneticae Medicae," September 7, 1953, *The Human Body,* p. 258.

16. The Sisters of Mercy of the Union and Sterilization

Richard A. McCormick, S.J.

This chapter first appeared in *Theological Studies* in 1984.

Margaret Farley, R.S.M., reveals an extremely interesting and in many senses troubling episode in recent American Church history.[1] Some of the more significant events could be detailed with the following chronology.

In 1978 the Sisters of Mercy of the Union, sponsors of the largest group of nonprofit hospitals in the country, began a study of the theological and ethical aspects of tubal ligation. The study resulted in a recommendation to the General Administration of the Sisters of Mercy that tubal ligations be allowed when they are determined by patient and physician to be essential to the overall good of the patient. The General Administrative Team accepted this recommendation in principle. In a Nov. 12, 1980, letter to their hospital administrators the General Administrative Team reported the results of the study and indicated a desire to draw concerned persons into dialogue on the issue. They did not, as was inaccurately reported to the bishops of this country, mandate a policy.

Copies of the original study, the position statement of the General Administrative Team, and the letter to the hospitals somehow fell into the hands of officials in Rome and of the Committee on Doctrine of the N.C.C.B. One thing led to another until finally a dialogue was initiated between a committee of five bishops (headed by James Malone of Youngstown) and six Sisters of Mercy, both groups with their theological consultants. Two meetings were held (Sept. and Dec. 1981). These were largely exploratory, get-acquainted-with-the-problem meetings. At the December meeting it was decided that the next meeting (March 1982) would enter the substance of the problem. The sisters were to present a single-page position paper stating why they thought that not all tubal ligations were morally wrong. The episcopal committee was to do the same, showing why they were.

Early in 1982 the sisters were informed that the dialogue was off and that a Committee of Verification had been appointed by Rome. The purpose of this committee (composed of three bishops, again head by Bishop Malone) was to verify the Administrative Team's answer to two questions: (1) Does it accept the teaching of the magisterium on tubal ligation? (2) Will it withdraw its circular letter (Nov. 12) to its hospitals?

On May 11, 1982, the Administrative Team addressed their response to Pope John Paul II. The pertinent answers read as follows:

> 1. We receive the teaching of the Church on tubal ligation with respectful fidelity in accord with *Lumen gentium* 25 (*obsequium religiosum*). We have personal disagreements as do others in the Church, including pastors and respectable theologians, with the formulation of the magisterium's teaching on sterilization. However, in light of present circumstances, we will not take an official public position contrary to this formulation.
>
> 2. We withdraw our letter of Nov. 12, 1980 and will notify the recipients of the letter of such withdrawal.[2]

The letter concluded by urging "continued study and consultation within the Church on this issue."

The Committee of Verification seemed quite pleased with the response. The Apostolic Delegate informed the Administrative Team that their response had been accepted. The matter seemed quietly put to rest. However, the sisters received a letter dated Aug. 30, 1982, from E. Cardinal Pironio (Prefect of the Congregation for Religious and Secular Institutes). In part it stated: "In light of all the sentiments expressed in your letter of May 11, as well as your letter of withdrawal, dated May 17, 1982, your reply is not considered fully satisfactory and, indeed, your interpretation of the *obsequium religiosum* is judged incomplete." The sisters were told by Cardinal Pironio that a "subsequent response" would be coming from the congregation.

This subsequent response was a letter from Cardinal Pironio to Sister M. Theresa Kane dated Nov. 21. The letter insisted that the religious submission of mind and will (*obsequium religiosum*) "calls for the Catholic not only not to take a public position contrary to the teaching of the Church but also to direct his or her efforts, by an act of the will, to a more profound personal study of the question which would ideally lead to a deeper understanding and eventually an intellectual acceptance of the teaching in question." The letter also requested the sisters to write another letter to their hospitals "clearly prohibiting the performing of tubal ligations in all the hospitals owned and/or operated by the Sisters of Mercy of the Union."

A letter dated July 6, 1983, was drafted by Sister Theresa Kane to the chief executive officers of the Mercy Sisters' hospitals and forwarded to Cardinal Pironio. It read as follows:

> On November 21, 1982, the Sacred Congregation for Religious and Secular Institutes (SCRIS) requested that we write you stating our reevaluation of tubal ligation and clearly prohibiting the performance of tubal ligations in Mercy hospitals owned and/or operated by the Sisters of Mercy of the Union.
>
> As requested by SCRIS to reevaluate, we, the Mercy Administrative Team, have spent additional time in study and consultation on tubal ligation. In obedience to the magisterium we will take no public position on this matter contrary to Church teaching. As you face pastoral problems regarding tubal ligation, we ask that you continue to work in close collaboration with your local ordinary in implementing Church teaching.

The Congregation for Religious responded to this draft in a letter to Bishop James Malone dated Aug. 22. The congregation insisted that the second and third sentences of paragraph 2 be changed to read as follows: "In obedience to the magisterium we will continue to study and reflect on Church teaching with a view to accepting it. We, therefore, direct that the performance of tubal ligations be prohibited in all hospitals owned and/or operated by the Sisters of Mercy of the Union." If any sister does not accept this, she is to specify the dissent in writing and with signature. Furthermore, Bishop Malone stated that¹ "upon enquiry I have learned that the letter from the congregation is indeed a 'formal precept' to you." That was specified to mean that "no further compromises or word changes . . . will be entertained by the congregation."

This happening is heavy with theological implications that invite explication. Margaret Farley's brief paper highlighted the powerlessness of women in the Church. Here three other points will be noted.

First, in the exchanges over a two-year period, the substantive issue was never discussed. Indeed, at the very point (March 1982) in the dialogue where the substantive issue (Is direct sterilization intrinsically evil?) was to be discussed, Rome (SCRIS) intervened to terminate the dialogue and appoint the Committee of Verification on the grounds that "there is nothing to be gained by further dialogue on this issue."

Is there really nothing to be gained by further dialogue? That would be the case only if it were antecedently clear and certain that the magisterial formulation was absolutely and unquestionably accurate. Yet, how can one sustain this in light of the very widespread theological questioning of that clarity and certainty? I have discussed this matter with very many established theologians throughout Europe and the United States and can report as a fact that most would endorse the approach and analysis of Johannes Gründel reviewed several years ago in these "Notes."³ Surely this fact needs discussion, unless we are to exclude in principle the relevance of theological analysis.

The second theologically pertinent issue is the notion of *obsequium religiosum*. The Mercy Administrative Team had responded that "we receive the teaching of the Church on tubal ligation with respectful fidelity in accord with *Lumen gentium* 25 (*obsequium religiosum*)." The Congregation of Religious responded to this by saying that it was incomplete because a Catholic must also "direct his or her efforts . . . to a more profound personal study of the question which would ideally lead to a deeper understanding and eventually an intellectual acceptance of the teaching in question.[22]

This raises a host of interesting issues. First, the assumption seems to be that the members of the Administrative Team have not so "directed their efforts." But what is the evidence for that? Surely it is not the simple fact of dissent. That would rule out dissent in principle and elevate the teaching to irreformable status—both theologically untenable. More positively, surely a group that has conducted a three-to-four year study, consulting opposing theological viewpoints and a variety of competences, has satisfied the demands of *obsequium religiosum.* If not, what more is required? Is this "direct his or her efforts" a duty with no time limit? Does it go on forever with no discernible *terminus?*

Next, the congregation uses the word "ideally" of the outcome of such directed efforts. What if it does not turn out that way? Furthermore, what if a group such as the Administrative Team discovers that many competent and demonstrably loyal theologians throughout the world have had similar problems? Are these simply regrettable but ultimately irrelevant failures? If magisterial inaccuracy or error is possible and if dissent is the vehicle that reveals this, is there not a point at which obligations begin to return to and weigh upon the proponents of the disputed formulation? Specifically, must they not re-examine *their* position if it is truth and not juridical position that is our dominant concern? To say anything else is to discount the significance of personal reflection in the teaching-learning process of the Church. In other words, it is utterly to juridicize the search for truth.

Finally, the "Mercy Affair" seems to have all the characteristics of an "enforcement of morals." Bishop Christopher Butler, O.S.B., distinguishing between the irrevocable and provisional in Church teaching, states of the latter: "To require the same adhesion for doctrines that are indeed taught by officials with authority but to which the Church has not irrevocably committed itself is to abuse authority, and if this requirement is accompanied by threatened sanctions it is also to abuse the power of constraint."[4] Whether these words fit this case in all respects, one need not judge. But if they do, their true theological importance should not be overlooked. One effect is to relieve bishops of their collegial task. An immediate implication of that relief is the undermining of authority in the Church. Those who treasure the magisterium as a privilege must view such a prospect, because of its generalizable implications, with profound sadness.

At the heart of this matter is the question of the proper response to authoritative noninfallible teaching. Vatican II described the response in the phrase *religiosum voluntatis et intellectus obsequium.* The best and most balanced treatment I have seen of this notion is that of Francis Sullivan, S.J.[5] Sullivan, after noting that free will can influence judgment, states that *obsequium* involves renunciation of attitudes of obstinacy and adoption of attitudes of docility. In sum, "an honest and sustained effort to overcome any contrary opinion I might have, and to achieve a sincere assent of my mind."

Sullivan then spells out two implications of this. First, since assent is an act of judgment, the magisterium must offer clear and convincing reasons for its teaching. "When the norm itself is said to be discoverable by human reasoning, it would be a mistake to rely too heavily on merely formal authority in proposing it for acceptance by thinking people." Why a mistake? Because the magisterium "will not be offering to the faithful the help that many of them will need to rid themselves of their doubts."

Second, if Catholics have made a sincere and sustained attempt to achieve assent but have failed to overcome their strong doubts, "I do not see how one could judge such non-assent, or internal dissent, to involve any lack of obedience to the magisterium. Having done all that they were capable of doing toward achieving assent, they actually fulfilled their obligation of obedience, whether they achieved internal assent or not." Therefore Sullivan regards it as "unjust to treat all dissent from the teaching of the ordinary magisterium as disobedience, or to turn agreement with this noninfallible teaching into a test of loyalty to the Holy See."

Certain aspects of the "Mercy Affair" lead to me to believe that these points can easily be overlooked. It must be remembered that *Dignitatis humanae* stated: "In the formation of their consciences, the Christian faithful ought carefully to attend to the sacred and certain doctrine of the Church."[6] An emendation was proposed for "ought carefully to attend to." It read: "ought to form their consciences according to." The Theological Commission rejected the emendation and stated: "The proposed formula seems excessively restrictive. The obligation binding on the faithful is sufficiently expressed in the text as it stands."[7]

Notes

1. Margaret Farley, R.S.M., "Power and Powerlessness: A Case in Point," *Proceedings of the Catholic Theological Society of America* 37 (1982) 116–19. Cf. also *National Catholic Reporter,* Nov. 11, 1983, 1.

2. These and subsequent citations are taken from documents kindly provided by the Sister of Mercy of the Union.

3. J. Gründel, "Zur Problematik der operativen Sterilisation in katholischen Kranken-haüsern," *Stimmen der Zeit* 199 (1981) 671–77. Recently Bernard Häring has endorsed a similar concept. He rejects the reduction of the problem to "a simple distinction between direct and indirect sterilization" and argues for the moral acceptability of "therapeutic" sterilization. "For some, sterilization is 'therapeutic' only if it is therapy concerning solely a sick sexual organ. In spite of the reality of psychotherapy as an important asset in today's medical world, these people would confine healing to organs alone. This not only leads to wrong and narrow-minded solutions in the case of sterilization, but is more dangerous because it betrays a wrong image of man and God. God does not care only for the health of discrete organs; he cares for the healthy person and for healthy relationships" (*Free and Faithful in Christ* 3 [New York: Crossroad, 1981] 20).

4. Cf. Charles Curran and Richard McCormick, eds. *Readings in Moral Theology* 3 (Ramsey: Paulist, 1982) 185.

5. Cf. n. 37 above.

6. *Documents of Vatican II* 694.

7. *Acta synodalia Conc. Vat. II* 4/6, 769.

17. Tubal Ligation: Good Medicine? Good Morality?

John R. Connery, S.J.

This chapter first appeared in *Linacre Quarterly* in 1981.

Once disillusionment set in regarding the "pill" and the IUD as "contraceptives," one had to expect a trend in the direction of tubal ligation. The only alternative was a step back to the old barrier type contraceptive with its higher failure rate as well as its other drawbacks. With a million sterilizations being performed annually, it would have been surprising if Catholic hospitals in this country experienced no pressure to follow the trend. Unfortunately, not all this pressure comes from outside sources. One finds Catholic "patients" and, even more often, Catholic doctors putting pressure on Catholic hospitals to allow tubal ligations. Some would limit such procedures to "medical" indications. Others would want an umbrella clause that would allow a tubal ligation for the "overall good of the patient."

The Church has always condemned sterilization for contraceptive purposes. In this it stands in a tradition that goes back to the Old Testament. Among Jews in the Old Testament, fertility was considered God's second greatest blessing, next to life itself, and barrenness was considered a curse. The thought of inducing barrenness or sterility was completely alien to Hebrew thinking. This tradition continued into the New Testament. St. Thomas expressed it very clearly when he stated that although tampering with the sources of human life is not the same as homicide, it is next (*secundo loco*) to it.

What the Church is saying in its condemnation of sterilization is that the power to give life is unique and unlike any other bodily function. It derives this special character from its relationship with life itself. The power to give life is sacred because life itself is sacred. Respect for life makes it inviolable.

Catholic doctors who want to do tubal ligations would like to consider the power to give life like any other bodily function. This would allow them to sterilize a patient whenever medical indications would warrant it, or more broadly, whenever the overall good of the patient would call for it. They would be applying what is called the principle of totality, allowing the sacrifice of a part (an organ or a member) for the good of the whole. In the Judeo-Christian tradition, the power to give life transcends the good of the person of its possessor and looks to the good of the person-to-be. It may not be reduced to a purely personal possession or disposed of as an ordinary body function (that is, according to the principle of totality). In a sense, however, one would wish that doctors who do contraceptive tubal ligations would accord the life-giving function even the respect they give other bodily functions. No doctor amputates a leg just to cripple a person. No doctor removes an eye just to blind a person. But doctors who do tubal ligations for contraceptive purposes do them precisely to destroy the power to procreate.

There is serious reason to ask today whether tubal ligation (contraceptive) is even good (much less "quality") medicine. One has to question the exercise of medical indications for tubal ligation. Thirty and even 40 years ago, the medical profession made the claim that there were practically no medical indications for abortion, since medicine had the capability of handling all the complications of pregnancy without abortion. If this was true then, how can there be medical indications for sterilization now? If there are no medical indications for abortion, it would seem to follow *a fortiori* that there are none for sterilization. It is hard to see how the medical profession can have it both ways.

Even if one wished to broaden the indications for tubal ligation to include the overall good of the patient, given the fact that, according to most recent studies, natural family planning can be just as effective as tubal ligation, one has to ask whether destructive surgery of this kind can be justified even from a medical standpoint. Or even if it could be considered necessary, the fact that it is less than 100% effective requires one to ask further whether it really solves the problem. It will reduce the possibility of pregnancy, but will not eliminate it. It would seem that the more serious the reason for avoiding a pregnancy, the less prudent it would be to rely on a tubal ligation. In other words, the kind of abstinence a tubal ligation is meant to avoid may still be the only sure way of avoiding a pregnancy, and without it the person with a tubal ligation will still be running a risk.

One wonders how carefully the above considerations are made today in hospitals where tubal ligations are performed. Even though consent forms may allude to them, one suspects that they are dealt with as a legal formality rather than a moral concern, and simply glossed over. Such glosses (with a touch of male chauvinism) may be the hidden factors in many, if not all, of the tubal ligations done today.

Even if there were medical indications for tubal ligation, and it was both necessary and effective, it would not automatically be permissible. Health is not the *summum bonum*. Nor is good medicine necessarily good morality, any more than is good plumbing, or good carpentry or good politics. One would hope that good medicine would not conflict with good morality, or that what would contribute to one's health would be morally good, but one cannot rule out the possibility that it would not. Thus, stealing or adultery would still be morally wrong even if somehow they might contribute to one's health. Or, more practically, an abortion would be morally wrong even if continuing a pregnancy would be a health burden. So, even if an individual doctor might want to consider a tubal ligation good medicine, it would not make it moral. As already pointed out, however, it is becoming increasingly difficult to defend the position that it is even good medicine. And empirical data beginning to come in from experience with tubal ligations is adding to the difficulty.

Part Four

ARTIFICIAL INSEMINATION AND IN VITRO FERTILIZATION

18. Address to the 4th International Convention of Catholic Physicians (September, 1949)

Pius XII

We have already had many occasions to speak on a good number of special points regarding medical morality, but now we have here a question of the first order which, with no less urgency than other questions, requires the light of Catholic moral doctrine: that of artificial insemination. We could not allow this present opportunity to pass without indicating briefly, along general lines, the moral judgment that must be made in this matter.

1) The practice of artificial insemination, when human beings are concerned, cannot be considered exclusively, or even principally, from a biological and medical point of view, leaving aside the claims of morality and law.

2) Artificial insemination outside of marriage is to be condemned purely and simply as immoral.

According to both the natural law and the divine positive law, the procreation of new life can be only the fruit of marriage. Marriage alone safeguards the dignity of the parties (principally, in the present case, of the woman) and their personal well-being. And it alone, by its nature, provides for the well-being and education of the child.

Consequently, there is no possibility of difference of opinion among Catholics as regards the condemnation of artificial insemination outside the conjugal union. The child conceived under these conditions would be, by that very fact, illegitimate.

3) Artificial insemination in marriage, but effected by means

of the active element of a third party, is equally immoral and, as such, is to be summarily rejected.

It is the spouses alone who have a mutual right over their bodies for generating a new life, and this right is exclusive, nontransferable, inalienable. And so it must be also out of consideration for the child. By virtue of this same bond, nature imposes on whoever gives life to a little one the responsibility for its preservation and education. But between the lawful husband and the child who is the fruit of an active element derived from a third party (even should the husband consent) there is no bond of origin, no moral and juridical bond of conjugal procreation.

4) As for the morality of artificial insemination within marriage, let it suffice for the present to recall these principles of the natural law: the simple fact that the desired result is attained by this means does not justify the use of the means itself; nor is the desire to have a child—perfectly lawful as that is for married persons— sufficient to prove the licitness of artificial insemination to attain this end.

It would be false to think that the possibility of resorting to this method might make valid a marriage between persons who are unfit to contract a marriage by reason of the impediment of impotence. Also, it is needless to observe that the active element can never be procured licitly by acts that are contrary to nature.

Although one may not *a priori* exclude new methods for the sole reason that they are new; nevertheless, as regards artificial insemination, there is not only reason for extreme reserve, but it must be entirely rejected. To say this is not necessarily to proscribe the use of certain artificial means designed only to facilitate the natural act or to enable that act, performed in a normal manner, to attain its end.

We must never forget this: It is only the procreation of a new life according to the will and plan of the Creator which brings with it—to an astonishing degree of perfection—the realization of the desired ends. This is, at the same time, in harmony with the dignity of the marriage partners, with their bodily and spiritual nature, and with the normal and happy development of the child.

Discourse on Moral Problems of Married Life (October 29, 1951)

Pius XII

These translations appeared in *Medico-Moral Problems* in 1957.

To reduce the cohabitation of married persons and the conjugal act to a mere organic function for the transmission of the germ of life would be to convert the domestic hearth, sanctuary of the family, into nothing more than a biological laboratory. Hence, in our address of September 29, 1949, to the international congress of Catholic doctors, we formally excluded artificial insemination from marriage. The conjugal act in its natural structure is a personal act, a simultaneous and immediate cooperation of the spouses which, by the very nature of the participants and the special character of the act, is the expression of that mutual self-giving which, in the words of Holy Scripture, effects the union "in one flesh."

This is much more than the mere union of two life-germs, which can be brought about also artificially, that is, without the natural action of the spouses. The conjugal act, as it is planned and willed by nature, implies a personal cooperation, the right to which the parties have mutually conferred on each other in contracting marriage.

Instruction on Respect for Human Life in its Origin and on the Dignity of Procreation (1987)

Congregation for the Doctrine of the Faith

Homologous Artificial Fertilization

Since heterologous artificial insemination has been declared unacceptable, the question arises of how to evaluate morally the process of homologous artificial fertilization: IVF and ET and artificial insemination between husband and wife. First a question of principle must be clarified.

4. What Connection Is Required from the Moral Point of View Between Procreation and the Conjugal Act?

a) The Church's teaching on marriage and human procreation affirms the "inseparable connection, willed by God and unable to be broken by man on his own initiative, between the two meanings of the conjugal act: the unitive meaning and the procreative meaning. Indeed, by its intimate structure, the conjugal act, while most closely uniting husband and wife, capacitates them for the generation of new lives, according to laws inscribed in the very being of man and of woman."[38] This principle, which is based upon the nature of marriage and the intimate connection of the goods of marriage, has well-known consequences on the level of responsible fatherhood and motherhood. "By safeguarding both these essential aspects, the unitive and the procreative, the conjugal act preserves in its fullness the sense of true mutual love and its ordination towards man's exalted vocation to parenthood."[39]

The same doctrine concerning the link between the meanings of the conjugal act and between the goods of marriage throws light on the moral problem of homologous artificial fertilization, since "it is never permitted to separate these different aspects to such a degree as positively to exclude either the procreative intention or the conjugal relation."[40]

Contraception deliberately deprives the conjugal act of its openness to procreation and in this way brings about a voluntary dissociation of the ends of marriage. Homologous artificial fertilization, in seeking a procreation which is not the fruit of a specific act of conjugal union, objectively effects an analogous separation between the goods and the meanings of marriage.

Thus, *fertilization is licitly sought when it is the result of a "conjugal act which is per se suitable for the generation of children to which marriage is ordered by its nature and by which the spouses become one flesh."*[41] *But from the moral point of view procreation is deprived of its proper perfection when it is not desired as the fruit of the conjugal act, that is to say of the specific act of the spouses' union.*

b) The moral value of the intimate link between the goods of marriage and between the meanings of the conjugal act is based upon the unity of the human being, a unity involving body and spiritual soul.[42] Spouses mutually express their personal love in the "language of the body," which clearly involves both "spousal meanings" and parental ones.[43] The conjugal act by which the couple mutually express their self-gift at the same time expresses openness to the gift of life. It is an act that is inseparably corporal and spiritual. It is in their bodies and through their bodies that the spouses consummate their marriage and are able to become father and mother. In order to respect the language of their bodies and their natural generosity, the conjugal union must take place with respect for its openness to procreation; and the procreation of a person must be the fruit and the result of married love. The origin of the human being thus follows from a procreation that is "linked to the union, not only biological but also spiritual, of the parents, made one by the bond of marriage."[44] Fertilization achieved outside the bodies of the couple remains by this very fact deprived of the meanings and the values which are expressed in the language of the body and in the union of human persons.

c) Only respect for the link between the meanings of the conjugal act and respect for the unity of the human being make possible procreation in conformity with the dignity of the person. In his unique and irrepeatable origin, the child must be respected and recognized as equal in personal dignity to those who give him life. The human person must be accepted in his parents' act of union and love; the generation of a child must therefore be the fruit of that mutual giving[45] which is realized in the conjugal act wherein the spouses cooperate as servants and not as masters in the work of the Creator who is Love.[46]

In reality, the origin of a human person is the result of an act of giving. The one conceived must be the fruit of his parents' love. He cannot be desired or conceived as the product of an intervention of medical or biological techniques; that would be equivalent to reducing him to an object of scientific technology. No one may subject the coming of a child into the world to conditions of technical efficiency which are to be evaluated according to standards of control and dominion.

The moral relevance of the link between the meanings of the conjugal act and between the goods of marriage, as well as the unity of the human being and the dignity of his origin, demand that the procreation of a human person be brought about as the fruit of the conjugal act specific to the love between spouses. The link between procreation and the conjugal act is thus shown to be of great importance on the anthropological and moral planes, and its throws light on the positions of the Magisterium with regard to homologous artificial fertilization.

5. Is Homologous 'In Vitro' Fertilization Morally Licit?

The answer to this question is strictly dependent on the principles just mentioned. Certainly one cannot ignore the legitimate aspirations of sterile couples. For some, recourse to homologous IVF and ET appears to be the only way of fulfilling their sincere desire for a child. The question is asked whether the totality of conjugal life in such situations is not sufficient to ensure the dignity proper to human procreation. It is acknowledged that IVF and ET certainly cannot supply for the absence of sexual relations[47] and cannot be preferred to the specific acts of conjugal union, given the risks involved for the child and the difficulties of the procedure. But it is asked whether, when there is no other way of overcoming the sterility which is a source of suffering, homologous *in vitro* fertilization may not constitute an aid, if not a form of therapy, whereby its moral licitness could be admitted.

The desire for a child—or at the very least an openness to the transmission of life—is a necessary prerequisite from the moral point of view for responsible human procreation. But this good intention is not sufficient for making a positive moral evaluation of *in vitro* fertilization between spouses. The process of IVF and ET must be judged in itself and cannot borrow its definitive moral quality from the totality of conjugal life of which it becomes part nor from the conjugal acts which may precede or follow it.[48]

It has already been recalled that, in the circumstances in which it is regularly practised, IVF and ET involves the destruction of human beings, which is something contrary to the doctrine on the illicitness of abortion previously mentioned.[49] But even in a situation in which every precaution were taken to avoid the death of human embryos, homologous IVF and ET dissociates from the conjugal act the actions which are directed to human fertilization. For this reason the very nature of homologous IVF and ET also must be taken into account, even abstracting from the link with procured abortion.

Homologous IVF and ET is brought about outside the bodies of the couple through actions of third parties whose competence and technical activity determine the success of the procedure. Such fertilization entrusts the life and identity of the embryo into the power of doctors and biologists and establishes the domination of technology over the origin and destiny of the human person. Such a relationship of domination is in itself contrary to the dignity and equality that must be common to parents and children.

Conception *in vitro* is the result of the technical action which presides over fertilization. *Such fertilization is neither in fact achieved nor positively willed as the expression and fruit of a specific act of the conjugal union. In homologous IVF and ET, therefore, even if it is considered in the context of "de facto" existing sexual relations, the generation of the human person is objectively deprived of its proper perfection: namely, that of being the result and fruit of a conjugal act* in which the spouses can become "cooperators with God for giving life to a new person."[50]

These reasons enable us to understand why the act of conjugal love is considered in the teaching of the Church as the only setting worthy of human procreation. For the same reasons the so-called "simple case," i.e. a homologous IVF and ET procedure that is free of any compromise with the abortive practice of destroying embryos and with masturbation, remains a technique which is morally illicit because it deprives human procreation of the dignity which is proper and connatural to it.

Certainly, homologous IVF and ET fertilization is not marked by all that ethical negativity found in extra-conjugal procreation; the family and marriage continue to constitute the setting for the birth and upbringing of the children. Nevertheless, in conformity with the traditional doctrine relating to the goods of marriage and the dignity of the person, *the Church remains opposed from the moral point of view to homologous "in vitro" fertilization. Such fertilization is in itself illicit and in opposition to the dignity of procreation and of the conjugal union, even when everything is done to avoid the death of the human embryo.*

Although the manner in which human conception is achieved with IVF and ET cannot be approved, every child which comes into the world must in any case be accepted as a living gift of the divine Goodness and must be brought up with love.

6. How Is Homologous Artificial Insemination To Be Evaluated from the Moral Point of View?

Homologous artificial insemination within marriage cannot be admitted except for those cases in which the technical means is not a substitute for the conjugal act but serves to facilitate and to help so that the act attains its natural purpose.

The teaching of the Magisterium on this point has already been stated.[51] This teaching is not just an expression of particular historical circumstances but is based on the Church's doctrine concerning the connection between the conjugal union and procreation and on a consideration of the personal nature of the conjugal act and of human procreation. "In its natural structure, the conjugal act is a personal action, a simultaneous and immediate cooperation on the part of the husband and wife, which by the very nature of the agents and the proper nature of the act is the expression of the mutual gift which, according to the words of Scripture, brings about union 'in one flesh.' "[52] Thus moral conscience "does not necessarily proscribe the use of certain artificial means destined solely either to the facilitating of the natural act or to ensuring that the natural act normally performed achieves its proper end."[53] If the technical means facilitates the conjugal act or helps it to reach its natural objectives, it can be morally acceptable. If, on the other hand, the procedure were to replace the conjugal act, it is morally illicit.

Artificial insemination as a substitute for the conjugal act is prohibited by reason of the voluntarily achieved dissociation of the two meanings of the conjugal act. Masturbation, through which the sperm is normally obtained, is another sign of this dissociation: even when it is done for the purpose of procreation, the act remains deprived of its unitive meaning: "It lacks the sexual relationship called for by the moral order, namely the relationship which realizes 'the full sense of mutual self-giving and human procreation in the context of true love.' "[54]

7. What Moral Criterion Can Be Proposed with Regard to Medical Intervention in Human Procreation?

The medical act must be evaluated not only with reference to its technical dimension but also and above all in relation to its goal which is the good of persons and their bodily and psychological health. The moral criteria for medical intervention in procreation are deduced from the dignity of human persons, of their sexuality and of their origin.

Medicine which seeks to be ordered to the integral good of the person must respect the specifically human values of sexuality.[55] *The* doctor is at the service of persons and of human procreation. He does not have the authority to dispose of them or to decide their fate. A medical intervention respects the dignity of persons when it seeks to assist the conjugal act either in order to facilitate its performance or in order to enable it to achieve its objective once it has been normally performed.[56]

On the other hand, it sometimes happens that a medical procedure technologically replaces the conjugal act in order to obtain a procreation which is neither its result nor its fruit. In this case the medical act is not, as it should be, at the service of conjugal union but rather appropriates to itself the procreative function and thus contradicts the dignity and the inalienable rights of the spouses and of the child to be born.

The humanization of medicine, which is insisted upon today by everyone, requires respect for the integral dignity of the human person first of all in the act and at the moment in which the spouses transmit life to a new person. It is only logical therefore to address an urgent appeal to Catholic doctors and scientists that they bear exemplary witness to the respect due to the human embryo and to the dignity of procreation. The medical and nursing staff of Catholic hospitals and clinics are in a special way urged to do justice to the moral obligations which they have assumed, frequently also, as part of their contract. Those who are in charge of Catholic hospitals and clinics and who are often Religious will take special care to safeguard and promote a diligent observance of the moral norms recalled in the present Instruction.

8. The Suffering Caused by Infertility in Marriage

The suffering of spouses who cannot have children or who are afraid of bringing a handicapped child into the world is a suffering that everyone must understand and properly evaluate.

On the part of the spouses, the desire for a child is natural: it expresses the vocation to fatherhood and motherhood inscribed in conjugal love. This desire can be even stronger if the couple is affected by sterility which appears incurable. Nevertheless, marriage does not confer upon the spouses the right to have a child, but only the right to perform those natural acts which are *per se* ordered to procreation.[57]

A true and proper right to a child would be contrary to the child's dignity and nature. The child is not an object to which one has a right, nor can he be considered as an object of ownership: rather, a child is a gift, "the supreme gift"[58] *and the most gratuitous gift of marriage, and is a living testimony of the mutual giving of his parents. For this reason, the child has the right, as already mentioned, to be the fruit of the specific act of the conjugal love of his parents; and he also has the right to be respected as a person from the moment of his conception.*

Nevertheless, whatever its cause or prognosis, sterility is certainly a difficult trial. The community of believers is called to shed light upon and support the suffering of those who are unable to fulfill their legitimate aspiration to motherhood and fatherhood. Spouses who find themselves in this sad situation are called to find in it an opportunity for sharing in a particular way in the Lord's Cross, the source of spiritual fruitfulness. Sterile couples must not forget that "even when procreation is not possible, conjugal life does not for this reason lose its value. Physical sterility in fact can be for spouses the occasion for other important services to the life of the human person, for example, adoption, various forms of educational work, and assistance to other families and to poor or handicapped children."[59]

Many researchers are engaged in the fight against sterility. While fully safeguarding the dignity of human procreation, some have achieved results which previously seemed unattainable. Scientists therefore are to be encouraged to continue their research with the aim of preventing the causes of sterility and of being able to remedy them so that sterile couples will be able to procreate in full respect for their own personal dignity and that of the child to be born.

Notes

38. POPE PAUL VI, Encyclical Letter *Humanae Vitae,* 12: *AAS* 60 (1968) 488–489.

39. *Loc. cit., ibid.,* 489.

40. POPE PIUS XII, *Discourse to those taking part in the Second Naples World Congress on Fertility and Human Sterility,* 19 May 1956: *AAS* 48 (1956) 470.

41. *Code of Canon Law,* Can. 1061. According to this Canon, the conjugal act is that by which the marriage is consummated if the couple "have performed (it) between themselves in a human manner."

42. Cf. Pastoral Constitution *Gaudium et Spes,* 14.

43. Cf. POPE JOHN PAUL II, *General Audience on 16 January 1980: Insegnamenti di Giovanni Paolo II,* III, 1 (1980) 148–152.

44. POPE JOHN PAUL II, *Discourse to those taking part in the 35th General Assembly of the World Medical Association,* 29 October 1983: *AAS* 76 (1984) 393.

45. Cf. Pastoral Constitution *Gaudium et Spes,* 51.

46. Cf. Pastoral Constitution *Gaudium et Spes,* 50.

47. Cf. POPE PIUS XII, *Discourse to those taking part in the 4th International Congress of Catholic Doctors,* 29 September 1949: *AAS* 41 (1949) 560: "It would be erroneous . . . to think that the possibility of resorting to this means (artificial fertilization) might render valid a marriage between persons unable to contract it because of the *impedimentum impotentiae.*"

48. A similar question was dealt with by POPE PAUL VI, Encyclical *Humanae Vitae,* 14: *AAS* 60 (1968) 490–491.

49. Cf. *supra:* I, 1 ff.

50. POPE PAUL II, Apostolic Exhortation *Familiaris Consortio,* 14: *AAS* 74 (1982) 96.

51. Cf. *Response of the Holy Office,* 17 March 1897: *DS* 3323; POPE PIUS XII, *Discourse to those taking part in the 4th International Congress of Catholic Doctors,* 29 September 1949: *AAS* 41 (1949) 560; *Discourse to the Italian Catholic Union of Midwives,* 29 October 1951: *AAS* 43 (1951) 850; *Discourse to those taking part in the Second Naples World Congress on Fertility and Human Sterility,* 19 May 1956: *AAS* 48 (1956) 471–473; *Discourse to those taking part in the 7th International Congress of the International Society of Haematology,* 12 September 1958: *AAS* 50 (1958) 733; POPE JOHN XXIII, Encyclical *Mater et Magistra,* III: *AAS* 53 (1961) 447.

52. POPE PIUS XII, *Discourse to the Italian Catholic Union of Midwives,* 29 October 1951: *AAS* 43 (1951) 850.

53. POPE PIUS XII, *Discourse to those taking part in the 4th International Congress of Catholic Doctors,* 29 September 1949: *AAS* 41 (1949) 560.

54. SACRED CONGREGATION FOR THE DOCTRINE OF THE FAITH, *Declaration on Certain Questions Concerning Sexual Ethics,* 9: *AAS* 68 (1976) 86, which quotes the Pastoral Constitution *Gaudium et Spes,* 51. Cf. *Decree of*

the *Holy Office,* 2 August 1929: *AAS* 21 (1929) 490; POPE PIUS XII, *Discourse to those taking part in the 26th Congress of the Italian Society of Urology,* 8 October 1953: *AAS* 45 (1953) 678.

55. Cf. POPE JOHN XXIII, Encyclical *Mater et Magistra,* III: *AAS* 53 (1961) 447.

56. Cf. POPE PIUS XII, *Discourse to those taking part in the 4th International Congress of Catholic Doctors,* 29 September 1949: *AAS* 41 (1949), 560.

57. Cf. POPE PIUS XII, *Discourse to those taking part in the Second Naples World Congress on Fertility and Human Sterility,* 19 May 1956: *AAS* 48 (1956) 471–473.

58. Pastoral Constitution *Gaudium et Spes,* 50.

59. POPE JOHN PAUL II, Apostolic Exhortation *Familiaris Consortio,* 14: *AAS* 74 (1982) 97.

19. Artificial Insemination

Gerald Kelly, S.J.

This chapter first appeared in *Medico-Moral Problems* in 1957.

> The use of artificial means to enable the natural marital act
> to be fertile (e.g. the cervical spoon) is permitted. No other
> form of artificial insemination is in accord with the divine
> plan for human procreation. Especially objectionable are
> donor insemination and unnatural methods of obtaining
> semen. *Directive 39.*

This directive is based upon two official statements of Pope
Pius XII. The first of these was made to the fourth international
convention of Catholic doctors, held in Rome in September, 1949.
During this convention there was much discussion of artificial insemination. At the conclusion of the convention, the delegates assembled at Castelgandolfo to hear an address by Pope Pius XII. The
first part of this address dealt with the attitude of the Christian doctor toward the progress of medicine and the part he is to take in it;
the second part was specifically concerned with the judgment of
natural and Christian morality on the practice of artificial
insemination.

This was the first official pronouncement of the Holy See since
1897, when the Sacred Congregation of the Holy Office had answered a question with the brief statement that artificial insemination is illicit. And it is undoubtedly the most important of all Catholic statements on the subject. Some time later (Oct. 29, 1951), in his
discourse on the moral problems of married life,[1] Pope Pius XII
referred to his former address.

COMMENTARY

These two papal statements give the essential points on the morality of artificial insemination so completely that a theologian can do little more than supply explanatory background and perhaps indicate more specifically some practical conclusions. This I shall try to do by considering both donor insemination and insemination within the conjugal union itself.

I. DONOR INSEMINATION (HETEROLOGOUS INSEMINATION)

In condemning donor insemination, the Pope was officially confirming the unanimous opinion of moral theologians. Among Catholic moralists, there has never been the slightest disagreement regarding the morality of donor insemination, whether the woman be married or unmarried. From the time when this topic was first brought up for discussion, theologians have consistently opposed donor insemination for the following reasons: it is contrary to the divine plan for marriage; it is the product of a false philosophy of life; it generally involves the immoral procurement of sperm; and its consequences on social life are apt to be disastrous. A word about each of these points.

1. Contrary to The Divine Plan for Marriage:

One way of learning the Creator's plan is to make a careful analysis of the natures He creates. Certainly His plan for human propagation must be judged according to human nature and not according to mere animal nature. And, whatever may be said of cats and dogs and horses, the well-being of the human child normally demands the care of father and mother over a considerable number of years. Moreover, the parents also, if they are to rear their children in a manner consonant with human dignity, need mutual support and security. Because of such facts, Catholic theologians have unwaveringly held to the principle that reproductive acts are permissible only between two persons who are united in the firm bond of marriage. It is the contract of marriage that gives the child the guarantee of father-mother care that his genuine well-being requires and that gives to the parents themselves their much-needed comfort and security. This principle—that the right to generate children belongs only to husband and wife—is not only deduced from an analysis of human nature; it is also an integral part of the Christian tradition. Whatever may have been the lapses in practical life, the principle has never been seriously challenged by Catholics nor—as far as I have been able to discover—by any recognized Christian society.

In a word, the Catholic theologian maintains that the well-being of the parents themselves and especially the well-being of the child demand that generative activity be restricted to the conjugal union. These points were briefly stated by Pope Pius XII in his condemnation of donor insemination. The same points were stated more completely by Pope Pius XI in his encyclical on Christian marriage. As regards the welfare of the child, Pope Pius XI said:

> The blessing of offspring, however, is not completed by the mere begetting of them, but something else must be added, namely, the proper education of the offspring. For the most wise God would have failed to make sufficient provision for children that had been born, and so for the whole human race, if He had not given to those to whom He had entrusted the power and right to beget them, the duty also and the right to educate them. For no one can fail to see that children are incapable of providing wholly for themselves, even in matters pertaining to their natural life, and much less to those pertaining to the supernatural, but require for many years to be helped, instructed, and educated by others.
>
> Now it is certain that both by the law of nature and of God [i.e., by nature and divine positive law] this right and duty of educating their offspring belongs in the first place to those who began the work of nature by giving them birth, and they are indeed forbidden to leave unfinished this work and so expose it to certain ruin. But in matrimony provision has been made in the best possible way for

this education of children that is so necessary, for, since the parents are bound together by an indissoluble bond, the care and mutual help of each is always at hand. . . .

Nor must We omit to remark, in fine, that since the duty entrusted to parents for the good of their children is of such high dignity and of such great importance, every use of the faculty given by God for the procreation of new life is the right and the privilege of the marriage state alone, by the law of God and of nature, and must be confined absolutely within the sacred limits of that state.

In the encyclical, Pope Pius XI followed St. Augustine's plan of considering marriage according to its three "blessings": offspring, conjugal fidelity, and indissolubility. The words just quoted are in the section dealing with the blessing of offspring, and they show how the true welfare of the child requires that the right to generate children belongs exclusively to the married. The subsequent section explains more in detail the Christian concept of marriage with reference to the welfare of the parents themselves; and it is also pertinent to the question of artificial insemination. It reads in part:

The second blessing of matrimony which We said was mentioned by St. Augustine, is the blessing of conjugal honor which consists in the mutual fidelity of the spouses in fulfilling the marriage contract "so that what belongs to one of the parties by reason of this contract sanctioned by Divine Law, may not be denied to him or permitted to any third person, nor may there be conceded to one of the parties that which, being contrary to the rights and laws of God and entirely opposed to matrimonial faith, can never be conceded."

Wherefore, conjugal faith, or honor, demands in the first place the complete unity of matrimony which the Creator Himself laid down in the beginning when He wished it to be not otherwise than between one man and one woman. And although afterwards this primeval law was relaxed to some extent by God, the Supreme Legislator, there is no doubt that the law of the Gospel fully restored that original and perfect unity, and abrogated all dispensations, as the words of Christ and the constant teaching and action of the Church show plainly.

With reason, therefore, does the sacred Council of Trent solemnly declare: "Christ Our Lord very clearly taught that in this bond two persons only are to be united and joined together when He said: 'Therefore they are no longer two but one flesh. . . .' "

This conjugal faith, however, which is most aptly called by St. Augustine the "faith of chastity" blooms more freely, the more beautifully, and more nobly when it is rooted in that more excellent soil, the love of husband and wife which pervades all the duties of married life and holds pride of place in Christian marriage.

I have given these lengthy quotations because I think it is imperative to note how the Christian concept of marriage insists that the divine law concerning marriage provides for the welfare of both child and parents. This twofold purpose of marriage requires that generative activity be absolutely restricted to man and wife. The inherent wrongness of fornication and adultery are deduced from this principle; and from the same principle we deduce the immorality of donor insemination. It is true that donor insemination is not the same as fornication or adultery in the ordinary sense of these terms. Nevertheless, donor insemination is a generative act—that is precisely the reason why it is used—and the donor and recipient are not man and wife; hence it is immoral for the same basic reason that fornication and adultery are immoral. This idea is quite well expressed, it seems to me, in the following quotation from a speech made by the Archbishop of Canterbury (an Anglican, not a Roman Catholic) in a debate in the House of Lords:

Adultery is the surrender, outside the bonds of wedlock and in violation of it, either of the sexual organs alone by the use of contraceptives, or of the reproductive organs alone by A.I.D., or, of course, of both, as in normal intercourse. If that be so, A.I.D. is adultery. I do not wish thereby to stigmatize A.I.D. as having the same moral tur-

pitude which attaches to the word adultery in ordinary use
... there is certainly a moral difference between adultery in
the ordinary sense and A.I.D., yet in fact A.I.D. is adultery.
Lord Dunedin, in *Russell v. Russell,* said bluntly: "fecundation *ab extra* [which I take to mean from another party]
is, I doubt not, adultery. Other legal judgments have supported that. It is a mere fact, whether you like to use the
word or not, that by the introduction of semen *ab extra*
outside wedlock there is an intrusion into, and a breach of,
the natural relations of husband and wife—and that is
what adultery means; and the exclusive union set up by
marriage between husband and wife is violated—and that
is what adultery means.[2]

2. *Product of a False Philosophy of Life:*

I cannot dwell on this reason, but I wish at least to point out
that donor insemination makes a logical piece with the false philosophy that has long been working for the degradation of the family.
One of the ingredients of this false philosophy is a crude liberalism
that claims for every man the "right to be happy" and which really
means the right to do as one pleases. A second ingredient is sheer
materialism, which denies the spiritual and thus puts man on the
same plane as brute animals. The same subversive principles apparently underlie the "proxy" father propaganda. People want a child;
they need it "to be happy"; therefore, let them have it in any way
they can. And since artificial insemination is a good way of breeding
animals, it should be satisfactory for men, too.

3. *Immoral Procurement of Sperm:*

The point I wish to make here is aptly expressed by an extract
from an Anglican paper:

Artificial insemination usually depends on masturbation.

This is condemned by all Christian moralists, because it implies the solitary and essentially individualistic use of sexual activities intended to be used in association. It disregards the truth that with those powers God provides physiological means for exercising them in a joint and common act.[3]

The statement that masturbation is condemned by all Christian moralists may be somewhat exaggerated. At any rate, I have seen statements made by supposedly Christian leaders that masturbation is no more immoral than picking the nose. One can hope that these men were merely expressing their own opinion, and not the view of any definite Christian group.

As for the Catholic moralists, they have constantly taught with a practical unanimity that masturbation is against the natural law and the divine positive law, and that there is no exception to the law. In proving that masturbation is against the natural law, they have advanced various arguments, the simplest of which, I believe, is the one indicated in the Anglican statement just quoted. This argument is based on an analysis of the physical sex mechanism. The very configuration of the male and female bodies and the biological processes pertaining to reproduction make it clear that the psycho-physical processes culminating in orgasm should be directed to and find their fulfillment in coitus. Solitary orgasm makes a mockery of this entire mechanism. Thus runs the principal argument. Besides this there is the plain fact that, if a solitary act is not against nature, then no other sexual act is against nature. In a word, there are no perversions and there is no natural basis for sex morality. That, of course, is just the conclusion that the materialists would like us to draw; but one can reach such a conclusion only by blinding oneself to the divine plan as manifested in human nature.

The argument from revelation is based principally on St. Paul, who says that "effeminates . . . shall not inherit the kingdom of heaven" (cf. I Cor., ch. 6). Early Christian tradition has interpreted "effeminates" (the Latin word is *molles*) to mean those practicing self-abuse; and this interpretation squares perfectly with the context, in which various acts of impurity are enumerated.

4. *Consequences on Social Life:*

An eminent Jewish scholar speaks thus of donor insemination: "Such human stud-farming exposes society to the gravest dangers which can never by outweighed by the benefits that may accrue in individual cases."[4] Catholic theologians would agree with this general statement, though they might, with a very realistic scepticism, underscore the word "may" and even follow it with a very large question mark. Enthusiasts for donor insemination speak and write glowingly about the great happiness that this procedure has brought to many couples. They admit that they cannot prove this because of the secrecy necessarily involved. Moral theologians, who are not mere armchair philosophers but men who must constantly face the realities of life, consider themselves justified in questioning these glowing reports as long as proof is wanting. However, granted for the sake of argument that the reports are true, theologians would still say that the social evils and dangers inherent in the practice are such that there would be no sound moral justification for it, even if it were not in itself contrary to the divine law.

Only rank sentimentalists and the exceptionally boastful "liberals" are willing to plead the case for insemination of an unmarried woman. No one who has had to deal with the problems of unmarried motherhood would seriously argue for insemination of unmarried women. Usually the case for donor insemination concerns the married couple who want a child but cannot have one because of sterility of the husband. The following remarks are made principally with a view to this case.

First of all there is the effect on society when this practice is encouraged and propagated. I have already indicated that the practice is apparently an offshoot of the materialistic attitude that reduces man to the level of the brute animal. It does not stop here; it also fosters the growth of the same attitude. This is aptly expressed by the strong (but not too strong) expression chosen by the Jewish scholar, "human stud-farming."

Then there is the question of the donor. The literature favoring insemination always stresses the splendid qualifications of the donor, his intellect, his character, etc. Alan F. Guttmacher, M.D., a professed advocate of the practice, gives this simple test of the ideal donor: "Is that the kind of a man I would like my daughter to marry?"[5] Let the readers answer the question for themselves. Personally, I can give my own necessarily conditional answer without any hesitation. If I had a daughter, I would not want her to marry a man whose sense of moral values was such that he could calmly enter a doctor's office or laboratory and ejaculate semen into a glass jar for a sum of money. As a confessor, I can understand and sympathize with the young man who masturbates because of outbursts of passion that he has not yet learned to control; I confess that I have little appreciation of the mentality of the donor. Moreover, to return to the question of my hypothetical daughter, I would not want her to marry a man whose realization of the responsibilities of parenthood was so slight that he would be willing to father a child, or many children, whom he would never see and towards whom he would have no duty—and this, moreover through a woman he does not even know. The donor, whatever be his other qualifications, can hardly be either psychologically or morally normal. The policy of portraying such men as ideal progenitors of human beings is a menace to the true welfare of society.

Next there is the family itself, composed of the lawful husband, the wife and her child conceived through donor insemination. Theologians must admit that they cannot point to actual facts, just as the insemination enthusiasts who claim facts cannot prove them. Nevertheless, from their experience with human beings, theologians can point to some very real dangers inherent in the practice of donor insemination. The child is flesh of his mother's flesh, but not of his supposed father's. He is born a stepson, and worse. To the supposed father he is a constant reminder of the intense humiliation of his sterility.[6] (One wonders, incidentally, how often the husbands who give "consent" to donor insemination do so merely out of a sense of hurt pride, and not with genuine willingness.) To the mother, the developing child will bring none of the joy that comes to women as they see the characteristics of a beloved husband bud forth in the child; all that she will know about the child's father is that he is the kind of man who will masturbate for a price and assume the function of parenthood with neither the love nor the responsibility that parenthood normally entails. By nature's plan, children should be a bond of union between their parents, and bring them joy and a sense of mutual fulfillment; the donor-child is much more likely to be a source of humiliation, jealousy, and anxiety.

The foregoing are some of the dangers and evils inherent in the practice of donor insemination. With these in mind, the theologian seems perfectly justified in saying that, even if the practice were not wrong in itself, it would still be morally unjustifiable because of its actual and potential effects on society. But, as I have previously pointed out, it is wrong in itself, partly because it usually entails masturbation as the means of procuring the semen and mainly because it is contrary to the divine law which requires that "the procreation of new life can be only the fruit of marriage." It was this divine law that Pope Pius XII stressed in his address to Catholic doctors.

II. WITHIN THE CONJUGAL UNION (HOMOLOGOUS INSEMINATION)

In chapter 26, I spoke of the cervical spoon, invented by Joseph B. Doyle, M.D.[7] One use of the spoon, it will be recalled, is to aid sperm migration through the cervical os. Obviously, this procedure is not artificial insemination in the ordinary sense of the expression; it is merely a technique for aiding marital intercourse to be fertile by overcoming certain physiological obstacles. Some might call it "assisted insemination." Another form of assisted insemination sometimes discussed by theologians concerns a case like this: husband and wife have normal coitus, and after coitus the semen is collected in a syringe and placed further into the wife's genital tract. Although there was some theological controversy over the latter method, yet the general practical rule before the papal address to doctors was that the various forms of assisted insemination could be permitted. This practical rule may still be followed, because the Pope made it clear that he wished to make no official statement either for or against assisted insemination when he said: "To say this [that artificial insemination is to be entirely rejected] is not necessarily to proscribe the use of certain artificial means designed only to facilitate the natural act or to enable that act, performed in a normal manner, to attain its end."

As regards homologous insemination, therefore, the Pope's

words of warning or condemnation refer only to substitutes for intercourse. Three points call for special attention.

1. *The Impediment of Impotence:*

Canon 1068 of the Code of Canon Law reads as follows:

1. Impotence, antecedent and perpetual, whether on the part of the man or the woman, whether known to the other party or not, whether absolute or relative, invalidates marriage by the law of nature itself.

2. If the impediment of impotence is doubtful either in law or in fact, the marriage is not to be hindered.

3. Sterility neither invalidates marriage nor renders it illicit.

A full explanation of this canon would carry me far beyond the scope of this chapter. I have cited it merely as background for the Pope's statement that the possibility of recurring to artificial insemination would not remove the impediment of impotence. By impotence is understood the inability to have coitus. If this condition certainly exists before a marriage and if it is also certain that the condition is perpetual, and not merely temporary, the person so afflicted is incapable of contracting marriage. An example would be a man whom some accident has permanently deprived of the power of erection. It is quite possible that such a man might have fertile semen and that he could have a child by means of artificial insemination. This would not, according to the Pope, make the man capable of contracting marriage.

2. *Acts Contrary to Nature:*

With reference to homologous insemination, Stuart Abel, M.S., M.D., once wrote: "The semen specimens for insemination from husband to wife are collected by condomistic intercourse, coitus interruptus, or again, and preferably from a practical standpoint, masturbation."[8] Later in the same article, Dr. Abel pointed out that the Catholic Church would apparently object to all these methods of obtaining germ cells. This observation is correct. And it was undoubtedly to such methods that Pope Pius XII was referring when he said: "Also, it is needless to observe that the active element can never be procured licitly by acts that are contrary to nature."

Why do we consider these methods to be unnatural sex acts? The reason, as I have already explained in the preceding chapter and in this chapter when speaking of masturbation, is that the psychophysical processes leading to sexual orgasm are used in such a way that the orgasm itself takes place outside of coitus. It is true that there is an appearance of coitus in condomistic intercourse and coitus interruptus. But it is only an appearance. The determining factor of true coitus is ejaculation into the vagina; and that factor is missing in all three procedures.

I realize that some non-Catholics who might agree with all that has been said here about donor insemination would not agree that these methods of obtaining the husband's germ cells for insemination are always immoral. Even among prominent Catholic theologians there have been a few attempts to justify these means of accomplishing homologous insemination. To practically all theologians, however, and certainly to the Pope himself, such attempts mean the sacrifice of principle for the sake of sympathy. It is a basic principle of sexual ethics that an unnatural act is never permitted, even for a laudable purpose; and, if ejaculation into the vagina is not taken as the minimum norm of determining a natural sex act, there seems to be no sound way of determining such an act.

3. Is Any Substitute for Intercourse Justifiable?

The following interesting quotation from the *Year Book of Obstetrics and Gynecology,*[9] can serve as an apt introduction to a final point of discussion:

Adler and Makris (Fertil. & Steril. 2:459, 1951) reported the first case of artificial insemination with use of testicular tissue. A man with aspermia had a testicular biopsy and the wife was prepared for insemination in an adjoining room. The specimen was placed in Ringer's solution and an emulsion of the tissue made. This showed active spermatozoa. Insemination was performed in the usual way and a healthy baby was delivered.

If I understand this procedure correctly, it is an example of homologous insemination in which the husband's germ cells were obtained without any unnatural sex act and then transferred to the wife. Granted that my interpretation is correct, the case may be used as a concrete illustration of a problem debated by theologians for many years before the Pope's address to the Catholic doctors. The question was: would homologous insemination without intercourse be permissible, provided the husband's germ cells could be obtained in some licit manner? The majority of theologians held that even this would not be permissible. It was their view that husband and wife have no right to generate offspring except through coitus. They contended that coitus is the means established by nature, and the only means of generation in keeping with human dignity and with the traditional notion of the marriage contract. In a word, this majority opinion was that no substitute for conjugal intercourse is permissible. There was, however, a minority opinion that the right of a validly married couple to generate children is not limited to intercourse but might include the use of any artificial means not in itself immoral.[10]

The Pope made no explicit reference to this controversy in his official statements on artificial insemination; but there can be little doubt that the last part of his address on Sept. 29, 1949, and especially his further statement on Oct. 29, 1951, adopt the majority view: viz., that no substitute for intercourse is justifiable.

Summary

The official teaching of the Catholic Church on artificial insemination, as expressed by Pope Pius XII in the statements quoted at the beginning of this chapter, may be briefly summarized in these points:

1. Since donor insemination is contrary to the divine law that procreation must be only the fruit of marriage, it is never permitted.
2. The use of acts contrary to nature to obtain germ cells for insemination is always immoral.
3. The possibility of having children by means of homologous insemination does not remove the impediment of impotence.
4. No substitute for intercourse is in harmony with the divine plan that children should be the fruit of a personal union by which the parents become two in one flesh.
5. The use of artificial means to help natural conjugal relations to be fruitful is permitted.

Notes

1. Pope Pius XII discussed artificial insemination again in his address to participants in the Second World Congress on Fertility and Sterility, which was mentioned in the last chapter. On this occasion he merely confirmed his previous teaching. He did, however, briefly touch on the interesting question of artificial insemination *in vitro,* and he stated unequivocally that this procedure "must be rejected as immoral and absolutely illicit."

2. Quoted by Fr. Henry Davis, S.J., in *Artificial Human Fecundation* (London: Sheed and Ward, 1950), p. 13. The Archbishop's speech was given March 16, 1949. Fr. Davis quotes from the official debates in the House of Lords. The letters, "A.I.D.," stand for donor insemination.

3. Quoted by Fr. Davis, *op. cit.,* p. 13.

4. The Very Rev. I. Jakobovits, B. A., *Problems in Jewish Family Life* (London, 1953), p. 14.

5. See *Transactions of the Conference on Sterility and Fertility of the American Society for the Study of Sterility,* Vol. 3, p. 10.

6. I mention sterility because it is the most common reason alleged for resorting to donor insemination. Other reasons sometimes advanced are unfavorable genetic history and a previous erythroblastotic fetus. The first of these would be at least as humiliating to the husband as consciousness of his sterility.

7. It should be noted that the cervical spoon is not the same as the cervical cap. As regards the latter, cf. M. James Whitelaw, M.D., "Use of the Cervical Cap to Increase Fertility in Cases of Oligospermia," *Fertility and Sterility,* Jan., 1950, pp. 33–39. In Dr. Whitelaw's article, there is question of artificial insemination between husband and wife, the purpose of the procedure being to place the husband's entire ejaculate close to the cervix. The purpose, therefore, is the same as that of the spoon when the latter is used to promote sperm migration. But there are two pronounced differences from the moral point of view. In the Whitelaw method, the semen is obtained "either by withdrawal or masturbation" and is placed in a cup-like container (the cap), which is then fitted over the cervix. This method is a substitute for intercourse, and it implies the obtaining of semen by illicit methods. The Doyle procedure is merely an aid to natural intercourse.

8. "The Present Status of Artificial Insemination," p. 4. This is a reprint from *International Abstracts of Surgery,* Dec. 1947, pp. 521–531. The article gives an excellent survey of the medical, legal, and theological aspects of artificial insemination up to 1947.

9. 1952, p. 337.

10. Those interested in studying the trend of the theological debate should consult *Theological Studies,* March, 1947, pp. 106–110; March, 1949, pp. 113–114; March, 1950, pp. 67–68.

20. Human Fertility Control

John Mahoney, S.J.

This chapter first appeared in *Bioethics and Belief* in 1984.

Of the various remarkable achievements and advances in medicine in the past half-century, many can be seen as important developments in the discipline, and others as revolutionary turning-points for human society. The break-throughs, such as the discovery of penicillin, kidney and heart transplants, intensive care and laser surgery, may all, of course, be seen as possessing social implications in terms of improving the individual lives of countless individuals. Other advances, however, may be seen as offering completely new options to the human race, and of opening up new social horizons, such as the discovery of DNA and the expanding field of microbiology, with its implications for genetic manipulation, human and otherwise, giving man a biological power comparable to the nuclear energy generated by the splitting of the atom. Another, which may not be far from us, will be the capacity to determine in advance the sex of children and hence of future generations, with all the social repercussions which that will entail. At present the most sensational, and the most debated, revolutionary turning-point which the advance of medical science has offered to society is the developing technique of *in-vitro* fertilisation, whose applications and implications for society are being urgently considered by various professionally sponsored working parties, and particularly by the interdisciplinary Government Committee of Enquiry into Human Fertilisation. This newly acquired expertise in controlling human fertilisation is one which poses important questions for religious belief, and equally stimulates belief to address to it various considerations relating to human life and relationships in society. The purpose of this opening chapter is to engage both belief and medicine in a dialogue concentrated on the subject of human control of fertilisation.

It may be helpful at the outset to introduce a distinction between positive and negative control of human fertilisation, and to consider the former as covering procedures aimed at achieving fertilisation in a variety of medical and personal situations. By contrast, negative control considers the variety of contraceptive techniques directed towards preventing human fertilisation. One objection to such a distinction may be that it appears to overlook the question of how certain techniques commonly termed contraceptive may achieve their effect, such as intra-uterine devices and various types of post-coital pills, but if there is ambiguity in this area it centres on whether certain techniques should more properly and accurately be termed abortifacient than contraceptive, and this we shall consider later. For the present we shall concentrate on positive methods of achieving fertilisation, with the possible consequence that consideration of this area may also throw light on the whole vexed question of contraception.

It was in 1951 that Roman Catholic moral teaching first officially took note of human *in-vitro* fertilisation, in an address of Pope Pius XII which took up the condemnation he had directed two years previously against human artificial insemination, even by the husband, and which he was to repeat in 1956 in a speech to participants at the World Congress on Fertility and Sterility.[1] In 1978, when the first completely successful "test-tube baby," Louise Brown, was safely delivered, such official reaction as was expressed in the Roman Catholic Church came from a few individual bishops in varying degrees of favour (including the Patriarch of Venice, later Pope John Paul I, who was reported as being delighted for the mother), with other bishops objecting to what they considered to be at variance with the Church's moral teaching. No statement on the subject has been made by the Vatican, and the present situation may be usefully compared with official Church teaching on the morality of transplantation of organs such as the kidney from living donors, a practice which many thought condemned by Pope Pius XII in his day, but which appears to have become since then increasingly, if tacitly, countenanced in Roman Catholic moral thinking, despite the continued disapproval of various individuals.

In objecting to artificial insemination, even by the husband, and to *in-vitro* fertilisation, even using material obtained exclusively from husband and wife, Pope Pius XII appealed to two fundamental considerations which may still today express at least some of the misgivings felt in the minds of those who react adversely to these new methods of fertilisation, quite irrespective of the various ways in which they can be applied, and which we shall examine later. The technique itself appeared to him to offend on two counts: that the semen used is obtained by masturbation, a practice which has long been considered morally reprehensible; and that the fertilisation procedure itself disrupts the intrinsic relationship between loving marital intercourse and the emergence of a new human being as the expression of such love. Reflection on these two considerations, however, in the context of positive control of human fertilisation, reveals certain weaknesses which call for consideration.

Pius XII's moral objection to masturbation as a method for providing semen was based on a philosophical consideration of the human reproductive system and organs and what he considered their obvious and inherent purpose, that of contributing to the production of a new human individual. This being so, the wrongness of masturbation lay in its "frustrating" this purpose, in setting in train the male reproductive potential in circumstances which clearly did not favour its achieving its effect. Masturbation was a reproductive contradiction, an action which, as the 1976 Vatican Declaration on Sexual Ethics explained, "essentially contradicts" the purpose of human reproductive organs. It may be noted, of course, that all reference to the sexual faculty as designed with an inherent and built-in purpose, that of procreation, relies heavily on religious belief in a Creator who has so fashioned man that from his very constitution he is able to deduce that the God who made him wishes him to comport himself in certain ways by respecting the data of human bodily existence. In the area of sexual conduct this would include a recognition of God's purpose in creating man with sexual characteristics and a respect for their divinely-ordained nature and function, such that any behaviour at variance with that nature and purpose would not only contravene the wishes and intentions of the Creator but would at the same time be a misuse of man's sexual powers.

Such a traditionally Roman Catholic expression of 'natural

law' has come under considerable fire in recent years, largely, it is interesting to note, in connection with the conclusions concerning contraception to which it appears to lead. Even for the believer reflecting within a Christian context, it may be considered an unduly minute application of a form of argumentation from the divine purpose in creation which is more compelling in its more general conclusions relating to human individuals as a whole. But even within the particular argumentation against masturbation, to which Pius XII appealed, and which considers such behaviour in general as morally wrong on the grounds that it actuates man's sexuality to no good reproductive purpose, what this line of argument does not take into account is that in some circumstances the practice is resorted to precisely to achieve procreation and to correct the process of human reproduction in cases where it has repeatedly failed. It is difficult also to avoid the conclusion that, had another term than "masturbation" been used to describe such behaviour in a context of attempting to achieve human fertilisation, then the moral reprobation of the procedure on philosophical grounds would not appear to be so strong or convincing. The term itself, it is sometimes suggested, may derive from a Latin phrase meaning manual defilement, and without going into the question of religious feelings deeply connected with matters of ritual hygiene and cleanliness, there can be no doubt that the word bears an aura of sexual shame connected with the practice being resorted to for sexual pleasure and relief in solitary circumstances. The intensity of pleasure associated with male emission in privacy is at least as operative in all condemnation of masturbation as any more philosophical considerations, and contributes an element of emotional distaste to any verdict passed on the practice even when it is not self-centred. It is, in fact, the centring of the action which gives it moral significance as an expression of sexuality. Human sexuality is essentially relational and interpersonal, so much so that the major ethical problems concerning contemporary sexual behaviour can be seen as situated in the connections between sexual activity and love, and between sexual love and marriage. This being so, the disordered element in masturbation lies in its being a form of sexual behaviour which denies the interpersonal dimension of human sexuality and turns it in on itself as a form of self-love. But if this is the case, then what is termed masturbation to produce male semen is anything but the exercise of self-directed love. It is not undertaken for its pleasurable accompaniment, and it is essentially other-directed, orientated towards the production of a new human being who will literally embody the generous love between husband and wife.

The fundamental objections, then, which have been or might be put to the action of masturbation in general are its biological futility and its emotional futility. But neither of these considerations is applicable to the cases which we have been considering, where the production of semen is directed towards reproduction and is a physical expression of marital and parental love. It might be objected, however, that this and other stages of artificial insemination or *in-vitro* fertilisation cannot be appropriate expressions of married love, or suitable "carriers" of the interpersonal love between husband and wife. And this brings us to the second of Pius XII's arguments against these medical techniques for producing a child, that they divorce the conception of the child from its normal and natural context of loving marital intercourse and so prevent it from being the fruit of the totally expressed love of husband and wife. It is interesting to note that essentially the same line of argument has been recently expressed more succinctly and in more explicitly religious terms by the Archbishop of Melbourne, responding to developments in Australia where work on *in-vitro* fertilisation is being actively pursued. One must begin, he argues, from "the fundamental principle: God has bound the transmission of human life to the conjugal sex act . . . [I]f science seeks to exclude or substitute the marital act, the scientific action is not licit."[2]

There are two difficulties about this argument, with its latent appeal to the teaching of Jesus on divorce that what God has joined together man may not put asunder. The first is a difficulty from which many arguments claiming the weight of "natural law" suffer, that because things have always been thus, this is the way in which they must continue to be. It makes a silent transposition from the factual truth that in the past there has been only one way of achieving certain effects to a moral truth that for the future, despite the development of alternatives, there can be only one morally permissible way to achieve those effects. Frequently such a line of thought springs from a mentality which will prefer to canonise the past and the familiar than to explore the unknown and the future; and as such it is, of course, profoundly at variance with the scientific mentality and, it may be added, with the general modern mentality which feels increasingly at home with change and does not consider it necessarily disquieting. The more static mentality will tend to think of the spontaneous and the customary way as more "natural" and more characteristically human than the "artificial," the calculated and the contrived, not to mention the clinical. And in this it is profoundly mistaken, for the characteristically human qualities are intelligent control of the environment coupled with respect, and simple human ingenuity in finding means to ends. In more religious terms, the difference is one between the passive acceptance of God's gifts and finding in them the challenge of active stewardship, so that the ultimate religious defence for any status quo, including the biological or the human, cannot be an appeal to the doctrine of creation as the divinely guaranteed blueprint for human nature and human living for all time. If that doctrine is to be appealed to, it is more in terms of the human values which man owes ultimately to God and the ways in which those values may be enhanced or endangered by human developments and activities. Moreover, so static a view of things is ill-equipped to handle the process of human evolution, whether before the appearance of man or since that time, or to accept that the bodily functions which the human species has inherited from its forebears may now be used in more characteristically human and intelligent ways, and be called upon to express relationships not just between individuals but between persons.

Within the present context, although it may also have implications for contraception, this line of thinking leads one to enquire why it is that only loving marital intercourse may be the context and the cause of human procreation. To this question no answer appears to be forthcoming, except to reassert it as a God-given datum which appears to be claimed as in some sense self-evident. Such an objection to artificial insemination by the husband and to *in-vitro* fertilisation simply discounts the possibility that other actions between husband and wife can be, in the circumstances, equally expressive of their mutual love and equally fruitful. The Roman Catholic Church has taught that at times, such as sickness or pregnancy, abstinence can be at least as equally loving as marital relations. It is clear that the production of a child should be expressive of the loving personal interchange between husband and wife, and not just an impersonal, clinical contribution by each of the ingredients required for conception; and it was this consideration which led Pope Pius XII to warn against "turning the sanctuary of the family into nothing more than a biological laboratory." But it is equally clear that the frustrations of childless couples and all the disruption and inconveniences entailed by clinical procedures for artificial insemination and *in-vitro* fertilisation can also be expressions of deep mutual love and of a shared longing to give each other a child as the fruit of their married life and love expressed in manifold ways from day to day. It is one thing to state that a child must be the expression of marital loving actions, but quite another to state that only through the marital act itself may loving union be expressed and made effective. And if science can now bring to birth this living expression of the love between husband and wife which would otherwise simply not exist, this too, it would appear, must be seen as part of the Creator's loving plan for all his children.

In the absence of more cogent objections, then, we may conclude that there is nothing morally wrong in principle about resorting to artificial insemination by the husband or to *in-vitro* fertilisation within a marriage when the genetic material is provided by husband and wife. What this tells us, however, is that in certain circumstances the application of these procedures is morally legitimate and even desirable. The procedures themselves are neither moral nor immoral, like so many other scientific and medical techniques or developments. The process of generating nuclear power, for instance, which is such a controversial issue today, is in itself morally neutral, and receives its moral tone or coloration from the uses to which it is applied, whether constructively to meet the energy needs of man or destructively to blot out whole areas of the globe with their inhabitants. Similarly, as a solution to problems of infertility in a marriage, the application of artificial insemination and *in-vitro* fertilisation procedures utilising husband-semen and wife-ovum appears a legitimate and laudable procedure, but new problems and considerations arise when the material drawn upon is not specific to the marriage partners, but is donated from an outside source, whether male semen, as in artificial insemination by a donor, or female ovum, as in egg transfer from a donor or in surrogate motherhood.

To what is seen as the intrusion of a third party into a marriage as a means of remedying its infertility the Christian, and particularly the Roman Catholic, response has been on the whole uniformly hostile. Apart from social and legal considerations pertaining to secrecy of true parentage and even falsification of public documents and records, and apart also from the charge that the so-far-anonymous donor is either unwilling or unable to exercise parental responsibility towards the child produced, the basic religious objection to such intervention of a third party is that it trespasses upon the covenant and exclusive relationship between husband and wife who are, as Genesis describes it, "one flesh," as well as intruding into the parent–child relationship of the family. As evidence and confirmation of this much is often made in some arguments of the biological imbalance introduced into the parent–child relationship when only the mother or, in egg transfer, the father is completely a parent. Much is also made of the resultant stress between husband and wife when a child who ideally should be the fruit and the physical embodiment of their love and union can constitute rather a perpetual reproach of personal inadequacy. It should be noted, however, that if attention is concentrated on this evidence alone, as the harmful personal and interpersonal consequences which are predicted as the inevitable result of donor contribution, then such consequences are in principle verifiable by follow-up studies of families which are the result of such procedures. It might, for instance, turn out that not all marital and parental relationships are undermined in such cases. It is also worth noting that, if biological and relational imbalance between the genetic parent and the social parent is urged as the major objection, then there is a rather close parallel in the case of second marriages to which one partner may bring children of a previous marriage, of whom the other partner would be only the step-father or step-mother. Despite the popular image of cruel step-parents, similar perhaps to that of mothers-in-law, there are many instances of successful and loving, if difficult, adjustment to such circumstances.

What these considerations lead to is a warning, if not a reproof, which belief can receive from science, with its concentration on strict accuracy in verifying hypotheses and on precise proofs and arguments, not to translate its present revulsion automatically into unproven predictions of future disaster. If the application of some new procedure is convicted of wrongness because of the harmful consequences to which it will lead, the accuracy of such prediction can be checked, and perhaps even the possibly harmful consequences can be avoided or controlled by some other means. To appeal to consequences in cases of artificial insemination by a donor, and of egg transfer from a donor, is implicitly, on pain of dishonesty, to submit to a testing of such consequences, and to the possibility of being proved wrong. It may be, however, that in such cases of predicting disastrous consequences from contemplated behaviour there is a hidden step in the argument, which is taken for granted by the believer and not suspected or adverted to by the more empirical scientist. It is the conclusion that if something is known to be morally wrong on grounds other than the consequences to which it will lead, then it is ipso facto harmful and this will inevitably show itself in the results of the behaviour. Prediction here partakes more of an implicit belief that the sinner cannot enjoy a happy life, than of a scientific projection into the future. And in many instances it is simply disproved by the facts, to the bafflement of some believers who may then resort to a difference between leading a happy and enjoyable life and being "really" happy, in an attempt to deny or undermine the facts of the case. What is also at issue here, of course, is the difference between doing something wrong by objective standards to which, in a particular case, an individual may not subscribe, and acting wrongly in free acknowledgment of one's moral guilt. In the former case one may experience considerable psychological discomfort through having acted at variance with the views of others whom one respects and whose esteem is valued. And in the latter case this may also be accompanied with feelings of personal guilt or remorse for one's behaviour. But in neither case does it automatically follow that the ensuing consequences of one's action will be invariably and totally harmful, either to oneself or to others. One outstanding instance of this today is the case of those who may have remarried after divorce, and some of whom at least are prepared to brave the disapproval of their fellow-believers and even to tolerate considerable personal misgivings about the rightness of their action, as a price worth paying for the happiness and fulfillment which they now experience, perhaps for the first time. If beliefs, in other words, are to be worthwhile, they are to be valued and esteemed for their own sake and not simply on the grounds of a questionable corollary that the absence of belief is accompanied by an absence of human happiness and wellbeing.

For the believer, then, it would be more consistent and more acceptable to base his objection to the use of donor material not simply on allegedly damaging personal consequences as that which makes such use morally objectionable in principle, but only as confirmation and evidence (when and only to the extent that such is forthcoming) that it is already wrong in itself for other reasons and regardless of consequences, whether good or bad. Such reasons can only be the religious ones of the exclusive covenant relationship which God established between man and woman at creation as the institution of marriage, a divinely ordained relationship which mirrors and in some way partakes of the union between God and his people and, for Christians, of the union between Christ and the Church. It is within that closest of personal unions, lived at various levels and expressed in numerous ways, that new human beings are brought into existence and, the believer may maintain, it is only as the expression of such unions that children may morally be brought into existence in the image of God, as the fruit of his creative love and of the co-creative mutual love of husband and wife.

It could no doubt be argued that to make this moral stipulation on the ground of a firm belief in the God-given nature of marriage and the family is to fall victim to objections similar to those which we considered cogent against the unproven assertion that only as a consequence of marital intercourse expressive of interpersonal love may children be brought into existence. It might also be argued that advances in medical science have the function of pressing upon beliefs and of refining their content of all purely human components resulting from ignorance, presumptions and familiar habits of thought. And belief must pay science the courtesy of taking such counter-arguments seriously without too readily or too quickly seeking refuge in mystery. It may be that underlying the circumstantial stress on marriage and the family, which is characteristic of Christian teaching, is the fundamental conviction, with which many more than Christians would agree, that human life is a gift whose transmission should be motivated by love and whose flourishing requires an environment of love. To claim that only between married couples and only within the close community of the family can such creative and nurturing love be found is not, of course, to assert that every marriage and every family will satisfy these requirements. And as an absolute and exclusive factual claim it clearly goes beyond the evidence of various situations which disprove it. What it may be held to urge, however, is that, for all the weaknesses and faults of the institutions of marriage and the family as they exist today, they do continue to provide the most favourable circumstances for the loving transmission and nurturing of human life.

Such theological and social considerations on the introduction of a third party as a solution to marital infertility can also throw light on other applications for which *in-vitro* fertilisation and donor insemination are being considered, or to which they are already being directed, as well as on an argument frequently advanced in support of these applications. The argument is that every woman has an absolute right to have a child, should she so wish; and the conclusions drawn are that this would justify the use of *in-vitro* fertilisation or donor insemination to give a child to an unmarried woman or to a lesbian couple. It is clear that the implications of belief about marriage and the family which we have explored would militate against such applications of modern medical science. And it appears also that to argue against these applications from foreseen harmful consequences is to occupy considerably firmer empirical ground than in the case of donor contribution to an infertile marriage. One of the growing social phenomena causing increasing concern to various bodies in society, including the Churches, is that of the one-parent family, which is not only socially disadvantaged in many ways but in which, it seems fair to say, there is also psychological and emotional disadvantage, particularly for the child. It appears to be the case that children are in danger of being emotionally and sexually (in a broad sense) deprived, or perhaps even harmed, in their upbringing if both a father and a mother are not at hand to cooperate in that delicate and demanding task. No doubt there are, of course, individual instances where such dangers are met with considerable success or perhaps with qualified success, but this does not appear to affect the conclusion that deliberately to set about creating one-parent families is a line of action which will not be in the best interests of the child in such families.

Concentrating attention on the interests and future rights of the offspring is also salutary in considering questions surrounding proposals to enable lesbian couples to have a child, whether by adoption or at the much earlier stage of fertilisation. In such cases there is the particular factor that one can predict with a fair measure of certainty what kind of environment and what positive, if not approving, attitude to homosexual behaviour will influence the upbringing and education of the child. And one would be justified, should such influences be considered undesirable, in concluding with even more force that to bring a child into existence in such conditions would inevitably result in a serious infringement of its natural rights.

In any consideration, then, of the basic argument which underlies the advocacy of these applications of *in-vitro* fertilisation and artificial donor insemination, that it is every woman's right to have a child, should she so wish, it appears that one major qualification must be in terms of the rights of such a child once it is brought into existence. It would, of course, be nonsense to argue that a child could have a right not to be brought into existence, that is, not even to be conceived, but it can be strongly argued that if a child will be born into circumstances which will be seriously harmful or detrimental to it, then there is a moral obligation not to initiate that process. If a married woman, for instance, has a medical history which makes it highly probable that, should she conceive, she will produce a severely handicapped child, then, far from claiming that she has a right to have such a child, one would have to conclude that, on the contrary, she has an obligation not to conceive and produce such a child. Similarly, the growing acknowledgement in Roman Catholic teaching that there can be cases when a married couple decide they would be justified in not having a child, and therefore in having recourse to the infertile period in their marital relations, includes the implication that in some circumstances the right of a woman not to be fertilised arises not only from a right that her life not be endangered or that the interests of the existing family not be seriously harmed on economic or other grounds, but also from a present obligation not to submit a future child to an existence which will impair its human flourishing and development. In other words, to urge as a principle without qualification that every woman has a right to have a child is to advocate a principle of self-fulfillment to the exclusion of other moral considerations, and to incur the danger of viewing such a child not as an end, but rather as a means to an end. And to these considerations arising from the infringement of human rights belief would also add that it is only, but not infallibly, within the covenant of the heterosexual union of marriage that such rights of the person can be respected as the embodiment of interpersonal and lifegiving love, which is the image in marriage of the interpersonal divine reality which we point to when we speak of the Trinity of Persons in God.

What the procedure of *in-vitro* fertilisation has raised as a fundamental and urgent question is the connection between procreation and parenthood. The new possibility of separating genetic parenthood from social parenthood, and of separating both from physiological parenthood, as in the case of host-mothers or womb-leasing, an agreement to carry a child of another woman and to return it at birth, raises questions for society of the utmost gravity and importance, and questions for religious belief which are no less urgent. One temptation for belief is to identify new questions as really old questions in new guise and as a reaction to advance once again old answers. Earlier in this chapter we have seen one instance of this in the moral verdict delivered on the procedure for providing human semen, and perhaps this should alert belief to such a general tendency to consider that there is nothing new under the sun. Another instance arose from the development of transplant surgery and the desirability of living kidney donors, when the Roman Catholic tradition reached for the "principle of totality," which had been enunciated to condemn punitive or contraceptive sterilisation as a mutilation of bodily integrity which might be justified only if it served the interests of the organism as a whole. The result was to condemn organ-donation as a similar mutilation, without considering that such a term is a wholly inadequate description of the surgical exchange achieved by transplantation and that it leaves entirely out of account the generosity of which such a gift is the expression. It may equally be that developments in *in-vitro* fertilisation, which are having the effect of identifying different types or stages of parenthood, which has hitherto on the whole been a simple concept, will force belief to acknowledge and evaluate individually such elements of parenthood against the background of human love and generosity which it considers morally indispensable to the production and nurturing of new human beings. So, for instance, for all the justifiable concern about financial abuses surrounding recourse to host-mothers acting as a physiological parent to bring to term the child of a marriage which might not otherwise be possible, and for all the undoubted emotional strains involved in such an agreement, the practice itself, as a matter of principle, does not necessarily appear morally improper. Were an artificial placenta or an artificial womb to be devised, the case for its desirability in certain circumstances could be morally justified, and indeed incubators for children born or delivered prematurely already constitute a rudimentary form of an artificial womb. The use of such a resource in circumstances where, for whatever reason, a woman's womb was unable to function properly and safely would be similar to the generally accepted and morally routine recourse to kidney or to heart-lung machines to supply for a failure of other bodily functions. Moreover, recourse to a living and related source of organ donation as highly desirable in some cases of renal failure provides a further parallel to considering the morality of host-mothering. If organ donation can be morally justified, then function donation can be morally justified, with this significant difference than even those who might traditionally object that kidney donation was an unwarranted mutilation which does not serve the interests of the whole organism, and which is irreparable, could not advance the same objection against providing the services only of a bodily function, and only for so long as they were required.

With the human element, of course, psychological and emotional factors are introduced which require careful scrutiny. But psychological and emotional traumas may not be gratuitously prophesied, and it is not difficult to envisage circumstances, perhaps as rare as those indicating the need for live kidney donation, in which the inability of a wife to carry the child of her and her husband might be compensated by the generous offer of physiological motherhood on the part of a sister.

Parenthood shared in this way is a novel concept, for belief as well as for society, but novelty is not an invariable indication of moral wrongness. And the same may be said of the new-found ability arising from *in-vitro* fertilisation techniques to space out parenthood, not just between pregnancies but also within the course of one pregnancy. The freezing and banking of human semen, and proposals to freeze and bank human embryos, are enterprises which shock many people, and yet when they are looked at carefully and within the context of the family, it does not appear that their use must be absolutely condemned on moral grounds. There are, of course, many considerations arising from experimentation and from risks of failure or genetic deformity, and these we shall examine in our fourth chapter. Given, however, that such reservations can be met, there appears no inherent objection on moral grounds to a process of what could be called delayed, or suspended, parenthood in families where particular circumstances might favour it. Short-term freezing and holding of husband semen might be indicated until all the other conditions are present for artificial insemination by the husband. And such treatment of semen may also be desired if a husband's health is such that it may in course of time lead to sterility or castration at a stage when he and his wife would wish to increase their family. Freezing and banking human embryos, and thus introducing a pause between genetic and physiological parenthood, clearly has for some people many much more serious implications, including fundamental questions about the beginning of human life and, particularly for the believer, about the existence of the human soul and its direct creation by God. Granted, however, that such questions can be satisfactorily answered, then such treatment of human embryos in the short term might be a necessary part of waiting for the woman to receive the embryo in the most favourable conditions, or of using healthy semen rather than possibly endangering it by freezing it. And in the long term other considerations might arise, such as the fact that ova in particular can begin to deteriorate genetically during the reproductive span of life, to result in disorders such as mongolism, or Down's syndrome, in a future child. For various reasons, then, and not least the desire to produce a healthy child of a marriage, fertilisation and production of an embryo early, or at a particular stage, in a marriage might appear desirable with the purpose of resuming the process of active parenthood in due and appropriate time. Nor does it appear that such an adoption of prolonged parenthood is necessarily in itself morally objectionable.

If the fundamental question central to all these considerations on the application of *in-vitro* fertilisation techniques is the connection between procreation and responsible parenthood, then another equally basic issue which calls for close scrutiny is the connection between the exercise of human sexuality and procreation. Earlier in this chapter we have argued that recourse to artificial insemination and *in-vitro* fertilisation are in principle morally acceptable using only the contributions of husband and wife, since their actions can be seen as motivated by, and expressive of, their mutual love and their shared desire for a child as the fruit and the culmination of their union. The major thrust of Pope Pius XII's argument against the use of these techniques even within marriage was that they are a method of producing a child who is not the result of a loving interpersonal union, or, in other words, that procreation which is contrived without love is morally unacceptable.

Notes

1. Cf. AAS 41 (1949) pp. 559–560; 43 (1951) pp. 849–851; 48 (1956) pp. 470–474.
2. W. Walters and P. Singer (Eds.), *Test-Tube Babies,* Oxford, 1982, p. 40.

21. What the Churches Are Saying About IVF

Kevin T. Kelly

This chapter first appeared in *Life and Love* in 1987.

What the different churches say about the morality of IVF as currently practised will depend, to a large extent, on how they interpret the status of the embryo. This will be the theme of Chapter 3. The present chapter focuses on IVF viewed precisely as a method of human procreation. The first question it faces is: prescinding from the fate of surplus embryos, do the churches accept IVF *in principle* as a method of human procreation? Moreover, since all the churches acknowledge a God-given link between procreation and marriage, there is a second question which must also be faced in this chapter. It is this: even if the churches are prepared to view IVF as ethically acceptable in principle, how do they react to IVF when it includes some form of donor-involvement?

I. Is IVF Acceptable in Principle?

The Position of Most Churches—IVF Is Acceptable in Principle

Apart from the Roman Catholic Church, all the churches whose statments on IVF I have been able to study arrive at a favourable judgement *in principle* regarding IVF. They see no moral objection to IVF as a procedure, although some churches have reservations about how this procedure may actually work in practice. Examples of the kind of positions adopted are:

THE CHURCH OF ENGLAND

"The responsible use of IVF to remove the disability of childlessness within marriage will not threaten to undermine the interweaving of procreational and relational goods in general within marriage. In fact, in specific marriages, it may offer an enrichment of the marriage relationship which both partners gladly accept" (*Personal Origins*, n. 106).

THE FREE CHURCH FEDERAL COUNCIL
AND THE BRITISH COUNCIL OF CHURCHES

"*In vitro* fertilisation of a woman's ovum by her husband's sperm, and implantation of the embryo at a suitable time in her womb, in principle pose no moral problems. They are an extension of AIH. In practice, however, a moral objection arises if this procedure involves unjustifiable risk to the future life and well-being of the human being conceived in this way. The risk ought not to be greater than that involved in normal processes of conception and birth" (*Choices in Childlessness*, pp. 54–55, cf. also p. 47).

THE BAPTIST UNION OF GREAT BRITAIN

"There seem to be no critical moral objections to this technique, together with embryo-transfer, where the ovum and sperm of a married couple are involved. Contrary factors would be: (a) the danger as with any genetic manipulation of treating human life as mere genetic material; (b) the question of the cost of the process in the light of just distribution of resources. But in many situations these factors could be outweighed by the benefit of relieving the pain of childlessness and the responsibility of man to co-operate with God in the enrichment of life" (*Evidence*, p. 8).

THE CHURCH OF SCOTLAND

"As a technique to relieve infertility within the husband/wife relationship, IVF raises no moral questions. However, when superovulation is used to produce more embryos than will be transferred to the mother's uterus, questions arise concerning the deliberate creation of new life without hope of its potential being realised" (p. 290, n. 6).

Why IVF Is Acceptable

What sort of analysis has led to this clear consensus among most of the churches in favour of IVF?

Christians believe that marriage is a God-given human institution. The will of God can be clearly discerned in its basic "goods." *Personal Origins* spells out the "goods" of marriage:

> The union of two people in the completeness of marriage involving sexual, social, emotional and relational aspects, is seen as promoting three central goods of human life: namely, the transmission of life in the human community, a disciplined structure of living in which the individual may grow to moral maturity, and a strong and enduring relationship between them. In short we may speak of the "procreational," "moral" and "relational" goods of marriage" (n. 99).

Since the procreation of children is one of the "goods" of marriage, Christians will naturally welcome ways to remedy childlessness in marriage. Such remedies will enable married couples to live and enjoy the fullness of their marriage in all its three "goods."

The Christian view of marriage does not view its different "goods" as entirely separate from each other. They are intimately related. Christians do not see it as a mere accident of evolution that it is the act of "making love" which can initiate the life-giving process leading to the conception and eventual birth of a new human person. Children are seen as the "fruit" of married love. Married love is "life-giving" love. As well as empowering the couple to live more fully themselves, it also has the potentiality to create new human beings to share in their parents' love and to grow and develop themselves as loving persons. That is why the "life-giving" role of the parents' love is not restricted to "giving life" in the sense of "conceiving and giving birth to a new life." The whole process of nurturing and education is an equally essential part of "giving life." The whole climate of being wanted, of trust and acceptance, created by the parents' love in the home is crucial if children are to be given life in the full sense of the word—that is, if they are to grow and develop as persons able to love and be loved. It is in this very full sense that the Christian view of marriage believes that the procreational and relational goods of marriage should be held together. That is why, at least in principle, it welcomes any new development which can render fertile a marriage which is deprived of the procreational good.

The Artificiality of the Process Is No Objection

In exploring the ethics of IVF the fundamental issue which can give rise to concern is not the "artificiality" of the process. What is artificial will normally be welcomed as good insofar as it remedies some natural deficiency or even improves on what is natural. Ethical question-marks only begin to appear when it is thought that an artificial procedure might in fact be having a dehumanising effect. Then, however, it is the alleged "inhumanity" of the process that gives cause for concern, not its artificiality. There will be few Christians who would disagree with the position of *Choices in Childlessness* regarding the relationship between what is "artificial" and what is "human."

> . . . the popular ethical distinction between the "natural"
> and the "unnatural" is a distinction between what is in
> keeping with human nature and what is not. It is not a
> distinction between the natural and artificial. Since, then,
> human beings are by nature intelligent and creative, and
> the adaptation of the environment to their needs is an ex-
> pression of their intelligence, human artifice, such as that
> developed in medical technology, is in principle ethically
> natural. It is a mistake to condemn some piece of medical
> intervention as "unnatural" simply because it is artificial

and sophisticated. On the other hand, the ethical distinction between the natural and the unnatural does recognise that there are limits beyond which human intervention ought not to go. These limits are transgressed when such intervention renders our humanity less than human. Where and what these limits are in any specific case is matter for moral assessment and judgment (p. 42).

Therefore, if there is an objection to be faced regarding IVF, it will not be because it is "artificial." It can only be because some people consider it "inhuman."

Holding Together the Procreational and Relational "Goods" of Marriage

Can it be argued that IVF is "inhuman" because it fails to hold together sufficiently the procreational and relational "goods" of marriage by separating procreation from the human act of intercourse? The question of holding together the procreational and relational "goods" is usually discussed in the context of contraception. Does that discussion throw any light on how these two "goods" might be held together in the case of IVF?

The Church of England and other Christian churches have argued that, even when contraceptives are used, the procreational and relational "goods" of marriage are still held together in a loving marriage. That is because these two "goods" inspire the couple's whole relationship. They devote themselves to each other and to their children. Consequently, it is precisely within the couple's marriage relationship itself that these two "goods" are held together essentially. *Personal Origins* states:

> . . . the important points are: that procreation should not occur entirely outside the loving relationship; and that the loving relationship should issue in the good of children, unless there are strong reasons to the contrary (like genetic defect of a grave kind) (n. 103).

However, it is not essential that this "holding together" of the procreational and relational "goods" of marriage be fully expressed symbolically in every single act of intercourse. Even contraceptive intercourse is still truly "life-giving" as well as loving, since it expresses and deepens the couple's life-giving love for each other and their family.

Personal Origins sees this line of argument as relevant to its discussion of IVF. It argues that if the use of contraceptives does not violate the essential "holding together" of the procreational and relational goods of marriage, neither does the use of artificial techniques of procreation. "As long as such techniques are not used entirely outside the context of a loving relationship" their use can be justified by an extension of this same line of argument; and the report continues: ". . . in such cases, the technique is offered as an aid to the restoration of a good proper to the marriage, which through some handicap has been impeded. So it is calculated to strengthen the relational good, and the bond between the various goods which go together to make a proper Christian marriage." (p. 37) It is this line of argument which enables *Personal Origins* to conclude finally:

A Christian couple may decide that, if it is permissible to plan responsibly the number and timing of children, by the use of contraceptives, then we are already seeking and achieving a greater mastery over the processes of reproduction without reducing anything to the status of an object. They will know that it is not true that in each act of sexual intercourse they engender children as well as delighting in each other. And so they will not hesitate in situations where they are not otherwise able to have children of their own to engender children by artificial means, within the context of their own loving relationship. They will certainly wish to guard against any undermining of commitment to the goods of marriages which, they believe, have been willed by God himself. Yet the responsible use of IVF to remove the disability of childlessness within marriage will not threaten to undermine the interweaving of procreational and relational goods in general within marriage. In fact, in specific marriages, it may offer an enrichment of the marriage relationship which both partners gladly accept (n. 106).

I have been outlining the argument in favour of IVF as it is presented in the Church of England report, *Personal Origins.* That is because, on this aspect of the matter, it develops the line of argument more thoroughly than do the reports of the other church bodies. However, my impression is that its main line of argument would be acceptable to the other Christian churches who are able to accept the prior position that the relational and procreational goods of marriage are adequately "kept together" when contraceptive measures are employed to prevent particular acts of intercourse being open to procreation. Since this approach believes that the holding together of the procreational and relational "goods" is situated more essentially in the loving relationship within marriage than in the act of intercourse expressing this relationship, it is able to accommodate an artificially produced conception as long as it is still within the confines of the marriage relationship itself.

The Roman Catholic Position

The Roman Catholic church is in fundamental disagreement with the other churches as regards their acceptance of responsible contraception within marriage. It maintains that the relational and procreational "goods" are not adequately kept together when the openness of the sexual act to procreation is deliberately impeded. If *Personal Origins* is correct in its judgement that the argument in favour of IVF is related to the same basic issue which underlies the argument in favor of responsible contraception, one would expect the Roman Catholic position to have some objections to IVF. In fact, the position is not quite as clear-cut as that.

An objection is certainly raised and it is elaborated at length in the evidence submitted to the Warnock Committee by the Catholic Bishops' Joint Committee on Bio-Ethical Issues speaking on behalf of the Roman Catholic Bishops of Great Britain. The argumentation underlying this objection is found in Part III of their evidence under the heading, *Possible Moral and Social Implications.* It should be stressed that this section of the Joint Committee's Evidence acknowledges that it "includes arguments which go beyond definitive Catholic teaching" and it claims no greater authority than that "it represents an approach favoured by most of the Joint Committee." (n. 19) We are not told why some of the Committee did not favour this approach. However, I have been reliably informed that "the minority did not find the "product" argument a convincing reason for rejecting IVF; they did not regard accepting IVF as incompatible with *Humanae Vitae's* teaching on contraception." It would appear that this minority view is shared by the bishops of England and Wales. There is no reason to believe that, as a body, they do not stand firmly behind the teaching of *Humanae Vitae*. Yet at the end of their November 1984 meeting they concluded a statement on the Warnock Report with the remark that "they see no reason to consider "the simple case" of IVF as morally unacceptable." (*Briefing,* 23/11/84, p. 6) What they mean by 'the simple case,' as explained in an explanatory note attached to their statement, is the case in which the sperm and egg are obtained from the husband and wife respectively and not from a third party (or "donor") and no intentional destruction of embryos is involved. To forestall possible misunderstandings a further "clarification" was issued shortly afterwards:

> The bishops did not give approval to the present practice of *in vitro* fertilisation within marriage. This they consider to be unacceptable because the process involves the intentional destruction of human embryos.
>
> The bishops recognised that there are also serious questions about the compatibility of these practices with the Church's teaching concerning marital intercourse as the proper context for the transmission of human life. Their intention was not to engage in a comprehensive treatment of questions at this stage but to exercise prudent discernment in an area full of complex possibilities and far-reaching pastoral implications.
>
> The bishops did not wish to exclude the possibility that future developments in *in vitro* fertilisation could eliminate those factors which make current practice immoral (*Briefing,* 14/12/84, p. 3).

Neither the "minority" of the Joint Committee nor the Bish-ops' Conference have issued any official documentation laying out the argumentation in favour of their position. Consequently, it seems best to leave aside consideration of this division of opinion until Chapter 6. For the present, therefore, it would seem more in line with the methodology I am following to examine more closely the objection raised against IVF by the "majority" of the Catholic Bishops' Joint Committee on Bio-Ethical Issues.

IVF Makes a Child's Relationship to its Parents One of "Product" to "Makers"

The Committee do not argue from the intentions of the IVF parents. In fact, far from presuming any unworthy motives on the part of the parents, they actually envisage them to be acting from the highest motivation—

> . . . we have been envisaging parents whose motives are good motives, whose desire to have a child of their own is human and good, whose choice of IVF had none of the serious wrongfulness of choices against human life in be-ing or human life in its transmission, and whose subse-quent dedication in nurturing and educating their child together may well enhance and strengthen their marital relationship (n. 27).

Instead, their argument is founded on what they consider to be the inbuilt significance of the IVF process and the effect that this will inevitably have on the IVF parents themselves, despite their highest motivation.

> To choose to have a child by IVF is to choose to have a child as the product of a making. But the relationship of product to maker is a relationship of radical inequality, of profound subordination. Thus, the choice to have or to create a child by IVF is a choice in which the child does not have the status which the child of sexual union has, a status which is a great good for any child: the status of radical

equality with parents, as partner like them in the familial community (n. 25).

The Key Lies in the Intrinsic Meaning of Sexual Intercourse

The flaw they see in the IVF process lies precisely in the separation of procreation from sexual intercourse. The conjunction of the two is needed if the child is to come into existence as an equal partner in the life of the couple—

> (24) . . . the IVF child comes into existence, not as a gift supervening on an act expressive of marital union, and so not in the manner of a new partner in the common life so vividly expressed by that act, but rather in the manner of a product of a making (and indeed, typically, as the end-product of a process managed and carried out by persons other than his parents). . . .

> (26) . . . The act of sexual intercourse profoundly embodies, expresses and enacts this submission to membership in a partnership. In this respect there is a profound difference between procreation by intercourse, even an act of intercourse which the spouses hope and expect will result in procreation. Such an act, even if engaged in at a time calculated by them most likely to be fertile, will properly be an act inherently expressive of the marital partnership and thus quite different from any human acts of making, producing or acquiring a possession. Freely chosen by the spouses, it has nonetheless a physical and emotional structure making it inherently apt to be experienced by each partner as a giving of self and receiving of the other, a giving which may be complemented by the gift of a child. That gift of a child will have come, then, not from any act of mastery, even jointly agreed mastery, over extraneous materials, even natural biological materials. Rather, the child will have come from an act of mutual involvement between persons (involvement at all levels, physical, emotional, intelligent and moral).

In thus giving and submitting themselves each to the other, these partners in marriage are opening themselves up (and submitting themselves) both to the profound source of life from which the child (they hope) can come, and to service of the child and of each other in the unforeseeable contingencies of their new role as parents . . . That . . . is why the child of such a union, although weak and dependent, enters the community of the family not as an object of production but as a kind of *partner* in the familial enterprise; and as such this child has a fundamental *parity or equality with the parents* (nn. 24 & 26).

The proponents of this view state their position very moderately. They recognise that good IVF parents will try to avoid the danger they are highlighting but they see this as a deeper issue than mere good-will. "If the parents are to be good parents, they will strive to assign the child his or her true status as a member of the human race and of their own family. But in so doing, they will be labouring against the real structure of the decisive choices and against the deep symbolism of all that was done to bring that child into being." (n. 27) Their final conclusion is not expressed in terms of an absolutist prohibition of IVF but as a warning against the harmful consequences of the "logic" of radical domination involved in IVF and against its "morally flawed procedures, which inherently undermine fundamental human good and the attitudes appropriate to it" (n. 27).

Similar Positions Outside the Roman Catholic Church

Many people right across the spectrum of the Christian churches and beyond have reservations about IVF which are at least remotely linked to the separation of procreation from intercourse. These reservations concern the effect that IVF might be having on our perception and appreciation of parenthood. Such reservations need not lead to an absolutist stance against IVF. Remedying infertility is good and IVF can be welcomed insofar as it is a form of infertility therapy. The reservations are focused more on the possibility of a new "norm" of parenthood becoming accepted, as advances in reproductive technology open out new styles of parenthood to parents or even to single women, and possibly even to single men.

A line of argument which has a certain affinity to the "majority" position of the Roman Catholic committee is mentioned in the Church of England Board of Social Responsibility Report, *Personal Origins* (1985), n. 105—

> It is thought that we may be attempting to achieve a mastery over human nature itself, possibly involving a reduction of it to the status of an object to be made and manipulated, in encouraging a technological way of thinking about procreation. The natural processes embody and express much larger patterns and relationships on which our whole experience of the world and each other depends . . . What is feared is the impact on our culture of a technological way of thinking about sexual intercourse and procreation. Those who feel this strongly will be reluctant to embark on such a procedure. They feel that sexual intercourse forms the centre of a network of instinctive family relationships which is complex and deep-rooted, and that nothing should be countenanced which threatens this complex network (p. 38).

It is not clear whether any on the Committee would identify themselves with this position. The previous paragraph has already stated that for anyone who accepts "the permissibility—and indeed the desirability—of sundering procreative and relational acts in particular cases," there is no problem about the artificiality of IVF in marriage since it is "an aid to the restoration of a good proper to the marriage, which through some handicap has been impeded." There is nothing to suggest that all the Committee do not agree with this. In fact, even their statement of the "human technology" objection seems to say that this will have no harmful effect on a rightly-motivated couple. "It is clearly possible for a mature and thoughtful couple to use a technical procedure in procreation without coming to think any differently about each other and about their children than they would otherwise have done." (n. 105) Were the *Personal Origins* Committee, therefore, merely voicing a view which they recognised to be peculiar to the Roman Catholic Church or was there some sympathy for this view on the Committee itself? The evidence would seem to suggest that the latter is true.

One of the members of the Committee responsible for *Personal Origins* was Professor Oliver O'Donovan. His book, *Begotten or Made?* (Oxford University Press, 1984), leads me to think that he might have been mainly responsible for the inclusion of n. 105 in *Personal Origins*. O'Donovan discusses IVF specifically in Chapter 5 of *Begotten or Made?*, though his general remarks in Chapter 1 are very relevant. Although he cannot accept the Roman Catholic Joint Committee's position since it puts too much emphasis on the *act* of sexual intercourse rather than on the over-all sexual relationship, yet he shares their fear about the "product" mentality. Clearly, therefore, in O'Donovan's mind the Roman Catholic "product" argument is not inseparably bound up with its position on the holding together of the procreational and relational "goods" of marriage in "the one intentional act" of intercourse. Moreover, O'Donovan believes that the embryo enjoys an equal status with any other human being. Hence, he regards IVF as seriously flawed because it has developed from and is still dependent on experimental research on embryos and also because it involves being prepared to take unknown risks with human beings. O'Donovan concludes his examination of the issue of IVF by expressing a concern very akin to the Roman Catholic Report and n. 105 of *Personal Origins:*

> I confess that I do not know how to think of an IVF child except (in some unclear but inescapable sense) as the *creature* of the doctors who assisted at her conception—which means, also, of the society to which the doctor belongs and for whom he acts.
>
> . . . If our habits of thought continue to instruct us that the IVF child is radically equal to the doctors who produced her, then that is good—for the time being. But if we do not live and act in accordance with such conceptions, and if society welcomes more and more institutions and practices which implicitly deny them, then they will soon appear to be merely sentimental, the tatters and shreds which remind us of how we used once to clothe the world with intelligibility (pp. 85–86).

Is the IVF Child the Fruit of Its Parents' Love?

Could the objection we have been examining be expressed more simply as: the IVF child is not the fruit of its parents' love. Although it may have had its origin in an instinctive feeling of that kind, such a simple statement does not do justice to the far more sophisticated version of the objection presented, for instance, by the Roman Catholic Bishops' Bioethical Committee. In fact, it is probably accepted by most people nowadays, even those opposed to IVF, that it is precisely the infertile couple's mutual love and their desire to share that love which drives them to seek a child by IVF. It could even be said that their actual decision to try to have an IVF child is itself an expression of their love. Their willingness to undergo both personal and material hardship to have a child is a clear indication of how self-sacrificing their love is prepared to be. It is probably true to say that an IVF baby is likely to be even more a "wanted" baby than a child conceived normally. The fact that the IVF child is not the fruit of the specific act of love which is sexual intercourse does not mean that it is in no way the fruit of its parents' love.

Although acts of sexual intercourse can express and even deepen a couple's love for each other, yet their love lies essentially in them as persons and in their relationship to one another. It is true that, for this love to stay alive and grow, they need to express it to each other in all sorts of ways. It is also true that sexual intercourse holds a special place in the language of love. Nevertheless, it still remains only one expression of love among many within marriage. Even refraining from intercourse can be an expression of love on occasion. Even the sufferings that the woman has to go through in infertility treatment and the feeling of helplessness experienced by the man throughout the process can be transformed into expressions of self-sacrificing love. The same is true of the sacrifice of creature comforts they might need to accept together to cover the costs of treatment. There are many different ways in which a couple can express their love for each other and their desire to share their mutual love with a child of their own. Any children they have are the fruit of that love and not simply of specific acts expressing that love.

The Roman Catholic Report does not doubt that the IVF couple are motivated by love; rather it expresses the fear that the IVF process will inevitably have an eroding effect on their love. Despite their best intentions the IVF process is such that they will experience their child as a "product." They provide the raw materials, as it were, but the crucial stages of the process are controlled by people extrinsic to their relationship. Though these "third parties" are genuinely committed to helping the couple with their infertility problem, the very nature of the process with its in-built canons of efficiency and quality-control creates a climate in which much of the wonder of new life is lost and in which the quality of the life produced becomes predominant. Unconsciously, so the argument goes, the couple will be looking for a "good quality" baby which the technicians, acting as third parties, will produce from the selection of embryos available to them. This almost imperceptible shift to "quality" thinking will inevitably put at risk the total and unconditional acceptance of a child by its parents which would seem to be the one essential pre-requisite if a child is to grow and develop in the secure family atmosphere created by its parents' love. Without any specifically Christian point of reference, this argument is put very forcefully by Barbara Katz Rothman—

> Parenthood demands such total acceptance from us. We expect mothers to love, to accept their babies unreservedly, with the fullness of their hearts, no matter what. We joke about: "A face only a mother could love." It is not that women have always been able to achieve that unconditional love. Indeed, the fear of having a child one cannot love is one of the more common fears that haunt pregnancy. But never before have we asked women to make rational, intellectual determinations based on that fear. What does it do to motherhood, to women, and to men as fathers too, when we make parental acceptance conditional, pending further testing? We ask the mother and her family to say, in essence, "These are my standards. If you meet these standards of acceptability, then you are mine and I will love and accept you totally. After you pass this test" (Rothman 1985, p. 190).

It is this totally accepting love, it is claimed, that is threatened by IVF and other processes in reproductive technology.

Whose Needs Does IVF Serve—the Parents' or the Children's?

The Roman Catholic position as found in the Evidence to the Warnock Committee from the Bishops' Joint Committee on Bioethical Issues insists that the needs of the children are primary. It is not sufficient that prospective parents want to have children. Their desire for children is unreasonable if the situation into which the child will be born is likely to be harmful to the child's personal development:

> . . . children have the right to have been brought into the world in the context which tends best to promote their individuality and responsibility and their sense of identity, and which characteristically affords them the most all-round and discriminating support in the crises of development and even of later life . . . (n. 16).

In their Response to the *Warnock Report* the Joint Committee make this one of their major objections. They argue that the War-nock Commission has subordinated the interests of the prospective child to the interests of the adults involved:

> The interests of embryo and child, i.e. of the new human being who is either being envisaged and planned for or who actually exists, are systematically subordinated to the interests of the adults who (very understandably) want a child. And those interests and rights of the newly generated are subordinated to the optimisation of a technique for fulfilling that adult want (n. 11).

The other Christian churches are not inattentive to the needs of the children, especially since they "are unable to look after their own interests for themselves." (*Choices in Childlessness,* p. 20) However, they believe that the deepest interests of the children are inseparably linked to the love and stability of the marriage itself. Hence, they refuse to isolate the welfare of the children from "the good of Christian marriage." (*Personal Origins,* p. 113) The interests of the parents and the interests of the children are mutually dependent each on the other.

It could be argued that the difference of emphasis here between the Roman Catholic position we have been examining and the other Christian churches comes back to the same key issue which has been high-lighted in this chapter. The other Christian churches emphasise the importance of the parents' relationship for the good of the children and in that sense locate the holding together of the relational and the procreational "goods" essentially in the relationship itself. The Roman Catholic position does not accept that. Consequently, it is more inclined to think that "because the parents want a child" is a reason which only looks to the parents' needs and not one which will normally be answering the future child's needs as well.

Why is there such a major difference between the Roman Catholic position and the other Christian churches on this issue of whether within marriage the holding together of the procreational and the relational "goods" occurs essentially in the act of sexual intercourse or in the couple's relationship of life-giving love? That question will be examined further in Chapter 2.

II. IS IVF WITH DONOR INVOLVEMENT ACCEPTABLE? THE INTRUSION OF THIRD PARTIES INTO THE MARRIAGE RELATIONSHIP AND PARENTHOOD

The third parties under consideration here are the donors of sperm or ova or embryos and surrogate mothers or women who are prepared to carry in their womb a child which is not their own. While it is true that third parties can also take the form of the medical personnel and scientists involved in the IVF procedures, the possible impact of their involvement has already been touched on in the previous section.

Some Questions Raised by Donor Involvement in IVF

The involvement of a third-party as donor in IVF raises a number of questions for the Christian churches:

(1) Does third party involvement offend against the exclusive character of the marriage relationship? Is it a new form of adultery?

(2) When donor sperm or donor ova are used, does the non-contributing partner feel alienated by the process and does this seriously affect his or her sense of being a true parent of the child? Is this likely to be a greater difficulty for the father in the case of sperm-donation, if he feels reduced to the role of a non-involved on-looker throughout the whole process?

(3) Since donor involvement creates a situation of multi-parentage (with greater or lesser complexity, depending on the circumstances), is this exposing the resulting child to the danger of a major psychological crisis regarding personal identity and all the harmful consequences flowing from this?

(4) Does the process foster an attitude of genetic irresponsibility on the part of donors?

How do the various Christian Churches respond to these questions?

THE CHURCH OF ENGLAND

The Anglican Board for Social Responsibility has twice expressed itself on the question of donor involvement since the publication of the *Warnock Report*. The first occasion was when it published its Response to the *Warnock Report*. In this Response, while acknowledging that the contrary position had previously been the "official" teaching of the Church of England, it expressed a strong majority position accepting AID and argued its case as follows:

AID introduces a third party into the intimacies of married life. Marriage is the union of one man and one woman for life. The Memorandum of Evidence submitted on this issue in 1959 on behalf of the Church of England reaffirmed the finding of the Archbishop of Canterbury's Commission of 1948 that "artificial insemination with donated semen involves a breach of the marriage. It violates the exclusive union set up between husband and wife" (n. 3, p. 58). There are those who hold that when a couple become "one flesh" in marriage, they belong to one another in such a close and exclusive way that nothing and no one else should take their place both in sexual union and in the procreation that normally results from it. For such people union and procreation are indissolubly linked. There can be, however, a proper development of Anglican ethical thinking on matters concerning sex (cf. the development of Anglican thinking on contraception). It is possible for a couple today to hold in good conscience the conviction that the semen of a third party imports nothing alien into the marriage relationship and does not adulterate it as physical union would. It is a possible view of the exclusiveness of the marital relationship that it concerns physical congress rather than the giving and reception of semen which is its normal accompaniment. *The majority of us agree with the Report that "those engaging in AID are, in their own view, involved in a positive affirmation of the family"* (4.14) *and hence AID may be regarded as an acceptable practice* (5.2).

The Board for Social Responsibility spoke again on this issue in its more comprehensive report on human fertilisation and embryology entitled *Personal Origins* (1985). This report acknowledges that gamete donation (i.e. donation of sperm and/or ova) has certain features which are in common with adoption and certain features in common with adultery. Yet all its members agree that it should not be equated with either. Unlike adoption, the prospective parents' decision is not about an already existing child. Theirs is a "much more consciously responsible role." (n. 108) They are actually deciding to bring a child into existence. Although the child is not genetically their own as a couple, the situation is very different from adultery since "there is no breaking of the relationship of physical fidelity and there is no real relationship with a person outside the marriage." (n. 109) Nevertheless, there is a problem here that divides the Committee. They all recognise that in gamete donation "procreation is separated from relationship completely, at the genetic level, even though the connection between the two is preserved at the social level" (n. 107) but they cannot agree about how morally significant this is—

We differ on this, depending on whether we see the genetic as the most basic manifestation of the personal and find the alienation of genetic parenthood from marriage a development which undermines the Christian understanding; or whether we judge that, although everyone is fundamentally influenced and limited by his or her genetic endowment, nevertheless the overriding factor is the social context which can assure proper love, respect and care. To this extent the question of genetic origin is not of fundamental moral importance, when compared with the question of how the child will be loved and cared for (n. 109).

The Committee also divide on whether the "dominion over nature" problem is further aggravated by the introduction of a donor element. To some it "introduces an element of dominion over nature which appears unjustifiable . . . and possibly even threatening to human values." (n. 110) To others it is simply a further extension of responsible control over procreation and any dangers involved should be coped with by appropriate safeguards rather than by prohibition.

However, the Committee are in full agreement over their practical rejection of surrogate motherhood—"In surrogate motherhood the Christian institution of the family is fundamentally endangered, and thus . . . it cannot be morally acceptable as a practice for Christians." (n. 112)

In the final analysis it is not easy to determine where precisely *Personal Origins* stands on the basic issue of donor involvement. For instance, it repeats almost verbatim the whole passage from n. 5.2 of the Response to the *Warnock Report* quoted [. . .] above. Yet very significantly it omits the final sentence in that quotation. In its chapter headed *Conclusions for Practice* it admits that it has been divided as a Working Party but, unlike in the Response, no indication is given as to the relative numerical strength of support for the two positions.

Nature is God-given, but is flawed. Human beings are called to co-operate with God in treating and (so far as possible) remedying any natural deficiency. We gratefully acknowledge the blessings that come from a right use of medical technological to assist a couple in founding a family. In considering embryo donation we have had to determine the boundaries beyond which we should not transgress in altering the course of nature. We have found here, as we have experienced elsewhere, a theological division concerning the extent to which nature is given by God with its ends determined, and the extent to which we may regard it as "raw material" to fashion for our own good ends. Some would argue, particularly in the case of embryo donation, that technological interference with the course of nature goes far beyond the remedying of a natural defect. They believe that the fertilisation of an ovum by artificial means from an anonymous donor, to be implanted in a mother and reared by parents who have no genetic relationship with the child, entails treating that child too much as a product. Opponents of the practice fear that knowledge about his or her totally anonymous origins might have a deleterious effect on a person born in this way. Nevertheless, the distinction between implanting an embryo with a donated ovum, one with donated semen, and one where both ovum and semen are donated, seems one of degree. Once the principle of donation is granted, some would see little reason to insist that at least 50 per cent of the embryo's genes should be those of one social parent. When genetic and social parentage have been sundered in principle, it seems an uneasy compromise to try to reaffirm a partial link between the two (n. 125).

Perhaps the most accurate statement of the Working Party's final stance on donor involvement is the following:

Finally, we would wish to reiterate that our fundamental concern in these matters is for the preservation of the good of Christian marriage, as instituted by God himself, and for the welfare of children, who are to be brought up in the fear and love of the Lord. It will need much observation and discussion before we can come to a clear mind about whether these practices threaten marriage or the true welfare of children, or conversely if they are a blessing in marriage. But it is above all important to recognise the new situation in which we stand, with possibilities now open to us which have never before existed. In this situation, our traditions of moral thought need to be extended and re-thought. It may well be that previous ways of thinking will not be sustainable on reflection. On the other hand, we should not give up too lightly positions which have been important to generations of Christians (n. 113).

The British Council of Churches and Free Church Council Report, *Choices in Childlessness* (1982), also admits to a division of views among its members. Their division is concerned with whether or not the involvement of a donor violates the exclusivity of the marriage covenant.

> Some of us from the outset took the view, from which no further argument or reflection dislodged us, that there is a specifically Christian objection to the practice of AID. This rested on the conviction that marriage is a covenant-relationship between husband and wife exclusive of all others, not only in sexual intercourse, but also in the pro-creation of children. If there is going to be a child by the one, then so long as the covenant relationship endures, it shall be a child by both; if it is not to be by both, then it shall be by neither. This is part of the meaning of marriage "for better, for worse." A covenant-relationship of this kind does not, of course, rule out adoption, but it rules out AID as much as it rules out adultery.
>
> Others of us took the view that the full and informed consent to AID of both husband and wife materially altered the case. Such consent cannot in principle be invalidated by the existence of a covenant-relationship. It can be incorporated within the covenant and may in certain circumstances support and even strengthen it (p. 43).

The Report also expresses "anxiety" over the possible harmful effects of gamete donation on the resulting child's sense of personal identity, linking this with such practical questions as mixing donor and husband sperm and the anonymity of the donor.

> Ancestry may not be altogether irrelevant to identity. If

our primary concern is really for the interests of the child, we should be sure that the risks to which we are subjecting an AID child are not substantially greater than the risks to which we should be willing to subject any other child. So far we do not have the evidence necessary for making reliable comparisons (p. 44).

Like *Personal Origins* the BCC-Free Church Report is in no doubt about its condemnation of surrogate motherhood—

The surrogate mother ... provides more than the ovum ... (She) has ... a deepening relationship which, begun before birth, would in the normal course of events be expected to continue after birth. Deliberately to disrupt this relationship is totally to alter its character and to damage its potentiality. It is to act irresponsibly and inhumanly. It is to reduce procreation to nothing more than a biological process. Surrogate motherhood is hardly motherhood at all (p. 48).

The final conclusion of *Choices in Childlessness* is far more against than in favour of any donor involvement—"Although, as a group, we are not prepared to condemn AID outright, nevertheless we are sufficiently impressed by the objections raised against it to wish to register our disquiet, and call for a public inquiry" (p. 45).

THE ROMAN CATHOLIC CHURCH

Donor involvement in all forms is regarded as morally unacceptable by the Roman Catholic Bishops' Joint Committee on Bio-Ethical Issues. They state the principle that "children have a right to be born the true child of a married couple, and thus to have an unimpaired sense of identity." (n. 17, p. 11) Their position is clearly based on what they see to be in the best interests of the prospective child. "The rights and interests of the prospective child ... should systematically prevail over the understandable desires of men or women who want a child." (n. 18, p. 11) Nevertheless, they are careful to state that this line of argument does not justify abortion, once conception has taken place. "Even when the cause of their conception involved serious wrong-doing or unwisdom, children once conceived are not "better off dead" (n. 17, p. 11).

THE CHURCH OF SCOTLAND

The Church of Scotland, likewise, is opposed to any form of donor involvement and sees "in AID the unwarranted intrusion of a third party in the marriage relationship, which it cannot support." (p. 290) Hence, it states: "Profound as feelings associated with infertility unquestionably are, the experience of infertility should not be taken to advocate practices such as AID, embryo transfer or egg donation which imply either the introduction of a third party into the marriage relationship or treat women as merely incubators or men as disinterested donors of sperm" (p. 289).

THE BAPTIST UNION OF GREAT BRITAIN AND IRELAND

One of the clearest and most thorough moral considerations of donor involvement is that found in the evidence submitted to the Warnock Committee on behalf of the Baptist Union of Great Britain and Ireland. Regarding AID they list the "strong contrary factors which a Christian ethic would urge"—

(a) the use of unknown sperm or ova intensifies the tendency to treat human genetic material as objects to be manipulated, and even sold commercially, rather than as the basis for personality. There are dangerous implications for social awareness here;

(b) the use of unknown sperm or ova means that the procreator has no responsibility for his/her offspring. The conception of children is thus divorced from the context of responsible relationships. While this may unfortunately happen in other circumstances in which a child is conceived normally, here it is built into the process as an inevitable element;

(c) the use of sperm and ova "banks" encourages the selection of certain genetic types as "desirable" and opens the door to a programme of positive eugenics. This is offensive to Christian morality, which believes that God gives value to human life rather than man;

(d) the child is deprived of the right to know the identity of its father/mother. While this may happen in normal instances of conception, here again it is built into the process;

(e) while AID or egg-donation could hardly be defined as "adultery" or "unfaithfulness" within the Christian ethic, it does disturb the principle of "one flesh" within Christian marriage, where sexual union is understood to be the active symbol of a covenantal relationship.

In the light of the above "strong contrary factors" the conclusion drawn is: "A Christian ethic would be likely to resist the development of AID and egg-donation as a normally available method for overcoming infertility. Supporting factors would have to be very strong indeed to outweigh the contrary ones" (n. 13).

The Baptist Union evidence also gives a similar list of "strong contrary factors" against the practice of womb leasing—

(a) the surrogate mother is treated as a mere incubator, ignoring the effect upon her personality and physiology of carrying and bearing a child . . .

(b) The foetus is also being regarded as less than a potential personality, ignoring the interaction between mother and child in the uterine stage. Stimuli from the uterine environment influence the development of the nervous system as well as probably producing feelings that may have a long-lasting effect;

(c) . . . Some psychiatrists say that the first three months of pregnancy are crucial to the psychological development of the unborn child. The mother's feelings of well-being, contentment, rejection, love or unlove, can be transferred to the foetus and remembered in his subconscious for the rest of his life . . . Although nothing is conclusive in this area, it does indicate that whereas in terms of the physical we are beginning to understand the start of life, when it comes to the psyche we still have a lot of research to do. What we are considering in this re-

> port are processes that could cause untold psycho-
> logical harm;
> (d) . . . in the USA . . . it is reported that frequently the
> surrogate mother refuses to give up the baby . . .
> (n. 14).

Consequently, womb leasing is rejected by this Baptist Union report as "normally unacceptable to a Christian ethic."

THE CHURCH IN WALES

The Church in Wales, in their response to the *Warnock Report,* have a long section on AID. They express grave concern about "the involvement of a 'third party,' an anonymous and non-responsible third person, into what ought to be an exclusive marriage covenant" but they are far from suggesting that there is anything akin to adultery in this. Far from it: when both partners fully consent to AID it could be a very rich expression of their mutual fidelity:

> When AID is undertaken out of such a freely-given mutual consent, when it is decided on as an act of love expressing the inner meaning of the marriage covenant, when it ex-presses the desire for a child of the wife's own flesh who will be the child of the parenthood covenant of the hus-band as well as the wife, then AID hardly constitutes adul-tery. To the contrary, it may well express the very opposite: fidelity in the richest sense of the term (p. 4).

They also express concern about "the psychological factors re-lating to AID." They recognise that the husband and wife will be affected differently:

> Undoubtedly the husband usually has the greater psycho-logical adjustment to make in these procedures. He is the 'deficient' one, a difficult role for many in a society with exaggerated masculine virility images. The effect on the woman is not by any means less smooth. Somehow she must cope both with her husband's deficiency and with the potential guilt of carrying "another man's baby" in her womb (p. 4).

Summing Up

Can we draw any final conclusion concerning the position of the various Christian churches on the moral acceptability of IVF with donor involvement?

All the questions mentioned [above] are considered by most of the churches. Their conclusions can be summarised as follows:

(1) No church condemns donor involvement in IVF as a form of adultery but some churches believe that it is not really in accord with the exclusivity of the marriage covenant. However, not all the churches who adopt this position would go on to draw the conclusion that AID is to be rejected in all circumstances.
(2) The possibility of the non-contributing partners feeling alienated is acknowledged but this is not viewed as a major objection to the practice. It is merely a negative factor to be borne in mind.
(3) The potential harm to the IVF child due to confusion or ambiguity over personal identity and anonymous parentage comes over as the objection which carries most weight among the churches. Nevertheless, the lack of empirical evidence needed to substantiate this objection is acknowledged.
(4) Genetic irresponsibility is acknowledged as a further contributory negative factor. There is total agreement over the rejection of surrogate motherhood or womb-leasing on the grounds that this violates the personal dignity of the woman involved and might also have harmful effects on the child.

As regards arriving at any kind of clear over-all moral evaluation, no church, among those whose statements I have been able to examine, is unreservedly in favour of IVF with donor involvement. The Roman Catholic church and the Church of Scotland are quite definite in their rejection of it. The Baptist Union also comes out against it but is less absolute in its judgement. The Church in Wales expresses serious reservations but does not arrive at any definite moral judgement on the issue. The Church of England is divided in its report, *Personal Origins.* Although it is never stated explicitly in the Report, one senses that within the Working Party it is the majority who consider that IVF with donor involvement is morally acceptable. *Choices in Childlessness,* the Report sponsored by the Free

Church Federal Council and the British Council of Churches, reflects a division of opinion among its members. However, in the end they seem to lean more towards rejection than acceptance.

References

Personal Origins, The Report of a [Church of England] Working Party on Human Fertilisation and Embryology of the Board for Social Responsibility (CIO Publishing, 1985).

Choices in Childlessness (1982), The Report of a Working Party under the auspices of The Free Church Federal Council and The British Council of Churches.

Oliver O'Donovan, *Begotten or Made?* (Oxford: Clarendon Press, 1984).

Barbara Katz Rothman, "The Products of Conception: The Social Context of Reproductive Choice." in *Journal of Medical Ethics* (1985), 188–193.

Full citations for other church documents can be found in the original volume, *Life and Love* (1987).

Part Five

HOMOSEXUALITY

22. Letter to the Bishops of the Catholic Church on the Pastoral Care of Homosexual Persons (1986)

Congregation for the Doctrine of the Faith

---

1. The issue of homosexuality and the moral evaluation of homosexual acts have increasingly become a matter of public debate, even in Catholic circles. Since this debate often advances arguments and makes assertions inconsistent with the teaching of the Catholic Church, it is quite rightly a cause for concern to all engaged in the pastoral ministry, and this Congregation has judged it to be of sufficiently grave and widespread importance to address to the Bishops of the Catholic Church this Letter on the Pastoral Care of Homosexual Persons.

2. Naturally, an exhaustive treatment of this complex issue cannot be attempted here, but we will focus our reflection within the distinctive context of the Catholic moral perspective. It is a perspective which finds support in the more secure findings of the natural sciences, which have their own legitimate and proper methodology and field of inquiry.

However, the Catholic moral viewpoint is founded on human reason illumined by faith and is consciously motivated by the desire to do the will of God our Father. The Church is thus in a position to learn from scientific discovery but also to transcend the horizons of science and to be confident that her more global vision does greater justice to the rich reality of the human person in his spiritual and physical dimensions, created by God and heir, by grace, to eternal life.

It is within this context, then, that it can be clearly seen that the phenomenon of homosexuality, complex as it is, and with its many consequences for society and ecclesial life, is a proper focus for the Church's pastoral care. It thus requires of her ministers attentive study, active concern and honest, theologically well-balanced counsel.

3. Explicit treatment of the problem was given in this Congregation's "Declaration on Certain Questions Concerning Sexual Ethics" of December 29, 1975. That document stressed the duty of trying to understand the homosexual condition and noted that culpability for homosexual acts should only be judged with prudence. At the same time the Congregation took note of the distinction commonly drawn between the homosexual condition or tendency and individual homosexual actions. These were described as deprived of their essential and indispensable finality, as being "intrinsically disordered," and able in no case to be approved of (cf. n. 8, § 4).

In the discussion which followed the publication of the Declaration, however, an overly benign interpretation was given to the homosexual condition itself, some going so far as to call it neutral, or even good. Although the particular inclination of the homosexual person is not a sin, it is a more or less strong tendency ordered toward an intrinsic moral evil; and thus the inclination itself must be seen as an objective disorder.

Therefore special concern and pastoral attention should be directed toward those who have this condition, lest they be led to believe that the living out of this orientation in homosexual activity is a morally acceptable option. It is not.

4. An essential dimension of authentic pastoral care is the identification of causes of confusion regarding the Church's teaching. One is a new exegesis of Sacred Scripture which claims variously that Scripture has nothing to say on the subject of homosexuality, or that it somehow tacitly approves of it, or that all of its moral injunctions are so culture-bound that they are no longer applicable to

contemporary life. These views are gravely erroneous and call for particular attention here.

5. It is quite true that the Biblical literature owes to the different epochs in which it was written a good deal of its varied patterns of thought and expression (*Dei Verbum* 12). The Church today addresses the Gospel to a world which differs in many ways from ancient days. But the world in which the New Testament was written was already quite diverse from the situation in which the Sacred Scriptures of the Hebrew People had been written or compiled, for example.

What should be noticed is that, in the presence of such remarkable diversity, there is nevertheless a clear consistency within the Scriptures themselves on the moral issue of homosexual behavior. The Church's doctrine regarding this issue is thus based, not on isolated phrases for facile theological argument, but on the solid foundation of a constant Biblical testimony. The community of faith today, in unbroken continuity with the Jewish and Christian communities within which the ancient Scriptures were written, continues to be nourished by those same Scriptures and by the Spirit of Truth whose Word they are. It is likewise essential to recognize that the Scriptures are not properly understood when they are interpreted in a way which contradicts the Church's living Tradition. To be correct, the interpretation of Scripture must be in substantial accord with that Tradition.

The Vatican Council II in *Dei Verbum* 10, put it this way: "It is clear, therefore, that in the supremely wise arrangement of God, sacred Tradition, sacred Scripture, and the Magisterium of the Church are so connected and associated that one of them cannot stand without the others. Working together, each in its own way under the action of the one Holy Spirit, they all contribute effectively to the salvation of souls." In that spirit we wish to outline briefly the Biblical teaching here.

6. Providing a basic plan for understanding this entire discussion of homosexuality is the theology of creation we find in Genesis. God, by his infinite wisdom and love, brings into existence all of reality as a reflection of his goodness. He fashions mankind, male

and female, in his own image and likeness. Human beings, there-fore, are nothing less than the work of God himself; and in the complementarity of the sexes, they are called to reflect the inner unity of the Creator. They do this in a striking way in their coopera-tion with him in the transmission of life by a mutual donation of the self to the other.

In *Genesis* 3, we find that this truth about persons being an image of God has been obscured by original sin. There inevitably follows a loss of awareness of the covenantal character of the union these persons had with God and with each other. The human body retains its "spousal significance" but this is now clouded by sin. Thus, in *Genesis* 19:1–11, the deterioration due to sin continues in the story of the men of Sodom. There can be no doubt of the moral judgement made there against homosexual relations. In *Leviticus* 18:22 and 20:13, in the course of describing the conditions necessary for belonging to the Chosen People, the author excludes from the People of God those who behave in a homosexual fashion.

Against the background of this exposition of theocratic law, an eschatological perspective is developed by St. Paul when, in *1 Cor.* 6:9, he proposes the same doctrine and lists those who behave in a homosexual fashion among those who shall not enter the Kingdom of God.

In *Romans* 1:18–32, still building on the moral traditions of his forebears, but in the new context of the confrontation between Christianity and the pagan society of his day, Paul uses homosexual behaviour as an example of the blindness which has overcome hu-mankind. Instead of the original harmony between Creator and creatures, the acute distortion of idolatry has led to all kinds of moral excess. Paul is at a loss to find a clearer example of this dishar-mony than homosexual relations. Finally, *1 Tim.* 1, in full continu-ity with the Biblical position, singles out those who spread wrong doctrine and in v. 10 explicitly names as sinners those who engage in homosexual acts.

7. The Church, obedient to the Lord who founded her and gave to her the sacramental life, celebrates the divine plan of the loving and live-giving union of men and women in the sacrament of marriage. It is only in the marital relationship that the use of the

sexual faculty can be morally good. A person engaging in homosexual behaviour therefore acts immorally.

To choose someone of the same sex for one's sexual activity is to annul the rich symbolism and meaning, not to mention the goals, of the Creator's sexual design. Homosexual activity is not a complementary union, able to transmit life; and so it thwarts the call to a life of that form of self-giving which the Gospel says is the essence of Christian living. This does not mean that homosexual persons are not often generous and giving of themselves; but when they engage in homosexual activity they confirm within themselves a disordered sexual inclination which is essentially self-indulgent.

As in every moral disorder, homosexual activity prevents one's own fulfillment and happiness by acting contrary to the creative wisdom of God. The Church, in rejecting erroneous opinions regarding homosexuality, does not limit but rather defends personal freedom and dignity realistically and authentically understood.

8. Thus, the Church's teaching today is in organic continuity with the Scriptural perspective and with her own constant Tradition. Though today's world is in many ways quite new, the Christian community senses the profound and lasting bonds which join us to those generations who have gone before us, "marked with the sign of faith."

Nevertheless, increasing numbers of people today, even within the Church, are bringing enormous pressure to bear on the Church to accept the homosexual condition as though it were not disordered and to condone homosexual activity. Those within the Church who argue in this fashion often have close ties with those with similar views outside it. These latter groups are guided by a vision opposed to the truth about the human person, which is fully disclosed in the mystery of Christ. They reflect, even if not entirely consciously, a materialistic ideology which denies the transcendent nature of the human person as well as the supernatural vocation of every individual.

The Church's ministers must ensure that homosexual persons in their care will not be misled by this point of view, so profoundly opposed to the teaching of the Church. But the risk is great and there are many who seek to create confusion regarding the Church's position, and then to use that confusion to their own advantage.

9. The movement within the Church, which takes the form of pressure groups of various names and sizes, attempts to give the impression that it represents all homosexual persons who are Catholics. As a matter of fact, its membership is by and large restricted to those who either ignore the teaching of the Church or seek somehow to undermine it. It brings together under the aegis of Catholicism homosexual persons who have no intention of abandoning their homosexual behaviour. One tactic used is to protest that any and all criticism of or reservations about homosexual people, their activity and lifestyle, are simply diverse forms of unjust discrimination.

There is an effort in some countries to manipulate the Church by gaining the often well-intentioned support of her pastors with a view to changing civil-statutes and laws. This is done in order to conform to these pressure groups' concept that homosexuality is at least a completely harmless, if not an entirely good, thing. Even when the practice of homosexuality may seriously threaten the lives and well-being of a large number of people, its advocates remain undeterred and refuse to consider the magnitude of the risks involved.

The Church can never be so callous. It is true that her clear position cannot be revised by pressure from civil legislation or the trend of the moment. But she is really concerned about the many who are not represented by the pro-homosexual movement and about those who may have been tempted to believe its deceitful propaganda. She is also aware that the view that homosexual activity is equivalent to, or as acceptable as, the sexual expression of conjugal love has a direct impact on society's understanding of the nature and rights of the family and puts them in jeopardy.

10. It is deplorable that homosexual persons have been and are the object of violent malice in speech or in action. Such treatment deserves condemnation from the Church's pastors wherever it occurs. It reveals a kind of disregard for others which endangers the most fundamental principles of a healthy society. The intrinsic dignity of each person must always be respected in word, in action and in law.

But the proper reaction to crimes committed against homosexual persons should not be to claim that the homosexual condition is not disordered. When such a claim is made and when homosexual activity is consequently condoned, or when civil legislation is introduced to protect behaviour to which no one has any conceivable right, neither the Church nor society at large should be surprised when other distorted notions and practices gain ground, and irrational and violent reactions increase.

11. It has been argued that the homosexual orientation in certain cases is not the result of deliberate choice; and so the homosexual person would then have no choice but to behave in a homosexual fashion. Lacking freedom, such a person, even if engaged in homosexual activity, would not be culpable.

Here, the Church's wise moral tradition is necessary since it warns against generalizations in judging individual cases. In fact, circumstances may exist, or may have existed in the past, which would reduce or remove the culpability of the individual in a given instance; or other circumstances may increase it. What is at all costs to be avoided is the unfounded and demeaning assumption that the sexual behavior of homosexual persons is always and totally compulsive and therefore inculpable. What is essential is that the fundamental liberty which characterizes the human person and gives him his dignity be recognized as belonging to the homosexual person as well. As in every conversion from evil, the abandonment of homosexual activity will require a profound collaboration of the individual with God's liberating grace.

12. What, then, are homosexual persons to do who seek to follow the Lord? Fundamentally, they are called to enact the will of God in their life by joining whatever sufferings and difficulties they experience in virtue of their condition to the sacrifice of the Lord's Cross. That Cross, for the believer, is a fruitful sacrifice since from that death come life and redemption. While any call to carry the cross or to understand a Christian's suffering in this way will predictably be met with bitter ridicule by some, it should be remembered that this is the way to eternal life for *all* who follow Christ.

It is, in effect, none other than the teaching of Paul the Apostle to the Galatians when he says that the Spirit produces in the lives of the faithful "love, joy, peace, patience, kindness, goodness, trustfulness, gentleness and self-control" (5:22) and further (v. 24), "You cannot belong to Christ unless you crucify all self-indulgent passions and desires."

It is easily misunderstood, however, if it is merely seen as a pointless effort at self-denial. The Cross *is* a denial of self, but in service to the will of God himself who makes life come from death and empowers those who trust in him to practise virtue in place of vice.

To celebrate the Paschal Mystery, it is necessary to let that Mystery become imprinted in the fabric of daily life. To refuse to sacrifice one's own will in obedience to the will of the Lord is effectively to prevent salvation. Just as the Cross was central to the expression of God's redemptive love for us in Jesus, so the conformity of the self-denial of homosexual men and women with the sacrifice of the Lord will constitute for them a source of self-giving which will save them from a way of life which constantly threatens to destroy them.

Christians who are homosexual are called, as all of us are, to a chaste life. As they dedicate their lives to understanding the nature of God's personal call to them, they will be able to celebrate the Sacrament of Penance more faithfully and receive the Lord's grace so freely offered there in order to convert their lives more fully to his Way.

13. We recognize, of course, that in great measure the clear and successful communication of the Church's teaching to all the faithful, and to society at large, depends on the correct instruction and fidelity of her pastoral ministers. The Bishops have the particularly grave responsibility to see to it that their assistants in the ministry, above all the priests, are rightly informed and personally disposed to bring the teaching of the Church in its integrity to everyone.

The characteristic concern and good will exhibited by many clergy and religious in their pastoral care for homosexual persons is admirable, and, we hope, will not diminish. Such devoted ministers should have the confidence that they are faithfully following the will of the Lord by encouraging the homosexual person to lead a chaste life and by affirming that person's God-given dignity and worth.

14. With this in mind, this Congregation wishes to ask the Bishops to be especially cautious of any programmes which may seek to pressure the Church to change her teaching, even while claiming not to do so. A careful examination of their public statements and the activities they promote reveals a studied ambiguity by which they attempt to mislead the pastors and the faithful. For example, they may present the teaching of the Magisterium, but only as if it were an optional source for the formation of one's conscience. Its specific authority is not recognized. Some of these groups will use the word "Catholic" to describe either the organization or its intended members, yet they do not defend and promote the teaching of the Magisterium; indeed, they even openly attack it. While their members may claim a desire to conform their lives to the teaching of Jesus, in fact they abandon the teaching of his Church. This contradictory action should not have the support of the Bishops in any way.

15. We encourage the Bishops, then, to provide pastoral care in full accord with the teaching of the Church for homosexual persons of their dioceses. No authentic pastoral programme will include organizations in which homosexual persons associate with each other without clearly stating that homosexual activity is immoral. A truly pastoral approach will appreciate the need for homosexual persons to avoid the near occasions of sin.

We would heartily encourage programmes where these dangers are avoided. But we wish to make it clear that departure from the Church's teaching, or silence about it, in an effort to provide pastoral care is neither caring nor pastoral. Only what is true can ultimately be pastoral. The neglect of the Church's position prevents homosexual men and women from receiving the care they need and deserve.

An authentic pastoral programme will assist homosexual persons at all levels of the spiritual life: through the sacraments; and in particular through the frequent and sincere use of the sacrament of Reconciliation, through prayer, witness, counsel and individual care. In such a way, the entire Christian community can come to recognize its own call to assist its brothers and sisters, without deluding them or isolating them.

16. From this multi-faceted approach there are numerous advantages to be gained, not the least of which is the realization that a homosexual person, as every human being, deeply needs to be nourished at many different levels simultaneously.

The human person, made in the image and likeness of God, can hardly be adequately described by a reductionist reference to his or her sexual orientation. Every one living on the face of the earth has personal problems and difficulties, but challenges to growth, strengths, talents and gifts as well. Today, the Church provides a badly needed context for the care of the human person when she refuses to consider the person as a "heterosexual" or a "homosexual" and insists that every person has a fundamental identity: the creature of God, and by grace, his child and heir to eternal life.

17. In bringing this entire matter to the Bishops' attention, this Congregation wishes to support their efforts to assure that the teaching of the Lord and his Church on this important question be communicated fully to all the faithful.

In light of the points made above, they should decide for their own dioceses the extent to which an intervention on their part is indicated. In addition, should they consider it helpful, further coordinated action at the level of their National Bishops' Conference may be envisioned.

In a particular way, we would ask the Bishops to support, with the means at their disposal, the development of appropriate forms of pastoral care for homosexual persons. These would include the assistance of the psychological, sociological and medical sciences, in full accord with the teaching of the Church.

They are encouraged to call on the assistance of all Catholic theologians who, by teaching what the Church teaches, and by deepening their reflections on the true meaning of human sexuality and Christian marriage with the virtues it engenders, will make an important contribution in this particular area of pastoral care.

The Bishops are asked to exercise special care in the selection of pastoral ministers so that by their own high degree of spiritual and personal maturity and by their fidelity to the Magisterium, they may be of real service to homosexual persons, promoting their health and well-being in the fullest sense. Such ministers will reject theological opinions which dissent from the teaching of the Church and which, therefore, cannot be used as guidelines for pastoral care.

We encourage the Bishops to promote appropriate catechetical programmes based on the truth about human sexuality in its relationship to the family as taught by the Church. Such programmes should provide a good context within which to deal with the question of homosexuality.

This catechesis would also assist those families of homosexual persons to deal with this problem which affects them so deeply.

All support should be withdrawn from any organizations which seek to undermine the teaching of the Church, which are ambiguous about it, or which neglect it entirely. Such support, or even the semblance of such support, can be gravely misinterpreted. Special attention should be given to the practice of scheduling religious services and to the use of Church buildings by these groups, including the facilities of Catholic schools and colleges. To some, such permission to use Church property may seem only just and charitable; but in reality it is contradictory to the purpose for which these institutions were founded, it is misleading and often scandalous.

In assessing proposed legislation, the Bishops should keep as their uppermost concern the responsibility to defend and promote family life.

18. The Lord Jesus promised, "You shall know the truth and the truth shall set you free" (*Jn* 8:32). Scripture bids us speak the truth in love (cf. *Eph* 4:15). The God who is at once truth and love calls the Church to minister to every man, woman and child with the pastoral solicitude of our compassionate Lord. It is in this spirit that we have addressed this Letter to the Bishops of the Church, with the hope that it will be of some help as they care for those whose suffering can only be intensified by error and lightened by truth.

During an audience granted to the undersigned Prefect, His Holiness, Pope John Paul II, approved this Letter, adopted in an ordinary session of the Congregation for the Doctrine of the Faith, and ordered it to be published.

Given at Rome, 1 October 1986.

Joseph Cardinal Ratzinger
Prefect

✠ Alberto Bovone
Titular Archbishop of Caesarea in Numidia
Secretary

23. Arguments from Revelation and Reason in Favor of the Official Teaching of the Church

John F. Harvey, O.S.F.S.

This chapter first appeared in *The Homosexual Person: New Thinking in Pastoral Care* in 1987.

1. Arguments Against Homosexuality Based on Scripture

It should be noted that Church teaching is concerned primarily with homosexual acts, not the homosexual condition, which the person most probably did not will; furthermore, it is concerned primarily with free acts as opposed to compulsive acts, although the compulsive person does have responsibility to do something about his addiction. With these distinctions in mind, I turn to the Church's understanding of Holy Scripture in her condemnation of homosexual acts. I have already described how the opponents of Church teaching try to explain away the obvious meaning of the classical texts referring to homosexuality (on male homosexuality: Lev 18:22; 20:13; Rom 1:27; 1 Cor 6:9–10; 1 Tim 1:9–10; on female homosexuality: Rom 1:26).

But without denying the probative force of these specific texts, I think it better to begin with a scriptural argument against homosexual acts that is rooted in the Church's constant understanding of marriage in the Scriptures. As the October 1, 1986, document points out, homosexuality must be understood within the theology of creation described in Genesis, chapters 1 and 2: "He fashions mankind, male and female, in His own image and likeness. Human beings, therefore, are nothing less than the work of God Himself; and in the complementarity of the sexes, they are called to reflect the inner

unity of the Creator. They do this in a striking way in their cooperation with Him in the transmission of life by a mutual donation of
the self to the other." [1]

Thus only in marriage is found the proper place for genital
sexual expression. From the first chapter of Genesis to the Book of
Revelation the twofold meaning of sexual-genital expression—
namely, procreation and union—is clearly manifest. In Genesis
1:27–28 it is said: "God created man in the image of Himself, in the
image of God He created him, male and female He created them.
God blessed them, saying to them, 'Be fruitful, multiply, fill the
earth and conquer it.' " In the second account of creation God presents Eve to Adam, and Adam exclaims, " 'This at last is bone from
my bones, and flesh from my flesh. This is to be called woman, for
this was taken from man.' This is why a man leaves his father and
mother and joins himself to his wife, and they become one body"
(Gen 2:23–24).

Despite deviations from the original norm of monogamous
marriage, including polygamy and divorce, the norm for sexual activity remained a permanent heterosexual union. Yahweh is portrayed as the faithful bridegroom, and Israel, the faithless bride,
indicating that heterosexual love can be the basis for expressing the
mystery of God's loving the human race.[2] Throughout the Old Testament, however, the truth about persons being the image of God
was obscured by original sin. Men and women lost their awareness
of the covenantal character of the union these people had with God
and with each other. Among other places, this is indicated in Genesis 3 and in Genesis 19:1–11.[3] Then in the New Testament Jesus
Himself reaffirms the norm of Genesis.

The context is the Pharisees questioning Jesus whether a man
may divorce his wife on any pretext whatever. Jesus answered:
"Have you not read that the creator from the beginning *made them
male and female* and that He said: *'This is why a man must leave
father and mother and cling to his wife, and the two become one
body?* They are no longer two, therefore, but one body. So then what
God has united, man must not divide.' " When the Pharisees, then,
asked Him why Moses allowed divorce, Jesus replied that it was
"because you were so unteachable . . . but it was not like this from
the beginning" (Mt 19:3–8).

Here Jesus reaffirms the monogamous, heterosexual norm of sexuality found in Genesis. Note that He quotes both Genesis 1:27 and 2:24, thereby repeating their teaching about the meaning of human sexuality.

The author of Ephesians, moreover, reiterates the same revealed truth about human sexuality in the context of the sublime comparison in which the husband is compared with Christ and the wife with the Church. When the author wishes to express the love that Christ has for His Church, he turns to the heterosexual love of husband and wife: "Husbands should love their wives just as Christ loved the Church and sacrificed Himself for her to make her holy. . . . In the same way husbands must love their wives as they love their own bodies . . ." (Eph 5:25, 28). Then the author adds: *"For this reason a man must leave his father and mother and be joined to his wife and the two will become one body"* (Gen 2:24). Once again the Genesis norm of permanent heterosexual union is reaffirmed (Eph 5:30).

One could go on referencing other passages of Holy Scripture to demonstrate its teaching that sexual activity ought to be heterosexual and marital, but this has already been done by scholars throughout the centuries, as I have indicated.[4] Indeed the Second Vatican Council's document, *The Church in the Modern World,* 47–52 and *Humanae Vitae,* 11–14 sum up the teaching of Holy Scripture, of the Fathers of the Church, and of previous magisterial statements of popes and councils that the moral norm of sexual activity is a permanent union of husband and wife for the essentially inseparable purposes of love and union. This is the perennial teaching of the Church. Taken as a whole, it is at least authoritative; but the divine origin of marriage is a teaching of Faith.

In his July 25, 1986, letter to Father Charles Curran, Cardinal Ratzinger, Prefect of the Congregation for the Doctrine of the Faith, said that Father Curran had not given due consideration to the Church's position on the indissolubility of sacramental and consummated marriage. Father Curran had argued that the Church's position ought to be changed, but Cardinal Ratzinger points out that this "was in fact defined at the Council of Trent and so belongs to the patrimony of the faith."[5] It should be noted that Father Curran regards the Church's condemnation of homosexual activities as a non-infallible teaching, from which one has a right of responsible dissent. To this position Ratzinger replies that the teaching of Vatican II does not confine the infallible Magisterium "purely to matters of faith nor to solemn definitions." Quoting *Lumen Gentium,* 25, Ratzinger adds: "Besides this, the Church does not build its life upon its infallible magisterium alone but on the teaching of its authentic ordinary magisterium as well." [6]

From all this one may logically conclude that homosexual activity is objectively always seriously immoral, inasmuch as it in no way fulfills the essential purposes of human sexuality. The Catholic teaching flows *necessarily* from the *whole scriptural vision of the meaning of sexuality* and of the *complementarity* of man and woman. Specific biblical texts, moreover, confirm this general thrust of Holy Scripture.

I have already discussed the way in which Kosnik et al., McNeill, and others attempt to explain away the specific texts of both the Old and New Testaments. Since the argument against homosexual activity would stand on the basis of the Church's teaching on sexual activity in general, I do not see the need to develop the argument from specific texts at great length. I shall begin with the Sodom story (Gen 19:4–11).[7]

In 1956 Derrick Sherwin Bailey argued in *Homosexuality and the Western Christian Tradition* that Sodom was destroyed for inhospitable treatment of the angel visitors sent by the Lord. In this interpretation the homosexual overtones of the story are minor, while the predominant meaning centers on the violation of hospitality.

His argument is not convincing. In my judgment the Genesis passage does refer to attempted homosexual rape, and the effort to interpret the passage primarily in terms of hospitality is forced, because taking the sexual element out renders the rest of the narrative nonsensical. As Ruth Tiffany Barnhouse observes, "If the men of Sodom had no sexual intentions toward Lot's visitors, why would Lot have replied, 'I beg you, my brothers, do no such wicked thing. Listen, I have two daughters who are virgins. I am ready to send them out to you, to treat as it pleases you. But as to the men, do nothing to them, for they have come under the shadow of my roof' " (Gen 19:7–9).[8]

John Mahoney, S.J., also believes that the effort to weaken the force of the Sodom narrative is unsuccessful, because "there can be little reasonable doubt that the story of Sodom and Gomorrah expresses a judgment, however dramatic, of divine displeasure upon the homosexual behavior of its inhabitants and in so doing only serves to echo the explicit condemnation of such behavior in The Holiness Code of Leviticus." [9]

John Boswell claims that numerous other references in Holy Scripture do not identify the sin of Sodom as homosexual activity, but it may be assumed that the readers of these passages knew what the sin was. Again, there is no reason why the sin of Sodom cannot denote homosexual behavior, inhospitality, and wickedness.[10] When Boswell attempts to reduce the explicit prohibitions of Leviticus (18:22; 20:13) to the level of ritual impurity, he is confronted by the objection of scriptural scholar George Montague: "Sexual morality is often connected with the cult, but this does not prove that sexual sins, such as homosexual acts and bestiality, were condemned only because they were part of the Canaanite worship. While the book of Leviticus does have a cultic framework, the legislation of Leviticus does not give idolatry as the reason for avoiding the sexual practices of the Canaanites. Quite the contrary. The reason given why the Lord is driving the nations out of the land is not their worship of false gods, but their abominable sexual practices (Lev 18:24–30; 20:28). The strict prohibition of the sexual practices of the Canaanites indicates that more than the cult was at issue. . . . To say that the concern of Leviticus is not ethical, but cultic (or in Boswell 'ritual impurity') is a gross oversimplification and even more misleading is the statement: 'The condemnation of homosexual activity in Leviticus is not an ethical judgment.' " [11]

With regard to the classical text of the New Testament, Boswell does not deny that the text is concerned with homosexual activity, but he maintains that it is describing heterosexuals performing homosexual acts, and only this is immoral—the same position as that of McNeill, to which I have already responded. Without qualification St. Paul condemns homosexual acts, whether they are performed by heterosexual or homosexual persons; he does not attempt to analyze subjective dispositions, but only to condemn the act. Thus Boswell's efforts to do away with the meaning of Genesis 19, Leviticus 18 and 20, and Romans 1 is a failure. The first and obvious meaning of all three passages cannot be explained away.[12] In concluding my scriptural analysis I refer the reader to an overlooked verse in the Letter of Jude. "The fornication of Sodom and Gomorrah and the other nearby towns was equally unnatural; and it is a warning to us that they are paying for their crimes in eternal fire" (verse 7). In my judgment this indicates that the sin of Sodom and Gomorrah was unnatural and homosexual. It should be noted that whenever homosexual activity is described in Holy Scripture it is condemned, but nowhere is the homosexual person condemned.[13] I turn now to considerations of the nature of homosexual activity.

2. ARGUMENTS AGAINST HOMOSEXUAL ACTIVITY BASED UPON ITS NATURE

From Church documents such as *The Church in the Modern World, Humanae Vitae, The Declaration concerning Certain Questions in Sexual Ethics,* and the *Letter on the Pastoral Care of Homosexual Persons* of October 1, 1986, we hold that sexual activity is both life-giving and person-uniting. We have seen that both these purposes of sexual-genital activity are found in the Scriptures. Sex is life-giving by its very nature. This does not mean that every genital act must lead to new life, but that it must not be structured in ways that rob it of its life-giving power. But homosexual activity can in no way fulfill this procreative power of human sexuality, which "transcends the activity itself and is essential for its human significance." [14]

Genital activity also has a life-uniting meaning: it joins two persons by a special kind of love. "This is marital love—a love that has an exclusive and enduring quality about it, precisely because it has reference to the life-giving end or meaning of genital sexuality. This is a love which opens those whom it units to what is other than themselves, to a transcendent goal or good toward which they can commit themselves and their shared lives. But this sort of love is simply incapable of being expressed in homosexual activity." [15] Referring to this impoverished form of complementarity, André Guindon writes, "It is therefore easy to see how the homosexual relation fails as a totally human relationship. The authentic human sense of the other, as nourished by the enriching and complementary otherness of the other sex, is conspicuously absent. The other side of the bed is occupied, as it were, only by more of the same—the same half of humanity instead of the other half for whom each person is constitutionally seeking." [16]

It is useful to contrast the man-woman relationship in marriage with the steady-lover relationship of homosexual persons. The man-woman relationship is in accord with the aspirations and needs of both sexes. This is the way nature's God meant things to be. In his commentary on the two creation accounts, Helmut Thielicke describes beautifully the complementarity of man and woman. God did not want the man to be alone, so He created a partner for him. Then comes the poetic expression of the man upon seeing the woman: "Bone of my bone, and flesh of my flesh. For this reason a man shall leave father and mother, and cleave to his wife, and they shall be two in one flesh." These words are in harmony with present natural moral law reasoning. The complementarity between man and woman is physical (two in one flesh), psychological (the male's joy in the presence of the female), and spiritual (he leaves his own family to commit himself to her). Think of Jacob's love for Rachel; the Valiant Woman of Proverbs 31 or the two lovers in the Canticle of Canticles.

The kind of complementarity, however, between two homosexual persons in a steady relationship is much inferior in terms of its structure, strength of commitment, and consequences. To speak of the physical structure of the homosexual union is to raise the question of whether homosexuals can really achieve a true physical union. Consider the three common forms of sexual activity between homosexual persons. Mutual masturbation in no way constitutes a physical union. In the present AIDS crisis this is the practice recommended by the gay community. Among female homosexuals some form of genital massage is used to bring the partner to orgasm, but this is not a physical union. In anal or oral intercourse between males the intromission of the penis in an opening of the body not meant to be used for the genital expression of sexuality cannot be called a true physical union. It is also an unsanitary and pathological act, as Gene Antonio points out in *The AIDS Cover-up?*[17] It is really a vain attempt to imitate heterosexual intercourse—a form of bodily massage. By way of contrast, the heterosexual union aptly symbolizes the psychological and spiritual union that ought to exist between a man and a woman. To be sure, in many instances union on these levels is merely symbolized and not realized, but there is a congruency of the physical, psychological, and spiritual levels in the permanent commitment of the man to the woman, and vice versa.

It is not surprising, moreover, that the strength of commitment between a man and a woman in marriage is stronger than the steady homosexual relationship. The main reason for this stronger commitment is the procreational meaning of marriage. Even if the marriage is sterile on the biological level, nonetheless a yearning for children often causes such a couple to adopt children or to take care of relatives' children. There is also greater meaning in their sexual intercourse, as if the act were saying, "If we could have a child, we would have one." There is an affinity between husband and wife who complement each other's qualities on all levels. They see each other in terms of covenant. If they are bonded in Christ, the commitment should be that much stronger.

Thus even the best homosexual genital relationship is seriously flawed. It is "essentially disordered because it cannot be directed toward nor have a proper respect for the goods of human sexuality. Recall that the lovemaking of spouses is either directed toward having children or is expressive of a love that essentially includes an orientation toward the fruitfulness of procreation. The love of spouses can and must be enduring, because it is essentially related to enduring goods; but homosexual love simply is not ordered to any transcendent good that requires of the partners utter self-giving and faithfulness until death. A marital kind of friendship cannot obtain among homosexuals; their sexual act cannot express a marital kind of love, for they cannot be what spouses are. . . ." [18]

As to consequences, consider two female homosexuals who bring in a guru from the East to witness their "holy union." They have a few witnesses. They go back to their domicile and live together. Presumably they love each other, but there are only the two of them, nothing more. In a sense, there is no past, no future—only the present. Now consider the ordinary wedding. Man and wife come from different families, each with its own history that gives identity to each spouse. At the wedding are the families of each spouse. They look forward to the new family that the bride and the bridegroom will form. In short, in this wedding there is meaning that transcends the two persons, a meaning relating to family and children and symbolizing the union of Christ with His Church. Obviously, the homosexual union lacks these transcendent meanings. It is closed in—just the same two persons with nothing beyond them.[19]

This fact leads many homosexual persons to admit the overwhelming sterility of such unions, very few of which are permanent, and even fewer, faithful. In working with homosexual persons in spiritual support groups in New York City I have discovered that the consideration of such frustrating sterility is a persuasive argument for giving up the active homosexual lifestyle.

The homosexual lifestyle finds a common focus in the "ultimate commitment to unrestricted personal sexual freedom. Whatever other values individual homosexuals may hold and pursue, this liberation conviction is at the heart of their common identity with other homosexuals. To accept homosexuality as a way of life is to call into question any attempt to enforce sexual standards of a more restrictive sort, whether based on political, social, or religious grounds." [20]

There is a reason for this commitment to sexual freedom and sexual pleasure. If one concentrates on achieving orgasm, usually with many partners, one deprives the act of achieving any genuinely and authentically satisfying human good. As one becomes hell-bent on such pleasure, one also isolates oneself from any deep relationships with anyone. One becomes a loner, looking for intimacy but afraid of it and seeking it in the wrong way. This manner of life is characteristic of many male homosexuals. ". . . to organize one's life around the pleasure of orgasms in acts which separate sexual activity from its precious human goods is unreasonable and immoral." [21]

In *City of Night* (New York: Grove Press, 1963) John Rechy

describes this lifestyle in all its alienation and loneliness; in *Numbers* (New York: Grove Press, 1967) he continues the description; and in *Sexual Outlaw* (New York: Dell Press, 1977) he further details the promiscuous lifestyle of many male homosexuals. Although Rechy's purpose is to show how an unfeeling society drives homosexual persons into compulsive and senseless copulation, he also demonstrates what happens when sexual activity is separated from its purposes. Were one to read the ads in the weekly homosexual newspaper the Los Angeles *Advocate,* one would gain deeper insight into the mentality of the promiscuous homosexual male—a frenetic search for new forms of genital pleasure. In short, *unrestricted personal sexual pleasure leads to loss of control over one's life.*

Throughout this work the reader may have noticed that I seldom use the term *gay* to describe the homosexual person: and this with good reason. In thirty-two years of counseling homosexual persons, I have yet to meet a practicing homosexual person who could be called "gay" in the sense of joyful.[22] In a penetrating article Samuel McCracken shows by a critical analysis of data in prohomosexual books that the claim that homosexuals are as happy as other people has not been established; in particular, he points to data that show that suicide attempts are significantly higher among homosexuals than among others—for example, 3% for white non-homosexual males, 18% for white homosexual males.[23]

The unhappiness of so many so-called gay persons is rooted in their mania for sexual pleasure, coupled with their unwillingness to accept responsibility. Again, McCracken points out: "The fact is that homosexuality generally entails a renunciation of responsibility for the continuance of the human race and of a voice in the dialogue of the generations. This is a renunciation made also by some heterosexuals and indeed by some married heterosexuals. There is, however, a still greater renunciation made by homosexuals, and that is of the intricate, complicated, and challenging process of adjusting one's life to someone so different from oneself as to be in a different sex completely." [24] One notes in McCracken's line of reasoning a similarity with Catholic teaching on the meaning of sexuality as a loving union of two persons for the purpose of progeny and family.

There is one final argument against homosexual acts: Some have held that for the sake of what is called psychic intimacy, feeling close to the beloved, one may violate the physical structures of heterosexual intercourse, as it is meant to be, a physical union of man and woman, through penetration of the vagina by the penis, and the pouring in of the seed of the man. On the plea that one can violate physical structures of the body for the sake of intimacy, it is proposed that one may ignore the due physical structure of the genital act between the sexes, to say nothing of the inherent meaning of such acts. This is *dualism,* i.e., the failure to recognize the essentially composite structure of the human person which makes the psychic and the physical inseparable. One will find in the writings of Pope John Paul II concerning the nuptial meaning of the human body a powerful repudiation of such dualism.[25]

Thus the arguments against homosexual activity proposed by cited Church documents are found to be rooted in Sacred Scripture as understood by the Church; in natural moral law reasoning; in psychological and sociological considerations; and in the experiences of many homosexuals whom I have counseled over the years, about which I shall say more in the pastoral section. There is no way one can justify homosexual acts. The homosexual lifestyle cannot be reconciled with a truly Christian way of life, as Edward Malloy points out in his book. Having established the *objective* immorality of homosexual activity, it is now necessary to consider the *subjective* responsibility of the homosexual person for his acts.

3. SUBJECTIVE RESPONSIBILITY OF HOMOSEXUAL ACTIVITY

The Vatican Declaration on Sexual Ethics, paragraph 8, reminds us that the culpability of the homosexual person must be judged with prudence, and the 1973 Pastoral Statement of the National Conference of Catholic Bishops (U.S.A.) states that in assessing the responsibility of the homosexual person "the confessor must avoid both harshness and permissiveness." [26] The subjective responsibility of the homosexual person may be considered under two aspects: (1) the origin of the tendency and (2) the manner in which the person controls it.

1. *Origin of the tendency:* As we have already seen (Chapter Three) in considering Moberly's and van den Aardweg's analyses of the origins of homosexual tendencies, it can be said safely that a man or woman does not will to become homosexual. At a certain point in his psychosexual development one discovers his homosexuality and usually suffers a certain amount of trauma in the discovery. Sometimes he is young and desires to find a program where he can have some hope of reorienting his sexual desires; sometimes, because he has allowed himself to be convinced by gay liberation propaganda, he has already given up hope of changing his sexual orientation; sometimes he has spent so many years in homosexual activity that he feels too old to benefit by such treatment, or he cannot afford to pay for it. In every case he *discovers* an already-existing condition.

Since in more recent years there is more evidence that persons can change their sexual orientation (though the evidence is by no means sufficient to constitute a probable argument in favor of any specific therapy), it seems that the spiritual counselor or confessor should at least keep his mind open to the possibility that the person, particularly the young person, can change sexual orientation and that counselors should encourage homosexual persons to look into the possibility of changing from a homosexual to a heterosexual orientation.[27] I shall say more about this important question in Chapter Seven; now I consider the manner in which the homosexual person controls his tendency.

2. *Controlling the tendency:* Admittedly, responsibility for controlling the homosexual tendency is a complex question. Persons vary in the degree of freedom they possess in controlling their sexual desires. At one extreme are homosexuals who have as much control over their tendencies as normal heterosexuals; at the other extreme are homosexuals who are as compulsive as alcoholics or drug addicts. Each person has the obligation to control his tendency by every means within his power, particularly by psychological and spiritual counsel; and, if his homosexual activity has become com-

pulsive, he has an obligation to seek the means that are truly adequate to control compulsive activity, namely, some form of group therapy that integrates the psychological and the spiritual, such as A.A. or Courage (the latter is a spiritual support group for homosexual men and women).

Since I have already treated compulsion in homosexuals,[28] I should like to add the caution that the counselor, or the confessor, however compassionate one may want to be, should not convey to the compulsive person the impression that he is not responsible for his actions. Nothing is more devastating to the dignity and freedom of the homosexual person than the feeling that he has not only lost control of his life but is unable to regain it. The assessment of responsibility for past actions done apparently under the force of compulsion is often almost impossible and is usually a purely academic exercise. The best the confessor can do is to point out that the compulsive person does have a modicum of freedom left and that he should use that freedom to become involved in a spiritual support group system.

The assessment of responsibility, however, in the non-compulsive homosexual is similar to the responsibility of the heterosexual person in sexual matters, with some differences. It is more difficult for the homosexual person to remain chaste in his environment—one in which, generally speaking, he is unable to share his difficulties and temptations with others for fear of ridicule; there is loneliness as well as the attraction of homosexual companions; and, unlike the heterosexual person who usually can look forward to marriage, the homosexual person cannot do so as long as his orientation continues. In many homosexual persons there is also a terrible sense of inferiority.[29]

Thus, while the non-compulsive homosexual person is morally responsible for his actions, his freedom is nonetheless very often diminished, more in some situations than in others. One may speak of a weakened will, but at the same time one must be careful not to excuse the homosexual person's past activity. As already observed, the chief responsibility of the homosexual person is to discover ways of strengthening the power of the will through renewed vision and fresh motivation, particularly through group-support systems. The accent should be on the future and on the need to develop an ascetical plan of life so as to be able to lead a celibate Christian life. The person with homosexual orientation, however, should be made aware that, despite the resolution to begin a new way of living, very probably there will be relapses because of the psychosomatic effects of long-standing sexual indulgence, but this must not be allowed to be the occasion of sterile self-pity.[30]

4. CIVIL LAW, MORAL LAW, AND THE RIGHTS OF HOMOSEXUAL PERSONS

Readers are familiar with the media's frequent coverage of homosexual-rights issues in various parts of the country, particularly in New York City. Questions arise concerning what are the rights that numerous homosexual organizations are fighting for. Are their rights, like those of heterosexual persons, not already adequately protected by the Constitution? Do their claims to unrestricted housing and employment come in conflict with the rights of other citizens, and if so, how are these conflicts to be resolved? These are some of the questions one needs to discuss. Before getting into any specific issues it will be profitable to review recent history on the civil law concerning homosexual acts.

In 1957 *The Wolfenden Report* in England suggested that homosexual acts taking place in private between consenting adults should no longer be subject to the criminal law.[31] Previously (1955) the Model Penal Code had made a similar proposal. Both proposals precipitated widespread discussion of the merits of such a revision of civil law, and the controversy continues to the present. In 1967 after considerable debate the main features of *The Wolfenden Report* became law in the *Sex Offenses Act*. While decriminalizing consensual acts done in private by adult males, the *Report* made three types of situations punishable by the law: (1) offenses against minors; (2) offenses against public decency; and (3) exploitation of vice for the purposes of gain. In the United States only a few states have followed the example of England, although the Gay Liberation Task Force continues to seek the repeal of state laws that make punishable by law homosexual acts freely done by adults in private.[32] What are usually illegal are acts of oral or anal intercourse, but in many states these acts were also forbidden to heterosexuals.

Notes

1. PCHP, 6. See also Ronald Lawler, O.F.M., Cap., Joseph Boyle, Jr., and William E. May, *Catholic Sexual Ethics* (Huntington, Ind.: Our Sunday Visitor, Inc., 1985), p. 197: "The Bible teaches that the sexual differentiation of the human race into male and female is divinely willed, that male and female complement each other, and that marriage, rooted in the irrevocable consent of man and woman to be 'one flesh', alone respects the goods of human sexuality."

2. Pierre Grelot, *Man and Wife in Scripture* (New York: Herder and Herder, 1965), pp. 34–37; Edward Schillebeeckx, *Marriage,* pp. 14–16, 20–21; John L. McKenzie, *The Two-Edged Sword* (New York: Doubleday, 1966). Grelot gives a full treatment of this question.

3. PCHP, 6.

4. See previous references to Pierre Grelot, Edward Schillebeeckx, and John L. McKenzie (*The Two-Edged Sword*). The latter holds that Genesis 1 and 2—the story of the creation of mankind as male and female—is also the story of the creation of marriage. See also *Summa Theologiae,* II–II, q. 154, aa. 11–12.

5. Excerpt from Cardinal Ratzinger's Letter in *The Philadelphia Catholic Standard and Times,* Thursday, Aug. 21, 1986, p. 2.

6. *Ibid.*

7. The Vatican document of Oct. 1, 1986, stated that "the deterioration due to sin continues in the story of the men of Sodom. There can be no doubt of the moral judgment made there against homosexual relations" (PCHP, 6).

8. *Homosexuality: A Symbolic Confusion,* p. 190.

9. *The Month,* May 1977, p. 167.

10. *Christianity, Social Tolerance, and Homosexuality,* pp. 93–98.

11. "A Scriptural Response to the Report on Human Sexuality," *America,* Oct. 1977, pp. 284–285.

12. See my review of Boswell's book in *The Linacre Quarterly,* Aug.

1981, pp. 265–275, particularly pp. 267–289, where I look at Boswell's use of Scripture.

13. The Oct. 1, 1986, Vatican document also interprets Lev 18:22 and 20:13, 1 Cor 6:9, and 1 Tim 1:10 as condemning homosexual acts.

14. *Catholic Sexual Ethics,* p. 200.

15. *Ibid.*

16. *The Sexual Language* (Ottawa: The University of Ottawa Press, 1977), p. 339.

17. (San Francisco: Ignatius Press 1986). See also Chapter Eight, Section 3, below, where AIDS is considered.

18. *Catholic Sexual Ethics,* p. 201.

19. See my reflections on complementarity: "Homosexuality" in *The Supplement to the New Catholic Encyclopedia,* vol. 17, pp. 271–273.

20. Edward Malloy, *Homosexuality and the Christian Way of Life,* p. 181.

21. *Catholic Sexual Ethics,* p. 201.

22. Herbert F. Smith, S.J., and Joseph Dilenno, *Sexual Inversion* (Boston: Daughters of St. Paul, 1979), p. 63, point out that there is a touch of irony in the typology of gay, gaiety, gayety. "Although the first meaning is merriment, gay can also mean 'loving forbidden pleasure, wanton', as in Funk and Wagnalls *New Standard Dictionary* (rev. ed., 1919) or again 'dissipated; immoral' in the *World Book Dictionary* (1976 Edition). Thus, 'gay' contains an element of license and forbiddenness as well as merriment in its very conception."

23. "Are Homosexuals Gay?" *Commentary,* Jan. 1979, pp. 20–22. See also *Catholic Sexual Ethics,* p. 269, nn. 65–67.

24. *Ibid.,* p. 27.

25. See *Original Unity of Man and Woman* (Boston: Daughters of St. Paul, 1981); *Reflections on Humanae Vitae* (Daughters of St. Paul, 1984).

26. *Principles to Guide Confessors in Questions of Homosexuality* (Washington, D.C.: U.S. Catholic Conference, 1973), pp. 8–9.

27. Irving Bieber et al., Samuel Haddon, Lawrence Hatterer, Colin Cook, Elizabeth Moberly, and Gerald van den Aardweg and others hold that sexual reorientation is possible in certain instances, provided the person stays with the program. With the exception of Moberly, the others present empirical evidence. Moberly's theory needs further verification, which we hope will come.

28. See Chapter Two, Section 3: distinction between compulsive and non-compulsive activity.

29. *To Live in Christ Jesus* (Washington, D.C.: National Conference of Catholic Bishops, Nov. 11, 1976), asks that the homosexual person be pro-

vided with a special grace of pastoral understanding and care. Van den Aardweg (*On the Origins and Treatment of Homosexuality*) sees the sense of inferiority linked to the origin of homosexual orientation. See our Chapter Three, Section 2, on van den Aardweg's thought.

30. *Principles to Guide Confessors in Questions of Homosexuality,* p. 9.

31. (London: Scottish Home Department, 1957). An excerpt from the Roman Catholic Archbishop of Westminster's comment on *The Wolfenden Report* appears in *Homosexuality and Ethics,* ed. Edward J. Batchelor, Jr., appendix, pp. 239–240. It draws the distinction between moral and civil law and states the issues but does not draw any conclusions.

32. See Edward Malloy, *op. cit.,* ch. 6, "Homosexuals and the Civil Law", pp. 145–162, for a brief history of the civil-rights controversy and his personal view.

24. Epilogue

John J. McNeill

This article first appeared in *The Church and the Homosexual.* 3rd ed. 1988.

Three major theses have traditionally dominated the thinking of moral theologians concerning homosexuality. As we have seen, each one of these theses is open to serious question today. In fact, in each case a new understanding of human sexuality and new evidence concerning the life-style of homosexuals seem to support the contradictory thesis.

The first thesis is the traditional belief that the homosexual condition, and subsequently all homosexual activity, is contrary to the will of God. It was God's intention that all humans should be heterosexual. Consequently, we must search for an etiological explanation of the homosexual condition in sin, whether that be original sin, the sin of the parents, or the personal sin of the individual homosexual.

In contradiction to that thesis, I have argued that the homosexual condition is according to the will of God. God so created humans that their sexuality is not determined by their biology. We are born male and female; we become men or women by a process of education that is unconscious for the most part. We now know from psychology that a homosexual phase is a normal phase of the sexual maturing process; that there is a homosexual as well as a heterosexual component in every human being; that always and everywhere a certain percentage of humans emerge from that complex learning process as predominantly homosexually oriented through no fault of their own. We have seen that in the light of today's knowledge of the Bible and of human sexuality, the traditional effort to prove from Scripture and from the natural law that such an orientation is contrary to the will of God no longer has any validity.

The second traditional thesis sprang from the first. Granted that the homosexual condition is contrary to the will of God, the presence of the homosexual in the human community is a menace to that community, and especially a threat to the values of the family. Consequently, everything should be done to isolate and "cure" the individual homosexual; or, failing that, to deny him or her any right to exercise their sexuality.

Over against that thesis I have proposed that, granted the homosexual is here according to God's will, God had a divine purpose in so creating human nature that a certain percentage of human beings are homosexual. In other words, homosexuals frequently are endowed with special gifts and a divinely appointed task in the construction of a truly human society. Rather than being a menace to the community in general and the family in particular, they have an important role to play in preserving and strengthening values such as interpersonal relations between the sexes and the development of a moral understanding of human sexuality outside the procreative context; values which are essential to the community and the family.

Finally, moral theologians have traditionally believed that the love which unites two homosexuals in a sexual union is a sinful love which separates them from the love of God and places them in danger of eternal damnation. In recent times theologians have attempted to buttress that judgment with so-called empirical evidence coming from certain psychiatrists to the effect that homosexuals are necessarily mentally ill and all homosexual relationships are humanly destructive.

In contrast to that thesis—and perhaps most controversially—I have posed the thesis that there is the possibility of morally good homosexual relationships and that the love which unites the partners in such a relationship, rather than alienating them from God, can be judged as uniting them more closely with God and as mediating God's presence in our world. The new empirical evidence in support of this thesis is, first of all, the psychological evidence that homosexuality is not necessarily an illness and the empirical evidence that there are many homosexual couples in stable unions whose relationship provides the context for mutual growth and fulfillment. Further, there is evidence of the work of the Spirit bringing into existence believing communities of homosexuals who in a spirit of love and forgiveness are seeking dialogue with that same institutional Church which so often in the past and in recent times has been their persecutor.

I have been asked frequently to clarify further what I mean by "ethically responsible homosexual relationships." Obviously what I mean first of all is to distinguish between a homosexual relationship that is built on selfishness and mutual destructiveness and a relationship that is unselfish and constructive. I agree with Thielicke that the primary moral problem in sexual relationships is sex as a depersonalizing force versus sex as a fulfillment of human relationship.

Further, I do maintain that there are objective values and moral norms governing the constructive human use of sexuality. These norms are objective in the sense that they are intimately related to the nature of the human person as such, and thus have universal validity wherever there is growth toward the fullness of human personality. There are the negative norms involving a relationship based on the value of justice—e.g., any sexual relationship that involves exploitation of another person is immoral. The positive norms are based on the value of interpersonal love as the ideal human context for sexual expression. These positive norms must be derived from the concept of the human person as an end in himself, or herself, and from the necessary conditions of possibility for a genuine interpersonal love relationship. Among these conditions I personally believe are such norms as mutuality, fidelity, unselfishness, etc.

I hope in the near future to explore a new ethical understanding of human sexuality as a form of human play—where play is understood as any action which has its meaning in itself in the here-and-now; that is to say, an action that is end-in-itself, just as the person is end-in-himself or -herself.

Beyond these general principles I believe it is impossible for me at this point to define more clearly or to lay down a priori what the nature of an "ethically responsible homosexual relationship" should be. This is a task which necessarily must be reserved to the Christian homosexual community and its own communal discernment of its experience. As John Milhaven said in his letter concerning my manuscript to the *National Catholic Reporter:*

> If anything is clear about human sexuality, it is that Christians today are experiencing values in it that were generally unknown to the traditional Christian. . . . Can one presume that there are no similar developments in homosexual experience? Can one expound the "meaning of human sexuality" without having a clear idea of what actually takes place in homosexual love in our culture? Can one pronounce moral judgments on homosexual behavior without ever taking a long, unblinking look at the actual experience of homosexual love in our times?
>
> May more and more of the real experiences of Christian homosexuals find through brave men . . . expression in the forum of the Church. It is up to the Church, all of us, to speak and listen and gradually, carefully, form a helpful consensus on this agonizing question.
>
> We will be doing only what the Christian community has done on troubling issues many times in the past.

25. An Ethic for Same-Sex Relations

Margaret A. Farley, R.S.M.

This chapter first appeared in *A Challenge to Love: Gay and Lesbian Catholics in the Church* in 1983.

Nearly every traditional moral rule governing sexual behavior in Western culture is today being challenged. Longstanding prohibitions have become so problematic that nations and states debate legal changes, and major religious traditions struggle with new formulations of ethical teachings. In the midst of all of this, there may be no question more intensely probed, more politically volatile, more personally troubling or liberating, than that of the moral status of same-sex relations. Like other questions of contemporary sexual ethics, it has emerged in a context shaped by new understandings of human sexuality, changing patterns of relationship between women and men, and increased control—through technology—of human fertility and reproduction.

Homosexuals today find themselves living in a society still greatly influenced by the Christian churches. Moreover, persons with homosexual or lesbian orientation have often been nurtured by the Christian community, and they seek to continue to give and receive life within it. In acknowledgment of these facts, official groups within many of the Christian churches, as well as individual Christian theologians, have struggled to review and reconstruct Christian views of homosexuality. Major attention in such studies has centered on the fundamental question of whether or not homosexuality offers one of the possible ways for Christians to live out the sexual dimension of their lives; whether or not same-sex relations and sexual activity have a place within the Christian community. My concern in this essay is to move beyond this question to another: What norms should govern same-sex relations and activity? It is to move, then, from the question of whether homosexuality can be morally justified to what must characterize it when it is justified. In order to make this move, however, I need to consider, at least briefly, the fundamental question of the general moral status of homosexual relations and activity.

When Christians look for light on an ethical question, they turn to basic sources: scripture, tradition (in the sense of the history of Christian belief discernible in the teachings and practice of the church and in the history of Christian theology), and other disciplines of knowledge (in this case, for example, philosophy and the biological and behavioral sciences), and contemporary experience. These are the sources, then, to which the Christian community must turn for an understanding of human sexuality in general and homosexuality in particular. But what have we thus far found by studying these sources?

NOT AN ABSOLUTE PROHIBITION

Scriptural Sources[1]

Although there is some pessimism in the Old Testament about the body as a hindrance to the life of the spirit and some fear of sex as a source of defilement, overall there is a clear affirmation of sex as a positive element in human life. Sexuality and sexual activity are natural, created by God, necessary for the well-being of human persons, and even a religious imperative. Central to the Old Testament tradition of sexual morality is the command to marry. Marriage is a religious duty, affirmed by all the codes of Jewish law. Two elements in the concept of marriage account for many other major laws regarding sexuality. The first of these is the command to procreate, which is at the heart of the command to marry. The second is the patriarchal model upon which the Old Testament ideas of marriage and society were institutionally based. These two elements provide a rationale for prohibitions against adultery and regulations regarding divorce, prostitution, polygamous marriage, concubinage, and to some extent, homosexuality. Thus, for example, adultery was considered a violation of a husband's property rights; polygamy and concubinage were accepted for a long time as a remedy for barrenness in a wife; homosexuality was looked upon as demeaning to males in part because it made them passive like females or at least did not allow them dominance over a female.

A third factor was influential in shaping Old Testament sexual rules: a concern to distinguish the practices of the Old Testament people from the idolotry of neighboring nations. The Leviticus prohibition against males lying "with a male as with a woman" is associated with this concern, as is the proscription of "improper emission of seed," whether through masturbation or homosexual activity. It is only later developments which tend to escalate specific prohibitions into paradigms of moral evil, obscuring the original intention of the laws. This seems to be true even in the case of the story of Sodom and Gomorrah, where the basic sin of the cities is described in other Old Testament texts as lack of hospitality, injustice, pride—but not as sexual sin in particular.

It is, of course, all too easy to explain away certain meanings of texts, or to relativize otherwise unambiguous passages by subordinating them to a larger context. Nonetheless, the simple recognition of the influence of factors such as patriarchalism, a concern for procreation, and a salutary fear of idolotry, alerts us to the problems we must encounter in any efforts to find in the Old Testament definitive answers to our questions regarding homosexuality.

The New Testament, too, sets problems for our search. It provides no systematic code of sexual ethics. The teachings of Jesus and his followers provide a central focus for the moral life of Christians in the command to love God and neighbor. Some fundamental virtues and principles fill out our understanding of this love. Beyond this, there are grounds in the New Testament for a sexual ethic which values marriage and procreation on the one hand and celibacy on the other, and which affirms a sacred symbolic meaning for sexual intercourse yet both subordinates it as a value to other human values and finds in it a possibility for evil. More specific guidelines for sexual morality appear in the New Testament only as responses to specific questions arising in specific situations. These responses have been used to support varying positions regarding such questions as divorce and remarriage, the status and role of women, and homosexual acts. Particular texts on homosexuality all offer problems for interpretation—whether because of our uncertainty about the meaning of terms, or ambiguity in the use of rhetorical devices, or disparity between the meaning of homosexuality during the time of Saint Paul and our own time (disparity between understandings of homosexuality as chosen debauchery or innate stable sexual orientation).

Whether one enters the battle of proof-texts, or stands before the biblical revelation as a whole, a modest conclusion that might be drawn is that neither the Old Testament or the New Testament offers us solid ground for an absolute prohibition or a comprehensive blessing regarding same-sex relations and activity. Rather, determining the meaning and import of the scriptures themselves in relation to this particular ethical issue (as others) has been and is a part of the unfolding history of Christian doctrine regarding human sexual activity.

Tradition

Like other religious and cultural traditions, the teachings within the Christian tradition regarding human sexuality are complex, subject to outside influences, and expressive of change and development through succeeding generations. Within this tradition, however, two dominant motifs have been particularly relevant to the moral evaluation of homosexuality: procreation as the purpose of sexual intercourse, and male-female complementarity as the essential ground for sexual activity.

Christianity emerged in the late Hellenistic age when even Judaism with its strong positive valuation of marriage and procreation was influenced by the dualistic anthropologies of Stoic philosophy and the Gnostic religions. Early writers in the church were persuaded by theories which idealized human virtue in terms of reason controlling emotion, mind controlling body. Thus, while they affirmed the basic goodness of sex (because it is a part of creation), they were deeply suspicious of the power of sex to overwhelm the mind and to introduce disorder contrary to reason into the attitudes and actions of the person. The disorder which characterizes sexual

334 / Margaret A. Farley, R.S.M.

desire as a consequence of sin could only be corrected, they thought, by bringing it once again under the rule of reason. This was possible only if it could be given a rational purpose, an overriding value as its goal. Procreation served as this purpose and goal. Moreover, as medieval theologians argued, procreation could be discovered by reason as the natural goal of the physical organs of human reproduction. With a procreative norm, then, sex could be affirmed as good, and it could also be disciplined by restriction to a circumscribed sphere—the sphere of marriage. Only in marriage could there be adequate provision for the support and education of children.

Protestant Reformation theologians relativized the procreative ethic and prepared the way for a growing emphasis on male-female complementarity in sexual activity and gender roles. They shared the traditional pessimistic view of fallen nature in which human sexual desire is no longer ordered as it should be within the complex structure of the human personality. In their view, so great is the power of sexual desire that it cannot be ordered—even by giving it the rational purpose of procreation; it can only be restrained. Marriage is the remedy of restraint. Through marriage, sex can be channeled into the meaningful whole of human life (which includes the good of offspring); in marriage, sinful elements in sexual passion can be forgiven. New emphasis on the givenness of sexual desire and the almost universal need to institutionalize it in marriage deflected attention from procreation and turned it to an interpretation of sexuality as relational. What was "natural" was now not so much the proper functioning of reproductive organs but the need of man for woman, and vice versa, and the proper structuring of that need in complementary roles.

So long as the Christian tradition continued to justify sex primarily as a means for the procreation of children, or sex in marriage primarily as a corrective to disordered sexual desire, there was little room for any positive valuation of homosexuality. Heterosexual marriage had to be not only the general norm for Christian life, but along with celibacy the only acceptable choice for Christians regarding human sexuality. The twentieth century, however, has seen dramatic developments in both Roman Catholic and Protestant sexual ethics. The tradition has been deeply affected by historical studies which reveal the early roots of Christian sexual norms, biblical research which questions direct recourse to explicit biblical sexual norms, and new philosophical and theological anthropologies. The procreative norm (as the sole or even primary justification of sexual activity) is gone. Even in Roman Catholic ethics a wedge was introduced between procreation and sexual intercourse by the acceptance of the rhythm method of contraception, and new understandings of the totality of the human person have tended to support a radically new concern for sexuality as an expression and cause of love.[2] The view of sexuality as fundamentally disordered is also gone. Though Christian theologians still underline the special potential which sexuality has for evil, the almost total suspicion of its destructive power has been seriously modified. Rigid views of male-female complementarity have been softened; equality and mutuality, shared capabilities and responsibilities, now appear as central elements in Christian theologies of marriage and family. Finally, traditional notions of Christian friendship,[3] not dictated by gender lines, have received new attention, and there is a growing sense of the need to understand more clearly the dimensions and the criteria of friendship.

Although the Christian tradition has offered absolute prohibitions of homosexual activities (and sometimes relationships) in the past, it has not done so on the basis of arbitrary commands. Negative rules have depended upon rational justifications. However, past justifications, as we have just seen, no longer appear with the same clarity. They have sometimes been widely abandoned or changed. Those who stand within Christianity as a living tradition must either find new justifications for former prohibitions, or modify the prohibitions. Without offering the last word for the tradition, another modest conclusion may be drawn: Just as it is certainly not possible to draw from the tradition, at this point, a comprehensive blessing on same-sex relations and activity, so it is also not possible to draw an absolute prohibition. The wisdom of the tradition requires more labor if its best insights are to be brought to bear on contemporary questions of homosexuality.

Secular Disciplines

One reason why the separation of sources for Christian ethics into "tradition" and "other disciplines of knowledge" is not wholly satisfactory is that Christian theology has traditionally incorporated secular disciplines into its reflection on Christian faith. The ongoing presence of natural law theory within Christian theological ethics is striking evidence of this. Protestant ethics has, it is true, often understood natural law as "revealed natural law," whose conclusions about human nature are drawn from a biblical doctrine of creation. Roman Catholic ethics, on the other hand, has considered natural law to be discernible by human reason itself—aided and healed by revelation and grace, but human reason nonetheless. In this sense of natural law, secular disciplines can be important, constituting the ways of reason as it tries to interpret human reality.

Various human sciences have contributed to contemporary understandings of homosexuality. Chromosomes and hormones, behavioral patterns and psychological problems and adjustments, statistical deviations and cultural differences have all been studied. As a result of such studies, there exists today a variety of theories regarding the etiology of homosexuality and its status as a human phenomenon. Many Christian ethicists have drawn from this array some provisional, and minimal, conclusions: (1) The empirical sciences have not determined homosexuality to be of itself, in a culture-free way, harmful to human persons (nor have they finally ruled out this possibility). (2) Same-sex orientation may be natural for some persons if by "natural" is meant a given characteristic, impossible to change without doing violence to one's nature as a whole. (3) Same-sex preference in sexual relations may be an option for many persons since human persons have generally a greater or lesser capacity to respond emotionally and sexually to persons of both the opposite or the same sex. Persons exist on a continuum of possibilities in this regard—those on one extreme able to respond only to the same sex, and those on the other able to respond only to the opposite sex. (4) Same-sex orientation need not entail the denial of one's given gender or failure to accept the givenness of human embodiment. Members of the contemporary gay community tend to reject an artificial adoption of heterosexual stereotypes as the model for their relations, and to affirm their own maleness or female-ness in same-sex relations.

Perhaps even more important to a moral evaluation of homo-sexuality than the reports of the empirical sciences regarding homo-sexuality in particular have been the new interpretations of sexuality in general. The emergence of psychoanalytic theory brought with it new perceptions of the meaning and role of sexuality in the life of each person. What the Christian tradition had thought to be an indomitable need and desire, distorted by sin, has come to be inter-preted as a natural drive, importantly constitutive of the dynamism at the base of the human personality. What for centuries was under-stood as an effort to order sexuality according to rational purposes has come to be understood as repression. However, psychoanalytic theory raised as many questions as it answered. Freud argued for liberation from sexual taboos, and from the hypocrisy and sickness which they entailed; but he also maintained the need for sexual restraint. Without the use of free choice to restrain sexuality, for Freud as for Augustine, the human spirit would be bound to lesser objects and occupations. Analysts, philosophers, sociologists, and criminologists have found connections between sex and violence, sex and exploitation, sex and insecurity.

Shifts have come in both contemporary psychology and philo-sophy regarding the meaning of human sexuality. Classical libido theory considered sexual desire a search for pleasure to be found in the relief of libidinal tension. Contemporary object-relations theory argues that the ultimate aim of libido is relationship with an object, not simple gratification of an impulse.[4] Contemporary philosophi-cal theories have focused on sexuality as relational; as such, it can function for human conflict or union. It can destroy individuals and groups, but it can also serve both the individual and the common good. Sexual desire had been suspect because of what was thought to be its power to distract and cloud the mind; now it is maintained that sex not only need not be distracting but may enable a harmoni-zation and concentration of powers so that the deepest and most creative springs of action are tapped close to the center of personal life. There is nothing in such theory that restricts sexual desire or activity to heterosexual relationships.

The last word is not in from reason's efforts to understand

sexuality or homosexuality. At this point, however, it is difficult to see how on the basis of sheer human rationality alone, and all of its disciplines, an absolute prohibition of same-sex relations or activity could be maintained. On the other hand, the ambiguity of sex remains, so that it is equally difficult to argue that all sexual expression is for the benefit of human persons. We are pressed once more to the task of discerning what must characterize same-sex relations if they are to conduce to human flourishing.

Contemporary Experience

The final source for Christian ethical insight is as apt to be misleading in its designation as the others. Scripture, tradition, and secular disciplines all must reflect on experiences, past and present. What differentiates the source I am calling "contemporary experience" is the unsystematic way we have access to it. In this context, I am referring primarily to the testimony of women and men whose sexual preference is for others of the same sex. Here, too, we have as yet no univocal voice putting to rest all of our questions regarding the status of same-sex relations. We do, however, have some clear and profound testimonies to the life-enhancing possibilities of same-sex relations and the integrating possibilities of sexual activity within these relations. We have the witness that homosexuality can be a way of embodying responsible human love and sustaining Christian friendship. Without grounds in scripture, tradition, or any other source of human knowledge for an absolute prohibition of same-sex relations, this witness alone is enough to demand of the Christian community that it reflect anew on the norms for homosexual love.

HOMOSEXUALITY AND JUSTICE

I began this essay by saying that my concern was to move beyond the question of whether or not same-sex relations and sexual activity can ever be justified. By arguing that no absolute prohibition and no absolute blessing can be established from the sources of

Christian ethics, I have meant, of course, to imply that *some* same-sex relations and activity can be justified. I have not tried to settle questions of whether homosexual relations are as humanly fulfilling as heterosexual, or whether they can be justified only as exceptions to what is otherwise normative. I have focused on what I have called a "modest conclusion" because there is greater possibility of agreement with it, and because I am convinced that it is sufficient to move us on to what is the most important task for Christian ethics in regard to homosexuality. That is the task of articulating an ethic *for* same-sex activity and relations. This task, in my view, is finally the same as the task of articulating an adequate contemporary ethic for heterosexual relations and activity.

One way to begin to identify ethical norms for sexual activity is to refine a justice ethic for the sexual sphere of human life. This may prove to be only preliminary to a more adequate sexual ethic, but it has the advantage of moving sexuality away from a taboo morality, without assuming a contentless ethic of love. Moral criteria for homosexual relations must serve in particular as a corrective to remaining tendencies in the culture to associate sex with defilement in relation to taboos. (The culture's marginalization and oppression of homosexuals has at times manifested the worst of these tendencies.) On the other hand, it will not do to end all ethical discernment by saying simply that sexual relations and activities are good when they express love; for love is the problem in ethics, not the solution. The question ultimately is, "What is a right love, a good love?" The articulation of norms of justice will begin to answer that question, for these will be the norms of a just love.

Justice, of course, can have many meanings. The classic meaning of rendering to each her or his due can be, I think, most helpfully translated into the fundamental formal principle that persons and groups of persons ought to be affirmed according to their concrete reality, actual and potential. The formulation of material principles of justice depends, then, on our interpretation of the reality of persons. Contemporary efforts to develop a sexual ethic must take into account new interpretations not only of human sexuality but of the human person. Thus, for example, new emphasis on the element of freedom in the complex structure of the person must give rise to norms for sexual behavior which place great emphasis on the need for the free consent of both sexual partners. Similarly, new under-standings of the nature and role of women must challenge tradi-tional understandings of an order of justice in which men and women were affirmed (each given his or her due) in relations marked by hierarchy and subordination. Identification of such fairly obvious norms for sexual relations suggests a way of organiz-ing a sexual ethic.

Contemporary concern for the nature of the person leads to a focus on at least two essential features of human personhood: auton-omy and relationality. These two features ground an obligation to respect persons as ends in themselves and forbid the use of persons as mere means.[5] Moreover, together they provide the central con-tent of the obligation to respect persons. Norms for a general sexual ethic, then, must not only satisfy the demands of these two features of personhood; they must serve to specify the meaning of the features.

The obligation to respect the autonomy of persons sets a mini-mum but absolute requirement for the free consent of sexual partners. This means, of course, that rape, violence, or any harmful use of power against unwilling victims is never justified; and seduc-tion or manipulation of persons who have limited capacity for choice because of immaturity, special dependency, or loss of ordi-nary personal power, is ruled out. It also means that other general ethical principles such as the principles of truth-telling, promise-keeping, and respect for privacy are fundamental to an adequate sexual justice ethic. Whatever other rationales can be given for these principles, their violation hinders the freedom of choice of the other person. Deception and betrayal are ultimately coercive, ultimately not a just affirmation of persons as autonomous ends in themselves.

Relationality is equiprimordial with autonomy as an essential feature of human personhood. Individuals do not just survive or thrive in relation to others; they cannot exist without some form of fundamental relatedness to personal others. In relation, awareness of autonomy is born, and freedom either grows or is diminished. Insofar as sexuality qualifies the whole personality of persons, it also qualifies the relation of persons to one another. Sexual activity and sexual pleasure are instruments and modes of relation; they can enhance relation or hinder it, contribute to it and express it. Sexual activity and sexual pleasure are optional goods for human persons (in the sense that they are not absolute, peremptory goods which could never be subordinated to other goods or for the sake of other goods be let go), but they can be very great goods, mediating relationality and the general well-being of persons.

In so far as one person is sexually active in relation to another, sex must not violate relationality but serve it. Another way of saying this is that it is not enough to respect the free choice of sexual partners. Respect for persons together in sexual activity requires mutuality of participation. This, of course, can be expressed in many ways, but it entails activity and receptivity on the part of both persons—mutuality of desire, of action, and of response.[6]

Underlying a norm of mutuality is a view of sexual desire which does not see it as a search only for the pleasure to be found in the relief of libidinal tension, although it may include this. Human sexuality, rather, is fundamentally relational; sexual desire ultimately seeks what contemporary philosophers have called a "double reciprocal incarnation," or mutuality of desire and embodied union.[7] No one can deny that sex may, in fact, serve many functions and be motivated by many kinds of desire, but central to its meaning, necessary for its fulfillment, and normative for its morality when it is within an interpersonal relation is some form of and some degree of mutuality.

This leads to yet another norm, however. Freedom and mutuality are not sufficient to respect persons in sexual relations. A condition for real freedom and a necessary qualification of mutuality is equality. The equality which is at stake here is equality of power. Inequities in social and economic status, age and maturity, professional identity, etc., render sexual relations inappropriate and unethical primarily because they entail power inequities—hence, unequal vulnerability, dependency, and limitation of options. Jean-Paul Sartre describes, for example, a supposedly free and mutual exchange between two persons, but an exchange marked by unacknowledged domination and subordination: "It is just that one of them pretends . . . not to notice that the Other is forced by the constraint of needs to sell himself as a material object."[8]

Strong arguments can be made for a third norm regarding relationality in a Christian sexual ethic. At the heart of the Christian community's understanding of the place of sexuality in human and Christian life has been the notion that some form of commitment, some form of covenant, must characterize relations that include a sexual dimension. In the past, this commitment, of course, was identified with heterosexual marriage. It was tied to the need for a procreative order and a discipline for unruly sex. Even when it was valued in itself as a realization of the life of the church in relation to Jesus Christ it carried what today are unwanted connotations of inequality in relation between men and women. It is possible, nonetheless, that when all the meanings of commitment for sexual relations are sifted, we are left with powerful reasons to retain it as an ethical norm.

As we have already noted, contemporary understandings of sexuality point to different possibilities for sex than were seen in the past—possibilities of growth in the human person, the gathering of creative power with sexuality as a dimension not an obstacle, the mediation of human relationship. On the other hand, no one argues that sex necessarily leads to creative power in the individual or depth of union between persons. Sexual desire left to itself does not even seem able to sustain its own ardor. In the past, persons feared that sexual desire would be too great; in the present the rise in impotency and sexual boredom makes persons more likely to fear that sexual desire will be too little. There is growing general evidence that sex is neither the indomitable drive that early Christians thought it was nor the primordial impulse of early psychoanalytic theory. When it was culturally repressed, it seemed an inexhaustible power, underlying other motivations, always struggling to express itself in one way or another. Now that it is less repressed, more and more free and in the open, it is easier to see other complex motivations behind it, and to recognize its inability in and of itself to satisfy the affective yearning of persons. More and more readily comes the conclusion that sexual desire without interpersonal love leads to disappointment and a growing meaninglessness. The other side of this conclusion is that sexuality is an expression of something beyond itself. Its power is a power for union and its desire a desire for intimacy.

One of the central insights from contemporary ethical reflection on sexuality is that norms of justice cannot have as their whole goal to set limits to the power and expression of human sexuality. Sexuality is of such importance in human life that it needs to be nurtured, sustained, as well as disciplined, channeled, and controlled. There seem to be two ways which persons have found to keep alive the power of sexual desire within them. One is through novelty of persons with whom they are in sexual relation. Moving from one person to another prevents boredom, sustains sexual interest and the possibility of pleasure. A second way is through relationship extended sufficiently through time to allow the incorporation of sexuality into a shared life and an enduring love. The second way seems possible only through commitment.

Sobering evidence of the inability of persons to blend their lives together, and weariness with the high rhetoric that has traditionally surrounded human covenants, yield a contemporary reluctance to evaluate the two ways of living sexual union. At the very least it may be said, however, that while brief encounters open a lover to relation, they cannot mediate the kind of union—of knowing and being known, loving and being loved—for which human relationality offers the potential. Moreover, the pursuit of multiple relations precisely for the sake of sustaining sexual desire risks violating the norms of autonomy and mutuality, risks measuring others as apt means to our own ends, risks inner disconnection from any kind of life-process of our own or in relation with others. Discrete moments of union are not valueless (though they may be so, and may even be disvalues), but they serve to isolate us from others and from ourselves.

On the other hand, there is reason to believe that sexuality can be the object of commitment, that sexual desire can be incorporated into a covenanted love, without distortion and loss. Given all the caution learned from contemporary experience, we may still hope that our freedom is sufficiently powerful to gather up our love and give it a future; that thereby our sexual desire can be nurtured into a tenderness that has not forgotten passion. We may still believe that to try to use our freedom in this way is to be faithful to the love that arises in us or even the yearning that rises from us. Rhetoric should be limited regarding commitment, however, for commitment is itself only a means, not an end. As Robin Morgan notes regarding the possibility of process only within an enduring relation, "Commitment gives you the leverage to bring about change—and the time in which to do it."[9]

A Christian sexual ethic, then, may well identify commitment as a norm for sexual relations and activity. Given a concern for the wholeness of the human person, and for a way of living that is conducive to the integration of all of life's important aspects, and for the fulfillment of sexual desire in the highest forms of friendship, the norm must be a committed love. This, of course, raises special problems in an ethic for homosexual love—problems to which I will return.

While the traditional procreative norm of sexual relations and activity no longer holds absolute sway in Christian sexual ethics, there remains a special concern for responsible reproduction of the human species. Traditional arguments that if there is sex it must be procreative have changed to arguments that if sex is procreative it must be within a context that assures responsible care of offspring. These concerns appear at first glance to have little to do with a sexual ethic for same-sex relations. Yet they suggest an important last norm for homosexuals as for heterosexuals in regard to relationality. Interpersonal love, in so far as it is just, must be fruitful. That is to say, it violates relationality if it closes in upon itself and refuses to open to a wider community of persons. The new life within it may move beyond it in countless forms (nourishing other relationships, providing goods and services for others, informing the work lives of the partners in relation, etc.), but all of them can be understood as the fruit of a love for which the persons in relation are responsible.

The articulation of this norm, however, moves us to another perspective in the development of a sexual ethic for same-sex relations. There are obligations in justice which others in the Christian community and the wider society have toward those persons who choose same-sex relations. Just as homosexual men and lesbian women must affirm one another and themselves in terms of autonomy and relationality, so they have claims to respect from the wider society and the Christian churches. Given no grounds for an absolute prohibition of same-sex relations, and none for an absolute blessing, homosexuals have the same rights as others to equal protection under the law, to self-determination, to a share in the goods and services available to all. Their needs for incorporation into the wider community, for psychic security, for basic well-being, make the same claims for social cooperation among us as do those of us all. The Christian community, in particular, is faced with serious questions in this regard. If, for example, a norm of commitment is appropriate for sexual relations among Christians; and if such a norm belongs to a homosexual ethic as much as to a heterosexual ethic, then the problems of institutional support must (like the questions of a sexual ethic) be addressed anew.

What I have tried to offer here is a beginning response to the question of what norms should govern same-sex relations and activities. My answer has been: the norms of justice—those norms which govern all human relationships and those which are particular to the intimacy of sexual relations. Most generally, the norms are respect for persons through respect for autonomy and relationality; respect for relationality through requirements of mutuality, equality, commitment, and fruitfulness. More specifically one might say things like: sex between two persons of the same sex (just as two persons of the opposite sex) should not be used in a way that exploits, objectifies, or dominates; homosexual (like heterosexual) rape, violence, or any harmful use of power against unwilling victims (or those incapacitated by reason of age, etc.) is never justified; freedom, integrity, privacy are values to be affirmed in every homosexual (as heterosexual) relationship; all in all, individuals are not to be harmed, and the common good is to be promoted. The Christian community will want and need to add those norms of faithfulness, of forgiveness, of patience and hope, which are essential for any relationships between persons within the Church.

It is not an easy task to introduce considerations of justice into every sexual relation and the evaluation of every sexual activity. Critical questions remain unanswered, and serious disagreements are all too frequent, regarding the reality of persons and the meaning of sexuality. What is harmful and what helpful to individual persons and societies is not always clear. Which sexual activities contribute to and which prevent the integration of sexuality into the whole of human life is not in every case evident. What can be normative and what exceptional is sometimes a matter of all too delicate judgment. But if sexuality is to be creative and not destructive in personal and social relationships, then there is no substitute for discerning ever more carefully the norms whereby it will be just.

Notes

1. For a more detailed study of these sources, see my article, "Sexual Ethics," *Encyclopedia of Bioethics,* 4 (New York: Free Press, 1978), pp. 1575–89. See also similar treatments in A. Kosnik, et al., *Human Sexuality* (New York: Paulist Press, 1966), pp. 7–78; Lisa Cahill, "Moral Methodology: A Case Study," *Chicago Studies* 19 (Summer, 1980): 171–87, reprinted in this book. The Cahill essay comes to a somewhat different conclusion than I do.

2. The history of this shift, and continued concern for a procreative ethic, is much more complicated than this brief reference to it suggests. For slightly more detail, see my article, "Sexual Ethics," p. 1582.

3. See, for example, Aelred of Rievaulx, *Spiritual Friendship,* trans. M. E. Laker (Kalamazoo, Mich.: Cistercian Publications, 1977).

4. See, for example, W. R. D. Fairbairn, *Psychoanalytic Studies of the Personality* (London: Routledge and Kegan Paul, 1952), pp. 137–42.

5. See my article, "Obligating-features of Personhood," to be published by Medicine in the Public Interest, 1983.

6. The best analysis of sex in these terms that I have found is that by Sara Ruddick, "Better Sex," in R. Baker and F. Elliston (eds.), *Philosophy and Sex* (Buffalo: Prometheus Publishers, 1975), pp. 83–104.

7. See T. Nagel, "Sexual Perversion," *The Journal of Philosophy* 66 (1969): 5–17; R. Solomon, "Sexual Paradigms," *The Journal of Philosophy* 71 (1974): 336–45; J. Moulton, "Sexual Behavior: Another Position," *The Journal of Philosophy* 73 (1976): 537–46.

8. Jean-Paul Sartre, *Critique of Dialectical Reason,* trans. A. Sheridan-Smith (London: NLB, 1976), p. 110.

9. Robin Morgan, "A Marriage Map," *Ms.* 11 (July–August, 1982): 204.

Part Six

MASTURBATION

26. Masturbation

Anthony Kosnik, William Carroll, Agnes Cunningham, Ronald Modras and James Schulte

This chapter first appeared in *Human Sexuality* in 1977.

There is no clear explicit moral prohibition of masturbation in either the Old or New Testament. Several passages are occasionally cited as condemning this practice (Lev 15:16; Dt 23:9–11; Gen 38;1 Thes 4:3–4; Rom 1:24 and 1 Cor 6:10), but contemporary biblical exegesis finds no convincing proof that the authors were addressing themselves in these texts to the morality of masturbation.[1] The testimony from tradition on the other hand is quite consistent in regarding masturbation as a serious moral wrong. Authors, however, have not always been in agreement regarding the reason for the evil of masturbation.

Originally, the deliberate wasting of the seed of life was deemed by most as the reason for the grave and intrinsic evil of masturbation. Because the male seed was regarded as the only active element in the procreative process, many authors even into the present century concluded on this basis that female masturbation did not share in the same moral evil as that of the male.[2] Other authors placed greater emphasis on the deliberate pursuit of complete venereal pleasure outside the marriage act as the source of the moral evil.[3] When it was realized that some prostitutes find no pleasure in their involvement in sexual activity but engage in sex for other reasons, this argumentation too was found to be inadequate. They were still judged guilty for their willingness to provide pleasure for others for monetary gain.[4] Still others considered masturbation as evil because it constituted a threat to propagation of the human race; it was supposed that if masturbation were permitted, men would not be anxious to enter marriage and procreate children. Most recently, there seems to be emerging a consensus that places the moral malice of masturbation in a "substantial inversion of an order of great importance."[5]

Throughout most of Catholic tradition every act of masturbation was regarded as gravely and intrinsically evil; if performed with full knowledge and consent, it was considered a mortal sin. But the widespread and repeated practice of masturbation, especially among males, created serious difficulties for many when drawing the logical conclusions. Human experience and common sense seem to be in sharp conflict with the formulations of theology. On the pastoral level, this clash was often mitigated and harsh judgments tempered by maintaining that full knowledge and consent were often lacking in such activity and consequently mortal sin was not committed.

During the last decade much discussion has centered around the question as to whether a single act of masturbation constitutes such a substantial inversion of the sexual order that it must always be regarded as intrinsically grave matter. The discussion stemmed from the theological developments regarding the nature of mortal sin and from an improved understanding of the complex nature of the phenomenon of masturbation. In what must be regarded as a significant theological breakthrough in this matter, Charles Curran successfully argued that every act of masturbation of itself need not be considered as constituting a deordination "which is always and necessarily grave."[6] This is not meant to imply that masturbation is not sinful or that masturbation can never involve serious sin. It maintains simply that not every deliberately willed act of masturbation necessarily constitutes the grave matter required for mortal sin. The vast majority of contemporary theologians would seem to agree with Curran's conclusion.

MAGISTERIUM

A review of some of the magisterial pronouncements on masturbation reflects much of the historical development:

1054—Pope Leo IX issued the first official teaching on masturbation, when he declared that "masturbators should not be admitted to sacred orders."[7]

1679—Pope Innocent XI condemned as at least scandalous and dangerous in practice the opinion of Caramuel that "masturbation is not forbidden by the law of nature; therefore, if God had not forbidden it, it would be good and sometimes gravely obligatory."[8]

1904—The Sacred Penitentiary declared that complete masturbatory acts of a woman during the absence of her husband are gravely illicit and that any confessor who approves this practice should be denounced to the Holy See.[9]

1929—The Holy Office responded to an inquiry as follows: Q. "Whether direct masturbation is permitted for the purpose of obtaining semen for the scientific detection of the contagious disease 'blenorragia' and its cure." A. In the negative.[10]

1952—Pius XII in his encyclical on the *Christian Education of Youth* made the following statement:

We reject, therefore, as erroneous the affirmation of those who regard lapses as inevitable in the adolescent years, and therefore as not worthy of being taken into consideration, as if they were not grave faults, because, they add, as a general rule, passion destroys the liberty requisite if an act is to be morally imputable.[11]

1961—The Sacred Congregation for Religious issued the following instruction to spiritual directors of candidates for the religious life:

Any candidate who has the habit of solitary sins and who has not given well-founded hope that he can break this habit within a period of time to be determined prudently, is not to be admitted to the novitiate . . . A much stricter policy must be followed in admission to perpetual profession and advancement to Sacred Orders. No one should be admitted to perpetual vows or promoted to Sacred Orders unless he has acquired a firm habit of continency and has given in every case consistent proof of habitual chastity over a period of at least one year. If within this year . . . doubt should arise because of new falls, the candidate is to be barred from . . . Sacred Orders.[12]

1971—*The Ethical and Religious Directives for Catholic Health Care Facilities* promulgated by the National Conference of Catholic Bishops states:

The use of the sex faculty outside the legitimate use by married partners is never permitted even for medical or other laudable purposes, e.g., masturbation as a means of obtaining seminal specimens.[13]

1974—The Sacred Congregation for Catholic Education in *A Guide to Formation in Priestly Celibacy* gives the following advice:

One of the causes of masturbation is sexual imbalance. The other causes are generally of an occasional and secondary nature, albeit contributing to its appearance and continuation. In education, efforts should be directed rather towards the causes than to attacking the problem directly. Only in this way can one promote the effective development of boyish instincts—which means an interior growing up towards domination of instinct. This is the growth that the causes mentioned above tend to obstruct.

Fear, threats, physical or spiritual intimidation are best avoided. These could encourage the formation of obsessions and compromise the possibility of a balanced sexual attitude, making him turn further in on himself instead of opening himself to others. Success as always will depend on the degree of awareness of the real causes of the problem. This is what formation needs to be particularly concerned with.

Self-abuse upsets the kind of life which is the educator's aim. He cannot remain indifferent to the close-up attitude which results from this. Nevertheless, he should not overdramatize the fact of masturbation nor lessen his esteem and goodwill for the individual afflicted. As he comes into deeper contact with the supernatural and self-sacrificing love of the educator, the youth is bound to be aware of his place in the communion of charity and will begin to feel himself drawn out of his isolation.

In trying to meet each difficulty, it is better not to offer a readymade take-it-or-leave-it solution. Rather, using the occasion for real interior growth, help and encourage the sufferer in such a way that he finds his own remedy. Not only will he then solve this one problem, but will learn the art of resolving all other problems which eventually he will have to face.[14]

1975—The Vatican *Declaration on Certain Questions Concerning Sexual Ethics* prepared by the Sacred Congregation for the Doctrine of the Faith states as follows:

The traditional Catholic doctrine that masturbation constitutes a grave moral disorder is often called into doubt or expressly denied today. It is said that psychology and sociology show that it is a normal phenomenon of sexual development, especially among the young. It is stated that there is real and serious fault only in the measure that the subject deliberately indulges in solitary pleasure closed in on self ("ipsation"), because in this case the act would indeed be radically opposed to the loving communion between persons of different sex which some hold is what is principally sought in the use of the sexual faculty.

This opinion is contradictory to the teaching and pastoral practice of the Catholic Church. Whatever the force of certain arguments of a biological and philosophical nature, which have sometimes been used by theologians, in fact both the Magisterium of the Church—in the course of a constant tradition—and the moral sense of the faithful have declared without hesitation that masturbation is an intrinsically and seriously disordered act. The main reason is that, whatever the motive for acting in this way, the deliberate use of the sexual faculty outside normal conjugal relations essentially contradicts the finality of the faculty. For it lacks the sexual relationship called for by the moral order, namely, the relationship which realizes "the full sense of mutual self-giving and human procreation in the context of true love." All deliberate exercise of sexuality must be reserved to this regular relationship. Even if it cannot be proved that Scripture condemns this sin by name, the tradition of the Church has rightly understood it to be condemned in the New Testament when the latter speaks of "impurity," "unchasteness" and other vices contrary to chastity and continence.[15]

CURRENT THEOLOGY

In reviewing the current theological literature, one can find three widely varying approaches to the morality of masturbation:

(1) *Masturbation is an objectively grave evil.*

This position maintains that every act of masturbation objectively constitutes a grave moral deordination and hence serious sin. It often appeals subjectively to mitigating circumstances to lessen imputability for repeated falls. Generally, however, it insists on the regular confession of each individual act in an attempt to eradicate this practice entirely from the life of the individual. The following excerpt from a recent publication exemplifies this approach:

> Self-abuse is a serious rejection of God's plans for the individual. Aside from the harm to the individual, each of us—from God's point of view—is a kind of window. If we are to give a clear view of him, we cannot pull the shades down on our personality and its development. And yet, this is exactly what self-abuse does. It constitutes a closing off of self to others and to real self. It is playing a game with life. This has to be a serious rejection of God and his designs, even if such persons claim they are not rejecting God or his plans.
>
> Where do we stand? Of itself, the act of self-abuse is an

intoxication or poisoning from within. Obviously, this is seriously offensive to self and God. However, since responsibility is measured by people's knowledge and strength of character, it could well be that because of their lack of awareness or weakness they suffer little or no guilt from their actions. It would be similar to a child or dazed person pulling the trigger of a loaded gun. The action is deadly but little or no guilt can be assigned to the one who pulled the trigger.

Such persons have, however, a responsibility to seek out help. Not to seek help, because of shame or attachment to their actions, could be serious, providing they have sufficient awareness and strength to seek help. As we have said, perhaps the final weighing of morality must be left to God. Those who are guiding such persons must not compromise on the goal. The way can be made smooth with kindness and understanding, but self-abuse should not be made light of. The goal is self-liberation not self-imprisonment.[16]

(2) *Masturbation, generally speaking, is objectively neutral.*
This position would maintain that occasional masturbation (with some periods of greater frequency and intensity caused by anxiety) is statistically, psychologically, and morally normal. As one writer puts it: "Masturbation is no less inevitable and no less a part of the psycho-physical development of adolescence than is nocturnal emission."[17] Some psychologists and educators suggest that the only thing wrong with masturbation is the misinformation, the myths, and religious taboos that surround it.

Some authors have even waxed poetic in their defense of masturbation, concluding that far from being the vice combatted by teachers and moralists, it is "the natural passage by which is reached the warm and generous love of youth and later the calm and positive matrimonial love of maturity."[18] Another outspoken author defending this view of masturbation as amoral, states:

It is necessary to have the courage to speak frankly to the child about masturbation and to recognize what are its rights. For the benefit of both parents and child, it must be said once and for all that the masturbation of the child and of the adolescent is a normal act which has no unfavorable consequences, either physical or moral, as long as one does not make the mistake of placing these acts on a moral plane, with which they have nothing to do.[19]

Those who hold this view of masturbation thus advise youngsters that it is a perfectly natural and normal sexual outlet, and that they need not fear any harmful consequences or experience feelings of guilt for having expressed themselves in this manner.

(3) *Masturbation is a "symptom" capable of many meanings.*

This approach regards masturbation as a symptom that must be carefully read to discern its true human and moral meaning. The 1974 statement from the Sacred Congregation for Catholic Education reflects this approach, which is very much in accord with the finding of the behavioral sciences, recent theological developments, and the judgment of human experience. It insists that any attempt to change or eliminate masturbatory activity will be successful only to the extent that one discovers and responds to the underlying cause or source of such activity.

The following categories would be illustrative of the varying meanings that masturbation can have and indicate the varying pastoral responses that are needed in dealing with this phenomenon:

(a) *Adolescent Masturbation:* Puberty signals the onset of important changes in the life of the adolescent. The curiosity awakened by the first experience of the sexual tension that arises in the adolescent quite naturally leads to a process of self-discovery that results in a certain tendency to close in on oneself. The fact that at this age sexuality is not oriented as yet toward a partner of the opposite sex complicates the problem and quite often leads to a search for release and satisfaction for these tensions within oneself. The youngster at this stage needs support and direction that will bring reassurance and foster growth and development in terms of reaching out to others. Directing attention to each act of masturbation can hamper this development by focusing attention on self and deepening the youngster's sense of inadequacy. Directing the young person to activities that strengthen self-confidence and encourage growth and interrelationship with others is the most important help that can be given. As the adolescent reaches out to others and progresses in personal development, the masturbation in most instances will gradually disappear.

(b) *Compensatory Masturbation:* Where youngsters find their healthy growth toward autonomy and personal responsibility repressed by tyrannical parents or smothered by oversolicitous ones, it is not unusual for them to turn to masturbation as a sign of reaction. The root of the problem in these instances is the unhealthy family life, which needs to be changed if the problem is to cease. Where changing the family atmosphere is impossible, teachers and friends can be of great help by showing interest and encouraging involvement in activities that provide opportunity for self-expression and autonomy.

(c) *Masturbation of Necessity:* The very strength of the biological urge that is part of human sexuality especially for some persons or at least at certain times for others finds in masturbation a relief from the tremendous sexual tensions that may be deprived of their normal outlet. Early habits may add to the difficulty of dealing with this tension by simple resistance. Celibates, married men away from home on business or in military service or prison, or spouses who for health or other reasons must abstain from intercourse for long periods of time often find themselves in this predicament. The use of masturbation to obtain reasonable relief from excessive sexual tension or to preserve fidelity would seem to be a matter of prudent choice of values. Moral malice in such instances ought not be imputed.

(d) *Pathological Masturbation:* Psychological maladjustment can at times be the root cause of masturbatory behavior. This is especially indicated when the impulse to masturbation seems to be a compulsion, bringing little or no satisfaction and yet frequently repeated even though there is no rational explanation for the behavior. Likewise, persons who regularly prefer masturbation even in the presence of opportunities for intercourse are seen to be operating out of a sexuality that has not been fully integrated. Counseling to help discover the deeper causes of such behavior would be appropriate.

(e) *Medically Indicated Masturbation:* Masturbation is generally accepted as the standard clinical procedure for obtaining semen for fertility testing or for diagnosing certain venereal infections. Such procedures do not constitute a substantial inversion of the sexual order but rather serve to preserve or promote the life-serving quality of human sexuality. In keeping with our understanding of human sexuality and the principles indicated for evaluating such behavior, procedures of this kind should not be viewed in any way as sinful or immoral.

(f) *Hedonistic Masturbation:* Masturbation simply for the sake of the pleasure involved, without any effort at control or integration, can be indicative of self-centeredness, isolation, and evasion of relational responsibility. Cases of this type deserve the serious attention of the counselor-confessor. Exploitation of one's sexuality freely, deliberately, and consistently in this manner creates a serious obstacle to personal growth and integration and constitutes the substantial inversion of the sexual order—an inversion that is at the heart of the malice of masturbation. Pastoral prudence will indicate that little can be gained by simply highlighting and condemning the sinfulness of each individual act. A far more radical conversion is needed in regard to the very nature and meaning of human sexuality and human personhood.

PASTORAL REFLECTIONS

1. Masturbation is a subtle and complex phenomenon. To condemn every act of masturbation harshly as mortal sin or to dismiss it lightly as of no moral consequence fails to do justice to the symptomatic nature of masturbation capable of many meanings. The sensitive pastoral approach outlined in the Sacred Congregation's *Guide to Formation in Priestly Celibacy* (1974), which insists on discovering and responding to the cause of such behavior, deserves serious consideration and implementation.

2. A single act even of willful masturbation seldom achieves that substantial deordination in a matter of great importance, which is generally considered to constitute the serious moral malice of masturbation. Such substantial deordination requires a consistent,

deliberate, self-centered pursuit of pleasure, which refuses to acknowledge or respond to one's relational responsibility toward others. Persons who occasionally masturbate must not, therefore, be automatically judged as being in the state of mortal sin.

3. Persons seriously struggling with the task of integrating their sexuality, especially adolescents, should be encouraged to receive the eucharist at every opportunity even though occasional incidents of masturbation may occur. The presumption should be that such persons have not sinned gravely and consequently have not lost their right to receive the sacraments. The regular celebration of the sacrament of reconciliation and the wise counsel of a prudent confessor can provide additional support in the struggle toward integration.

4. Little benefit appears to be gained from focusing directly on the masturbatory behavior. Highlighting the malice of each act of masturbation only serves to compound the problem and drive the person further into self. For this reason, directing the counselee to activities that are other-centered appears to be the most effective remedy for treating adolescent masturbation. Immediate confession after each act of masturbation ought not to be encouraged, though periodic discussion of one's progress in this area can prove helpful to the counselee or penitent.

5. Professional psychological consultation should be recommended only in those instances in which it is clear that the masturbatory behavior stems from serious psychological maladjustment and the counselee could benefit from such professional therapy.

Notes

1. T. C. de Kruijf, *The Bible on Sexuality* (Wisconsin: St. Norbert's Abbey Press, 1966) 40; J. Dedek, *Contemporary Sexual Morality* (New York: Sheed and Ward, 1970) 49–51; J. Fuchs, *De Castitate et Ordine Sexuali* (Rome: Gregorian University, 1963) 63.

2. H. Noldin, S.J., "De Sexto Praecepto et De Usu Matrimonii" *Theologia Moralis* (Austria, 1922) 76.

360 / Anthony Kosnik, et al.

3. *Ibid.*, 30, n. 29.

4. *Ibid.*, 21–23, n. 18.

5. Fuchs, 68.

6. Charles Curran, "Masturbation and Objectively Grave Matter," in *A New Look at Christian Morality* (Notre Dame: Fides, 1968) 214.

7. H. Denziger, A. Schönmetzer, *Enchiridion Symbolorum,* 33^d Ed. (Rome: Herder, 1965) n. 688.

8. *Ibid.*, n. 2149.

9. Reprinted in Marcellinus Zalba, *Theologiae Moralis Summa* (Madrid: Biblioteca de Autores Christianos, 1957) 160, n. 39.

10. Denziger, n. 3684.

11. AAS 44 (1952) 275.

12. Religiosorum institutio, n. 30.

13. *Ethical and Religious Directives* (Washington: U.S.C.C., 1971) n. 21, p. 7.

14. *Declaration on Certain Questions Concerning Sexual Ethics,* n. 9, cf. chapter 28 of this volume.

15. Russell Abata, C.S.S.R., *Sex Sanity in The Modern World—A Guidebook for Everyone* (Missouri: Liguorian Pamphlet Books, 1975) 48.

16. Cf. William Bausch, *A Boy's Sex Life: Handbook of Basic Information and Guidance* (Notre Dame: Fides, 1969).

17. Silves Venturi, cited in Havelock Ellis, *Psychology of Sex* (London: Pan Books Limited, 1959) 97.

18. Dr. Cherbuliez, cited in Paulo Liggeri, *Morale e Difficolta Attuali* (Milano: Istituto La Casa, 1958) 293.

27. Masturbation

Ronald Lawler, O.F.M.Cap.,
Joseph M. Boyle, Jr., and *William E. May*

This chapter first appeared in *Catholic Sexual Ethics* in 1985.

Masturbation is the deliberate stimulation of the genital organs to the point of orgasm which is not a part of sexual intercourse.[1] Thus understood, masturbation can be done either by a person acting on himself or herself (thus, its frequent description as "self-abuse"), or by one person acting on another. Throughout her history the Church has consistently held that masturbation, when it is a freely chosen act, is seriously wrong, for it always involves a failure to respect the human goods which all sexual activity should take into account. The Fathers of the Church,[2] the medieval Scholastics, and all moral theologians[3] until most recent times have been unanimous in condemning every deliberate act of masturbation as a serious violation of the virtue of chastity.[4] This same teaching has been proposed by the magisterium of the Church from the time when it was discussed by Pope Leo IX in 1054 to the present.[5]

In 1975, responding to the questions that had been raised by some contemporary theologians regarding the malice of masturbation, the Sacred Congregation for the Doctrine of the Faith firmly reasserted this teaching of the Church:

> ... both the Magisterium of the Church—in the course of a constant tradition—and the moral sense of the faithful have declared without hesitation that masturbation is an intrinsically and seriously disordered act. The main reason is that, whatever the motive for acting in this way, the deliberate use of the sexual faculty outside normal conjugal relations essentially contradicts the finality of the fac-

ulty. For it lacks the sexual relationship called for by the moral order, namely the relationship which realizes "the full sense of mutual self-giving and human procreation in the context of true love." All deliberate exercise of sexuality must be reserved to this regular relationship.[6]

The Church's certainty that of its very nature masturbation is gravely wrong is first of all rooted in divine revelation. Theologians have frequently cited certain key texts as witnesses to the scriptural condemnation of masturbation—for example, the Onan text in Genesis 38.8–10, or 1 Corinthians 6.9, where St. Paul lists among those who are excluded from the kingdom the *malakoi* or the "soft," or Romans 1.24, where he points out that those who reject God come to dishonor their own bodies.[7]

Contemporary scholarship points out that these texts do not *unambiguously* refer specifically to masturbation.[8] But in condemning irresponsible uses of sex generally, Scripture certainly does include a condemnation of masturbation. As the 1975 *Declaration on Certain Questions Concerning Sexual Ethics* states: "Even if it cannot be proved that Scripture condemns this sin by name [masturbation], the tradition of the Church has rightly understood it to be condemned in the New Testament when the latter speaks of 'impurity,' 'unchasteness,' and other vices contrary to chastity and continence."[9]

The Church has rightly understood Scripture to teach that genital activity should take place only within marriage in ways that rightly express marital love. From St. Paul (1 Thessalonians 4.1–5, 1 Corinthians 6.15–20) Christians have learned that their bodies are the temples of the Holy Spirit, that their flesh has become one with the flesh of Christ. Our genital organs, Christians have thus rightly concluded, are not playthings or tools that we are to employ simply for pleasure. Rather, they are integral to our persons, and our free choice to exercise our genital powers is thus to be in service of human persons and of the goods perfective of human persons. The goods to which sexual activity is ordered, as we have seen throughout this work, include procreation, marital friendship, and chaste self-possession. By respecting these goods when we use our genital powers, we honor the body that has, through baptism, become one body with Christ and a temple of his Spirit. When we do not respect these goods in our genital activity we act immorally, and we desecrate the temple of the Holy Spirit and abuse the body-person who has been purchased at such great price. It is this deeply biblical vision of human sexuality and of the human person that is at the heart of the Church's teaching on the immorality of masturbation.

This vision does not exclude a more purely ethical analysis of the immorality of masturbation, for one who chooses to masturbate exercises his or her genital powers of sexuality in a way that does not take into account the precious human goods that these powers are meant to serve. These are life-uniting and life-giving powers. And in choosing to masturbate we use these meaningful powers in ways which ignore or disdain their life-uniting or life-giving meaning. Psychologists note that there is a sort of narcissism involved in such acts, a turning in on oneself, in the use of powers which should serve one to go beyond oneself. This reason takes on added significance for the Christian, who is to regard him- or herself as a "vessel" consecrated to the Lord and a temple of his Spirit.

Objections. Despite the overwhelming weight of a tradition rooted in the scriptural view of sexuality, and the seriousness of the reasons presented in the tradition, some recent moralists have rejected the Church's teaching on masturbation. Three distinct lines of argument have been made: (1) some have argued that the constant teaching of the Church that divine revelation condemns masturbation as seriously wrong is simply mistaken; (2) others have argued that the Church is mistaken in teaching that all acts of masturbation are wrong, for only some masturbatory acts are really lustful; and (3) others actually hold that masturbation is of itself morally neutral and not in fact a bad kind of act. We will consider these objections in order.

The first objection is that the weight of traditional teachings on masturbation is not a reliable indication of God's revelation because this tradition is based upon a misunderstanding of Scripture. According to this view the true bases of the traditional condemnation of masturbation are found in Stoicism with its view that procreation alone is the purpose of sex, and in Manicheanism with its dualism and consequent denial that bodily life is good.[10]

This objection includes several unacceptable claims. The first is that Scripture does not condemn masturbation. This is altogether unacceptable, for it goes far beyond the denial that some specific texts unequivocally condemn masturbation, and proposes instead that the scriptural vision of man does not exclude masturbation. The Church, the authentic interpreter of Scripture, draws a contrary conclusion; and, as we have seen, her judgment is entirely sound.

The second unacceptable component of this objection is that the Church is radically mistaken in her most firm and insistent interpretations of Scripture. This overlooks the fact that the Church is guided by the Holy Spirit in proposing moral truths as part of what is necessary for salvation. A teaching so seriously proposed over so many centuries is certainly authoritative for believers. In fact, it would not be implausible to count her teaching on masturbation as part of the infallible exercise of the ordinary magisterium of the Church.[11]

The third disputable component in this first objection is that the Church's teaching on masturbation is based on Stoicism and a version of Manichean mind-body dualism. This is far from true. In fact, dualism of a pernicious sort seems to underlie the arguments which revisionists use to justify masturbation and other sexual activity that the received tradition has rejected.[12]

Those who accept masturbation cannot consistently regard their bodies and sexual activities as integral parts of their own selves and their personal lives, for such persons cannot regard their bodies as governed by the concerns central to their being, as sharing fully in the pursuit of intelligible goods. Their sexual organs and activities are taken, rather, as instruments for pleasure. The Church is not dualistic; permissive sexual morality is.

Nor is the Church's position based on a Stoic view that procreation is the only legitimate purpose of sexual activity. We have seen how the Church has grown in her explicit appreciation of the fact that sexual activity serves other human goods as well. The development of this appreciation has in no way been accompanied by any tendency to abandon her absolute prohibitions of masturbation, for masturbation serves none of the great goods to which human sexuality is ordered, and fails, in its pursuit of pleasure, to respect any of them adequately.

Obviously, the person-uniting and procreative aspects of sexual activity are ignored and undercut in solitary masturbation. These values are trivialized in homosexual masturbation, and, less clearly, though nevertheless really, in masturbation even between spouses. One reason for this inadequacy is found in the fact that normally the immediate purpose of masturbation is the pleasure associated with orgasm. It is this pleasure alone that is sought in such acts and not the pleasure in doing substantially good acts. Seeking pleasure in this way—as part of a kind of unsatisfactory self-integration—is necessarily incompatible with concern and respect for all the human goods.[13]

The second objection to the Church's teaching on masturbation is that it is not a grave moral disorder in some circumstances. Some who make this objection distinguish various kinds of masturbation: adolescent, compensatory, of "necessity," pathological, medically indicated, and hedonistic. Masturbation in most of these categories is held, contrary to the teaching of the Church, not to be seriously wrong.[14]

Now the Church has always acknowledged that circumstances alter cases. To perform an act of masturbation in some circumstances may be far more reprehensible than in others. Moreover, the Church recognizes that not all acts of masturbation are done with the full consent and knowledge necessary for grave personal guilt. Nevertheless, the Church has consistently maintained that objectively every act of masturbation is seriously wrong. To distinguish several different kinds of masturbation is not to provide any reasonable ground for thinking that some forms of masturbation are not gravely wrong. But reflection on some of these kinds, such as pathological masturbation, does correctly suggest that masturbation is at times not a fully voluntary human action.

"Medically indicated masturbation" may appear to be a genuine exception to the Church's general condemnation of masturbation. (This would mean, for example, procuring a solitary orgasm solely to obtain a specimen of semen for medical examination.) This type of activity could seem to be directed toward a morally upright and nonlustful purpose. It should be noted, first of all, that if this type of act were morally permissible it would be so not because there is an act of masturbation essentially like other acts of masturbation but one which can be morally justified because of its motive. Rather, it would be permissible because the act would be morally speaking a different kind of act—a medical act. Hence, there is in no case any reason for concluding that there are exceptions to the Church's firm judgment that all acts of masturbation are wrong. Still, it is by no means clear that medical masturbation is not in fact an act condemned by the Church's teaching on masturbation, or that, if it is in fact a different kind of act, it is an act which is not also morally wrong.

The designation of medically indicated masturbation as a medical act appears to be a rhetorical redefinition of the act based on the purpose of the masturbation. The inducing of orgasm seems to be of the essence of the act as a moral act—it is by inducing the orgasm that the sperm is procured. Thus, we have, in fact, a disordered sexual act—one directed toward orgasm outside of marital intercourse. The fact that there is a good purpose for such an act does not remove its disorder.[15] Moreover, even if medically indicated masturbation could be shown to be a different sort of act than lustful masturbation—that it is simply an act of obtaining semen for medical purposes and not the performance of a distinctively sexual act— it still does not follow that acts of this type would be permissible. There are, after all, other effective and practical ways to procure sperm. This activity, even if not essentially directed toward sexual pleasure outside of marriage, ordinarily so stimulates such pleasure, and so inclines the agent to delight in sexual pleasure unrelated to the real goods of sexuality, that it may be an unreasonable way to pursue the medical end. Thus, Pope Pius XII's authoritative condemnation of medically indicated masturbation is realistic and well founded.[16]

We turn to the third objection to the Church's teaching on masturbation: that masturbation is objectively a neutral act which *by itself* lacks any moral disorder. There are several versions of this thesis. One is that no *single* act of masturbation can be seriously wrong; if masturbation is wrong it is only because of the larger lifestyle in which it occurs.[17] Another version is that masturbation cannot be seriously wrong because masturbation is natural or normal, an inevitable phase in personal growth.[18]

The first version of this position—that a single act of masturbation cannot be gravely wrong, that only a sustained practice of masturbation as an essential part of one's life could have such gravity—is based on a view of human action we have shown in Chapter 4 to be mistaken, for the primary locus of moral responsibility is in freely chosen actions, not in patterns of behavior. One's freely chosen acts are what establish one's moral personality; one's character is established by these acts and can be radically changed by one of them.[19]

Of course, one can hold that a single act of masturbation cannot be seriously sinful because masturbation is just not the sort of thing that can be seriously sinful—that is, masturbation is not concerned with "grave matter." This is the second version of the view that masturbation is objectively neutral from the moral perspective. Although it is not surprising that many secular writers on sex regard masturbation as innocent or even good, and hold that the only evil associated with it is the mistaken guilt feeling induced by allegedly wrong moral teaching,[20] it is surprising that some Catholic moralists approximate this view. The reason why some Catholic moralists deny that masturbation is concerned with grave matter appears to be their conviction that something so statistically common cannot be seriously wrong.[21]

Now it appears to be the case that masturbation is very common, especially among adolescent males.[22] The moral significance of the statistics in this matter, however, is anything but clear. They report that many people have engaged in this behavior, but they do not indicate the nature of the individual's responsibility for such acts. Nor do they indicate the extent to which those who have masturbated do so frequently, or do so with or without judging their actions to be immoral or shameful, and so on.

Surely, these statistics do not contradict the experience of many confessors over the centuries which shows that those who earnestly desire to turn away from such practices find the resources to do so. It must be remembered that true moral norms state what ought to be the case, not what statistically is the case. A moral norm is not therefore a statistical generalization and cannot be refuted by information about what is statistically common. Thus, it does not follow from the fact that because the normal attitudes of a certain population are racist, the racism of the population is not objectively immoral. Nor would it follow from the fact that because most believers denied their faith during a certain persecution, it is not seriously wrong to deny one's faith. This argument therefore does nothing to undercut the common teaching of the Church that deliberate masturbation, like other sexual sins, is *seriously* wrong. The received teaching of the Church is only too clear. From the perspective of faith, there is no ground to doubt that masturbating is gravely wrong. Christian tradition has taught this constantly,[23] and the reasons for this teaching are integral to the Church's understanding of sexuality, chastity, and human life.

But the statistical information on which this invalid argument is based may suggest that masturbation is often not a fully human act.[24] As we have already indicated, the Church recognizes that even when a person does what is seriously wrong, the agent is not always fully responsible for the act. The act may be compulsive behavior for which the agent bears only indirect responsibility; moreover, an act can be in some measure deliberate and still not be fully free if it proceeds from weakness of the will. Whether or not a given act is truly a human act is determined by an empirical consideration of the circumstances of the act and the agent's state of mind and heart at the time. Nevertheless, the results of behavioral sciences can be very helpful in making these often difficult determinations. Moreover, the knowledge gained from behavioral sciences can be very useful in helping people to deal with compulsive behavior or morally bad habits. It would be a mistake, however, to assume that, in general, individuals or certain types of individuals are not responsible for their sexual behavior: "This would be to misunderstand people's moral capacity."[25]

To sum up: the Church has always taught that masturbation is seriously wrong. Even though the Church recognizes that sins of this type are sometimes not fully imputable, and pastors have shown great gentleness and understanding in helping those who wish to overcome sins of this type, the Church has never qualified her authoritative teaching on the serious wrongness of masturbation. Moreover, the objections to this teaching are based on poor arguments or perspectives contrary to the received teachings of the faith. There is no doubt therefore that the Christian ideal of chastity excludes masturbation, and that it is possible for Christians to acquire the ability to live in accord with this teaching.

Notes

1. See Joseph J. Farraher, S.J., "Masturbation," *New Catholic Encyclopedia* (New York: McGraw-Hill, 1965), 9.438, for a general discussion; for a more thorough discussion with several classical definitions, see *Dictionaire de Théologie Catholique,* ed. A. Vacant, E. Manganot, and A. Amann (Paris: Librairie Letouzy et Ane, 1902–1905), 15 vols., 9.1346–1347. See also Marcellinus Zalba, S.J., *Theologiae Moralis Compendium,* vol. 1, (Madrid: Biblioteca de Autores Cristianos, 1958), pp. 771–775, for a modern definition and discussion. Zalba defines pollution as the complete, separate use of the generative faculty. By *complete* he means to orgasm, by *separate* he means outside of sexual intercourse. He goes on to argue that all directly and perfectly voluntary pollution is intrinsically a grave sin.

2. See, for instance, Augustine, *Opus Imperfectum Contra Julianum,* 4, 11, 10 (PL 44.74); 3, 20, 38 (PL 44.72) and *De Nuptiis et Concupiscentia,* 2, 26, 42 (PL 44.460). The penitentials in use from the sixth through ninth centuries strongly condemned masturbation. See, for example, *Paenitentiale Aquilonale* (Canon 2) and *Luci Victoriae* (Canon 8), cited in Josef Fuchs, S.J., *De Castitate et Ordine Sexuali,* 2nd ed. (Rome: Gregorian University, 1960), p. 49. See also the references in John T. Noonan, Jr., *Contraception: A History of Its Treatment by Catholic Theologians and Canonists* (Cambridge, Mass.: Harvard University Press, 1965), pp. 70–77, for a discussion of patristic and Jewish views on masturbation.

3. For medieval thought, see, for instance, Thomas Aquinas, *Summa Theologie,* II-II, q. 154, a. 5. Zalba and Fuchs, cited above in Notes 22 and 23, are representatives of the manualist tradition.

4. It should be noted that not only in the Catholic theological tradition has masturbation been regarded as seriously immoral but also in the whole Christian tradition until relatively modern times. For Protestant thought on this subject, see references given by Derrick S. Bailey, *The Male-Female Relationship in Christian Tradition* (New York: Harper and Row, 1968).

5. See Leo IX, Epistola "Ad Splendidum Nitentis" ad Petrum Damiani, 1054, DS 687–688; Alexander VII, "Errores Doctrinae Moralis Lax-

ioris," September 14, 1665, DS 2044; Innocent XI, "Errores Doctrinae Moralis Laxioris," March 2, 1679, DS 2149; Pius XI, "Decree of Holy Office on Masturbation," July 24, 1929, DS 3684; addresses of Pius XII, October 8, 1953, AAS 45.677–678; May 19, 1956, AAS 48.472–473; Sacred Congregation for the Doctrine of the Faith, *Declaration on Certain Questions Concerning Sexual Ethics,* no. 9; Sacred Congregation for Catholic Education, "Educational Guidance in Human Love," November 1, 1983, no. 98.

6. *Declaration on Certain Questions Concerning Sexual Ethics,* no. 9.

7. On the use of the Onan texts, see the discussions in Noonan, *Contraception,* under Onan in the index.

8. See Fuchs, *De Castitate et Ordine Sexuali,* pp. 47–48; John L. McKenzie, "Onan," in his *Dictionary of the Bible* (Milwaukee: Bruce, 1965).

9. *Declaration on Certain Questions Concerning Sexual Ethics,* no. 9.

10. See, for example, Michael Valente, *Sex: the Radical View of a Catholic Theologian* (New York: Bruce-Macmillan, 1970).

11. See John C. Ford, S.J., and Germain Grisez, "Contraception and the Infallibility of the Ordinary Magisterium," *Theological Studies,* 39 (1978), 263–277, for an exposition of the conditions under which the ordinary magisterium teaches infallibly; these conditions are set out in *Lumen Gentium,* no. 25. In the remainder of this article Ford and Grisez apply these conditions to the teaching on contraception; some of this material is directly relevant to the teaching on the morality of masturbation; their analysis suggests that a similar argument can be made concerning the received teaching on masturbation.

12. See Germain Grisez, "Dualism and the New Morality," *Atti del Congressa Internazionale Tommaso D'Aquino nel Suo Settimo Centario,* vol. 5, *L'Agir Morale,* (Naples: Edizione Domenicane, 1977), pp. 323–330.

13. See *Dictionnaire de Théologie Catholique,* "Luxure: Especes," 9.1347–1349, for a critical summary of the theological arguments against masturbation. Plainly these arguments do not assume that procreation is the only legitimate goal of sexual activity.

14. See Kosnik et al., *Human Sexuality,* pp. 219–229.

15. See "Decree of the Holy Office, August 2, 1929," DS 3684; Henry Davis, S.J., *Pastoral and Moral Theology,* vol. 2, *Commandments of God: Precepts of the Church,* 8th ed. (New York: Sheed and Ward, 1959), p. 259.

16. See citations from Pius XII, in Note 26 above.

17. See Kosnik et al., *Human Sexuality,* pp. 227–229; Charles E. Curran, "Masturbation: An Objectively Grave Matter?" in *A New Look at Christian Morality* (Notre Dame, Ind.: Fides, 1968), pp. 200–221.

18. See Charles E. Curran, *Contemporary Problems in Moral Theology* (Notre Dame, Ind.: University of Notre Dame Press, 1970), pp. 159–188; Keane, *Sexual Morality,* pp. 62–68.

19. See Sacred Congregation for the Doctrine of the Faith, *Declaration on Certain Questions Concerning Sexual Ethics,* no. 10: "According to the Church's teaching, mortal sin, which is opposed to God, does not consist only in formal and direct resistance to the commandment of charity. It is equally to be found in this opposition to authentic love which is included in every deliberate transgression, in serious matter, of each of the moral laws."

20. Among the authors taking this perspective are: Albert Ellis, *Sex Without Guilt* (New York: Grove Press, 1965), pp. 10–19; Eleanor Hamilton, *Sex Before Marriage* (New York: Bantam Books, 1970), pp. 6–7, 13–16; James L. McCary, *Human Sexuality,* 2nd ed. (New York: Van Nostrand, 1979), pp. 183–184; Herant A. Katchadourian and Donald T. Lunde, *Fundamentals of Human Sexuality,* 3rd ed. (New York: Holt, Rinehart, and Winston, 1980), pp. 291–308. It is not surprising that these authors regard masturbation in such a casual way because they have adopted an extremely separatist view of human sexuality. They regard its procreative meaning merely as a biological function, and regard sex as simply one way for a lonely individual to break out of his or her prison of loneliness.

21. See the works of Curran and Keane cited above in Note 39, and that of Kosnik et al., previously cited so frequently in these pages.

22. André Guindon, *The Sexual Language* (Ottawa: The University of Ottawa Press, 1976), pp. 251–252, gives a variety of statistics from Kinsey and other sources. See also Farraher, "Masturbation," 438.

23. See *Dictionnaire de Théologie Catholique,* "Luxure: Gravité," 9.1340–1345, for a survey of biblical, theological, and magisterial discussions of the gravity of sexual sin.

24. For a sound, complete discussion on these points, see John C. Ford, S.J., and Gerald Kelly, S.J., *Contemporary Moral Theology,* vol. 1 (Westminster, Md.: The Newman Press, 1969), pp. 174–247.

25. See *Declaration on Certain Questions Concerning Sexual Ethics,* no. 9: "On the subject of masturbation modern psychology provides much valid and useful information for formulating a more equitable judgment on moral responsibility and for orienting pastoral action. Psychology helps one to see how the immaturity of adolescence (which can sometimes persist after that age), psychological imbalance or habit can influence behavior, diminishing the deliberate character of the act and bringing about a situation whereby subjectively there may not always be serious fault. But in general, the absence of serious responsibility must not be presumed; this would be to misunderstand people's moral capacity."

Part Seven

CHASTITY, SIN, AND SEXUALITY OUTSIDE OF MARRIAGE

28. Declaration on Certain Questions Concerning Sexual Ethics (1975)

Congregation for the Doctrine of the Faith

---

1. The human person, present-day scientists maintain, is so profoundly affected by sexuality that it must be considered one of the principal formative influences on the life of a man or woman. In fact, sex is the source of the biological, psychological and spiritual characteristics which make a person male or female and which thus considerably influence each individual's progress towards maturity and membership of society. Sex, as everyone is aware, is a topic which nowadays is frequently and frankly discussed in books, magazines, newspapers and other media.

In the meantime, morals are becoming increasingly corrupt. One of the most ominous signs of this is the unrestrained glorification of sex. The media and the entertainment world have spread the corruption to the field of education and the mentality of the age has become infected.

In this matter, some educators and moralists have contributed to an improved understanding of the values proper to each of the sexes and thus have helped people give expression to these values in their lives. On the other hand, others have proposed opinions and patterns of behaviour which are contrary to the true moral needs of the human person. Indeed they have been paving the way for hedonism.

All this has led, in the space of a few years, to the vigorous challenging, even by Christians, of doctrines, moral criteria and patterns of behaviour which had gone unquestioned hitherto. Many people, confronted with so many opinions contrary to what the Church had taught them, nowadays wonder what truths they must still cling to.

2. The Church cannot remain indifferent to this confusion of minds and corruption of morals. It is a matter of the utmost importance both for the personal lives of Christians and for the life of society today.[1]

Bishops know from daily experience that it is becoming increasingly difficult for the faithful to obtain sound moral instruction, especially in sexual matters, and that pastors are finding it increasingly difficult to expound moral doctrine effectively. Bishops know well that their pastoral office obliges them to meet the needs of the faithful in this important regard. Some of them have published important documents on the matter and so have episcopal conferences. However, false opinions and the immoral conduct to which they lead have continued to spread. Consequently, the Sacred Congregation for the Doctrine of the Faith judged it necessary to publish this declaration, in view of its function in the universal Church[1] and at the behest of the Supreme Pontiff.

3. Nowadays people are increasingly convinced that man's dignity and destiny, and indeed his development, demand that they should apply their intelligence to the discovery and constant development of the values inherent in human nature and should give practical effect to them in their lives.

However, man may not make moral judgments arbitrarily: "Deep within his conscience man discovers a law which he has not laid upon himself, but which he must obey. . . . For man has in his heart a law inscribed by God. His dignity lies in observing this law and by it he will be judged."[3]

Moreover, God has revealed his plan of salvation to us Christians and has held up to us the teaching and example of Christ, the Saviour and Sanctifier, as the supreme and unchangeable law of life. Christ said: "I am the light of the world. No follower of mine shall wander in the dark; he shall have the light of life."[4]

Therefore, man's true dignity cannot be achieved unless the essential order of his nature be observed. It must, of course, be recognized that in the course of history civilization has taken many forms, that the requirements for human living have changed considerably and that many changes are still to come. But limits must be set to the evolution of mores and life-styles, limits set by the unchangeable principles based on the elements that go to make up the human person and on his essential relationships. Such things transcend historical circumstances.

These fundamental principles, which can be perceived by human reason, are contained in "the divine law itself—eternal, objective and universal, by which God orders, directs and governs the whole world and the ways of the human community according to a plan conceived in his wisdom and love. God has enabled man to participate in this law of his so that, under the gentle disposition of his divine providence, many may be able to arrive at a deeper and deeper knowledge of the unchanging truth."[5] This divine law is accessible to our minds.

4. Consequently, it is wrong to assert as many do today that neither human nature nor revealed law provide any absolute and unchangeable norms as a guide for individual actions, that all they offer is the general law of charity and respect for the human person. Proponents of this view allege in its support that the norms of the natural law, as they are called, and the precepts of sacred scripture are to be seen rather as patterns of behaviour found in particular cultures at given moments of history.

Since revelation and, in its own sphere, philosophy have to do with the deepest needs of mankind, they inevitably at the same time reveal the unchangeable laws inscribed in man's nature and which are identical in all rational beings.

The Church was founded by Christ as "the pillar and bulwark of the truth."[6] It preserves without ceasing and transmits without error the truths of the moral order. It interprets authentically both revealed positive law and "the principles of the moral order which spring from human nature itself"[7] and which relate to man's full development and sanctification. Throughout its history the Church has always held a certain number of precepts of the natural law to be absolute and unchangeable and in its eyes to disobey them is to go against the teaching and spirit of the gospel.

5. Since sexual ethics have to do with certain fundamental values of human and Christian life, this general teaching applies equally to sexual ethics. There are principles and norms in sexual

ethics which the Church has always proclaimed as part of her teaching and has never had any doubt about it, however much the opinions and mores of the world opposed them. These principles and norms in no way owe their origin to a particular culture, but rather to knowledge of the divine law and of human nature. They do not therefore cease to oblige or become doubtful because cultural changes take place.

These are the principles on which the Second Council of the Vatican based its suggestions and directives for the establishment and the organization of a social order in which due account would be taken of the equal dignity of men and women, while respecting the difference between them.[8]

In speaking of "man's sexuality and the faculty of reproduction," the Council noted that they "wondrously surpassed the endowments of lower forms of life."[9] It then dealt one by one with the principles and rules which relate to human sexuality in marriage and which are based on the specific purpose of sexuality.

With regard to the matter in hand, the Council declares that when assessing the propriety of conjugal acts, determining if they accord with true human dignity, "it is not enough to take only the good intention and the evaluation of motives into account. Objective criteria must be used, criteria based on the nature of the human person and of human action, criteria which respect the total meaning of mutual self-giving and human procreation in the context of true love."[10]

This last quotation summarizes the Council's teaching on the finality of the sexual act and on the principal criterion of its morality: when the finality of the act is respected the moral goodness of the act is ensured. This teaching is explained in greater detail in the same Constitution.[11]

This same principle, which the Church derives from divine revelation and from its authentic interpretation of the natural law, is at the core of its traditional teaching that only in legitimate marriage does the use of the sexual faculty find its true meaning and its probity.[12]

6. It is not the intention of this declaration to deal with all abuses of sex, nor with all that is involved in the cultivation of chastity. Its object is rather to re-state the Church's norms with

regard to certain points of doctrine. It would seem that it has become a matter of urgent necessity to oppose the grave errors and depraved conduct which are now widespread.

7. Nowadays many claim the right to sexual intercourse before marriage, at least for those who have a firm intention of marrying and whose love for one another, already conjugal as it were, is deemed to demand this as its natural outcome. This argument is put with particular insistence when the celebration of marriage is impeded by external circumstances or when this intimate relationship is judged necessary for the preservation of love.

This opinion is contrary to Christian teaching, which asserts that sexual intercourse may take place only within marriage. No matter how definite the intention of those who indulge in premarital sex, the fact is that such liaisons can scarcely ensure mutual sincerity and fidelity in a relationship between a man and a woman, nor, especially, can they protect it from inconstancy of desires or whim. Jesus willed that such a union be stable and he restored it to its original condition, based on the difference between the sexes: "Have you not read that the creator from the beginning made them male and female and that he said: 'This is why a man must leave father and mother, and cling to his wife, and the two become one body. They are no longer two, therefore, but one body. So then, what God has united, man must not divide.' "[13] St Paul was more explicit, when he taught that if the unmarried or widows are unable to remain continent they have no alternative but to marry: "Better be married than burn with vain desire."[14] In marriage the love of a couple for each other becomes part of Christ's unfailing love for the Church.[15] An incontinent union of bodies defiles the temple of the Holy Spirit which the Christian himself has become.[16] Sexual intercourse is not lawful, therefore, save between a man and a woman who have embarked upon a permanent, life-long partnership.

The Church has always understood this and taught it[17] and has found the fullest confirmation of its teaching in natural philosophy and the testimony of history.

Experience teaches that love must be protected by the stability of marriage if sexual intercourse is really to meet the demands of its own finality and of human dignity. For this to be achieved there is need of a contract sanctioned and protected by society. The marriage contract inaugurates a state of life which is of the greatest importance. It makes possible a union between husband and wife that is exclusive and it promotes the good of their family and of the whole of human society. In fact, pre-marital liaisons very often exclude the expectation of a family. The love which, wrongly, is portrayed as conjugal will not be able to develop into paternal and maternal love, as it certainly should. Or, if children are born to partners in such a union it will be to their detriment. They will be deprived of a stable family-life in which to grow up properly and through which to find their place in the community.

Those who wish to be united in matrimony should, therefore, manifest their consent externally and in a manner which the community accepts as valid. The faithful, for their part, should declare their consent to marry in the way prescribed by the laws of the Church. This makes their marriage one of Christ's sacraments.

8. In our day there are those who, relying on the findings of psychology, have begun to judge homosexual relationships indulgently and even to excuse them completely. This goes against the constant teaching of the Magisterium and the moral sense of the Christian people.

They draw a distinction, not, without reason, between two kinds of homosexuals. The first kind consists of homosexuals whose condition is temporary or at least is not incurable. It can be due to a faulty education, a lack of normal sexual development, to habit or bad example or other similar causes. The second type consists of homosexuals whose condition is permanent and who are such because of some kind of innate impulse or because of a constitutional defect presumed to be incurable.

Many argue that the condition of the second type of homosexuals is so natural that it justifies homosexual relations for them, in the context of a genuine partnership in life and love analogous to marriage, and granted that they feel quite incapable of leading solitary lives.

Certainly, pastoral care of such homosexuals should be considerate and kind. The hope should be instilled in them of one day overcoming their difficulties and their alienation from society. Their culpability will be judged prudently. However, it is not permissible to employ any pastoral method or theory to provide moral justification for their actions, on the grounds that they are in keeping with their condition. Sexual relations between persons of the same sex are necessarily and essentially disordered according to the objective moral order. Sacred scripture condemns them as gravely depraved and even portrays them as the tragic consequence of rejecting God.[18] Of course, the judgment of sacred scripture does not imply that all who suffer from this deformity are by that very fact guilty of personal fault. But it does show that homosexual acts are intrinsically disordered and may never be approved in any way whatever.

9. The traditional teaching of the Catholic Church that masturbation is gravely sinful is frequently doubted nowadays if not expressly denied. It is claimed that psychology and sociology show that, especially in adolescents, it is a normal concomitant of growth towards sexual maturity and that for this reason no grave fault is involved. The only exception is when a person deliberately indulges in solitary pleasure focussed exclusively on self (*ipsatio*), since such an action would be totally opposed to that loving partnership between persons of opposite sexes which, indeed, they claim to be the principal object of sexual activity.

The opinion, however, is contrary to both the teaching and the pastoral practice of the Church. Whatever force there may be in certain biological and philosophical arguments put forward from time to time by theologians, the fact remains that both the magisterium of the Church, in the course of a constant tradition, and the moral sense of the faithful have been in no doubt and have firmly maintained that masturbation is an intrinsically and gravely disordered action.[19] The principal argument in support of this truth is that the deliberate use of the sexual faculty, for whatever reason, outside of marriage is essentially contrary to its purpose. For it lacks that sexual relationship demanded by the moral order and in which "the total meaning of mutual self-giving and human procreation in the context of true love"[20] is achieved. All deliberate sexual activity must therefore be referred to the married state. Although it cannot be established that sacred scripture condemned masturbation by name, the tradition of the Church has rightly taken it to have been condemned by the New Testament when it speaks of "uncleanness" and "unchastity" and other vices contrary to chastity and continence.

Sociological investigations can disclose the incidence of masturbation in this or that region, among this or that people, in any circumstances of time or place that are chosen for investigation. That is how facts are collected. But facts do not furnish a rule for judging the morality of human acts.[21] The incidence is linked, it is true, with the weakness implanted in man by original sin. But it is also linked with the loss of the sense of God, with the corruption of morals caused by the commercialization of vice, with the unrestrained licence of so many public entertainments and publications, with the neglect of modesty, which is the guardian of chastity.

Modern psychology has much that is valid and useful to offer on the subject of masturbation. It is helpful for gauging moral responsibility more accurately and for directing pastoral activity along the right lines. It can enable one to understand how adolescent immaturity, which sometimes outlasts adolescence, the lack of psychological balance and ingrained habit can influence a person's behaviour, diminishing his responsibility for his actions, with the result that he is not always guilty of subjectively grave fault. But the absence of grave responsibility must not always be presumed. If it were it would scarcely be a recognition of men's ability to behave morally.

In the pastoral ministry itself, when there is a question of reaching a sound judgment on an individual case, the habitual general conduct of the person concerned should be taken into account, not only the practice of justice and charity but also the care given to the observance of the special precept of chastity. In particular, one should ascertain whether necessary natural and supernatural helps are being used which age-long Christian ascetical experience recommends for curbing passion and making progress in virtue.

10. There is nowadays a considerable threat to the observance of the moral law on sexual matters and to the practice of chastity, especially among less fervent Christians. The threat is posed by the current tendency to minimize the reality of grave sin as much as possible, at least in the concrete, and even at times to deny its existence altogether. Some have gone on to assert that mortal sin, which

separated man from God, is to be found only in the direct and formal refusal of God's call, or when a person deliberately chooses self-love, to the total exclusion of the neighbour. They say that only then is there question of a "fundamental option"—that is, a decision of the will which involves the person totally and without which there is no mortal sin. For it is by this option that from the depths of his personality a man adopts or ratifies a fundamental attitude towards God or people. On the contrary, they say, actions which are termed "peripheral" (in which, they say, the choice is often not definitive) do not succeed in changing a person's fundamental option. Indeed, since they are often done out of habit, there is then even less chance of their doing so. Therefore, while such actions can indeed weaken a person's fundamental option, they cannot change it completely. Now, according to these authors, it is more difficult to change a fundamental option for God in sexual matters, where normally it is not by fully deliberate and responsible actions that a person violates the moral order, but rather under the influence of passion or because of weakness or immaturity; sometimes it happens because a person wrongly thinks he can thus express love for his neighbour. Social pressures are often a further cause.

It is true that it is a person's fundamental option which ultimately defines adequately his moral stance. But it can be radically altered by individual actions, especially when, as often happens, they have already been prepared for by previous less deliberate actions. However that may be, it is scarcely correct to say that individual actions are not sufficient to constitute mortal sin (*mortale peccatum*).

According to the Church's teaching, mortal sin, which is opposed to God, is not found solely in the formal and direct refusal to obey the precept of charity. It is also found in that opposition to true love which is involved in every deliberate transgression of the moral law in a grave matter (*in re gravi*).

Christ designated the double law of charity as the foundation of moral life. "Everything in the law and the prophets hangs on these two commandments."[22] They include therefore the other individual commandments. To the young man who asked him: "What good must I do to gain eternal life?" Jesus replied: ". . . if you wish to enter into life, keep the commandments . . . Do not murder; do not commit adultery; do not steal; do not give false evidence; honour your father and your mother; and love your neighbour as yourself."[23]

A person commits mortal sin, therefore, not only when his actions stem from direct contempt for God and his neighbour, but also when knowingly and willingly, for whatever reason, he makes a choice which is gravely at variance with right order (*aliquid graviter inordinatum*). For in that choice, as has been said, contempt for the divine precept is already implied: it involves turning away from God and losing charity. According to Christian and the Church's teaching, and as right reason acknowledges, sexual morality encompasses such important human values that every violation of it is objectively grave (*objective . . . gravis*).[24]

It must be acknowledged that, granted their nature and causes, totally free consent may easily be lacking in sins of sex. Prudence and caution are needed therefore in passing any judgment on a person's responsibility. The words of scripture are relevant here: "Man looks at appearances, but God looks at the heart."[25] However, while prudence is recommended in judging the subjective gravity of an individual sinful action (*actus pravi*), it in no way follows that there are no mortal sins in matters of sex.

Pastors of souls must therefore be patient and kind. However, they may not set God's commandments at naught nor diminish men's obligations more than is right. "It is a great charity to souls to refuse to minimize any of the saving teaching of Christ, but this attitude must always go hand in hand with tolerance and charity. The Redeemer himself gave an example of it when talking to people and when dealing with them. He came not to judge but to save the world. He was unsparing in his condemnation of sin, but was patient and merciful towards sinners."[26]

11. As has already been said, the purpose of this declaration is to put the faithful on their guard against certain current errors and patterns of behaviour. The virtue of chastity, however, does not at all consist solely in avoiding these faults. It demands something more as well: achievement of higher goals. It is a virtue which affects the whole person, both inwardly and in external behaviour.

People should cultivate this virtue in a way that is suited to their state of life. Some profess virginity or consecrated celibacy which enables them to give themselves to God alone with undivided heart in a remarkable manner.[27] Others live in the way prescribed for all by the moral law, whether they are married or single. However, in every state of life, chastity is not confined to an external bodily quality. It must purify the heart, as Christ said: "You have learned that they were told, 'Do not commit adultery.' But what I tell you is this: If a man looks on a woman with a lustful eye, he has already committed adultery with her in his heart."[28]

Chastity is part of that continence which St Paul numbers among the gifts of the Holy Spirit. Impurity, however, he condemns as a vice particularly unworthy of a Christian and as one which merits exclusion from the kingdom.[29] "This is the will of God, that you should be holy: you must abstain from fornication; each one of you must learn to gain mastery over his body, to hallow and honour it, not giving way to lust like the pagans who are ignorant of God; and no man must do his brother wrong in this matter. . . . For God called us to holiness, not to impurity. Anyone therefore who flouts these rules is flouting, not man, but God who bestows upon you his Holy Spirit."[30] Fornication and indecency of any kind, or ruthless greed, must not be as much as mentioned among you, as befits the people of God. No coarse, stupid, or flippant talk; these things are out of place; you should rather be thanking God. For be very sure of this: no one given to fornication or indecency, or the greed which makes an idol of gain, has any share in the kingdom of Christ and of God. Do not let anyone deceive you with shallow arguments; it is for all these things that God's dreadful judgment is coming upon his rebel subjects. Have no part or lot with them. For though you were once all darkness, now as Christians you are light. Live like men who are at home in daylight, for where light is, there all goodness springs up, all justice and truth."[31]

Further, St Paul indicates a specifically Christian motive for practising chastity. He condemns the sin of fornication, but not merely because the action injures a persons' neighbours or the social order. He condemns it because the fornicator offends Christ, by whose blood he was saved and whose member he is, and he offends the Holy Spirit, whose temple he is: "Do you know that your bodies are limbs and organs of Christ? . . . Every other sin that a man can commit is outside his own body; but the fornicator sins against his own body. Do you know that your body is a shrine of the indwelling

Holy Spirit, and the Spirit is God's gift to you? You do not belong to yourselves, you were bought at a price. Then honour God in your body."[32]

The more the faithful appreciate the importance of chastity and its necessary role in their lives, the more clearly will they perceive, by a kind of spiritual instinct, its directives and counsels. It will also be easier for them, in obedience to the magisterium of the Church, to accept and comply with the dictates of a right conscience in individual instances.

12. The apostle Paul has a vivid description of the bitter interior struggle, experienced by a man enslaved to sin, between "the law that . . . (his) reason approves" and another law, which is in his "bodily members" and which holds him captive.[33] Man, however, can be liberated from "this body doomed to death" through the grace of Jesus Christ.[34] This grace is given to men. They are justified through it and in Christ Jesus the life-giving law of the Spirit has set them free from the law of sin and death.[35] St Paul therefore implores them: "So sin must no longer reign in your mortal body, exacting obedience to the body's desires."[36]

However, while it is true that this liberation fits us for the service of God in a new life, it does not remove the concupiscence which comes from original sin, nor does it remove the inducements to evil provided by this world which lies wholly "in the power of the evil one."[37] Thus St Paul encourages the faithful to overcome temptations by the power of God,[38] to "stand firm against the devices of the devil,"[39] by faith, watchful prayer[40] and austerity of life, by which the body is brought into subjection to the Spirit.[41]

The Christian life, which consists in following in the footsteps of Christ, requires of every one that "he must leave self behind; day after day must take up his cross,"[42] sustained by the hope of reward, for "if we died with him, we shall live with him; if we endure, we shall reign with him."[43]

Granted the forcefulness of these admonitions, Christians of today—indeed, today more than ever before—should use the means which the Church has always recommended for living a chaste life. They are: discipline of the senses and of the mind, vigilance and prudence in avoiding occasions of sin, modesty, moderation in amusements, wholesome pursuits, constant prayer, frequent recourse to the sacraments of Penance and the Eucharist. Young people especially should diligently develop devotion to the Immaculate Mother of God and should take as models the lives of the saints and of other Christians, especially young Christians, who excelled in the practice of chastity.

It is particularly important that everyone should hold the virtue of chastity in high esteem, its beauty and its radiant splendour. This virtue emphasizes man's dignity and opens man to a love which is true, magnanimous, unselfish and respectful of others.

13. It is for the bishops to instruct the faithful in sexual morality, however difficult this may be today because of the thinking and behaviour-patterns which are everywhere prevalent. The traditional teaching must be studied more deeply. It must be communicated in a way that will enlighten the consciences of people confronted with new situations. Lastly, it must be wisely enriched with whatever can truly and usefully be adduced about the meaning and power of human sexuality. The bishops must faithfully hold and teach the principles and norms on the moral life which have been reaffirmed in this declaration. In particular, it will be necessary to convince the faithful that the Church holds these principles not as old and unchangeable objects of superstition, nor, as is often alleged, as a Manichaean prejudice; that the Church, rather, knows for certain that these principles are in complete harmony with the divine order of creation and with the spirit of Christ, and therefore with human dignity also.

It will also be for the bishops to ensure that in theological faculties and in seminaries sound doctrine is expounded, in the light of faith and under the guidance of the magisterium of the Church. They must also ensure that confessors enlighten people's consciences and that catechetical instruction be imparted in perfect fidelity to Catholic doctrine.

It is for the bishops, priests and their collaborators to warn the faithful against erroneous opinions in books, reviews and public meetings.

Parents, first of all, and then teachers must try to lead their charges—their children or their pupils—by means of a complete education, to proper mental, affective and moral maturity. Thus, they will teach them about sex prudently and in a manner suited to their age. They will form their wills in accordance with Christian behaviour, not only by giving them advice but also by the powerful example of their own lives, supported by God's help, obtained through prayer. They will protect them from the many dangers whose existence the young do not suspect.

Artists, writers and all in whose hands are the means of social communication should use their skills in ways that are in keeping with their Christian faith and with a clear awareness of the great power that is theirs to exercise over men. They should bear in mind that "all must accept the absolute primacy of the objective moral order"[44] and that it is wrong to give priority to what are known as[45] aesthetic considerations, to material advantage or success. Whether it be question of art or literature, entertainment or communication, each person in his or her province must be circumspect, prudent and moderate and must display sound judgment. In this way, far from increasing the growing permissiveness, each will help control it and make the moral climate of society more wholesome.

All lay people should do likewise, because of their rights and duties in the apostolate.

Finally, it will be helpful to remind everyone of the following statement of the Second Council of the Vatican: "Similarly, the sacred Synod affirms that children and young people have the right to be stimulated to make sound moral judgments based on a well-formed conscience and to put them into practice with a sense of personal commitment, and to know and love God more perfectly. Accordingly, it earnestly entreats all who are in charge of civil administration or in control of education to make it their care to ensure that young people are never deprived of this sacred right.[46]

Notes

* Translated from the Latin, *Osservatore Romano,* 16 January 1976, by Austin Flannery, O. P.

1. See Second Vatican Council, Constitution on the Church in the Modern World, *Gaudium et Spes,* 47.

2. See Apostolic Constitution, *Regimini Ecclesiae Universae,* 29 (15 August 1967).

3. *Gaudium et Spes,* 16.

4. John 8:12.

5. Second Vatican Council, Declaration on Religious Liberty, *Dignitatis Humanae,* 3.

6. 1 Tim. 3:15.

7. *Dignitatis Humanae,* 14; See Pius XII, *Casti Connubii,* AAS 1930, pp. 579–580; Allocution of 2 November 1954, AAS 1954, pp. 671–672; John XXIII, *Mater et Magistra,* AAS 1961, p. 457; Paul VI, *Humanae Vitae,* 4, AAS 1968, p. 483.

8. See Second Vatican Council, Declaration on Christian Education, *Gravissimum Educationis,* 1, 8; 726–727, 732–733; *Gaudium et Spes,* 29, 60, 67: ibid., pp. 929–930, 964–965, 972–973.

9. *Gaudium et Spes,* 51: ibid., p. 955.

10. *Gaudium et Spes,* 51; see also 49: ibid., pp. 955, 952–953.

11. *Gaudium et Spes,* 49, 50: ibid., pp. 952–954.

12. The present declaration does not go into further detail regarding the norms of sexual life within marriage; these have been clearly taught in the encyclical letters *Casti Connubii* and *Humanae Vitae.*

13. See Matt. 19:4–6.

14. 1 Cor. 7:9.

15. See Eph. 5:25–32.

16. Sexual intercourse outside marriage is formally condemned: 1 Cor. 5:1; 6:9, 7:2; 10:8; Eph. 5:5, 1 Tim. 1:10; Heb. 14:4; and with explicit reasons: 1 Cor. 6:12–20.

17. See Innocent IV, Letter *Sub catholica professione,* 6 March 1254, Denz. Schon., 835; Pius II, *Propos. damn. in Ep. Cum sicut accepimus,* 14 Nov. 1459, Denz. Schon., 1367; Decrees of the Holy Office, 24 Sept. 1665, Denz. Schon., 2045; 2 March 1679, Denz. Schon., 2148; Pius XI, *Casti Connubii,* 31 Dec. 1940, AAS 1930, pp. 558–559.

18. Rom. 1:24–27, "for this reason God has given them up to the vileness of their own desires, and the consequent degradation of their bodies, because they have bartered away the true God for a false one, and have offered reverence and worship to created things instead of to the creator, who is blessed for ever; amen. In consequence, I say, God has given them up to shameful passions. Their women have exchanged natural intercourse for unnatural, and their men in turn, giving up natural relations with women, burn with lust for one another; males behave indecently with males, and are

paid in their own persons the fitting wage of such perversion." See also what St Paul says of those "guilty of homosexual perversion" in 1 Cor. 6:10; 1 Tim. 1:10.

19. See Leo IX, Letter *Ad splendidum nitentis,* in 1054, Denz. Schon. 587–688; Decree of the Holy Office, 2 March 1679, Denz. Schon., 2149; Pius XII, Allocution, 9 Oct. 1953, AAS 1953, pp. 677–678: AAS 1956, pp. 472–473.

20. *Gaudium et Spes.*

21. ". . . sociological surveys help disclose the thought patterns of a particular people, the anxieties and needs of those to whom we proclaim the word of God, and also the opposition of modern thought to it, based on the widespread notion that no legitimate knowledge exists outside of science. However, the conclusions drawn from such surveys could not of themselves provide criteria for determining truth." Paul VI, Apostolic Exhortation, *Quinque jam anni,* 8 Dec. 1970, AAS 1971, p. 102.

22. Matt. 22:38, 40.

23. Matt. 19:16–19.

24. See notes 17 and 19 above: Decree of the Holy Office, 18 March 1666, Denz. Schon., 2060; Paul VI, Encyclical Letter *Humanae Vitae,* 13, 14.

25. 1 Sam. 16:7.

26. Paul VI, Encyclical Letter *Humanae Vitae,* 29: AAS 1968, p. 501.

27. See 1 Cor. 7:7, 34. Council of Trent, Session 24, can. 10: Denz. Schon. 1810; Second Vatican Council, Constitution *Lumen Gentium;* Synod of Bishops, *De Sacerdotio Ministeriali,* Part II, 4, b: AAS, 1971, pp. 915–916.

28. Matt. 5:28.

29. See Gal. 5:19–23; 1 Cor. 6:9–11.

30. 1 Thess. 4:3–8; see Col. 3:5–7.

31. Eph. 5:3–8; see 4:18–19.

32. 1 Cor. 6:15, 18–20.

33. See Rom. 7:23.

34. See Rom. 7:24–25.

35. See Rom. 8:2.

36. Rom. 6:12.

37. 1 John 5:11.

38. See 1 Cor. 10:13.

39. Eph. 6:11.

40. See Eph. 6:16, 18.

41. See 1 Cor. 9:27.

42. Luke 9:23.

43. 2 Tim. 2:11–12.

44. Second Council of the Vatican, Decree *Inter Mirifica,* 6: Flannery, p. 286.

45. Vatican Press Office version, "so-called."

46. Second Council of the Vatican, Declaration *Gravissimum Educationis,* 1: Flannery, p. 727.

29. Practical Moral Principles

Gerald Kelly, S.J.

This chapter first appeared in *Modern Youth and Chastity* in 1941.

Are engaged people allowed any special liberties? Is it a sin to go to a somewhat objectionable or suggestive movie? When is kissing sinful? These are but a few of an almost endless stream of questions proposed to priests at various times. The questioners always ask them with the hope of a brief, definite answer, and they perhaps seldom advert to the fact that these are among the most difficult questions to answer. The preceding chapters of this book should have indicated that such questions cannot be answered without taking into account a large number of factors. In the present chapter we are going to indicate as briefly, yet as adequately, as possible the main points that a priest always has to consider before he can answer such questions. In doing this we shall formulate certain practical principles that must be applied to these various cases. This should help the reader to appreciate some of the difficulty the priest faces, and at the same time it should be of some service in the solution of one's own problems.

DIRECTLY VENEREAL ACTIONS

In answering any question concerning chastity, the first point to be determined concerns the action itself. In this respect, it should already be clear to our readers that there are two quite distinct classes of actions. In the first class are those actions which of their very nature are so closely connected with the sexual appetite that they serve the single purpose of stimulating or promoting the generative function. Such are the actions spoken of in the last chapter:

sexual intercourse; intimate, passionate kissing and embracing which form the natural preliminary to intercourse; unnatural acts such as self-abuse or sexual intimacies with a person of the same sex. We may call these acts *directly venereal,* because their one direct and exclusive effect is to stimulate or further venereal passion.

These directly venereal actions are always unchaste for unmarried people. No "good intention" can make them right; for instance, a girl may not indulge in unchaste intimacies to avoid leading a lonely life or losing a man she loves, and so forth. The law of God in this matter is absolute, and to do such things for some so-called good purpose is simply to do evil in order to obtain some good. With these unequivocal notions in mind, we can formulate our first practical principle of extra-marital chastity:

FIRST PRACTICAL PRINCIPLE:
"Every directly venereal action is against the law of God, and a serious sin of impurity."

NOTE: When we say that such things are mortal sins, we mean that they are objectively serious sins. That is, the *matter* is serious. As we know from our catechism, for a person to commit a full-fledged mortal sin, three things are necessary: a) serious matter; b) sufficient reflection; c) full consent of the will. It happens now and then that an impure action is performed in a sudden burst of passion, or without forethought, or through ignorance of the real evil of the action, or when one is only half-awake, and so forth. In such cases, the second or third element for a subjective mortal sin is lacking, and one may incur little or no guilt before God. But such subjective excuses do not change the nature of the action.

INDIRECTLY VENEREAL

Besides the actions that we have called directly venereal, there are almost countless other actions and situations in life which do frequently stimulate the sexual appetite, but which also serve another purpose *entirely distinct* from venereal stimulation. We are referring to such things as the following: the study of physiology or medicine; decent dancing; modest kissing and embracing; motion pictures, plays, and books containing an occasional suggestive scene or description; and so forth. Now, it is true that (as we said) these things often do arouse venereal passion to a greater or less degree; but they also and *primarily* serve another distinct purpose. The study of physiology or medicine provides useful or even necessary information; dancing, plays, and motion pictures provide recreation for the mind; the modest kiss or embrace is a sing of affection; and so on. The venereal passion aroused by these things may be called a by-product, and for this reason we label them *indirectly venereal.*

The moral problem involved in these indirectly venereal actions may present itself in these two ways:

1) *Before doing something,* one is conscious that it will very likely be a source of sexual passion. For instance, a boy may know that if he dances, or embraces a girl he loves, his passions will be aroused; a girl may know that if she reads a certain book or magazine or thinks about her future married life, she will be sexually disturbed; a young medical student (or a nurse) may realize that his studies will have a stimulating effect on him. The question that each must answer before acting is: May I dance, embrace, read, study, etc., without violating chastity?

2) *While doing something* one becomes conscious that the action is sexually stimulating. He may not have thought of it before, but now he must answer the question: May I continue to dance, read, study, etc., without violating chastity?

In deciding whether such actions may be begun or continued, one must keep in mind that they are not like directly venereal actions; they are not necessarily wrong. They will be sinful or not sinful according to certain circumstances, and these circumstances may be reduced to three.

1. Impure Intention

Everyone will readily see that if a boy kisses a girl *in order to* arouse his passion, or *in order to* prepare the way for some directly venereal action, his act is against chastity. Even though the kiss be externally quite modest he is really turning it into an impure act. And so of other things, to read a book, to look at pictures, to attend plays in order to arouse or further venereal passion is to turn them into violations of chastity. This would hold whether the action is *begun* for that purpose or *continued* for that purpose; hence we come naturally to our:

SECOND PRACTICAL PRINCIPLE:
"Any action is a serious sin against chastity when it is performed with the intention of stimulating or promoting venereal pleasure."

2. DANGER

Perhaps what we have to say about the second circumstance may be made clear by some examples. From our first two principles we know that these two things are always seriously wrong: i) the performance of a directly venereal action, and ii) the intentional seeking or promoting of venereal pleasure. Now, let us suppose this case: A boy kisses a girl. Externally, the kiss is quite modest and when he kisses her, his intention is not impure. Therefore, he does not violate either of the first two principles. Yet, let us suppose further that the boy knows that this apparently chaste action *generally leads him to go too far,* for example, to try to perform some directly venereal action.

Or suppose another case: A girl reads a magazine. It is not a bad magazine, though it does contain a few parts that are sexually stimulating for her. However, we can suppose she does not read for that purpose, that she merely wants some information, or some recreation. Hence, she too avoids the violation of the first two principles. But in her case too we are making the further supposition that this seemingly justifiable reading *generally leads her to lose control of herself;* her good intention wavers and she consents to the venereal pleasure aroused by the reading.

These two examples illustrate the second very important circumstance that must be considered when there is question of indirectly venereal actions. For both the boy and the girl referred to in our examples these actions, though not wrong in themselves, involve what is termed the *proximate danger of serious sin.* In other words, in performing these actions they are practically certain to sin. Everyone must avoid a danger like that; one who knowingly courts such a danger is already showing a will to sin.

Situations that involve the proximate danger of sin are termed *proximate occasions of sin.* For instance, in the examples we have just cited, the apparently decent kissing is a proximate occasion of serious sin for the boy, and the reading of that particular type of magazine is a proximate occasion of serious sin for the girl. It is seriously wrong for one to expose oneself rashly to such dangers. Ordinarily we are obliged under pain of serious sin to avoid such occasions. If the occasion cannot be avoided, as may happen in certain rather rare instances, then we must find some means which will fortify us against the danger. Expert counsel is usually required in such cases.

OBSCENITY

To a great extent, proximate occasions of sin differ with different individuals; hence the difficulty of solving cases for a group. However, there are some things which are commonly and practically universally proximate occasions. For instance, the modern burlesque show is planned along such sexually stimulating lines that it is a proximate occasion for almost anyone. In fact, we may say in general that real *obscenity* usually constitutes a proximate danger of sin. The term, *obscenity,* is frequently used with a rather wide and vague meaning, but with the moral expert it is very technical. Let us illustrate from things to which the term is especially applicable, namely, obscene "literature" and theatrical productions. For such things to be obscene, two elements are required: a) their theme, or content, is of an impure or sexually-exciting nature; and b) their manner of presentation is such as to throw an attractive emphasis on that impure or sexually-exciting element. For instance, adultery is a sin of impurity; so when a book or play not only centers about adultery but portrays it in an attractive manner, such a play or book is obscene. Again, excessive nudity, and especially disrobing by a woman in the presence of a man are commonly recognized as strongly stimulating to the sexual passions. Hence, when such things are alluringly emphasized and advertised, as they are in most modern burlesque shows, the shows must be called obscene.

This rather lengthy discussion of the meaning of proximate danger was necessary for our purpose. We can now summarize it in our:

THIRD PRACTICAL PRINCIPLE:
"It is mortal sin for one to expose oneself freely and knowingly to the proximate danger of performing a directly venereal action or of consenting to venereal pleasure."

3. INSUFFICIENT REASON

In the first three principles we have indicated the three possible sources of mortal sins against purity: a) impure *action;* b) impure *intention;* c) willful *proximate danger* of either. One who guards against these three things avoids mortal sin. However, that does not necessarily mean that he avoids all sin. It is possible to commit a venial sin in this matter by acting *without a relatively sufficient reason.* This statement calls for a brief explanation; then we can formulate it into a practical principle.

In the second principle, we stated that one commits a mortal sin if his intention is impure. This implies that to avoid mortal sin one must have some reason for acting which is not impure. Now evidently such "pure" reasons are very numerous and they vary in value. A school teacher who must read a mystery story that contains some sexually-disturbing passages surely has a better reason for reading than a person who reads the same story merely for recreation. Engaged people have a better reason for decent affectionate embracing than those who are not engaged. A medical student has a better reason for reading a medical treatise than a person who is interested in medicine merely as a hobby or who is just curious to know the contents of the book.

Again, consider the third principle. In it we considered the case of proximate danger, and we explained this as referring to a situation in which one generally loses control of oneself and commits an impure action or fully consents to venereal passion. For instance, John knows that when he reads his father's medical books, he suffers violent temptations and generally gives in. The direct opposite of proximate danger is *remote danger,* which may be explained as referring to situations in which one generally does not lose self-control. For example, James reads the same books, is very little disturbed by them, and they seldom or never prove a source of sin to him.

Everyone should see that between the two extremes (proximate and remote) there lies a wide zone which might be termed *intermediate danger.* For example, Joseph also reads the medical books. He cannot say they are a proximate occasion of sin for him, nor can he say simply that the danger of sin is thoroughly remote. In other words, he does *occasionally* lose control of himself.

Now, the point we wish to make here is a simple one: Joseph is obliged to exercise more caution in regard to this reading than is James. For Joseph takes some risk, James practically none. And the cases of Joseph and James are only examples. They illustrate the point that some actions or thoughts need a greater reason for perfect justification than do others. In other words, for an indirectly venereal action to be perfectly justifiable, that is, not even venially sinful, one must have a *relatively sufficient* reason. Without such a reason he takes a needless risk and is guilty of some negligence or insincerity.

Obviously, the determination of what constitutes a sufficient reason is not a question of mathematics. Nevertheless, the normal rule is about as follows: The more stimulating the thought or action, the stronger must be the reason, because usually the danger of sin and insincerity increases with the vehemence of passion.

Usually this lack of a sufficient reason constitutes a venial sin. Examples might be: curious and imprudent looks and reading; delaying on dangerous thoughts through idle curiosity; unduly prolonged or repeated kisses by lovers, even though they intend no passion; kissing from frivolous motives; and so forth. In such cases there is no outright willful impurity, and no mortal sin, but there is a lack of due caution or some degree of insincerity. These cases can all be comprised under this:

FOURTH PRACTICAL PRINCIPLE:
"It is a venial sin to perform an indirectly venereal action with-
out a relatively sufficient reason."

(NOTE: In this last principle we have not referred to those cases in which there is really a complete fundamental lack of sincerity. But it does happen at times that people merely deceive themselves in the matter of impurity. They want venereal pleasure, but they do not like to admit it, even to themselves. Hence, they read strongly stimulating things, dwell on stimulating thoughts—always with a certain pretense that they have some other motive. In reality, they violate the second principle but rationalize themselves out of guilt, at least serious guilt. It is often difficult to estimate these cases, as mental quirks develop easily in one who is not sincerely devoted to chastity.)

SINLESS ACTIONS

The four preceding principles have taken care of anything that might be sinful in regard to chastity. It remains merely to indicate what is *sinless.* Practically speaking, our actions are sinless when they are *reasonable.* In other words, when we have a good reason for our thoughts or actions, we may think or act, and ignore the sexual-stimulation that may accidentally result. Thus, necessity permits the intimate actions of a medical examination. The acquisition of useful or necessary knowledge permits young doctors, nurses, theologians, and instructors to study things which might at times be strongly stimulating. Normal recreation is sufficient to justify things which are only slightly stimulating (as some people may notice regarding dancing, slightly suggestive motion pictures, generally decent picture magazines, and so forth). Hypersensitive people, that is, those who are bothered by things which do not disturb others and greatly bothered by things which only slightly disturb others, may live as others do in this matter, so long as their intention is good. Sometimes it is better for them to live as others do; sometimes the more advisable course is to lead a more careful life. They need sound personal direction.

What we have said about sinlessness can now be summarized in our:

FIFTH PRACTICAL PRINCIPLE:
"Indirectly venereal actions are not sinful if one has a good and sufficient reason for beginning or continuing such actions."

THE LAW OF CHARITY

The foregoing principles are norms of conduct in regard to one's *personal chastity.* In things that involve other people, however, we must always have regard for another great law of morality, the *law of charity.* By this law **we are bound not to induce others to sin or to help them to sin, and we must also take reasonable means to prevent their sinning when** we can do so. What these "reasonable means" are depends largely on circumstances, and complicated situations require the expert direction of a priest. But it should be clear that in general in regard to such things as kissing, conversation, and choosing forms of entertainment for oneself and others, we cannot simply settle the matter by saying: "It doesn't bother me; therefore it's all right."

It is difficult to give any absolute rule for judging the reactions of others. A fair presumption is that they will be about the same as our own, unless either party happens to be extraordinarily callous or sensitive, or unless some special circumstance such as adolescence indicates greater danger. Particularly in the matter of kissing, a girl must keep in mind that a boy is more responsive physically than she; but if there is some good reason for a decent manifestation of affection, she may presume that he has proper control of himself unless he attempts or suggests immodesty.

SUMMARY: FOUR QUESTIONS

If one understands the principles explained, he can then reduce them to practice by answering four questions:

1) *What* am I doing, or about to do?
2) *Why* am I doing it or about to do it?
3) What *dangers* are involved for myself or others?
4) Have I a sufficient reason to render my action perfectly justifiable?

These four questions will solve all the ordinary problems involving our voluntary conduct with respect to chastity. One who knows them learns to apply them spontaneously without any need of a formal, mechanical process. They furnish definite rules for determining what is of obligation and what is not; though we must constantly remember that often the *better* things to do will be to go beyond these rules and avoid things which might in themselves be done without sin. Moreover, there are certain special circumstances which might make even chaste actions inappropriate, and perhaps even unjust and scandalous. Married people, for instance, have a special obligation to reserve their demonstrations of tender affection to themselves. The girl who trespasses upon a wife's right to the affection of her husband does wrong, even though no real unchastity be involved; so too the man who disregards a husband's right to his wife's affection. And it goes without saying that those who are consecrated to God have renounced their right even to such expressions of affection as might be permissible to other unmarried people of different sexes.

We mentioned these examples to indicate that at times special factors must be considered which are not included in our principles concerning chastity. In our summary in this chapter and in the practical cases in the next, we shall presume that no such special factors are present.

SIXTH COMMANDMENT

It may now be helpful to summarize the principal conclusions of this chapter in terms of the Sixth and Ninth Commandments of God. The Sixth Commandment commands us to be pure in our external actions, and forbids all actions against purity; therefore in terms of what is sinful or not sinful it may be visualized as follows:

Mortal Sin a) All directly venereal actions. (Principle I)

              b) All other actions performed for the purpose of stimulating or promoting venereal pleasure. (Principle II)

              c) All actions involving the proximate danger of performing a directly venereal action or of consenting to venereal pleasure. (Principle III)

Venial Sin: Indirectly venereal actions performed without a relatively sufficient reason. (Principle IV)

No Sin: Indirectly venereal actions performed with a relatively sufficient reason. (Principle V)

In this summary we give only the points that pertain to one's personal chastity. It should not be forgotten that if others are concerned in these external actions, charity demands that we consider them; also at times other factors must be considered, such as the special obligations of one's state of life, as indicated before.

NINTH COMMANDMENT

The Ninth Commandment prescribes chastity of thought, and forbids unchaste thoughts. In this matter of thoughts, some preliminary explanation is necessary before formulating our summary because the question of sinful thoughts is frequently misunderstood. In the first place, it should be clear to everyone that a *thought which is not willful cannot be sinful.* We have no absolute control over our imaginations; they frequently retain disturbing images, no matter what we try to do about it. There is simply no question of sin when that occurs.

It should also be clear (though it frequently is not) that not all willful thinking about sexual matters is sinful. Thoughts differ vastly from external actions in this: There are some kinds of external actions (directly venereal) which may never be done by unmarried people; there is no action which may not be *thought about.* For instance, in studying or reading a book of this kind, one necessarily thinks about many impure actions. The mere thinking about them does not make them sinful.

The one thing which is absolutely wrong in regard to thoughts is to think about a sinful action, *with approval of what is sinful.* In general, this might be done in three ways; and a few examples should illustrate the point clearly:

a) John thinks about the sin of fornication, with the willful desire or intention of committing it. In this case he gives his approval of sin by desiring or intending to commit it.

b) Mary once committed the sin of fornication, and now she thinks about that action, and willfully rejoices over the fact that she committed it. In other words, Mary, instead of having sorrow for the sin as she should have, here and now goes over it again in her mind with willful approval of what she did.

c) James also thinks about the sin of fornication. He has no intention of actually performing the external action; he is not approving of anything he did in the past, but here and now he willfully delights in imagining that he is performing the act. James is giving his approval of a sinful act by willfully taking complacency in the thought of doing it.

Note that in each of these cases the sin consisted in willfully approving of an act which it would be sinful to perform. If one should approve of an act which is not sinful for him to perform, then such approval would not be sinful. For instance, marital relations are certainly not sinful for married people; hence they may desire them beforehand and rejoice over them afterwards. It might be dangerous for even married people to dwell long on such thoughts because they might prove strongly stimulating to passion and bring about temptations to self-abuse; but the thoughts of approval would not be wrong for them because the acts they think about are permissible for married people.

Note that we have stressed the point that thoughts are sinful when they express *willful* approval of evil (willful desires, willful complacency, willful rejoicing). This is quite different from the involuntary sense of approval or desire that comes upon almost anyone who has to think of various sexual acts. Such things are naturally attractive to the lower appetites but that mere natural urge is not an act of the free will.

With this preliminary explanation of the particularly difficult points concerning thoughts, we can now summarize our principles as they apply to the Ninth Commandment:

Mortal Sin: a) The *willful approval* of unchaste actions. (Cf. foregoing explanation and Principle I.)

      b) The willful entertaining of any thoughts *for the purpose of* stimulating or promoting venereal passion. (Principle II.—This kind of thinking is about the same as self-abuse.)

      c) The willful harboring of thoughts which involve *the proximate danger of* performing an unchaste action, approving of such an action, or consenting to venereal pleasure. (Principle III)

Venial Sin: Thinking about sexually-stimulating things without a sufficient reason. (Principle IV)

No Sin: Thinking about sexually-stimulating things with a sufficient reason. (Principle V)

30. Sexuality and Sin: A Current Appraisal

Charles E. Curran

This chapter first appeared in *Contemporary Problems in Moral Theology* in 1970.

The Roman Catholic theology of sexuality has been frequently criticized in the past because it was too negative and gave an undue importance to sexuality. In the last few years the renewal in moral theology has stressed the primacy of love and service of the neighbor and not sexuality as the hallmark of Christian life. An appreciation of human sexuality based on the theology of creation, incarnation and bodily resurrection at the end of time has replaced the antimaterial and antisexual prejudices of an older theology. A total Christian view of sexuality also sees the limitations of human sexuality: the imperfections involved in time and space, the fact that sexuality is just one aspect of human life, and the reality of human sinfulness which affects sexuality and all human life.[1]

However, there remain many questions about sexual ethics. One very important obstacle in the attempt to arrive at a more balanced view of human sexuality and its role in the life of the Christian is the teaching that all sins against sexuality involve grave matter. Is that statement true? What was the reasoning process that led to such a conclusion? Will a changed understanding of the gravity of sins against chastity change any of our other teaching on sins against sexuality? This article will attempt to explain the older approach in Catholic theology to sins against chastity and their gravity. The older approach will be criticized, and then the final section will survey some general and particular guidelines for an understanding of sins against sexuality in contemporary Catholic moral theology. There remain many other even more important aspects of human

405

sexuality which Catholic theology must consider, but first of all it is necessary to show the inadequacies in the older way of understanding sins against sexuality and their gravity and to point out newer approaches.

I. The Older Teaching and Its Development

In general, Catholic moral theology has approached the question of sexuality in the light of a natural law methodology. Such a methodology recognizes that there exists a source of ethical wisdom and knowledge apart from the explicit revelation of God in the Scriptures. Whereas individual texts from the Scriptures were used by the theologians in pointing out the malice of certain actions, Catholic theology realized the insufficiency of the revealed Scriptures for furnishing a complete and adequate understanding of the way in which the Christian should view human sexuality. Natural law methodology as such does not necessarily imply the existence of any absolute norms. Since natural law in its best understanding is right reason, such a methodology is deliberative rather than prescriptive.[2] Unfortunately, the natural law approach to sexuality in Catholic theology illustrates the problems developed at great length in Chapter Two including the ambiguity in the very concept of natural law.

In the natural law understanding of sins against chastity, nature does not mean right reason. In this context nature means the physical, biological, or natural processes which are common to man and all the animals. Theology textbooks from Thomas Aquinas until a very few years ago divided the sins against sexuality into two classes —sins against nature (*peccata contra naturam*) and sins according to nature (*peccata iuxta naturam*).[3] Nature in this distinction refers to the physical, biological process common to man and all the animals in which male semen is deposited in the vas of the female. Sins against nature are those in which this natural process does not take place and are generally listed as masturbation, sodomy, homosexuality, bestiality, and contraception. Sins according to nature are sexual actuations in which the biological or "natural" structure is observed, but they are opposed to the distinctively human aspects of sexuality. These sins include fornication, adultery, incest, rape, and sacrilege.[4] Chapter Two has shown that this understanding is logically and historically influenced by the ideas of Ulpian.[5]

A second inadequacy in the textbook natural law approach to sexuality is the over-emphasis on procreation as the primary end of marriage and also of sexuality.[6] Such an understanding of the primary end of marriage theoretically follows from the natural law understanding of Ulpian. Ulpian himself gives the example of procreation and education of offspring as the classical example of natural law as that which is common to man and all the animals.[7] Ulpian's theory would of necessity relegate the love union aspect of marriage and sexuality to a secondary end. The primary or fundamental in man is what he shares with the other animals. The human aspect is something which is another layer merely placed on top of the primary layer of animality. Since relationality and love union do not enter into animal sexuality, these aspects are relegated to secondary ends of sexuality and marriage.

The emphasis on procreation and education shows through in the arguments proposed for the malice of certain sexual sins. Sins against nature are wrong because they violate the order of nature and thus impede the procreation of offspring.[8] However, even the sins according to nature are wrong primarily because they are against the primary end of procreation and education. Even though there may be no other circumstances present, such as the injustice to another marriage in adultery or the lack of consent in rape, all sins according to nature partake in the basic malice of fornication. Simple fornication is a grave sin because both parents are needed to provide for the proper education and upbringing of the child who might be born as a result of such an act.[9]

Imperfect medical and biological knowledge merely heightened the importance attached by the older theologians to the physical and procreational aspects of sexuality. Contemporary Catholic theologians too often forget the recent and rapid advances in scientific knowledge about human reproduction and sexuality. The very word "semen," taken from the agricultural metaphor of seed, indicates that the male semen merely had to be put in the fertile spot provided by the female. The classical authors in moral theology knew nothing of the exact contribution of the female to the human reproduction process. Very little progress in any type of anatomic knowledge was made until the sixteenth century because of the difficulty in obtaining corpses. In the sixteenth century, Gabriele Falloppio discovered the fallopian tubes in the woman, but he did not understand their true purpose.[10] In 1672 De Graaf described the female ovaries and the follicle which bears his name, but he made the mistake of identifying the ovum with the entire follicle. Only in the nineteenth century was the theory of De Graaf revived and corrected by the realization that the ovum is contained within the follicle.

In 1677, Van Leeuwenhoek, the great microscopist, discovered spermatozoa. Even after the discovery of spermatozoa a number of scientists thought that the male element was the only active element in reproduction. Some of Van Leeuwenhoek's over-zealous followers even published pictures of the "homounculus" or little man which they found outlined in the spermatozoa![11] Obviously, such an understanding would attach great importance to human semen and spermatozoa.

Less than a century ago (1875), Oscar Hertwig showed that fertilization was effected by the union of the nuclei of ovum and sperm. Thus, only within the last hundred years or so has science realized that the woman is not fertile for the greater part of her menstrual cycle. Procreation is not possible after every act of sexual intercourse but only during a comparatively short time each month.[12] Thinkers like the classical moral theologians who lacked the knowledge of modern medicine necessarily would give too great a value to human semen and see too strong a connection between the individual sexual actuation and procreation.

Catholic theologians generally followed the teaching of St. Thomas that sins against sexuality are grave because they go against an important order of nature or because the absence of marriage between the parties fails to provide for the education of the child who might be born of such a union. Thomas also considered the question whether touches and kisses are grave sins. Thomas responded that an embrace, a kiss or a touch is not mortal *secundum speciem* because such actions can be done for some reasonable cause or necessity. However, something can be mortal because of its cause; and if these actions are done for a libidinous reason, they are mortal sins. Thomas had earlier argued that consent to the pleasure of a mortal sin is itself a mortal sin; therefore, if such actions are done from a libidinous intention, they are mortal sins.[13]

The commentators on St. Thomas approached the question of embraces, kisses, etc. in this Thomistic context. Martin Le Maistre (1432–1481) disagreed with Thomas.[14] Martin denied that such actions *secundum quod libidinosa sunt* are mortal sins. If such a kiss is done for the pleasure involved in the kiss and is not ordered to fornication, such a kiss is not a mortal sin. There remains the problem of what is meant by libidinous. However, for the purpose of our present study, the stage is thus set for the famous question of the existence of parvity of matter in sins against sexuality. Martin of Azpilcueta, the famous Doctor Navarrus (1493–1586), was apparently the first theologian to affirm that in matters of sexuality there can be parvity of matter.[15] Navarrus proves his point by merely stating that the transgression of any precept is excused from grave sin because of parvity of matter and the precept governing chastity should be no different.[16] The opinion of Navarrus was accepted by Thomas Sanchez (1550–1610) who maintained there could be a slight venereal pleasure which would not involve lethal guilt provided there is no danger of pollution and no danger of consent to a carnal act.[17]

In 1612, the General of the Society of Jesus, Claudius Aquaviva forbade Jesuits to maintain the existence of parvity of matter in deliberately willed, imperfect sexual actuation or pleasure. This was later extended to imperfect sexual actuation which may have arisen indirectly but was later consented to. The opinion proposed by Sanchez was ordered to be changed in all the editions of his work.[18] (In 1659, the Revisores of the Society of Jesus did admit that the opinion affirming the existence of parvity of matter in questions of chastity was still extrinsically probable and penitents holding such a position could be validly absolved.)[19] The teaching denying the existence of parvity of matter in the sixth commandment gradually became so strong that contemporary theologians claim it is temerarious to deny it.[20] The ruling by Father Aquaviva has obviously prevented any true discussion of the question by the Jesuit theologians who have been most influential in the area of moral theology.

Since the issue was not allowed to be discussed, one can and should seriously question the validity of the apparent consensus of Catholic theologians on this point.

Jose M. Diaz Moreno recently published a protracted historical study of eighty theologians from Cajetan to St. Alphonsus to determine if the opinion admitting parvity of matter ever enjoyed probability. Only nine of these authors affirmed that parvity of matter excuses from grave sin in matters of sexuality.[21] However, the author concludes his lengthy investigation by saying that the arguments advanced by the proponents of parvity of matter are so generic or open to other interpretations that they do and did not constitute a solidly probable opinion. Nor do the nine theologians who maintained such a teaching constitute an extrinsically probable opinion either because many of them do not enjoy great esteem or because the reasons proposed by some (e.g. Navarrus and Sanchez) are not convincing.[22]

There have been no definitive interventions of the hierarchical magisterium concerning the question of parvity of matter.[23] Some statements definitely indicate and even presuppose the teaching denying the existence of parvity of matter in sexual sins.[24] A number of statements have condemned those who would assert that kisses, embraces, and touches that are done for carnal pleasure are only venial sins.[25] Also one response of the Holy Office presupposes there is no parvity of matter in the sixth commandment.[26] All of these are comparatively minor statements and must be judged today in the light of many different circumstances.

Since the seventeenth century theologians have generally taught that even imperfect sexual actuation or pleasure outside marriage does not admit of parvity of matter. There was some dispute, but only concerning the ultimate reason for such a teaching. Was the teaching based on intrinsic and theoretical reasons or merely practical and moral reasons?[27] Just a decade ago theologians maintained that the teaching denying parvity of matter was so certain that the contrary opinion was temerarious.[28] The reasons proposed by theologians for their opinion denying parvity of matter in the sixth commandment have taken different forms. Diaz Moreno summarizes the two arguments proposed by the authors he studied from Cajetan to St. Alphonsus. The first argument is based on the fact that all these imperfect sexual actuations are ordered to sexual intercourse, and thus all venereal pleasure, even the smallest, is the beginning of copula or pollution. The second argument consists in the danger of consent to a complete act which is intimately connected with these previous acts.[29] Fuchs proposes what he considers to be the best intrinsic argument in this way: in incomplete sexual actuation outside marriage there is a substantial breaking of an order of great importance, insofar as the individual desires for himself that which was ordained by the creator for the good of the species.[30]

In fairness to the theologians one must carefully examine what is meant by the axiom that there is no parvity of matter in sexual matters. According to the best interpretations, the axiom means this: imperfect sexual actuation or pleasure outside marriage, which is directly willed, whether purposely procured or consented to, is by reason of matter always a grave sin.[31] Note well that the axiom denying parvity of matter in the sixth commandment does not mean that every sin against the sixth commandment constitutes a mortal sin. Sexual actuation or pleasure within marriage and indirect sexual actuation outside marriage are not grave matter. Although the matter is always grave in the other cases, the theologians constantly taught that sufficient reflection and full consent of the will are necessary for mortal sin. St. Thomas very wisely remarked that libido in the sensitive appetite diminishes sin because passion reduces culpability. Thomas admits that passion in sexual matters is very strong and difficult to overcome.[32]

II. EVALUATION OF THE OLDER TEACHING

What about the teaching of the theologians that complete sexual actuation outside marriage is always grave matter and that direct, imperfect sexual actuation or pleasure outside marriage is always grave matter? I believe that such opinions and axioms are not true.

Contemporary moral theology views mortal sin in the light of the theory of the fundamental option which has been developed at great length in Chapter One. The difference between mortal and venial sin does not reside primarily in the difference between grave and light matter. Mortal sin involves the core of the person in a fundamental choice or option, a basic orientation of his existence. Venial sin is an action which tends to be more peripheral and does not involve such a change in basic orientation. At best the distinction between grave matter and light matter is a presumption. The presumption is that grave matter will usually call for an involvement of the core of the person whereas light matter tends to call for only a peripheral response. If grave and light matter are at best presumptive guidelines, then such axioms as *ex toto genere suo gravis* or *non datur parvitas materiae* lose much of their rigidity.[33] However, my contention is that one cannot maintain the presumption that all complete sexual actuations outside marriage and all directly willed, imperfect sexual actuations outside marriage constitute grave matter. In the following arguments much of the attention will be directed to the case of complete sexual actuation outside marriage. However, if such complete sexual actuation outside marriage does not always involve grave matter, *a fortiori* directly willed, imperfect sexual actuation does not always involve grave matter.

The older view of the theologians rests upon a very inadequate notion of natural law which has exaggerated the importance attached to actions against sexuality. The Christian should be especially alert to a theological axiom which would seem to give primary importance to sexuality and chastity and not to the primary element of Christian love. Negative attitudes towards sexuality have definitely accented the over-emphasis on the importance of sexual sins. However, our discussion will center on the concept of natural law underlying the meaning and appreciation of sexuality and sexual sins in the teaching of the Catholic theologians before the last few years.

The manualistic concept of natural law applied to questions of sexuality distorts the meaning and importance of sexuality because it sees sexuality only in terms of the physical, biological process. No mention is made of the psychological which is just as objective an aspect of human sexuality as the physical. The older theologians can be excused because man has become aware of the psychological only within the last century. However, to deny the value and importance of the psychological distorts the meaning of human sexuality. For example, psychology reminds us that masturbation is not a very important matter in the life of some people such as the developing adolescent.[34]

The natural law concept underlying sexual morality in the manuals also fails to see the individual action in relation to the person. The Pastoral Constitution on the Church in the Modern World calls for theology to take into consideration the person and his acts.[35] The older approach viewed just the act in itself. There is a danger in some ethical thinking today which tends to give little or no importance to individual actions. However, it is equally fallacious to consider the act apart from the person placing the action. Masturbation may mean many different things depending on the person placing the action.

The exclusive emphasis on the physical aspect and the individual act apart from the person fails to do justice to the full meaning of human sexuality. One cannot brand all premarital sex under the same blanket condemnation of fornication. There is quite a bit of difference between sexual relations with a prostitute and with a spouse to be. Criteria which cannot come to grips with the differences involved in such cases do not seem to be adequate criteria. An emphasis on the physical and the natural, as opposed to the personal aspect of the action, also fails to see the need of growth and development as a person gradually strives to achieve a mature sexuality. Growth and development might even involve temporary problems along the way, but these are to be seen in view of the overall effort to reach the goal of an integrated human sexuality.

Perhaps the greatest error in the older approach is the close connection seen between every sexual actuation and procreation. Procreation is a very important human value. If every sexual actuation outside marriage involves a direct going against actual procreation, then there would be reason to assert the generic gravity of sins against sexuality. However, Catholic theology now realizes the overimportance attached to the relationship between sexuality and procreation in the past. The more recent statements of the hierarchical magisterium no longer mention procreation and education of offspring as the primary end of marriage.[36] Even the acceptance of the rhythm system of responsible parenthood argues that not every sexual actuation is closely connected with possible procreation. Ironically, an approach to sexuality exclusively in terms of procreation could logically lead to interesting consequences. Thomas Aquinas saw the generic grave malice of fornication in the harm done to the child who might be born of that union. The use of contraception would destroy the primary argument of St. Thomas asserting the generic malice of fornication!

Older biological notions also exaggerated the importance attached by Catholic theologians to the connection between sexual actuation and procreation. Even from a physical viewpoint the vast majority of sexual acts will not result in procreation because the woman is sterile for the greater part of her period. Modern science with its knowledge of the prodigality of nature in giving spermatozoa and the realization that semen is not the only active element in procreation indicates that human semen is not as important as older theologians seemed to think. Contemporary medical knowledge thus argues against the reasons assigned for the generic importance attached to sins of sexuality in the past.

From the pastoral viewpoint, it is most important to discard the older view denying parvity of matter in sexual sins. Such a view gave an undue importance to sexuality in the overall view of the Christian life. In addition such a teaching tended to stifle a proper understanding of human sexuality and human sexual development. Sex was always connected with the fear of mortal sin. Such fear impeded the development of a proper attitude toward human sexuality on the part of many Catholics and even brought about grave repercussions in their adult attitude to sexuality.

Notes

1. For a non-technical but well-balanced approach to sexuality from within a Catholic context, see Sidney Cornelia Callahan, *Beyond Birth Control* (New York: Sheed & Ward, 1968).

2. Thomas Aquinas, *Summa Theologiae, Ia Ilae,* q. 91, q. 94. Josef Fuchs, *Natural Law,* tr. Helmut Reckter and John A. Dowling (New York: Sheed & Ward, 1965), distinguishes both an ontological and a noetic ele-

ment in the Thomistic concept of natural law. For a description of natural law ethics and Thomistic ethics as deliberative rather than prescriptive, see Edward LeRoy Long, Jr., *A Survey of Christian Ethics* (New York: Oxford University Press, 1967), pp. 45–52.

3. *IIa IIae,* q. 154, introduction and a. 11. E.g., H. Noldin et al., *Summa Theologiae Moralis: De Castitate,* 36th ed. (Innsbruck: Rauch, 1958), pp. 21–40.

4. Thomas Aquinas has practically the same enumeration as found in the more recent manuals of moral theology.

5. Ulpian's definition and theory is briefly cited in Justinian's *Digest,* 1. I, tit. I, I.

6. For a survey of the teaching on procreation as the primary end of marriage and sexuality, see John C. Ford, S. J., and Gerald Kelly, S. J., *Contemporary Moral Theology:* Vol. II: *Marriage Questions* (Westminster, Maryland: Newman Press, 1963), 1–127.

7. Ulpian, *loc. cit.*

8. *IIa IIae,* q. 154, a. 1, *in corp.;* a. 11, *in corp.* Note that Thomas does speak about such actions as also being against right reason, but Ulpian's notion of natural law appears to have been the determining factor of what Thomas considered against right reason in this area. Lottin admits that Thomas in his attitude toward earlier definitions of natural law definitely "shows a sympathy for the formulae of Roman Law." Odon Lottin, *Le Droit Naturel chez Saint Thomas d'Aquin et ses prédécesseurs,* 2nd ed. (Bruges: Charles Beyaert, 1931), p. 67.

9. *IIa IIae,* q. 154, a 2, *in corp.* Noldin, p. 23, like Thomas, mentions that fornication is wrong because it is against the good of offspring and the propagation of the human race. No mention is made of the unitive or love union aspect of sexuality.

10. The historical information on the development of knowledge of human reproduction is taken from the following sources: George Washington Corner, "Discovery of the Mammalian Ovum," *Publications from the Department of Anatomy, School of Medicine and Dentistry, University of Rochester,* II (1930–33), No. 38, 401–423; Richard A. Leonardo, *A History of Gynecology* (New York: Forben Press, 1944); Harvey Graham, *Eternal Eve: The History of Obstetrics and Gynecology* (Garden City, N.Y.: Doubleday, 1955); Harold Speert, *Obstetric and Gynecologic Milestones* (New York: Macmillan, 1958).

11. Leonardo, p. 202.

12. The rhythm method of family planning, which is based on this comparatively recent information, only became scientifically acceptable through the independent work of Ogino and Knaus in the late 1920's.

13. *IIa IIae,* q. 154, a. 4, *in corp.*

14. Martinus DeMagistris, *Quaestiones Morales,* Vol. II (Paris, 1511), *De temperantia, Quaest. de luxuria,* fol. 54.

15. In the historical development of the question of parvity of matter in the sixth commandment, I am following quite closely the work of Jose M. Diaz Moreno, S.I., "La doctrina moral sobre la parvedad de materia 'in re venerea' desde Cayetano hasta S. Alfonso," *Archivo Teologico Granadino,* 23 (1960), 5–138.

16. *Operum Martini ab Azpilcueta (Doct. Navarri),* Vol. II (Rome: 1590), *Commentaria in Septem Distinctiones de Poenitentia,* d. 1, cap. *si cui,* n. 17. Navarrus here admits that he has found no other theologians who admit "a small venereal pleasure."

17. Thomas Sanchez, *Disputationum de Sancto Matrimonii Sacramento,* Vol. III (Venice, 1606), lib. 9, dis. 46. n. 9. Compare this with the change made in the later editions of his work in accord with the order of Father Aquaviva—e.g., the Antwerp edition of 1626.

18. Josephus Fuchs, S. I., *De Castitate et Ordine Sexuali,* 3rd ed. (Rome: Gregorian University Press, 1963), p. 139; Diaz Moreno, 42–47.

19. Arthurus Vermeersch, S. I., *De Castitate et De Vitiis Contrariis* (Bruges: Charles Beyaert, 1919), n. 352, p. 357.

20. Marcellino Zalba, S. I., *Theologiae Moralis Summa,* Vol. II: *De Mandatis Dei et Ecclesiae* (Madrid: Biblioteca de Autores Cristianos, 1953), pp. 340, 341.

21. Diaz Moreno lists the following as arguing in favor of parvity of matter in the sixth commandment: Navarrus, Thomas Sanchez, Cunha-freytas, John Sanchez, Marchant, Caramuel, Bassaeus, Hurtado and Verde. However, four of these authors treated the question only indirectly in the context of the question of sollicitation in confession.

22. Diaz Moreno, 135.

23. This statement is made by the contemporary manualist M. Zalba, p. 340. Waffelaert maintains that the opinion admitting parvity of matter was not condemned by the Pope or rejected as improbable. G. J. Waffelaert, *De Virtutibus Cardinalibus: De Prudentia, Fortitudine et Temperantia* (Bruges, 1889), n. 188, p. 303. Obviously this statement is limited to the time before Wafflelaert wrote his manual.

24. Response of the Holy Office of February 11, 1661, concerning the denunciation of sollicitation in confession: "Cum in rebus venereis non detur parvitas materiae, et, si daretur, in re praesenti non dari (detur?), censuerunt esse denuntiandum, et opinionem contrariam non esse probabilem." *DS, 2013.*

25. One of 45 propositions condemned by decree of the Holy Office,

March 18, 1666, as at least scandalous. *D.S.* 2060. For the order issued under Clement VIII and Paul V to denounce to the inquisitors those who assert that a kiss, an embrace, or a touch done for carnal pleasure is not a mortal sin, see Zalba, p. 340.

26. A decree of the Holy Office of May 1, 1929, withdrew from commerce the book of P.A. Laarakkers, *Quaedam moralia quae ex doctrina Divi Thomae Aquinatis selegit P.A. Laarakkers* (Cuyk aan de Maas, 1928) in which the author argued in favor of parvity of matter in the sixth commandment. For details, see Benedictus Merkelbach, *Questiones de Castitate et Luxuria* (Liege, 1936), pp. 28–31.

27. Fuchs, p. 139.

28. Fuchs, p. 139; Zalba, p. 341. Bernard Häring, *The Law of Christ*, III, (Westminster, Maryland: Newman Press, 1966), p. 291, says that it would be presumptuous to place the traditional thesis in doubt.

29. Diaz Moreno, pp. 135–137.

30. Fuchs, p. 141. Note the emphasis here on procreation and the good of the species. The same explanation with the same emphasis is found in Noldin, pp. 16, 17 and Zalba, pp. 342, 343.

31. The authors mentioned in note 30 all agree with this interpretation.

32. *IIa IIae,* q. 154, a. 3, ad. 1.

33. Anton Meinrad Meier, *Des Peccatum Mortale Ex Toto Genere Suo* (Regensburg: Verlag Friedrich Pustet, 1966).

34. As an example of such assertions made by Catholic psychologists, see Frederick von Gagern, *The Problem of Onanism* (Cork: Mercier Press, 1955), p. 95; George Hagmaier, C.S.P., and Robert Gleason, S. J., *Counseling the Catholic* (New York: Sheed and Ward, 1959), p. 81.

35. n. 51.

36. The Pastoral Constitution on the Church in the Modern World does not mention the question of the ends of marriage and their mutual relationship in its consideration of marriage, sexuality and responsible parenthood. The addresses of Paul VI on the precise question of responsible parenthood (June 23, 1964; March 27, 1965; October 29, 1966) seem to studiously avoid the question of the relationship between the ends of marriage. Even the encyclical *Humanae Vitae* does not speak of procreation as the primary end of marriage.

31. Heterosexual Expression, Marriage and Morality

Philip S. Keane, S.S.

This chapter first appeared in *Sexual Morality: A Catholic Perspective* in 1977.

Though this chapter will be our longest, it will be impossible to take up all aspects of heterosexual activity and marriage. Rather our purpose will be to treat a few key questions about heterosexual activity and marriage. We will begin with a basic statement about heterosexual genital activity and marriage, and then move on to treat premarital and extramarital sexual activities, sexual communion in marriage, means of controlling birth, and finally divorce and remarriage.

THE FUNDAMENTAL CATHOLIC CHRISTIAN VALUES ON HETEROSEXUAL ACTS AND MARRIAGE

The Beginning Point: Genital Sexual Acts and Marriage Go Together

As this book has unfolded, many of the wonderful and deeply significant aspects of human sexuality have been touched upon. We have seen how profoundly human sexuality affects our capacity for physical intimacy, for meaningful personal relationships, for the creation of new life (both physical and spiritual), for insertion into society as a whole and for relationship to the mystery of God. Across the centuries Christianity has deepened and is still deepening its appreciation of all these aspects of human sexuality. While no one insight or value can ever completely integrate all the aspects of our sexuality, the Roman Catholic tradition has constantly offered one key insight, that, perhaps more than any other insight, has served to unify and give coherence to the many values pertinent to human sexuality.

This key insight is that genital sexual activity so deeply involves all the potentials of the human person that it is best expressed and protected in a stable and enduring union between a man and a woman. To put it in other terms, the meaning of genital sexual activity is such that it calls for the personal union we know as marriage. Only in the context of marital fidelity can genital sexual acts have the possibility of accomplishing all the goodness for which such acts are apt. This is not to say that all types of marriage concretely structured in modern societies sufficiently reflect and give to people the opportunities that genital sexual union calls for. Nor is it to say that all marriages are automatically accomplishing more than other unions involving explicitly sexual activity, e.g., premarital unions or homosexual unions. But the point is that Roman Catholicism (and I think all of Christianity) has a clear value system in which genital sexual activity is linked with marriage.[1]

The insight of our faith on this point is not something that has come down upon humanity strictly from on high with no foundation in human life and experience. Rather there has been the experience of countless persons throughout the ages on the value of uniting genital sexual activity and marriage. Granted the many issues and difficulties of our own times (premarital sex and the divorce rate), the personally experienced intuition that genital sexual acts and marriage ought to be united remains quite prominent today. It is true that in our era many persons have more of a need to try a variety of adjustments out (in all areas of life) so as to decide for themselves what really seems to be most meaningful. Such experimentation has gone on in the area of genital sexual activity. Very interestingly, the experiments in the area of genital sexual activity have tended to lead many of the experimenters to discover on an inductive or experiential basis that monogamous marriage works better for most human beings. The work of Carl Rogers and other authors summarizes some of the inductively made discoveries of the value of monogamous marriage.[2]

Deeper Christian Insights into Marriage

What we have so far described about the union between genital sexual activity and marriage might be said to have a primarily natural basis. We have talked about the conjugal love of spouses for each other and indicated that the character of the conjugal love union between spouses argues for the union of sexual acts and permanent marriage. If we reflect more deeply on the Christian tradition, we can find an even deeper basis for our insight about heterosexual activity and marriage. This deeper basis is that the conjugal love of a married couple mysteriously and wonderfully symbolizes and makes real in this world the covenantal love God has for all of us. Earlier it was stated that Yahweh's covenant of love for his people is the most ultimate basis from which to understand the mystery of human sexuality. Our present position on marriage (and on sexual acts in marriage) as a sign of God's love explicates this connection between human sexuality and God's covenant love.

Additional metaphors and images besides covenant can also be used to make the point about sexuality and marriage as a mirror of God and his love for us. St. Paul uses Christ's love for the Church as the theological point to which marriage ought to be compared. "Husbands love your wives as Christ loved the Church" (Eph. 5,25). Those theologians who hold that the Trinity is a profound teaching on the existence of dynamic and intimate personal relationships in God would see marriage as a beautiful symbol of the trinitarian life of God. Other theologians would make the highly significant point that the married couple give love as growing members of the communion of saints. Their love is not only for themselves but for all people.[3] In the final analysis, married love proclaims that the whole people of God is called to newness of life in the resurrection. Hence, the married couple's covenantal love is a proclamation of hope for the whole communion of saints.

In Roman Catholicism, and in other Christian communities as well, all these insights about marriage (its witness to God's covenantal love, to the inner life of the Trinity, to Christ's love for the Church, and to our resurrection destiny in the communion of saints) have led to our key faith consciousness on marriage, namely that marriage is a sacrament. It took the Church a number of centuries to recognize clearly the sacramentality of marriage, but this recognition is essential in our faith perspective concerning marriage. The fact that marriage existed as a very meaningful human good before the time of Christ probably explains why it took so long for the explicitly religious aspects of marriage to be distinguished in such a way that we could perceive the sacramentality of marriage.[4]

Because the context of this book is human sexuality, it is especially important for us to note that everything about a marriage, including its explicitly sexual aspects, is part of the sacrament. Sometimes there is too much of a tendency to think of the sacrament of matrimony as only the ceremony that begins the marriage, not the whole marriage. Past fear of human sexuality may have been part of the reason why the marriage ceremony, rather than the whole marriage, popped into mind when we spoke about the sacrament of marriage. But all of the married couple's giving to one another and to their children is part of the sacrament of marriage.[5] Sexual intercourse, as a major sign of the total union of spouses, is surely to be conceived of as a significant element in the sacramental life of married couples. In this context, sexual intercourse can be understood as a liturgical or worshipful action.

The Purposes or Ends of Marriage

As we have reflected on the natural and religious aspects (which are never fully separable in the concrete) of heterosexual acts and marriage, mention has been made of both the union between the spouses and their openness to having children. The question might be asked as to how these elements or ends of marriage (mutual love, children) and indeed other aspects of a marriage are best integrated into a synthesis. Past Catholic teaching used to express its synthesis of the ends of marriage by the statement that the procreation of children is the primary end of marriage. This teaching was not, however, used by the Second Vatican Council,[6] so it seems that we are free to search for other formulations in our effort to integrate all the values pertinent to sexual activity and marriage.

Our purpose in these pages has been to be wholistic, human, and Christian in our approach to sexuality. With this in mind it seems best to take the union between the spouses as the most integrating factor in our description of the meaning and purposes of sexuality and marriage. It is this conjugal union of the couples that makes possible all the values at stake in marriage. The man/woman relationship which is so meaningful in life as a whole is most deeply realized by the personal union of spouses in marriage. The capacity for physical intimacy, which is a universal human need, is most fully able to be realized through the union of spouses in marriage. Creative life-giving service and witness to others comes as a result of the personal union of the spouses in marriage. This life-giving creativity includes but goes far beyond the procreation of children. In other words, all the values at stake in sexuality and marriage (physical, personal, social, and spiritual values) seem to have roots in the total union of the couple and in their experience of loving each other in their differences. When a couple marries, their clear commitment is to each other; this commitment (which witnesses God's love and gift of resurrection) will continue even if there are no children or even after the children have moved away. This commitment or two-in-oneness of the married couple is what society and individuals concretely and really have in mind when they think of conjugal or married love. For Christians, this commitment sacramentalizes God's love for the human family.[7]

Properly understood, this description of married love in no way minimalizes the place of children in marriage. Children are the supreme concrete manifestation of the physical, personal, and social union of the spouses. But marriage is still marriage even when there are no children, (e.g., in cases of sterility). And unless children spring from the kind of total personal and permanent union of spouses just described, the life situation of children will be sadly lacking. Thus it seems essential that we declare the union of the spouses in their otherness to be the focal point from which marriage is to be understood both humanly and Christianly. If we too quickly move to the children in defining marriage, values essential to the marriage and to the children may be lost sight of.

In a way this question about synthesizing the ends of marriage reflects a false problem, brought on by the popular Catholic impression (for which the Church must bear some responsibility) that children were far more important than anything else in marriage. For the couple who have a dynamically growing and wholistic view of their marriage, all the various "ends" of marriage (each other, their children, if any, and union with all of God's people) fit together integrally into a total pattern of life that emerges out of lived experience and does not require a lot of theorizing. Our reflections have made covenantal, conjugal love the focal point of marriage since it is from this love that the whole picture of marriage flows and toward this love (ultimately consummated in our resurrected life) that the whole picture of marriage moves.

Some Problems with the Current Catholic Proclamation of Marriage

The past few pages have described the beauty and sacramentality of marriage, and the Christian insight that genital sexual activity belongs in marriage. Yet in today's world the incidence of premarital sex and divorce is very high. One may wonder why, if the Church's viewpoint is as sound as we have argued, there is not more appreciation of the approach to sexuality and marriage just outlined. There are a number of reasons why many persons in our society disagree with the Church's approach to sexuality and marriage. The selfishness and sinfulness of various persons and social structures certainly cannot be omitted from any list of reasons to be proposed on this point. From our vantage point, however, it might be well to develop at more length one particular reason why the Church's views on sexuality and marriage are less appreciated than they ought to be. The reason we shall develop is the failure of the Church (and here we mean all in the Church, not simply those in authority) to make her teaching on sexuality and marriage stand out as clearly as possible.

Several factors enter into the Church's failure to make her fundamental position on sexual acts and marriage more clear to people at large. First, the Church has spent too much time making one-sided and unnuanced condemnations of sexual acts that fall short of her basic position on sexual acts and marriage. The result is that people have to spend so much time wrestling with the Church's approach to non-marital sexual acts that they do not appreciate the positive strength of what the Church has to say about marriage and sexuality. If the Church more carefully nuanced its stands on other sexual questions, people would be more free to appreciate the positive side of the Church's teaching on the normativity of heterosexual acts in marriage. This book has attempted to develop more nuanced positions on masturbation and homosexuality and will later do so on premarital sex and divorce. The recent Vatican document on sexual ethics did attempt to be more pastoral on the matters it treated, though it could have gone further. Individual leaders such as Bishop Mugavero of Brooklyn have tried to develop sensitive positions on issues such as homosexuality.[8] The Canon Law Society of America and the Catholic Theological Society of America have done the same in the whole area of second marriages.[9] More steps need to be taken in this direction so that a harshness on particular problems does not continue to be an obstacle keeping people from seeing the basic strength of the Church's insight that genital sexual acts are best protected in stable marriages. Those who simply and unqualifiedly repeat traditional condemnations of various sexual matters may in fact be helping to undermine the Church's teaching on marriage.

Another way in which the Church can obscure the value of her position on sexuality and marriage is by being too physical in her explanation of marriage. Marriage is a personal union of the couple, a union that of its very nature calls out for fidelity and, therefore, for personal maturity. If the notion that marriage is basically for physical sex and for children is stressed without emphasis on the notions of union, human fidelity, and maturity, there are bound to be difficult marriages, many of which end in divorce. The Church, of course, knows that there is more to marriage than physical sex and children, but she does sometimes leave the popular impression that these are the main values at stake in marriage.[10] Since marriage calls for fidelity and commitment, the Church has a responsibility to sponsor careful education and preparation for marriage, especially in an era when human maturity seems on average to come at an older age than in the past.[11] We will talk later about the Church's stand on divorce, but it should be noted now that the real issue raised by divorce is the Church's need to attain to a deeper vision of marriage and prepare people for marriage on the basis of such a vision.

Needed: A Richer Theology of Marriage

These last comments indicate the greatest single task for the Church to undertake if her approach to sexuality and marriage is to win wider acceptance. This task is the building of a well-articulated theology of marriage, a theology that will give a more substantial grounding to the basic insight that genital sexual acts best take place in marriage. It was mentioned earlier that it took the Church centuries to understand that marriage is a sacrament in the first place. This fact, plus the various currents of misunderstanding that have surrounded human sexuality, make it no surprise that we do not have a very extensive theology of marriage. A great deal of material has been written on particular sexual questions and problems both in and outside of marriage. But there has been relatively little written on the theology of marriage itself.[12]

This lack must be overcome. We live in a world that has come of age, to use Bonhoeffer's phrase. In such a world we are much more conscious of the dignity and worth of human persons. We are also conscious of the great richness and variety in human relationships, a richness available to all persons including married couples.[13] Simple stereotyped descriptions of marriage that do not treat it as a relational reality and that tend to close the development of the marriage partners both toward each other and toward all persons will not work. Much of the theology we do have on marriage still comes from the era of arranged marriages, i.e., from the era when older relatives made marital decisions with a view to inheritances, etc., not with a view to whether the married couple themselves loved each other and wanted to foster each other's personal dignity and worth through their marriage.[14] In our age, which has transcended these past customs, there exists both the possibility and the necessity of enunciating a richer theology of marriage that will be more widely understood and accepted on the popular level.

Some of the bare rudiments of this in-depth theology of marriage have been suggested herein. We have noted for instance that human sexuality opens up avenues to personal growth both in and outside of the marriage union itself. We have tried to suggest that the awesome and enriching character of human sexual intercourse calls for fidelity and commitment,[15] with these notions not being as old-fashioned as they sometimes sound. We have stressed the central importance (though not absolute necessity) of children to marriage, an importance that in itself demands marital stability for the sake of the best human development of the children. Finally, we have asserted that marriage as a human reality and as a sacrament bears witness to God and enriches the lives of all people by proclaiming our resurrection destiny. Hopefully others will pick up these rudiments and build a theology of marriage. The present author is convinced that the Church has the necessary roots for sound theology of marriage and that the explication of this theology will serve to increase significantly the acceptance of a Christian viewpoint on sexuality and marriage.

Many of the remarks made so far in this chapter have stressed the beauty and goodness of Christian marriage. It might be well to close this section on a note of realism so that the foregoing will not be written off as pie in the sky. Marriage is hard work. For all its value it will not cure people of all their problems as some seem to think when they enter it. Indeed, it would be very foolish to look upon marriage as a solution to problems. No marriage will ever fully actualize all the values described above. Every marriage will have its difficult times. But many marriages, for all their limitations, will be very good marriages that do go a long way toward realizing the values of marriage described above.

PREMARITAL AND EXTRAMARITAL SEXUAL ACTIVITIES

Premarital and Extramarital Intercourse: Definitions and Statistics

One issue that must be treated in light of the above remarks on heterosexual activity and marriage is premarital and extramarital intercourse. In our present context premarital sexual intercourse refers to any intercourse before marriage, whether with one's future marriage partner or someone else. Extramarital sexual intercourse refers to that extramarital intercourse taking place when there is an existing, functioning marriage. The case of someone who marries a second time after a first marriage has broken up (and who is thus guilty of adultery and extramarital sex in the traditional Catholic view) will be considered later.

Before getting into some specific types of cases of premarital and extramarital sexual intercourse, a few statistical reflections might help set a context. There is a very widespread opinion that the rates of premarital and extramarital intercourse have increased enormously in the last decade or so. Stories about college campuses, wife-swapping parties, etc., promote this opinion. The statistics we have available show that the rate of premarital sexual intercourse in the United States has increased gradually over our century instead of all at once in recent years. The really big change in participation in premarital sex in the United States in our century has involved women, inasmuch as the percentage of twentieth-century American males having premarital sexual intercourse has always been quite high (eighty to ninety percent in most surveys). Of American women born before 1900 only fourteen percent had premarital intercourse. About thirty-six percent of women born around 1925 had premarital intercourse. Of those women born in the World War II era, sixty-five percent have had premarital sexual intercourse, with the figure reaching eighty-one percent in the youngest age group surveyed.[16]

One interesting aspect of the fact that the number of women having premarital intercourse has come to almost equal the number of men doing so is that premarital sexual intercourse seems to have become more affectionate and personal than it was earlier in the century when the many men having premarital intercourse had to do so with fewer available women, often with prostitutes. In addition, while much premarital sex has been narrowly premarital (only with one's fiancé) throughout the twentieth century, even more premarital sexual intercourse is limited to fiancés only today than was the case earlier in our century.[17] This seems to imply that premarital intercourse is more connected with permanent commitment today than it was in past decades. Another important point is that the statistical research done so far has failed to show any clear correlation, positive or negative, between premarital intercourse and the success or failure of marriages. It should also be noted that premarital intercourse is less frequent among the very devout in all religious groups.[18]

These statistics are not presented to condone premarital sexual intercourse but simply to bring us abreast of the results of some admittedly limited surveys of premarital sexual intercourse. Possibly these surveys indicate a change for the better in the context in which premarital intercourse is occurring. The statistics also suggest that older generations in our society ought not to cry out against premarital intercourse as if it had never happened before the sixties and seventies.

As far as extramarital sexual intercourse is concerned it is harder to get a complete picture since statistics are much less available and reliable. In general however, extramarital intercourse happens a lot less often than premarital intercourse. Kinsey's report placed the extramarital intercourse rate at fifty percent for men and twenty-six percent for women, and noted that among devoutly religious people the rate was much less than this.[19] There appears to have been very little change on this issue since Kinsey's time except that the adultery rates for both sexes are equalizing.[20] Those Americans who have been involved in adultery have generally found the experience notably less satisfying than they find sexual intercourse in marriage.[21] The adultery that does happen in our country is only very rarely of the wife-swapping, group-sex, swinging-orgy variety that gets so much publicity. Only about two percent of American men and even fewer women have ever been involved in these so called "swinging" activities.[22] All in all, therefore, the statistics suggest that twentieth-century America's opposition to extramarital intercourse remains fairly high. If our society has shifted somewhat in its attitude toward premarital intercourse, it has not done so on any large scale in regard to extramarital intercourse.

Casual Premarital Intercourse and Adultery

With the background of Roman Catholicism's basic position on heterosexual acts and marriage, and with the statistical facts in mind, we can now consider the morality of premarital and extramarital intercourse. Our considerations will cover three types of non-marital intercourse, two of which will be fairly easy to handle since the Church's teaching and the statistical input tend to support one another. The first of our cases has to do with the casual use of sexual intercourse by the unmarried, i.e., with intercourse for physical fun or pleasure. This type of intercourse falls very far short of the Church's insight that intercourse is best expressed in the personal union known as marriage.[23] Since this form of intercourse is so lacking in personal commitment, it seems impossible to justify it. The data in our statistics suggest that society is still quite opposed to this sort of intercourse on an experiential or practical level. If anything, there is even less of this casual intercourse practiced today per capita than fifty years ago. Hence in the case of casual premarital intercourse, the best judgment seems to be that there are no circumstances in which the ontic evil contained in such intercourse does not become a moral evil. To put it in another way, the Church's traditional opposition to casual premarital intercourse is still quite coherent in our times.[24]

The statement that casual premarital intercourse always involves a moral as well as an ontic evil should not be taken as meaning that every couple who engages in casual premarital intercourse is guilty of mortal sin, i.e., guilty of breaking their fundamental option for God. Regrettably, there are sources in our society that strongly promote casual premarital intercourse, and thus pressure some of our young people (e.g., college students) into acts of premarital intercourse for which they are not fully personally responsible. At times this pressure is such that young unmarried women can feel "out of it" if they are not having intercourse. All this means that we must be pastorally sensitive in dealing with young people who are having casual premarital intercourse. Some of them may not be involved in the total turning away from God that is necessary for the breaking of their fundamental options. In no way, however, should our pastoral sensitivity lead us to give the impression that there is any moral justification for casual premarital intercourse.

Our second case of non-marital sexual intercourse is the case of adultery, i.e., the case of a married person having intercourse with someone other than his or her spouse. As indicated above, we are not including in this case those persons who are in second marriages that are invalid from the Church's viewpoint. Our focus is on those acts of extramarital intercourse that are engaged in by partners in concretely existing marriages. The trust, openness, and self-giving to one's spouse that marriage calls for seems clearly to exclude acts of intercourse outside the marriage, since such acts indicate a division of the deep, personal self-giving that belongs in marriage. The act of sexual intercourse inherently contains a meaning level involving personal fidelity and commitment. Human beings cannot deny this meaning level in sexual intercourse and act as if any meaning whatever can be attached to intercourse.[25] One of our key theses in this book is that body and soul are inseparable in the human person. This thesis means that sexual intercourse will never achieve its real human potential except in the context of the personal commitment we call marriage. The statistical fact that so many married persons who have tried extramarital intercourse have found it to be less satisfying than married intercourse seems to bear out this fundamental philosophical and Christian insight. Hence we must conclude that in normal life there are virtually no circumstances that would give moral justification to the ontic evil inherent in extramarital sexual intercourse.[26] As with casual premarital intercourse, this position does not imply that all adulterers are guilty of broken fundamental option and personal mortal sin. At the same time, in the case of extramarital intercourse we are ordinarily dealing with persons older than the young adults who might be led to engage in casual premarital intercourse. Thus the possibility of extramarital intercourse's involving someone's fundamental option seems more likely than in the case of casual premarital intercourse, especially when there are repeated instances of extramarital intercourse over an extended period of time.

The Dilemma of Committed Premarital Intercourse

The third and by far the most difficult case of sexual intercourse outside of marriage is the case of sexual intercourse by a man and a woman who are deeply personally committed to each other and whose intercourse takes place in this context of personal commitment. In this case the union of the partners has much of the personal and human reality of marriage. Often the partners in such intercourse intend to marry and will do so if and when their circumstances permit. These factors do make this sort of intercourse complex and challenging to evaluate. Our review of statistics has suggested that society at large is rather open to this particular type of intercourse, which, as we shall see, may never have existed in former societies in quite the way it exists today.

Several perspectives need to be developed to evaluate fully this case of premarital intercourse with personal commitment and affection. First, it must be said that even in this case the Church's basic norm that genital sexual activity is best protected and expressed in marriage remains clearly in place. Marriage has about it an inherent social dimension as well as a personal dimension. Thus a deep heterosexual love union between two persons needs to be publicly witnessed. Such a union by its very nature is apt to contribute to the growth and development of society. As long as the union remains on a purely private level it is not achieving its fullness, it is not clearly sacramentally witnessing to society the love of God for his people.[27] Part of the reason, but by no means the whole reason, why such a union is not witnessing to society is because it is not open (most probably through birth control) to the procreation of children. When all of these factors are put together, the conclusion to be drawn is that there is no case of premarital intercourse, even in the best of circumstances, that does not contain a morally significant level of ontic evil or lack of due fullness of being. This conviction about ontic evil will be an element in all our evaluations of premarital intercourse.

A second point to be made is that many of these cases of committed premarital sexual intercourse are not as good as they look at first glance. A lot of the rhetoric about love and commitment in these cases is simply rhetoric and it can cover a fair degree of selfishness and immaturity. Part of the problem here is that one partner can never be sure that the other partner's words of commitment—which are not public—are genuine. It all too often and all too traumatically happens that one deeply committed partner in such a union discovers that the other person's commitment, though spoken, was really not meant.[28] Admittedly this problem could also happen after marriage, but the social character of marriage does help make such a problem less likely.

Third, it must be acknowledged that, in our highly complicated and industrialized society, loving heterosexual unions of people are sometimes affected by some very difficult circumstances. For centuries, the Church has taught that people have a right to marry, a right that society cannot unreasonably infringe upon.[29] With this in mind, it can be argued that in our times there are perhaps some cases in which society does unreasonably impede people's right to marry. One example is the situation of a widow who falls in love and wishes to marry, but faces significant financial problems (loss of pension benefits, etc.) if she does so. In an older, simpler society, this widow and her first husband probably would have saved their own retirement income so that she would have had no financial problems relative to a second marriage. In our society, with its socialized retirement programs, she does have a problem. Another example would be the case of a young man and woman in their later twenties who are mature, deeply committed to each other, and fully intending to marry. Before they are free to do so, the young man is having to work through a whole series of socially structured delays: college, military service, graduate school, the achievement of financial independence, etc. These factors might not delay all couples from marriage, but they tend to do so for some of our best young people. If all the delay factors just mentioned operate in a given case, marriage might be postponed ten full years beyond the time when the couple is physically prepared for it, ten years beyond the time when people married in an older, more agrarian type of society. It is perhaps no surprise that society began to adopt a new attitude toward committed premarital intercourse at about the same time that our industrial society altered the usual age and financial conditions necessary for marriage (cf. our statistics showing that the change on this matter began early in our century). It may also be quite possible that the delay in achieving maturity that many notice in our young adults is related to the fact that many young adults cannot achieve financial independence until they near the age of thirty.[30]

Both of the examples just given make the same key point: our society has established a socioeconomic structure for marriage and family life that may unreasonably restrict some persons' fundamental freedom to marry. Because of this situation, the present author's position is that, in a limited number of cases, the circumstances surrounding the intercourse of a couple who are deeply committed to each other and who fully intend to marry may render their premarital intercourse an ontic evil but not a moral evil.[31] The possibility of such intercourse being an ontic but not a moral evil would seem to be present especially when the committed couple whose marriage rights are unreasonably prejudiced by society do not experience themselves as genuinely free to take the more ideal route of abstaining from that intercourse that cannot be publicly proclaimed as part of a marriage. In these cases the intercourse's lack of public proclamation is not due to any defect in the intention of the couple; it is due rather to certain problematic characteristics of modern society. The couple in such a situation needs to have the humility to recognize that their intercourse is still lacking an important dimension; morally speaking, however, their intercourse may not be wrong.

From a pastoral viewpoint, the most important thing to recognize about the cases we have just described is that they are rare. The great problem is that when we admit the existence of such rare cases, all sorts of people will conclude that their case is one of the rare cases.[32] Ways must be found to avoid this difficulty. Of the issues we treated earlier, masturbation is obviously a transitional phase of sexual development and homosexual acts based on a permanent homosexual orientation are relevant for only a small (but significant) portion of humanity. Thus there is little danger that our positions on certain cases of masturbation and homosexual activity will be applied permanently to the larger part of the human race. But with premarital intercourse the danger of our carefully outlined cases being carelessly extended to large segments of humanity is quite real.

In terms of what we might do to cut down on the increased occurrence of such unwarranted premarital sex, the first priority is a theme we have already touched on: the deepening of our theology of marriage. With a richer vision of marriage, perhaps more people would freely respond to the ascetic challenge to abstain from intercourse until marriage. Besides this step we should clearly assert once again that the only cases where premarital intercourse seems morally justifiable are the cases where there is a real maturity and commitment including the intention to marry when and if the interfering social obstacles are removed. If in such cases the couple breaks up or fails to marry when the opportunity comes, they ought to be judged by moral standards similar to those that apply to formally married couples who break up.

We should also note that there may be cases of committed premarital intercourse in which, while the degree of commitment and social pressures do not offer a moral justification, the emotional attachment of the couple and the attitudes of our society are such as to bring about a situation in which the couple do not break their fundamental option for God through their intercourse. This, in other words, is the objectively grave but subjectively not culpable case. The case in which we would offer a moral justification for premarital intercourse (ontic evil but not moral evil) is very rare. The objectively grave but subjectively not culpable case seems likely to happen somewhat more often.[33]

Three issues ought to be raised as a follow-up to our whole approach to premarital intercourse. First, some might pose the question whether those few cases where premarital intercourse does seem morally justifiable could be handled through the traditional notion of a secret marriage (i.e., a marriage secretly witnessed by the priest) since in these cases the couple's intention toward each other is basically the same as if they were married. There is a somewhat unfortunate legalism underlying this question, a legalism assuming that the problem involved in premarital intercourse is completely solved when a priest blesses a genuine intention to marry that is frustrated by unreasonable external factors. Some would even suggest that fully committed premarital intercourse is not premarital intercourse at all, but only preceremonial intercourse. To those who would assert such a distinction or who would hold that a secret ceremony would take care of such a case,[34] it must be asserted that public proclamation (so that the couple can witness God's love) is an essential element in marriage. Thus even a secret marriage is an ontic evil; it is not a complete solution to the difficulty that committed but not publicly marriageable couples face.

Also, while the cases of justifiable premarital intercourse, even in our times, are few, our dealing with them on the basis of secret marriages would lead to significantly more secret marriages than in past nonindustrial societies. This in turn could lead to a variety of social and legal problems. Hence, a secret marriage might be used in cases of grave pastoral necessity (e.g., the case of an elderly couple having weighty problems of conscience about their love relationship), but it does not seem wise to expand the notion of secret marriages too greatly.

Another issue has to do with the use of birth control devices by those whose premarital intercourse may be morally justifiable or even by those whose premarital intercourse is not morally justifiable. It used to be said that the employment of birth control devices always added to the wrong of premarital intercourse. Our more complete treatment of birth control will come later in this chapter. For now we can briefly anticipate that treatment by saying that if a premarried couple is truly justified in having intercourse, their use of birth control devices does not seem morally wrong provided that they are open to having children when the right opportunity comes. As for those who premarital intercourse does not seem morally justified, it might be suggested today that such a couple, by using birth control devices, is actually lessening the wrong in their intercourse since at least they are avoiding the procreation of new life for which they are unable to take responsibility.

Finally, nothing that has been said about some cases of premarital sexual intercourse gives any credibility at all to the notion of trial marriage. Our basic notion is that marriage is permanent and the few exceptions we did make concerning premarital intercourse were made precisely because these exceptions involved the basic reality of a permanent marital commitment. Married love is difficult to achieve amid life's ups and downs. Trial marriage for a few years would almost guarantee that marriage would not work. Without permanent commitment, too many couples would take the easy way out when they ran into problems. The growth that is part of committed marriages would not take place. There is a big difference between being open to a few premarital dilemmas such as those described above and setting up a legal-social structure that literally invites marriage to fail. The Church, in its tradition on marriage, must remain steadfastly opposed to trial marriages.

Premarital Petting

Our past theology, with its position that all sexual arousal outside of marriage is an objectively grave moral evil, tended to place premarital sexual petting in more or less the same category of condemnation as premarital intercourse. Perhaps a bit more refinement is called for on this matter. For one thing, statistical surveys seem to suggest that petting has increased in our industrially and socially complicated century because persons whose marriage has been delayed beyond the age when they are physically ready to marry (college students, etc.) have turned to petting precisely as a means to avoid sexual intercourse.[35] In other words, some petting is an effort by physically mature young people to deal with their sexual tensions in a way that respects the fact that intercourse ought to be reserved for marriage. Another point is that not all petting is the same. Some of it is very mild, really intended more as a sign of affection than as a means to intense sexual arousal. Other petting is more intense, perhaps involving protracted lying together, deep and erotic kissing, fondling of the breasts or genitals, partial or total nudity, and possibly even organsm. Some would say that a distinction should be made between deep petting that is not orgasm-producing and deep petting that leads to orgasm. Others might see this particular distinction as based on an overly physical understanding of human sexuality.[36] Regardless of the exact distinctions made, premarital petting is a complex enough issue that it deserves some comment in addition to what has already been said about premarital intercourse.

As far as mild petting activities (kisses, brief embraces, etc.) are concerned, it should be acknowledged that the signs of human affection involved in such mild petting are signs that are not exclusively oriented toward marriage or sexual intercourse. All persons in all states of life have a need for affection and support. Thus, in situations when close human affection is appropriate, mild gestures of embrace and kissing are certainly acceptable. Such mild gestures are acceptable not only for premarried couples, but also for married couples with persons other than their spouses, for celibates, and indeed for everyone. These gestures are part of the basic human need for intimacy; growing comfortable with them is an important human learning process. It is a bit difficult to draw an exact line between petting that is mild and not directly intended for sexual arousal (though it may indirectly cause some arousal) and petting that is not so mild and more clearly arousing. The level of response and stimulation from the activities we are discussing can vary greatly from individual to individual, meaning that different persons (possibly in consultation with a confessor or other counselor) will have to make their own best decisions on what is acceptable for them in this area. Some cases of acceptable human kissing and embracing outside the context of marriage (funerals, weddings of good friends, etc.) should be fairly obvious to all of us.

The position that there are clear instances in which mild forms of petting are acceptable in non-marital contexts does not mean that these mild forms of petting should be taken for granted. Such petting can easily incline people toward sexual involvement and, even apart from this fact, human embrace and the respect for the other that it bespeaks should never be treated lightly. There are persons who seem almost too ready to make use of the gift of embrace in practically any circumstances. People, their backgrounds, and their cultures do differ, but the importance of human embrace ("the theology of hugging") is such that we ought to be careful not to cheapen it.

On the subject of deeper and more protracted petting, the clear orientation of this petting toward sexual intercourse and marriage suggests that this kind of petting falls under our basic norm that genital sexual activity is best expressed in marriage. Thus heavy petting before marriage should always be understood as involving ontic evil, i.e., as not being a fully satisfactory form of human sexual expression. We noted earlier that there may be some cases in which the ontic evil of premarital intercourse does not become a moral evil. This same judgment should be applied to heavy premarital petting. In the same sort of circumstances in which premarital intercourse might not be a moral evil, premarital petting might also not be a moral evil.

Moreover, if we seek to compare the ontic evil involved in heavy premarital petting with the ontic evil involved in premarital intercourse, it seems reasonable to assert that the ontic evil in premarital petting, while quite important, is not as significant as the ontic evil involved in premarital intercourse. In the special circumstances of a societally hindered commitment to marry, the couple who limit themselves to heavy petting (possibly including orgasm) are trying, in their difficult situation, to respect the fact that intercourse is best expressed in marriage. It is this which suggests that the ontic evil involved in heavy premarital petting may be somewhat less significant than the ontic evil in premarital intercourse. If this line of argument is correct, the proportionate reasons necessary to give moral justification to heavy premarital petting may not be quite as weighty as the proportionate reasons necessary to justify premarital intercourse. A couple who find themselves in a borderline situation might keep this in mind.

We might also argue that, even in those cases (and there are many) where the ontic evil of heavy premarital petting cannot be given any objective moral justification, the fact that the ontic evil in heavy petting is less significant than the ontic evil in premarital intercourse implies that there may be more likelihood of heavy premarital petters not breaking their fundamental option for God than would be the case with those engaging in premarital intercourse. Of course, in both of these matters (heavy premarital petting and premarital intercourse), the breaking of a fundamental option is more prone to occur when there is a series of actions rather than one act or incident alone.

In applying these remarks about heavy premarital petting, we should note that the psychological implications of heavy petting (in many ways a practice new to the twentieth century) without intercourse are not fully understood. For instance, might the interruption of sexual arousal before it leads to intercourse cause psychological problems for the persons involved? This does not seem very likely in occasional instances of petting, since petting can be understood as part of a learning process that will eventually and integrally lead one to intercourse. But regular non-coital petting over a lengthy period of time might possibly be a cause of notable psychological frustrations. We really do not know the answer on this matter, and until we do caution is called for, especially in regard to petting over protracted periods of months and years. If it should emerge that certain types of premarital petting situations do lead to significant psychological problems, our above-stated tentative conclusion about the weight of the ontic evil of heavy premarital petting would have to be revised, at least for the pertinent cases.[37]

Notes

1. For a recent statement of this basic value system, cf. Richard A. McCormick, "Sexual Ethics: An Opinion," *NCR* (January 30, 1976), p. 9. McCormick also developed this notion in "NMT," *TS* 34 (1973), pp. 90–91.

2. Carl Rogers, *Becoming Partners: Marriage and Its Alternatives* (New York: Delacorte Press, 1972).

3. Cf. Karl Rahner, *The Trinity* (New York: Herder and Herder, 1970); Wilhelm Breuning, "The Communion of Saints," *SM* 1, pp. 391–394.

4. The theme of the above sentence is contained in the title of Edward Schillebeeckx's *Marriage: Human Reality and Saving Mystery* (cf. abbreviation *MHR*).

5. For a fuller development of this notion, cf. Leonard F. Gerke, *Christian Marriage: A Permanent Sacrament* (Washington: The Catholic University of America Press, 1965: Doctoral Dissertation).

6. On Vatican II's omission of the terms primary and secondary, see the *Pastoral Constitution on the Church in the Modern World,* no. 48 (*DV2,* p. 250, note 155). Actually, if the word primary is not taken to mean most important or most fundamental, but rather as meaning "what is most concretely unique about the possibilities available in marriage as compared to other love relationships,"·children could still be called the primary end of marriage. The problem is that the word is too seldom understood in this very precise and specific sense.

7. The notion of conjugal commitment as the basic focal point of marriage was developed very significantly by Hubert Doms in *The Meaning of Marriage* (New York: Sheed and Ward, 1939). More recently this theme (with a healthy stress on the physical values present in conjugal love) has

been taken up by John Giles Milhaven in "Conjugal Sexual Love," *TS* 35 (1974), pp. 692–710.

8. Cf. Francis Mugavero, "Pastoral Letter: The Gift of Sexuality," *Origins* 5 (1976), pp. 581–586.

9. For examples of the continuing work of the Canon Law Society of America see *The Jurist* 30 (1970), pp. 1–74; Lawrence G. Wrenn, ed., *Divorce and Remarriage in the Catholic Church* (New York: Newman Press, 1973). For the work of the Catholic Theological Society of America, see "Appendix B: The Problem of Second Marriages," *CTSA* 27 (1972), pp. 233–240.

10. An opposite sort of danger can also exist. Some of those who want to move away from the overly physical approaches become so spiritual in their approaches to marriage that the physical and emotional values of marriage are lost sight of. Cf. John Giles Milhaven, "Conjugal Sexual Love," *TS* 35 (1974), p. 700.

11. Material on marriage preparation is relatively limited. One program is Martin Olsen and George Kaenel, *Two as One: A Christian Marriage Preparation Program* (Includes Workbook and Manual, New York: Paulist Press, 1976). Also very helpful is J. Murray Elwood, *Growing Together in Marriage* (Notre Dame, Indiana: Ave Maria Press, 1977).

12. Besides Schillebeeckx, *MHR*, other works on the theology of marriage include Karl Rahner, "Marriage as a Sacrament," *TI* 10 pp. 199–221; Franz Bockle, ed. *Concilium* 5, no. 7 (1970), Issue title: *The Future of Marriage as an Institution;* Rosemary Haughton, *The Theology of Marriage* (Notre Dame, Indiana: Fides Publishers, 1970); William Bassett and Peter Huizing, eds., *Concilium* 7, no. 9 (1973), Issue title: *The Future of Christian Marriage;* Bernard Häring, *Marriage in the Modern World* (Westminster, Maryland: The Newman Press, 1965).

13. While questions might be raised about some of its specific approaches, the basic outlook of the bestseller *Open Marriage,* with its stress on the variety of relationships possible for a married couple, seems quite sound. Nena and George O'Neill, *Open Marriage: A New Lifestyle for Couples* (New York: M. Evans, 1972).

14. For an historical background, cf. Schillebeeckx, *MHR,* pp. 231–380. Thomas Aquinas held that the bethrothal could take place at the age of seven (*ST* III, 43, 2). My comments on the limitations and impersonalism of some aspects of the medieval view of marriage should not be construed as denying the social nature of marriage, as denying that society can place some legitimate social expectations on couples planning to marry.

15. Important recent works on commitment include John Haughey, *Should Anyone Say Forever? On Making, Keeping and Breaking Commit-*

ments (Garden City, New York: Doubleday, 1975); Margaret A. Farley, *A Study in the Ethics of Commitment Within the Context of Theories of Human Love and Temporality* (New Haven: Yale University, 1974, Doctoral Dissertation).

16. The first of the figures given for women having premarital intercourse (14%) comes from Alfred Kinsey *et al., SBF,* p. 298. The more recent figures come from Morton Hunt, *SB70,* p. 150. For no group of American males born at any time during the twentieth century did Hunt find less than eighty-four percent who had had premarital intercourse.

17. *K&L,* p. 314.

18. *K&L,* p. 313.

19. Kinsey *et al., SBF,* p. 437.

20. Morton Hunt, *SB70,* pp. 258–261. For the oldest group Hunt surveyed, (55 or older in 1972), forty-three percent of men and fifteen percent of women had had extramarital intercourse. For the youngest group he surveyed (age 25 and under), the respective figures were thirty-two percent and twenty-four percent. Figures for this youngest group will probably increase as their years of marriage increase.

21. Hunt, *SB70,* pp. 215–278.

22. Hunt, *SB70,* pp. 271–274.

23. In rejecting the theory of premarital intercourse for fun only, there is no denial that intercourse, when it is morally appropriate, can and should be fun. The point is that there must be more to sexual communion than the fun aspect.

24. One of the most widely read statements of the traditional case against premarital intercourse is Evelyn Millis Duvall, *Why Wait Till Marriage?* (New York: Association Press, 1968). Other statements of the case against premarital intercourse include Peter A. Bertocci, *SLP;* Robert O'Neill and Michael Donovan, *SMR,* pp. 129–168.

25. The human being does impose meaning on the world, but he or she also lives in a world where there is a level of pregiven meaning. Keeping the balance between receiving meaning from the world and giving it back to the world is the art we all must learn. Extreme situationalism which says that philosophy is utterly useless and there is no continuity of meaning in our world must be rejected. Karl Rahner has aptly called such extreme situationalism "massive nominalism" (in "On the Question of a Formal Existential Ethics," *TI* 2, p. 219). To attach any meaning whatever to sexual intercourse would be such a massive nominalism. On this point of sexuality and meaning, cf. Peter Chirico, *ICD,* p. 275.

26. I say "virtually no circumstances in normal life" to hold open the possibility that in some unusually bizarre circumstances proportionate rea-

sons for extramarital intercourse might exist. Scholars sometimes debate the case of Mrs. Bergmaier, the concentration camp inmate who wishes to rejoin her husband and children and who can only do so by becoming pregnant. Cf. Joseph Fletcher, *Situation Ethics: The New Morality* (Philadelphia: Westminster Press, 1966), pp. 164–165. Without solving Mrs. Bergmaier's case, it does seem wise to suggest that our prohibition of extramarital intercourse is a virtually exceptionless norm, i.e., that the exceptions to it would exist only in the rarest of cases, cases that hardly ever happen in normal life.

27. While marriage's social witness is a natural value, it is also very much a Christian faith value. Pastors and parents who wish to help young people see the arguments against premarital intercourse should concentrate on developing a lively sense of Christian faith in such young people. Such a faith will be at least as valuable, and probably more valuable, than the rational arguments against premarital intercourse.

28. For a summary of the flaws in some of the arguments proposed for this kind of premarital intercourse see Charles E. Curran, "Sexuality and Sin: A Current Appraisal," *CP*, pp. 177–179.

29. Historically this notion of a person's having a right to marry emerged especially in the Church's insistence that parents could not force a marriage on children. Cf. Thomas Aquinas *ST* III, 47, 6. In the twentieth century the right to marry was clearly asserted by Pius XI in *Casti Connubii* no. 68 (in *Seven Great Encyclicals,* Glen Rock: N.J.: Paulist Press, 1963, p. 96). To say that people have a right to marry does not mean that every person has achieved the necessary maturity to exercise this right. Hence society and the Church can impose restrictions on who can exercise the right to marry (restrictions based on age, etc.). Perhaps pastors should be more ready than they are at present to refuse to marry obviously unprepared couples. In the text we are, therefore, speaking only of cases where couples truly are prepared to marry and society unreasonably and unjustly restricts their right to marry.

30. Based on this whole issue of delayed maturity in our society, the Church in the future may have to give serious consideration to postponing the usual age for marriage (and also for ordination and religious profession) till about thirty. The pros and cons of such a postponement are not, however, resolved.

31. While I have not seen anyone use the exact language I propose here, similar sensitive approaches to this type of premarital intercourse include Charles E. Curran, "Sexuality and Sin . . . ," *CP*, p. 179–180; John F. Dedek, *CSM*, p. 42; Richard A. McCormick, "NMT," *TS* 34 (1973), p. 89–92; Bernard Häring, *"Voreheliche geschlechtliche Vereinigung," Theologie der*

Gegenwart 15 (1972), pp. 63–77. For a position that opposes the type of calculation I suggest, see John M. Finnis, "Natural Law and Unnatural Acts," *Heythrop Journal* 11 (1970), pp. 365–387.

32. This problem of the exception being taken as the norm happens with many moral issues today. Those teaching moral values must take care to avoid giving the impression that the exception is the norm. Cf. Paul Ramsey, "The Case of the Curious Exception," *Norm and Context in Christian Ethics,* Gene Outka and Paul Ramsey, eds., (New York: Charles Scribner's Sons, 1968), pp. 67–135.

33. *DSexEth,* no. 10, p. 11, would seem to allow this interpretation.

34. For the premarital/preceremonial distinction see Paul Ramsey, "A Christian Approach to the Question of Sexual Relations Outside of Marriage," *The Journal of Religion* 45 (1965), pp. 110–118. For a critique of the legalism involved in assuming that a hindered firm intention to marry or a secret marriage removes completely the evil of premarital intercourse see Richard A. McCormick, "NMT," *TS* 34 (1973), pp. 88–90. McCormick suggests here a point we have already made, that the real answer to the dilemma of premarital intercourse is to enhance our theology of and preparation for marriage so that people will freely want to choose to wait for marriage to have intercourse.

35. Cf. Alfred Kinsey *et al., SBM,* pp. 344–346, 365–373.

36. As we have already noted (chapter four, especially notes 16–20), much of the historical dispute about parvity of matter in the sexual sphere concerned a possible moral difference between those forms of sexual arousal that involve orgasm and those that do not. The fact of this historical dispute may suggest that we need to be especially open to rethinking our moral stance on mild and moderately arousing forms of petting.

37. Many theological interpretations of petting (cf. Peter A. Bertocci, *SLP,* pp. 94–97) hold that there is a more or less inevitable progression from petting to intercourse. Kinsey's data, on the other hand, might imply that there is enough new about twentieth century petting that we cannot be sure how to evaluate it. Thus there is an uncertainty that makes our remarks in the text tentative. For contemporary theological treatments of premarital petting, cf. John F. Dedek, *CSM,* pp. 42–43; Robert O'Neill and Michael Donovan, *SMR,* pp. 137–144.

32. Marriage Under Threat

Jack Dominian

This article first appeared in *The Tablet* in 1992.

In this article a Catholic psychiatrist who has spent a lifetime studying the institution of marriage looks at the increasing trend towards cohabitation and premarital sex. He asks the Church to respond with understanding, and to see that the wedding is only part of the support which a couple require.

The huge changes in sexual behaviour which have occurred in the last few decades have left priests and ministers of all denominations puzzled and confused. What was frowned on has today become the norm. Couples who present themselves for marriage preparation have frequently been sleeping together first, or cohabiting. Both practices offer challenges to traditional sexual teaching. In this article I want to examine cohabitation and premarital sexual intercourse from both the social and the moral point of view.

Cohabitation has become much more common in the last 15 years. More and more couples are sharing a common social and sexual life under one roof for a variable period. According to a recent publication, "The Relationship Revolution," from the marriage organisation One plus One which I founded, half of those now marrying for the first time in England and Wales cohabited first and by the year 2000 four out of five couples could well do so. Marriage usually follows, but not always. A similar pattern of cohabitation is emerging in northern Europe, the United States and other Western countries. In some Scandinavian countries cohabitation is well established.

I would see four main reasons for this rise in cohabitation. The first is the significant increase in marital breakdown and divorce since 1960. Young people have seen their parents end their marriages in large numbers. They have suffered as a result. In response, they have decided that they themselves will, in effect, enter a trial marriage. It seems to them common sense that if a couple who cohabit have a satisfactory relationship, it will continue when they marry.

In this they are mistaken. Contrary to what is so often popularly supposed, we now have evidence that cohabitation does not protect a subsequent marriage from breaking down. There have always been anecdotal reports of couples who cohabited happily, but then were unable to sustain a subsequent marriage. No one, however, knew for sure. Now we do. A study by John Haskey, published in the summer issue of *Population Trends,* shows that of couples who married for the first time early in the 1980s, those who had previously cohabited were 50 per cent more likely than the others to have divorced after five years of marriage, and 60 per cent more likely to have divorced after eight years of marriage.

Many people have been surprised by the findings of this excellent study, but the most elementary understanding of contemporary marriage would have predicted exactly this result. Where traditional marriage was a contract, modern marriage is an unfolding relationship, based on mutual compatibility in its succeeding phases. Couples do not remain married, as in the past, independently of the underlying state of their relationship. So a relationship which works while they cohabit is of no value in predicting how they will get on when it develops later into marriage.

Nevertheless, cohabitation is going to remain a feature of modern society. The first of the reasons for it may be faulty, but it will continue to exert its pressure. None of the other three reasons is going to disappear either.

The second reason is the ever increasing dissatisfaction of women with marriage. Hardly a week seems to pass without some eminent woman complaining that marriage renders women subservient to men, with a loss of dignity and status. Cohabitation, then, is felt to be a protection against these undesirable consequences. The emancipation of women is a fact, and marriage may be seen as a yoke by them unless society and the Churches bring marriage laws up to date and ensure that the dignity, equality and value of both parties is preserved.

The third reason is social and sexual. The average age for marriage is now the late twenties. Most young people view abstinence from sexual activity for nearly a decade as a virtually impossible requirement. In addition, economic circumstances and considerations of housing add to the arguments for living together.

The complete sexual abstinence asked of previous generations is never likely to be re-established. All the psychological discoveries of the last 100 years about the significance of sex point the other way. This is a dilemma that Christianity has to face. Youthful marriages are bad for the stability of marriage. Just as those entering the priesthood are encouraged to be older and more mature, so marriages need the same maturity. Sexual energy, however, is at its peak in the late teens and early twenties.

The fourth reason is the decrease in religious practice, and the scepticism of young people that a ceremony or a piece of paper will make any difference if they are in love. The most persistent question I am faced with as I travel round the country is what difference a wedding ceremony or a piece of paper makes to the love a couple have for each other. The traditional answers often fall on deaf ears: that marriage is a lifelong commitment which needs to be made publicly, that the legal consequences of marriage have profound social and economic significance for the couple, that children need committed stability, that the presence of a sacrament transforms the relationship, and that the vows and the ceremony bring all this about. Rather, young people and the married have to be shown that the ceremony does indeed make a difference socially, emotionally and spiritually. That means that the wedding cannot be the conclusion of the Church's involvement but part of a journey alongside married people so as to support them in every phase of their life.

All these four factors, singly or combined, constitute a powerful challenge to traditional Christian marriage, which has faded under the onslaught. The Churches have not known how to respond adequately. John Haskey's research finding confirms what I have repeatedly said, that it is urgent for the Church to supply preparation for the whole of the marriage and to support it throughout. Such a strategy has yet to emerge in every diocese, and the price we are paying is heavy. In addition we need a theology of marriage which makes people see that their marital relationship is a minute-to-minute encounter with God which transforms their life.

Premarital sexual intercourse is, of course, implicit in cohabitation, but may frequently occur nowadays without cohabitation. In the second part of this article, I want to examine the official teaching that all premarital sexual intercourse is wrong. As in the case of contraception, official teaching which is widely ignored simply erodes the authority of the Churches.

It is often put to me that a teaching which is widely ignored may still be correct. Let us therefore look at the Scriptures, natural law teaching and tradition to see what an integrated approach of the three has to say about sex and love.

In all my writings I have questioned the wisdom of rejecting all premarital sex as equally wrong and uniformly describing it as fornication. It is absurd to equate casual sexual intercourse with a prostitute with intercourse the night before an engaged couple marry. All we know about sex, love and relationships suggests that, broadly speaking, the greater the commitment and love, the more appropriate sexual intercourse will be.

Starting with the Scriptures and the teaching of Our Lord, we can see that there is no direct reference to these matters, but there is plenty of indirect evidence. The teaching of Our Lord was that love is the supreme criterion by which human relationships should be conducted. Furthermore, human beings should be treated as persons, not objects or things. Thus in sexual intercourse persons, not just bodies, should unite. Finally, Our Lord held such a high view of human beings that he suggested that fornication may be committed through a mere look of lust. Human beings reflect the image of God and are not to be used or manipulated. Casual sex, promiscuity, or sex with a prostitute is incompatible with human integrity.

Sex in Courtship

But what if we are concerned with couples committed to each other in love, with marriage as their object—in other words, in a state of betrothal? It is they who make the marriage, not the Church;

their commitment to one another is the marriage. The wedding is the public witnessing by the Church and society of that mutual commitment which they have made to one another.

Today sexual intercourse is widely practised as part of the courtship. Some scholars believe that the Scriptures do provide us with such a situation. In their view, the Song of Songs is a celebration of physical and sensuous communion between what is most likely to be a betrothed couple. But this text is open to many interpretations.

Turning next to the natural law, which has been such a powerful force in the shaping of sexual morality, we come across a view developed by St Thomas Aquinas which eventually became the standard argument in Catholic manuals of theology against premarital sex: that it is opposed to the natural purpose of sexual intercourse, which needs a stable marriage unit—the generation and education of children. Perhaps more than any other, however, this argument has lost its force today. Biologically and psychologically we know that most acts of sexual intercourse are unitive, a powerful expression of love, not procreative. Procreation will follow only a few sexual acts, a minute part of the totality. Vatican II greatly strengthened the link between sex and love, and although Pope Paul VI's encyclical, *Humanae Vitae,* insists on the procreative element being present in each sexual act, and rules out contraception, the Church accepts natural family planning as licit. There is no doubt that the prevention of pregnancy has revolutionised sexual intercourse, both premarital and marital. Contraceptives have added to the sum total of permissiveness, but the answer to that is greater understanding of sexual integrity.

A further veto on premarital sexual intercourse comes from Christian tradition. But the obligation to marry before a priest and witnesses in church, and to avoid all premarital sex before, is a late phenomenon after the Council of Trent. Sex following betrothal and before marriage, as a way of expressing commitment to each other, has a long history.

I do not see, in the light of these three sources of moral teaching, that premarital sexual intercourse as part of a committed, exclusive and faithful relationship leading to marriage can be condemned categorically as intrinsically wrong. A number of theologians concur with this view: they prefer to say that premarital sexual intercourse of this kind contains ontic, but not moral, evil. Such a view would in no way approve casual, promiscuous, adulterous or prostituted sex.

The key issues are not legal, as in the past, but personal and scriptural. Marriage is a state that mirrors the covenant of love between God and his people, Christ and the Church. Sexual intercourse is the seal of that covenant, and belongs only to marriage, but it is false to identify marriage as something static, as though it began with the wedding. Marriage offers a unique opportunity for love to grow over a lifetime in the unity of the couple and their children. So the Church too needs to see marriage as a process, the operation of an inner grace made visible by external preparation and support, so as to manifest to the couple the precious gift of their state.

Part Eight

NORTH AMERICAN SCENE

33. American Catholic Sexual Ethics, 1789–1989

Leslie Griffin

This chapter first appeared in *Perspectives on the American Catholic Church, 1789–1989* in 1989.

In his 1785 description of American Catholicism, John Carroll reported that:

> The abuses that have grown among Catholics are chiefly those, which result with unavoidable intercourse with non-Catholics, and the examples thence derived: namely more free intercourse between young people of opposite sexes than is compatible with chastity in mind and body; too great fondness for dances and similar amusements; and an incredible eagerness, especially in girls, for reading love stories which are brought over in great quantities from Europe.[1]

Carroll's text illustrates a number of concerns of American Catholic sexual ethics from 1789 until the twentieth century. As Catholics worked out their relationship to the new United States, they struggled to live and to interpret a Catholic sexual ethic amid the mores of the general non-Catholic public. Throughout these centuries, a constant worry of Catholic clergy and hierarchy was that Catholics would be corrupted by their association with those outside the faith. "Keeping company" with non-Catholics, e.g., in their dances, festivities and amusements, or in dating or marriage, might undermine appropriate moral standards for Catholic youth and adults.

The history of American Catholic sexual ethics is of course part of a larger story, in which Catholics have struggled to be at the same time loyal Americans and loyal Catholics. In the field of Catholic sexual ethics, a division between American and Catholic interpretations of sexuality erupts after the Second Vatican Council; up to that point, the story is one of basic continuity in teaching an ethic whose content remains fairly constant from 1789 to 1965.

In the later eighteenth century, and in the early years of the nineteenth century, the official Catholic sexual ethic clearly identified heterosexual marriage as the sole appropriate locus for sexual activity, and heterosexual marriage between Catholics as the norm. American Catholic sexual ethics arose from European interpretations of sexuality. In the eighteenth and nineteenth centuries, European moral theology consisted primarily of moral manuals. These manuals were rooted in the writings of Hermann Busenbaum and Alphonsus Liguori, and served primarily to guide confessors in the sacrament of penance. As such, their purpose was to explore the level of sinfulness of certain actions.[2]

A perceived strength of these manuals was precisely their lack of originality. New manuals were necessary over time which could include the pressing questions arising in later ages. Yet a similarity in format, style and content persists among these manuals. Continuity rather than innovation is the hallmark of Catholic sexual ethics.

Francis P. Kenrick, Archbishop of Baltimore, wrote the first American manual of moral theology, *Theologia Moralis,* in 1841, in imitation of the Liguori approach. Kenrick wrote his volumes because the seminary students were in need of texts responsive to the American context. In France, Jean Gury's *Compendium Theologiae Moralis* (1850) also reproduced Liguori's basic organization and style of argumentation, and became an important source for American moral theology. It was updated in 1865, and was revised again by Antonio Ballerini. The Gury manual was the standard for the *Compendium Theologiae Moralis* of Aloysius Sabetti, an American Jesuit who taught moral theology at Woodstock. Sabetti's volumes (later edited by Timothy Barrett) became one of the standard manuals used in seminaries throughout the United States. Both Kenrick and Sabetti employed American and English legal sources, including non-Catholic sources. Both tomes were used during the nineteenth century.[3]

John Noonan argues that Gury (in 1869) is the first moral theologian to mention love as a rational purpose for marital coitus. Peter Gardella, however, in *Innocent Ecstasy: How Christianity Gave America an Ethic of Sexual Pleasure,* states that Noonan is only "formally correct"; Kenrick anticipates Gury by 26 years. Kenrick opens his section on marriage with a discussion of love. Gardella attributes this to the American context of Kenrick's writings; given the constant migration life in the United States, Gardella believes that personal love is especially important in the American context. Gardella asserts: "Until the 1920's, no Catholic moralist equaled Kenrick in relating sex to a larger pattern of marital behavior centered on love."[4]

Gury, Sabetti-Barrett, and Kenrick are in agreement on certain fundamentals in sexual ethics. Sexual ethics is treated in certain key locations in the manuals: under the sixth and ninth commandments, under the sacrament of matrimony, and (less frequently) under the cardinal virtue of temperance. The sixth and ninth commandments prohibit sins of impurity (in deeds and in thoughts, respectively). As manuals for confessors, the texts identify sexual sins in terms of their gravity. A pivotal argument is that there is no *parvitas materiae,* no small or slight matter, in the sixth and ninth commandments; all sexual sins contain grave matter. Patrick Boyle explains the concept of parvity of matter:

> The manualists classified sin according to the seriousness of the matter. Mortal sins *ex toto genere suo* are sins whose matter is so evil that there is no possible situation in which gravity of the evil can be lessened. The matter is intrinsically evil. Mortal sins *ex genero suo* are sins whose matter can be either serious or light depending upon the circumstances which specify the act. In this category sins within the same species may be mortal or venial depending upon the seriousness of the matter. . . . It has been a long established teaching in pre-Vatican II moral theology that the matter in every sexual sin falls into the *ex toto genere suo* category. For centuries moral theologians and the papal magisterium of the Church held that there can be no parvity of matter in sins against the sixth and ninth commandments.[5]

A definition of venereal pleasure often opens the discussion of these commandments. Next, sins of impurity are divided into consummated and non-consummated acts. All sins of impurity are mortal if they are direct and voluntary. They may be venial if indirect or involuntary. (This means that sexual pleasure in marriage and indirect pleasure outside marriage are not necessarily mortal sins.) The consummated sins of impurity are fornication, adultery, incest, rape, abduction and sacrilege. Consummated sins which are in addition against nature are masturbation, sodomy and bestiality. Intentional non-consummated sins of impurity are also mortally sinful. These include a catalogue of touches, looks, reading and conversation, all dangerous, because all could lead to venereal pleasure. The teaching on parvity of matter guarantees that if venereal pleasure, however slight, is willed in these actions they are mortally sinful. Carroll's criticism of dances, love stories and association of young men and women is comprehensible in such a context.

In the sections on marriage, there is a lengthy treatment of the rite of marriage, including, e.g., what counts as an engagement, how to announce the banns, what an impediment is, what a valid marriage is, what the priest's responsibilities are. An additional feature of this section is frequently a discussion of the marital debt, including some analysis of when it is reasonable for spouses to refuse sexual relations (danger of venereal disease, risk to life, unreasonable frequency of demands). Here are also listed the prohibitions of any interference with the proper end of the marital act, namely, of contraception or of "onanism."

In the United States in the nineteenth century, both priests and moral theologians warned that occasions of sins of impurity and dangers to the sacrament of matrimony were posed by the non-Catholic presence. For example, in clerical discussions of the nineteenth century (as evident, e.g., in the *American Ecclesiastical Review*) proper preparation for and participation in marriage are a constant concern. The cases of conscience presented and analyzed by priests often focus on the special problem of mixed marriages. These cases of conscience become a familiar forum for discussions of sexual (i.e., marital) activity. In such cases, for example, priests try to resolve whether a baptized person whose first marriage was to a non-baptized person can marry a Catholic, or whether a Catholic and a non-Catholic Christian can wed, or whether Catholics can be bridesmaids in Protestant weddings. Throughout, there are severe warnings against the dangers of mixed marriages as threats to the faith.[6]

These cases of conscience provide an interesting perspective on the moral theology and pastoral guidance of the age. First, it is clearly priests who are to resolve these cases. Sexual and marital cases are presented in Latin, with an explanation that this is the usual procedure and that the cases have international appeal. Moreover, the editors of an early issue of the *American Ecclesiastical Review* explain that they try to limit subscriptions to priests and students of theology.[7] In sexual ethics, there is also concern that certain suggestive materials should not be accessible to lay readers. Second, the style of moral reflection is casuistical, a casuistry which cites the manualists in support of its conclusions. Moreover, it is a casuistry which relies on theological opinions for questions which are open to dispute.[8] Finally, attention is paid to acts and to the sinfulness of certain acts.

Parallel approaches to sexual sin are found in Catholic revival movements of the nineteenth century. According to Jay Dolan, its preachers taught a "rigorous moralism," with drunkenness and *impurity* identified as the two major sins. Preachers (like moralists) had to approach the topic of sexuality with caution: "Whatever the people do not know in reference to this vice . . . they need not and should not learn from the missionary." The preacher could "express, in two or three sentences, his abhorrence of it, and then dismiss it in disgust, as being too abominable to be treated before a Christian audience."[9] Dolan notes that the dance hall received the harshest criticism; also prohibited were "bad reading," "excursions and picnics, shows and the theatre" and the "company of people of different sexes."[10]

At the same time, in the eighteenth and nineteenth centuries, the synodal and conciliar legislation of the American Church, in addition to the national pastorals of the American Bishops, demonstrate the resolution of the U.S. hierarchy to defend the indissolubility of marriage and to prevent the dangers of mixed marriages. The longest decree of the first National Synod in 1791 is on the sacrament of matrimony. In addition to a discussion of the banns, and of the marriage rite, there is strong opposition to mixed marriages. "Mixed marriages were to be discouraged as much as possible. The Fathers of the Synod realized how difficult it would be to avoid marriages with non-Catholics, especially in those places where few Catholics resided, but the pastors were urged to exercise every holy influence to prevent these unions."[11] The synodal statement makes some provisions if these marriages should occur: e.g., the children should be raised Catholic, the priests should not be so antagonistic to the marriage that the parties turn to a Protestant minister, the standard wedding blessing cannot be announced.

Councils and pastorals of 1840, 1866 and 1884 condemn such marriages, and there are ringing condemnations of divorce in the 1866 Second Plenary Council. These conclusions are summarized in the Baltimore Catechism (1889) which states that

> The Church does forbid the marriage of Catholics with persons who have a different religion or no religion at all because such marriages generally lead to indifference, loss of faith, and to the neglect of the religious education of the children.[12]

Dolan adds:

> Catholic fiction stressed the peril, especially to children, of such mixed marriages; spiritual guidebooks somberly discussed this "grave question," and only in exceptional cases could such a marriage be allowed. Though the numbers did increase during the twentieth century, religiously mixed marriages were not common during the nineteenth century.[13]

A more homely illustration of the opposition of mixed marriages is found in an 1880 issue of a Catholic magazine, *The Ave Maria*. The editors offer a series of letters from the 1854 *Catholic Telegraph*, citing them as "An example of Moral Heroism" rare for this age. A (Presbyterian) fiancé writes to his (Catholic) beloved, asking her to worship with him in a Protestant church, since "in our happy country all religions are alike." (He also adds that the Protestant service will be better for business than the Catholic.) She refuses, saying that she has yielded her heart but not her soul to him, and that she cannot "surrender God to win a husband."[14] He writes back a more formal letter, requiring that they be married by a minister only; she refuses, and ends the engagement. Such is Catholic heroism in a religiously pluralistic society.

One explanation for the style and substance of Catholic sexual ethics for much of the nineteenth century is that it is the era of the immigrant Church. Dolan estimates that in 1830, there were 318,000 Catholics in the U.S. By 1850, that number had risen to one and one half million; by 1860 to 3,103,000 and by 1890 to close to nine million.[15] Overwhelming numbers of Catholics taxed Catholic clergy, with a severe priest shortage as the outcome. This scarcity resulted in the entrance of foreign priests into the U.S.; moreover, American priests were sent abroad to study, and returned to staff the seminaries. European modes of thought were thus perpetuated in the United States. John Tracy Ellis characterizes the first foreign priests as French and Irish, inheritors of a rigorist, Jansenist tradition, especially in sexual ethics. As the nineteenth century progresses, the Church was "Europeanized." By the mid-nineteenth century, Ellis notes

> so strongly had the textbooks of Roman Jesuits established themselves in American seminaries, that even the works of Francis Patrick Kenrick, then Bishop of Philadelphia, were making a relatively slow progress in spite of the recommendation they had received from the bishops of the Fifth Provincial Council of Baltimore in May, 1843.[16]

Jay Dolan's conclusion is that the Republican movement of the 1790's (American Catholicism's first "romance with modernity") was drowned by the waves of immigrants.[17] Adding to the difficulty of American Catholic relationships is the growth of anti-Catholicism in the United States in response to immigration. Such anti-Catholicism made it easier for Catholics to view "keeping company" with Protestants as corruptive, and to turn with more loyalty to Roman teaching.

By the end of the nineteenth century, however, some significant changes occur. The American Church appears poised to provide intellectual leadership, and another "Catholic romance with modernity" occurs in the 1890's.[18] Robert Cross traces the roots of liberal Catholicism to this era.[19] In moral theology, Thomas Bouquillon, the Belgian-born priest who is the first professor of moral theology at Catholic University, questions the traditional role of moral theology in identifying sins, and brings social scientific analysis to his moral theology.[20] Yet the developments do not extend to changes in the field of sexual ethics. The papal condemnations of Americanism and Modernism occur in 1899 and 1907, and the work of many American theologians and clerics is viewed with suspicion. Gerald Fogarty reports,

> With the condemnation of Americanism a new spirit was breathed into the American Church, a spirit of Roman authority and discipline, of loss of American independence and episcopal collegiality. With it also came the stifling of intellectual life in the new nation.[21]

Both Fogarty and Ellis agree that American theology would not be renewed until the 1940's.

In sexual ethics, Peter Gardella argues that by the turn of the twentieth century, American theologians are even more conservative than their European counterparts. By this point, Adolphe Tanquerey, at St. Mary's Seminary in Baltimore, authors what Gardella calls the "second moral theology that drew on American materials and experiences." But this moral theology is "prudery triumphant," according to Gardella, because sexual questions are treated in separately bound volumes, and in the appendix, and not in the central parts of the text as in the past. Moreover, Tanquerey's conclusions are even stricter than those of Liguori.[22] Tanquerey fails to include a section on the sixth and ninth commandments, and even within the section on marriage, Tanquerey omits the usual treatment of the marital debt.

The first moral manual written in English, Thomas Slater's *A Manual of Moral Theology for English-Speaking Countries,* appears in 1908. Yet, the sections which treat sins of impurity remain in

Latin. Slater rejects those who argue that moral theology should be a discipline of ideals; it is for confessors, and for discerning sin.[23]

In 1911 the sterilization of criminals and of the mentally defective becomes a pressing question for Catholic moralists, as laws supporting such practices are promulgated in a number of states (the first, in Indiana, in March 1907). There is room for discussion of the issue because theologians find ambiguity in the papal texts. An essential question is: Does the prohibition against direct sterilization apply only to the innocent? John Ryan describes a "discussion which involved a dozen writers, twenty-four articles, one hundred and sixty-six pages and more than 62,000 words in the *American Ecclesiastical Review,* vols. 42–47 in the years 1910–1912."[24] Ryan views sterilization as a question of human welfare, and opposes it. It is not intrinsically wrong, but Ryan finds the arguments which support it unpersuasive. His approach to the subject is informative; he clearly identifies this as a subject open to discussion and disagreement. Moreover, he uses an analysis of proportionate good, which takes into account the numbers of persons who have been and will be affected by the problem.

John Ryan is also the earliest American moral theologian[25] to address the new subject of "birth control" in an *American Ecclesiastical Review* article in 1916.[26] On this subject, he says there is "no possibility of a difference of opinion." Again the American influence: Ryan worries that non-Catholics will persuade Catholics that birth control is not sinful, and that many Catholics already use it because they are unaware of its sinfulness. Ryan concedes that "chaste abstention" can be used to limit family size.[27] The 1919 National Pastoral addresses the subject of contraception, arguing that "the selfishness which leads to race suicide with or without the pretext of bettering the species is, in God's sight, 'a detestable thing'."[28] The letter opposes a double standard in sexual ethics, arguing that both men and women must maintain *purity* before marriage. There is also a strong argument against divorce, identifying it as "our national scandal."[29]

William Halsey's *The Survival of Innocence: Catholicism in an Era of Disillusionment, 1920–1940* identifies the era after the First World War as a time of Catholic innocence, an innocence which included a belief that there are clear-cut standards of morality.

While Protestant Americans are disillusioned after the war, Catholicism begins to establish itself in American life, in part because of its stable interpretation of life.

> The problem with American innocence and the Catholic involvement with it, however, was the tendency to absolutize answers and narrow premises. In cultural forms it tended to repress the possibility of doubt, preventing moments of healthy unease.[30]

In Catholic sexual ethics, certainties abound. A new moral manual appears in 1929, *Moral Theology* by John McHugh and Charles Callan. McHugh and Callan are critical of manuals which refer too much to theologians' opinions, and prefer to give principles and rules rather than opinions. They argue that moral theology and moral manuals are not just about sin. Instead, they proposed an ideal understanding, a positive view, of the moral life, in the spirit of Thomas Aquinas. That is, they want to help readers "escape from moral disease and death," but also "to live the life of grace and virtue."[31]

Yet there are only minor changes in sexual ethics, and portions of the text remain in Latin. First, sexual questions are treated under the virtue of temperance, in the section on sins of impurity. The listing of sins remains unchanged, although contraception has moved into the same section with other sexual sins, after pollution. Gardella calls attention to the text which argues that "sex pleasure has been ordained by God as an inducement to perform an act which is both disgusting in itself and burdensome in its consequences." He comments, "Catholic theology fell from the liberality of Kenrick, with his Liguorian tolerance for nature and his personal concern for love, to the repugnance of McHugh in less than a hundred years."[32] Gardella finds this approach more restrictive than that favored by European theologians of the same era, and blames it on the strong Protestant environment surrounding American Catholic sexual ethics.

In the 1940's American theology reawakens; several new sources shed light on sexual ethics in the United States. In 1940, *Theological Studies* commences publication, and includes an annual (sometimes semiannual) feature entitled "Notes on Moral Theology." Throughout the 1940's and 1950's, Jesuits John Lynch, Gerald Kelly, John Ford, John Connery and Joseph Farraher review Catholic moral theological literature, both European and American. In 1946 the Catholic Theological Society of American is founded and its *Proceedings* are published annually. The journals are a record of the multitude of issues that confront moral theologians in the twentieth century. Rhythm and other means of birth control take center stage; other prominent topics include sterility tests, sterilization, courtship and marriage (and proper limits/conditions to them), artificial insemination, the problem of divorce, *amplexus reservatus* (vaginal penetration without orgasm) and *copula dimidiata* (partial vaginal penetration), homosexuality, psychiatry and the Kinsey reports.

In *Theological Studies,* the authors review the opinions of moral theologians on these questions, in which discussion and disagreement can take place among moralists on a number of issues. An article in the first volume of *Theological Studies* discusses sex morality and chastity, reviews the manualist tradition on the subject, and urges avoidance of direct venereal pleasure.[33] Chastity and sex morality, and the delineation of mortal and venial sins in this area, remain a concern of the Jesuit authors in the years following 1940.[34]

Gerald Kelly's 1941 text, *Modern Youth and Chastity,* illustrates the era's sexual ethic. It is a textbook for college students; it thus places the manualist tradition in a broader context, although the basic content has not changed. Sexual expression is appropriate only in the context of marriage. Unmarried Catholics must be wary of any actions which could lead to venereal pleasure. Kelly distinguishes between direct (always unchaste) and indirect (sinful or not according to circumstances) venereal actions. Catholic youth are warned to distance themselves from serious relationships in which there is no possibility of marriage (and from non-Catholics). Young people should act with restraint around members of the opposite sex, and should avoid proximate occasions of sin.

Kelly also includes a traditional formulation of the sixth and ninth commandments. According to the sixth commandment, the following division of sins is employed:

Mortal Sin: a) All directly venereal actions.

              b) All other actions performed for the purpose of stimulating or promoting venereal pleasure.

              c) All actions involving the proximate danger of performing a directly venereal action or of consenting to venereal pleasure.

Venial Sin: Indirectly venereal actions performed without a relatively sufficient reason.

No Sin: Indirectly venereal actions performed with a relatively sufficient reason.

For the ninth commandment, the following categories apply:

Mortal Sin: a) The *willful approval* of unchaste actions.

              b) The willful entertaining of any thoughts *for the purpose of* stimulating or promoting venereal passion.

              c) The willful harboring of thoughts which involve the *proximate danger of* performing an unchaste action, or consenting to venereal pleasure.

Venial Sin: Thinking about sexually-stimulating things without a sufficient reason.

No Sin: Thinking about sexually-stimulating things with a sufficient reason.[35]

Modern Youth and Chastity also includes a more positive context for sexuality. Kelly describes friendship, general sexual attraction, personal sexual attraction and physical sexual attraction. He explains what makes a good marriage partner, and connects marriage to sexual attraction and friendship.

Certain gender expectations also figure in Kelly's analysis. Men are attracted to grace, emotional susceptibility, beauty, tenderness; women to strength, courage, energy and calm deliberation.[36] When he is looking for a wife, a man should ask "Can she cook, and make the house a home? Has she that womanly quality that instinctively puts things in order?"[37] He praises the *Notre Dame Bulletin* story of a man who left a broom on the floor of his room. Five women stepped over it; one picked it up. Kelly concludes: "The wise man proposed [to the sixth]—and there is much to be said for his wisdom."[38]

Given the long history of American Catholic opposition to "keeping company," the *Theological Studies* discussion of this issue in the 1940's and 1950's is of interest. In 1948 Gerald Kelly (writing in agreement with Francis Connell) states: "it is a mortal sin to keep company with a non-Catholic with a view to marriage unless one has good reason to believe that one has or will have before the marriage a justifying cause for entering the union."[39] "Justifying cause" here means reason to believe that the partner will convert, or that a dispensation is possible. By the 1950's, moral theologians are still assessing certain social events. European texts (including Liguori) had limited visits between unmarried persons of the opposite sex and remained critical, for example, of dances. The concern, of course, is that such events may be occasions of sin. While Francis Connell defends such strict standards, John Connery, John Ford and Gerald Kelly disagree. Connery argues that American conditions are different and justify a less strict standard; in the United States, dancing is certainly not an occasion of sin. On this issue, then, the American environment causes moral theologians to distinguish themselves from a European standard.[40] However, "going steady" remains suspicious; while Connell opposes it, Ford and Kelly would prefer to assess it on an individual basis. On the other hand, certain "social" events remain reprehensible; in 1963 Joseph Farraher warns against attendance at non-Catholic weddings; even Catholic parents should not attend a child's wedding outside the Church.[41]

In *Theological Studies* and the *CTSA Proceedings* in the 1940's and 1950's, there are hints of the changes that will occur after the Second Vatican Council. By 1942, the personalism of Herbert Doms is well-known in the U.S., but Francis Connell's rejection of Doms provides occasion for him to reiterate the traditional ranking of the ends of marriage: procreative, primary; unitive, secondary.[42] In 1953 Gerald Gilleman's *The Primacy of Charity in Moral Theology* is assessed, as is Bernard Haring's *The Law of Christ* in 1957–1958. Both Gilleman and Haring wished to expand the purview of moral theology through emphasis on charity and on a Christ-centered life. The leading American moral theologians are cautious about such enterprises, preferring to leave these issues to ascetic and pastoral theology.[43]

Another perspective on the moral theology of the 1950's can be found in a summary of the moral seminar at the Catholic Theological Society of America in 1950. The participants studied seminal tests and artificial insemination. Their overview provides some indication of the act-centered, probabilistic, casuistic approach to moral theology dominant in this era. For sterility tests, the conclusions run as follows:

> Objectionable methods—masturbation, interrupted intercourse, condomistic intercourse, use of a vaginal sheath or of a contraceptive pessary. Licit to a greater or lesser degree —puncture of testicle, rectal massage, post-coital aspiration of vagina, use of a tassette, perforated condom, cloth condom, use of semen accidentally deposited outside of the vagina, as well as of that adhering to penis after intercourse, use of the emission produced during an involuntary pollution, also of the semen found in the male urethra after normal coitus, and lastly the use of a cervical spoon.[44]

A similar listing follows for judging methods of artificial (i.e., assisted) insemination.

The predominant and representative moral text of the 1950's is John Ford and Gerald Kelly's *Contemporary Moral Theology,* volume one (1958) on fundamental moral questions; volume two (1963) on marriage questions. These volumes incorporate much of the material from Ford and Kelly's "Notes," yet also add original material. They stake out a middle ground approach to morality: They are responsive to contemporary criticisms of past manuals, but they warn against the excesses of new approaches to moral theology. Noteworthy is their tremendous reliance on magisterial teaching; the theologian must not only accept magisterial teaching but also incorporate it into his writing. In addition, they argue that good moral theology requires good casuistry. They retain as well a concern for identifying levels of sinfulness; they include in volume one a discussion of occasions of sin which rehearses the Connell-Connery discussion about company-keeping and dancing. In sexual matters, they are critical of Marc Oraison's psychiatric evaluation of sexual actions because it identifies acts such as masturbation, homosexuality, fornication, adultery and conjugal onanism as only materially mortal sins, instead of as formally mortal. However, more attention is paid to psychiatric developments and their implications for human action than in the past.[45]

In volume two, the input of contemporary theology is evident. The first half of the book is devoted to the ends of marriage. Here Ford and Kelly acknowledge the importance of personalist insights into the unity of the couple in marriage, but their aim "is to vindicate, theologically and canonically, for the so-called personalist (secondary) ends of marriage the essential place they deserve, while at the same time *defending their essential subordination to the primary ends.*"[46] Such an approach enables them to view marriage in a positive light (emphasize, e.g., marriage as vocation) while retaining traditional prohibitions. Mixed marriages are still *"per se hindrances to the realization of the vocational ideal of marriage,"*[47] although Ford and Kelly do not wish to exclude them in all cases, since they may serve to propagate the faith.

Part two of *Contemporary Moral Theology: Marriage Questions* treats practical questions of marital sexuality: orgasm, *amplexus reservatus* and *copula dimidiata,* oral-genital acts, incomplete sexual acts, contraception and periodic continence, and sterilizing drugs. Ford and Kelly employ traditional analyses of the marital act, and reinforce their prohibitions by including papal pronouncements on sexuality.

The constant subject of the 1940's and 1950's, whether in journals or magazines, or in works like *Catholic Moral Theology,* is birth control. In *Theological Studies,* in 1942, the issue is whether or not a wife may cooperate with *coitus interruptus* on the part of her husband. The survey of recent literature suggests that she can do so only with grave reason (such as abandonment) but she must actively resist condomistic intercourse.[48] By 1944, Planned Parenthood is identified as "one of the most powerful attacks on the chastity of the nation" and Catholic doctor John Rock (later a major player in the debate over the pill) is criticized for the use of masturbation in research.[49] By the 1950's, the licitness of rhythm is the cynosure, as moral theologians distinguish between moral and immoral uses of rhythm. "How long can one practice rhythm?" as well as "Can one practice rhythm without sufficient reason?" are pressing questions. In 1957 Connery and Kelly discuss how many children is "enough," and whether Catholics are obliged to bear a certain number of children.[50] *Amplexus reservatus* is at times advocated as a permissible method for couples, but is later prohibited. The focus, then, is on what circumstances justify Catholic couples in limiting family size by the rhythm method.

Throughout these years, there is constant, vigorous opposition to artificial methods of birth control. By 1960, John Lynch calls contraception "tiresome," "theologically, a dead issue."[51] Theologians discuss whether a Catholic president should sign laws permitting contraceptives.[52] In the early 1960's, moral theologians criticize Catholic doctor John Rock's espousal of the birth control pill for Catholics; Rock publishes these views in a 1963 book, *The Time Has Come.* In chapter thirteen of *Contemporary Moral Theology,* "Can the Catholic Teaching Change?," Ford and Kelly assess the status of church teaching on contraception. After a lengthy review of theological opinions on the subject, they conclude:

1) The Church is so completely committed to the doctrine that contraception is intrinsically and gravely immoral that no substantial change in this teaching is possible. It is *irrevocable.*

2) It is not easy at present to assign a technical dogmatic note to the doctrine. But it is safe to say that it is "*at least* definable doctrine," and it is very likely already taught infallibly *ex iugi magisterio.*

3) Since the doctrine is at least definable, it must be included in some way within the object of infallibility. At the minimum, therefore, it is a part of the secondary object of infallibility and may be proposed as a truth which is absolutely *tenenda.* And there are good, though not yet convincing, reasons for holding that this doctrine is a part of the *depositum fidei* and can thus be infallibly taught as *credenda.*[53]

They join the criticism of Dr. John Rock, asserting in a (footnote) comment that "Dr. Rock's opinions in this matter have no standing whatever with Catholic theologians and directly contravene the authoritative teaching of the Catholic Church, which is binding on all Catholics."[54]

By 1964, however, there are dramatic developments in the birth control controversy. John Lynch warns of "a threat of moral schism within our own ranks,"[55] because people are questioning what Lynch views as the unquestionable teaching on contraception. Two articles, from *European* theologians W. van der Marck and Louis Janssens,[56] justify the use of the pill by Catholics. Lynch describes this as the first time in church history that Catholic moral theologians have opposed the common teaching of the Church.

By 1964, the Second Vatican Council begins to influence American theology. In that year, an issue of *The Commonweal* devoted to the subject of birth control appears, with Daniel Callahan's essay "Authority and the Theologian."[57] The title is significant; from this point on, sexual ethical questions are inextricably linked to ecclesiological questions about church authority. Callahan concedes that "there was a remarkable harmony among the ideals of the magisterium, the theologians and the married laity"[58] until the mid-1950's. However, social factors, including overpopulation and the changing role of women, have changed this consensus, while new theological insights (including those from the Council) have made the old manuals "appear dangerously inadequate, if not altogether misleading."[59] In the midst of a "theological revolution," the "Center Party" (Callahan's description of Ford and Kelly) had "remained firmly imbedded in the atmosphere of the past," fearful of change, "years behind the revolution," like "government civil servants" trying to put the best light on official teaching.[60] Callahan urges theologians to maintain their integrity by taking stances contrary to the magisterium on birth control, if necessary.

1965 witnesses some telling changes in two journals, *Studies* and the *CTSA Proceedings,* which have recorded developments in the American theological community since the 1940's. For example, in the *CTSA Proceedings* of 1965, Charles E. Curran brings a new analysis to the subject of masturbation, rejecting the traditional approach which examined the act "statically," apart from the person. Curran reviews masturbation in light of fundamental option theory and empirical evidence (especially from psychology), and asserts that masturbation does not always involve grave matter. Because of fundamental option theory (which views individual choices in relationship to one's whole orientation toward God) Curran argues that the traditional teaching on parvity of matter must be rethought. Curran concludes:

> In the past, we moralists spent most of our time interpreting the documents of the magisterium for the Christian people. Today the Vatican Council and theologians are beginning to recognize the importance of the experience of Christian people. Theologians must also interpret the experience of Christian people for the magisterium. Previous teachings must be examined in the light of the circumstances of the times in which they were formed.[61]

In the same year, Richard McCormick publishes his "Notes on Moral Theology" in *Theological Studies.* In 1965, McCormick states that if Paul VI fails "to speak soon and authoritatively" about contraception, Catholics may be justified in applying "principles of probabilism" to the questions. From 1965 to 1968, McCormick weighs the teaching on contraception in connection to this question of doubt. McCormick's "Notes" exemplify the ecumenical openness and the critical engagement of magisterial thought which characterize American Catholic moral theology after the Council.[62]

While Curran and McCormick lead a new generation of American Catholic moral theologians, other U.S. Catholics participate in the papal birth control commission. In addition to the presence of American Bishops and American Jesuit moral theologian John Ford, the lay scholar John Noonan, and Patrick and Patricia Crowley, leaders of the Christian Family Movement, are included as expert consultants. Even the Vatican recognizes the importance of the experience of married persons, as lived and studied by the Crowleys, as a source of ethical insight. Within the committee, John Noonan's historical analysis of contraception provides powerful scholarly impetus for a change in official church teaching, while John Ford is an ardent advocate of the *status quo,* and defender of papal authority.[63]

In his 1968 presidential address to the Catholic Theological

Society of America, Walter Burghardt, S.J., chides the members for their failure to develop an American theology

> whose neuralgic problems arise from our soil and our people; a theology with a distinctive style and rhetoric; a theology where not only is the Catholic past a critique in the American present, but the American present challenges and enriches the Catholic past; where the Catholic theologian is heard because he is talking to living people, about themselves, in their own tongue.[64]

One month later, on July 29, 1968, Pope Paul VI issues his statement on birth control, *Humanae Vitae*. While neither an American Catholic theology nor an American Catholic sexual ethic yet exists, the new papal encyclical provokes an American response. At a press conference in Washington, DC, on July 30, Charles Curran presents a statement with 87 (later 600) signatures of theologians which justifies dissent for Catholics from the birth control teaching. In September of 1968, the Board of Trustees of Catholic University authorizes an investigation into Curran and other professors who had signed the statement. Curran was not new to such controversy; already in 1967, the Trustees had blocked Curran's promotion to tenure and associate professor. Curran was reinstated in 1967 after a strike by students and faculty; in 1968, the Board of Inquiry cleared Curran and his fellow professors.[65]

In post-*Humanae Vitae* sexual ethics, then, Catholics are divided over their relationship to magisterial teaching. For while many theologians signed the Washington statement, other theologians, joined by numerous bishops, defend Paul VI. Meanwhile, studies show that in 1965, 77% of American Catholic women under 45 used some form of birth control, with only 14% employing rhythm. Although in 1955, "only 30 percent of Catholic women younger than 30 had been using contraception," by 1970 "two-thirds of U.S. Catholic women, and three-fourths of Catholic women younger than 30, were using birth control methods disapproved by the church."[66] Many theologians critical of official teaching cite this lay practice as evidence of the magisterium's error. *Humanae Vitae* is a watershed in American Catholic history, as it ushers in an era in which individual conscience and experience grow in importance as sources of norms for sexual ethics, and in which Catholics openly debate the merits of magisterial teaching.

One way to understand sexual ethical developments after 1968 is to realize that most of the actions outlawed as sins of impurity in the manuals are open to question in the American theological community. Even a glance at McCormick's "Notes on Moral Theology" over the past twenty years demonstrates that divorce and remarriage, premarital sexual relations, reproductive technology, homosexuality, and the roles of men and women in marriage and the family, are controverted questions. Jesuit John McNeill's 1976 book, *The Church and the Homosexual,* alerts Catholics to reconsider traditional prohibitions on all homosexual activity. McNeill is silenced after the book's publication, and is dismissed from the Jesuits in 1988 when he breaks his silence to criticize a 1986 Vatican letter on homosexuality.[67] Philip Keane employs a person-centered approach to criticize act-centered assessments of sexual conduct.[68] Throughout the 1970's, Catholic hospital policies, especially those which regulate sterilization, are challenged by a number of Catholic theologians.[69] In the 1970's and 1980's, many ethicists move to a limited acceptance of reproductive technologies by married couples.

Meanwhile, the entire history of Christian thought on sexual ethics is called into question by the rise of feminist scholarship. Feminist scholars demand that sexual norms promote the well-being of women as well as men. Traditional assumptions about women's sexuality and sexual desire, about women's roles in marriage, family and reproduction, are challenged. Many feminist theologians reject self-sacrifice as a norm for Christian women in the family, and propose instead a standard of "mutuality" in relationship. Finally, feminist thought argues that the experience of women (so long ignored in the Christian tradition) is a resource and a starting point essential to ethical reflection on sexuality. Margaret Farley identifies the "moral revolution" that emerges from "new patterns of relationship" between women and men. This revolution changes the assessment of sexual conduct; for Farley, human actions must be measured by the standard of a "just love," which respects the concrete reality of the person, and not by abstract assessments of human acts. In a work such as *Between the Sexes,* Lisa Sowle Cahill presupposes the equality of women and men, and then moves to identify norms which promote such equality. Cahill relies on a revised natural law approach, which is reluctant to provide *absolute* norms for human sexual conduct.[70] Moreover, by 1985, it is Cahill who takes over the review of sexual ethical literature in *Theological Studies.*

Curran's publications and career after 1968 exemplify many of the developments in contemporary Catholic sexual ethics. Curran employs a revised natural law approach, which rejects a physicalist interpretation of human sexuality. Fundamental option theory leads him to reject "no parvity of matter." His anthropology accepts the reality of sinfulness in human life. His ethical stance is historically conscious and inductive, and questions the existence of absolute prohibitions of identifiable acts. Over the past twenty years, he has challenged absolute prohibitions of premarital sex, divorce, sterilization, and artificial insemination, as well as contraception and masturbation, while insisting that sexual conduct must still be guided by moral standards of responsibility and relationality. His theory of compromise permits a limited acceptance of homosexual relations. Amidst his lengthy corpus of theological and ethical arguments, in his 1988 book, *Tensions in Moral Theology,* Curran argues that "the primary questions or problem in developing a sexual ethic today is not the ethical question itself but the ecclesiological question of dissent and authoritative church teaching."[71] The 1986 Vatican ruling that finds him "not suitable nor eligible to teach Catholic theology" cites his writings on contraception, masturbation, abortion, euthanasia, premarital sex, homosexuality, sterilization and artificial insemination.[72]

The challenge to traditional moral norms after 1968 is also evident in the 1977 book, *Human Sexuality.* In 1972, the Catholic Theological Society of America appointed a committee to study sexual ethics; William Carroll, Agnes Cunningham, Anthony Kosnik, Ronald Modras and James Schulte are appointed members. In the tradition of Kenrick, Sabetti, Slater, Ford and Kelly, *Human Sexuality: New Directions in American Catholic Thought* seeks to relate the Christian tradition of sexual ethics to the North American context.

The text bears witness to many of the crucial differences in post-conciliar American Catholic theology; even the ecclesial status of the composers (two laymen and one woman religious, in addition to two priests) reflect a change. New interpretations of theological and ethical methodology are present as well. The authors employ Scripture, the Christian tradition and empirical sciences as sources for Christian ethics, and examine them in light of biblical scholarship and historical consciousness. The traditional moral manuals are given brief treatment. Kosnik *et al.* reject a strict act-centered analysis of sexuality as well as the teaching on parvity of matter. Instead, they take their "universal principle" or "fundamental criterion"[73] from Vatican II: it is the "nature of the person and his acts." They replace the traditional ends of marriage, "procreative" and "unitive," with "creative" and "integrative" goals; sexuality should foster "creative growth toward integration."[74] The commission members next identify particular values that contribute to creative growth toward integration. These are that sexual expression be self-liberating, other-enriching, honest, faithful, socially responsible, life-serving and joyous. Only at a third level (after the fundamental principle and these values) does the question of concrete rules or norms for specific actions (e.g., masturbation, premarital sex) emerge. However, the authors prefer to employ the term "guidelines" for this level. The fourth level of analysis is the individual person's decision, which must not be viewed merely as conformity to pre-existing rules.

It is under the rubric "guidelines," then, that Kosnik *et al.* treat the specific actions, the sins of impurity, so important to the manualist tradition. They review homosexual relations, masturbation, premarital sex, bestiality, sterilization, artificial insemination, adultery and other actions. While they are critical of some of these activities, they insist that these actions cannot be assessed independently of persons.

It would be a mistake, however, to interpret the CTSA report as a definitive statement of American Catholic sexual ethics. For the "epiphenomenon"[75] over the book—loud praise *and* loud protest— illustrates the pluralism of opinion in the American Catholic moral theological community. On the ecclesial front, Anthony Kosnik is disciplined for his participation in the project.[76]

Yet American Catholic voices also laud and protest a work which reiterates the traditional prohibitions of the sixth and ninth commandments, the 1975 Declaration on Sexual Ethics, *Persona Humana,* issued by the Congregation for the Doctrine of the Faith. That document reaffirms prohibitions on masturbation, homosexuality and premarital sex, as intrinsically evil actions, and reasserts the traditional teaching on parvity of matter.[77] Some members of the American theological community continue to criticize "revisionist" sexual ethics and to defend official magisterial teaching. For example, a 1985 book by Donald Lawler, Joseph Boyle and William E. May defends official magisterial teaching on sexuality, not only against the secular influences of American society (whose permissiveness trivializes sex), but against "the work of these Catholic writers [which] suffers from the same essential shortcomings as that of their secular counterparts."[78] Their solution is to explain the positive, personalistic interpretations of sexuality in the Catholic tradition that render the traditional prohibitions of certain types of conduct meaningful.

Many challenges, then, are posed to traditional Catholic sexual ethics after *Humanae Vitae,* even as it retains defenders in Rome and in the United States. Many ethicists abandon an act-centered analysis for a focus on persons in relationship. Many reject a physicalist, "order of nature" approach to sexuality, and lean toward "order of reason" approaches in which persons transcend biology. Absolute norms are questioned, and proportionalist modes of assessment become popular. The field of moral theology expands to include women as well as men, laity as well as priests. Experience is recognized as an important source of ethical reflection. Andre Guindon argues that over the past twenty years, much American Catholic ethics has undergone a

> substantial paradigmatic shift. The new model recognizes that human sexuality is more than a corporeal reality and, consequently, that human sexual acts cannot be reduced to "genital acts." This change of perspective has been buttressed by a prevailing awareness of the inadequacy of a deontological, confession- and act-centered approach to ethics in a Christian context.[79]

Moreover, the new model is historically conscious, employs a wide range of sources, views sexuality in a broad context, and respects theological as well as scriptural developments. While Guindon is appreciative of these changes, however, he warns that contemporary Catholic moralists are still

> embedded, like everyone else, in a culture which construes "sex" as genital acts. This embeddedness is so compelling that, though they assert their critical distance, most Catholic moralists seem to buy the inventory of sexual activities wholesale from the old textbooks which they denigrate in their theoretical considerations.[80]

The manuals may still exert strong influence on American Catholic sexual ethics, even as ethicists struggle to develop new frameworks, such as Guindon's "sexual lifestyles" or Margaret Farley's "just love," capable of encompassing the changes in traditional ethical analysis.[81]

As we have seen, according to Jay Dolan, American Catholics have twice before confronted modernity. In the late 1790's the influx of immigrants and a foreign clergy stopped the development of a republican Church. In the 1890's the condemnations of Americanism and Modernism uprooted a burgeoning American Catholic theological community. In the 1990's the American Church again confronts modernity, and in sexual ethics its romance appears to be with the experience of Christians as a central source of ethical reflection on sexuality.

In sexual ethics, however, modernity confronts American Catholics with many challenges. In their book *Intimate Matters: A History of Sexuality in America,* John D'Emilio and Estelle B. Freedman argue that

> over the last three and a half centuries, the meaning and place of sexuality in American life have changed: from the family-centered, reproductive sexual system in the colonial era; to a romantic, intimate, yet conflicted sexuality in nineteenth-century marriage; to a commercialized sexuality in the modern period, when sexual relations are expected to provide personal identity and individual happiness, apart from reproduction.[82]

It is not yet clear if the lived experience of American Catholics conforms to these stages. As Anne Patrick notes,

> our historical narrative has focused on professional, clerical moral theology . . . a full account of the American experience in moral theology should . . . [do] justice to the efforts and contributions of lay women and men, or religious sisters and brothers, and of ordinary parish priests.[83]

So too, the full story of American Catholic sexual ethics, of the experience of Catholics through two centuries of this country's history, awaits retrieval.

It is clear, however, that Catholic moral theological reflection on sexual ethics does not correspond to these stages. Personalism makes a late entry into American Catholic sexual ethics in the 1950's, and most moral theologians remain critical of a sexual ethic which is too individualistic in focus. As American Catholics begin to highlight the lived experience of women and men as a valid source of moral norms, the American milieu and its interpretation of sexuality, will have a profound impact on their discussions. They will need to take account of the demands of the "stage three" lifestyle of their compatriots. For example, in a climate in which sexual relations furnish great possibilities for personal meaning, they also carry the prospect of meaninglessness, and persons may need to learn to "discipline sexuality precisely in order to prevent it from contributing to a general personal apathy."[84] As in the days when they struggled with the influence of mixed marriage, divorce, dances and other socials, in the next century the struggle will be for American Catholics to discern the proper relationship between the values embodied in the Christian tradition on sexual ethics and the daily experience of individual Catholics in the United States.

Notes

1. *Documents of American Catholic History,* John Tracy Ellis, ed. (Wilmington: Michael Glazier, 1987), Vol. I, p. 149.

2. See Hermann Busenbaum, *Medulla Theologiae moralis* (Munster, 1650); Alfonso Maria de Liguori, *Theologia moralis,* 3 vols. (Bassani: Suis Typis Remondini Edidit, 1822).

3. For the history of the use of manuals in American Catholic moral theology, see the fine article by John P. Boyle, "The American Experience in Moral Theology," in Catholic Theological Society of America, *Proceedings of the Forty-First Annual Convention* 41 (1986), pp. 23–46; Paul McKeever, "75 Years of Moral Theology in America," *American Ecclesiastical Review* 152 (1965), pp. 17–32; David F. Kelly, *The Emergence of Roman Catholic Medical Ethics in North America: An Historical-Methodological-Bibliographical Study* (New York: The Edwin Mellen Press, 1979). See also Joanne Petro Gury, S.J., *Compendium Theologiae Moralis* (Lyons: J.B. Pelagaud, 1859); *Theologiae moralis [volumina] concinnatae a Francisco Patricio Kenrick,* 3 vols. (Philadelphiae apud Eugenium Cummiskey, 1841–1843; 2nd ed. Mechlin: Dessain, 1860–1861); Aloysius Sabetti, S.J., *Compendium Theologiae Moralis* (Ratisbon: Fr. Pustet, 1897; rev. ed., 1906, 1924). References to sexual ethics in the manuals can be found in sections on the sixth and ninth commandments and on the sacrament of matrimony.

4. (New York: Oxford, 1985), p. 23. See John T. Noonan, Jr., *Contraception: A History of Its Treatment by the Catholic Theologians and Canonists* (New York: New American Library, 1967), pp. 583–584.

5. Patrick J. Boyle, S.J., *Parvitas Materiae in Sexto* in *Contemporary Catholic Thought* (Lanham, MD: University Press of America, 1987) pp. 2–3.

6. Volume I of the *American Ecclesiastical Review* appears in 1889; see also *The Casuist: A Collection of Cases in Moral and Pastoral Theology,* 5 vols. (New York: Joseph F. Wagner, 1906; rev ed. 1924).

7. "Conferences," *American Ecclesiastical Review* 9 (1983), p. 367.

8. Probable opinions are clearly important to these authors. See the *New Catholic Encyclopedia* (New York: McGraw-Hill, 1967), articles on "Probabilism" and "Probabiliorism," in vol. 11, pp. 814–815, and on "Equiprobabilism," in vol. 5, pp. 502–503. See also John Mahoney, *The Making of Moral Theology: A Study of the Roman Catholic Tradition* (Oxford: Clarendon Press, 1987), ch. 4.

9. From Joseph Wissel, *The Redemptorist on the American Missions* (New York: John Ross and Son, 1875), pp. 83–84, cited by Jay P. Dolan, *Catholic Revivalism: The American Experience 1830–1900* (Notre Dame: University of Notre Dame Press, 1978), p. 110. See also Jay P. Dolan, *The*

American Catholic Experience: A History from Colonial Times to the Present (Garden City, NY: Doubleday & Co., 1985), p. 227.

10. *Ibid.,* p. 111.

11. Peter Guilday, *A History of the Councils of Baltimore, 1791–1884* (New York: Arno Press, 1969), p. 67. See also his *The National Pastorals of the American Hierarchy (1792–1919)* (Washington, DC: National Catholic Welfare Council, 1923).

12. Third Plenary Council of Baltimore, *Baltimore Catechism, No. 3* (New York: Benziger Brothers, 1885), p. 228.

13. Dolan, *American Catholic Experience,* p. 228.

14. N.A., "A Beautiful Example of Moral Heroism," *The Ave Maria* 16 (1880), pp. 191–192.

15. Dolan, *Catholic Revivalism,* p. 25.

16. John Tracy Ellis, "The Formation of the American Priest: An Historical Perspective," in *The Catholic Priest in the United States* (Collegeville: St. John's University Press, 1971), p. 32; see also pp. 19–22. Kenrick writes to his brother that seminaries are not taking his books lest "they appear to hurt the majesty of the city [Rome] by introducing the work of a stranger" (p. 32).

17. Jay Dolan, "A Catholic Romance with Modernity," *The Wilson Quarterly* 5 (1981), pp. 120–133.

18. *Ibid.*

19. Robert D. Cross, *The Emergence of Liberal Catholicism in America* (Cambridge: Harvard University Press, 1958).

20. On Bouquillon, see Cross, *Liberal Catholicism,* pp. 96–98, 142–144; Boyle, "American Catholic," pp. 32–33.

21. Gerald P. Fogarty, S.J., *The Vatican and the American Hierarchy from 1870 to 1965* (Wilmington: Michael Glazier, 1985), p. 190. On Americanism and Modernism, see also Dolan, *American Catholic Experience,* ch. 11; Ellis, "The Formation," pp. 57–74.

22. Gardella, *Innocent Ecstasy,* p. 37. Gardella attributes this to anti-Catholicism, as well, and argues that Protestant discomfort with discussions of sexuality restricted American Catholic discussions. See A. Tanquerey, *Synopsis Theologiae Moralis et Pastoralis,* 3 vols. (Rome: Desclee, 1908).

23. Thomas Slater, S.J., *A Manual of Moral Theology for English-Speaking Countries,* 2 vols. (New York: Benziger Brothers, 1912).

24. John A. Ryan, *Moral Aspects of Sterilization* (Washington, DC: National Catholic Welfare Conference, 1930), p. 3.

25. According to Noonan, *op. cit.,* p. 502.

26. John A. Ryan, "Family Limitation," *American Ecclesiastical Review* 54 (1916), pp. 684–696.

27. Ryan also discussed the circumstances under which a wife could refuse intercourse with her husband.

28. Guilday, *National Pastorals,* p. 313.

29. *Ibid.,* p. 315.

30. (Notre Dame, IN: University of Notre Dame Press, 1980), p. 7.

31. John A. McHugh, O.P., and Charles J. Callan, O.P., *Moral Theology: A Complete Course,* 2 vols. (New York: Joseph Wagner, 1929; rev. ed., 1958), Vol. 1, p. iv.

32. Gardella, *op. cit.,* p. 38. McHugh and Callan, pp. 484–565, 596–624. By 1958, McHugh and Callan have revised the text to read: "Now, sex pleasure has been ordained by God as an inducement to perform an act which has for its purpose the propagation and education of children" (p. 518).

33. Gerald Kelly, S.J., "A Fundamental Notion on the Problem of Sex Morality," *Theological Studies* 1 (1940), pp. 117–129.

34. See. e.g., John C. Ford, S.J., "Notes on Moral Theology, 1942," *Theological Studies* 3 (1942), pp. 593–598.

35. Gerald Kelly, S.J., *Modern Youth and Chastity* (St. Louis: The Queen's Work, 1941), pp. 82, 84.

36. *Ibid.,* p. 14.

37. *Ibid.,* p. 35.

38. *Ibid.*

39. "Notes on Moral Theology, 1947," *Theological Studies* 9 (1948), p. 120.

40. See John C. Ford, S.J., and Gerald Kelly, S.J., *Contemporary Moral Theology, Volume One, Questions in Fundamental Moral Theology* (Westminster, MD: The Newman Press, 1958), ch. 9, for a summary of this discussion. See also John R. Connery, "Notes on Moral Theology," *Theological Studies* 16 (1955), p. 584; Francis J. Connell, C.SS.R., "Juvenile Courtships," *American Ecclesiastical Review* 132 (1955), pp. 181–190.

41. "Notes on Moral Theology," *Theological Studies* 24 (1963), pp. 58–59.

42. Francis J. Connell, C.SS.R., "The Catholic Doctrine of the Ends of Marriage," The Catholic Theological Society of America, *Proceedings of the Foundation Meeting* 1 (1946), pp. 34–45.

43. Gerald Kelly, "Notes on Moral Theology," *Theological Studies* 14 (1953), pp. 31–38; John R. Connery, "Notes on Moral Theology," *Theological Studies* 18 (1957), p. 562.

44. The Catholic Theological Society of America, "Summary of the

Moral Seminar," *Proceedings of the Fifth Annual Meeting* 5 (1950), p. 157. It is no wonder that James Hennesey, S.J., *American Catholics: A History of the Roman Catholic Community in the United States* (New York: Oxford, 1981), notes of this era: "A pervasive moralism characterized American Catholics of the 1950's. . . . Moral theology, curiously immune to the influence of Christian history and dogma and heavily influenced by the legalistic approach of canonists and the abstractions of scholastic philosophers, dominated the scene. On the popular level, long lines at Saturday afternoon and evening confessions gave impressive witness to the phenomenon. Legalism, too, loomed large, reflected in and assisted by the willingness of churchmen (Pius XII in the van) to legislate the tiniest minutiae of church observance. Moralism was confused with religiousness, ethics with theology" (p. 288).

45. There are some sections in which they cite other moral theologians and the traditional manuals at length, and some in which they do not.

46. Ford and Kelly, *Contemporary*, p. v., my emphasis.

47. *Ibid.,* p. 161.

48. John C. Ford, "Notes on Moral Theology, 1942" *Theological Studies* 3 (1942), pp. 596–598. There is long rooting in the manual traditions on the marital debt to allow this limited cooperation.

49. John C. Ford, "Notes on Moral Theology, 1944" *Theological Studies* 5 (1944), p. 506.

50. See, e.g., *Theological Studies* 11 (1950), pp. 71–77; 14 (1953), pp. 54–57; 18 (1957), pp. 593–595; see also Orville Griese, *The "Rhythm" in Marriage and Christian Morality* (Westminster, MD: Newman Press, 1944) and "Objective Morality of the Rhythm Practice," *American Ecclesiastical Review* 120 (1949), pp. 475–479.

51. "Notes on Moral Theology," *Theological Studies* 21 (1960), p. 227.

52. John Connery, "May A Catholic President Sign. . . ?" *America* 102 (December 12, 1959), pp. 353–354.

53. Ford and Kelly, *Contemporary*, Vol. 2, p. 277.

54. *Ibid.,* p. 377.

55. "Notes on Moral Theology," *Theological Studies* 25 (1964), p. 232.

56. This lends support to Fogarty's (*The Vatican*, p. 193) assertion that "the stifling atmosphere following the condemnation of Modernism had perhaps more effect in the United States than in Europe. In Europe critical scholarship went underground; in the United States it was nipped in the bud."

57. 80, no. 11 (June 5, 1964), pp. 319–323. Other authors in this volume include Richard McCormick, Bernard Haring, George Casey, Thomas Burch, E. Schillebeeckx and Louis Dupre.

58. *Ibid.,* p. 320.

59. *Ibid.*

60. *Ibid.,* p. 321.

61. "Masturbation and Objectively Grave Matter," reprinted in *A New Look at Christian Morality* (Notre Dame: Fides Publishers, 1968), p. 215. Curran employs Richard McCormick's analyses; see Richard A. McCormick, S.J., "The Priest and Teen-Age Sexuality," *Homiletic and Pastoral Review* 65 (1964–1965), pp. 379–387; "Adolescent Masturbation: A Pastoral Problem," *Homiletic and Pastoral Review* 60 (1959–1960), pp. 527–540.

62. Richard A. McCormick, S.J., *Notes on Moral Theology 1965–1980* (Lanham, MD: University Press of America, 1981), p. 51; see also pp. 38–51, 109–116, 164–168. Notes from later years are found in *Notes on Moral Theology 1981–1984* (Lanham, MD: University Press of America, 1984).

63. For history of the commission, including a list of the other American members, see Robert Blair Kaiser, *The Politics of Sex and Religion: A Case History in the Development of Doctrine, 1962–1984* (Kansas City, MO: Leaven Press, 1985).

64. *Proceedings of the Twenty-Third Annual Convention* 23 (1968), p. 22.

65. See Kaiser, *op. cit.,* pp. 208ff; see also William H. Shannon, *The Lively Debate: Response to* Humanae Vitae (New York: Sheed & Ward, 1970), and Charles E. Curran, Robert E. Hunt, and the "Subject Professors" with John F. Hunt and Terrence R. Connelly, *Dissent In and For the Church: Theologians and* Humanae Vitae (New York: Sheed & Ward, 1969).

66. Kaiser, *op. cit.,* p. 218; see also Andrew M. Greeley, *The American Catholic: A Social Portrait* (New York: Basic Books, 1977).

67. (Kansas City, KS: Sheed, Andrews and McMeel, 1976); see also *Taking a Chance on God: Liberating Theology for Gays, Lesbians, and Their Lovers, Families and Friends* (Boston: Beacon Press, 1988).

68. Philip S. Keane, *Sexual Morality: A Catholic Perspective* (New York: Paulist Press, 1977).

69. Richard McCormick, "Sterilization and Theological Method," *Theological Studies* 37 (1976), pp. 471–477; John P. Boyle, *The Sterilization Controversy* (New York: Paulist Press, 1977).

70. Margaret A. Farley, "New Patterns of Relationship: Beginnings of a Moral Revolution," in *Woman: New Dimensions,* Walter J. Burghardt, S.J., ed. (New York: Paulist Press, 1975), and *Personal Commitments: Beginning, Keeping, Changing* (San Francisco: Harper & Row, 1986); Lisa Sowle Cahill, *Between the Sexes: Foundations for a Christian Ethics of Sexuality* (Philadelphia: Fortress Press and New York: Paulist Press, 1985).

71. (Notre Dame: University of Notre Dame Press, 1988), p. 77.

72. *Ibid.,* p. 7. For Curran's sexual ethics, see also *A New Look at Christian Morality* (Notre Dame: Fides, 1968); "How My Mind Has Changed, 1960–1975," in *Horizons* 2 (1975), pp. 187–205; *Catholic Moral Theology in Dialogue* (Notre Dame: University of Notre Dame Press, 1976); *Themes in Fundamental Moral Theology* (Notre Dame: University of Notre Dame Press, 1977); *Issues in Sexual and Medical Ethics* (Notre Dame: University of Notre Dame Press, 1978); *Transition and Tradition in Moral Theology* (Notre Dame: University of Notre Dame Press, 1982).

73. (Garden City, NY: Doubleday, 1979), p. 116. See also Dennis Doherty, ed., *Dimensions of Human Sexuality* (Garden City, NY: Doubleday, 1979).

74. *Ibid.,* p. 106.

75. Daniel Maguire, "Human Sexuality: The Book and the Epiphenomenon," The Catholic Theological Society of America, *Proceedings of the Thirty-Third Annual Convention* 33 (1978), pp. 54–76.

76. See Curran, *Tensions,* p. 76.

77. Sacred Congregation for the Doctrine of the Faith, *Declaration on Sexual Ethics* (Washington, DC: United States Catholic Conference, 1977); see also Boyle, *Parvitas,* pp. 84–85.

78. Rev. Donald Lawler, O.F.M.Cap., Joseph Boyle, Jr., and William E. May, *Catholic Sexual Ethics: A Summary, Explanation, and Defense* (Huntington, IN: Our Sunday Visitor, 1985), p. 12. For an explanation of the moral/theological perspective which undergirds their argument, see Germain Grisez, *The Way of the Lord Jesus, Volume One, Christian Moral Principles* (Chicago: Franciscan Herald Press, 1983).

79. Andre Guindon, "Sexual Acts or Sexual Lifestyles: A Methodological Problem in Sexual Ethics," *Eglise et Theologie* 18 (1987), p. 315. Guindon's essay studies the writings of Charles Curran, Philip Keane, Lisa Sowle Cahill and Anthony Kosnik (in the CTSA report).

80. *Ibid.*

81. Guindon urges an approach which examines sexual lifestyles—conjugal, familial, gay and celibate—and which espouses a "sexual language which is integrated, relational, generous, and responsible" (p. 329). See also *The Sexual Creators: An Ethical Proposal for Concerned Christians* (Lanham, MD: University Press of America, 1986). Another ethicist who avoids the act-centered approach is Margaret Farley. She proposes norms of justice for sexuality. "Most generally, the norms are respect for persons through respect for autonomy and relationality; respect for relationality through requirements of mutuality, equality, commitment, and fruitfulness." See "An Ethic for Same-Sex Relations," in *A Challenge to Love: Gay and Les-*

bian Catholics in the Church, edited by Robert Nugent (New York: Crossroad, 1983), p. 105.

82. (New York: Harper & Row, 1988), pp. xi–xii.

83. Anne E. Patrick, "A Response (II) to John Boyle," The Catholic Theological Society of America, *Proceedings of the Forty-First Annual Convention* 41 (1986), p. 50.

84. Margaret A. Farley, "Sexual Ethics," in the *Encyclopedia of Bioethics,* 4 vols. (New York: The Free Press, 1978), p. 1587.

34. Congregation for the Doctrine of the Faith on Anthony Kosnik et al., *Human Sexuality.* July 13, 1979

The book *Human Sexuality: New Directions in American Catholic Thought,* a study commissioned by the Catholic Theological Society of America and edited by the Reverend Anthony Kosnik, has been given wide publicity through its distribution not only in the United States but elsewhere, both in the English version and in various translations.

The Sacred Congregation for the Doctrine of the Faith wishes to commend the actions of the American bishops, who exercised their pastoral ministry as authentic teachers of the faith by calling to the attention of their priests and people the errors contained in this book, particularly in regard to the unacceptability of its "pastoral guidelines" as suitable norms for the formation of Christian consciences in matters of sexual morality.

The Congregation particularly wishes to commend the National Conference of Catholic Bishops' Committee on Doctrine for its statement of November, 1977, which gives an evaluation of the book that can serve the bishops and the Catholic community at large not only in the United States but wherever this book has made its appearance. The enclosed *Observations* of this Congregation may also be useful to the bishops for their continued prudent guidance of their people on this delicate pastoral question.

At the same time, the Congregation cannot fail to note its concern that a distinguished society of Catholic theologians would have arranged for the publication of this report in such a way as to give broad distribution to the erroneous principles and conclusions of this book and in this way provide a source of confusion among the people of God.

I would be grateful to Your Excellency for bringing this letter to the attention of the members of the Episcopal Conference. With kind regards and personal best wishes for you.

OBSERVATIONS

The book *Human Sexuality* has already received substantial criticism on the part of theologians, of numerous American bishops, and of the Doctrinal Commission of the American Episcopal Conference. It would seem clear that the authors of this book, who speak of "encouraging others to join us in the continuing search for more satisfying answers to the mystery of human sexuality" (p. XV), will have to give rigorous reconsideration to the position they have assumed in the light of such criticism. This is all the more important, since the topic of the book—human sexuality—and the attempt to offer "helpful practical guidelines to beleaguered pastors, priests, counsellors and teachers," charge the authors with an enormous responsibility for the erroneous conclusions and the potentially harmful impact these ideas can have on the correct formation of the Christian consciences of so many people.

This Sacred Congregation, considering the fact that this book and its opinions have been given wide distribution within the U.S.A. throughout the English-speaking world, and elsewhere through various translations, considers it a duty to intervene by calling attention to the errors contained in this book and by inviting the authors to correct these errors. Here we limit our considerations to some of these errors which seem to be the most fundamental and to touch the heart of the matter; this limitation should not lead to the inference that other errors of a historical, scriptural, and theological nature are not to be found in this book as well.

1. A most pervasive mistake in this book is the manipulation of the concept or definition of human sexuality. "Sexuality then is

the mode or manner by which humans experience and express both the incompleteness of their individualities as well as their relatedness to each other as male and female. . . . This definition broadens the meaning of sexuality beyond the merely genital and generative and is so to be understood in all that follows" (p. 82). This definition refers to what may be called *generic* sexuality, in which "sex is seen as a force that permeates, influences, and affects every act of a person's being at every moment of existence." In this generic sense the book quotes the Vatican *Declaration on Certain Questions concerning Sexual Ethics,* which acknowledged this basic human differentiation saying "it is from sex that the human person receives the characteristics which, on the biological, psychological and spiritual levels, make that person a man or a woman, and thereby largely condition his or her progress towards maturity and insertion into society" (*Persona Humana,* 1).

It is not, however, in this area of generic sexuality that the moral problematic of chastity is engaged. This occurs rather within the more specific field of sexual being and behaviour called *genital* sexuality, which, while existing within the field of generic sexuality, has its specific rules corresponding to its proper structure and finality. These do not simply coincide with those of generic sexuality. Hence while *Human Sexuality* cites the first paragraph of *Persona humana,* as noted above, it fails to refer to the rest of this document's teaching on human sexuality, especially n. 5, which clearly states that "the use of the sexual function has its true meaning and moral rectitude only in true marriage."

It is equally evident that Vatican II, in n. 51 of *Gaudium et Spes,* speaks clearly of genital rather than generic sexuality when it indicates that the moral character of sexual conduct "does not depend solely on sincere intentions or on an evaluation of motives. It must be determined by objective standards. These, based on the nature of the human person and his acts, preserve the full sense of mutual self-giving and human procreation in the context of true love. Such a goal cannot be achieved unless the virtue of conjugal chastity is sincerely practised." While the first part of this quotation is often cited in *Human Sexuality,* the last part is regularly omitted, an omission extended also to the following sentence in GS 51, which states, "Relying on these principles, sons of the Church may not undertake methods of regulating procreation which are found blameworthy by the teaching authority of the Church in its unfolding of the divine law." While this book speaks in fact exclusively about genital sexuality, it sets aside the specific norms for genital sexuality and instead attempts to resolve questions by the criteria of generic sexuality (cf. n. 2 below).

Furthermore, in regard to the teaching of Vatican II, we note here another mistaken notion. This book repeatedly states that the Council deliberately refused to retain the traditional hierarchy of primary and secondary ends of marriage, opening "the Church to a new and deeper understanding of the meaning and value of conjugal love" (p. 125 and passim). On the contrary, the Commission of the Modi declared explicitly, replying to a proposal brought forward by many Fathers to put this hierarchical distinction into the text of n. 48, "In a pastoral text which intends to institute a dialogue with the world, juridical elements are not required. . . . In any case, the primordial importance of procreation and education is shown at least ten times in the text" (cf. nn. 48 and 50).

2. In the view of sexuality described in *Human Sexuality,* the formulation of its purpose undergoes a substantial change with respect to the classical formulation: the traditional "procreative and unitive purpose" of sexuality, consistently developed in all the magisterial documents through Vatican II and *Humanae Vitae,* is substituted by a "creative and integrative purpose," also called "creative growth towards integration," which describes a broad and vague purpose applicable to any generic sexuality (and practically to any human action). Admitting that procreation is only one possible form of creativity, but not essential to sexuality (cf. p. 83 sq.), is a gratuitous change in the accepted terms without any substantial argument, a change which contradicts the formulation used in Vatican II and assumed in *Persona humana.* This change of purpose and consequently of the criteria for morality in human sexuality evidently changes all the traditional conclusions about sexual behaviour; it even precludes the possibility of fruitful theological discussion by removing the common terminology.

3. The authors of this book try to give more concrete content to the formal criterion "creative growth towards integration" (p. 92 sq.), but hardly anything in this development seems to refer specifi-

cally to genital sexual activity. It is true that they intend to give only some "particularly significant" values (cf. p. 92); nevertheless, those cited (e.g., honest, joyous, socially responsible) may be postulated equally well of most human activity.

The authors pretend that these are not purely subjective criteria, though in fact they are: the personal judgments about these factors are so different, determined by personal sentiments, feelings, customs, etc., that it would be next to impossible to single out definite criteria of what exactly integrates a particular person or contributes to his or her creative growth in any specific sexual activity.

Thus in chapter five, the criteria for discerning "creative growth towards integration," when applied to specific areas of sexual activity, yield no manageable or helpful rules for serious conscience formation in matters of sexuality. In the book, moreover, they are called "guidelines" which can never be regarded as "absolute and universal moral norms" (p. 97).

4. The practical applications proposed in chapter five show clearly the consequences of this theory of human sexuality. These conclusions either dissociate themselves from or directly contradict Catholic teaching as consistently proposed by moral theologians and as taught by the Church's magisterium. The intention expressed in the preface—"The fifth chapter . . . attempts to provide information and assistance for leaders in pastoral ministry to help them form and guide consciences in this area according to the mind of Jesus"—is sadly unfulfilled, indeed even reversed.

The authors nearly always find a way to allow for integrative growth through the neglect or destruction of some intrinsic element of sexual morality, particularly its procreative ordination. And if some forms of sexual conduct are disapproved, it is only because of the supposed absence, generally expressed in the form of a doubt, of "human integration" (as in swinging, mate-swapping, bestiality), and not because these actions are opposed to the nature of human sexuality. When some action is considered completely immoral, it is never for intrinsic reasons, on the basis of objective finality, but only because the authors happen not to see, for their part, any way of making it serve for some human integration. This subjection of theological and scientific arguments to evaluation by criteria primarily derived from one's present experience of what is human or less than human gives rise to a relativism in human conduct which recognizes no absolute values.

Given these criteria, it is small wonder that this book pays such scant attention to the documents of the Church's magisterium, whose clear teaching and helpful norms of morality in the area of human sexuality it often openly contradicts.

Congregation for the Doctrine of the Faith on John McNeill, *The Church and the Homosexual.* Summer, 1978

During the summer of 1978, the Congregation for the Doctrine of the Faith sent a letter to the Jesuit Superior General Pedro Arrupe, S.J., regarding Father John McNeill, S.J., and a book McNeill had published entitled The Church and the Homosexual.

I

The congregation first intends to clarify certain points concerning the nature and publication of this book.

1. The book, *The Church and the Homosexual,* clearly and openly advocates a moral position regarding homosexuality which is contrary to—in theory as well as in practice—the traditional and actual teaching of the church.

In his own words, the author presents an "advocacy theology" (p. 23) for "ethically responsible homosexual relationships" (p. 196 and *passim*). The contents of this book are arranged to show that there is no proven moral obligation to refrain from "ethically responsible homosexual relationships" and that, therefore, both church and civil norms must accept these relationships as legitimate. The author describes the spirit and content of the book in the following words:

In their traditional presentation of moral obligation, Aquinas and Alphonsus Liguori, among others, always maintained *nulla obligatio nisi sit certa.* Given, as I believe, (1) the uncertainty of clear scriptural prohibition, (2) the questionable basis of the traditional condemnation in moral philosophy and moral theology, (3) the emergence of new data which upset many traditional assumptions, and (4) controversies among psychologists and psychiatrists concerning theory, etiology, treatment, and so on, there obviously is a need to open up anew the question of the moral standing of homosexual activity and homosexual relationships for public debate. (cf. pp. 20, 21).

2. The book was published with the *imprimi potest* of the Jesuit provincial superior, Father Eamon Taylor; the *imprimatur* was not requested because, according to the judgment of the canonist consulted, "permission is recommended but not prescribed," and in this case "the purpose of the recommendation has already been fulfilled through the extensive process of examination . . . , and the further delays which would be entailed in requesting diocesan approval would constitute a disproportionate inconvenience to the author, the publisher. . . ."

This point is important: What is the *purpose* of the *imprimi potest* which was given? Although the *imprimatur* is strongly recommended in a case of this sort (cf. this congregation's *Decretum de Ecclesiae Pastorum vigilantia circa libros* of March 19, 1975), it is not required; the permission of the competent superior, however, is required according to the constitutions of the Jesuit Order. The *imprimi potest* given would normally indicate that the contents of the book were judged to be sound, in accord with the church's teaching, and safe to follow in practice. This is clearly not the case with Father McNeill's book.

Father McNeill explains in the Preface to his book his understanding of the significance of the *imprimi potest:*

It is important for the reader to understand what is implied in the granting of an ecclesiastical *imprimi potest,* i.e. permission to publish, by my religious superiors and what is not implied. First, the authorities that grant the permission in no way commit themselves as agreeing or disagreeing with the content of the book. Rather, all that is implied is that authorities have assured that the book is a prudent work that meets the standards of scholarship for publication of a book on a controversial moral topic. Secondly, the "permission to publish" in no way implies that the conclusions stated in this book are accepted by the Catholic Church as part of its official teaching; only the Pope and the bishops have the authority to teach officially in the name of the church (cf. pp. xii–xiii).

Normally, however, the *imprimi potest* is the superior's permission based on the censor's judgment that the book does not contain errors or advice which would be harmful to its readership.

For this reason, it seems important to note the explanation given by the provincial superior, Father Eamon G. Taylor, S.J., in granting the *imprimi potest*. His reason in departing from the customary norms governing the granting of the *imprimi potest* seems to be based on the fact that he envisions a *restricted readership* for the book—one for whom the danger of scandal could be reasonably said not to exist. Father Taylor's prepared statement on his *imprimi potest* stated:

> The permission to publish granted by ecclesiastical superiors does not imply any judgment of the content or opinions expressed in the book. It does imply that the work has been judged competently and responsibly written, and therefore, *suitable for presentation to and evaluation by scholars.* . . . The ultimate judgment upon Father McNeill's method and conclusion will come from *his peers among professional moral theologians,* and from the magisterial authority of the church, to which Father McNeill defers. (Italics ours).

In this explanation, Father Taylor appeals to "scholars" and "peers" in the field of moral theology as the intended readership justifying the permission to publish.

On the other hand, it seems apparent to us that the kind of scholarly and peer-group readership envisioned by the provincial superior was not at all the audience Father McNeill and his publishers had in mind. We conclude this both from his stated intention in the Preface of his book, and from the speeches and lectures he has given in city after city to promote the book's sale and its thesis on homosexuality. The intention of Father McNeill is clear; he says:

> The *imprimi potest* was important to me, first of all, because it is my hope that this book will help foster an all-out discussion of the church's moral understanding and pastoral practice concerning the homosexual. Secondly, I *particularly want to reach, and open up new, hopeful possibilities for, all those Catholic homosexuals* who are struggling to put together their dual identities as Catholics and as homosexuals. Therefore it was important to me that the book should be accepted into the *mainstream of Catholic debate* and reflection (p. xii; Italics ours).

Father McNeill further indicated his intention of giving the widest possible publicity to his theological and pastoral opinions, when he comments on the developments leading up to publication in this way:

> Almost simultaneously with the offer of publication I received a notice from my Jesuit superiors that Father General Pedro Arrupe, S.J., had written from Rome ordering me not to publish anything in the popular press and not to address homosexual groups. (At a later date, officials told me that with the appearance of the article in the National Catholic Reporter, pressure was brought to bear on Father General by various Roman congregations to take some action against me in the matter.) I was particularly upset by this prohibition, first because *the implication of the letter that the moral debate could be carried on outside the notice of the public media and exclusively on a peer-group level* seemed to me to be totally impracticable; and secondly because I was convinced that it was *only through*

open discussion, with the Catholic homosexual community participating as an equal partner, that any real advance could be made in the church's moral understanding
of homosexuality and consequent pastoral practice (p. x;
Italics ours).

Father McNeill indicates he took the attitude of some of the
scholars on the commission which the Jesuit authorities set up to
judge his work as encouragement to pursue a course of publicizing
his ideas among the entire Catholic and secular community, rather
than aim for the community of scholarship:

. . . a majority of the commission reported that they found
the manuscript a serious and scholarly work worthy of
publication. Several felt strongly that *there should be a
public debate* on all the issues involved and that my manuscript would be an important contribution to that debate
(p. xi).

It seems clear that Father Taylor's stated purpose and the purpose and course of action of Father McNeill do not coincide. Therefore, even apart from a judgment about the wisdom of granting the
imprimi potest in the first place, it seems altogether reasonable and
necessary to withdraw it now.

3. We find it extraordinary that a book so clearly contradicting
the moral teaching of the church would be published a few days after
the publication of *Persona humana,* a document of this congregation treating in part of the same question; no reasonable person
could imagine that time for serious study and evaluation had been
given to the declaration of the authentic magisterium of the church
in this case. Such an action cannot but indicate the gravest sort of
disregard for the mature study of and loyal support for the teachings
of the church expected of her sons, especially those who have positions of responsibility through the reception of holy orders. The
following extract from the article in *Time* magazine (Sept. 20, 1976)
is an example of how well this situation is understood by society
at large:

When the Congregation for the Doctrine of the Faith issued its 5,000-word statement on homosexuality, premarital sex and masturbation, it was responding in part to complaints that the church was not providing sufficient guidelines for sexual behavior and attitudes. Days later, Father John McNeill, a Jesuit priest and former teacher of moral theology at the now defunct Woodstock College and at Fordham University, won the designation *imprimi potest* (it can be printed) for a book strongly attacking the church's views on homosexuality.

4. Finally, we think it important to clarify the issue regarding the scandal caused by this book. This scandal comes from the content of the book itself—ideas and suggested pastoral practice clearly at variance with the teaching and practice of the church; from the circumstances of publication—the *imprimi potest* gives the aura of ecclesiastical approval, and the publication of the book within days after *Persona humana* gravely damages the respectful attitude toward the teaching of the authentic magisterium of the church in the public view; and from the publicity and promotion given to the book and its ideas by Father McNeill himself through his tour of public lectures and press conferences.

One measure of the seriousness of this scandal is the extraordinary step taken by the president of the episcopal conference in the United States, Archbishop Joseph Bernardin of Cincinnati, on the occasion of the publicity given to Father McNeill's scheduled appearance in his archdiocese:

> This weekend Father John McNeill, S.J., will be in the city to speak about his new book, *The Church and the Homosexual*. Because his visit has already been given public notice and because his lecture will also be given publicity, I wish to restate the church's position regarding homosexuality so there will be no confusion in the minds of people. . . . No one can take it upon himself to alter this clear teaching. While it is legitimate for theologians to explore this moral question like any other, it is a disservice to challenge this teaching publicly in such a way as to give the impres-

sion that some radical change has taken place or is about to take place.

Such appearances by Father McNeill in various cities throughout the United States continue to be a source of scandal, both in the false hopes given to Catholic homosexuals and in the confusion caused in the community at large. These public appearances clearly indicate that the purpose originally stated for granting the *imprimi potest* by Father Taylor—"its presentation to and evaluation by scholars"—has long been set aside.

II

After the explicit clarification of the facts of the case by the above considerations, we are best able to address the second point: What steps or actions would be suitable to avoid further scandal? It seems to us that the following actions should be taken as a minimum:

1. Father Taylor should be required to withdraw the *imprimi potest,* so that it would not appear in any possible second printing, second edition, or translation of the book. It is clear that more than adequate distribution has already been given for purposes of scholarly study of the book.
2. It is important that the withdrawal of the *imprimi potest* and the reasons for it be communicated both to Father McNeill and to the publisher of the book lest a situation develop again in which the fact that preparations had advanced so far might prompt local authorities to concede a further printing (edition or translation) with ecclesiastical approval.
3. It seems urgent that Father McNeill be prohibited from any further appearance or lecture on the question of homosexuality and sexual ethics, or in promotion of the book.

Congregation for the Doctrine of the Faith on André Guindon, *The Sexual Creators.* January 30, 1992

On Jan. 30, 1992 the Congregation for the Doctrine of the Faith publicly released a note on the book The Sexual Creators: An Ethical Proposal for Concerned Christians *by Father André Guindon, O.M.I., of St. Paul's University, Ottawa. It follows.*

PREFACE

The Congregation for the Doctrine of the Faith, which is entrusted with the responsibility "of promoting and safeguarding the doctrine of faith and morals in the whole Catholic world" (apostolic constitution *Pastor Bonus,* art. 48), has completed an examination of the aforementioned book by Father André Guindon according to the ordinary procedure of its *Ratio Agendi.* After a dialogue with the author conducted through the mediation of the superior general of the Oblates of Mary Immaculate from November 1988 to September 1991, the congregation publishes this Note which indicates points in which the volume conflicts with the doctrine of the church in the area of sexual morality. At this same time, the congregation again extends the author the opportunity within a reasonable period of time to furnish clarifications which would exemplify his stated desire to be faithful to the teaching of the magisterium. The dialogue with the author is being pursued in conjunction with the Congregation for Institutes of Consecrated Life and Apostolic Societies and the Congregation for Catholic Education in respect to the areas of each's competence.

I. OBSERVATIONS ON THE BOOK

Introduction

The book seeks to be more than a study of sexology. The author intends to offer the church a personal contribution toward the development of a new doctrine regarding what he calls "sexual fecundity," proposed as "a contribution toward the construction of an alternative to the unsatisfactory fecundity-fertility view" (p. ix). We are not just dealing then with a rethinking of the moral norms concerning human sexuality, but with the proposal of a new anthropology and an "agenda for the forthcoming revolution of the sexual creators" (p. 236).

The volume is not lacking in a number of praiseworthy goals and positive aspects, for example its desire to overcome a legalism which is merely exterior and negative (p. 9ff), its avowed opposition to a contraceptive or hedonistic mentality which considers sexual pleasure an end in itself (pp. 36, 74, 94), its efforts to attain a unified vision of the human being (pp. 22ff), its resolve to be attentive to persons beyond their moral faults (p. 164) and its investigation of the Christian meaning of human affectivity (pp. 100, 105).

A careful examination of the text, however, has shown that it also contains a number of serious and fundamental disagreements, not only with more recent teachings of the magisterium, but also with the traditional doctrine of the church. These disagreements regard the general understanding of sexuality, the understanding of the human person in his relationships with others and with God the creator, as well as the moral judgment of particular forms of sexual behavior. These disagreements are ultimately rooted in an inadequate and at times erroneous approach on the level of theological method.

2. *Particular Problems*

2.1. GENERAL UNDERSTANDING OF SEXUALITY

The author uses the terms *sexual* and *sexuality* in so wide a sense so as to designate all that characterizes the affective activities of the human being as sexual (cf., for example, pp. 23, 71, 120–121). "Sexuality is that which gives human beings an interpersonal and social history and that which makes them responsible for its development" (p. 34). One can hardly imagine a broader definition. Sexuality is described in terms of the two components of "sexuality" and "tenderness," which are linked respectively to the bodily and spiritual dimensions of the human being. But to designate as sexual every expression of affection with the claim that it is inevitably marked by the sexual nature of the person is not only a confusing inflation of the word *sexual,* but also a violation of the elementary rules of logic. From the fact that every affective relationship is marked by the sexual character of the partners, it does not follow that every affective relationship is a sexual one. It becomes ambiguous and confusing, then, when all affective relationships, even those of parents with their children, those of celibates and so on are characterized as sexual (pp. 66–67, 120–121).

Corresponding to this enlarged notion of sexuality is the author's proposal of a new and more fundamental understanding of "sexual fecundity," which is to become the basis for illuminating "all the instances of sexual interaction" (pp. 66–67). This new criterion of reference is presented as independent of "biological fecundity," which traditional Catholic moral teaching, it is claimed, mistakenly assumed to be the only norm. Thus the principle regulating human sexuality would no longer be the inseparability of the unitive and procreative meanings of the sexual act, but rather the inseparability of "sensuality" and "tenderness" (pp. 66–68). The primary meaning of the "transmission of life" would be a "new quality of human life which is communicated in and through an integrated sexual experience . . . from one love to the other" (p. 67). Procreation is treated as secondary and dispensable. The integration of sensuality and tenderness is proposed as the criterion for judging any kind of sexual activity, not only conjugal, nor heterosexual only, but also homosexual (p. 67). As a result, "it is assumed that the moral journey in the sexual lives of spouses, parents, sons and daughters, lesbians and gays or celibates does not differ substantially from one lifestyle to another" (p. 79).

It is right to recognize the author's intention to base his notion of sexuality and fecundity on an integral anthropology ("a holistic view of selfhood," p. 23), one which would not forsake the composite nature of the human being, but be able to reformulate it in truly integrated terms without lapsing into dangerous dualisms resulting in biologistic or spiritualistic reductions which lead in turn to the production of a seriously distorted sexual ethics. But one searches in vain in the book for even a summary statement of such an anthropology, the lack of which reduces the anthropology to a sort of declaration of intent. Furthermore, the equivocal definition of sexuality, together with the erroneous vision of fecundity, actually leads to what was sought to be avoided, namely, an anthropological dualism. In the first two chapters, the notion of sexuality held by Father Guindon requires a strong emphasis on the bodily nature of the human person. But in the third and fourth chapters, when it comes to defining fecundity in and of itself, independently of fertility, bodily nature, which apparently has become cumbersome for the author, is neglected or sacrificed in order to avoid what the author sees as the age-old reduction of sexuality and fecundity to mere biology.

A unified and fitting understanding of the human person, one which takes account of all the levels of his being (biological, psychological and spiritual), would not permit the author to speak of fertility as follows:

> As long as we maintain that the result intended must be a child, we are no longer talking about an aspect of a sexual source (fecundity) or of a sexual product. We are dealing with substances: chromosomes (the source) producing a child (the effect) (p. 65).

The procreative meaning of fecundity is reduced to the level of making copies of the species. At the same time, the anthropological meaning of sexuality is located mostly in its experiential components of sensuality and tenderness, which can thus be creative and make use of the body as an instrument lacking inherent moral values and thus completely manipulatable according to subjective intentions. The separation of the experiential or psychological elements of sensuality and tenderness, on the one hand, from the bodily elements of reproduction, on the other, is indisputably dualistic. Both, in fact, are integral parts of one and the same person. But the same charge of dualism cannot be leveled against the principle, precisely that of church teaching, that the unitive and procreative meanings of the sexual act are inseparable.

2.2. INTERPERSONAL RELATIONS

In Father Guindon's phenomenology of sexual relationships, emphasis is repeatedly placed on the "self expressing the self" (for expressions of this kind, see pp. 11, 14, 22, 23, 26, 27, 31, 33, 34, 65–67, 71, 90, 102). We have here a personalism centered on the self and self-expression. How is this to be reconciled with the requirements of loving another person, taking into account the other person's reality and autonomy? Why does the book make practically no reference to the fact, surely part of the Christian tradition, that the law of love includes the law of the cross? According to Vatican Council II, the vocation of marriage requires "outstanding virtue" and "a spirit of sacrifice" (*Gaudium et Spes,* 49). Father Guindon hardly makes reference to the need for such virtue. He does not take account of the fact that sexual impulses are not easily integrated with a genuine love so that chastity and self-restraint become a necessary and difficult part of human love—unless one assumes that the desire to express oneself sexually is always matched by the availability of a willing partner to whom one can express oneself.

Although the author proposes the values of "loving fecundity" (pp. 72–74) and "responsible fecundity" (pp. 74–78) as third and fourth criteria for evaluating "sexual fecundity" and even asserts that "human sexuality is fecund when it promotes humanly tender/sensuous life, self-identity, personal worth and community (p. 78)," no adequate explanation is given as to how the experiences of tenderness and sensuality might lead to the building up of a community.

2.3. THE RELATIONSHIP BETWEEN THE HUMAN PERSON AND THE CREATOR

A more basic deficiency underlying the erroneous positions pointed out in the work is the substitution of a concept of creativity for creaturehood (pp. viiff). God, in creating the creature's freedom, is said to have given man and woman the capability to liberate their own humanity, and so man and woman are to be seen as "sexual creators." The author does not recognize that God has placed a meaning and an intrinsic order within created reality, whose truth as the objective norm for human behavior is to be recognized and followed (cf. *Gaudium et Spes,* 48). Instead, God is said to have entrusted to men and women the creative power to develop a sexual language which expresses and structures meaningful human relationships (p. viii). For the author, therefore, there is no truth which precedes and directs action (*agere*). There is only the production, through subjective spontaneity, of creative models of meaning (the author makes reference to the epistemology of T.S. Kuhn, pp. 4, 15–16). Moral goodness, no longer a quality of the will which chooses in harmony with the truth of being, is reduced to a product of subjective intentions. For example, we read that "the moral task consists in making one's own truth or in making sense of one's own life" (p. 163). Furthermore, Father Guindon states that homosexually oriented persons should act homosexually since *agere sequitur esse* (p. 161). Here, *esse* seems to be reduced to subjective inclination. The truly revolutionary aspect of the book is to be found precisely here in the way it ignores the anthropological bases required by any objective morality, and by Christian morality in particular.

2.4. PROBLEMS OF MORAL METHOD

The erroneous positions arrived at in this book are a consequence of the adoption of a deficient method.

First, the author makes a general reference to experience without adducing any phenomenological analysis of the nature and dynamics of human sexuality, in other words, of that which is to constitute the substance of what is new in his work. On this point he confines himself to bibliographical references. Nevertheless, he maintains that it is from experience that one discovers the nature of sexuality as the integration of sensuality and tenderness (p. 23). He goes on to make a brief presentation of a linguistic model of apparently structuralist derivation which allows him further to explore the meaning of sexuality (pp. 26–30). Nonetheless, this model, as the author expressly declares, can be replaced by others (p. 15).

The author understands moral reflection not only as a reflection upon lived experience (p. ix) but as an articulation of the meaning inherent in that same experience (p. 13), since "no one knows the good and values it if one does not 'live' it" (p. 13). Thus what is affirmed is the primacy of the "lived," which becomes the true criterion for making moral judgments. The "lived" is mainly conceived in terms of qualities of subjective experience like sensuality and tenderness. The result is a morality based on a kind of blind faith in human spontaneity. Little or nothing is said of the basic dichotomy in the human heart (cf. *Gaudium et Spes,* 10), of the consequences of this dichotomy in the sexual realm or of the role of grace and human perseverance in dealing with this conflict. As a result, the notion of experience is presented in a very selective way, so too the choice of psychological sources is highly selective. There are many psychologists—not to mention philosophers and theologians—who would not agree that subjective experiences like tenderness and sensuality are able to lead automatically by themselves to genuine human love, responsibility and self-transcendence.

With these presuppositions, the author also uses the classical sources of moral theology (Scripture, tradition and magisterium) in a way that is partial, reductive and inadequate. Invoking the historico-critical method, the author holds that the moral norms contained in sacred Scripture should be referred back to their historical context in such a way that they are to be considered "inconclusive" with regard to making a moral judgment today, for example, on homosexual acts (p. 160). Sacred Scripture then would be seen not to convey concrete norms but intentions. And the only intentions to which Jesus appealed are love and freedom, interpreted subjectively (cf. p. 175). In direct contrast with these very principles, however, we find distorted interpretations of the Bible, for example the author's purported discovery of edifying examples of lesbians and male homosexuals (pp. 164–165), which the author adduces in support of his own positions.

Tradition and magisterium, frequently presented in caricatured fashion (e.g. pp. 4–10, 43–53), are neither accorded their proper authority nor their normative value for theological reflection. They serve rather as the polemical prelude to the author's presentation of his "alternative," developed from the fourth chapter onward. It is true that the author sometimes quotes the magisterium favorably, even showing his approval (p. 120) for the statement of *Gaudium et Spes* (50) that "children are really the supreme gift of marriage." Nonetheless, he sets himself up as the judge of which parts of the teaching of the tradition and of the magisterium are acceptable and which are not. Such a role implies superiority in the one judging over the one judged.

2.5. MORAL JUDGMENTS ON PARTICULAR KINDS OF BEHAVIOR

The Sexual Creators contains moral judgments in opposition to what sacred Scripture and tradition have constantly and consistently affirmed and the magisterium has authoritatively taught even quite recently. Furthermore, these positions are not incidental to the book but emerge successively in a form coherent with the author's repeated emphasis of his intention to make sexual fecundity, understood as the integration of sensuality and tenderness, autonomous with respect to procreation.

First of all, the author treats Scripture, tradition and the declarations of the magisterium in a highly selective fashion, often to the point of complete distortion. One would have to conclude from the third chapter titled "The Dualistic Tradition of Fertility," especially from pages 44–53, that traditional sexual morality has been in large part mistaken for almost two millennia in regard to its emphasis on procreation, which the author describes as "natalist ideology" (pp. 44ff). Concerning the teaching of *Gaudium et Spes* (47–52) on the dignity of marriage and the family, we read in the fourth chapter:

> We could probably pick out, in the constitution, statements which would support a reproductive interpretation

of sexual fecundity. This should not surprise us. There is general agreement today that one finds, in the council documents, texts which are the result of a compromise between what are sometimes theoretically irreconcilable positions. Paradigmatic transitions are always marked by the simultaneous presence of contradictory views (p. 65).

This cannot but mean that *Gaudium et Spes* is in part erroneous and can be understood correctly only by excluding the mistaken part of its doctrine, that is to say, the considerable part not in keeping with the ideas expressed in *The Sexual Creators. Humanae Vitae* is criticized for invoking biological laws (p. 47). *Familiaris Consortio* is said to make a "mere nominal distinction" between "observance of rhythm" and "obstacle to birth" as if this were a distinction of moral relevance (pp. 49–50). *Persona Humana* is criticized for considering procreation as the "essential and indispensable finality" (of fecundity) (p. 43).

Contrary to the teaching of the magisterium (cf. *Persona Humana,* 7; also *Familiaris Consortio,* 80), the author, in considering premarital sexual relations, the possibility of "pre-ceremonial" cohabitation, and "marriage by phases" (pp. 87–89) observes: "One could even argue that, theologically, such a 'marriage by phases' is not unthinkable." He also refers here to other writings of his (p. 110, Note 5). Contrary to church doctrine, the author asserts the irrelevance of the public celebration of the marital covenant and of the canonical form of marriage between Catholics. The author discredits the necessity for the church's consent on the basis of a flawed presentation of history (p. 88). He, in fact, gives one to understand that the liturgical celebration of marriage represents a late development in the church, confusing thereby the obligation of observing the required canonical form for the validity of marriage with the existence of a liturgical ceremony which is in fact quite ancient.

In brief, the author proposes (pp. 87–89) a sweeping redefinition of the sacrament of matrimony.

In regard to homosexuality, the author tends to liken, from the moral point of view, the homosexual situation and the heterosexual situation on the basis of an abstract conception of sexual fecundity, applied univocally to specifically different kinds of sexual conduct (pp. 159–160, 172, 177). In some respects a homosexual relationship would indeed seem to be superior to a heterosexual relationship. On Page 165, we read:

> This gratuitous celebration of love (as in the Song of Songs: cf. above on the same page) is characteristic of gay sexuality. . . . A woman does not make love to another woman, or a man to another man, because that is what is expected of everyone; or because that is what must be done to get a provider or a homemaker, or again, because that is how babies are made. Healthy gay persons are sexually active with a partner because they wish to express their affection to someone to whom they are attracted.

Father Guindon defends the "sexual fecundity" of homosexuals, claiming to prescind thereby from any judgment on the objective morality of erotic or genital acts they may perform (p. 163)—a claim which is difficult or impossible to reconcile with the obvious sense of expressions like "make love" and "(being) sexually active" on Page 165, as just quoted—and appealing in a vague and equivocal way to the norm of interpersonal love proclaimed in the Gospel (pp. 174–175). Not only is there no recognition of any objective disorder in the homosexual condition as such, but homosexual behavior, in opposition to *Persona Humana,* 8, is even justified as being "the only sane choice" for one who is naturally and irreversibly homosexual (pp. 160–161). To sustain this the author appeals to the principle *agere sequitur esse* (p. 161), which is applied indiscriminately and univocally to the ontological and moral orders. He does not seem to allow homosexual persons much freedom concerning their sexual orientation or the possibility of sexual abstinence: "The only options they (moralists) seem to be able to offer them (a heterosexual or asexual lifestyle), are, as they themselves must recognize, unachievable for healthy homosexual persons" (p. 162). The possibility of a homosexual person changing to a heterosexual orientation through psychotherapy is ridiculed and dismissed (p. 161). Homosexuals are presented as a source of witness to our society in their celebration of gratuitous love (pp. 174ff).

II. THE NEED FOR CLARIFICATION

In letters to his superior general, written after having received a previous critique of *The Sexual Creators* from the Congregation for the Doctrine of the Faith and subsequently forwarded to this same congregation, and especially in a letter dated Aug. 15, 1990, Father Guindon states that apart from the question of contraception his book is meant to be faithful to the richness of the Catholic tradition, and that one will not find in it any passage denying the role of the magisterium in Catholic ethics. These statements seem irreconcilable with the way in which he in fact presents and criticizes the tradition and the magisterium. Father Guindon has also stated in these letters that at no point in the book does he contradict the teaching of *Persona Humana* (5) "that the use of the sexual function has its true meaning and moral rectitude only in true marriage." He maintains instead that in *The Sexual Creators* he has not questioned any of the positions of *Persona Humana* regarding specific genital actions.

Needless to say, what is taught in *Persona Humana* does not exhaust all of Catholic sexual morality. The document constitutes, nonetheless, a convenient point of reference and one chosen by Father Guindon in his own defense and thus may be given closer attention here. This line of defense chosen by the author is, to say the least, surprising.

First, the book proposes an extremely broad definition of human sexuality: "Sexuality is that which gives human beings an interpersonal and social history and that which makes them responsible for its development" (p. 34). But then, according to what Father Guindon states in his defense, his treatment of sexuality does not take into consideration genital acts, as if one could write a book on sexual morality prescinding completely from the morality of such acts. We are asked to believe that the author discusses different sexual lifestyles, including premarital cohabitation (pp. 87–88) and homosexual relationships (pp. 159–204), in a way that does not imply that these types of relationships may include genital expression, at least as a question to be confronted.

Second, the declaration that he does not mean to contradict *Persona Humana* on this aspect of the problem does not agree in various points with the text of *The Sexual Creators* itself. It is the author himself who emphasizes the importance of sexual intercourse: "As each other's existence is confirmed by requited acknowledgement in the coital embrace, subjects are born to themselves as subjects" (p. 93). Taking terms employed by the author like "preceremonial" cohabitation (pp. 87–88), "make love" and "sexual expression" (p. 165, in the context of homosexuality) in the sense in which these are now commonly used, the obvious meaning of the text indicates an approval of genital union even outside the context of true marriage. The very least that one can say is that the morality of genital union is a question which practically everyone must confront and answer, and to write a book on sexual ethics while professing to set aside this question seems a very strange approach indeed. How can one affirm the need for a unified vision of human nature as the basis for understanding human sexuality and then assume that the notion of sexuality, however it is to be understood, does not involve facing the question of the morality of genital union, when referring, for example, to premarital cohabitation or to homosexuality? In this case, the refusal to take an explicit position is in effect to take an implicit position.

The dialogue with Father Guindon has not yet led to satisfactory clarification of his positions, and so further clarification must be solicited.

III. THE CLARIFICATIONS REQUESTED

In the interest of the spiritual well-being of the faithful, the Congregation for the Doctrine of the Faith is charged with the responsibility of promoting and defending authentic Catholic doctrine. For this reason, the congregation has deemed fit to publish these points of criticism of Father Guindon's book *The Sexual Creators*.

The congregation further requests that Father Guindon publicly confirm and explain the significance of three important statements which were made privately in his letter to his superior general (Aug. 15, 1990), namely, (1) that he sought, in writing *The Sexual Creators,* to be faithful to the riches of the Catholic tradition in the area of sexual morality; (2) that at no point did he intend the book to deny the authoritative role of the magisterium in Catholic ethics; and (3) that he does not contradict the constant teaching of the church, recently reaffirmed in *Persona Humana,* that the use of the sexual function has its rightful place only in true marriage.

The congregation further requests that Father Guindon resolve in a public statement the contradiction pointed out in this Note between the statements made to his superior general and the text of *The Sexual Creators,* developing thereby his thought in a more consistent way, resolving the incongruities within the text of *The Sexual Creators* (such as its selective and variable use of tradition and magisterium), and according the doctrine of the magisterium its proper place and true authority.

Editors' note: In 1986, the Congregation for the Doctrine of the Faith informed Charles E. Curran that because of some of his positions on dissent and sexuality he was neither "suitable nor eligible to exercise the function of a Professor of Catholic Theology." For the correspondence about and discussion of this case, see our *Readings in Moral Theology No. 6: Dissent in the Church,* pp. 357–539.

Part Nine

OVERALL EVALUATION

35. The Liberating Truth of Catholic Teaching on Sexual Morality

William E. May

This article first appeared in *Homiletic and Pastoral Review* in 1983.

"No unwanted child ought ever to be born" is the slogan of proponents of contraception and abortion. "No human being ought ever to be unwanted" is the truth proclaimed by the Catholic Church in the name of Jesus Christ. The only way to shape human choices and human actions—and through them human persons and human societies—so that human beings will be wanted as they ought to be wanted is by ordering them in accordance with true and objective norms. It is within this context that the Church's teaching on sexual morality and marriage is presented, and this context must first be understood if the truth of that teaching is to be grasped.

I propose, therefore, to do the following: (1) to provide the reasons why it is true to say that *no human being ought ever to be unwanted;* (2) to describe the dignity to which human beings, as intelligent entities capable of determining their own lives through their own free choices, are called; (3) to propose a normative framework for making true judgments and good choices about what one is to do if one is to be fully the being human beings are called to be; and (4) to examine, within this framework, the free choice to exercise one's genital sexuality.

The Church, in proclaiming the Gospel and bringing to humankind the saving truth of God's revealing and redemptive word, teaches that each human being is an irreplaceable, priceless person, a being of moral worth. Of each of us it has been written, "Does a woman forget her baby at the breast, or fail to cherish the son of her womb? Yet even if they forget, I will never forget you. See, I have branded your name on the palms of my hands" (Isa. 49:15–16). Every human being is a living image of God himself, an icon or living representative of the all-holy and all-loving God. Every one of us is, as it were, a "word" uttered by God himself; in fact, each one of us is the "created word" of God that his Uncreated Word became (John 1:1, 14) precisely to show us how deeply God loves us and cherishes us as irreplaceable and precious persons: "Who will separate us from the love of Christ? Trial, or distress, or persecution, or hunger, or nakedness, or danger, or the sword? . . . For I am certain that neither death nor life, neither angels nor principalities, neither the present nor the future, nor powers, neither height nor depth nor any other creature, will be able to separate us from the love of God that comes to us in Christ Jesus, our Lord" (Rom. 8:35, 37–39).

EACH PERSON IS AN ICON OF GOD

Every human person, moreover, is called to a life of friendship with God himself. God made us to be the kind of beings capable of sharing his own inner life, and to enable us actually to receive this life God himself became, in the person of his only begotten Son, one with us and for us. He came to share in our humanity—a humanity that had, because of original sin, been wounded and rendered impotent even of receiving the gift for which it had been, by God's grace, originally created—precisely so that we might be actually capable of participating in his own divine life. In and through baptism we actually become children of God himself, members of his family, with the right to call him, in union with his only begotten Son Jesus Christ, "Abba," "Father." Thus we are *to be* his children, intimate members of his divine family, alive with his own life. This life begins in us in baptism, and it is to be fulfilled in the resurrection, when we become fully the persons we are meant to be. Thus it is that the Risen Lord Jesus *is now* the human being *we* are called to be. He is the "firstfruits of the dead," living now the life to which we are called and for which we are now capacitated because of him who is "our best and wisest friend."[1]

To be a human being, therefore, is to be a being of incalculable worth, of irreplaceable value, of precious dignity. To be a human being, moreover, is to be a bodily being, living flesh. This means that to be a human being is to be a sexed being,[2] for in the beginning "God created man in his own image . . . *male* and *female* he created them" (Gen. 1:27). Every living human body is a person, and every living human body is inescapably a male or a female person, a man or a woman, a boy or a girl, a boy-baby or a girl-baby (born or unborn; cf. Ps. 139:13–14; Luke 1:41–42). And every living human body, every human person, whatever its age or sex or race or condition, is a being of precious worth, irreplaceable and non-substitutable, a being that *ought* to be wanted. Every human person ought to be wanted precisely because we ought to want what is truly good and valuable, and every human being is, by virtue of being a "word" or icon of God himself, truly good and valuable.[3]

This is the point emphasized by Karol Wojtyla (Pope John Paul II) in proposing what he calls the "personalistic norm": "This norm, in its negative aspect, states that the person is the kind of good which does not admit of use and cannot be treated as an object of use and as such the means to an end. In its positive form the personalistic norm confirms this: the person is a good towards which the only proper and adequate attitude is love."[4]

CHOOSING LIFE IS THE CHALLENGE

There is, in brief, an inherent, inalienable, inviolable dignity or sanctity in every human life. But in addition to this inherent dignity of the human person, there is another human dignity of which the Church speaks, and this is the dignity to which we are called as intelligent beings capable of determining our own lives by our own choices. This is the dignity we give to ourselves when, with the help of God's grace, we inwardly shape our choices and actions by con-forming them to the requirements of what Vatican Council II called the "highest norm of human life." This norm is the "divine law itself—eternal, objective, and universal, by which God orders, di-rects and governs the whole world and the ways of the human com-munity according to a plan conceived in his wisdom and love" (*Dig-nitatis Humanae,* 2). God has so created us that we are able, through the mediation of our conscience, to "recognize the demands of this divine law" (*Dignitatis Humanae,* 2). Indeed, as the Council put the matter elsewhere,

> Deep within his conscience man discovers a law which he has not laid upon himself but which he must obey. *Its voice, ever calling him to love and to do what is good and to avoid evil,* tells him inwardly at the right moment, do this, shun that. For man has in his heart a law written by God. *His dignity lies in observing this law,* and by it he will be judged (*Gaudium et Spes,* 16; emphasis added).

"Conscience," continued the Council, quoting Pope Pius XII, "is the most secret core and sanctuary of a man, where he is alone with God, whose voice echoes in his depths" (*Gaudium et Spes,* 16). Fidelity to conscience means a "search for truth" and for *true* solutions to moral problems; conscience can indeed err "through invincible ignorance without losing its dignity" (so long as there is sufficient "care for the search for the true and the good"); but "to the extent that a correct conscience holds sway, persons and groups turn away from blind choice and seek to conform to the objective norms of morality" (*Gaudium et Spes,* 16).

In short, as John M. Finnis, professor of jurisprudence at Oxford University, has so well said:

> It was the Council's unwavering teaching that the dignity of conscience consists in its *capacity* to disclose the objective truth about what is to be done, both in particular assessments and in general norms, and that that truth has its truth as an intention of God whose voice is our law. This law is knowable by us because we "participate in the light of the divine mind" (*Gaudium et Spes,* 15).

Thus human persons, who *are,* by virtue of being humans to begin with, beings of incalculable dignity, are summoned to give to themselves, with the help of God's grace, the added dignity of persons who choose in accordance with the truth, who in effect say "yes" to God's offer of divine life, who choose life, not death.

LIFE IS A REAL GOOD OF THE PERSON

Yet how are we to make true judgments about what we are to do and, in the light of these judgments, good moral choices? Every intelligent person can assent to the truth of the practical proposal that *good is to be done and pursued and evil is to be avoided,*[6] and thus everyone would agree with Karol Wojtyla (who here merely echoes an age-old wisdom) that the purpose of our education as moral agents is at heart a "matter of seeking true ends, i.e., *real goods* as the ends of our actions, and of finding and showing to others the ways to realize them."[7]

But what are the real goods of human existence, goods that serve as purposeful ends of human choices and actions and make intelligent human activity possible? St. Thomas Aquinas suggested a triple-tiered set of human goods, which, when grasped by practical reason, function as first principles of intelligent human activity. The first set includes being itself, a good that human persons share with all other entities, and since the being (*esse*) of living things is life itself (*vivere*), the key good at issue here is human life itself, which human persons seek to protect and nourish and defend. The second set includes the union of male and female in order to transmit the good of life to progeny, who need education and care if they are to flourish, and this is a set of goods that human persons share with other animals, but, of course, in their own unique way. The third set includes those goods that are unique to human persons, for instance the goods of truth and knowledge and of living in harmony with others in society, (goods that we could term the goods of justice and peace and friendship).[8] Modern commentators on St. Thomas, among them Germain G. Grisez[9] and John M. Finnis,[10] seek to specify more precisely and exhaustively the basic goods of human persons, goods that contribute to the flourishing of human persons and communities. But the point is that there are indeed real goods of human existence, and among them must surely be included the good of life itself (including health, bodily integrity, and the handing on of life to new human persons), of truth, and of human friendship. Such goods are *real goods* of persons; they are goods that human persons prize and do not price. They serve, when intelligently grasped, as principles or starting points for deliberating about what one is to do and they make purposeful human activity possible. No matter what we choose to do, whether what we choose to do is morally good or morally bad, we choose to do it ultimately for the sake of goods of this sort.

But where does morality enter in, and how can we make true moral judgments and good moral choices? In short, what is the basic normative principle in morality (as distinguished from the set of first premoral principles such as *good is to be done and pursued, life is a good to be protected and its opposite is to be avoided,* etc.)? Vatican Council II suggested a basic normative principle for human choices and actions. After noting that human activity is important not only for its results but also and even more importantly because it develops human persons and gives to them, because it is self-determining and free, their identity as moral beings, the Council declared:

> Hence, the norm of human activity is this: that in accord with the divine plan and will, it should harmonize with the *genuine good of the human race,* and allow men as individuals and as members of society to pursue their total vocation and fulfill it (*Gaudium et Spes,* 35; emphasis added).

This basic normative proposal suggested by Vatican Council II is, I think, another way of articulating the "personalistic norm" proposed by Karol Wojtyla and noted previously. It can perhaps be clarified if it is put in this way (as suggested by Germain G. Grisez): "In freely acting for human goods, that is, those goods of human persons that contribute to their fullness of being and their flourishing, and avoiding what is opposed to them, one ought to choose and otherwise will those and only those possible actions whose willing is compatible with a willing affirmation of every real good of human persons."[11]

If we are to choose in accordance with this basic normative truth, certain specific requirements in making true practical judgments and good moral choices are, upon reflection, clearly demanded. First of all, we are required to take into account the real goods of human persons in judging and choosing what we are to do; simply to disregard them or to put them out of mind is to manifest a will that is not seriously concerned with them and with the persons in whom they are to be. Second, every one of these goods demands of us that, when we can do so as easily as not, we avoid acting in ways that inhibit its realization and prefer ways of acting which contribute to its realization. Third, every one of the good demands of us that we make an effort on its behalf when its significant realization in some person is in peril. Other requirements necessary if we are to shape our choices and actions according to this basic norm can be spelled out; but one that is surely necessary, if we are to have an upright will and a heart open to the goods of human existence, to the goodness of human persons, and to the *Summmum Bonum,* God, from whom persons and the goods of persons derive, is the following: we ought not to choose, with deliberate and direct intent, to set these goods aside, to destroy, damage, or impede them either in ourselves or in others.[12]

It is within the context of the foregoing understanding of the human person as irreplaceably precious and as a being that ought always to be wanted and of our summons to choose in such a way that we give ourselves the added dignity of persons whose hearts are open to the goods of human existence and of persons that the Church's teaching on sexual morality is presented.

INTERCOURSE LEADS TO PROCREATION

This teaching is well-known. Its major claim is that the choice to engage in genital coition can rightly be made only by a man and a woman who have made themselves to be husband and wife by the covenant of marriage, and that it can be made rightly by them only when they respect, in their choices to unite coitally, the goods of life and marital friendship.[13] When coition is not marital, or when it violates the marital goods of life-giving love or of love-giving union, it is, as Pope John Paul II said in *Familiaris Consortio,* "a lie."[14]

This specific teaching of the Church is today widely regarded as repressive and inhibiting, an unwarranted infringement upon human liberty. My claim is that it is a liberating truth, one that needs to be recognized if "no human being ought ever to be unwanted," and that it will be recognized as true if examined within the perspective set forth in the previous sections of this essay.

What are the goods that come into focus when one considers the possibility of engaging in sexual coition? The goods in question are those of life itself and of human friendship. They are inescapably brought into focus when one considers this possible way of acting, and hence one simply cannot intelligently and freely choose this deed without taking a stance toward these basic human goods.

As far as the good of life itself being at stake when one considers the possibility of sexual coition, the observations of John M. Finnis seem pertinent. He observed:

> an intelligent choice to engage in sexual intercourse has to take into account a plain fact . . . viz. that intercourse may bring about procreation; that a child may be conceived; that intercourse is procreative (cause and effect, nothing more). One can accept this fact and seek to capitalize on it, or one can ignore this fact and proceed regardless, or one can by simple means prevent the effect from following the cause. But in any case, one is willy nilly engaged, in sexual intercourse, with the basic human value of procreation.[15]

With respect to the good of friendship and its stake in this possible course of action, I think it sufficient to note that a human being simply cannot have sexual intercourse with himself or herself. Another human person—an irreplaceable being of incalculable worth—is inescapably included in this possible way of acting.

Thus the goods that come into focus when one considers the possibility of having sexual relations are inescapably the goods of life itself (the life that can be transmitted in and through the act) and of friendship with the person with whom one can choose to have sexual relations. Since both of these goods are goods of the *persons* involved (including the child that can possibly be begotten), it seems to me that one's acceptance of the truth that *no human being ought ever to be unwanted* is also at stake in considering the possibility of having sexual relations.

No Partner Should Ever Be Unwanted

The sex act *unites.* But if the individuals it unites are not joined to one another already by the consent that makes them spouses and hence irreplaceable and nonsubstitutable in each other's life, then the choice to engage in it can hardly respect authentic human friendship and the irreplaceable and non-substitutable value of the human person. It is rather the choice to join two beings who are *in principle* replaceable and substitutable, disposable. It is the choice to use the other as a means, and not a choice to respect the other as an end. It is thus a choice that fails to take seriously into account the irreplaceable value of the human person and the good of human friendship that values the person and wills for the person only what is good.[16] There may be some sentimental affection between those who choose to have sexual intercourse while unmarried, but sentimental affection is by no means the same as human love and friendship.[17]

The sex act is, whether one wants it to be so or not, a life-giving sort of act. It is precisely because it is this sort of act that some people today choose to contracept, for the precise point of contraception is to make the act one chooses to do, i.e., the sort of act open to the transmission of human life, to be a different sort of act, namely, one closed deliberately to the transmission of human life. Yet as we know, all contraceptives have their "failure rates," due both to the methods, none of which is foolproof, and to their users.

It seems to me that a proper respect for the good of human life itself would require that no one freely choose to have sexual relations unless one is willing to be a mother or father,[18] to care for the life that can be begotten and to care, too, for the person with whom one chooses to engage in the act that is life-giving. One can ask oneself, do I regard the life that this act can bring into being as a human being that ought to be wanted or not? If one is not disposed to accept this human being and to contribute to its *bene esse* as well as its *esse,* then one ought not to choose to engage in this act. To do so is to be heedless of and disrespectful to the life that can be begotten.

It also seems to me that a proper respect for the irreplaceable value of human persons requires that one not choose to have sexual relations with a person whom one has not already made, by virtue of the choice that constitutes marriage, irreplaceable in one's own life. The person with whom one chooses to have sexual relations is, as a person, a being that ought to be wanted and never unwanted. In and through sexual relations one comes to "know" this other in a unique and unforgettable way, and one reveals oneself to this other in a unique and unforgettable way. Our "private parts" are not called such for nothing. As Dietrich von Hildebrand once said, "sex occupies a central position in the personality. It represents a factor in human nature which essentially seeks to play a decisive part in man's life. Sex can indeed keep silence, but when it speaks it is no mere *obiter dictum,* but a voice from the depths, the utterance of something central and of utmost significance. In and with sex, man, in a special sense, gives himself."[19]

From this it should be evident why the specific teaching of the Church on the morality of sexual coition is a teaching that is rooted in a profound grasp of the goodness of human persons and of the human goods of life itself and friendship. If one freely chooses inwardly to shape his/her choices and actions in accordance with the truth that no human being ought ever to be unwanted, one will choose to engage in sexual relations only with that person who is irreplaceable and nonsubstitutable and with whom one is willing and able to welcome new life and give to it the home where it can take root and grow.

* *A cassette recording of the above article may be obtained from: Cardinal Communications, 20 Milton Road, Quaker Hill, Conn. 06375. Price $3.50 postpaid (Canada: add 50¢).*

Notes

1. St. Thomas Aquinas, *Summa Theologiae,* 1–2, 108, 4: "Christus maxime est sapiens et amicus."

2. Cf. Pope John Paul II, *Familiaris Consortio,* n.11: "sexuality . . . is by no means merely biological but concerns the innermost being of the human person as such."

3. Here I have expressed in religious language and in the light of divine revelation the priceless dignity and sanctity of human life. Yet even from the perspective of philosophical inquiry one can come to know that human

beings are radically different in kind from other kinds of material creatures and that they possess a dignity that surpasses the whole of the material universe. On this see, for instance, Mortimer Adler, *The Difference of Man and the Difference It Makes* (New York: Meridian, 1968).

4. Karol Wojtyla (Pope John Paul II), *Love and Responsibility* (New York: Farrar, Straus, and Giroux, 1981), p. 41.

5. John M. Finnis, "The Natural Law, Objective Morality, and Vatican II," in *Principles of Catholic Moral Life,* ed. William E. May (Chicago: Franciscan Herald Press, 1981), p. 119. Finnis's entire essay (pp. 113–149) is most important for understanding the normative ethical position set forth in the Documents of the Second Vatican Council.

6. St. Thomas Aquinas, *Summa Theologiae,* 1-2, 94, 2.

7. *Love and Responsibility,* p. 27; emphasis added.

8. St. Thomas Aquinas, *Summa Theologiae,* 1-2, 94, 2.

9. Germain G. Grisez has set forth his developments of St. Thomas's natural law theory in many works. See in particular his *Contraception and the Natural Law* (Milwaukee: Bruce Publishing Company, 1964), in particular ch. 2; *Abortion: The Myths, the Realities, and the Arguments* (New York: Corpus, 1970), chapter 6; "Toward a Consistent Natural Law Ethics of Killing," *American Journal of Jurisprudence* 15 (1970) 64–96; (with Russell Shaw), *Beyond the New Morality* (Notre Dame, Ind.: University of Notre Dame Press, 1981, second edition).

10. John M. Finnis, *Natural Law and Natural Rights* (Oxford: Oxford University Press, 1980), chapters 3 and 4.

11. This way of formulating the basic normative principle is adumbrated in some of Grisez's earlier works (see note 9) and in the way provided here is most thoroughly presented in a new work that is in progress, *A Summary of Christian Moral Theology.* Vol. I, *Christian Moral Principles.*

12. On the requirements of "practical reasonableness" or "modes of responsibility" see Grisez, *Contraception and the Natural Law,* chapter 4, *Abortion . . . ,* pp. 318–319; Finnis, *Natural Law and Natural Rights,* chapter 5.

13. On this see Pope Paul VI, *Humanae Vitae,* in particular nn. 13 and 14; *Persona Humana* (Vatican Declaration on Certain Questions of Sexual Ethics, December 29, 1975), the section on premarital sex; Pope John Paul II, *Familiaris Consortio,* n. 11.

14. Pope John Paul II, *Familiaris Consortio,* n. 11.

15. John M. Finnis, "Natural Law and Unnatural Acts," *Heythrop Journal 11* (1970), 383.

16. On this see Wojtyla, *Love and Responsibility,* pp. 73–84.

17. On this it is important to read what Wojtyla has to say on the subject of sentiment and love in *Love and Responsibility,* pp. 109–114.

18. Cf. *Ibid.,* pp. 224–237; see also *Familiaris Consortio,* nn. 11, 28–32.

19. Dietrich von Hildebrand, *In Defense of Purity* (New York: Sheed and Ward, 1935), pp. 12–14 (reprinted by Franciscan Herald Press, 1968).

36. Current Teaching on Sexual Ethics

Lisa Sowle Cahill

This article first appeared in *Studies* in 1987.

Many of the problems that loom large on the horizon of controversy in Catholic ethics today come from the realm of what traditionally has been called "personal ethics." The examples which spring readily to mind—due to the attention that they have received within the Church—have to do with sexual norms: contraception, sterilization, infertility therapies, abortion, divorce. In my view, these problems no longer can be handled adequately (if ever they could be) apart from the larger social contexts in which they arise, or apart from a more general consideration of the sorts of evidence or arguments to be used in "Catholic" approaches to moral questions. A most important factor in the social context is the changing role of women in the family and in society. In addition, Catholic moral theology is undergoing a shift in method, so that it is becoming more experiential, social, and biblical. Both facts have tremendous implications for the contemporary Catholic discussion of sexual morality.

What Has the Tradition Taught?

It is difficult to interpret controversy in the Church today without at least a general understanding of what has preceded and contributed to it. The characteristic Catholic approach to questions of ethics has for several centuries been based on Thomas Aquinas's hypothesis of a "natural moral law." Drawing on the philosophy of

Aristotle, Aquinas taught that there are certain human values—such as respect for life, co-operation in society, and education of the young—which are known in all cultures. A natural morality common to all persons can be derived from reasonable reflection on these values, although Aquinas did acknowledge that as we approach the more particular details of natural-law morality (how to apply the basic principles), there can be variation from person to person and culture to culture.

In the realm of sexual behaviour, the proper way to discover moral norms would be to ask the natural human "ends" or purposes of sexual acts. The most obvious biological purpose of sex is procreation, and so this became its primary purpose from a natural law point of view. Aquinas also relied on the thought of St. Augustine, who not only held that procreation is the primary purpose of sex, but that it is a venial sin to seek sexual intercourse without that purpose explicitly in mind. Augustine was especially suspicious of the uncontrollability of sexual passions, and suggested that even marital intercourse is so tainted that it is the vehicle for the passing on of original sin. Augustine's views are more understandable when we realize that he was engaged in a constant struggle with the dualism which plagued many ancient philosophies and religions, and which succeeded in infiltrating Christianity. The source of dualism is a simple and universal problem: often the body seems not to co-operate with the spirit or the mind, whether due to limitation of agility and strength, or the urgency of physical needs and drives. The dualist explanation of this reality is to say that the body is evil or at least inferior, tends to drag the spirit down, and must be disciplined or subjugated. Against the militant dualist religions of his day (especially Manicheism, which he followed in his youth), Augustine insisted that the body is created by God and is good. He capitulated to the dualist temptation to the extent that he tended to see sexual passions in any form as negative and even sinful. But even sex has a good and justifying purpose (children). Moreover, marriage serves the goods of sexual fidelity (avoiding illicit sexual outlets), and sacramental indissolubility (*On the Good of Marriage*). Thus we have the tradition of the three goods of marriage: *fides, proles, sacramentum* (fidelity, offspring, sacrament). Less prominently, Augustine mentions the partnership or companionship of the spouses.

Aquinas takes up Augustine's three goods, but emphasizes domestic partnership more centrally (*Summa Theologiae,* Supplement, Q.49). He abandons the view that sex is somehow tainted, and says instead that the passions can have a rightly ordered place in human life. When sexual passion occurs in marriage, and for the purpose of procreation, then it follows the natural moral law and is even commendable. Perhaps the most important contribution of Aquinas to the theology and ethics of marriage—one which deserves more attention—is his description of marriage as the "greatest friendship" (*Summa Contra Gentiles* III/2.123). Further, Aquinas sees marital love as the most "intense" love possible between humans, precisely because of the union of spouses "in the flesh" (ST II–II. Q.26. a 11). Even though Aquinas still focuses on procreation as the key objective of intercourse, he expresses great appreciation of the interpersonal dimensions of marriage, and of the contribution that sexuality makes to this relationship. These shifts were to reemerge in the twentieth-century Church, at the time of the Second Vatican Council.

CURRENT TEACHING ON SEXUAL ETHICS

Up until the middle of the present century, the prevailing view was that procreation was the primary purpose of sexual acts (Pius XI, *Casti connubii,* 1930). With the Council's *Pastoral Constitution on the Church in the Modern World (Gaudium et Spes, 1965),* a change occurred which also was to be reflected in Paul VI's *On Human Life (Humanae vitae, 1968).* Procreation and the love or union of the spouses were given as the two natural purposes of sexual acts, with no ranking of these ends. This opened the door to seeing sexuality much more in relation to the interpersonal qualities of the relationship of wife and husband, and of interpreting the morality of sex in this light. It meant that the goal of procreation was no longer the dominant moral standard in Catholic sexual ethics. This fact is highlighted by the affirmation by Paul VI of "responsible parenthood" and of family planning to be carried out by natural means. Some ethicists maintain that the morally crucial difference between natural and artificial means still has not been explicated convincingly, especially since the legitimacy of avoiding conception is acknowledged. Although the reputation of *Humanae vitae* derives mostly from its negative prohibition of all artificial means of controlling births, its positive contribution is to recognize that the needs of the marriage partners and of family members can justify and even demand the avoidance of procreation. Moreover, marital intimacy itself and sexual relations as enhancing the marital partnership are portrayed in a much more positive light.

To summarize the current magisterial teaching on sexual morality, as represented in *Humanae vitae* and subsequent official statements, there are two intrinsic, natural meanings or goals of sexual acts: procreation and the love union of the sexual partners. Permanent, monogamous marriage is stipulated as the only appropriate context for the fulfillment of these meanings. Sexual acts must always represent a love commitment; procreation may be avoided, but not artificially. Immediately directed at contraception (and its permanent form, sterilization), this norm has implications for recently developed medical interventions as well. Before, sexual acts were regarded as a sort of "given" or point of departure for moral analysis. Thus it was asked what their purposes are, and whether sexual acts could be performed morally when those purposes were lacking. Now, sex acts themselves have become a "variable," rather than a given. It is possible not only to have sex without procreation or love, but also to have procreation without sex (AIH, IVF with the gametes of spouses) or without either sex *or* love between the genetic parents (AID, IVF with donor sperm or ovum, surrogate mothers). By insisting that *all three variables* (sex, love, procreation) be kept in unity, Catholic teaching resists not only contraception, but also any infertility therapy which circumvents natural conception, even if it involves spouses only.

CHANGING ROLES OF WOMEN

Catholic views of sexual ethics cannot be understood apart from the roles of men and women in relation to which the meaning of sex is defined. The German theologian Lorenz Wachinger recently gave a wonderful example of traditional gender roles and their implications for sexual ethics (*Stimmen der Zeit,* 1985). In pious Catholic German households of the past generation, it was customary to hang over the marriage bed a framed portrait of the Holy Family. In this picture, a blue-robed Mary is seated, cradling on her lap a golden-haired child. Joseph, standing protectively behind her, holds a tool of his carpenter's trade. In this romanticized, hierarchical vision, the woman is placed in the home, caring for the children, the man in his profession. The upright posture of the husband suggests that he has the responsibility of leadership, and that it is to his prudent authority that the wife is gratefully obedient. The fact that the picture is enshrined in the spouses' bedroom also gives eloquent testimony: it is to this ideal of family that marital sexuality is to contribute. The woman is ready to bear, receive, and serenely nurture as many children as the good Lord and nature deign to send; the husband through his industry will provide the economic resources necessary to sustain in middle-class security the family to which he is faithfully devoted. Wachinger notes at length the many challenges to this ideal which arise from twentieth-century Western culture. Among them are changes in our views of the roles of women and men, both inside and outside the home. Certainly women are gaining increasing access to education and the professions in Western societies, although the pace of change will vary from nation to nation, and among rural and urban populations. Sometimes the work of women outside the home is due to sheer economic necessity, but the ideal is to provide opportunities for both women and men to make contributions in economic and political life, as well as in the domestic sphere. The social encyclicals of the modern popes and the documents of Vatican II all affirm the equal dignity of all persons. Gone at least from official writing is Aquinas's belief that women are less rational, more susceptible to the passions, weaker, and more passive than men. Once the basic equality of men and women is recognized, it becomes less and less credible to maintain the position that women are not capable of leadership and authority —or that men are not capable of self-sacrifice and service to others. But more flexible views of male and female roles in society seem to require new interpretations of sexuality and gender roles within the family. In modern Catholic teaching, shifting views of gender roles and of sexual ethics have not been fully worked out or co-ordinated.

An example is The Apostolic Exhortation *On the Family* of John Paul II (*Familiaris Consortio,* 1981). In this address, the Pope recognizes the importance of the roles of both mother and father in raising children; but it is only the *mother's* parental role that he sees as having more value in relation to all her other roles. He also recognizes that women should have access to "public functions," and to a just wage. Yet at the same time, he reiterates his position that the very nature of marital love and fidelity make it immoral to rely on artificial means of effectively and reliably controlling birth. Does this genuinely regard marital intimacy as an experience which is interpersonal and relational before it is biological? How serious is the suggestion that domestic and parental roles are important for men, and that professional and public roles are important for women?

CONTEXT: SHIFTS IN MORAL THEOLOGY SINCE VATICAN II

Ambiguity in Church teaching on the roles of women (and men) and debate over its conclusions on sexual matters also need to be understood in the light of three shifts in moral theology generally in the post-Vatican II Church. Many problems arise from the fact that these shifts have been gradual, and that their significance has not been understood fully in relation to the older natural law method. Catholic ethics (moral theology) has become increasingly *experiential, biblical* and *social.*

1. *Experience.* In a phrase of Pope John XXIII, repeated in *Gaudium et Spes,* the Church in the modern world is called to read "the signs of the times." This means attention to the concrete actualities of contemporary society, culture, and human experience. Traditional natural law ethics had aimed at a transcendent rationality, universality, and certainty; at universal and absolute moral norms which could be applied to specific situations invariably, with only a few closely-defined exceptions. While these norms were supposed to have been formulated after reasonable human reflection on the universal elements in concrete experience, they eventually took on a life of their own, and were applied rigidly to experience even when the experience in question had changed. Examples from the areas of

sexuality are plentiful. Paul VI, recognizing that "responsible parent-hood" and the personal relation of spouses are important in the modern world, was still committed to the traditional system of norms for sexual morality in marriage. A major relevant problem is that the appeal to experience, especially prominent in the present Pope's interpretation of "the language of the body" (Wednesday audience talks on "The Theology of the Body," 1979–81) and of marital intimacy, calls out for clarification of the standards by which "experience" is to be validated. Whose experience is to be examined? Who defines what the experience is, and gives the authoritative interpretation? One can hardly avoid the impression that the experience of married persons and of women in general has not been heard with real openness, if references to their experience are used by celibate, male theologians, clergy, and Church authorities to support conclusions which are in all essential points unvarying. Speaking more generally, the importance of the experience of those who have not yet been given a full voice in the Church is the basis of theologies of liberation, including Latin American political theology and feminist theology.

2. *Scripture.* The Second Vatican Council also represents a commitment to use the Bible as a more integral resource, especially in moral theology. One important asset of natural-law moral theology is that it makes possible the discussion of moral questions and public policy in a "reasonable" manner and on the basis of "common human values." A difficulty from the perspective of Catholic ethics as Christian ethics, is that the natural-law approach necessarily downplays the importance of Scripture and of specifically Christian commitment. It will no doubt always remain difficult to integrate perfectly reason and revelation as sources of ethics. However, it may be helpful to explore very briefly the ways in which Scripture can enlarge Catholic views of sexuality and of women. Regarding the role of women, Jesus broke many of the racial, religious, class, and gender boundaries of his time. He spoke with women directly, and many were prominent among his followers. Christian feminist theologians draw attention to Mary Magdalene, whom all four gospels portray as a first witness to the resurrection, and whom Bernard of Clairvaux called "apostle to the apostles." It is arguable that, on the New Testament evidence, Mary Magdalene is among the most

prominent of Jesus' disciples, and that she is given special status for her qualities of courage, perseverance, and leadership. Qualities of faithfulness, obedience, humility, love and self-sacrifice are not held up in the New Testament as special qualities of women; they are above all the qualities of Jesus himself and so to be manifested in all Christians. Moreover, sexual conduct is not nearly as prominent an issue in the Bible, especially the New Testament, as it has been in Catholic moral theology. (It says something about our attitudes toward both sex and women that we traditionally identified Mary Magdalene as a prostitute—when the Bible calls her simply a "sinner"—Luke 8:3.) Only in Corinthians 7 do we find anything like an extended consideration of sexual morality. Jesus forgives the adulteress about to be stoned to death (John 8:1–11), and the only sex-related offence he forbids explicitly is divorce (Mark 10:2–11, Luke 16:18, Matthew 5:31–32, and 19:3–9; cf. 1 Corinthians 7:10–11). Matthew and Paul qualify Jesus' saying—although it was for them "authoritative teaching"—in order to meet the needs of their communities. The major moral criterion for biblical authors is that the Christian lives a life which is consistent with redemption in Christ, and with building up the Body of Christ through love and service, but they do not specify in great detail all the things in which such a life consists. If anything, the divorce texts give us a model of somewhat flexible application, rather than a legalistic system of moral absolutes.

3. *Social Justice*. Catholic ethics recently has given attention to questions of social justice such as the threat of nuclear war, violence and terrorism, human rights and international development. Perhaps more importantly, it has begun to draw connections among the issues of so-called "personal ethics" and "social ethics." The Bishops of the United States, following the lead of Cardinal Joseph Bernardin, have begun to talk about a "consistent ethic of life," and to use the metaphor of a "seamless garment" of life issues. This began as an attempt to see abortion and the arms race as both threats to innocent life, and to call for consistent non-violence toward that life. The consistent ethic of life has been extended to issues like health care, employment, care for the elderly, and genetic research. I believe that issues such as contraception, sterilization, and fertility

therapies cannot be seen apart from broader views of sexuality and of men and women, as not only sexual actors, but as persons in whom are united many relationships, responsibilities, and burdens. Merely to forbid certain sexual choices is not an effective response to the social, cultural, and economic factors which lead or force persons into situations in which decisions must be made. Church teaching on issues such as sterilization, abortion, and divorce will be neither credible nor effective if it cannot connect meaningfully with the real and often painful experiences of real people; if it isolates particular choices from the web of other events, decisions, and options or lack of options; or if it retreats from the complexity and compromises of life into an unyielding legalism having little in common with the gospel.

NEEDED: A CREDIBLE WITNESS

In my view, the Catholic Church needs to develop a "credible witness" on moral matters, including sexual morality. It needs to speak to the situation of moral confusion in the larger cultures in which it exists. In the West, especially in prosperous and industrialized nations, the prevailing moral attitude is one of pragmatism and individualism. The morally right choice is the one which accomplishes the goal desired, which is freely chosen by the agent, and which does not infringe on the personal autonomy of others. Lacking is a sense of community, of sacrifice for others, and of boundaries to what can be undertaken for the sake of good consequences. The Church needs to be a *witness.* It needs the courage to hold up ideals in sexual morality beyond personal fulfillment and individual autonomy. It needs to be said that commitment and children are somehow essentially connected to sexual relationships as important human meanings. There should be a bias in marriage in favour of children; children are not a merely incidental outcome of the marital relationship, to be excluded if spouses choose to be "child free." Conversely, children are not a "right" of all adults, even married ones, even though children are a great blessing. When a couple faces infertility, they usually undergo considerable suffering, and it is commendable to attempt its alleviation through medical means. But there may be limits to means which are acceptable. Certainly to go outside the marriage bond in the use of "donor" sperm or ova represents an intrusion into the commitment of spouses, which in the traditional Christian view should be at once interpersonal, physical and potentially parental. No less problematic is the willingness of the donor to procreate with a stranger, and with the explicit intention of abdicating responsibility for his or her offspring. The severance of reproductive acts from any sort of personal involvement represents a new sort of dualism of body and spirit.

If the witness of the Church is to be heard, it also has to be *credible*. The repetition of time-honoured dicta in no way guarantees credibility. The Church must speak to the modern world with sympathy, with genuine understanding of the situations to be addressed, and with willingness to learn new lessons, even to reformulate its moral wisdom. One of the biggest barriers to credibility is the tendency of Church teachers to lump all moral issues together, and to regard a threat to "the Catholic" position on one as a threat to the entire edifice of Catholic morality. How can the Church be credible as a witness against the so-called "contraceptive mentality," if it cannot be sensitive to the situation of a family for whom natural methods of birth control are not very effective, and which has serious medical or economic problems? How can it be a credible witness against the sterilization of young persons who have decided that they never want children if it cannot make an exception for a couple at risk from a devastating genetic disease, or for maternal death during pregnancy? How can the Church witness credibly against infertility therapies which use donors if it regards them as morally the same as therapies which involve only the spouses, or if it regards as equally morally serious the masturbation which may be necessary for infertility testing, diagnosis, and therapy? How can the Church credibly urge women to take their maternal responsibilities seriously, including responsibility for the unborn, when it does not urge equal responsibility upon fathers, nor truly support access for women as adult moral agents to leadership in the family, society, and Church? The Church's witness on moral issues generally will be a "credible witness" if it brings its tradition into true dialogue with modern human experience, if it attends to the social ramifications of every moral issue, and if it tests its teaching by the gospel imperative to "encourage one another and build one another up" (I Thessalonians 5:11).

37. Official Catholic Social and Sexual Teachings: A Methodological Comparison

Charles E. Curran

This chapter first appeared in *Tensions in Moral Theology* in 1988.

The official hierarchical teaching of the Roman Catholic Church in moral matters has importance not only for the church members themselves but also for others in society at large. The attention given to this moral teaching in the popular press illustrates the news worthiness attached to it. Thanks to the popular media people in the United States were widely alerted to the stance taken by the United States Roman Catholic bishops on war and the economy as well as the position of the Vatican on test-tube babies.

A general impression is in evidence both within and outside the Catholic Church that Catholic moral teaching in social and sexual areas appears to be somewhat different. From the perspective of the general public contemporary Catholic social teaching with its criticism of the United States economic system and of our nuclear war and deterrence policy falls into what is often called the "liberal camp." However, Catholic teaching in sexual matters is definitely in the more "conservative camp."

The impression of differences between official Catholic social and sexual teaching also exists within the Catholic Church itself. Many conservative and neoconservative Roman Catholics have objected strenuously to the recent social teachings of the United States bishops but seem to have no problems with the official church teaching on sexual ethics. On the other hand, liberal Catholics have applauded the recent social teachings while often dissenting from the sexual teachings.

The purpose of this chapter is not to discuss the relationship between social and sexual ethics; nor will I take sides in the dispute between "liberal" and "conservative" Catholics, even though my own position is well known. My purpose is to examine the ethical methodology employed in each of these two aspects of official Catholic moral teachings and to point out the clear differences between the methodologies.

CATHOLIC SOCIAL TEACHING

Today a body of official Catholic social teaching exists going back to Pope Leo XIII's encyclical *Rerum Novarum* in 1891.[1] Subsequent encyclicals and official documents were often issued on anniversaries of *Rerum Novarum*, such as Pope Pius XI's *Quadragesimo Anno*[2] in 1931, Pope John XXIII's *Mater et Magistra*[3] in 1961, Pope Paul VI's *Octogesima Adveniens*[4] in 1971, and Pope John Paul II's *Laborem Exercens*[5] in 1981. In addition there are other papal documents as well as documents from the Second Vatican Council and the synods of bishops which constitute this body of official Catholic social teaching.

One significant question about these documents and other hierarchical social teaching concerns the authoritative nature of such teaching and the response which is due to such teaching on the part of Roman Catholic believers. To discuss the nature, extent, and limits of authoritative teaching in the Catholic Church lies beyond the scope of the present considerations. However, one point should be made. There are many other hierarchical church teachings from Pope Leo XIII and later which are no longer remembered today. Leo's teaching on the political order is seldom read or even mentioned on the contemporary scene. Leo's political writings generally insist on at best a paternalistic or at worst an authoritarian view of society.[6] The unofficial canon of Catholic social teaching today has been brought about by the reception of the church itself—the voices of subsequent popes but also the response of the total church. The whole church has played a role in what is viewed today as constituting the body of official Catholic social teaching.

Within the documents themselves the popes and the episcopal

bodies explicitly stress the continuity with what went before. Popes are very fond of quoting their predecessors of happy memory. However, in reality much change and development have occurred within this body of social teaching. This section will study three important methodological issues which have experienced a very significant change in the less than 100-year historical span covered by this body of official Catholic social teaching. These methodological changes in social teaching will be contrasted in the following section with the official teaching on sexual ethics which has not experienced such changes. The three methodological areas to be considered are the shift to historical consciousness, the shift to personalism, and the acceptance of a relationality-responsibility ethical model. Each of these methodological developments will now be traced.

Shift to Historical Consciousness[7]

Historical consciousness is often contrasted with classicism. Classicism understands reality in terms of the eternal, the immutable, and the unchanging; whereas historical consciousness gives more importance to the particular, the contingent, the historical, and the individual. Historical consciousness should also be contrasted with the other extreme of sheer existentialism. Sheer existentialism sees the present moment in isolation from the before and the after of time, with no binding relationships to persons and values in the present. Historical consciousness recognizes the need for both continuity and discontinuity. This discussion about worldview tends to be primarily a philosophical endeavor, but there are relationships to the theological. The Catholic theological tradition has recognized historicity in its rejection of the axiom "the scripture alone." The scripture must always be understood, appropriated, communicated, and lived in the light of the historical and cultural realities of the present time. The church just cannot repeat the words of the scriptures. Catholicism has undergone much more development than most people think. While creative fidelity is necessary for any tradition, such creative fidelity is consistent with the philosophical worldview of historical consciousness.

These two different worldviews spawn two different methodological approaches. The classicist worldview is associated with the deductive methodology that deduces its conclusions from its premises, which are eternal verities. The syllogism well illustrates the deductive approach. Note that in such an approach one's conclusions are as certain as the premises if the logic is correct. Historical consciousness recognizes the need for a more inductive approach. However, the need to maintain both continuity as well as discontinuity argues against a one-sided inductive approach. An inductive approach by its very nature can never achieve the same degree of certitude for its conclusions as does the deductive methodology of the classicist worldview.

There can be no doubt that a significant development toward historical consciousness has occurred in the body of official social teaching. Pope Pius XI's 1931 encyclical *Quadragesimo Anno* is often called in English "On Reconstructing the Social Order."[8] In this encyclical the pope proposes his plan for this reorganization, which is often called moderate corporatism or solidarism. In keeping with the traditional emphasis in the Catholic tradition this papal plan sees all the different institutions that are part of society as working together for the common good of all. Catholic social teaching has insisted on the metaphor of society as an organism with all the parts existing for the good of the totality. According to such an outlook labor and capital should not be adversaries fighting one another, but rather they should work together for the common good. Moderate corporatism sees labor, capital, and consumers all working together and forming one group to control what happens in a particular industry. This group would set prices, wages, and the amount of goods to be produced. Then other such groups on a higher level would coordinate and direct the individual industries and professions.

Pope Pius XI proposed his plan for reconstruction as something applicable to the whole world. Of course, the world of Pius XI and his contemporaries was primarily the Euro-centric world. The deductive nature of the plan is quite evident in the encyclical. From a philosophical view of society as an organism the pope sketched out his approach as a middle course between the extremes of individualistic capitalism and collective socialism. In reality this plan had little chance of succeeding precisely because it did not correspond to any existing historical reality, and the popes never entered into the debate of making the plan work in practice. Pope Pius XII, the successor of Pope Pius XI, spoke less and less about this plan as his pontificate continued, and Pope John XXIII basically ignored the proposal.[9]

Such a deductive methodology is in keeping with the neo-Scholastic thesis-approach to theology. However, some developments gradually occurred. Pope John XXIII's 1963 encyclical *Pacem in Terris* still follows a generally deductive approach, but in this and in his earlier encyclical *Mater et Magistra* Pope John XXIII did not give attention to the plan for reconstruction proposed by Pope Pius XI. However, at the end of each of the four chapters or parts of *Pacem in Terris* there is a short section on the signs of the times— the special characteristics of the present day.[10] Two years later *Gaudium et Spes,* the Pastoral Constitution of the Church in the Modern World of the Second Vatican Council, gives a much greater emphasis to historical consciousness. Each of the five chapters in the second part of the document deals with a specific area of concern and each begins with the signs of the times.

Pope Paul VI's Apostolic Letter *Octogesima Adveniens* of 1971 shows a very heightened awareness of historical consciousness:

> In the face of such widely varying situations it is difficult for us to utter a unified message and to put forward a solution which has universal validity. Such is not our ambition, nor is it our mission. It is up to the Christian communities to analyze with objectivity the situation which is proper to their own country, to shed on it the light of the Gospel's unalterable words and to draw principles of reflection, norms of judgment, and directives for action from the social teaching of the church. . . . It is up to these Christian communities, with the help of the Holy Spirit, in communion with the bishops who hold responsibility and in dialogue with other Christian brethren and all people of good will, to discern the options and commitments which are called for in order to bring about the social, political, and economic changes seen in many cases to be urgently needed.[11]

Only forty years earlier Pope Pius XI had put forward a plan for social reconstruction which in his mind had universal validity. The difference between the approaches of these two popes is very great.

The more inductive methodology of *Octogesima Adveniens* gives great importance to contemporary developments. A large portion of the letter is devoted to two aspirations that have come to the fore in the contemporary consciousness:

> While scientific and technological progress continues to overturn human surroundings, patterns of knowledge, work, consumption, and relationships, two aspirations persistently make themselves felt in these new contexts, and they grow stronger to the extent that one becomes better informed and better educated: the aspiration to equality and the aspiration to participation, two forms of human dignity and freedom.[12]

It must be pointed out that the present pope, John Paul II, has pulled back somewhat from Pope Paul VI's insistence on historical consciousness. *Laborem Exercens,* the 1981 encyclical, is a philosophical reflection on work and its meaning that is intended to address all people. In his other writings John Paul II definitely moves away from the historical consciousness of Paul VI. His Christology, for example, is a Christology from above which begins with the eternally begotten Word of God and not with the historical Jesus.

Two reasons help to explain John Paul II's reluctance to embrace historical consciousness as much as his predecessor did. By temperament and training the present pope is a philosopher who studied, taught, and wrote in the more classical philosophical mode. Such thinking and writing are clearly congenial to him. In addition, historical consciousness can be seen as somewhat of a threat to the unity and central authority in the church. All today recognize the tensions existing between the church universal as represented by the bishop of Rome and the national and local churches. Local diversity and pluralism are seen as threats to the unity and authority of the church. There can be no doubt that these existing tensions have made Pope John Paul II very wary of historical consciousness.

However, the present pope does not use a more classicist approach to avoid making some very concrete and critical statements about existing social reality. *Laborem Exercens* does not shrink from criticizing many aspects of the plight of the worker today.

Recent Catholic social theology and ethics have embraced the concept of historical consciousness. Consider, for example, the whole field of liberation theology as well as the importance given to praxis and to social analysis in recent writings.

Shift to the Person with an Emphasis on Freedom, Equality, and Participation

Within the time frame of a one-hundred-year span there has been a very significant shift in Catholic social teaching away from an emphasis on human nature with a concomitant stress on order, the acceptance of some inequality, and away from obedience to the many controlling authorities to a recognition of the vital importance of the human person with the concomitant need for human freedom, equality, and participation.

In the nineteenth century the Catholic Church opposed freedom and the thought of the Enlightenment. Freedom in religion, philosophy, science, and politics threatened the old order in all its aspects. Individualistic freedom forgot about human beings' relationships to God, to God's law, to human society in general, and to other human beings. Continental liberalism with its emphasis on the individualistic freedom was seen as the primary enemy of the church.[13] Even in the nineteenth century official Catholic teaching did not condemn all slavery as always wrong.[14]

Pope Leo XIII was very much a part of this tradition. He stressed order and social cohesiveness rather than freedom. God's law and the natural law govern human existence. Leo's view of society was authoritarian or at least paternalistic. He often referred to the people as the ignorant multitude that had to be led by their rulers. (Such an approach is somewhat understandable in the light of the low state of European literacy at the time.) In social ethics freedom was seen as a threat to the social organism. Individualistic capitalism was condemned as a form of economic liberalism which claimed that one could pay whatever wage one could get away with.

Leo was also no friend of democracy because no majority could do away with God's law, and freedom of religion could never be promoted but at best only tolerated as the lesser evil in certain circumstances.[15]

Development occurred in the methodology of official Catholic social teaching precisely because of changing historical circumstances. The Catholic Church's enemy, or in more recent terminology, the dialogue partner, changed. In the nineteenth century the church opposed the individualistic liberalism of the day. As the twentieth century advanced, the central problem became the rise and existence of totalitarian governments. In this context the Catholic Church began to defend the freedom and dignity of the human person against the encroachments of totalitarianism. Pope Pius XI in the 1930s wrote encyclical letters against fascism, nazism, and communism.[16] In theory the Roman Catholic Church opposed all forms of totalitarianism, but there can be no doubt that the church was more willing in practice to tolerate totalitarianism from the right. After the Second World War Catholic teaching consistently and constantly attacked communism. (Note that in the 1960s a change occurred with Pope John XXIII, and there ensued a much more nuanced dialogical approach to Marxism.)[17] In the light of this polemic Catholic teaching stressed the freedom and dignity of the individual.

Pope John XXIII's *Pacem in Terris* in 1963 signals the Catholic acceptance of the role of freedom. In *Mater et Magistra* in 1961 John XXIII, in keeping with the Catholic tradition, insisted in a major part of this document that the ideal social order rests on the three values of truth, justice and love.[18] Two years later in *Pacem in Terris* the pope adds a fourth element—truth, justice, charity, and freedom.[19] *Pacem in Terris* develops for the first time a full-blown treatment of human rights in the Catholic tradition.[20] Before that time Catholic thought had been fearful of rights language precisely because of the danger of excessive individualism. Catholic social teaching had insisted on duties and obedience to the divine and natural law and not on rights. In its quite late embracing of the human rights tradition *Pacem in Terris* still recognizes the danger of individualism by including economic rights and by insisting on the correlation between rights and duties.

There was one major obstacle or inconsistency in Catholic social teaching in the early 1960s. While the tradition was now insisting on the importance of freedom and the dignity of the individual, official hierarchical teaching still could not accept religious freedom. One of the great accomplishments of the Second Vatican Council in 1965 was the acceptance of religious freedom as demanded by the very dignity of the human person. Religious freedom is understood as freedom from external coercion that forces one to act against one's conscience or prevents one's acting in accord with one's conscience in religious matters.[21] In accepting this teaching Vatican II had to admit that a significant development and even change had occurred in Catholic thinking because in the nineteenth and twentieth century before 1965 official Catholic teaching could not accept religious freedom.[22] In the light of present circumstances one appreciates all the more both the theoretical and the practical import of this change in Catholic teaching.

In 1971 Pope Paul VI in *Octogesima Adveniens* devoted a long section of the document to two new aspirations which have become more persistent and stronger in the contemporary context—the aspiration to equality and the aspiration to participation—two forms of human dignity and freedom.[23]

Pope John Paul II has strengthened and even developed the shift to personalism. *Laborem Exercens* in 1981 emphasizes that the subjective aspect of work is more important than the objective precisely because of the dignity of the human person. The personal aspect of labor is the basis for the priority of labor over capital.

Thus in the twentieth century a very significant shift has occurred in the methodology of Catholic social teaching through its emphasis on the importance of the dignity and freedom of the human person. Catholic personalism is the basis for many changes in particular teachings in the area of social, political, and economic morality.

Shift to a Relationality-Responsibility Ethical Model

In general there are three generic ethical models that have been used to understand the moral life in a more systematic way. The deontological model understands morality primarily in terms of law and obedience to the law. Deontological approaches are often castigated for being legalistic in a pejorative sense, but such is not necessarily the case. (Think, for example, of the legal model developed by Kant with its categorical imperative.) The teleological model understands morality in the light of the end or the goal and the means to attain it. One first determines what is the end or the goal. Something is good if it leads toward that goal and evil if it impedes attaining the goal. In the complexity of human existence there are many various types of goals and ends—the ultimate end less ultimate ends, subordinate ends, etc. The relationality-responsibility model sees the human person in terms of one's multiple relationships with God, neighbor, world, and self and the call to live responsibly in the midst of these relationships. In systematic understandings of moral theory one of the models will be primary. One word of caution is necessary. Although one of these models is primary, they should not be seen as mutually exclusive. Thus, for example, in a teleological model or in a relationality-responsibility model there will always be place for some laws and norms, but the law model will not be primary.

All agree that the manuals of Catholic moral theology which existed until the time of the Second Vatican Council employed the legal model as primary. According to the manuals of moral theology the proximate, subjective, and intrinsic norm of moral action is conscience. Conscience is the dictate of moral reason about the morality of an act. The remote, objective, and extrinsic norm of moral action is law. The function of conscience is thus to obey the law. Law is either divine law or human law. Divine law is twofold. First, the laws which necessarily follow from God as the author and creator of nature involve the eternal law, which is the order or plan existing in the mind of God, and the natural law, which is the participation of the eternal law in the rational creature. Second, divine positive law comes from the free determination of God as the author of revelation. Human law has human beings as its author and can be either church or civil law. Note that all law shares in the eternal law of God and that human law must always be seen in relationship to and subordinate to the natural law and the eternal law. Thus the manuals of moral theology view the moral life as conscience obeying the various laws.[24] More specifically, Catholic moral teaching has insisted that most of its moral teaching is based on the natural law, which in principle is knowable by all human beings since it is human reason reflecting on human nature.

The emphasis on the legal model as primary in Catholic moral theology before the Second Vatican Council is somewhat anomalous in light of the Catholic tradition. Thomas Aquinas (d. 1274) remains the most significant figure in the Roman Catholic theological tradition. However, Thomas Aquinas in his moral theory was not a deontologist but a teleologist.[25] It is true that Thomas does have a treatise on law and the different types of law just as is found in the manuals, but this treatise on law is comparatively small and appears only at the end of his discussion of ethical theory. Aquinas was an intrinsic teleologist. His first ethical consideration is the ultimate end of human beings. The ultimate end of human beings is happiness, which is achieved when the fundamental powers or drives of human nature achieve their end. The intellect and the will are the most basic human powers. To know the truth and to love the good constitute the basic fulfillment and happiness of the human being. This happiness occurs in the beautific vision. Morality in this view is intrinsic. Something is commanded because it is good for the individual and leads to the ultimate fulfillment and happiness of the individual. However, the neo-Scholasticism of the manuals of moral theology truncated Aquinas' moral thought and reduced it to a deontological model.

There can be no doubt that the Catholic social teaching in the nineteenth and early twentieth centuries basically worked out of a legal model. Even as late as 1963 *Pacem in Terris* recognized the law model to be the primary structural approach of the whole encyclical. *Pacem in Terris* begins by insisting that peace on earth can firmly be established only if the order laid down by God be dutifully observed. An astounding order reigns in our world, and the greatness of human beings is to understand that order. The creator of the world has imprinted on the human heart an order which conscience reveals and enjoins one to obey.[26]

> But fickleness of opinion often produces this error, that many think that the relationships between human beings and states can be governed by the same laws as the forces

and irrational elements of the universe, whereas the laws governing them are of quite a different kind and are to be sought elsewhere, namely, where the Father of all things wrote them, that is, in human nature.

By these laws human beings are most admirably taught first of all how they should conduct their mutual dealings among themselves, then how the relationships between the citizens and the public authority of each state should be regulated, then how states should deal with one another, and finally how, on the one hand, individual human beings and states, and, on the other hand, the community of all peoples, should act toward each other, the establishment of such a community being urgently demanded today by the requirements of universal common good.[27]

This introductory section sets the stage for the four parts of the encyclical which are the four areas mentioned above. Thus, the law model is highlighted as the approach still followed in *Pacem in Terris.*

Pope Paul VI's *Octogesima Adveniens* in 1971 well illustrates the shift from a legal model to a relationality-responsibility model. As noted above, Paul VI here strongly endorses a shift to historical consciousness. In such a perspective this document does not look for the order and laws inscribed in human nature. Here the historical character and the dynamism of the church's social teaching are stressed:

It is with all its dynamism that the social teaching of the church accompanies human beings in their search. If it does not intervene to authenticate a given structure or to propose a ready-made model, it does not thereby limit itself to recalling general principles. It develops through reflection applied to the changing situations of this world, under the driving force of the gospel as the source of renewal when its message is accepted in its totality and with all its demands. It also develops with a sensitivity proper to the church which is characterized by a disinterested will to serve and by attention to the poorest. Finally, it draws upon its rich experience of many centuries which enables it, while continuing its permanent preoccupations, to undertake the daring and creative innovations which the present state of the world requires.[28]

Octogesima Adveniens does not see conscience in the light of obedience to law. Chapter nine below will examine in greater detail the understanding of conscience in church documents on social questions. The most characteristic word to describe the function of conscience in this papal letter is discernment (n. 36). Pope Paul VI also introduces into Catholic social teaching the methodological importance of utopias:

> The appeal to a utopia is often a convenient excuse for those who wish to escape from concrete tasks in order to take refuge in an imaginary world. To live in a hypothetical future is a facile alibi for rejecting immediate responsibilities. But it must clearly be recognized that this kind of criticism of existing society often provokes the forward-looking imagination both to perceive in the present the discarded possibility hidden within it, and to direct itself toward a fresh future; it thus sustains social dynamism by the confidence that it gives to the inventive powers of the human mind and heart; and, if it refuses no overture, it can also meet the Christian appeal. The Spirit of the Lord, who animates human beings renewed in Christ, continually breaks down the horizons within which one's understanding likes to find security and the limits to which one's activity would willingly restrict itself; there dwells within one a power which urges one to go beyond every system and every ideology. At the heart of the world there dwells the mystery of the human person discovering oneself to be God's child in the course of a historical and psychological process in which constraint and freedom as well as the weight of sin and the breath of the Spirit alternate and struggle for the upper hand.[29]

Octogesima Adveniens ends with a recognition of shared responsibility, a call to action, and the realization of a pluralism of possible options.[30] Thus the letter definitely marks a decided shift toward the primacy of the relationality-responsibility model in Catholic social teaching. Development within official Catholic social teaching has thus occurred on three very important methodological concerns.

CATHOLIC SEXUAL TEACHING

The focus now shifts to official Catholic teaching in the area of sexual morality. Three recent documents will be examined—the "Declaration on Sexual Ethics" issued by the Congregation for the Doctrine of the Faith on December 29, 1975;[31] the "Letter to the Bishops of the Catholic Church on the Pastoral Care of Homosexual Persons" promulgated by the Congregation for the Doctrine of the Faith on October 1, 1986;[32] the "Instruction on Respect for Human Life in Its Origin and on the Dignity of Procreation" issued by the Congregation for the Doctrine of the Faith on February 22, 1987.[33] The present discussion centers on methodological issues, but something must be said briefly about the authoritative nature of these documents. There is a hierarchy of official Catholic Church documents. These three documents are not from the pope himself but from one of the Roman congregations. By their very nature such documents are not expected to break new ground. However, it is interesting that the documents have received wide public discussion. Catholics owe a religious respect to the teaching of these documents, but they are of less authoritative weight than the documents issued by the pope himself.

For our present purposes the focus is on the methodological approaches taken in these documents. This study will show that these methodological approaches differ sharply from the three methodological approaches found in the contemporary documents on Catholic social teaching. Each of these three methodological issues will be considered in turn.

Classicist Rather Than Historically Conscious

The "Declaration on Sexual Ethics" of 1975 shows very little historical consciousness. In the very beginning of the document the emphasis on the eternal and the immutable is very clear:

Therefore there can be no true promotion of human dignity unless the essential order of human nature is respected. Of course, in the history of civilization many of the concrete conditions and needs of human life have changed and will continue to change. But all evolution of morals and every type of life must be kept within the limits imposed by the immutable principles based upon every human person's constitutive elements and essential relations—elements and relations which transcend historical contingencies.

These fundamental principles which can be grasped by reason are contained in "the divine law—eternal, objective, and universal—whereby God orders, directs, and governs the entire universe and all the ways of human community by a plan conceived in wisdom and love. Human beings have been made by God to participate in this law with the result that under the gentle disposition of divine providence they can come to perceive ever increasingly the unchanging truth." This divine law is accessible to our minds. (n. 3)

The "Letter to the Bishops of the Catholic Church on the Pastoral Care of Homosexual Persons" in 1986 bases its teaching on "the divine plan" and "the theology of creation" which tells us of "the creator's sexual design" (nn. 1–7). The "theocratic law" (n. 6) found in the scripture also attests to the church's teaching. Emphasis is frequently put on the will of God which is known in the above-mentioned ways and is what the church teaches.

This letter points out that many call for a change in the church's teaching on homosexuality because the earlier condemnations were culture-bound (n. 4). The letter acknowledges that the Bible was composed in many different epochs with great cultural and historical diversity and that the church today addresses the gospel to a world which differs in many ways from ancient days (n. 5). In the light of this recognition of historical consciousness one is not prepared for the opening sentence of the next paragraph: "What should be noticed is that, in the presence of such remarkable diversity, there is nevertheless a clear consistency within the scriptures themselves on the moral issue of homosexual behaviour" (n. 5). Historical consciousness is mentioned only to deny it in practice.

The "Instruction on Respect for Human Life in Its Origin and on the Dignity of Procreation" promulgated in 1987 appeals to the unchangeable and immutable laws of human nature. The laws are described as "inscribed in the very being of man and of woman" (II, B, n. 4). These laws are "inscribed in their persons and in their union" (Introduction, n. 5).

This instruction describes its own methodology as deductive: "The moral criteria for medical intervention in procreation are deduced from the dignity of human persons, of their sexuality, and of their origins" (II, B, n. 7). "A first consequence can be deduced from these principles" of the natural law (Introduction, n. 3). In summary these documents show little or no historical consciousness in their approach to questions of sexuality.

The Emphasis Is on Nature and Faculties Rather Than on the Person

In the official hierarchical teaching on sexuality the methodology gives much more significance to nature and faculties than it does to the person. This has been a constant complaint against the older Catholic methodology in sexual ethics which has led to its teaching on masturbation, artificial contraception, sterilization, artificial insemination, homosexual acts, etc.[34] The manuals of moral theology based their sexual ethics on the innate purpose and God-given structure and finality of the sexual faculty. The sexual faculty has a twofold purpose—procreation and love union. Every sexual actuation must respect that twofold finality, and nothing should interfere with this God-given purpose. The sexual act itself must be open to procreation and expressive of love. Such an understanding forms the basis of the Catholic teaching that masturbation, contraception, and artificial insemination even with the husband's seed are always wrong.[35]

The popular mentality often thought that Catholic opposition to artificial contraception was based on a strong pronatalist position. However, such is not the case. Catholic teaching has also condemned artificial insemination with the husband's seed which is done precisely in order to have a child. In my judgment this condemnation points up the problematic aspect in the methodology of Catholic sexual teaching—the sexual faculty can never be interfered with and the sexual act must always be open to procreation and expressive of love. This natural act must always be present. The last chapter developed the position of many theologians that for the good of the person or the good of the marriage one can and should interfere with the sexual faculty and the sexual act. I have claimed that the official teaching is guilty of physicalism by insisting that the human person cannot interfere with the physical, biological structure of the sexual faculty or the sexual act. There is no doubt that the official documents under discussion here continue to accept and propose this basic understanding.

The "Declaration on Sexual Ethics" points out that the sexual teaching of the Catholic Church is based "on the finality of the sexual act and on the principal criterion of its morality: it is respect for its finality that ensures the moral goodness of this act" (n. 5). Sexual sins are described often in this document as "abuses of the sexual faculty" (n. 6, also nn. 8, 9). The nature of the sexual faculty and of the sexual act and not the person form the ultimate moral criterion in matters of sexual morality.

The letter on homosexuality cites the earlier "Declaration on Sexual Ethics" to point out that homosexual acts are deprived of their essential and indispensable finality and are intrinsically disordered (n. 3). This letter points out that it is only within marriage that the use of the sexual faculty can be morally good (n. 7). However, there does seem to be a development in this letter in terms of a greater appeal to personalism. The teaching claims to be based on the reality of the human person in one's spiritual and physical dimensions (n. 2). There are more references to the human person throughout this document than in the earlier declaration, but the change is only verbal. The methodology is ultimately still based on the nature of the faculty and of the act, which are then assumed to be the same thing as the person.

The instruction on some aspects of bioethics is very similar to the letter on homosexuality in this regard. There are references to the "intimate structure" of the conjugal act and to the conjugal act as expressing the self-gift of the spouses and their openness to the gift of life. The document also appeals to the meaning and values which are expressed in the language of the body and in the union of human persons (II, B, n. 4). Thus the terms, the finality of the faculty and of the act and the abuse of the sexual faculty, are not used, but the basic teaching remains the same. There are many more references to the person and to the rights of persons than in the earlier documents, but the change remains verbal and does not affect the substance of the teaching.

Ethical Model

There can be no doubt that the documents in official Catholic teaching on sexuality employ the law model as primary. The "Declaration on Sexual Ethics" in its discussion of ethical methodology insists on the importance of the divine law—eternal, objective, and universal—whereby God orders, directs, and governs the entire universe (n. 3). This document bases its teaching on the "existence of immutable laws inscribed in the constitutive elements of human nature and which are revealed to be identical in all beings endowed with reason" (n. 4). Throughout the introductory comments there is no doubt whatsoever that this declaration follows a legal model:

> Since sexual ethics concern certain fundamental values of human and Christian life, this general teaching equally applies to sexual ethics. In this domain there exist principles and norms which the church has always unhesitatingly transmitted as part of her teaching, however much the opinions and morals of the world may have been opposed to them. These principles and norms in no way owe their origin to a certain type of culture, but rather to knowledge of the divine law and of human nature. They therefore cannot be considered as having become out of date or doubtful under the pretext that a new cultural situation has risen. (n. 5)

The "Letter to the Bishops of the Catholic Church on the Pastoral Care of Homosexual Persons" is by its very nature more concerned with pastoral care than with an explanation of the moral teaching and the ethical model employed in such teaching (n. 2). However, the occasional references found in this pastoral letter indicate the deontological model at work. There are frequent references to the will of God, the plan of God, and the theology of creation. Traditional Catholic natural law is the basis for this teaching. The teaching of scripture on this matter is called "theocratic law" (n. 6).

The recent instruction on bioethics definitely employs a deontological ethical model:

> Thus the Church once more puts forward the divine law in order to accomplish the work of truth and liberation. For it is out of goodness—in order to indicate the path of life— that God gives human beings his commandments and the grace to observe them. . . . (Introduction, n. 1)
>
> The natural moral law expresses and lays down the purposes, rights, and duties which are based upon the bodily and spiritual nature of the human person. Therefore this law cannot be thought of as simply a set of norms on the biological level; rather it must be defined as the rational order whereby the human being is called by the Creator to direct and regulate one's life and action and in particular to make use of one's own body. (Introduction, n. 3)

This document also cites the following quotation from *Mater et Magistra:* "The transmission of human life is entrusted by nature to a personal and conscious act and as such is subject to the all-holy laws of God: immutable and inviolable laws which must be recognized and observed" (Introduction, n. 4). Biomedical science and technology have grown immensely in the last few years, but "science and technology require, for their own intrinsic meaning, an unconditional respect for the fundamental criteria of the moral law" (Introduction, n. 2).

A very significant practical difference between a law model and a relationality-responsibility model is illustrated by the teaching proposed in these documents. In a legal model the primary question is the existence of law. If something is against the law, it is wrong; if there is no law against it, it is acceptable and good. Within such a perspective there is very little gray area. Something is either forbidden or permitted. Within a relationality-responsibility model there are more gray areas. Here one recognizes that in the midst of complexity and specificity one cannot always claim a certitude for one's moral positions.

The contemporary official Catholic teaching on social issues with its relationality-responsibility model recognizes significant gray areas. *Octogesima Adveniens* acknowledges the pluralism of options available and the need for discernment. The two recent pastoral letters of the United States Roman Catholic bishops on peace and the economy well illustrate such an approach. The documents make some very particular judgments, but they recognize that other Catholics might in good conscience disagree with such judgments. The bishops' letters call for unity and agreement on the level of principles, but they recognize that practical judgments on specific issues cannot claim with absolute certitude to be the only possible solution. The pastoral letter on peace, for example, proposes that the first use of nuclear weapons is always wrong but recognizes that other Catholics in good conscience might disagree with such a judgment.[36]

In the contemporary official Catholic teaching on sexual issues there is little or no mention of such gray areas. Something is either forbidden or permitted. Even in the complex question of bioethics the same approach is used. Certain technologies and interventions are always wrong; others are permitted. Thus the very way in which topics are treated—namely, either forbidden or permitted— indicates again that a legal model is at work in the hierarchical sexual teaching.

The thesis and the conclusions of this chapter are somewhat modest, but still very significant. There can be no doubt that there are three important methodological differences between hierarchical Roman Catholic teaching on social morality and the official hierarchical teaching on sexual morality. Whereas the official social teaching has evolved so that it now employs historical consciousness, personalism, and a relationality-responsibility ethical model, the sexual teaching still emphasizes classicism, human nature and faculties, and a law model of ethics. The ramifications of these conclusions are most significant, but they go beyond the scope of this study.

Notes

1. Pope Leo XIII, *Rerum Novarum,* in Etienne Gilson, ed., *The Church Speaks to the Modern World: The Social Teachings of Leo XIII* (Garden City, NY: Doubleday Image Books, 1954), pp. 200–244.

2. Pope Pius XI, *Quadragesimo Anno,* in Terence P. McLaughlin, ed., *The Church and the Reconstruction of the Modern World: The Social Encyclicals of Pope Pius XI* (Garden City, NY: Doubleday Image Books, 1957), pp. 218–278.

3. Pope John XXIII, *Mater et Magistra,* in David J. O'Brien and Thomas A. Shannon, eds., *Renewing the Earth: Catholic Documents on Peace, Justice, and Liberation* (New York: Paulist Press, 1977), pp. 44–116.

4. Pope Paul VI, *Octogesima Adveniens,* in O'Brien and Shannon, *Renewing the Earth,* pp. 347–383.

5. Pope John Paul II, *Laborem Exercens,* in Gregory Baum, *The Priority of Labor* (New York: Paulist Press, 1982), pp. 95–152.

6. E.g., Pope Leo XIII, *Diuturnum,* in Gilson, *The Church Speaks to the Modern World,* pp. 140–161.

7. I have developed in greater detail this shift to historical consciousness as well as the shift to personalism in my *Directions in Catholic Social Ethics* (Notre Dame, IN: University of Notre Dame Press, 1985), pp. 6–22.

8. Gilson, *The Church Speaks to the Modern World,* p. 218.

9. For an interpretation that sees somewhat more continuity between Pope Pius XI and his successors see John F. Cronin, *Social Principles and Economic Life,* rev. ed. (Milwaukee: Bruce, 1964), pp. 130–140.

10. *Pacem in Terris,* nn. 39–45, 75–79, 126–129, 142–145, in O'Brien and Shannon, *Renewing the Earth,* pp. 133–135, 143, 154, 158–159.

11. *Octogesima Adveniens,* n. 4, in ibid., pp. 353, 354.

12. *Octogesima Adveniens,* n. 22, in ibid., p. 364.

13. John Courtney Murray, "The Church and Totalitarian Democracy," *Theological Studies* 13 (1952): 525–563.

14. John Francis Maxwell, *Slavery and the Catholic Church* (London:

Barry Rose Publishers, 1975), pp. 78, 79; Joseph D. Brokhage, *Francis Patrick Kenrick's Opinion on Slavery* (Washington: Catholic University of America Press, 1955).

15. John Courtney Murray, *The Problem of Religious Freedom* (Westminster, MD: Newman Press, 1965), pp. 52–66; Fr. Refoulé, "L'Église et les libertés de Léon XIII à Jean XXIII," *Le Supplément* 125 (mai 1978): 243–259.

16. McLaughlin, *The Church and the Reconstruction of the Modern World,* pp. 299–402.

17. Arthur F. McGovern, *Marxism: An American Christian Perspective* (Maryknoll, NY: Orbis Books, 1980), pp. 90–131.

18. *Mater et Magistra,* nn. 212–265, in O'Brien and Shannon, *Renewing the Earth,* pp. 102–114.

19. *Pacem in Terris,* nn. 35, 36, in ibid., p. 132.

20. *Pacem in Terris,* nn. 11–34, in ibid., pp. 126–132.

21. "Declaration on Religious Freedom," in ibid., pp. 285–306.

22. John Courtney Murray, "Vers une intelligence du dévelopment de la doctrine de l'Église sur la liberté religieuse," in J. Hamer and Y. Congar, eds., *Vatican II: La liberté religieuse, declaration "Dignitatis humanae personae"* (Paris: Éditions du Cerf, 1967), pp. 111–147.

23. *Octogesima Adveniens,* n. 22, in O'Brien and Shannon, *Renewing the Earth,* p. 364.

24. E.g., Marcellinus Zalba, *Theologiae Moralis Summa,* I: *Theologia Moralis Fundamentalis* (Madrid: Biblioteca de Autores Cristianos, 1952).

25. Thomas Aquinas, *Summa Theologiae, Pars I^a II^{ae}* (Rome: Marietti, 1952).

26. *Pacem in Terris,* nn. 1–5, in O'Brien and Shannon, *Renewing the Earth,* pp. 124, 125.

27. *Pacem in Terris,* nn. 6, 7, in ibid., pp. 125, 126.

28. *Octogesima Adveniens,* n. 42, in ibid., p. 375.

29. *Octogesima Adveniens,* n. 37, in ibid., p. 371.

30. *Octogesima Adveniens,* nn. 47–52, in ibid., pp. 378–382.

31. Congregation for the Doctrine of the Faith, "Declaration on Sexual Ethics," *Origins* 5 (1976): 485–494. References to this and the subsequent documents will be to the official paragraph numbers. These documents are also available from the Publications Office, National Conference of Catholic Bishops, 1312 Massachusetts Ave. NW, Washington, DC 20005.

32. Congregation for the Doctrine of the Faith, "Letter to the Bishops of the Catholic Church on the Pastoral Care of Homosexual Persons," *Origins* 16 (1986): 377–382.

33. Congregation for the Doctrine of the Faith, "Instruction on Respect for Human Life in Its Origin and on the Dignity of Procreation," *Origins* 16 (1987): 697–711.

34. Luigi Lorenzetti, "Tramissione della vita humana: da un'etica della natura ad un'etica della persona," *Rivista di Teologia Morale* 18, n. 71 (1986): 117–129.

35. E.g., Marcellinus Zalba, *Theologiae Moralis Summa,* II: *Tractatus De Mandatis Dei et Ecclesiae* (Madrid: Biblioteca de Autores Cristianos, 1953), pp. 314–420.

36. United States Catholic Bishops, "The Challenge of Peace: God's Promise and Our Response," *Origins* 13 (1983): 2, 3.

38. Commentary on the *Declaration on Certain Questions Concerning Sexual Ethics*

Richard A. McCormick, S.J.

This article first appeared in *Theological Studies* in 1977.

On January 15, 1976, the Sacred Congregation for the Doctrine of the Faith released the "Declaration on Certain Questions Concerning Sexual Ethics" (*Persona humana*). For lack of space and because the document is widely available,[1] it will not be summarized here. I will present quick references to the wide and swift response the Declaration received, then summarize in more detail the more systematic theological analyses.

The journalistic response was varied and predictable. Many of the negative responses are given in *Informations catholiques internationales.*[2] Thus, Jacques Duquesne (writing in *Le point*) sees the document as a "formidable retour en arrière." Odette Thibault (*Le monde*) regrets that "for the Catholic Church sin (with a capital S) is still and will always be sexual sin." Henry Fesquet (*Le monde*) deplored the morality of fear in the statement. P. Liégé, dean of the faculty of theology at Paris, stated (*La vie catholique*) that the Declaration lacks "human and gospel warmth. It is cold, it is abstract, it is sad."

A group of theologians comprising the "Organisation régionale pour le développement théologique" (ORDET) issued a statement highly critical of *Persona humana.*[3] "Its individualistic and legalistic character, its outdated philosophical categories, its abusive authoritarianism distance it from sincere scholarly inquiry and from the call of the gospel." In the document they found "neither truth, nor justice, nor love of God who, in Christ Jesus, has not destroyed the 'tyranny of the law' only to restore it in the Church."

Such severe criticisms were responded to by the bishop of Carcassone,[4] the Permanent Council of the French Episcopate,[5] Cardinal François Marty alone[6] and together with Roger Etchegaray, president of the French Episcopal Conference.[7] Bishop Armand Le Bourgeois of Autun noted that "Evangelization in the Modern World," released about the same time, met with a thundering silence, whereas *Persona humana* " 'caused a tilt' or better a 'boom'!"[8] He regretted that truly "necessary reminders" were not more positive and global. The Belgian bishops called the document "opportune and necessary."[9] The Dutch episcopate said the document must be considered a direction pointer ("indicateur de route").[10] They hoped that the reflexion provoked by the document would produce more "positive detailed teachings pastoral in character" in the future. Coadjustor Archbishop Franz Jachym of Vienna saw the Declaration as appropriately demanding but regretted its authoritarian tone.[11] The many supportive episcopal responses may be found in *L'Osservatore romano.*[12]

In England, the *Tablet* believed the response of many Catholics would be: *cui bono?*[13] "In this country, at any rate, it cannot be described as appropriate." Theologian D. O'Callaghan thought *Persona humana* places the loyal Catholic in a dilemma: the inability to subscribe to "moral absoluteness" and "intrinsic evil" because he knows these very verdicts are being questioned in our time.[14] In Canada, Gregory Baum was critical of the document as being "legalistic morality which judges acts of faculties rather than the total functioning of the person."[15] His comments elicited an immediate response from the Archbishop of Toronto.[16] In the United States, Arthur McNally, C.P., viewed the Declaration as a "masterpiece of pastoral teaching."[17] Paul McKeever, on the contrary, argued that it fails to communicate.[18] Paul Surlis, while agreeing with the basic value judgments, regretted the lack of a positive approach.[19] *America* scored the abstract language and outdated categories.[20]

L. Kaufmann and J. David of Switzerland regretted the secrecy of the Congregation, "for which the demand for greater openness still falls on deaf ears."[21] Whatever consultation was involved or reference made to previous episcopal documents, "nothing indicates that these were mined or anything learned from them." Where adolescent masturbation is discussed, they wondered what good is achieved by mentioning the "useful data" provided by psychology while immediately narrowing the question to a "serious violation of the moral order." The tone of the document when it speaks of premarital relations is regrettable, a tone quite different from that employed by the Swiss diocesan synods. Something very similar is true of the undifferentiated discussion of homosexuality. The authors conclude that the document is dominated by a narrow view of human actions and "a static ordering of commands and prohibitions, instead of a dynamic view of the assimilation of truth and realization of values. . . ."

Roman Bleistein, S.J., associate editor of *Stimmen der Zeit,* thought that anyone concerned about the Church's authority must wonder whether its institutions are not undermining their own authority.[22] He cited the differences in *Persona humana* and several documents of the German episcopate. In the latter the findings of contemporary sciences are not overlooked, whereas the Roman document leans above all on Church tradition and uncritical use of St. Paul ("oft ohne Rücksicht auf den jeweiligen Zusammenhang").

Beyond such differences in the over-all approach, substantive differences were noted by Bleistein. For instance, where masturbation is concerned, the pastoral letter of the German bishops (*Hirtenbrief der deutschen Bischöfe zu Fragen der menschlichen Geschlechtlichkeit,* 1973) states that it cannot be approved "as a self-evident actuation of sexuality." As for premarital relations, the German synodal document (*Christlich gelebte Ehe und Familie*) states: "These relations cannot be seen as corresponding to the ethical norm." *Persona humana* is much more abstract and apodictic. Nor can these differences be reduced, according to Bleistein, to the difference between moral theology and pastoral application. "There is revealed a different mentality in the judgment of sexual behavior." In the face of such different *official* mentalities, what is the Catholic to think? Bleistein thinks that one institution (clearly he means the Congregation) is undermining authority.

If one reads the Declaration with a tranquil soul, declared *Civiltà cattolica,* one will discover that the massive objections against it are unfounded.[23] *Civiltà* cited the "moral sexual revolution" as the cause for the difficult reception *Persona humana* received. It highlighted especially the theses of S. Pfürtner, the Swiss ex-Dominican, and argued that the Church must speak out against the "grave confusion" such misleading statements cause.

Razón y fe detected a mixture of pre-Vatican II and post-Vatican II ingredients in the Declaration.[24] There is a static notion of nature, and yet an openness to anthropological evidence and a compassionate pastoral tone. If the document itself does not achieve an adequate synthesis of pre- and post-Vatican II morality, it is the responsibility of the mature Christian to do so in his/her personal life.

Jorge Mejía believed that the Latin American reaction to *Persona humana* was calmer than the Western European and American because Latin Americans have maintained a greater discernment "as to what is good and what is bad in this delicate matter of sex."[25] He defended the document as a necessary corrective to contemporary confusion and saw its chief value as a witness value to a world that has lost its bearings.

For Jose A. Llinares, O.P., the argumentation is legalistic and the style abstract, elements that distract from the Declaration's power to persuade.[26] He sees the dominant point in the document in its constant emphasis on the need of focusing on the specific circumstances of each personal case. Firmness of principle does not release pastors and educators from the duty to learn from the human sciences.

Now to some of the more detailed studies.

John Harvey, O.S.F.S., is in agreement with the moral-theological conclusions and spends most of his time on pastoral applications.[27] Working within the objectively-wrong-but-not-always-culpable perspective, Harvey shows himself a compassionate counselor. I agree with his contention that the biblical norm ("heterosexual marriage is the proper form of sexual activity") does not depend on individual texts of Scripture. I make only two points. First, against those who are cautious about using Pauline texts (because Paul was unfamiliar with the *condition* of homosexuality, as we know it in at least some cases), he remains unconvinced because "the sacred writers did not attempt to analyze personal *motives* . . ." (emphasis added). I do not believe motivation is the point under discussion. Secondly, Harvey agrees with the document's reassertion that "every direct violation of this order is objectively serious." He paints the opposite attitude as follows: "After all, what harm to God . . . is found in deliberate masturbation, occasional fornication or acts of genital homosexuality between consenting adults?" If that is all the traditional thesis (no parvity of matter in direct violations) meant, there would be less problem with it. But it says that "*every* direct violation*," and this includes even the smallest. It is *this* that most theologians and pastoral counselors deny.

Daniel Maguire first points up the values of the Declaration.[28] It stresses the reality of guilt in a time when feigned or strained innocence is fashionable. It correctly rejects the idea that science is the only legitimate way of knowing. It rejects custom as normative, takes sexual encounter seriously, etc. But all in all, Maguire believes it does not do justice "either to the subject or to the Catholic tradition." Some of Maguire's specific criticisms: (1) the Declaration was developed in secrecy and represents only one view of things; (2) methodological shortcomings (e.g., the separation of the idea of moral disorder from the notion of harm; abstractionism; aloofness from the empirical basis of ethics); (3) lack of intellectual modesty in its claims to certainty; (4) dominance of the notion of sin; (5) unrealism of expectation when dealing with homosexuality. Maguire concludes with some suggestions about "what might have been" in the document. I think his suggestions make eminent good sense.

R. P. Spitz, O.P., has a very positive reaction to the document and a very negative reaction to its critics.[29] After noting that many criticisms concerned not the principles involved but the fact that Rome recalled them, he states: "To formulate such criticisms is to admit implicitly that one finds obedience to commands repugnant, even if one holds them to be acceptable and true." Spitz agrees with the Congregation's "principal criterion" (the finality of each act), a principle "which the Church holds from revelation and an authentic interpretation of natural law." The rest of his article is deeply homiletic, e.g., that we must not lose the sense of sin, of asceticism, of sacrifice. In this sense he does not enlighten the document but deals with the attitudes and practices it was targeted against.

G. Lobo, S.J., notes that as between traditional doctrine in traditional terms and exposing it in terms appealing to the present generation, the Congregation has chosen the first.[30] He feels there is no point in lamenting the style or tone but that our challenge is to present its content more persuasively. At one key point, however, Lobo would disagree with the content of *Persona humana*. He does not accept the statement that every act of masturbation must be considered an objectively serious violation, even though it is "undesirable . . . and sinful when practiced deliberately." His conclusion: "while permissiveness leads to disastrous results, too much rigidity also leads to equally harmful consequences."

Ph. Delhaye, secretary of the International Theological Commission, has a very long defense-commentary of *Persona humana*.[31] He first takes up some of the objections leveled against it. For instance, he insists on the right of the Holy Father to use his congregations for the ordinary, day-to-day administration of the Church. To those who claim that *Persona humana* was inopportune in its concentration on three practical problems, Delhaye responds that the whole purpose of the document was quite simple: to recall the doctrine of the Church on *certain particular points* to a world fast forgetting this doctrine. To those who are allergic to use of the natural law, Delhaye explains at length the notion as found in the scholastic tradition and insists that the nature of which the Declaration speaks "is not that of the cosmos or of philosophy alone but that of the human person."

I have the sense that Delhaye is answering a fair number of unasked questions. For instance, the question is not whether the Holy Father has a right to speak out through his congregations on moral or doctrinal questions. No well-informed Catholic theologian questions this. The issue is rather the nature of the input and consultative processes involved, so that the ultimate product is one that instructs, illumines, inspires. Similarly, the question is not whether the notion of natural law is appropriate; it is rather how it is to be interpreted, with what enrichment from behavioral sciences, with what theological perspectives. One does not respond to such questions by merely pointing to the long tradition of natural-law reasoning and comparing this to certain phrases in the Declaration. Again, Delhaye's lengthy rejection of the "neosociologism" of the sciences (which all theologians would share) hardly tells us much about just how the redactors of *Persona humana* did make use of contemporary scientific studies.

Throughout his essay Delhaye argues that the Declaration is trying to walk a middle path between extremes. Item: "*Persona humana* seems to me to keep an equal distance from two extremes: that which simply rejects the fundamental option, that which makes of it an unreal thing." Item: against pseudoscientific assertions that masturbation is not only permitted but necessary, Delhaye states that the response of *Persona humana* to this propaganda is contained in two major notions. "On the one hand, it recognizes that every material deviation is not necessarily a deliberate fault; on the other, the Declaration does not accept the idea of generalized sexual irresponsibility." At this point, and in many places throughout, I have to wonder whether we are reading the same document. In other words, are not Delhaye's repeated attempts to say what the document meant and was trying to do indicative of its failure?

Bernhard Stoeckle admits the need of the document.[32] He regrets its harsh tone and believes it suffers by comparison with the documents of the German episcopate. Several pluses he admits: its attempt to be restrained in using the natural-law notions that were criticized in *Humanae vitae;* attempts to deepen traditional teaching by advertence to the work of the sciences; a certain distance from the biological and philosophical arguments used in the past. But eventually he sees its arguments as insufficient. While accepting the conclusions, he believes that the arguments would have been legitimated and solidified if the double meaning of sexual conduct had been brought within the sphere of charity (agape) to be stamped by it. In a sense, he is concretizing in this sphere his attitude toward a specific Christian ethic. In my judgment he does not succeed.

A very critical response to the Declaration was drawn up by three theologians from Tübingen: Alfons Auer, Wilhelm Korff, Gerhard Lohfink.[33] Several other members of the Catholic theological faculty of Tübingen declared their agreement with the critique: H. Küng, W. Kasper, J. Neumann, and others. The critique takes the form of a comparison between the Declaration and a working paper drawn up for the German Synod (Würzburg): *Sinn und Gestaltung menschlicher Sexualität.* When *Persona humana* appeared, the head of the German episcopal conference declared that the Declaration confirmed the Würzburg Synod's document as well as the 1973 pastoral of the German bishops. The theologians from Tübingen contest that judgment and argue that a totally different climate is present in the Congregation's document. To show this, they lift out the sharp differences between the Würzburg working paper and *Persona humana.*

The working paper begins with the results of contemporary human and social sciences. It notes that all cultures have regulated sexual behavior and that, in spite of differences and qualifications, the norms achieved two goals: (1) institutionalization of sexual relations with the principles of permanence and exclusivity; (2) the concern of the partners for each other, for the continuation and well-being of the family. In the past the social aspects took precedence; now there is more emphasis on the meaning of sexuality for self-development and for a deep partnership.

The working paper then turns its attention to the many values of human sexuality, values which it sees as playing different roles at different periods of one's life. Then the biblical and theological evidence is used to put human experience in the broader context of faith. Against such a background the working paper faces practical issues. It evaluates promiscuous sexual relations differently from those between partners who are in love and "who are decided on a permanent bond but see themselves hindered from contracting it because of reasons felt to be grave." In treating of homosexuality, it speaks of a "narrowing of existential possibilities." Adolescent masturbation is seen as a phase-specific phenomenon to be passed through without an overload of guilt.

In contrast to this, *Persona humana* is entirely deductive, from eternal, objective, universal divine laws. The Tübingen theologians argue that the Declaration misuses Scripture (an "adventitious ornament for systematic assertions"), misuses its own tradition, and does not take scientific data seriously. By its moral positivism it "excludes itself from the scientific discussion." In the end, while achieving a certain stabilizing effect, it pays too great a price: not secession, but "a retreat to a position of partial identification with the Church will present itself as the only possibility for many." They conclude their severe criticism with the insistence that "the house of the Church ought to be, for people of our time, an intellectually and ethically livable place." Of the two documents studied and compared, it is clear to them that only the working paper of the Würzburg Synod passes this test.

Bernard Häring approaches the Declaration in three steps: (1) its good points; (2) the theological presuppositions; (3) evaluation of its pastoral attitudes.[34] At the outset and repeatedly thereafter, he expresses agreement with the underlying core-value judgments ("Kernerklärung") of the document, against those who would see no moral problem in premarital relations, homosexual activity, and masturbation. Furthermore, he insists that the Church must have the courage to say unpopular things. Finally, he welcomes the reference made to the insights of the sciences in these areas.

Häring faults the document for the following theological presuppositions. There is, he argues, an ahistorical and unrealistic tone and attitude toward the magisterium and its formulation of moral truth. The use of Scripture is highly questionable. It totally neglects the distinction between a substantive value judgment and its formulation. The language, arguments, and conceptual underpinning lead to undifferentiated condemnations. The natural-law perspectives of the contemporary consultors to the Congregation are "represented as *the* constant tradition and the teaching of the Church." Häring argues that "there speaks in the document not *the* preconciliar theology, but a very distinct preconciliar theology," the type rejected by the Council in its rejection of several preliminary drafts for *Gaudium et spes.*

Häring is particularly strong in his rejection of the Declaration's presumption that individual acts, especially of masturbation, involve serious guilt. He grants that some theologians have gone too far in their reaction to an earlier rigorism; but a too facile judgment of mortal sin in sexual matters harms the faith of people. "It must never for an instant be forgotten that conversation about mortal sin, especially the mortal sins of children, is conversation about God." The image of God inseparable from the perspectives of *Persona humana* is, he believes, that of an avenging policeman. The document refers to the letter of Leo IX in which he authorized Peter

Damian's *Liber gomorrhianus* as sexual teaching clean and free from error. Of that Häring says simply: "I certainly could not believe in the God who shines through that work."

Another problem Häring finds in the document is that its argument and language fail to allow for qualitative differences in human conduct. This is true of premarital intercourse, as well as masturbation, which is rejected "regardless of the motive." Häring's ultimate judgment is harsh: "The document of the Congregation, as a whole and in its individual formulations, goes far beyond the rigorism of past times. One can say that it represents the most logical and systematic piece of teaching, in so far as it brings tightly together all previous rigoristic teachings and presents them simply as *the* tradition."

In a careful and balanced study, Charles Curran reviews some of the literature recorded here and presents his own analysis of the Declaration.[35] First, Curran, like many others, faults the lack of consultation involved in its preparation. As for the criticism that followed its issuance, Curran sees it as a sign of greater maturity in the Church, "even though one wishes the negative criticism were unnecessary." I wish this last little point had been italicized in Curran's study; for there are many people in the Church who believe that criticism stems from a desire to criticize—as if truth and the good of the faithful were not one's motive, but rather victory within an imagined adversary relationship.

Curran's critique involves methodology and substance. As for methodology, he lists eight shortcomings: e.g., the deductive character; failure to use the nature of the person as a criterion; failure to pay sufficient attention to the experience of people. He concludes here with the judgment that the Declaration is "not in keeping with what . . . is the best in Catholic theological reflection."

In his substantive criticism, Curran singles out four points. First, the notion of fundamental option in the document is a caricature. E.g., the Congregation describes the opinions of some who see mortal sin only in a formal refusal directly opposed to God's call and not in particular acts. Curran rightly wonders what theologians hold this position. He knows of none; nor do I.

Secondly, Curran deals with premarital relations. He accepts the underlying substance of the Congregation on this matter. However, there could be times when the marriage ceremony is legitimately impeded. In these cases "there does not seem to be much of a problem from a moral viewpoint, although ordinarily such a covenant of love should be publicly witnessed and proclaimed." I believe many moral theologians would agree with that judgment. There even seems to be a foundation for this in canon law (can. 1098). But to prevent deleterious understanding of it, it might be well if we moralists emphasized the relative rarity of the occurrence and then struggled to specify more concretely what these circumstances are. Otherwise, little "covenants of marital love," like *entia,* risk being multiplied and consummated on warrants all of us would reject out of hand.

Curran next turns to homosexuality. The implication of the document's approach is that the irreversible homosexual "is asked to live in accord with the charism of celibacy." He then states his own well-known approach, based on a "theory of compromise," which proposes that for the irreversible homosexual "these actions are not wrong for this individual provided there is a context of a loving commitment to another." He regards this as a conclusion "on the level of the moral order," a phrase meant to distinguish it from an objectively-wrong-but-not-always-culpable analysis as well as one which regards homosexual actions as equivalent to heterosexual ones.

Curran's most marked disagreement with the Congregation is on masturbation. *Persona humana* sees it as an intrinsically and seriously disordered act. Curran denies this. "Individual masturbatory acts seen in the context of the person and the meaning of human sexuality do not constitute such important matter . . . providing the individual is truly growing in sexual maturity and integration." He sees the Congregation's approach as theologically inaccurate, psychologically harmful, and pedagogically counterproductive, and traces this to the methodology of the document, one whose approach is "limited to an analysis apart from the person."

This latter point is important and is certainly what distinguishes, and unfortunately divides, most contemporary theologians from those writing for the Congregation. Moral norms are generalizations about the meaning of our actions. But it is clear from many sources (contemporary sciences, Vatican II, wide pastoral experience) that sexual experiences *mean* far more than genital actuations of one sort or another. For instance, as Curran notes, masturbatory acts can be symptomatic of loneliness, of sexual tension, of prolonged absence from one's marital partner, of frustrated relationships and insufficient coping mechanisms in one's daily life, of growing selfishness, etc. It is only when the actions are seen from the viewpoint of the whole person that they reveal their *meaning*. While they are always a withdrawal from the full meaning (potential) of sexual behavior (and therefore an "intrinsic disorder"), in at least many of their meanings noted above, it is highly doubtful that this individual withdrawal is serious, scil., the type of action that is calculated to provoke the mature and sensitive person to a radical existential break with the God of salvation. And that is the meaning of "serious matter."

This point can be put in another, more systematic way. Two levels of moral rectitude are involved here. One we might call the general, the other the individual. The level of general rectitude prescinds from individual intentions, dispositions, qualities, and meanings, and states an over-all requirement. Thus we say that sexual expression finds its *full* meaning in the permanent relationship of covenanted love (marriage). However, while this tells us something, and something important, about the moral quality of our actions, it does not tell us everything; for it is quite possible to be objectively immoral once the requirement of general rectitude is satisfied. That is, it is possible to be *objectively* immoral within marriage (selfish, manipulatory, inconsiderate, uncommunicative, etc.). These qualities at the individual level of rectitude tell us much about the *meaning* of our activity. They fill out the meaning of our actions by viewing them within the context of the individual person. If, as Vatican II insisted, criteria for sexual activity are to be based on "the nature of the person and his acts" (*Gaudium et spes,* no. 51), then the meaning of our actions must be drawn from all dimensions of our personal life. By speaking as it does, on the level of general rectitude only, the Congregation prescinds from many aspects of the personal that yield the meaning of our actions, and therefore is able to condemn actions and assert seriousness in an undifferentiated way that does not correspond at key points with human experience.

This is, I think, the key substantive difference between the approach of the Congregation and the commentators on its document.

At this point I refer to two episcopal pastoral letters that have come to my attention: one by Bishop Francis J. Mugavero of Brooklyn, the other by Cardinal L. J. Suenens of Malines-Brussels.[36] Both are excellent, but let me concentrate briefly on Bishop Mugavero's statement here. It is difficult to cite from the pastoral, because its achievement is one of over-all tone that emerges from the totality. The tone is positive, compassionate, and supportive; the language is simple and "American." Sexuality is seen as a great gift. "It is a relational power which includes the qualities of sensitivity, understanding, warmth, openness to persons, compassion and mutual support. Who could imagine a loving person without these qualities?" The attitude is realistic and encouraging. Mugavero states simply and straightforwardly: "If we are honest with ourselves as were the Christians who lived before us, each of us will recognize that it is not easy to integrate sexuality into our lives."

Mugavero is theologically and pastorally superb in his treatment of each of the problems treated by the Congregation. E.g., he sees in masturbation "a prime example of the complex nature of sexual behavior." He then states: "We wish to encourage people to go continually beyond themselves in order to achieve greater sexual maturity and urge them to find peace and strength in a full sacramental life with the Christ who loves them."

The treatment of premarital relations is excellent. But let me cite homosexuality as another example. Mugavero notes that anthropological, psychological, and theological reasoning all contribute to the Church's conviction that "heterosexuality is normative. All should strive for a sexual integration which respects that norm, since any other orientation respects *less adequately* [emphasis added] the full spectrum of human relationships." This is a way, I submit, of formulating a moral statement that is both continuous with the deepest value judgments of our tradition and sensitive to what we know, and do not know, about homosexuality.

Mugavero's language and tone meet people where they are. Tone, in moral matters, is not everything, but it is enormously important; for it reveals attitudes toward persons, norms, conflicts,

God, the human condition. Because this is so, tone not only affects communicability; at some point it also cuts very close to the basic value judgments themselves, as the Tübingen theologians note. That is why a document that is tonally inadequate risks being substantively incomplete or even wrong.

These are just a sampling of the reactions to *Persona humana.* One could summarize them as follows. Nearly everyone believes a prophetic but compassionate statement from the Church on human sexuality is in place. Secondly, the actual response given by the Congregation finds both defenders and critics. By and large, the defenders highlight the right of the Church to speak authoritatively, the authority of the document, the clarity of the reassertion of traditional teaching, the sensitivity of *Persona humana* to contemporary studies in the behavioral sciences, and (defensively) the fact that it was not trying to give a full theology of sexuality. The critics—and in the theological world they far outnumber the defenders—go after the process (secret) which produced the document, the dated theology and language central to it, the failure to deal with the behavioral sciences adequately, the authoritarian tone, the misuse of Scripture, and some of the pastoral applications.

Some of the reactions, particularly but not exclusively the journalistic, seem extreme, even unfair. I see their excessive character as transparent of a deep sense of failed expectations, and of a profound discomfort with the Roman way of doing things. On the other hand, some of the positive reactions were quite uncritical; they are symptomatic of a felt need "to defend Rome." My own reaction to the document is presented elsewhere.[37] I have found little to alter in that statement except to say that the burden of the literature reported here is that we are dealing with a missed opportunity.

If one's judgment is that, all things considered, the Declaration missed its target, what happened to bring this about? Some explanation is given in an interview involving James McManus, C.SS.R., Sean O'Riordan, C.SS.R., and Henry Stratton.[38] Briefly it is this. Over the years two different schools of theological approach were involved in the consultations leading to the Declaration: (1) the personalist school; (2) the traditional, norm-centered school, which begins with abstract principles and uses a deductive method.

It was found impossible to develop a coherent document based on these two different methods. "Eventually," says O'Riordan, "the modern school was dropped from consultations." The document as we have it was mainly the work of three people: E. Lio, O.F.M., Card. Pietro Palazzini, and Jan Visser, C.SS.R. According to O'Riordan, "the document reproduces in large part a chapter in a book recently published by Cardinal Palazzini on Christian life and virtue. In this book the Cardinal follows the old methodology— principles are stated, and conclusions are drawn more or less independently of human persons and the complexities of human existence."[39]

There follows an extremely interesting discussion in which O'Riordan points out the deeply compassionate and flexible viewpoint of the older theology at the pastoral level. E.g., Visser would condemn homosexual acts as intrinsically evil. Yet, in an interview in *L'Europa* (Jan. 30, 1976) Visser stated that "when one is dealing with people who are so deeply homosexual that they will be in serious personal and perhaps social trouble unless they attain a steady partnership within their homosexual lives, one can recommend them to seek such a partnership, and one accepts this relationship as the best they can do in their present situation." Visser explains this on the grounds that the lesser of two evils is often the best thing for people in a particular situation, and he would see no incompatibility between this *pastoral* attitude and adherence to the abstract principle that homosexual acts are intrinsically evil.

O'Riordan, then, was asked this question: "So, in a sense, is the good theologian of the traditional school doing in pastoral theology and pastoral practice what the personalist theologian is doing in moral theology?" His answer was: "You have defined it exactly." That is, the personalist theology is simply "working out in a theoretical way what the good pastors have always instinctively known and done."

That may be the case; but let me offer this tentative probe. That formulation so identifies normative ethics with individual *potential* that the possibility of a general normative statement all but disappears. In other words, does it not simply identify the morally right with the individually *possible*—which means that no truly normative statement is possible except for the individual? Which could mean that it is not possible at all. We can and should distinguish between an abstract and deductive way of deriving moral norms, and one anchored in persons and their acts. But is distinguishing in this way the same as identifying a normative statement (personalistically derived) with a pastoral statement? I wonder. If we say the two are the same, we have, it would seem, abandoned any possibility of generalization, scil., of ethics. Therefore, to say that "the good theologian of the traditional school is doing in pastoral theology and pastoral practice *what the personalist theologian is doing in moral theology*" (my emphasis) could destroy the possibility of normative statements. Even if one does theology out of personalist perspectives, as one ought, must there not still remain the possibility that individuals cannot achieve this personalistically derived *norm?* In other words, must we not distinguish between a moral theology derived from "the nature of the human person and his acts" and an approach that considers only this or that *particular* person and his/her *possibilities?* If we must, then there still remains a norm and a pastoral practice. I raise this only as a question, in the hope that O'Riordan and others can cast light on it in the future.

Notes

1. Texts may be found in *Catholic Mind* 74, no. 1302 (April 1976) 52–65; *Documentation catholique* 73 (1976) 108–14; *Esprit et vie* 86 (1976) 33–39; *Herder Korrespondenz* 30 (1976) 82–87; *The Pope Speaks* 21 (1976) 60–73.

2. "Document sur l'éthique sexuelle: Réactions réservées," *Informations catholiques internationales,* Feb. 15, 1976, pp. 10–12.

3. *Documentation catholique* 73 (1976) 181.

4. *Ibid.,* p. 182.

5. *Ibid.,* p. 208.

6. *Ibid.,* pp. 334–35.

7. *Ibid.,* p. 180.

8. *Ibid.,* pp. 209–10. He noted: "Il a 'fait tilt' ou mieux 'boum'! Pensez donc, il parlait du sexe!"

9. *Ibid.,* p. 210.

10. *Ibid.,* pp. 178–79.

11. Cf. *Orientierung* 40 (1976) 15.

12. Essays and supportive documents on *Persona humana* may be found in the following issues of *L'Osservatore Romano:* Jan. 29; Feb. 5, 12, 19, 26; March 4, 11, 25; April 1, 8, 15, 29; May 6, 13; July 29; Aug. 19.

13. "A Roman Declaration," *Tablet* 230 (1976) 73–75.

14. D. O'Callaghan, "Comment," *Furrow* 61 (1976) 126–29.

15. Cf. *Ecumenist* 14 (1976) 64.

16. *Ibid.,* p. 64.

17. Arthur McNally, C.P., "Sexual Ethics," *Sign* 55, no. 6 (March 1976) 4–5.

18. Paul McKeever, "Sex in the News," *Priest* 32, no. 2 (March 1976) 12–13 (an unsigned editorial).

19. Paul J. Surlis, "Theology and Sexuality," *Priest* 32, no. 10 (Oct. 1976) 42–47.

20. "Sex Declaration: Half a Loaf," *America* 134 (1976) 63.

21. J. David and L. Kaufmann, "Zur Erklärung der Glaubenskongregation," *Orientierung* 40 (1976) 14–15.

22. Roman Bleistein, S.J., "Kirchliche Autorität im Widerspruch," *Stimmen der Zeit* 101 (1976) 145–46.

23. "Sessuofobia o difesa dell'uomo? La Chiesa e la sessualità," *Civiltà cattolica* 127 (1976) 209–17 (editorial).

24. "Sexualidad y moral cristiana," *Razón y fe,* no. 938, March 1976, pp. 198–201.

25. Jorge Mejia, "La Declaración de la Santa Sede sobre la ética sexual," *Criterio* 49 (1976) 110–12.

26. J. A. Llinares, "Etica sexual y magisterio de la Iglesia," *Ciencia tomista* 103 (1976) 465–78.

27. John F. Harvey, O.S.F.S., "Pastoral Insights on 'Sexual Ethics,' " *Pastoral Life* 25, no. 4 (April 1976) 2–8.

28. Daniel C. Maguire, "The Vatican on Sex," *Commonweal* 103 (1976) 137–40.

29. R. P. Spitz, O.P., "A propos de la déclaration de la Sacrée Congrégation pour la Doctrine de la Foi," *Pensée catholique,* no. 161 (March–April 1976) 11–19.

30. G. Lobo, S.J., "Document—Declaration on Sexual Ethics," *Vidyajyoti* 40 (1976) 269–77.

31. Ph. Delhaye, "A propos de 'Persona humana,' " *Esprit et vie* 86 (1976) 177–86, 193–204, 225–34.

32. Bernhard Stoeckle, "Erklärung zu einigen Fragen der Sexualethik," *Internationale katholische Zeitschrift* 5 (1976) 256–61.

33. Alfons Auer *et al.,* "Zweierlei Sexualethik," *Theologische Quartalschrift* 156 (1976) 148–58.

34. B. Häring, "Reflexionen zur Erklärung der Glaubenskongregation über einige Fragen der Sexualethik," *Theologisch-praktische Quartalschrift* 124 (1976) 115–26.

35. Charles E. Curran, "Sexual Ethics: Reaction and Critique," *Linacre Quarterly* 43 (1976) 147–64.

36. Francis J. Mugavero, "Sexuality—God's Gift: A Pastoral Letter," *Catholic Mind* 74, no. 1303 (May 1976) 53–58; L. J. Suenens, "Amour et sexualité aujourd'hui," *Documentation catholique* 73 (1976) 679–90.

37. Richard A. McCormick, S.J., Sexual Ethics—An Opinion," *National Catholic Reporter,* Jan. 30, 1976, and *Theologie der Gegenwart* 19 (1976) 72–76.

38. J. McManus, Sean O'Riordan, and Henry Stratton, "The 'Declaration on Certain Questions concerning Sexual Ethics': A Discussion," *Clergy Review* 61 (1976) 231–37.

39. *Ibid.,* p. 232.

39. Human Experience and Women's Experience: Resources for Catholic Ethics

Susan L. Secker

This article first appeared in *The Annual,* The Society of Christian Ethics, in 1991.

A frequent question I encounter among contemporary North American Catholics is something like the following: "I consider myself to be a good Catholic, but how can I follow my Church's teachings when they do not speak to my experience?" While this question is asked by women and men alike, in more recent years it has become a constant refrain among Catholic women—as the initial draft of the United States bishops' pastoral letter on women's concerns attests.[1] Many women claim that they simply cannot connect their own experience with many of the official teachings of the Roman Catholic Church concerning sexual and biomedical ethics. Sociological studies corroborate this anecdotal evidence of a considerable and growing discrepancy between the "moral sense" of thoughtful lay Catholics and the moral teachings of the Magisterium.[2]

Among American Catholic ethicists there has been a parallel tendency to accord experience a more central role in moral reflection, and ecclesial events suggest that the effort by scholars to be attentive to experience in their ethics produces ecclesiastical ramifications. For example, one thinks of the meeting in Rome between the pope and representative American bishops during which a Curial official identified the influence of "radical feminism" as an area of Vatican concern regarding the health of the American Church.[3] Another example is the censure of Milwaukee's Archbishop apparently because of his listening sessions to women's experience on abortion.[4] One has to wonder whether the fate of the U.S. bishops' pastoral on women's concerns resulted from its willingness to take seriously women's experience.[5] Appeals to human experience, especially as descriptive of women's experience, constitute a double-edged challenge to Catholic ethics: one substantive and the other procedural. From the perspective of those Catholic ethicists focusing their scrutiny on the function of human experience as an ethical resource, the challenge is a substantive one. That is, the end-result of their scholarship lies in articulating with greater precisions what can be known about human existence and how this knowledge ought to function in defining moral agency and in constructing ethical norms. On the other side, the Vatican response views the challenge as one questioning the authoritative teaching role of the Magisterium. Thus, the significance of the research of these ethicists is reduced to the differing ethical positions their arguments produce rather than to their substantive contributions to Catholic moral wisdom.

Why is there such a gap between what American Catholics mean when they appeal to experience and its meaning in hierarchical ethics? Why have the efforts of American Catholic ethicists to close this gap precipitated not only theoretical resistance but ecclesiastical censure? This is puzzling in an ethical tradition which has consistently maintained that the human reality is a preeminent source from within which to construct normative ethical frameworks. One expects from that tradition continued efforts accurately to describe the salient features of the human reality and adequately to prescribe its normative character.

The purpose of this essay is to explore these questions. What do American Catholic ethicists mean when they appeal to human experience as a source for ethics? Derivatively, what do Catholic feminists mean when they appeal to women's experience as an ethical source? What is its methodological function? Finally, what conclusions can be drawn in suggesting implications for Catholic moral reasoning?

In what follows I will pursue these questions by turning to the work of Lisa Sowle Cahill and Margaret A. Farley, two Catholic ethicists whose writings on sexual and biomedical ethics emphasize the role of human experience in general, and of women's experience in particular.[6] I will begin by providing a conceptual framework from within which to clarify the function of human experience. Second, I will show that Cahill and Farley appeal to experience in ways that illustrate different ethical functions. Finally, in drawing conclusions from their use of human experience, I will sketch some implications for the reformulation of Catholic ethics.

HUMAN EXPERIENCE: DESCRIPTIVE ACCURACY AND NORMATIVE ADEQUACY

Since the term *human experience* is employed ambiguously in the ethical literature, the following distinctions may prove helpful. The appeal to human experience functions in two different ways in ethical reflection. *First,* one finds empirically-based descriptions of the way things are. To appeal to human experience in this way is to attempt to achieve complete and reliable information about human persons and societies as a foundation for moral judgment. For example, an ethical evaluation of homosexuality first requires a comprehensive and unbiased examination of the fullest possible factual evidences (i.e., the psycho-social and biological features of homosexual human reality). In developing a full understanding of the situation, the ethicist may appeal to one or both of two different sources of information about experience: (1) knowledge which is public and consensual such as that provided by the human, natural, and social sciences, and (2) personal reports of individuals concerning the situation in which they find themselves and about which they can provide firsthand reflection; this is often referred to as "lived experience" or "personal story." The ethicist uses information from these sources to establish factually accurate characterizations of human persons and of their socio-cultural and politico-economic contexts, clarifying "what is." Once this kind of descriptive accuracy is achieved, sound ethical judgments can be made.

There is in the ethical literature a *second* and entirely different appeal to human experience. In usages of the second type, claims about experience are not introduced in order to clarify the factual aspects of the human situation about which an ethical evaluation is to be made. Rather, appeals to human experience are introduced to provide normative criteria according to which judgments can be made about situations once they are accurately and fully understood. In this form of ethical appeal, the ethicist attempts to conceptualize the very meaning of the human person as an aspect of human experience. The ethicist seeks to identify features of the human which are so fundamental that normative ethical arguments cannot ignore them. Experience in this sense (or some particular way of construing experience) functions as an ethical authority, i.e., as a type of truth claim.

Traditionally, this sort of ethical appeal characterized a kind of natural law reasoning. At the heart of that system was a presumption that there is a certain agreed-upon conception of the essential nature of the human person and of human experience which can be universalized. In the light of that normative conception, ethical positions are developed and ethical judgments are made. Indeed, in past centuries, those employing a normative concept of the nature of the human person or of human experience did not inquire from whence their conception arose; they took it to be self-evident truth. As Charles Curran has argued, such a classical worldview is no longer satisfactory to contemporary persons.[7] Critical studies and cross-cultural research have produced a quite different consciousness of reality. We are much more likely to develop our conceptions of the human person and human experience from within particular and identifiable sets of experiences and from within a particular cultural and communal tradition. The appeal to experience as a normative authority is therefore more problematic and often more contested. What it requires is more careful attentiveness to the particularity of the nature of human persons and human experience prior to normative universal claims.

In appealing to human experience as a norm governing moral judgments, the ethicist may employ one or both of two distinct knowledge sources: (1) authoritative claims arising from various philosophical and theological anthropologies, and (2) the collective wisdom of ordinary people based on commonalities discovered in their shared experience from which normative notions about the human reality are developed. This notion that moral weight should be given to the untutored moral reasoning of ordinary particular people is new and controversial. While this might appear to mistakenly legitimize idiosyncratic, egocentric, or subjectivist claims as normative, the force of this appeal to experience is actually quite different. In attending to the actual moral judgments people make about themselves and their experience, the ethicist is attending to a form of wisdom that is socially influenced and communally generated and that is thus shaped by the values of a religious and philosophical tradition.[8] At the same time, it constitutes a way of knowing human existence which has not been adequately captured by either philosophical or theological anthropologies. That is, it captures features of the normatively human which spring from attentiveness to particularities (i.e., of culture, race, gender, class, and sexual orientation). This type argues that patterns of meaning can be constructed from the collective reflections on their experience of groups whose perspectives have been previously absent from both theological and philosophical anthropologies.[9] Thus, the claim is that reflections of women, of persons from African, Hispanic, and Asian heritage, and of gay and lesbian persons, must be included within a conception of the normatively human.

Those who utilize human experience in this way are not content with correcting our understanding of the situation in which right action must be defined; the point of this usage is to correct the criteria and rules that guide moral judgment and define moral agency by refining them in light of an adequate conception of normative human reality. Further, since the historically received conception of the normatively human was formed by Western, celibate, highly educated and affluent men on the basis of men's experience, these thinkers insist that it now has to be adjusted. Within this generalized framework I now proceed to its illustration in the thought of Cahill and Farley.

THE FUNCTION OF EXPERIENCE IN THE WORK OF CAHILL AND FARLEY

First, I will examine the empirical function of appeals to human experience, showing that both Cahill and Farley have not only adjusted their ethics to take account of the findings of the human sciences but have also developed methods of moral analysis that require taking account of the concrete context of particular moral agents. Following that, I will explore the normative function of appeals to experience, concentrating on the special importance of attending to women's experience. This criterio-logical use of human experience (especially women's experience), which is present in Farley's ethics and absent from Cahill's writings, constitutes the most critical challenge to Catholic ethics. When taken seriously, it seems to put in question the possibility of a universalized notion of the normatively human in ways that the descriptive use does not.

Understanding the empirical usage of human experience requires locating it within Cahill's and Farley's ethical methodologies. Cahill's distinctive methodological contribution lies in the extent to which the four traditional Catholic sources (the Bible, tradition, philosophical accounts of the ideal or essential humanity, and descriptive accounts of the empirical sciences) critically correlate in a mutually corrective manner. Indeed, she contends that the standard of adequacy for Catholic ethics lies in "fidelity to these four mutually correcting sources, and success in judiciously balancing them."[10] According to Cahill, problems commonly arise when ethical argument exhibits (1) reliance on only one or two sources or (2) failure to place the sources in dialogue.[11] This does not preclude historical and cultural particularities from requiring an emphasis on one or two sources in order to correct past neglect or partial consideration. In fact, she argues that today "experience"—that is, descriptive empirical accounts—is the source requiring emphasis, especially in regard to sexual ethics.[12]

The distinguishing feature of Farley's sexual ethics is the importance which she attaches to the constitutive features of *concrete* human reality. Epistemological questions are in the forefront of her ethical contribution, whereas the focus of Cahill's writings is methodological. According to Farley, the way humans come to know the moral depends upon the way we define and circumscribe the human reality in which the moral becomes intelligible. Differences in ethical positions are thus importantly dependent upon what factors are understood accurately to describe and adequately to prescribe human reality. Such concrete factors as personal, relational, socioeconomic and cultural contexts, as well as the way these are embedded structurally in thought and institutions, constitute its proper delineation.[13] Failure to take into account the fullness and complexity of experience that these factors represent is the major weakness of Catholic sexual ethics in particular, but of ethical discourse in general. For Farley, the standard of adequacy is met in Catholic ethics when the traditional sources are interpreted in accord with fidelity to human reality, concretely defined.[14]

DESCRIBING "WHAT IS": EMPIRICAL EVIDENCES ON THE CONTEXT OF CHOICE

To take experience seriously as an ethical source means, for both thinkers, incorporating empirically accurate information about "what is" into moral reasoning about "what ought to be." The importance of this strategy and its impact on their way of thinking about moral problems only becomes clear, however, when we notice what sort of factual knowledge they are determined to take into account: knowledge about the systemic pressures, organizational structures, and social patterns that create the unchosen context within which individual agents struggle to make moral choices. Some illustrations will make this clear.

The use of information about human experience derived from the natural, human, and social sciences can be seen in Farley's critique of the narrow scope of the ethical discourse surrounding abortion.[15] She argues that the debate neglects precisely those elements of concrete reality which often encompass the moral situation, i.e., the socio-economic and institutional dimensions. The choice for or against an abortion confronts women not in abstraction, but in a social and relational context which itself is a component part of the full moral description. The object of ethical analysis cannot be limited to the choice itself, independent of contextual characteristics. With respect to the ethics of abortion, Farley's emphasis upon the "concrete" character of human reality means that what must be assessed in the moral calculus includes: (1) the ambiguity of fetal status; (2) the socio-economic, cultural, and religious influences both on views of human sexuality and marriage, and also on views of the nature of women; (3) the complex and intimate nature of women's experience of pregnancy; and (4) the larger social reality within which pregnancies occur.[16]

Vigilance regarding these features of experience leads Farley to the conclusion that the entire discussion needs to be recast. She develops a "beyond abortion" position, arguing for values and structures which transform relational definitions for both women and men and which are conducive to mutuality in child-rearing. Critical to Farley's argument is the formative influence upon moral agency of the way in which dimensions of the social context are interstructured.[17] Taking experience seriously therefore broadens the context within which moral imperatives emerge.[18] Further, it widens the scope of moral scrutiny. Thus, if contemporary Catholic ethics is to be in continuity with the tradition's emphasis on discernment of the natural law, recognizing the concrete character of the complex situation within which a woman weighs the morality of abortion (i.e., accurate information about the personal *and* social dimensions of human reality) has implications for prescriptive judgments.[19]

Farley highlights for Catholic ethics the consequences of appealing to human experience abstractly instead of contextually. In her essay "The Church and the Family," she examines the notion of family life advanced by John Paul II in *Familiaris consortio,* using it to provide an example of the problems which result from abstract conceptions of human realities. In her view he misses the mark in his description of the problems which challenge contemporary families. A concrete accounting of contemporary family life necessitates an emphasis on socio-economic and sociological evidences. For example, there are embedded in official Catholic ethics certain presumptions about parenting, family, and sexual love within a married relationship that are often irrelevant to "the questions and struggles which characterize the lives of individuals and families."[20] The real challenge to family morality may not be, as John Paul II asserts, a "contraceptive mentality." Careful attention to concrete particularities may rather reveal "a real powerlessness before vast economic and social forces outside the family" (51). In addition, he neglects to give due weight to such factors as the implications for family morality of sexism and the mounting evidences of domestic violence against women. The Church document is flawed to the extent that it does not take these features of experience into account. The ethical effect is that solutions are proposed which strike many Catholic families as addressing another reality (66–71).

Cahill's thought reveals a similar descriptive function for human experience. "Experience" is not accurately accounted for without data describing the interpersonal and social contexts of choice.[21] For instance, an accurate moral delineation of marriage, and of women's role in marriage, necessitates examining the socio-cultural factors which bear upon presuppositions about how marriage and women are defined. Official ethical positions which leave unexamined the undergirding patriarchal worldviews no longer reflect the reality for Western women.[22]

DESCRIBING "WHAT IS": THE VOICE OF THE MORAL AGENT

In striving to establish a complete and reliable appreciation of the situation that requires moral action, both Cahill and Farley appeal to another dimension of experience: reflections of persons on their actual lived realities, i.e., Cahill's "personal story" and Farley's "contemporary human experience."[23] It is important to stress that neither thinker means to give ethical credibility to subjective whims and desires.[24] Rather, they mean to take seriously particular experiential reports which are representative of a generalized reality. Though less systematic than scientific knowledge, this type of knowledge nonetheless functions in Farley's and Cahill's methodologies as empirical characterization of "what is." Several examples will serve to illustrate this function.

Cahill insists that marital experience (especially the reflections by women on their personal experience) must become an operative dialogical component in re-thinking Catholic ethical teaching. Her rationale is that the experience of married women (and men) relative to the role of children within their married relationship, and with respect to the place of the conjugal act within their sexual lives, simply does not match the "romanticized" presuppositions about married life that ground the official teachings of the Church. The presumptions about married life on the basis of which the Church constructs its ethical norms diverges disturbingly from the presumptions on the basis of which married persons themselves proceed to ethical considerations. This is especially the case for women. As an illustration, Cahill points to the Vatican document on reproductive ethics. She contents that the instruction appeals to a consensus on the meaning of marriage, sex, and parenthood which does not exist. Its argumentation is not persuasive because its underlying assumptions about married experience are inaccurate portrayals of reality. Indeed, she claims that the instruction's notion of married reality seems "almost naive."[25]

Similarly, Farley argues that Catholic family ethics would be more adequate if the actual stories of married persons served as sources in defining the moral questions which need attention. In fact, Farley argues that such problematic realities as family violence, tensions between partners, alienation of children and elderly, have ethical significance. This experience demonstrates that the family is a place where questions of justice are integral to notions of human dignity. It is imperative that Catholic ethical norms reflect an accurate account of the contemporary experience of family living.[26]

In summary, both Cahill and Farley appeal to empirical knowledge about human experience as they stress descriptive accuracy in analyzing the concrete case preliminary to the task of constructing prescriptive judgments. As Cahill argues, experience in this empirical sense constitutes a "window onto the normative."[27] Methodologically, its chief ethical function lies in its stress upon factual accuracy concerning the human reality under moral scrutiny. However, this methodological move has implications that extend beyond its value in sharpening the skill and wisdom with which we reason practically about particular cases. The work of both women is distinctive in the attention and emphasis given to the way in which the larger socio-economic and cultural contexts shape moral agency. This gives their work a critical edge in relation to existing Catholic moral teachings. What their work makes clear is the fact that an agent's range of moral choices is impacted by social factors in ways that official Catholic ethics has not yet fully recognized. To the degree that Catholic ethics is not cognizant of this fact, Catholic ethics is impaired in its ability accurately to describe contemporary moral situations in

Western culture. Moreover, Cahill and Farley make it plain that a person's self-understanding and worth—especially a woman's self-understanding and worth—are formed by these contextual factors in morally significant ways. For example, motherhood and a woman's moral obligations as a married partner have been importantly shaped by society and culture within worldviews which are now subject to critical scrutiny. For this reason, empirical examination of contemporary human experience (perhaps especially women's experience) can be expected to qualify the ethical role of biblical and theological texts which were themselves products of socio-cultural presuppositions. As I will argue in the next section, Farley gives this second implication a normative significance relative to the meaning of human dignity that Cahill does not.

WOMEN'S EXPERIENCE AND THE NORMATIVELY HUMAN

Going beyond the empirical function of human experience, Farley's ethics exemplifies a second and entirely different use of human experience. Unlike the previous form, this usage is specifically exemplified by appeals to women's experience. Farley argues that features of women's experience, if taken seriously, would alter the very moral norms that are being brought to bear in particular judgments. Women's experience brings into view a dimension of personhood which the theological tradition has ignored, distorted, or falsely characterized in its construal of the normatively human.[28] Here the appeal to experience grounds constitutive claims about human reality which differ materially and structurally from the role appeals to experience play in correcting empirical description. There are basic convictions persons have about their concrete reality, about their personhood (e.g., convictions women have about what it means to be a woman and fully human) which are so integral to our self-understanding that to deny them is tantamount to contradicting our own truth. These convictions spring from intrinsic values rooted in fundamental understandings of personhood. They reflect our understanding of the human *qua* human. Ethical appeals based on a notion of personhood which violates women's intrinsic self-understanding—i.e., our "experience" in this normative sense —cannot be legitimately claimed to have authority, even if such appeals are grounded in Scripture or theological tradition.[29]

Farley's argument here is consistent with natural law reasoning. An adequate notion of human reality must be concretely formed; abstract conceptions are deficient. Hence women's reality, adequately conceived, must accord with basic convictions women come to about ourselves in the context of sharing our life narratives.[30] As such, women's experience must have an authoritative function in interpreting biblical and theological sources, a function which she claims is in continuity with that of human experience within the Bible itself and throughout the development of the theological tradition.[31] The result is that Farley suggests a twofold hermeneutical function for women's experience. Negatively, borrowing from Rosemary Radford Ruether, she claims that "Whatever diminishes or denies the full humanity of women must be presumed not to reflect the divine or an authentic relation to the divine, or to reflect the authentic nature of things, or to be the message or work of an authentic redeemer or a community of redemption."[32] Positively, she calls for an objective construal of the normatively human which is inclusive of women's understanding of women's personhood as a component part of human personhood.

Women's experience in this sense has critical implications for official Catholic ethical teachings. It brings into sharp relief the partiality of its universalist presuppositions about the human and calls into question the normative standards built on these presuppositions.[33] Put simply, Farley argues that Catholic natural law principles were developed by men, built upon men's experience, and designed in large part to guide men's behavior. Refusal to recognize the limited character of such claims violates an adequate notion of women's humanity and perpetuates an objective conception of human reality which is distorted.

With this in mind, Farley outlines the distinctive features of a different Catholic ethics. Biblical images (such as the *imago Dei* and the New Testament love command) and the theological concepts which ground the Catholic notion of human dignity are rejected when they legitimate notions about women's concrete reality which diminish or deny this sense of women's experience. They are retrieved when they can be reformulated as positive ideals for a more comprehensive notion of humanity, i.e., when they incorporate this sense of women's self-understanding.[34] For example, ethical interpretations of human sexuality have employed these symbols so as to distort conceptions of women's nature and our gender roles. Such distortions demand conscious correction. Further, theological doctrines have supported notions of evil which identified women with defilement and sin. Within internal ecclesiastical practices these have grounded policies which exclude women from leadership roles and thus from full ecclesial participation.[35]

Farley asserts that women's lived experience—that is, knowledge gained from living as women—provides a perspective upon human reality which is itself a source for moral truth.[36] Women's experience in this sense supports and compels a critique of the philosophical principles defining the meaning of human dignity. For example, modern liberal philosophy's principles of equality and autonomy require corrective modification from the vantage point of women's concrete reality. This means that definitions of persons as autonomous agents must be qualified through the addition of principles of human embodiedness and relationality. Human sociality implies modes of relationality which must be refined by principles of basic equality and mutuality.

On the other hand, this sense of women's experience requires that social theories which emphasize organic notions of society and human relationality be modified by the inclusion of principles of autonomy and worth which transcend gender roles. Finally, insistence on basic human equality must be further specified by a principle of equitable sharing, so that equality is construed to demand more than the protection of individual rights to freedom. It requires a positive right to participation in an equitable share of the world's goods and in human solidarity.[37]

Farley's central thesis is that these normative philosophical principles, when corrected in light of the concrete character of women's reality, constitute *in combination* the normative content of full human dignity. These principles function negatively to qualify or reject past normative formulations when such formulations represent women's personhood as derivative of or complementary to that of men, and thus only partially included in the universal claims about the meaning of human personhood.[38] Positively, women's realization of the disparity between our own experience and the claims of past theological and ethical teachings inspires efforts to reformulate the content of the teachings.[39] These efforts have produced a more adequate (meaning inclusive) view of the normatively human.

Human reality is *accurately defined* by the inclusion of comprehensive empirical evidence; it is *adequately defined* by developing philosophical notions of personhood which reflect the fullness of human experience, as opposed to partial or mistaken claims about intrinsic human dignity and worth. Arriving at ethical norms for human reality thus requires attentiveness to what can be factually known about human existence *and* to what can be argued as intrinsic to it. For Farley, therefore, the concrete character of human existence means ethical norms must give justice to, or be fitting in regard to, human reality concretely depicted.[40] Women's experience illustrates this second type of normative sense for human experience thus constituting the more radical challenge to Catholic ethics.

IMPLICATIONS FOR CATHOLIC ETHICS

What implications for Catholic ethics can be drawn from the arguments that more attention must be paid to human experience in defining moral issues and that the distinctive experience of women not only must be taken seriously but also will require significant adjustments in the normative criteria that Church teachings have traditionally employed? Several methodological implications emerge. First, in regard to the descriptive type of appeals, attentiveness to the empirically accurate means greater appreciation for the role of the particular in the process of constructing the ethically normative. Empirically-based descriptions which include an assessment of socio-economic and cultural particularity must be the starting point from which to proceed to dialogue with the Bible, the theological content of the tradition, and normative philosophical views. Both Cahill and Farley argue that factual accuracy in describing human experience is instrumental in correcting distorted conceptions of situations to which moral principles are then applied. Human experience in this sense must be embraced as a necessary component in the Catholic ethical process; as such, it functions in a corrective role providing reliable evidences in relation to which biblical, theological, and philosophical views can then proceed to moral assessment. Treating empirical accounts dialectically prevents Catholic ethics from embracing absolute norms. In some instances, it justifies judging some human situations as only capable of limited realizations of the ethically ideal. Thus, this type of appeal has an important function at the level of specifying the normative ideal. Empirical data, for example, back an ethical norm which recognizes that the best possible realization of committed sexual relationships may involve for some fidelity to part of that norm.[41]

Further, in its evidence gathering, an adequate Catholic ethics must take into account more than the *personal* circumstances of an action. Ethics must attend to the *contextual features,* i.e., not only the relational factors of person's lives, but also the socio-economic and cultural factors which function in formative ways to circumscribe a notion of moral agency. The proper focus of evaluation is thus very considerably broadened. Human experience as empirically defined is not in and of itself ethically determinative; rather, the empirical description functions as a corrective element or as the imperative *concrete* starting point in the ethical reflection process. Catholic ethical teachings which do not consider in serious ways accurate scientific information and commonly held wisdom are inadequate because their evidence base is inaccurate.

A final implication of this descriptive type of appeal is an ecclesiological one. Attention to *what* is claimed about human reality requires a concomitant attentiveness to *who* does the claiming. Who names human experience? According to what criteria? By whom is experience interpreted? These questions are importantly connected to the ethical principles which result. Thus, whose voice has access and influence in the formulation of moral teachings has decisive impact on the content of those teachings. It is therefore imperative for Catholic ethics that the means by which official ethical teachings are developed and revised be critically examined.[42]

Farley has pointed out the inadequacies of official Catholic ethics in its normative anthropological moorings. The way women's experience functions in her ethics rivets our intellectual scrutiny on a central claim of Catholic natural law methodology. Such a method claims that there are features of being human which are universally shared and which can be appealed to as a common ground basis from which to construct objective standards. What Farley's appeal to women's experience highlights is the necessity of first clarifying the constitutive features of human diversity in its *concrete* historicality and culturally conditioned particularity *before* moving to claims about what is universally shared.

Such an argument for a truly inclusive construal of the normatively human is buttressed by considerable social-scientific research. For example, Carol Gilligan's work has shown how women experience a self-consciousness which differs from men's in that it is a product of social and relational formation in quite gender-specific ways.[43] Mary Field Belenky and her research associates have demonstrated how economic and cultural factors are interstructured in such a way that they block even a minimal sense of moral agency in some women.[44] Their work has confirmed that relationality and connected knowing are characteristic for many women of our moral development processes and, hence, of our way of arriving at moral truth.

Further, this insight is supported by many contemporary theologians who make analogous appeals to this normative and authoritative sense for women's experience. For example, Susan Brooks Thistlethwaite terms it, "truth-in-action," by which she means truth which emerges in the context of a communitarian practice but which does not too quickly move to harmonize the differences of race and class.[45] Indeed, Thistlethwaite, Bell Hooks, Katie Geneva Cannon, and Ada Maria Isasi-Diaz caution against the danger of making universal claims for all women when such claims may properly be characteristic of only white, middle-class, educated women.[46]

My final observation about the import of Farley's use of women's experience for Catholic ethics relates to the Catholic women whose claims about finding their own moral reflections absent in their Church's teachings prompted this essay. It is clarified in reference to a recent report of the International Theological Commission in Rome. The commission asserts that a key component of feminist thought consists in a shift in the hermeneutical center. According to them, feminism shifts the center from the truth of revelation (the truth of being) to the particularity of experience.[47] This claim is superficially plausible but untrue; what contemporary Catholic women are asserting when we claim Church teaching does not resonate with our experience is more nuanced than the report recognizes. Our claim is that women's experience must be a component part of the theological locus within which the content of revelation is discovered. Because past interpretations of revelation have not taken this source into account and have indeed constructed theological claims on what were only erroneously presumed to be universal features of human reality, these interpretations now require redefinition and rearticulation. Therefore, in our view, the hermeneutical center has not shifted in our arguments. Its meaning has rather been expanded upon and deepened. Appeals to women's experience call for redefinitions which broaden the perspective on the intrinsically human and underscore the component voices which an inclusive conception must represent. In other words, to use the report's language, the constitutive features of "being" require the richness of particularity in the process of capturing the commonalities which must undergird any universal claims. The focus must therefore be precisely upon those aspects of revelation which heretofore have either ignored, or falsely characterized, what can be claimed to be true about the human, and by analogy, the divine.

For Catholic ethics to attend with care to the experience of women does not necessarily imply the impossibility of objective standards. Nor is it fair to construe our claims as "radical," if by this is meant that they are dangerous threats to our common faith. On the contrary, incorporating the particularity of women's experience as an ingredient element of human experience outlines the conditions for the possibility of an objective standard and hence for the truth claims of Catholic tradition. The women whose lives and reflections on experience initially motivated my reflections are far from being "radical" Catholics. What forces women to the margins is a hierarchical unwillingness of Church leadership to heed our wisdom regarding the content of Catholic ethics and to incorporate our voices and perspectives into the process of its formulation. The fact is that women's experience in this authoritative sense constitutes for the Church a locus of truth about features of the normatively human which our heightened consciousness of our own integrity will not permit us to deny.

Notes

1. United States Conference of Catholic Bishops, "Partners in the Mystery of Redemption: A Pastoral Response to Women's Concerns for Church and Society," *Origins* 17/45 (April 21, 1988): 757–88; and "One in Christ Jesus: A Pastoral Response to the Concerns of Women for Church and Society," *Origins* 19/44 (April 5, 1990): 717–40.

2. See Andrew Greeley's interpretation of the General Social Survey Data as gathered by the National Opinion Research Center at the University of Chicago in *American Catholics Since the Council: An Unauthorized Report* (Chicago: Thomas More, 1985); Joseph Gremillion and Jim Castelli's summary of the data gathered by the Notre Dame Study of Catholic Parish Life in *The Emerging Parish: The Notre Dame Study of Catholic Life since Vatican II* (San Francisco: Harper & Row, 1987; George Gallup, Jr., and Jim Castelli, *The American Catholic People: Their Beliefs, Practices and Values* (New York: Doubleday, 1987).

3. See *Origins* 18/41 (March 23, 1989): 678–96, and *Origins* 18/42 (March 30, 1989): 697–728.

4. See "Listening Sessions on Abortion: A Response," *Origins* 20/3 (May 31, 1990): 34–39; Peter Steinfels, "Vatican Bars Swiss University from Honoring Archbishop of Milwaukee," *New York Times,* November 11, 1990, 12.

5. See "Vote on Women's Pastoral Delayed," *Origins* 20/10 (September 27, 1990): 250–51.

6. The question of whether or not there is a difference in appeals thinkers make in regard to human experience and women's experience is an important one for ethics. I argue that its importance hinges on whether the

appeals function descriptively or normatively. If thinkers tend to use experience descriptively in the sense of providing reliable factual information about human reality, then the terms can be employed interchangeably. If, however, a thinker uses the term to express a normative claim about the intrinsic features of human persons, then the distinction between women's experience and men's experience is pivotal to their arguments.

7. Charles E. Curran, *Directions in Fundamental Moral Theology* (Notre Dame: University of Notre Dame Press, 1985), 169–70.

8. See James M. Gustafson, *Ethics from a Theocentric Perspective,* vol. 1, *Theology and Ethics* (Chicago: University of Chicago Press, 1981), 129.

9. I am indebted to Marilyn Frye's method of pattern perception as a way to capture new webs of meaning from the diversity which constitutes women's experience. See Marilyn Frye, "The Possibility of Feminist Theory" in *Theoretical Perspectives on Sexual Difference,* ed. Deborah L. Rhode (New Haven: Yale University Press, 1990), 174–84.

10. Lisa Sowle Cahill, *Between the Sexes: Foundations for a Christian Ethics of Sexuality* (Philadelphia: Fortress Press, 1985), 6. See also Thomas A. Shannon and Lisa Sowle Cahill, *Religion and Artificial Reproduction: An Inquiry into the Vatican "Instruction on Respect for Human Life"* (New York: Crossroad, 1988), 25.

11. As an example of the too narrow approach, Cahill cites the 1975 Vatican *Declaration on Certain Questions Concerning Sexual Ethics;* see Lisa Sowle Cahill, "Moral Methodology: A Case Study," in *A Challenge to Love: Gay and Lesbian Catholics in the Church,* ed. Robert Nugent (New York: Crossroad, 1986), 79. For a discussion of the failure to place the sources in dialogue, see Cahill, *Between the Sexes,* 5.

12. Lisa Sowle Cahill, "Community and Couple: Parameters of Marital Commitment in Catholic Tradition," in *Commitment to Partnership: Explorations of the Theology of Marriage,* ed. William P. Roberts (New York: Paulist Press, 1987), 82–83.

13. Margaret A. Farley, *Personal Commitments: Making, Keeping, Breaking* (San Francisco: Harper & Row, 1986), 82.

14. Margaret A. Farley, "An Ethic for Same-Sex Relations," in *A Challenge to Love: Gay and Lesbian Catholics in the Church,* ed. Robert Nugent (New York: Crossroad, 1986), 99; and Farley, *Personal Commitments,* 82.

15. Margaret A. Farley, "Liberation, Abortion and Responsibility," in *On Moral Medicine: Theological Perspectives in Medical Ethics,* ed. Stephen E. Lammers & Allen Verhey (Grand Rapids, Mich.: William B. Eerdmans, 1987), 434–38. For similar examples of this empirical type of claim, see Margaret A. Farley, "Sources of Sexual Inequality in the History of Christian Thought," *Journal of Religion* 56 (April 1976): 162–76; Margaret

A. Farley, "New Patterns of Relationship: Beginnings of a Moral Revolution," *Theological Studies* 36/4 (1975): 627–46; Margaret A. Farley, "The Church and Family: An Ethical Task" *Horizons* 10/1 (1983): 50–71; Margaret A. Farley, "An Ethic for Same-Sex Relations," in *A Challenge to Love,* ed. Nugent, 93–106.

16. Farley, "Liberation, Abortion and Responsibility," in *On Moral Medicine,* ed. Lammers and Verhey, 436–37.

17. Anne Carr develops this in "Women, Justice and the Church," *Horizons* 17/2 (Fall 1990): 269–79.

18. Margaret A. Farley, "Moral Discourse in the Public Arena," in *Vatican Authority and American Catholic Dissent,* ed. William W. May (New York: Crossroad, 1987), 174.

19. Farley, "An Ethic for Same-Sex Relations," 98.

20. Farley, "The Church and Family," 51. For an English translation of *Familiaris consortio,* see John Paul II, *Apostolic Exhortation on the Family* (Washington, D.C.: United States Catholic Conference, 1982).

21. Along with other revisionists, Cahill argues that a disjunction in Catholic ethical methodology between personal and social ethics challenges not only its adequacy but its credibility. See Lisa Sowle Cahill, "Current Teaching on Sexual Ethics," *Studies* 76 (Spring 1987): 20, 28.

22. Cahill, "Community and Couple," in *Commitment to Partnership,* ed. Roberts, 81–99. The methodological import of cultural differences can be seen in Lisa Sowle Cahill, "Moral Theology and the World Church," *Catholic Theological Society of America Proceedings* 39 (1984): 35–51.

23. Cahill, *Between the Sexes,* 10; Farley, "An Ethic for Same-Sex Relations," in *Challenge to Love,* ed. Nugent, 99.

24. Cahill, "Community and Couple," in *Commitment to Partnership,* ed. Roberts, 95.

25. Shannon and Cahill, *Religion and Artificial Reproduction,* 114. She is commenting on: Congregation for the Doctrine of the Faith, *Instruction on Respect for Human Life in Its Origin and on the Dignity of Procreation* (Washington, D.C.: United States Catholic Conference, 1987).

26. Farley, "The Church and Family," 70.

27. Cahill, *Between the Sexes,* 10.

28. Margaret A. Farley, "Moral Imperatives for the Ordination of Women," in *Women and Catholic Priesthood: An Expanded Vision,* ed. Anne Marie Gardiner (New York: Paulist Press, 1976), 42.

29. Margaret A. Farley, "Feminist Consciousness and Scripture," in *Feminist Interpretation of the Bible,* ed. Letty M. Russell (Philadelphia: Westminster Press, 1985), 42–43.

30. Farley, "New Patterns of Relationship," 630.

31. Current historical and exegetical research demonstrates that Scripture and the theological tradition are themselves products of an interaction with human experience. See Farley, "An Ethic for Same-Sex Relations," in *Challenge to Love,* ed. Nugent, 97–98.

32. Margaret A. Farley, "Feminist Theology and Bioethics," in *Women's Consciousness, Women's Conscience: A Reader in Feminist Ethics,* ed. Barbara Hilkert Andolsen, Christine E. Gudorf, and Mary D. Pellauer (Minneapolis: Winston Press, 1985), 296.

33. John Mahoney reasons similarly about the role of concrete reality in the articulation of church positions on ethical matters. "But if there is a historical shift, through improvement in scholarship or knowledge, or through an entry of society into a significantly different age, then what that same fidelity requires of the Church is that it respond to the historical shift, such that it might be not only mistaken but also unfaithful in declining to do so." John Mahoney, *The Making of Moral Theology: A Study of the Roman Catholic Tradition* (Oxford: Clarendon Press, 1987), 327. Farley's claim is that such historical shifts have occurred in both knowledge and scholarship relative to the concrete reality of women persons.

34. Farley, "New Patterns of Relationship," 631; "Feminist Consciousness and Scripture," in *Feminist Interpretation of the Bible,* ed. Russell, 50.

35. Ancient myths, cultural suspicions of human bodiliness, and philosophical dualisms have all influenced Christian Scripture and theology in such a way that, not only are women rendered inferior, but doctrines of God and of the Church, as well as notions of women's nature and role, have been affected by sexist influence. The way to re-construct these notions lies in building upon Paul Ricoeur's distinction between the mythological level of pre-ethical symbolism and the ethical level of relationships and choice. Farley's point is that sin is a matter of choosing to rupture a covenant bond, i.e., a relationship. Thus the ethics governing sexuality ought to be consistent with those which regulate human behavior in general. They must accord with notions of justice and love. See Farley, "Sources of Sexual Inequality," 166–67, 169; see also Paul Ricoeur, *The Symbolism of Evil,* trans. E. Buchanan (New York: Harper & Row, 1967), 29.

36. According to Mahoney, many of the developments in post-Vatican II moral theology concern themselves with re-evaluating the traditional objective/subjective distinction in Catholic ethics; see Mahoney, *The Making of Moral Theology,* 329–30.

37. Margaret A. Farley, "Feminist Ethics," in *Westminster Dictionary of Christian Ethics,* ed. James F. Childress and John Macquarrie (Philadelphia: Westminster Press, 1986), 230–31; "Feminist Theology and Bioethics," in *Women's Consciousness,* ed. Andolsen et al., 290.

38. Farley, "New Patterns of Relationship," 633 ff.

39. Farley, "Feminist Theology and Bioethics," in *Women's Consciousness,* ed. Andolsen et al., 295.

40. Farley, *Personal Commitments,* 82.

41. Examples include "remarriage after divorce; committed but premarital ('preceremonial') sex; the avoidance of conception in conjugal sexual relations; and even the committed homosexual relationship." In these situations, strict adherence to the norm of procreative, heterosexual monogamy is either inappropriate, difficult, or impossible. See Cahill, *Between the Sexes,* 148–49.

42. Lisa Sowle Cahill, "Catholic Sexual Teaching: Context, Function, and Authority," in *Vatican Authority and American Catholic Dissent,* ed. May, 199; in the same volume, see Farley, "Moral Discourse in the Public Arena," 175 ff. Catholic theologians and pastoral ministers who signed the *New York Times* ad (October 7, 1984) were making the same point; they called Church leadership to dialogue on an ethical issue which continues to have special significance for women. See "Statement on Pluralism and Abortion," *Origins* 14 (December 6, 1984): 414. I have written on this subject elsewhere. See Susan L. Secker, "The Crisis within Official Catholic Sexual and Biomedical Ethics and American Revisionist Moral Theology: The Relationship between Selected Methodological and Ecclesiological Aspects" (Ph.D. dissertation, The University of Chicago, 1989); and Susan L. Secker, "Catholic Ethics: Whose Experience Counts? Which Church Do You Mean?" *New Theology Review,* 1993.

43. Carol Gilligan, *In a Different Voice: Psychological Theory and Women's Development* (Cambridge: Harvard University Press, 1982); Carol Gilligan, Janie Victoria Ward, and Jill McLean Taylor, eds., with Betty Bardige, *Mapping the Moral Domain: A Contribution of Women's Thinking to Psychology and Education* (Cambridge: Harvard University Press, 1988); Carol Gilligan, Nona P. Lyons, and Trudy J. Hanmer, eds., *Making Connections: The Relational Worlds of Adolescent Girls at Emma Willard School* (Cambridge: Harvard University Press, 1990).

44. Mary Field Belenky, Blythe McVicker Clinchy, Nancy Rule Goldberger, and Jill Mattuck Tarule, *Women's Ways of Knowing: The Development of Self, Voice, and Mind* (New York: Basic Books, 1986).

45. Susan Brooks Thistlethwaite, *Sex, Race, and God: Christian Feminism in Black and White* (New York: Crossroad, 1989), 24–26.

46. Bell Hooks, *Feminist Theory: From Margin to Center* (Boston: South End Press, 1984). Katie G. Cannon, *Black Womanist Ethics* (Atlanta: Scholars Press, 1988). Ada Maria Isasi-Diaz, "Toward an Understanding of *Feminismo Hispano* in the U.S.A.," in *Women's Conscious-*

ness, Women's Conscience, ed. Barbara Hilkert Andolsen, Christine Gudorf, and Mary D. Pellauer (Minneapolis: Winston Press, 1985), 51–61; Ada Maria Isasi-Diaz, "The Bible and *Mujerista* Theology," in *Lift Every Voice: Constructing Christian Theologies from the Underside,* ed. Susan Brooks Thistlethwaite and Mary Potter Engel (San Francisco: Harper & Row, 1990), 261–69.

47. The International Theological Commission, "On the Interpretation of Dogmas," *Origins* 20/1 (May 17, 1990): 5.

List of Contributors

John P. Boyle is Professor and former Chair of the School of Religion of the University of Iowa.

Joseph M. Boyle, Jr., is Professor of Philosophy at St. Michael's College of the University of Toronto.

Lisa Sowle Cahill is Professor of Christian Ethics at Boston College.

John R. Connery, S.J., was Professor of Moral Theology at Loyola University in Chicago.

Charles E. Curran is Elizabeth Scurlock University Professor of Human Values at Southern Methodist University.

Jack Dominion is an English psychiatrist who has worked and written extensively in the areas of marriage and sexuality.

Margaret A. Farley, R.S.M., is Gilbert L. Stark Professor of Christian Ethics at Yale University Divinity School.

John Finnis is Reader in Law, Oxford University and Fellow of University College, Oxford.

John Gallagher, C.S.B., taught moral theology for many years and is currently Superior General of the Basilian Fathers.

Leslie Griffin is a fellow in the Program in Ethics and the Professions at Harvard University.

Germain Grisez is the Rev. Harry J. Flynn Professor of Christian Ethics at Mount St. Mary's College in Emmitsburg, Maryland.

André Guindon, O.M.I., is Professor of Moral Theology at St. Paul University in Ottawa, Canada.

Bernard Häring, C.SS.R., is Professor Emeritus of Moral Theology at the Alphonsian Academy in Rome and currently resides in Germany.

John F. Harvey, O.S.F.S., taught moral theology at DeSales College in Washington and is currently director of Courage.

Philip S. Keane, S.S., is Professor of Moral Theology at St. Mary's Seminary and University in Baltimore.

Gerald Kelly, S.J., taught moral theology for many years at the Jesuit Theologate at St. Mary's in Kansas.

Kevin Kelly is a Lecturer in Moral Theology at Heythrop College in London.

John P. Kenny, O.P., taught for many years at Providence College in Providence, Rhode Island.

Anthony R. Kosnik is Professor of Ethics at Marygrove College in Detroit, Michigan.

Ronald D. Lawler, O.F.M.Cap., is Director of Education at the Pope John XXIII Medical-Moral Research and Education Center at Braintree, Massachusetts.

John Mahoney, S.J., is F. D. Maurice Professor of Moral and Social Theology at King's College of the University of London.

William E. May is Michael J. McGivney Professor of Moral Theology at the Pope John Paul II Institute for Studies on Marriage and Family in Washington, D.C.

Richard A. McCormick, S.J., is John A. O'Brien Professor of Christian Ethics at the University of Notre Dame.

John J. McNeill is adjunct professor at the Institutes of Religion and Health at Union Theological Seminary in New York and a psychotherapist in private practice.

John T. Noonan, Jr., has written extensively in the history of law and theology and is currently a judge on the United States Court of Appeals for the Ninth Circuit in San Francisco.

Rosemary Radford Ruether is the Georgia Harkness Professor of Theology at the Garrett Theological Seminary and member of the graduate faculty of Northwestern University in Evanston, Illinois.

Susan S. Secker is Assistant Professor of Christian Ethics at Seattle University.

Joseph A. Selling is Professor of Moral Theology at Katholieke Universitait Leuven in Belgium.

Joan H. Timmerman is Professor of Theology at the College of St. Catherine in St. Paul, Minnesota.

EADINGS IN

1ORAL THEOLOGY NO.6

issent in the Church

ONTENTS

READINGS IN
MORAL THEOLOGY NO. 7
Natural Law and Theology